Confronting Poverty

Confronting Poverty
PRESCRIPTIONS FOR CHANGE

EDITED BY

SHELDON H. DANZIGER

GARY D. SANDEFUR

DANIEL H. WEINBERG

RUSSELL SAGE FOUNDATION
New York

1994

HARVARD UNIVERSITY PRESS
Cambridge, Massachusetts, and London, England

Library of Congress Cataloging-in-Publication Data

Confronting poverty : prescriptions for change / edited by Sheldon H.
  Danziger, Gary D. Sandefur, and Daniel H. Weinberg.
      p. cm.
    "The chapters in this volume were initially presented at a
  conference held in May 1992 in Madison, Wisconsin, jointly sponsored
  by the Institute for Research on Poverty at the University of
  Wisconsin-Madison and the Office of the Assistant Secretary for
  Planning and Evaluation in the U.S. Department of Health and Human
  Services"—Pref.
    Includes bibliographical references and index.
    ISBN 0–674–16081–9 (cloth). — ISBN 0–674–16082–7 (paper)
      1. Poverty—United States—Congresses. 2. Public welfare—United
  States—Congresses. 3. United States—Social policy—Congresses.
  I. Danziger, Sheldon. II. Sandefur, Gary D., 1951– .
  III. Weinberg, Daniel H.
  HC110.P6C63 1994
  362.5′8′0973—dc20
                                                            93–50929
                                                                CIP

To Robert J. Lampman

in recognition of his contributions to the intellectual
foundations of the War on Poverty and the establishment
of the Institute for Research on Poverty

Contents

Preface

The chapters in this volume were initially presented at a conference held in May 1992 in Madison, Wisconsin, jointly sponsored by the Institute for Research on Poverty at the University of Wisconsin–Madison and the Office of the Assistant Secretary for Planning and Evaluation in the U.S. Department of Health and Human Services. Additional support was provided by the Russell Sage Foundation and the Ford Foundation.

Participants in the conference included analysts from the academic community, government agencies, and private foundations. The participants spent three days assessing and debating the achievements, failures, and diverse lessons of government efforts over the past thirty years to reduce poverty in America. The papers were revised in May 1993 to reflect the conference discussion, reviewer comments, and the policy reforms proposed during President Clinton's initial months in office.

We gratefully acknowledge the contributions of Elizabeth Evanson to the development of this volume, from conference planning and organization to the final editing of the chapters and the compilation of the consolidated reference list. We also thank Robinson Hollister, who provided insightful comments on the entire manuscript; the contributors, who responded carefully to detailed requests for revision; Eugene Smolensky, Christopher Jencks, and other members of the Institute's National Advisory Committee, who helped shape the contents of the volume; and Charles F. Manski and Robert M. Hauser, directors of the Institute, William Prosser, in the U.S. Department of Health and Human Services, and Michael Aronson, of Harvard University Press, all of whom gave valuable support to the project.

Any views expressed in this book are those of the contributors and should not be construed as representing the official position or policy of any sponsoring institution, agency, or foundation.

S.H.D.

G.D.S.

D.H.W.

Confronting Poverty

CHAPTER ONE

Introduction

SHELDON H. DANZIGER, GARY D. SANDEFUR,
AND DANIEL H. WEINBERG

In 1964 President Lyndon Johnson declared unconditional war on poverty and committed the American people to a campaign against economic deprivation. Poverty did lessen in the following decade, but by the mid-1970s progress against it had come to a halt. In 1992, 14.5 percent of Americans were poor. Although this proportion was lower than the 19 percent of the population that had been poor when the War on Poverty was declared, it was above the historic low point (11.1 percent) in 1973 and was the highest since 1983, when 15.2 percent of the population had incomes below the poverty line. Further, the number of poor in 1992, 36.9 million, was as high as the 1964 figure, 36.1 million.

Because poverty has remained a national problem, conventional wisdom tends to regard the War on Poverty as a failure. Such a conclusion, however, is somewhat simplistic. Poverty is a complex social problem. It has not been eliminated, but this does not mean that the war against it failed. Poverty continues to exist because the economy and society have changed in many ways that were not envisioned in 1964. These changes have generated more poverty at the same time that the public resolve to fight poverty has waned.

This volume seeks to establish a new conventional wisdom with regard to poverty and antipoverty policy. The contributors were asked to review the research of the past three decades to establish what we know and do not know about the causes of poverty and to formulate an antipoverty agenda for the years ahead. Was the War on Poverty a success or a failure? The consensus that emerges is that there is no single answer to this question. Some programs were very successful; others failed; some were never large enough to make a difference; others were not designed to deal with the unforeseen demographic and economic changes that have occurred since the mid-1960s. Can and should government today place greater emphasis on policies to reduce poverty? To this question the volume provides a simple and affirmative answer. Even though the contributors differ regarding specific programs and policies, all of the evidence they review points to the need for a renewed antipoverty policy agenda.

Three Decades of Antipoverty Policy

In 1964 no official estimates of the nature or extent of poverty in the United States existed, and poverty was not a focus of government studies or programs. Since the Great Depression of the 1930s, poverty had commanded little academic attention and few legislative initiatives were proposed explicitly to aid the poor. In the 1960s, however, the situation changed dramatically. President John Kennedy, influenced by the poverty he observed while campaigning in West Virginia and by contemporary accounts of the plight of the poor (Harrington, 1962; Macdonald, 1963), directed his Council of Economic Advisers to study the problem. After Kennedy's assassination, Lyndon Johnson accelerated the work of the council and, in his first State of the Union message in January 1964, declared war on poverty. Shortly thereafter he announced a set of companion programs designed to enhance the general welfare and create the "Great Society."

In the next decade, as a result of these initiatives, new social welfare programs were introduced and old programs were expanded; the emphasis of the federal budget shifted from military spending toward social spending. The prevailing view during that period was optimistic. With the maintenance of stable growth and the provision of sufficient resources, government actions could solve the poverty problem. Policymakers assumed that the economy would continue to grow, but they also acknowledged that economic growth could not serve as the sole antipoverty policy: "We cannot and need not wait for the gradual growth of the economy to lift this forgotten fifth of our Nation above the poverty line . . . We know what must be done, and this Nation of abundance can surely afford to do it" (Johnson, 1964, p. 15). This economic optimism was warranted; the economy had grown rapidly during the twenty years since World War II and living standards had increased throughout the income distribution.

Many of the programs that were introduced or expanded during the War on Poverty–Great Society era are still operating, including Medicare and Medicaid, Food Stamps, Head Start, elementary and secondary educational assistance, and manpower development (training) programs such as the Job Corps. As the chapters in this volume demonstrate, these programs have improved the lives and the economic well-being of the low-income population. Nonetheless, the optimism that characterized the mid-1960s soured as the war in Vietnam replaced the War on Poverty in the headlines and helped destroy faith in the government's ability to solve any problem (Aaron, 1978). Increasingly heard were arguments that social problems could not be solved by "throwing money" at them and that the antipoverty attempts had failed.

By the late 1970s, after oil shocks, slow economic growth, and high inflation rates, a pessimistic view had emerged. It held that government was incapable of dealing with the major issues confronting U.S. society. Although a decade earlier government could do "almost anything," now it could do "almost nothing." Proponents of this view argued that social welfare programs had grown too large and had become a drag on economic growth, that work incentives had been eroded for both the poor and the rich, and that the incentive to save had been weakened. These programs should therefore be scaled back or eliminated (Murray, 1984). By 1982 this perspective had become official policy: "With the coming of the Great Society, government began eating away at the underpinnings of the private enterprise system. The big taxers and big spenders in the Congress had started a binge that would slowly change the nature of our society and, even worse, it threatened the character of our people . . . By the time the full weight of Great Society programs was felt, economic progress for America's poor had come to a tragic halt" (Reagan, 1982, p. 1154). Rather than ask what government could do for the poor, official policy now emphasized what government could not accomplish and the ways in which its involvement could be counterproductive.

In retrospect, the official perspective on antipoverty policy was too optimistic at the outset of the War on Poverty and too pessimistic at the outset of the Reagan administration's attempts to scale back the social safety net. The experience of the 1980s provided a "pseudo-social experiment" for this hands-off policy. The federal government emphasized policies designed to promote economic growth, and antipoverty policy was not a priority. As a result, even though the 1980s saw a seven-year economic recovery, there was relatively little reduction in poverty. The decade was one of "uneven tides," as the poor and the middle class hardly benefited from the recovery (Danziger and Gottschalk, 1993). Average living standards increased, but the gaps between the poor and the rich and between the middle class and the rich widened.

At the same time that the economy was generating increasing hardship for the poor and for less-skilled workers, the federal government was also cutting back substantially on its antipoverty and labor market programs. In 1980 federal spending on employment and training programs amounted to $9.3 billion in constant 1986 dollars. By 1986 spending had fallen to $3.7 billion, and it remained at roughly this level through the end of the Bush administration (see Chapter 3). In addition, legislated changes in unemployment insurance and welfare reduced the antipoverty effectiveness of the federal safety net. It soon became apparent that holding the line on social spending and waiting for employers to hire the poor was not a viable antipoverty strategy.

The experience of high poverty rates during an economic recovery helped to shape a "new consensus" about the nature and prospects for a renewed anti-poverty effort. By the late 1980s Congress rejected the hands-off policy. The Tax Reform Act of 1986, the Family Support Act of 1988, and the Budget Summit Agreement of 1990 all reflected a bipartisan agreement to reform tax and welfare policies to aid the poor.

This new consensus recognized the diversity of the poor and the need for a multiplicity of strategies to aid them. The poverty problem of the elderly widow, for example, differs from that of the family whose head seeks full-time work but finds only sporadic employment; the poverty of the family head who works full time but at low wages differs from that of the family head who receives welfare and either cannot find a job or does not find it profitable to seek work.

A key aspect of this approach to poverty policy is the consensus that only the poverty of those not expected to work, such as the elderly and the disabled, should be addressed with expanded welfare benefits. This represents a dramatic shift from the consensus of the 1970s that cash welfare benefits should be universally available (for example, President Nixon's Family Assistance Plan and President Carter's Program for Better Jobs and Income).[1] This consensus was embodied in the new emphasis placed on increasing the work effort of welfare recipients in the Family Support Act of 1988 and is also seen in the arguments in several chapters here for an expanded federal emphasis on labor market policies.

In 1991 the National Commission on Children released its report, *Beyond Rhetoric: A New American Agenda for Children and Families,* which endorsed proposals to raise the standard of living of low-income working families, move welfare families from nonwork to work, subsidize child-care costs, increase child support awards and collections, and extend medical coverage. President Bill Clinton, then governor of Arkansas, was a commission member. During his 1992 presidential campaign and in his initial months in office, he advocated renewed policy efforts in these areas. He proposed reforming health care and welfare, expanding Head Start, subsidizing low-wage workers, and expanding access to higher education.

Thus the United States is on the verge of another major shift in thinking about antipoverty policy. This new view is based on the research and policy lessons of the past three decades and can be characterized as reflecting realism, rather than either the optimism that characterized the War on Poverty or the pessimism of the Reagan retrenchment. Rejected are the views that government can do almost anything *and* that government can do almost nothing. The contributors to this volume, reflecting the new view, propose many changes that, if undertaken, would reduce poverty. They realize that these policies would not totally eliminate poverty. They also recognize that there are other proposals that require additional research, experimentation, and demonstration trials. They are more confident about the ability of policies to raise the incomes of the working poor and to move some welfare families into the labor market, for example, than they are about revitalizing our most poverty-stricken inner-city neighborhoods. The goal of resolving the American paradox of "poverty amid plenty" remains.

Three Decades of Research on Poverty

As changes in antipoverty policy have taken place, there have also been changes in the direction of research on poverty. These changes are manifest in four volumes that have come out of the Institute for Research on Poverty during the past twenty years: *Progress against Poverty: A Review of the 1964–1974 Decade,* by Robert Plotnick and Felicity Skidmore (1975); *A Decade of Federal Antipoverty Programs: Achievements, Failures, and Lessons,* edited by Robert H. Haveman (1977); *Fighting Poverty: What Works and What Doesn't,* edited by Sheldon H. Danziger and Daniel H. Weinberg (1986); and this book. Each contains essays that assess existing knowledge about poverty and antipoverty policy and recommend changes in policy.

A review of these volumes reveals the themes and ideas that have been important throughout the past three decades. Contributors to each volume have focused on expenditures on antipoverty programs, trends in the official poverty rate and the impact of income transfers on poverty, and the issue of income inequality. Each volume has analyzed the role of macroeconomic changes and has included evaluations of the special problems of black poverty in the central cities, education and training programs, health care, and employment policies. Each volume has addressed the issues of whether public assistance programs create adverse incentives (for example, reducing work effort or encouraging the formation of single-parent families) and has examined the political issues that constrain antipoverty policies. The particular questions posed in these areas, the empirical results, and the recommended policies have changed considerably since 1964. But the topics continue to attract attention.

Other issues and themes appear in the earlier volumes, but not here. One difference across all four volumes concerns the relative importance of poverty and antipoverty policy in the hierarchy of public policy issues at the time each volume was being prepared. Haveman (1977, p. 18), after reviewing the optimistic post–War on Poverty decade marked by major reductions in the poverty rate, concluded that "the day of income poverty as a major public issue would appear to be past." Danziger and Weinberg (1986, p. 1), writing after the Reagan retrenchment on social programs, began their introductory chapter with the statement: "Poverty was at the top of the nation's agenda when the War on Poverty was declared twenty years ago. Now it is only one of several concerns." As this volume goes to press, poverty seems to be once again moving back toward the top of the national political agenda.

Other changes in focus in antipoverty research are also reflected in the earlier works. A contribution to the Haveman volume considered community action programs a major part of antipoverty efforts. Neither of the next two volumes pays much attention to such programs. The idea of a guaranteed income or a negative income tax receives serious consideration in the Plotnick-Skidmore and Haveman volumes, but is of little concern in the Danziger-Weinberg or this volume. The legal rights of and legal services for the poor were important topics in the earlier books but are not discussed here. Each of these policies—community action programs, a guaranteed income, and legal services—attempts to increase the power and voice of the poor and/or make it easier for needy individuals to get cash benefits. In the 1980s, more attention was focused on requiring the poor to take greater responsibility through increased work effort and support for their children.

Contributions in this volume are primarily devoted to issues that took center stage after the mid-1980s. Recent studies have emphasized the persistence of poverty and of welfare use for individuals over time and the extent of the intergenerational transmission of both. Although urban poverty has been a long-standing concern, this is the first of the four volumes to contain chapters on the urban underclass and urban policy. The poverty experienced by immigrants, their patterns of receipt of public assistance, and the impact of immigrants on the native-born also appear for the first time. In addition, education—from preschool through college, and including worker training and retraining—as a key to economic success has once again moved to the forefront of public debate.

Although some topics have changed, some have been dropped, and others have been added, the broad questions addressed by research on poverty are similar to the broad questions raised in the mid-1960s. The chapters that follow address the four major questions that have formed the core of research on poverty during the past three decades: What is the extent of poverty? How effective are antipoverty programs? How should we reform and expand antipoverty programs and policies? What are the political constraints within which antipoverty policy must be formulated?

What Is the Extent of Poverty?

Sheldon H. Danziger and Daniel H. Weinberg discuss trends in the level and distribution of family income and a series of alternative measures of poverty. They provide a historical perspective on what has happened to poverty in the United

States since its eradication first became a goal of public policy. They examine trends over time in the official poverty rate and in alternative poverty measures adjusted for deficiencies in the official definition such as the failure to account for the receipt of in-kind income and the payment of taxes. They also examine the severity of poverty, both the proportion of people with incomes below half the official poverty line and the poverty gap—the amount by which a poor family's income falls below its poverty line.

Whatever measures they use, they find that prior to 1973, family income grew rapidly, income inequality declined modestly, and poverty declined dramatically—from 19 percent of the population (official rate) in 1964 to a low of 11.1 percent in 1973. The period between 1973 and 1979 was characterized by stagnation in mean income and modest cyclical changes in poverty. Poverty and inequality then rose rapidly between 1979 and 1983 because of back-to-back recessions and falling average incomes. It is the post-1983 period that Danziger and Weinberg find anomalous. In these years mean income grew rapidly, but so did inequality. As a result, the poverty rate and the severity of poverty remained above their 1973 levels and the gap between the incomes of the poorest and richest families widened to levels not seen since the late 1940s.

Danziger and Weinberg conclude that economic growth still matters. Growth matters less to the trend in poverty now than in the past, however, because of increased income inequality. Looking at trends among various demographic groups, Danziger and Weinberg report that, in any year, non-Hispanic whites have lower poverty rates than blacks, Hispanics, and other minority groups; working-age adults have lower poverty rates than children and the elderly; men have lower poverty rates than women; and married-couple families have lower poverty rates than female-headed families. All of these demographic disparities in poverty have persisted over the past fifty years with one exception. Until 1973 the poverty rate for the elderly was substantially higher than the rate for children, whereas since 1973 it has been lower, and is now substantially lower.

Peter Gottschalk, Sara McLanahan, and Gary D. Sandefur examine the nature of persistent poverty and welfare use within and across generations. They show that most people who are poor at some point in their lives are poor for only a short period of time. Blacks experience longer spells of poverty on average than do whites. Patterns of income mobility and the likelihood of individuals' escaping poverty from one year to the next did not change much between the late 1960s and the late 1980s. The majority of people who use welfare (in particular, Aid to Families with Dependent Children, or AFDC) use it for less than two years in a row. Yet about half of first-time users return to welfare later. Blacks are on welfare longer on average than are whites, and are more likely than whites to return to the welfare rolls after an initial experience with welfare.

Gottschalk, McLanahan, and Sandefur also examine the evidence regarding the causal effect of welfare on poverty, a critical issue in recent public policy debates. They conclude that although welfare has small but measurable adverse effects on work effort, marriage, divorce, and childbearing, these effects are not large enough to lead to an increase in the poverty rate relative to what it would be without welfare. Indeed, the poverty rate would be significantly higher without the cash transfers from welfare programs, and a more generous welfare system would reduce poverty.

Research on the intergenerational transmission of poverty suggests that individuals who grow up in poor families are substantially more likely to experience poverty as adults than those who do not grow up in poor families. Poverty is not a "trap," however; over half of the people who grow up in the bottom quintile of the income distribution will not be there as adults. Although the evidence also supports the intergenerational correlation of welfare use, it does not yet permit sorting out the extent to which welfare use in one generation *causes* welfare use in the next generation. Gottschalk, McLanahan, and Sandefur also report that growing up in a single-parent family is associated with deleterious life-cycle events such as dropping out of high school and premarital pregnancy, which in turn are associated with poverty and welfare use later as adults.

Indications of the intergenerational transmission of poverty and welfare use raise the specter of a permanent underclass, mired in poverty, behaving in ways that further isolate them from the economic and social mainstream. Ronald B. Mincy examines the concept of the underclass, a term used to describe the combination of poverty and social problems such as violence, drug abuse, joblessness, out-of-wedlock childbearing, and dependence on welfare attributed to some residents of urban slums. He outlines the work of William Julius Wilson, the principal underclass theorist, who constructed a set of hypotheses to explain the emergence of an urban underclass: changing employment opportunities (reduced demand for low-skilled labor), declines in black marriage rates, and selective outmigration (movement of middle-class blacks from the urban ghettos).

Mincy explores the extent to which the Wilson hypotheses have been substantiated and questioned, and he points to other theories, such as one that lays greater stress on the role of race discrimination in marginalizing low-skilled minorities in our society. He concludes that though much controversy remains and measurement of the underclass is exceedingly inexact, the literature on the underclass has been valuable in reestablishing a broader debate about poverty and its causes.

How Effective Are Antipoverty Programs?

Gary Burtless examines historical trends in and economic limits on public spending on the poor. Burtless points out that most programs for the poor are successful in meeting most of their objectives. He suggests that it is easier to examine the intensity of our effort to help the poor than it is to examine our success, because intensity can be measured by looking at expenditures.

Burtless points to three major eras in public spending on the poor. The 1960–1975 period was marked by the initiation and/or expansion of many programs targeting the poor. It was followed by a period of skepticism about antipoverty programs and retrenchment in social spending. The third and current era began toward the end of the 1980s, with program liberalization that involved the reform and extension of existing programs rather than the initiation of new programs as in the 1960s.

Burtless also poses the question of whether spending money on the poor has adverse effects. He questions whether the effects are very large with reference to the experience of other industrialized countries. In many of these, generous redistribution policies have been compatible with much higher growth in real per capita gross domestic product than has occurred in the United States. He concludes that the choice of redistribution policy rests ultimately on political rather than on purely economic considerations. The United States has chosen modest redistribution and high rates of poverty primarily because of political considerations, particularly the view that government—to the greatest extent possible—should minimize its intervention in the market economy.

Yet the government has increased redistributive payments to individuals since 1960. What, exactly, has been the effect on the poor of this spending? Danziger and Weinberg emphasize several points. First they point out that most income transfers are not targeted on the poor. Social insurance spending represents about three-quarters of the total of $573 billion spent on transfers in 1990. Only the remaining quarter targets the low-income population. They further point out that since 1960, programs have increasingly provided assistance in forms other than cash—increases in Medicare, Medicaid, housing assistance, and Food Stamps. Within these constraints, in 1990, 37.2 percent of the pretransfer poor (8 percent of all persons) were removed from poverty by cash transfers, and about half of the pretransfer poor were taken out of poverty by cash plus noncash transfers.

Trends in the antipoverty effectiveness of cash income transfers over the 1967–1990 period differ markedly for the elderly and for persons living in families with children headed by a nonelderly male or female. The poverty rate for the elderly is now below average and has declined relative to the rates of nonelderly families with children, primarily because of the increasing antipoverty effectiveness of income transfers. Since 1973, when Social Security benefits were indexed for inflation, cash transfers have continued to remove more than three-quarters of the elderly pretransfer poor from poverty.

Poverty rose primarily for those most affected by adverse economic conditions—families with children—for whom inflation-adjusted spending increases after 1973 have been quite modest. Government spending on families declined in the 1980s: unemployment insurance and AFDC coverage were restricted and public employment was eliminated, despite the rising pretransfer poverty generated by recession. For female-headed families with children, for example, cash transfers in 1990 removed only about 10 percent of the pretransfer poor from poverty.

James Tobin examines the relationship between macroeconomic policies (and trends) and poverty. He asserts that the early efforts to reduce poverty during the 1940s, 1950s, and 1960s could rely on favorable macroeconomic trends. The migration and shift of labor from rural agriculture to urban industry were important factors in reducing poverty during the 1940s and 1950s. Economic growth was robust during the 1950s and 1960s; this "rising tide" contributed to reducing the poverty rate through increased employment and made it possible to expand spending on government programs.

Since 1973, macroeconomic performance has been disappointing, and when the economy has grown, poverty has not been very responsive to this growth. This lack of responsiveness is in part due to the failure of economic growth to provide "good" jobs for low-skilled individuals as it did in the past. Tobin argues that public investments in education, infrastructure, housing and inner-city development, improved health care, job programs, and welfare reform are all necessary in order to reduce poverty, and that this investment should take priority over reducing the federal debt. He feels, however, that "the Reagan administration succeeded all too well and all too permanently in its objective of crippling civilian government by giving away tax revenues, creating a political taboo against raising taxes, and generating a deficit and debt to brandish against civilian expenditures."

What Have We Tried and What Should We Do?

Chapters 7–13 recommend changes in antipoverty policy on the basis of an assessment of the research and policy experience of the past three decades. Rebecca M. Blank examines employment policies. She finds that widespread unemployment is not a serious problem for some groups, such as adult white males, but that there are specific groups, for example, blacks in central cities, for whom the availability of jobs is of critical concern. While aggregate employment grew during the 1980s, the inflation-adjusted wages of less-skilled male workers fell. In contrast, women's wages rose faster than men's during the 1980s and the earnings of less-skilled women either remained flat or increased. Yet women still earn substantially less than men with the same levels of education. Overall, these trends and the rise in the percentage of families with a single female head have made it harder for low-income families to earn their way out of poverty. Blank notes that in this situation "it is now probably more difficult to implement an 'employment strategy' as a way to reduce poverty than it has been at any time in the recent past."

Blank finds that over the past two decades, changes in welfare policies have tended to concentrate less on improving the earnings potential of welfare recipients and more on increasing their work effort, regardless of whether this increased work effort enhances their economic well-being. She summarizes the changing impact of AFDC program structure on work incentives in three points. First, a steady decline in the purchasing power of AFDC benefits has made AFDC an increasingly less attractive option. Second, legislation, such as the Omnibus Budget Reconciliation Act of 1981, has tightened eligibility, increasing work incentives for those families removed from AFDC by the changes. Many of the former AFDC recipients thus removed are worse off, because they have less time for parenting or other home-based activities and little or no increases in family income. Third, high benefit-reduction rates have caused work effort to decline among those who continue to utilize AFDC, because the added work produces little net income gain.

Blank then examines the effects of on-the-job training, job search assistance, and work experience programs on the work effort of the poor. Evaluations have shown that job search assistance leads to modest employment and income gains among female AFDC recipients, and that the social returns from some of these programs are greater than the costs. Yet there is no evidence that these programs move many families out of poverty. The evidence on job training programs for men and youth is more mixed: some programs show positive results while others appear less effective.

She concludes with a set of interrelated policy recommendations that involve the stimulation of economic growth, educational reform, expansion and experimentation with job training programs and other employment-related services, stronger work incentives for those on AFDC, the recent expansion of the Earned Income Tax Credit and spatial targeting to meet the needs of those in rural and inner-city areas with high unemployment rates.

Irwin Garfinkel and Sara McLanahan explore the economic problems of single-mother families. They point out that over half of the current generation of children will live in a family headed only by a mother before reaching age eighteen, and that most of these families experience economic and social insecurity that has a detrimental effect on the children later in their lives.

Other industrialized countries, particularly Canada and those in western Europe, do much more for single-parent families than does the United States. This observation leads Garfinkel and McLanahan to propose two alternatives to improve the financial situation of single mothers and their children. One is a refundable tax credit of $1,000 per child to replace the child exemption in the federal income tax. This is similar to a child allowance, in widespread use in Europe and Canada. The second proposal is for a Child Support Assurance System, under which a child living apart from a parent receives either child support paid by the nonresident parent or a minimum benefit provided by the government.

Jeffrey S. Lehman considers antipoverty policies that are targeted at the urban poor. He begins with the two urban strategies most commonly discussed: enterprise zones and guaranteed public job programs. He then argues for a broader urban policy that promotes social mobility through employment. He also advocates a limited experiment with "access-to-enterprise zones" (AEZs).

Lehman is critical of enterprise zone proposals, such as the one vetoed in 1992 by President George Bush, that make federal subsidies conditional on economic activity within a selected neighborhood. He reviews equity-based reasons that make him suspicious of spatially targeted antipoverty programs. He contends that the primary justification for an enterprise zone program derives from the externalities that flow from spatially concentrated unemployment, and he suggests a program that attends to where workers live, not where they work. Lehman concludes that the federal government should not replicate state-based enterprise zone programs, which have shown no significant increases in aggregate employment.

Lehman notes that modern guaranteed public job proposals must contend with the legacy of the Comprehensive Employment and Training Act of 1973 (CETA). Although CETA generated modest long-term earnings increases for white and minority women participants (though not for men), it fell victim to charges that (1) it cost more than it was worth; (2) it created make-work jobs; (3) its jobs merely substituted for other, preexisting ones; and (4) it gave jobs to people who would have otherwise found work in the private sector. He concludes that universal public jobs programs conflict with the politically powerful ideology of limited government.

Lehman emphasizes the significance of employment mobility as an aspiration. He calls for a greater government response to the direct mobility restrictions that follow from racial discrimination in employment and stresses the importance of educating citizens about the moral objectionability of "statistical discrimination." He also calls for enhanced responses to the *indirect* constriction of mobility opportunities that follows from residential segregation; such responses include extending urban transportation networks, creating computerized job banks and information centers, enforcing antidiscrimination laws, and expanding housing vouchers along the lines of the Gautreaux experiment.

Because mobility-based strategies are long-term approaches, Lehman suggests limited experimentation with AEZs in the most deprived neighborhoods. Residents would be eligible for wage subsidies in the form of employer tax credits and for guaranteed public sector jobs. The AEZ program would not require beneficiaries to work in their neighborhoods. Lehman rejects the idea (implicit in traditional enterprise zone proposals) that the zone should be a location for work; his proposal instead suggests that these areas should be a home for workers.

Barbara L. Wolfe examines the possibilities for reforming health care for the nonelderly poor. She concludes that reported health problems are greater for the poor than for the nonpoor, leading to a greater need by the poor for medical care. The lack of health insurance, the indirect costs of utilization, the limited hours of service by providers, and the limited number of private providers in low-income areas limit the access of the poor to health care.

A number of public programs are designed to help the poor with their health care needs. Medicaid greatly improved the poor's access to health care relative to what it had been prior to the existence of that program. Medicaid has a number of problems, however, including the fact that a substantial number of the poor are not covered by it. Other programs designed to assist those without means who need medical care, such as maternal and child health services, community health centers, migrant health centers, and the Indian Health Service, have experienced declining resources over time.

Wolfe reviews the major proposals for reform in the health care system, including requirements that employers provide some minimum level of coverage to their employees and their dependents ("pay or play"), expansion of Medicare and/or Medicaid, modifications in tax incentives, and nationalized health insurance. Wolfe argues that major reform is very difficult for several reasons, primarily political in nature. If the Clinton administration is unable to legislate the major overhaul proposed in 1993, steps can and should be taken to patch the current health care system and improve the position of those in poverty. One such step is Wolfe's proposal for a "healthy kid" program, which would cover all children under the age of nineteen for a specific set of services at community health care centers. Certain types of medical care would be available at no charge; other types would require income-conditioned co-payments and might be delivered at places other than the community care centers. To help the poor who are not children, she proposes a refundable tax credit to the poor and near poor and a loan-forgiveness approach to the expansion of community health centers, paid for by a cap on the tax subsidy for health insurance.

Richard J. Murnane points out that education can play an important role in reducing poverty. The 1973–1991 period was difficult for all Americans, but particularly for those with no more than a high school degree. Their average wage declined considerably more than did the average wage for college graduates. In addition, the employment of those with less education is considerably less stable than that of college graduates. These problems are even more serious for blacks than for whites. In addition to improving graduation and continuation rates, Murnane stresses the importance of improving basic or threshold math and reading skills.

Murnane finds two policies to have little merit: educational vouchers and merit pay for teachers. Existing research does not indicate that educational vouchers would improve educational opportunities for poor children. Merit pay plans have been expensive to administer, have not increased effort levels by individual teachers, and have militated against the teamwork that is a critical component of effective schooling. Murnane advocates an expansion of preschool programs for disadvantaged children, changes in the design of compensatory education programs in public schools, experimentation with the integration of vocational with academic training, programs to increase the availability of skilled teachers for urban schools, and monitoring the quality of education provided to poor children.

Charles F. Manski evaluates the likely effects of school vouchers, also known as school choice. He challenges the view that school choice is a panacea for our educational problems. He contends that qualitative arguments comparing the relative merits of voucher systems and public schooling are not sufficient for rigorous evaluation. Assessment of the implications of vouchers for the quality of education for low-income children requires quantitative analysis. He develops a model of local educational markets and then simulates the effects of alternative school choice programs. His simulations suggest that the likely impact of school choice will be a mixture of desirable and undesirable consequences that will vary with the characteristics of the community and the characteristics of the school choice program. Manski concludes that "a system of uniform vouchers would not, even in the most favorable case, come close to equalizing educational opportunity across income groups."

Marta Tienda and Zai Liang examine recent trends in immigration and provide a historical review of immigration policy. They point out that the volume of immigration during the 1980s was very high by historical standards and was not noticeably affected by the Immigration Reform and Control Act of 1986. They expect that recent legislation will probably lead to even higher levels of immigration during the 1990s.

Currently, different types of immigrants and refugees are eligible for different social programs. Most immigrants are not eligible for many of the programs in which citizens participate. The authors argue for a more simplified and consistent policy for all immigrants, including access to the same benefits and programs that are available to U.S. citizens, the expansion of the small business grant program to include immigrants with demonstrated business experience, tax incentives for immigrants to start businesses in the inner city and to hire disadvantaged inner-city workers, and expansion of the Job Training Partnership Act to target unskilled immigrants who enter under family reunification provisions.

What Are the Political Constraints on the Formation of Antipoverty Policy?

Having noted that public opinion has a genuine and consequential input into the policymaking process, Lawrence Bobo and Ryan A. Smith review studies of public opinion in an effort to determine what levels of support exist for different social policies. They find no sign whatever of a strong ideological turn to the right, against the welfare state. Rather, they find a relatively clear and stable hierarchy of support for social programs. Obtaining the highest levels of popular support are health care, education, and social security programs. A quite general item concerned with the level of spending on "assistance to the poor" also ranks in the top tier of social programs. At the bottom of the hierarchy are means-tested income transfer programs, that is, welfare. In the middle are jobs-related and housing programs.

From the late 1980s to the present there has been a significant increase in support for spending on health and medical care programs, fueled by the rising cost of medical care. Public support has also risen for spending of education. Relative to most other industrialized nations, however, public opinion in the United States reflects a weaker commitment to social programs. Bobo and Smith find that race and racism do play a considerable role in social welfare attitudes, and that some programs, such as welfare, are thought to be racial in nature. Programs directed at making up for disadvantages by developing the human capital of blacks are typically well supported by white Americans, but "policies that involve preferential selection or quotas confront a solid wall of opposition."

Hugh Heclo argues that we must take into account three basic facts about the politics of antipoverty policy. First, poor people have very little political power to use in influencing policies that affect them. Second, the poverty debate and the racial debate are now inseparable, and one cannot seriously discuss antipoverty policy without paying attention to its racial ramifications. Third, antipoverty efforts are affected by macroeconomic conditions, but the nature of this relationship is not consistent. That is, good times are not a sufficient condition for increased efforts to fight poverty.

Heclo goes on to analyze why the War on Poverty lost political support, the roots and nature of the "New Paternalism" in welfare reform, and the reasons why our politics typically focus on inner-city welfare recipients, even though they are only a small part of the poverty problem. He then discusses the political prospects for a renewed effort to fight poverty more broadly in the United States. The constraints that impede this renewed effort include general public cynicism about the political process and the ability of government to solve social problems, as well as the immense federal budget deficit and, paradoxically, the end of the Cold War.

Two other sets of factors may or may not push in the opposite direction for strengthening antipoverty efforts. First, we might be motivated to pay more attention to poverty because of the competitive need internationally for a fully productive work force. We may therefore become convinced that our own economic well-being depends on educating, training, and improving the lives of the poor, especially poor youth. But so far, Americans have seemed unmoved by economic reasons to help those left behind. Second, we might be motivated by the desire for greater social stability, as people associate improving living conditions for the poor with reductions in crime and other antisocial behavior. But more punitive, short-term responses are at least as likely, and social policies based on fear are rarely constructive. Heclo contends that, ultimately, developing a stronger antipoverty policy will require more powerful coalitions to fight for a politics of inclusion and on political leaders capable of eliciting the public's long-term understanding and moral commitment in attacking our social problems. Whether that is possible under modern conditions remains an open question.

What Are the Unanswered Questions?

Robert Haveman concludes with a review of the volume. He mentions several issues not given much attention: homelessness; the imbalance in the policy treatment of children relative to the elderly; behavioral pathologies, including drug use and crime; the treatment of the poor and minorities in the criminal and civil justice systems; and consumption patterns of the poor. He also points to several alternative policies that are *not* proposed by any of the contributors, primarily because those authors were asked to address only policy reforms that followed directly from available research and policy experience. Haveman extends his view beyond this constraint. His proposed policies for further consideration have been the subject of public discussion, but not rigorous analysis. These include strategies to give the poor more control over their housing and work options and a greater incentive to invest in their futures; the abolition of the current welfare system and replacing it with a different set of programs; a National Urban Corps to use the thousands of military personnel who will soon be discharged; large wage and employment subsidies to create jobs; and the redirection of policies toward children.

Why are the policy recommendations in this book more modest than Haveman proposes? Clues can be found in the chapters by Burtless and by Haveman. Burtless points out that many social programs have been very successful in meeting their limited goals, but, as Haveman states: "There also exist certain additional untested policy strategies—perhaps bolder and more draconian—that might change the way people behave, aspire, and attain." Most of the proposals for policy changes in this volume build on the success of existing programs or demonstration projects. If these suggestions were to be adopted, the resulting increased antipoverty effort would permit the United States to remedy some of the weaknesses revealed in its experience with antipoverty policy to date. In addition, many of the proposals suggested by Haveman could form the basis for a renewed research, demonstration, and experimentation agenda for the rest of the 1990s. After more careful research and evaluation of those suggestions, we will have the kind of evidence necessary to frame these more ambitious proposals.

.   .   .

We conclude by returning to the introduction to the 1977 volume. As he looked forward, Robert Haveman concluded: "If one were inclined to speculate, . . . it would not be unreasonable to forecast that, in 1985, analysts will attribute a modest reduction in income inequality during the 1975–1985 decade to some combination of (1) an overhauled and somewhat larger income support system, (2) a reformed federal revenue system resulting in increased effective tax rates on higher income recipients, (3) a significantly expanded public employment policy, and (4) a modest reduction of labor market rigidities, including a reduction in labor market discrimination against racial minorities" (p. 19).

All four of Haveman's expected policy changes were reversed in the 1980s. The income support system is now somewhat smaller in scope than in the late 1970s, effective tax rates on the wealthy are lower, most public service employment programs were eliminated in the early 1980s, and much recent attention has been focused on continuing labor market discrimination. Our own forecasts in this volume are more cautious and reflect the political and economic uncertainties discussed by the contributors. If we are correct in our prediction that the mid-1990s will see the enactment of a "realistic" antipoverty agenda that reflects many of the policies suggested in this volume, however, then Haveman's forecast for 1985 will not be a bad one for the year 2000.

The Historical Record: Trends in Family Income, Inequality, and Poverty

SHELDON H. DANZIGER AND DANIEL H. WEINBERG

Poverty in America in the early 1990s remains relatively high. It is high relative to what it was in the early 1970s; it is high relative to what analysts expected, given the economic recovery of the 1980s (for example, Blank and Blinder, 1986); it is high relative to what it is in other countries that have similar standards of living (Smeeding, 1992). The poverty rates for some demographic groups—minorities, elderly widows, children living in mother-only families—are about as high today as was the poverty rate for all Americans in 1949. This lack of progress over the past two decades—the fact that poverty in 1993 was higher than it was in 1973—represents an American anomaly. For the first time in recent history, a generation of children has a higher poverty rate than the preceding generation, and a generation of adults has experienced only a modest increase in its standard of living.

In addition, earnings inequality and income inequality increased during the 1980s. The gap between the earnings of less-skilled workers and college graduates widened dramatically, as did the gaps between the family incomes of the poor and the rich and of the middle class and the rich. What are the long-run trends in the level of family income, income inequality, and poverty? What is their sensitivity to economic, demographic, and public policy changes? As we shall see, economic growth was very beneficial to the poor and the middle class during the long period of rapidly rising incomes that extended from the end of World War II until the recession and inflation induced by the 1973 oil price shock. Similarly, the antipoverty effects of government income transfers grew rapidly until the early 1970s, as new programs were introduced and spending on existing programs expanded rapidly as well (see Chapter 3). As a result of this economic growth and rising government spending, the official poverty rate was cut in half between the late 1940s and the early 1960s and in half again by the early 1970s.

Since that time, however, economic growth has been anemic, failing to "trickle down" to the poor, and the antipoverty impact of transfers has been eroded by inflation and legislative reductions in the generosity of public programs. A smaller proportion of the pretransfer poor are now removed from poverty by government income transfers than was the case in the early 1970s. At the same time that these economic and income transfer trends have lifted a smaller fraction of the poor out of poverty, demographic changes, especially the trend toward single-parent families, have contributed to rising poverty rates.

In this chapter we pay particular attention to the very slow decline in poverty and the large increase in income inequality during the 1980s. The economic recovery that began in November 1982 and ended in July 1990 followed a decade of "stagflation"—high unemployment and high inflation rates. During that period, median family income fell and inequality and poverty increased. The recovery of the 1980s ended this stagnant period, and real median family income grew gradually, so that by 1990 it was slightly above its 1973 level. Among the poor and less-educated workers, however, the effects of the recovery were quite modest.

If the incomes of all American families had grown at the same moderate rate as did the median, poverty in 1992 would have been somewhat below the 1973 rate. If the poverty rate in 1992 were at its 1973 level, there would be 8.7 million fewer poor Americans—28.2 million, not 36.9 million. Furthermore, poverty rates have ratcheted upward across the business cycle since the 1973–1975 recession. That is, poverty rates rose more during recessions than they fell during the ensuing recoveries. And in the early 1990s, poverty again increased because of recession.

Whereas the income gains in previous recoveries had been widely shared across demographic groups, those of the recovery of the 1980s were highly concentrated among the most advantaged. Groups with below-average incomes and relatively high poverty rates benefited the least. The young gained less than the old; less-educated workers gained less than more-educated workers; single-parent families with children gained less than two-parent families; minorities gained less than whites.

The failure of poverty to fall back to levels achieved almost two decades ago, despite increased average income, and the dramatic divergence in the experiences of the "haves" and "have-nots" have stimulated debate about the economic polarization of America and potential remedies for the high poverty rates. The design of more effective antipoverty programs and policies is the focus of Chapters 7–13. Our primary task is to explain why income poverty remains so high and has fallen so little in recent years. Robert Lampman (1971), writing over two decades ago, expected that the elimination of poverty under its official definition would have been achieved by 1980. Yet given the experience of the recent past, we do not expect this goal to be achieved anytime soon if current economic, demographic, and public policy trends persist.

Trends in the Level and Distribution of Family Income

Data on median and mean family income, several measures of income inequality, and poverty are gathered by the annual March supplement to the Current Population Survey (CPS) and published each year by the U.S. Bureau of the Census in its Current Population Reports, Consumer Income, series P-60.[1,2] Family income is defined by summing money income from all sources during the previous calendar year over all family members residing in the household in March. Money income includes wages and salaries, self-employment income, property income (for example, interest, dividends, and net rental income), cash benefits received from government income maintenance programs (such as Social Security, unemployment compensation, and public assistance), and other cash receipts (for example, private pensions, alimony). Current money income does not include capital gains, imputed rents, government or private benefits provided in-kind (such as food stamps, Medicare benefits, employer-provided health insurance) nor does it subtract taxes paid, although all of these affect a family's ability to consume.

Time-series data on a more comprehensive income concept—money income plus noncash transfers less direct federal taxes paid—have recently become available (reported, for example, in U.S. House of Representatives [1992], and U.S. Bureau of the Census [1992c]), but only for the years since 1979.[3] We analyze this more comprehensive income measure in our discussion of the trend in poverty.

Trends in Median and Mean Income

Columns 1 and 2 of Table 2.1 and Figure 2.1 show the trend in median and mean family income for each year from 1947 through 1992. Incomes in the table are expressed in constant 1990 dollars, adjusted for inflation using the price index for urban consumers (CPI-U) from 1947 to 1966, and the CPI-U-X1 from 1967 to 1992.[4]

Median family income is the most common measure of the standard of living. It reveals how the "typical" American family is faring, because half of all families have lower and half have higher incomes than the median. As a measure of central tendency, the median is less affected by changes in the upper or lower ends of the distribution than is the mean. As long as income growth is relatively constant throughout the entire range of incomes, as it was for the three decades following World War II, then trends in the median and mean family income will be similar. But if, as was the case in the 1980s, the incomes of the poorest families are growing less than is the income of the average family, and the incomes of the rich are growing much more rapidly, then the mean will increase more rapidly than the median.

Median and mean family income grew almost continuously from 1949 through

1973. The median increased by 43 percent between 1949 and 1959 and by another 40 percent between 1959 and 1969. The mean increased a little less in the first decade, 37 percent, and by about the same amount in the next, 42 percent. Both median and mean family income doubled between 1949 and 1973.

The post–World War II boom was so robust that its continuation was taken for granted when the War on Poverty was declared. In its *Economic Report of the President, 1967*, the Council of Economic Advisers noted that "the United States is the first large nation in the history of the world wealthy enough to end poverty within its borders" (p. 16). Conventional wisdom held not only that the United States was much richer than it had been two decades earlier but also that it was much richer than any other country.

Neither of these statements holds true today. The oil shock of 1973 brought an end to this remarkable quarter-century of rising living standards and to the optimistic view that American incomes would continue to grow and would always exceed those of other countries. The economic history of the country since 1973 differs markedly. Even a casual inspection of Figure 2.1 reveals that income growth subsequently became erratic.

The recession that began in November 1973, lasting sixteen months, was the longest and steepest since the late 1930s,[5] and income gains during the subsequent recovery (March 1975–January 1980) were modest. The economy again slid into recession at the beginning of 1980. Although this downturn lasted only six months, the one-year recovery that succeeded it was followed by a severe sixteen-month recession. By its end in November 1982, median family income was 7.4 percent below its 1979 value and 4 percent below its 1973 value. Starting from this low base, the economy entered a recovery that continued until July 1990. Family income growth in this period was relatively rapid, though not nearly as rapid as during the recovery of the 1960s. And because of the recent recession, the median fell by 4.9 percent between 1989 and 1992. The net result is that the 1970s and 1980s brought almost no increase in average living standards—median family income in 1992 was just 2.8 percent above the 1973 level.[6] All families, however, did not experience the same change in living standards.

Trends in Income Inequality

We use two measures of inequality to describe trends over the 1947–1992 period. The first measure is the share of income received by each of the five income quintiles (arrived at by ranking families according to income, from poorest to richest, and then dividing them into five groups, each containing 20 percent of all families). The total income received by each fifth is expressed as a percentage of total family income.[7] For example, in 1992 the poorest fifth of families received

Table 2.1 The level and distribution of family income, 1947–1992 (1990 dollars[a])

Year	Median income	Mean income	Percentage distribution of aggregate income						Gini coefficient[b]
			Lowest fifth	Second fifth	Third fifth	Fourth fifth	Highest fifth	Top 5 percent	
1947	$16,345	$19,123	5.0	11.9	17.0	23.1	43.0	17.5	.376
1948	$15,903	$18,318	4.9	12.1	17.3	23.2	42.4	17.1	.371
1949	$15,699	$18,034	4.5	11.9	17.3	23.5	42.7	16.9	.378
1950	$16,562	$19,037	4.5	12.0	17.4	23.4	42.7	17.3	.379
1951	$17,155	$19,399	5.0	12.4	17.6	23.4	41.6	16.8	.363
1952	$17,653	$20,226	4.9	12.3	17.4	23.4	41.9	17.4	.368
1953	$19,106	$21,196	4.7	12.5	18.0	23.9	40.9	15.7	.359
1954	$18,629	$20,940	4.5	12.1	17.7	23.9	41.8	16.3	.371
1955	$19,825	$22,266	4.8	12.3	17.8	23.7	41.3	16.4	.363
1956	$21,134	$23,614	5.0	12.5	17.9	23.7	41.0	16.1	.358
1957	$21,253	$23,294	5.1	12.7	18.1	23.8	40.4	15.6	.351
1958	$21,168	$23,157	5.0	12.5	18.0	23.9	40.6	15.4	.354
1959	$22,386	$24,696	4.9	12.3	17.9	23.8	41.1	15.9	.361
1960	$22,833	$25,299	4.8	12.2	17.8	24.0	41.3	15.9	.364
1961	$23,066	$26,026	4.7	11.9	17.5	23.8	42.2	16.6	.374
1962	$23,717	$26,560	5.0	12.1	17.6	24.0	41.3	15.7	.362
1963	$24,559	$27,502	5.0	12.1	17.7	24.0	41.2	15.8	.362
1964	$25,483	$28,459	5.1	12.0	17.7	24.0	41.2	15.9	.361
1965	$26,560	$29,412	5.2	12.2	17.8	23.9	40.9	15.5	.356
1966	$27,956	$31,160	5.6	12.4	17.8	23.8	40.5	15.6	.349
1967	$28,563	$31,688	5.5	12.4	17.9	23.9	40.4	15.2	.348
1968	$29,926	$33,524	5.6	12.4	17.7	23.7	40.5	15.6	.348
1969	$31,292	$35,087	5.6	12.4	17.7	23.7	40.6	15.6	.349
1970	$31,226	$35,147	5.4	12.2	17.6	23.8	40.9	15.6	.353
1971	$31,189	$35,125	5.5	12.0	17.6	23.8	41.1	15.7	.355

4.4 percent of the total; the share of the richest fifth was 44.6 percent (Table 2.1). Note also that the income share of the richest 5 percent of all families in that year, 17.6 percent, exceeded that of the bottom 40 percent of families, 14.9 percent. According to this measure, the average income of a family in the highest quintile was ten times as large as the average income of a family in the poorest fifth.

The quintile shares in Table 2.1 demonstrate the stability of the income distribution in the two decades following World War II, when rapid growth in living standards formed a "rising tide that lifted all boats." Families at the bottom of the distribution gained even more than those at the top. The share of the bottom quintile increased from 4.5 to 5.5 percent between 1949 and 1973, that of the top

Table 2.1   (continued)

Year	Median income	Mean income	Percentage distribution of aggregate income						Gini coefficient[b]
			Lowest fifth	Second fifth	Third fifth	Fourth fifth	Highest fifth	Top 5 percent	
1972	$32,722	$37,164	5.4	11.9	17.5	23.9	41.4	15.9	.359
1973	$33,370	$37,720	5.5	11.9	17.5	24.0	41.1	15.5	.356
1974	$32,491	$37,047	5.5	12.0	17.5	24.0	41.0	15.5	.355
1975	$31,905	$36,154	5.4	11.8	17.6	24.1	41.1	15.5	.357
1976	$32,913	$37,120	5.4	11.8	17.6	24.1	41.1	15.6	.358
1977	$33,107	$37,771	5.2	11.6	17.5	24.2	41.5	15.7	.363
1978	$34,156	$38,902	5.2	11.6	17.5	24.1	41.5	15.6	.363
1979	$34,595	$39,415	5.2	11.6	17.5	24.1	41.7	15.8	.365
1980	$33,386	$38,073	5.1	11.6	17.5	24.3	41.6	15.3	.365
1981	$32,476	$37,481	5.0	11.3	17.4	24.4	41.9	15.4	.369
1982	$32,037	$37,448	4.7	11.2	17.1	24.3	42.7	16.0	.380
1983	$32,378	$37,819	4.7	11.1	17.1	24.3	42.8	15.9	.382
1984	$33,251	$39,062	4.7	11.0	17.0	24.4	42.9	16.0	.383
1985	$33,689	$40,017	4.6	10.9	16.9	24.2	43.5	16.7	.389
1986	$35,129	$41,648	4.6	10.8	16.8	24.0	43.7	17.0	.392
1987	$35,632	$42,436	4.6	10.7	16.8	24.0	43.8	17.2	.393
1988	$35,565	$42,655	4.6	10.7	16.7	24.0	44.0	17.2	.395
1989	$36,062	$43,749	4.6	10.6	16.5	23.7	44.6	17.9	.401
1990	$35,353	$42,652	4.6	10.8	16.6	23.8	44.3	17.4	.396
1991	$34,488	$41,491	4.5	10.7	16.6	24.1	44.2	17.1	.397
1992	$34,293	$41,439	4.4	10.5	16.5	24.0	44.6	17.6	.403

Source: U.S. Bureau of the Census, Current Population Reports, series P-60, various issues.

a. Inflation measured by the CPI-U (price index for urban consumers) from 1947 to 1967, and by the CPI-U-X1 (an experimental price index) from 1968 to 1982.

b. A measure of inequality: zero represents perfect equality; 1.000 represents total inequality.

quintile fell from 42.7 to 41.1 percent, and those of the three middle quintiles were mostly unchanged.

The origins of today's very large gap between those at the top and those at the bottom of the income distribution can be found in the late 1960s. The income share of the bottom quintile reached its postwar maximum, 5.6 percent, in the years between 1966 and 1969, years during which the share of the top quintile was at its minimum, 40.5 percent. Since 1969, the shares of the bottom three quintiles have dropped and that of the richest quintile has reached a post–World War II high. For example, between 1969 and 1992, the income share of the poorest quintile fell from 5.6 to 4.4 percent. In 1992, the average income of the poorest

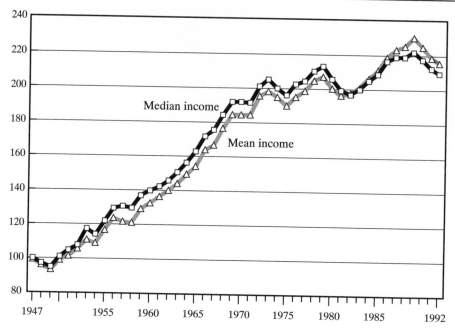

Figure 2.1 Median and mean family income, 1947–1992. (Data source: U.S. Bureau of the Census, Current Population Reports, series P-60, various issues.)

fifth of families was $9,708. If inequality had not increased after 1969 and they had received the same income share as in that year, 5.6 percent, their mean income in 1992 would have been $12,355, or 27 percent higher. Likewise, the income share of the richest fifth of families in 1992 was 44.6 percent and averaged $99,252. If their share had been at 40.6 percent, as in 1969, their average income would have been $90,350, 9 percent lower.

Those in the middle of the income distribution as well as those at the bottom have fared relatively poorly over the past two decades. The income shares of the second and third quintiles were lower in the last few years than in any other year in the post–World War II period. The income share of the second quintile, which was at least 11.9 percent in every year from 1949 to 1973, fell from 12.4 percent in 1969 to 10.5 percent in 1992. Similarly, the share of the third quintile fell from 17.7 percent in 1969 to 16.5 percent in 1992.

Most of the increase in the share of the richest quintile occurred after 1981, whereas the declines in the shares of the other quintiles were spread out over the two decades.[8] The gains of the highest quintile are even larger than those shown in Table 2.1, however, because the CPS data do not subtract taxes from income. Edward Gramlich, Richard Kasten, and Frank Sammartino (1993) have constructed a post-tax distribution of income for the 1980s. In any year, federal income and payroll taxes paid are slightly progressive—they raise quintile shares at the bottom and lower them at the top. The tax cuts of 1981, however, were very beneficial to the highest-income families. As a result, post-tax income inequality increased even more over the 1980s than did pretax inequality.[9]

The second measure of inequality presented in Table 2.1 is the Gini coefficient, which is affected by changes at all locations in the distribution of income and can be represented with a single number. If a family with income above the mean receives $1 less (more) and a family with income below the mean receives an extra $1 ($1 less), then the Gini will fall (increase). Although the Gini coefficient does not have a simple interpretation, it is a widely used summary measure of inequality. The closer it is to 1.000, the more highly are incomes concentrated among a smaller number of income recipients; the closer it is to zero, the more evenly are incomes distributed across families.[10]

The Gini coefficient of family income for 1947–1992 follows a pattern similar to that shown by the quintile shares. The Gini coefficient fell from the late 1940s to the late 1960s, with most of the decline in inequality occurring during the economic recovery of the 1960s. Since then, the Gini has moved up during recoveries as well as recessions. By 1982, inequality had increased to a level greater than that in any year back to 1947. Continuing to increase, the Gini coefficient reached its most unequal level of the forty years, .403, in 1992. The two decades following 1973 are thus very different from the prior two decades in terms of both increased inequality and very slow growth in average living standards.[11]

Most of the net increase in inequality over the past two decades was concentrated in the 1980s. This decade stands out as a historical anomaly, a period of rising family incomes and rising inequality. Part of this increase can be attributed to the two recessions of the early 1980s. Inequality usually increases during recessions, as the lowest-income families typically suffer the largest percentage declines in income. Inequality has historically declined during recoveries, however. It is the continued sharp increase in the Gini coefficient during the 1980s recovery, from .380 in 1982 to .401 in 1989, and the increase in the share of the richest 5 percent of families, from 16.0 to 17.9 percent, that ran counter to previous expectations.[12] This pattern plays a central role in explaining the high current poverty rate.

Trends in Poverty

The Official Poverty Rate

The federal government adopted an official definition of poverty after the declaration of the War on Poverty. The Census Bureau now publishes poverty rates for numerous demographic groups for the years since 1959. Scholarly studies over the past two decades have examined the suitability of the official poverty lines

Table 2.2   Alternative measures of the trend in poverty, 1959–1992

Year	Percentage poor under official measure (1)	Adding noncash income and subtracting taxes (2)	Official measure, using alternative adjustment for inflation (3)	Cumulative effect of columns 2 and 3 (4)	Pretransfer poverty (5)	Prewelfare poverty (6)
1959	22.4%	—	—	—	—	—
1960	22.2	—	—	—	—	—
1961	21.9	—	—	—	—	—
1962	21.0	—	—	—	—	—
1963	19.5	—	—	—	—	—
1964	19.0	—	—	—	—	—
1965	17.3	—	—	—	—	—
1966	14.7	—	—	—	—	—
1967	14.2	—	14.2%	—	19.4%	15.0%
1968	12.8	—	12.8	—	18.2	13.6
1969	12.1	—	11.9	—	17.7	13.3
1970	12.6	—	12.2	—	18.8	13.9
1971	12.5	—	12.1	—	19.6	13.8
1972	11.9	—	11.4	—	19.2	13.1
1973	11.1	—	10.7	—	19.0	12.4
1974	11.2	—	10.5	—	20.3	13.1
1975	12.3	—	11.5	—	22.0	13.7
1976	11.8	—	11.0	—	21.0	13.1
1977	11.6	—	10.7	—	21.0	13.0
1978	11.4	—	10.4	—	20.2	12.6
1979	11.7	8.9%	10.5	7.9%	20.5	12.9

and income concept. The most recent, by Patricia Ruggles (1990), concludes that the official poverty lines are too low because they are based on outdated consumption standards.[13] An opposing view (O'Neill, 1992) holds that official poverty rates are too high because the income concept used in computation—money income—excludes noncash income maintenance transfers, such as food stamps, Medicare, and other benefits that have increased in relative importance over the past three decades. Despite such controversies, the official measure is an important social indicator that has been used in most research studies since the late 1960s.

The federal government's official poverty measure, shown in column 1 of Table 2.2, compares a family's or an individual's money income during a calendar year with one among a set of income thresholds. If a family's total reported in-

Table 2.2   (continued)

Year	Percentage poor under official measure (1)	Adding noncash income and subtracting taxes (2)	Official measure, using alternative adjustment for inflation (3)	Cumulative effect of columns 2 and 3 (4)	Pretransfer poverty (5)	Prewelfare poverty (6)
1980	13.0	10.1	11.5	8.6	21.9	14.2
1981	14.0	11.5	12.2	9.8	23.1	15.1
1982	15.0	12.3	13.2	10.6	24.0	15.9
1983	15.2	12.7	13.7	11.0	24.2	16.1
1984	14.4	12.0	12.8	10.4	22.9	15.3
1985	14.0	11.7	12.5	10.1	22.4	14.9
1986	13.6	11.3	12.2	9.8	22.0	14.5
1987	13.4	11.0	12.0	9.5	21.8	14.3
1988	13.0	10.8	11.7	9.5	21.2	13.9
1989	12.8	10.4	11.4	8.9	20.9	13.8
1990	13.5	10.9	12.1	9.5	21.5	14.5
1991	14.2	11.4	12.7	9.9	22.9	15.2
1992	14.5	11.7	13.1	10.3	23.6	15.6

Source: U.S. Bureau of the Census, Current Population Reports, series P-60, for columns (1)–(4); authors' tabulations for columns (5) and (6).

Note: Column (2) counts government cash and noncash transfers, realized capital gains, and employer-provided health insurance as income and subtracts federal and state income taxes and payroll taxes from income; column (3) uses the experimental Consumer Price Index (CPI-X1) to adjust the poverty thresholds; column (4) combines the effects of columns (2) and (3); column (5) counts as income all private market cash income except government pensions, which are treated, like social security, as a government cash transfer; and column (6) adds cash social insurance payments and government pensions, but not public assistance (welfare) payments, to private market income.

come during the previous calendar year falls below this threshold, then all persons in the family are classified as poor. These cutoffs are adjusted for household size, the age of the head of the household, and the number of children under age 18.[14]

The cutoffs provide an "absolute" measure of poverty that specifies in dollar terms the income necessary to provide minimally decent levels of consumption. For 1992, the lines ranged from $6,729 for a single person over the age of sixty-four to $28,745 for a family of nine or more persons. The average threshold for a family of four was $14,335. The equivalence scales implicit in the poverty line were originally developed by Mollie Orshansky (1965) from information on dietary intake. As such, they reflect economies of scale in food consumption, not economies of scale measured over all consumer goods.[15]

The official poverty cutoffs are updated yearly by an amount corresponding to the change in the consumer price index, so that they represent the same purchasing power each year. This means that the poverty line for a family of four, $14,335 in 1992, should buy the same market basket of consumption goods as the comparable line, $2,973, in 1959: the difference is supposed to reflect increases in prices and not a rising standard of living. The Census Bureau also publishes an unofficial poverty series that uses the CPI-U-X1 from 1967 on to adjust poverty thresholds, rather than from 1983 on, as in the official CPI series (see column 3, Table 2.2). The poverty line for a family of four in 1992 according to this measure was $13,190.

The use of an absolute poverty line (one that is adjusted only for inflation and that does not change as real income changes) means that the poverty line falls further behind the average living standard during periods of economic growth. In contrast, a "relative" poverty measure is defined in some fixed relationship to the standard of living, for example, 50 percent of the median. In 1959, a nonfarm family of four at the poverty line had an income that was 55 percent as large as the median family income. Because real median family income grew over the next fifteen years, by 1973 this ratio had fallen to 38 percent. Because income growth has been so slow over the past two decades, this ratio was about the same in 1992 as in 1973. Thus, if the official poverty concept were a relative one instead, the current poverty line, and hence the poverty rate, would be substantially higher (see Danziger, Haveman, and Plotnick [1986] for a discussion of the trend in a "relative" poverty measure).[16]

Table 2.2 and Figure 2.2 present the percentage of all persons who were poor according to the official poverty definition from 1959 to 1992 (column 1) and according to several alternative definitions, available for a shorter time span. The poverty rate in 1959 (before the official thresholds were established) was 22.4 percent, and by 1964, when the War on Poverty was declared, it had fallen to 19.0 percent. It declined quickly during the remainder of the 1960s as the economy expanded, then fell more slowly in the early 1970s to a low of 11.1 percent in 1973, and stayed below 12 percent for the balance of the 1970s.[17] The poverty rate rose to its 1983 peak, 15.2 percent, because of the inflation and recessions of the late 1970s and early 1980s. Then it declined to 12.8 percent in 1989 as the economy expanded and rose to 14.5 percent in 1992 as the economy experienced a brief recession and the unemployment rate remained above 7 percent.

This simple relationship between the poverty rate and the state of the economy reveals only part of the story. Economic growth matters, but growth matters less to the trend in poverty now than in the past (Gottschalk and Danziger, 1985; Blank, 1991), because the poverty rate reflects changes not only in average living standards but also in the shape of income distribution. The trend in poverty mirrors the trend in median family income only when inequality is relatively constant.

% poor

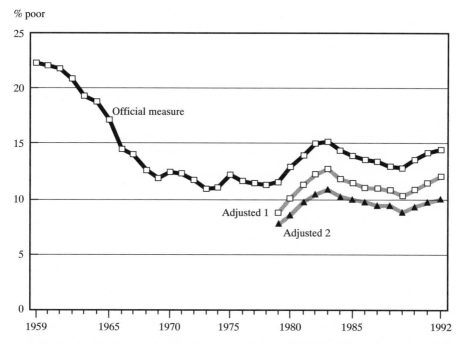

Figure 2.2 Poverty rates under alternative measures, 1959–1992. The top line shows the poverty rate under the official measure; the middle line, the rate as adjusted for noncash income and federal taxes; the bottom line, the rate as adjusted for noncash income, federal taxes, and an alternative inflation adjustment. (For data source, see Figure 2.1.)

If inequality had been constant, then all families would have experienced the same rate of income growth during each of these periods: poverty would have declined rapidly prior to 1973, stagnated during the 1970s, and risen during the 1982 recession. The trend in poverty did follow this pattern. The relationship between economic growth and the poverty rate changed, however, during the 1980s. Counter to the expectations of most researchers (for example, Blank and Blinder, 1986), inequality rose and, as a result, the poverty rate declined only a modest amount (see Cutler and Katz, 1991; Danziger and Gottschalk, 1993). The 1989 official poverty rate was 1.1 percentage points higher than in 1979, the previous cyclical peak, and 1.7 points higher than in 1973. The official poverty rate was the same in 1989 as in 1968.

This poverty rate is particularly high relative to the poverty rate in other industrialized countries. Timothy Smeeding (1992) has gathered similar data sets from a number of countries and estimated poverty rates on a consistent basis. In the mid-1980s, he finds a U.S. poverty rate of around 13 percent, rates of about 7 percent in Canada and Australia, 5 percent in France and the United Kingdom, and 4 percent or less in Sweden, Germany and the Netherlands (see Table 3.3).

We will show that, in addition to slow economic growth and rising inequality, demographic and public policy changes have also kept the official poverty rate from falling below the levels of the early 1970s. Before we do so, we examine several alternative time series that measure the severity of poverty, incorporate an alternative adjustment for inflation, and account for the receipt of in-kind income and the payment of taxes. This review allows us to demonstrate that the trend in the official rate is not an artifact of measurement issues.

Adjustments to the Official Poverty Measure

The official poverty rate does not reflect the value of in-kind benefits such as food stamps, Medicare, or public housing. When the official poverty definition was developed, the poor received few noncash transfers, so the official measure's comparison of cash income to the poverty line provided a fairly accurate picture of a family's situation. Noncash transfers have increased rapidly in recent years, however. The official measure also fails to account for taxes paid. Taxes paid by the poor, especially payroll taxes, have also increased in recent years.

The U.S. Bureau of the Census (1992c, 1993) has published poverty rates for the 1979–1992 period that are adjusted to include the value of public in-kind transfers received and state and federal income and payroll taxes paid. Since in-kind income increases command over resources, its exclusion upwardly biases the official poverty rate. Similarly, the failure to deduct income and payroll taxes leads to a downward bias. Because the poor receive substantially more in noncash benefits than they pay in income and payroll taxes, the net effect of including both is to lower the poverty rate.

Column 2 of Table 2.2 and Figure 2.2 show the Census series for the poverty rate adjusted to reflect noncash benefits and taxes.[18] According to these adjusted data, 11.7 percent of all persons, 29.7 million, were poor in 1992. This is 2.8 percentage points, or about 7.1 million people, below the official rate of 14.5 percent (36.9 million people).

There is controversy over many of the methods used by the Census Bureau to value noncash benefits, but the biggest controversy concerns medical transfers. The valuation of medical benefits is particularly difficult, because high payments for an ill person do not raise her above the poverty line (although they clearly make her better off). Even if the value of an equivalent insurance policy is calculated, these benefits (high in market value due to the large medical costs of the fraction who do get sick) cannot be used by the recipients to meet other needs of daily living. The Census Bureau has therefore developed a method, termed *fungible value,* that adjusts the value of benefits for those with low incomes.[19] Of the

7.2 million people moved out of poverty by the inclusion of noncash transfers, more than 3 million are removed through the valuation of Medicare and Medicaid (see U.S. House of Representatives [1992] for an alternative adjusted poverty series that does not value medical transfers).[20]

The official poverty series and the series that adjusts for the receipt of noncash transfers and the payment of taxes show very similar patterns over the 1979–1992 period (see Figure 2.2). Poverty in each series rises from 1979 to a post-recessionary high in 1983 and then falls gradually through 1989, the last business cycle peak. In each series, the 1989 rate was higher than the rate during the last business cycle peak, in 1979. Both rates also rose from 1989 to 1992.

Column 3 in Table 2.2 presents a measure of poverty for the 1967–1992 period that indexes the poverty threshold by the alternative inflation index CPI-U-X1 rather than by the CPI-U. The official and the CPI-U-X1 rates start out at the same level in 1967 and then diverge, because the CPI-U rose more rapidly than the CPI-U-X1. By 1992 the CPI-U-X1 poverty rate, 13.1 percent, was 1.4 percentage points lower than the official rate. An even lower poverty rate can be derived by combining the adjustments shown separately in columns 2 and 3—that is, using the CPI-U-X1 poverty line instead of the official line (for example, for a family of four, $13,190 instead of $14,335) and including the value of noncash transfers. This is shown in column 4 in Table 2.2 and in Figure 2.2. The resulting poverty rate for 1992 is 10.3 percent, a rate still higher than the 1979 rate for this measure, 7.9 percent.

The adjustments reflected in columns 2–4 of Table 2.2 lower the official poverty rate by reducing the poverty threshold and including in-kind transfers. In addition, the level and receipt of certain income sources is underreported to the Census Bureau. To the extent that the poor underreport their incomes, the official poverty rate is overstated.

There are several alternative adjustments that would raise the poverty rate. The official poverty counts do not include homeless individuals or persons living in institutions, such as jails, prisons, nursing homes, and mental hospitals. Both the homeless and the incarcerated populations increased during the 1980s (U.S. Bureau of the Census, 1991d). Although estimates of the number of homeless are imprecise, Martha Burt (1992) suggests that there were roughly half a million in the late 1980s. The number of persons in jails and prisons increased by about half a million during the 1980s, as well. Including an additional one million persons would raise the increase in poverty over the 1979–1989 period in any series shown in Table 2.2 by about 0.4 percentage points.[21] Other changes that could increase the poverty rate include reestimation of the minimum market basket or other revisions of the poverty line or a change in equivalence scales for the elderly (Ruggles, 1990).

The Severity of Poverty

The official measure of poverty counts a person as poor or not poor without regard to the severity of poverty. Yet a poor person with very little income is clearly worse off than one whose income is just a few dollars below the poverty line. One way to examine the severity of poverty is presented in Figure 2.3, which indicates trends from the 1975–1992 period in the percentage of the population below 50 percent of the official poverty threshold, the official poverty rate, and the percentage below 125 percent. For example, in 1992, the official poverty rate was 14.5 percent, with 5.9 percent of persons having incomes below half the poverty line and with 19.4 percent below 125 percent of the poverty line. The trends in all three series are very similar. The trends in the official series and that showing the "125 percent of the poverty line" standard move up and down with the business cycle. During the 1975–1992 period, each reached a low in 1978 and a high in 1983, fell somewhat by 1989 and rose in 1991 and 1992.

The proportion of "extremely poor"—those having incomes less than half the official poverty thresholds—is somewhat less responsive to economic conditions.

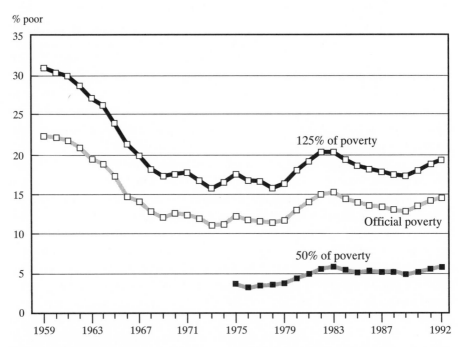

Figure 2.3 The trend in poverty under alternative thresholds, 1959–1992. (For data source, see Figure 2.1.)

There is no change in the proportion of extremely poor between 1975 and 1979; the percentage rises sharply during the 1979–1983 period, falls only slowly by 1989, and rises back to the 1982 level in 1991.

Another way to measure the severity of poverty is shown in Figure 2.4, which presents the trend in the income deficit (poverty gap) in constant 1990 dollars. The income deficit is the difference between a family's (or individual's) money income and its own poverty threshold. The deficit provides a means of determining whether the poor are getting poorer. This deficit per poor person fluctuated over a narrow band between 1959 and 1977 ($1,430 in 1959, falling to a low of $1,318 in 1966, and returning to $1,459 in 1977). The mean deficit increased by about 20 percent, to $1,751, in 1982, before peaking at $1,826 in 1987, 25 percent above the 1977 figure.

The severity of poverty is greater today than at any point since the late 1950s. Most of the increased severity occurred between 1977 and 1982, a period of high inflation and two recessions (see Littman, 1989), when the poor got poorer. More surprising is that the long economic recovery of the 1980s did not reduce the

Figure 2.4 The income deficit per poor person, 1959–1992 (1990 dollars). (For data source, see Figure 2.1.)

severity of poverty. The median poor family in 1992 had a poverty deficit of $5,073. The aggregate poverty deficit (summed over all poor persons) was about $71.5 billion (in 1992 dollars).

Trends Overall and among Specific Groups

The data reviewed thus far suggest that the trend in poverty can be broken down into several distinct periods. Prior to 1973, family income grew rapidly, income inequality declined modestly, and poverty declined dramatically. The period between 1973 and 1979 is characterized by stagnation in mean income and modest cyclical changes in poverty. The rapid rise in poverty between 1979 and 1983 is due to back-to-back recessions and falling average incomes. It is the post-1983 period that is an anomaly. During this period mean income grew, but so did inequality. These two forces were counteracting: by itself, the rising mean should have led to a historically low poverty rate; it was the rise in inequality that kept the poverty rate not only from reaching new lows but actually above the 1973 level. This aggregate story, however, does not fit the experience of all demographic groups. Children, for example, have fared worse than average and the elderly have fared better than average over the past two decades.

Poverty rates vary widely by race and ethnicity, by age, and by gender. In any year, non-Hispanic whites have lower poverty rates than blacks, Hispanics, and other minorities; prime-age adults have lower poverty rates than children and the elderly; men have lower poverty rates than women; and married-couple families have lower poverty rates than female-headed families.

All of these demographic disparities in poverty rates, with one major exception, have persisted over the past fifty years.[22] The major exception is that until 1973 the poverty rate for the elderly was substantially higher than the rate for children; since 1973 it has been lower, and it is now substantially lower.

Column 1 of Table 2.3 presents the official 1990 poverty rates for persons classified into twelve mutually exclusive groups by race and ethnicity—white non-Hispanics, black non-Hispanics, Hispanics, and persons of other races—and by their age—children, nonelderly adults, and the elderly.[23] Columns 2 and 3 disaggregate these groups further according to whether they live in a household headed by a man or by a woman with no spouse present. The data suggest that caution should be used in making generalized statements about children or the elderly, as there is great variation within these age groups by race/ethnicity and the marital status of the household head.

Holding marital status and race/ethnicity constant, the elderly have lower poverty rates than do children. Poverty rates vary to a greater extent by race/ethnicity and by marital status, however, than they do by age. For example, the poverty rate

Table 2.3 Percentage of persons in poverty within selected demographic groups, 1990

	All persons (1)	Persons living in households headed by	
		Men (2)	Women, no spouse present (3)
White non-Hispanic			
Children	12.4%	7.2%	41.2%
Nonelderly adults	7.3	5.1	19.0
Elderly	9.5	4.5	19.9
Black non-Hispanic			
Children	44.4	19.4	65.0
Nonelderly adults	24.2	14.7	38.4
Elderly	33.4	24.7	44.9
Hispanic			
Children	35.1	24.6	68.7
Nonelderly adults	21.3	16.8	40.6
Elderly	21.0	14.9	35.4
Other Races			
Children	22.3	16.3	51.4
Nonelderly adults	12.0	9.4	24.7
Elderly	14.8	13.0	19.1
Total	13.5%	8.1%	33.1%

Source: Computations by authors from March 1991 Current Population Survey, U.S. Bureau of the Census.

Note: Persons living in households headed by males, no spouse present, and persons living in married-couple families are included in column 2. Persons under the age of 18 are classified as children; those over 64, as elderly; and those 18–64, as nonelderly adults.

for elderly white non-Hispanics who live in households headed by males, 4.5 percent, is less than that of similar white children, 7.2 percent. But the rate for these white children is much lower than the poverty rate for persons living in households headed by elderly women—19.9 percent for whites, 44.9 percent for blacks, and 35.4 percent for Hispanics—and about half the rate for the minority elderly who live in married-couple households. At the same time, the poverty rate for white children living in female-headed families, 41.2 percent, is much higher than the rate for minority children living in married-couple families.

The differences in poverty rates shown in Table 2.3 can be traced to differences in income sources. The well-being of children and nonelderly adults is primarily determined by real wage rates and unemployment rates; the well-being of the elderly has become increasingly dependent on inflation-adjusted government benefits that are unaffected by the business cycle. Minorities fare less well than white non-Hispanics because of the lower wage rates and higher unemployment rates that minorities experience. Female-headed families fare more poorly than married-couple families because women earn less than men, because these families have fewer adult wage earners, and because their government benefits, which are not adjusted for inflation, have declined in real terms in the last two decades.

Table 2.4 provides additional demographic detail on the composition of the poor—that is, the percentage of all poor persons who fall into a variety of demographic groups—at the beginning of each of the four most recent decades. Also shown are the corresponding poverty rates for each of these groups.

The differences in poverty rates by age, race/ethnicity, and gender have already been discussed, and here we focus on compositional changes for these groups. Even though poverty rates of whites are much lower than those of blacks and Hispanics, most poor persons are white. Hispanics as a share of all poor persons have doubled between 1970 and 1990 to about 18 percent; blacks have composed about 30 percent of the poor over the last three decades. The data in Table 2.4, from published Census reports, do not represent mutually exclusive categories, because Hispanics may be of any race. Thus the published data show that about two-thirds of all the poor are white, and computations from the CPS computer tapes indicate that in 1990 about one-half of all the poor were white non-Hispanics.

The composition of the poor has also shifted away from persons living in married-couple families. The percentage of the poor living in female-headed families with no spouse present doubled, to about 38 percent, between 1960 and 1990; the percentage who were unrelated individuals also doubled, to about 22 percent. Both of these groups have above-average poverty rates, although the rate for unrelated individuals has declined substantially.

Although there have been dramatic changes in the poverty rates of children and the elderly, their share of the total poor population has changed very little, because the total number of children has fallen in recent years, while their poverty rate was rising, and the elderly population has expanded while its poverty rate has fallen. Children make up nearly 40 percent of the poor; the elderly, about 10 percent.

In 1960 most poor persons (56 percent) lived outside of metropolitan areas, and about one-fifth lived on farms. At the time, both these groups had very high poverty rates. By 1990 only about one-quarter of the poor lived outside of metropolitan areas and less than 2 percent lived on farms. Over these decades, their poverty rates fell dramatically. By 1980 the nonmetropolitan poverty rate had fallen below the central city rate. The increase in the percentage of the poor who live in

Table 2.4 Profile of the poverty population, 1960–1990

	Percentage of the poor population				Percentage poor			
	1960	1970	1980	1990	1960	1970	1980	1990
All persons	100.0%	100.0%	100.0%	100.0%	22.2%	12.6%	13.0%	13.5%
Race/Ethnicity								
White	71.0	68.5	67.3	66.5	17.8	9.9	10.2	10.7
Black[a]	29.0	30.0	29.3	29.3	55.9	33.5	32.5	31.9
Asian or Pacific Islander[b]	—	—	2.4	2.6	—	—	17.2	12.2
Amer. Indian, Eskimo, or Aleut[d]	—	1.2	1.2	1.9	—	38.3	27.5	30.9
Hispanic[c]	—	8.5	11.9	17.9	—	24.3	25.7	28.1
Family Structure								
In all families	87.6	80.0	77.2	75.1	20.7	10.9	11.5	12.0
In families with a female householder, no spouse present	18.2	29.5	34.6	37.5	48.9	38.1	36.7	37.2
Unrelated individuals	12.4	20.0	21.3	22.2	45.2	32.9	22.9	20.7
Young and Old								
Related children under 18	43.4	40.3	38.0	37.9	26.5	14.9	17.9	19.9
Adults 65 and over	14.1[e]	18.5	13.2	10.9	35.2	24.5	15.7	12.2
Residence								
Nonfarm	81.0	92.4	96.6	98.4	19.6	12.2	12.9	13.6
Farm	19.0	7.6	3.4	1.6	51.3	21.1	17.5	11.2
In metropolitan areas	43.9[e]	52.4	61.6	73.0	15.3	10.2	11.9	12.7
In central cities	26.9[e]	32.0	36.4	42.4	18.3	14.3	17.2	19.0
In suburbs	17.0[e]	20.4	25.2	30.5	12.2	7.1	8.2	8.7
Outside metropolitan areas	56.1[e]	47.6	38.4	27.0	33.2	17.0	15.4	16.3

Source: U.S. Bureau of the Census, Current Population Reports, series P-60, nos. 68, 81, 102, 133, 175.

Note: Data are from the Current Population Survey (CPS), except where noted. Population characteristics are as of March of the subsequent year.

a. Negro and other races in 1960.

b. Not computed as separate category from the CPS until 1990. Decennial census figures are presented for 1979.

c. Hispanics may be of any race; comparable statistics on non-Hispanics are not available.

d. Decennial census figures for the previous year. The geographic distribution of their poverty is important to note: in 1979, 41.3 percent of American Indians, Eskimos, and Aleuts living on reservations, in native villages, or on trust lands were poor; in 1989, 50.7 percent were poor.

e. Decennial census figures from 1979.

central cities from about one-quarter to about two-fifths of all the poor and the continuing high central-city poverty rate (19 percent in 1990) have contributed to concerns about the concentration of poverty and the emergence of an urban underclass (see Chapter 5). In sum, since 1960, a greater proportion of the poor are Hispanics, unrelated individuals, persons living in female-headed families with no husband present, and residents of metropolitan areas.

There is no simple or unique way to measure the effects of these demographic changes on the poverty rate.[24] We make use, however, of the fact that the 1990 poverty rate for all persons, 13.5 percent, can be expressed as the weighted sum of each of the twenty-four group-specific poverty rates shown in columns 2 and 3 of Table 2.3, where the weights are the population shares of each of the demographic groups. We computed a simple demographic standardization that simulates the 1990 poverty rate for all persons under the assumption that the demographic composition of the population in 1990 was the same for the twenty-four groups shown as it had been in 1973.[25] The simulated 1990 poverty rate is about 11.5 percent, instead of 13.5 percent. Taken together, these demographic changes increased poverty. Even if they had not occurred, however, there would still not have been a significant decline in poverty over the two decades.

Government Spending and the Antipoverty Effectiveness of Income Transfers

Spending

Having discussed the roles of economic and demographic changes, we turn to the antipoverty effects of government income transfers. As documented in Chapter 3, outlays for payments to individuals have increased rapidly since 1960. Outlays rose from nearly $16 billion (in 1990 dollars) in 1940 to $93 billion in 1960, and then to $573 billion in 1990. Social Security and Medicare account for the largest part of this increase, rising from $1.3 billion in 1940 (10 percent of the total) to $358 billion in 1990 (63 percent). Social insurance spending represents about three-quarters of the total; means-tested programs, targeted on those with low incomes, account for the remaining quarter.

The tilt of social spending toward the elderly has increased in recent years. Between fiscal years 1978 and 1987, federal expenditures targeted on children declined by 4 percent in real terms; those targeting the elderly increased by 52 percent.[26] Spending on children represents less than 10 percent of the federal total (U.S. House of Representatives, 1991).

In contrast to the relatively constant shares of the transfer budget that have been devoted to social insurance versus means-tested programs since 1960, the shares going to cash and noncash assistance programs have shifted radically. After staying at roughly one-tenth of the transfer budget from 1945 to 1965, the Great Society programs of Medicare and Medicaid, coupled with increases in housing assistance and Food Stamps, raised the noncash share to 43 percent in 1990.

Program Participation in Major Income-Tested Programs

Most transfer programs are designed to help specific demographic groups for specific purposes. None has the explicit goal of eliminating poverty. Consider the example of Aid to Families with Dependent Children, which operates as fifty-one different programs in the fifty states and the District of Columbia. Each state sets its own standard of need independent of the poverty line and then decides whether the benefits it will pay meet this need standard. In the median state, the AFDC benefit for single-parent families of three persons provides 41 percent of their poverty threshold ($10,913 in 1991); the combined AFDC and Food Stamp benefit equals 72 percent of the threshold (U.S. House of Representatives, 1992). The combined benefit in the median state was as high as 85 percent of the poverty line in the mid-1970s, but has fallen since then because AFDC benefits are not indexed for inflation.

The elderly poor benefit from a means-tested cash transfer program—Supplemental Security Income (SSI)—that is indexed for inflation and has a national minimum benefit level. SSI also provides benefits to poor blind and disabled persons and guarantees access to Medicaid. In most states, an elderly couple receives substantially more from SSI than a mother and two children receives from AFDC. Nonetheless, the SSI benefit levels ($5,064 per year for a single person and $7,596 per year for a couple in 1992, plus supplementation in some states) are typically below the corresponding poverty thresholds.[27]

Not all of those eligible for benefits receive them, for various reasons, including lack of information, reluctance to apply for "welfare" (stigma), and potential receipt of only a small benefit. Many of those not participating may be "income eligible," that is, their incomes may be low enough according to program rules, but they may be disqualified if their assets exceed program restrictions.[28]

Trends in program participation rates in relation to trends in the poverty rate provide a rough measure of how well the transfer system addresses the needs of the poor. Consider the situation of poor children. The ratio of children who receive AFDC to the total number of poor children increased rapidly after the declaration of the War on Poverty. This ratio, which was about 20 percent in 1965, peaked at about 80 percent in 1973, fell to about 50 percent in 1982, and then rose to about 59 percent in 1989 (U.S. House of Representatives, 1991). The SSI participation rate of the elderly poor also fell from 75.6 percent in 1975 to 53.6 percent in 1982, before rising to 60.1 percent in 1989.

Low-income households, including AFDC and SSI recipients, are eligible for food stamps that increase their food purchasing power. In the 1975–1990 period, the percentage of all persons receiving food stamps fluctuated between 6.5 percent (1978) and 9.2 percent (1983) of all persons, and was at 9.0 percent in 1991 (22.6 million persons). A smaller percentage of the poor now receives benefits: 68.1 percent in 1976, and 63.3 percent in 1991.

In contrast to AFDC, SSI, Food Stamps, and Medicaid, which, as entitlement programs, provide benefits to anyone who meets the appropriate income, assets, and demographic criteria, housing assistance benefits are limited. Many eligibles who wish to participate cannot do so. As a result, the number of poor housing assistance recipients is much smaller than the number receiving entitlements. The number of assisted renters rose from 2.1 to 4.5 million between 1977 and 1990; the number of assisted homeowners has remained roughly constant at about 1.0 million over the same period.

Receipt of Transfers by the Poor and the Nonpoor

Only rarely do the criteria for social welfare program participation involve the poverty thresholds explicitly, and almost never do programs restrict eligibility solely to the poor. Consequently, benefits from many programs that help the poor go in some part to the nonpoor. This is intentional—the bulk of Social Security payments (63 percent) are not misdirected simply because they are received by the nonpoor. Success in reducing poverty should not be the only way to judge program success, particularly for programs that have different goals. Yet the effectiveness of income transfer benefits in reducing poverty is directly relevant here. We begin our review of the antipoverty impact of income transfers by showing how the benefits of social insurance and means-tested transfers are distributed by income class. Benefits are shown for all families, poor families, families with incomes between one and three times the poverty line, and the remaining nonpoor families (those with incomes more than three times the poverty line) in Tables 2.5 and 2.6.[29]

Table 2.5 focuses on the receipt of social insurance transfers in 1989. Families are classified by their pretransfer private money income, defined simply as cash income minus cash government transfers.[30] Nearly one-third of all families received a social insurance transfer; about one-fifth received Social Security and/or Medicare. About 54 percent of all pretransfer poor families received a social insurance benefit. These benefits, 35.2 percent of all social insurance, removed 36.8 percent of pretransfer poor families from poverty and eliminated 37 percent of their income deficit.

As already mentioned, social insurance spending disproportionately benefits the elderly (not shown in table). Nearly all families with an elderly householder

Table 2.5 Receipt of social insurance transfers among families, 1989

	All	Private money income below 100% of poverty line	Private money income 100–299% of poverty line	Private money income 300% or more of poverty line
All families (in thousands)	66,624	12,051	21,000	33,573
Percentage	100.0%	18.1%	31.5%	50.4%
Percentage Receiving Benefits				
Social Security	22.9%	46.6%	24.7%	13.3%
Unemployment Compensation	6.7	4.9	8.7	6.2
Workers' Compensation	1.5	1.7	2.0	1.2
Medicare	20.3	43.4	21.1	11.6
All social insurance[a]	31.1	54.2	34.5	20.8
Percentage of Benefits Received				
Social Security	100.0%	37.4%	34.5%	28.1%
Unemployment Compensation	100.0	14.4	40.7	44.9
Workers' Compensation	100.0	26.2	43.8	30.0
Medicare	100.0	33.6	36.5	29.9
All social insurance	100.0	35.2	35.5	29.3
Percentage of Families Removed from Poverty by				
Social Security	5.9%	32.5%		
Unemployment Compensation	0.2	0.9		
Workers' Compensation	0.1	0.7		
Medicare	2.5	13.8		
All social insurance	6.7	36.8		
Percentage of Income Deficit[b] Eliminated				
Social Security	33.5%	33.5%		
Unemployment Compensation	1.2	1.2		
Workers' Compensation	1.0	1.0		
Medicare	15.9	15.9		
All social insurance	36.8	36.8		

Source: Unpublished U.S. Census Bureau tabulations from the March 1990 Current Population Survey.

Note: Private money income equals wages and salaries, self-employment income (including losses), interest, dividends, rents, royalties, government employee and private pensions, alimony, child support, and any other cash income regularly received.

a. Includes black lung benefits.

b. The income deficit is the amount of money needed to raise the incomes of all families in poverty up to their poverty threshold. In 1989 the income deficit before government cash transfers was $79.03 billion.

Table 2.6 Receipt of means-tested transfers among families, 1989

	All	Prewelfare income below 100% of poverty line	Prewelfare income 100–299% of poverty line	Prewelfare income 300% or more of poverty line
All families (in thousands)	66,624	7,708	22,417	36,499
Percentage	100.0%	11.6%	33.7%	54.8%
Percentage Receiving Benefits				
AFDC and other cash welfare	5.4%	37.8%	2.7%	0.3%
SSI	2.9	13.2	3.1	0.8
All cash welfare[a]	7.7	46.3	5.5	1.0
EITC	13.5	40.5	26.1	1.2
Food stamps	7.5	50.5	5.0	0.2
School lunch	9.0	43.3	12.0	0.3
Public/Subsidized housing	3.1	19.2	2.6	0.1
Medicaid	10.5	55.3	9.5	2.1
All means-tested transfers[b]	24.5	86.2	39.3	4.0
All means-tested transfers and Medicare	40.2	90.8	60.1	19.6
Education assistance[c]	3.7	5.9	4.9	2.8
Percentage of Benefits Received				
AFDC and other cash welfare	100.0%	86.1%	12.0%	1.9%
SSI	100.0	57.9	29.5	12.6
All cash welfare[a]	100.0	76.5	17.9	5.6
EITC	100.0	41.1	55.0	3.9
Food stamps	100.0	87.2	12.2	0.6
School lunch	100.0	59.7	39.0	1.3
Public/Subsidized housing	100.0	83.8	14.8	1.4
Medicaid	100.0	41.0	44.2	14.8
All means-tested transfers[b]	100.0	65.8	27.6	6.6
All means-tested transfers and Medicare	100.0	35.3	36.7	28.0
Education assistance[c]	100.0	14.1	37.5	48.4

Percentage of Families Removed from Poverty by

AFDC and other cash welfare	0.4%	3.6%
SSI	0.4	3.5
All cash welfare[a]	0.9	7.5
EITC	0.5	4.4
Food stamps	0.3	2.3
School lunch	0.2	1.9
Public/Subsidized housing	0.2	1.7
Medicaid	0.6	5.0
All means-tested transfers[b]	3.4	29.6
All means-tested transfers and Medicare	3.6	31.2
Education assistance[c]	0.1	1.1

Percentage of Income Deficit[d] Eliminated

AFDC and other cash welfare	22.0%	22.0%
SSI	6.7	6.7
All cash welfare[a]	28.3	28.3
EITC	3.8	3.8
Food stamps	13.3	13.3
School lunch	3.8	3.8
Public/Subsidized housing	6.2	6.2
Medicaid	7.2	7.2
All means-tested transfers[b]	54.6	54.6
All means-tested transfers and Medicare	54.8	54.8
Education assistance[c]	1.4	1.4

Source: Unpublished Census Bureau tabulations of the March 1990 Current Population Survey.

Note: Prewelfare equals private money income plus cash social insurance (social security, unemployment and workers' compensation, and black lung). AFDC = Aid to Families with Dependent Children; EITC = Earned Income Tax Credit; SSI = Supplemental Security Income.

a. Aid to Families with Dependent Children, other cash welfare, and Supplemental Security Income.

b. Includes means-tested veterans payments and home energy assistance; excludes education assistance.

c. Includes Pell grants, GI bill, and other educational assistance.

d. The income deficit is the amount of money needed to raise the incomes of all families in poverty up to their poverty threshold. In 1989 the income deficit after government social insurance cash transfers was $49.41 billion.

received benefits (97 percent), as did 99 percent of poor elderly families. These transfers removed 83 percent of the elderly poor from poverty and filled 89 percent of their income deficit. Benefits to the poor elderly were about 5 times larger than their private money income.[31]

The primary social insurance transfers received by the nonelderly, unemployment and workers' compensation, were much less effective against poverty. They each removed less than 1 percent of all poor families from poverty.

Table 2.6 examines the receipt and antipoverty effectiveness of means-tested transfers. Families are classified by their prewelfare income, defined as total family income less public assistance transfers.[32] Means-tested programs paid out a much smaller amount of benefits, but about 90 percent of all prewelfare poor families received some benefit. These benefits eliminated 55 percent of the income deficit, and removed 31 percent of prewelfare poor families from poverty. The addition of means-tested benefits nearly doubled these families' incomes.

Nearly 94 percent of poor single-parent families with related children received means-tested benefits, but the benefits are so low relative to their poverty gap that only 28 percent of them were removed from poverty by cash and noncash transfers.

Trends in the Antipoverty Effectiveness of Income Transfers

The adjusted and official poverty series reveal how much poverty remains after the receipt of all income sources. To distinguish between the effects of market income growth and that of government income transfers, we now focus separately on their relative antipoverty impacts. The time series on pretransfer poverty reveals the impact of market income sources. The difference between the pretransfer and the official series provides a measure of the antipoverty effect of cash transfers; the difference between the pretransfer and the adjusted series, the antipoverty effect of cash plus in-kind transfers.[33]

Columns 5 and 6 of Table 2.2 and Figure 2.5 present the time series for pretransfer and prewelfare poverty from all persons from 1967 through 1990. In 1990 the official poverty rate was 13.5 percent; the pretransfer rate was 21.5 percent. Thus 8.0 percent of all persons, or 37.2 percent of the pretransfer poor ($[21.5 - 13.5] \div 21.5$), were removed from poverty by cash transfers; about half of the pretransfer poor were taken out of poverty by cash plus noncash transfers.

Table 2.7 and Figure 2.6 show that trends in the antipoverty effectiveness of cash income transfers over the 1967–1990 period differ markedly for the elderly and for persons living in families with children headed by a nonelderly male or female.[34] Tables 2.3 and 2.4 demonstrated that the poverty rate for the elderly is now below average. Table 2.7 shows that their poverty rate has declined relative to those of nonelderly families with children primarily because of the increasing antipoverty effectiveness of income transfers.

% poor

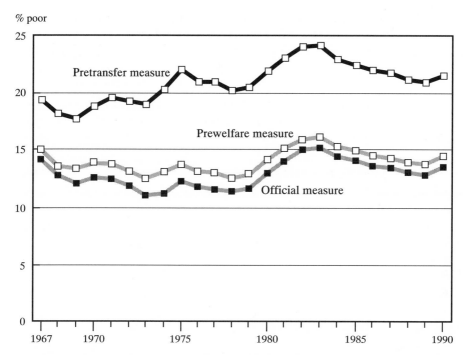

Figure 2.5 The trend in poverty, 1967–1990: (1) "pretransfer"—as poverty would have been in the absence of all government cash transfers; (2) "prewelfare"—as poverty would have been in the absence of public assistance (welfare) payments; and (3) as officially measured. (Data sources: for "pretransfer" and "prewelfare," authors' tabulations; for official measure, see Figure 2.1.)

For the elderly, pretransfer poverty rates were relatively constant from 1967 through 1982. This reflected their greater nonwage, nongovernment income, as a greater percentage of them were retired in the later years of this period. On its own, increasing retirement would raise pretransfer poverty, but this effect was offset by rising pension incomes and rising property incomes (both part of pretransfer income). Property income increased even more during the 1980s because of high real interest rates, and pretransfer poverty fell among the elderly. Nonetheless, most of the change over the almost quarter-century shown in the table is due to rising Social Security benefits and their increasing antipoverty effectiveness.

Columns 4 and 5 of Table 2.7 and Figure 2.6 show that cash transfers removed about half of the elderly pretransfer poor from poverty in 1967, but about three-quarters by the early 1970s. This period was one of rising Social Security benefits that culminated in their indexation for inflation in 1972. Since 1973 cash transfers

Table 2.7 Poverty rates and the antipoverty impact of cash transfers for elderly persons and persons living in families with children, selected years, 1967–1990

	Pretransfer proverty (1)	Prewelfare poverty (2)	Official poverty (3)	Percentage of pretransfer poor persons removed from poverty by	
				Cash social insurance[a] (4)	Cash public assistance[b] (5)
Elderly					
1967	58.3%	31.8%	29.7%	45.5%	3.6%
1969	55.6	27.8	25.4	50.0	4.3
1973	58.0	18.5	16.1	68.1	4.1
1979	58.9	17.3	15.1	70.6	3.7
1982	57.0	16.0	14.6	71.9	2.5
1989	51.9	13.1	11.4	74.8	3.3
1990	51.0	13.3	12.1	73.9	2.4
Nonelderly Male-Headed Families					
1967	11.5	10.3	10.0	10.4	2.6
1969	9.1	8.0	7.5	13.6	5.5
1973	8.7	7.0	6.5	19.5	5.8
1979	9.6	7.8	7.2	18.8	6.3
1982	14.5	11.8	11.3	18.6	3.5
1989	11.1	9.6	9.0	13.5	5.4
1990	11.4	10.0	9.3	12.3	6.1
Nonelderly Female-Headed Families					
1967	58.8	52.4	49.1	10.9	5.6
1969	61.0	54.4	48.5	10.8	9.7
1973	60.8	54.0	46.8	11.2	11.8
1979	53.5	48.6	43.3	9.2	9.9
1982	58.5	54.2	51.3	7.4	5.0
1989	52.2	48.9	46.5	6.3	4.6
1990	54.5	51.5	48.3	5.5	5.9

Source: Computations by authors from March Current Population Survey computer tapes, U.S. Bureau of the Census.

Note: Cash social insurance transfers include social security, railroad retirement, unemployment compensation, workers' compensation, government employee pensions, and veterans' pensions and compensation. Cash public assistance transfers include Aid to Families with Dependent Children, Supplemental Security Income, and general assistance.

a. Defined as ([column 2 − column 1] ÷ column 1) × 100.

b. Defined as ([column 3 − column 2] ÷ column 1) × 100. The total antipoverty effect of cash transfers, shown in Figure 2.6, is the sum of columns 4 and 5.

% pretransfer poor
removed from poverty

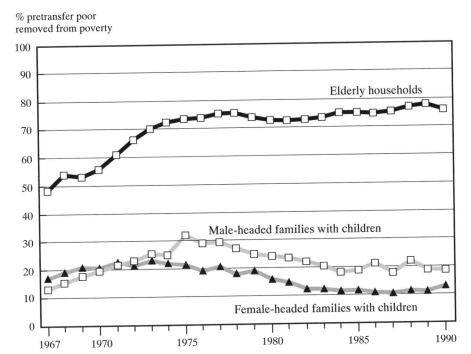

Figure 2.6 The antipoverty effects of cash transfers, 1967–1990. (Computations by the authors from March Current Population Survey computer tapes, U.S. Bureau of the Census.)

have continued to remove more than three-quarters of the elderly pretransfer poor from poverty.

Pretransfer poverty fell for male-headed families between 1967 and 1973 and the antipoverty impact of transfers increased. After that time, pretransfer poverty increased and the antipoverty impact of transfers decreased. For this group, poverty in 1990 was higher than in 1973, primarily because of increased pretransfer poverty. Had the mothers in married-couple families not substantially increased their labor force participation rates and earned a greater share of their families' income over the past two decades, the pretransfer poverty rate for this group would have gone up by an even greater amount.

Female-headed families with children have very high poverty rates because women earn less than men and receive fewer transfers than do the elderly. For these families, the antipoverty impact of cash transfers rose slowly from the late 1960s to the early 1970s, and then declined. In 1990 cash transfers removed only about 10 percent of the pretransfer poor in this group from poverty (see Table 2.7 and Figure 2.6).

Poverty for female-headed families with children was higher in 1990 than in 1973 primarily because of the declining effectiveness of social welfare transfers. The pretransfer poverty rate for this group actually declined somewhat. If the antipoverty effectiveness of cash transfers in 1990 had been the same as in 1973, then the official rate for these persons in 1990 would have been 42.0 percent instead of 48.3 percent.

A major reason child poverty is so much higher in the United States than in Canada and Western European countries is shown in columns 4 and 5 of Table 2.7. Social welfare programs in the United States remove a much smaller percentage of pretransfer poor children from poverty than do the others' (see Smeeding [1992], for comparative data). In these other countries, one-half to three-quarters of the pretransfer poor are removed from poverty by social transfers that treat children as generously as they do the elderly.

The trend in the pretransfer poverty rate (Figure 2.5) and the trend in the antipoverty effectiveness of cash and noncash transfers for all persons (Figure 2.7) are consistent with a story that emphasizes the roles of economic and public policy changes in the failure of poverty to decline after 1973. From the declaration of the War on Poverty through 1973, the economy and social spending both grew rapidly. The official poverty rate fell because of the rapid growth in market income and because the antipoverty effect of cash transfers increased from about 25 to about 45 percent.

Between 1973 and 1979, social spending continued to grow, but the economy slowed dramatically. For the remainder of the 1970s, the increasing transfers managed to offset most of the increased poverty generated by the market economy. That the official poverty rate was virtually constant while spending was rising, however, led to a major shift in public opinion. Government social programs, instead of being seen as helping to hold back the negative effects of a stagnant economy, came to be blamed for the high official poverty rates (Murray, 1984). This view minimized the problem of reducing poverty in a slowly growing economy and neglected the major success of antipoverty policy—the rapid decline in poverty for the elderly, on whom most of the spending increase of this period was targeted. Poverty rose primarily for those groups most affected by the adverse economic conditions—families with children—for whom inflation-adjusted spending increases after 1973 have been quite modest.

The pessimistic view about the efficacy of government antipoverty efforts provided an intellectual rationale for some of the cutbacks in social programs legislated in the early 1980s. Unemployment insurance and AFDC coverage were restricted, and public service employment was eliminated, despite the rising

% pretransfer poor
removed from poverty

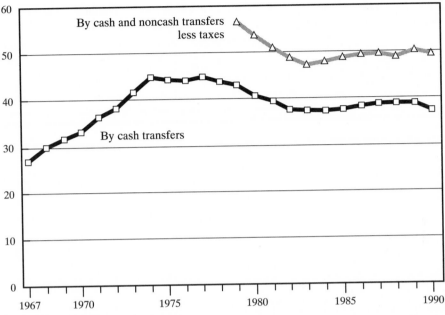

Figure 2.7 The antipoverty effects of cash and noncash transfers, 1967–1990. (For data source, see Figure 2.6.)

pretransfer poverty generated by the recession. As a result, the percentage of the poor removed from poverty by transfers declined as well. Post-transfer poverty fell by a smaller amount during the 1980s recovery than did pretransfer poverty, in part because of the reduced antipoverty impact of transfers attributable to these program restrictions.

The election of President Clinton in 1992 marked a rejection of the pessimistic view that the persisting high poverty rate was caused by government programs. It was clear by then that an economic recovery on its own could not replace antipoverty policies. Within his first one hundred days in office, the President announced a set of progressive tax changes and social policy changes designed to reduce poverty and to encourage more rapid wage and employment growth. Which proposals might actually be enacted were as yet unknown. But if economic growth could be sustained and antipoverty and labor market policies vigorously pursued, the likelihood was great that the antipoverty effects of government would begin to increase.

.   .   .

In the early 1990s, one in seven Americans was poor. The previous two decades constituted a period of very slow growth in average living standards and of rising earnings inequality and family income inequality. Three major factors contributed to this poor performance. The first is economic: real wages for less-skilled workers have fallen, and the gap between the wages of college graduates and other workers has increased. Sources of this growing wage inequality include technological changes that increased the demand for higher-skilled and decreased the demand for less-skilled workers, the globalization of markets, and the increased supply of immigrants and new labor market entrants. The continued transformation from an industrial to an information economy is likely to have further negative effects on less-skilled workers. The second factor is government programs, which are no longer as effective in reducing economic hardship because benefit levels in some programs have not kept up with inflation and because changes in program rules have reduced recipiency rates. The third factor is demographic: the composition of the population has shifted away from married-couple families, who have lower-than-average poverty rates, toward female-headed families and unrelated individuals, who have higher-than-average rates.

Similar economic and demographic changes have occurred in most industrialized countries. Other nations, however, have done more to offset the rising economic hardship through expanded government social policies. Government can affect the size of the work force through immigration policy, can supplement low wages through an expanded earned income tax credit, can raise the minimum wage, can reform welfare and the child support system, can increase access to health care, and can raise workers' skills by expanding education, employment, and training opportunities. Chapters 7–13 examine the specific components of these policy initiatives. The historical record makes clear that if the uneven nature of economic growth in the 1980s continues, poverty will not fall very much in the 1990s unless major changes are made in a variety of public programs and policies.

CHAPTER THREE

Public Spending on the Poor:
Historical Trends and Economic Limits

GARY BURTLESS

The conventional wisdom is that public programs intended to help the poor do not work. In spite of the government's best efforts, or perhaps because of them, the poor are drifting further and further away from the American mainstream. This perception is encouraged by conservative analysts, who routinely condemn government redistribution, and reinforced by official statistics, which show that poverty has climbed since the early 1970s even though public spending on the poor has soared (see Figure 3.1).

Although there is some truth in the conventional wisdom for some government programs, an accurate assessment would be much more complicated. Most programs for the poor achieve their objectives to at least a limited degree. Public assistance succeeds in making families who would otherwise be destitute a little less destitute. Food Stamps and other nutrition programs raise the food intake of people living in poor households. Medicaid improves poor families' access to decent health care. Job Corps, adult training and job search assistance, and other programs to improve the employability of workers with few skills are usually judged moderately successful by competent evaluators. None of these programs achieves spectacular results. But spectacular results are, of course, difficult to achieve.

More important, many of the most costly social programs do not even aim to reduce poverty as it is officially defined. They have specific objectives, such as improving diet, basic medical care, and housing conditions, which are not measured by a family's money income. The conventional poverty statistics thus provide a notoriously inaccurate yardstick for evaluating the success or failure of many of these programs. Finally, many social programs are designed to support the living standards of the nonpoor as well as the poor. Social Security and Medicare do not specifically target the poor. When spending on social insurance pro-

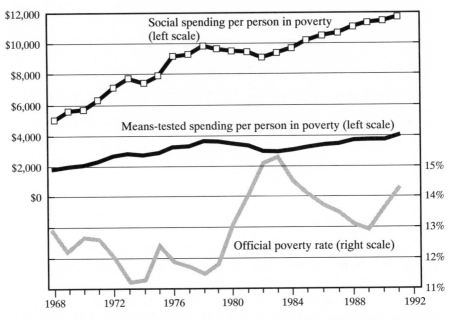

Figure 3.1   U.S. social spending and poverty rates, 1968–1991 (in 1990 dollars). "Person in poverty" is someone who is poor before receiving transfers. (For data source on social spending and means-tested spending, see Table 3.1; data on number of persons poor before receiving transfers from unpublished statistics supplied by Sheldon Danziger; official poverty rate data from published reports of the U.S. Bureau of the Census.)

grams is subtracted from total social spending, the increase in expenditures per person in poverty appears much more modest. (Note the comparative trends in means-tested and all social spending shown in Figure 3.1.)

But if it is easy to criticize the yardstick we use to measure success, it is harder to argue that we cannot measure the intensity of the effort. The nation's efforts can be gauged rather easily—by the money it spends. Spending on programs that aid the poor soared between 1960 and 1990. In the fifteen years after 1960, the U.S. government mounted or expanded numerous programs targeted on the poor: Medicaid, Food Stamps, subsidized housing, Supplemental Security Income, targeted student grants and loans, training for poor adults, an earned income tax credit, and work incentives for able-bodied welfare recipients. Transfer programs for the nonpoor, such as Social Security and Medicare, were also liberalized, but many of the extra benefits were showered on the poor.

The trend toward increased public generosity to the poor came to an abrupt halt at the end of the 1970s. Although total outlays continued to mount, almost all of the increase was due to rising poverty. None was due to more generous government provision for the low-income population. Many programs, including the main cash assistance program for indigent children, were severely curtailed. Despite increased outlays, spending per poor person did not rise.

The timing of these cutbacks was hardly accidental. The generosity of poverty programs grew when the general economy prospered but was curbed not long after economic growth slowed. American income growth fell off dramatically starting in 1974, whether growth is measured in terms of average or median family income. Many voters and politicians were no doubt persuaded that antipoverty programs had to be trimmed because the real incomes of working taxpayers were static or shrinking. In addition, the 1980s witnessed a ferocious attack on the underlying logic of antipoverty programs. Critics argued that many programs, especially income redistribution programs, created more problems than they solved. Extending help to the poor not only did not help them escape poverty, it undermined incentives that spurred them to improve their own lives. Charles Murray (1984) argued that most social programs for the poor actually produced net harm; they worsened the condition of people whose lives they were designed to improve.

Near the end of the 1980s, retrenchment in social welfare programs ended. The nation entered a new era of program liberalization. Few new programs were initiated, but some old ones were reformed and others expanded. After a decade of stagnation, poverty spending began to climb. Policymakers did not reach any consensus on the nature of desirable reform. Instead, under a variety of legal, political, and economic pressures, individual programs were liberalized in an uncoordinated way. Court rulings extended some benefits to new groups of the poor; Congress and state legislatures forced agencies to offer medical benefits and cash benefits to more people; and enthusiasm for tax reform led to a surge in refundable income tax benefits for the working poor. Although the press and public were largely unaware of the change, a significant liberalization of poverty programs was under way by the early 1990s. Of course, some state governments curbed spending on the most unpopular aid programs—cash public assistance—but cutbacks were outweighed by increased spending on Medicaid, Medicare, and Disability Insurance.

The Trend in Poverty Spending

The United States offers three categories of programs to help equalize incomes and reduce poverty: means-tested income transfers, social insurance, and targeted education and training programs. Means-tested programs distribute money and other resources directly to poor or near-poor families. Participation in these programs is limited; the affluent need not apply. In certain cases benefits are restricted even more narrowly to particular classes of the poor—the elderly, disabled, single parents and their children. Using traditional measures of antipoverty effectiveness, means-tested programs are highly efficient. A high proportion of benefits reaches families that would otherwise be poor or near-poor, and little help is received by families significantly above the poverty line.

A second type of redistribution takes place in the far more popular and costly social insurance programs—Social Security, Medicare, workers' compensation, and unemployment insurance. Financed by payroll taxes paid by those currently employed and their employers, benefits are provided to people with low current earnings—the retired, temporarily or permanently disabled, dependents of deceased workers, and insured unemployed. As a whole, these recipients are poorer than wage earners, at least as measured by current money income. If we judge the comparative affluence of contributors and beneficiaries by money income received in the most recent year, social insurance programs undeniably appear to redistribute income from the better off to the less affluent.

This charitable view of social insurance must be modified, however, if we take a longer-term perspective. Viewed over an individual's lifetime, social insurance redistributes income from periods of high earned income to periods of unemployment, disability, or retirement when wage income is low. Benefits received in lean times are thus assumed to be a rightful repayment of taxes paid in flush times. This lifetime redistribution takes place for insured workers whether they are poor, middle class, or wealthy. From this vantage-point, even though social insurance formulas are tilted to favor workers with low annual earnings, the amount of lifetime redistribution from rich to poor is much smaller than it seems when redistribution is viewed year by year.

The third form of redistribution aims at reducing poverty in the future rather than in the present. Instead of redistributing current incomes, these programs provide special education, training, and employment help that is intended to increase the future earnings of disadvantaged children and adults. Head Start, targeted aid to elementary schools, basic educational opportunity grants, the Job Corps, and the Job Training Partnership Act (JTPA) are among the better-known human capital enhancement programs. In theory, they should be far more popular among voters and politicians than means-tested income transfers. Their goal is to reduce poverty and public dependency by increasing the ability of current and future workers to earn more money. But when domestic spending was trimmed in the 1980s, education and training programs aimed at the poor were cut sharply. Means-tested transfers suffered much smaller proportional cuts.

Social scientists, and economists in particular, are usually more enthusiastic about programs to improve earnings ability than they are about income transfers.

In part this preference arises from a natural kind of bias. The case for pure income redistribution leaves many economists uneasy. Taking a dollar from rich Mr. Smith to give to poor Mr. Jones presumably decreases the well-being of Smith and increases that of Jones, but the act has an unknown effect on their combined well-being, even if their total income remains unchanged. And there are good economic reasons to believe that income will not remain unchanged; it may fall, possibly *lowering* their combined well-being.

The case for investment in training the disadvantaged appears stronger. Rich Mr. Smith is required to contribute one dollar toward training or educating poor Mr. Jones, and in consequence Jones becomes a better earner. Because the combined income of Smith and Jones may thereby be raised, economists have found it easier to persuade themselves that the combined well-being of the two has improved. But combined after-tax income can only be increased if poor Mr. Jones's earnings are ultimately raised by more than one dollar. If they are raised by less, Smith has paid more for the training than it has been worth to Jones. Smith could have raised Jones's income more cheaply simply by transferring money to him directly. In practice, the return on investing in human capital programs is uncertain, which may explain why the nation invests so little in such programs when they are directed at the poor, although lip service is paid to the idea that they are preferable to the dole. Both the poor and the nonpoor may prefer that society help impoverished breadwinners earn their way out of poverty, but there is no guarantee that education and training programs can achieve that goal, in either the short or the long run.

Means-Tested Transfers

Means-tested transfers are paid out by programs specifically aimed at raising money incomes or consumption of poor families. State, local, and federal government agencies distribute the transfers in two forms—cash grants and in-kind transfers. Programs popularly referred to as *welfare* distribute cash payments; the main ones include Aid to Families with Dependent Children, general assistance, and categorical aid programs for the blind, disabled, and destitute elderly. These last programs were combined in the federally administered Supplemental Security Income program in 1974. The federal government also offers means-tested cash aid to impoverished veterans and their families. All the cash assistance programs, except general assistance and means-tested veterans' benefits, trace their origins to the Social Security Act of 1935. Until the mid-1960s cash transfers accounted for an overwhelming part of means-tested transfers. In 1965, for example, 83 percent were distributed in the form of cash aid.

Cash assistance. Since 1960, spending on cash assistance programs has gone through several distinct phases (see Figure 3.2 and Table 3.1). Between 1960 and 1973 federal, state, and local spending on AFDC rose more than 400 percent, as average benefit levels and participation in the program soared.[1] Real spending surged again in 1975 and 1976 in response to the severe 1973–1975 recession. But in the 1970s eligibility conditions were tightened and nominal benefit levels failed to keep pace with inflation; in the eight years after 1976 real outlays declined 15 percent. The decrease is all the more striking because the number of American children officially classified as poor jumped 40 percent between 1978 and 1983. AFDC spending fell more than 10 percent in those years.

In 1988 a conservative President and a Democratic Congress agreed to a modest package of reforms in the Family Support Act. Although the reforms were intended to increase the percentage of AFDC recipients participating in work and training programs, some features of the package liberalized eligibility require-

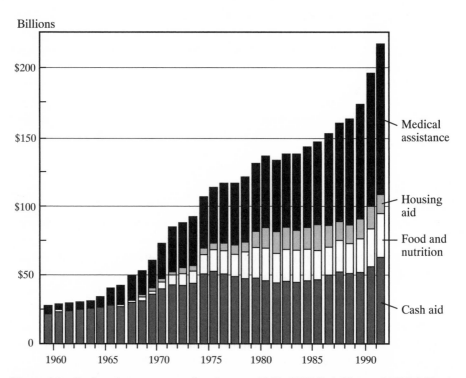

Figure 3.2 Outlays for means-tested assistance, 1960–1992 (in billions of 1990 dollars). (Data sources: U.S. Department of Health, Education and Welfare, 1971; U.S. House of Representatives, 1984, 1991, 1992; U.S. Department of Health and Human Services, Social Security Administration, 1984; U.S. Office of Management and Budget, *Budget of the U.S. Government,* various years.)

Table 3.1 Spending on U.S. welfare state programs, 1960–1992 (in billions of 1990 dollars)

	1960	1965	1970	1975	1980	1985	1990	1992
Income-Conditioned Transfers								
Cash assistance								
AFDC	$4.9	$7.7	$16.1	$22.7	$21.8	$20.6	$21.2	$22.9
SSI/Aid to aged and disabled	10.1	11.0	10.6	14.6	13.7	14.4	16.2	22.8
EITC	0.0	0.0	0.0	3.0	3.2	2.6	6.9	9.9
All other cash aid	7.3	8.9	9.8	10.5	9.1	9.1	8.5	8.0
Total cash assistance	$22.3	$27.6	$36.5	$50.9	$47.9	$46.6	$52.8	$63.6
In-kind assistance								
Food stamps	0.0	0.1	2.0	11.5	15.4	16.5	17.1	23.7
Other food and nutrition	1.0	1.0	1.2	3.8	7.1	6.6	7.4	8.3
Housing and energy aid	0.6	0.9	1.5	4.9	11.5	16.4	14.5	14.1
Medicaid	0.0	1.0	15.7	30.3	41.8	50.3	72.5	96.9
Other medical assistance	3.3	3.6	5.2	6.4	8.5	7.6	11.1	11.8
Total in-kind assistance	$4.8	$6.7	$25.6	$56.9	$84.3	$97.4	$122.6	$154.9
Total means-tested transfers	$27.1	$34.3	$62.1	$107.8	$132.1	$144.0	$175.4	$218.5
Social Insurance								
Old-Age and Survivors	46.0	61.5	88.7	135.9	167.5	207.8	223.5	238.0
Disability Insurance	2.2	5.8	9.6	19.1	24.9	23.7	25.1	28.4
Unemployment insurance	11.0	9.9	10.9	32.3	29.3	21.5	18.9	31.5
Workers' compensation	5.9	7.4	9.4	13.3	19.6	25.7	36.3	41.1
Black Lung	0.0	0.0	0.0	2.3	2.9	2.0	1.5	1.7
Medicare	0.0	0.0	23.2	35.5	56.8	87.7	109.7	120.4
Total social insurance	$65.2	$84.6	$141.8	$238.4	$301.0	$368.4	$415.0	$461.1
Education and Training								
Head Start	0.0	0.5	1.3	1.2	1.5	1.6	1.9	2.6
Targeted federal aid to K–12	0.5	0.6	5.6	5.7	7.8	6.5	6.2	8.2
Higher education (except GSL)	0.0	0.6	2.0	4.6	6.0	5.1	5.9	6.0
Guaranteed Student Loans	0.0	0.0	0.0	0.6	2.3	4.3	4.4	3.6
Total education	$0.5	$1.7	$8.9	$12.1	$17.5	$17.6	$18.4	$20.4
Federal targeted training	0.0	1.3	4.0	7.8	9.6	5.0	4.2	3.5
Public service jobs	0.0	0.0	0.0	0.8	6.0	0.0	0.0	0.0
Total labor market programs	$0.0	$1.3	$4.0	$8.6	$15.6	$5.0	$4.2	$3.5
Total education and training	$0.5	$3.0	$13.0	$20.8	$33.1	$22.6	$22.6	$23.8
Total Spending, All Programs	$92.8	$121.9	$216.9	$367.0	$466.2	$535.0	$613.0	$703.5
As a percentage of GNP	4.4%	4.7%	6.7%	10.1%	10.8%	11.0%	11.2%	12.9%

Sources: U.S. Office of Management and Budget, *Budget of the U.S. Government,* various years; *Social Security Bulletin, Annual Statistical Supplement* (January), various years; U.S. House of Representatives, Committee on Ways and Means (1991, 1992).

Note: Workers' compensation includes benefit payments only; administrative costs are excluded. Workers' compensation includes payments made by private and public insurance carriers. AFDC = Aid to Families with Dependent Children; EITC = Earned Income Tax Credit; GSL = Guaranteed Student Loans; SSI = Supplemental Security Income.

ments. States that previously restricted benefits to single-parent families were obligated to extend benefits to two-parent families with an unemployed parent. At the end of the 1980s, participation in the program—and its cost—once again began to rise. Pushed up by the effects of the 1990–91 recession, AFDC caseloads and spending levels reached record highs in the early 1990s. Still, spending was only modestly higher than in the mid-1970s, when 2 million fewer people were collecting benefits.

Spending on cash assistance programs other than AFDC grew much more slowly after 1960. After 1975, outlays shrank for nearly a decade. Means-tested veterans' payments have decreased steadily since the early 1970s. Means-tested cash transfers for the low-income aged, blind, and disabled remained relatively flat between 1960 and the late 1980s, except during the two years after 1973 when they jumped more than one-third as the federal government assumed almost complete responsibility for providing assistance to these groups.

Most means-tested cash assistance programs provide benefits to people with little or no wage earnings. An exception is the Earned Income Tax Credit (EITC), passed by Congress in 1975 to offset Social Security taxes and encourage job holding among poor breadwinners with children. Parents who have no earnings are ineligible to receive the credit, so it provides a modest incentive for unemployed parents to find work. As recipients' earnings rise above a moderate threshold (about $11,000 in 1992), the credit is gradually phased out. (It is eliminated altogether when a family's income exceeds about $21,000 a year.) Since its introduction in the mid-1970s, the program has enjoyed steady popularity in Congress. Liberalized in 1986 and 1990, the EITC now transfers about 40 percent as much money to low-income families as does the AFDC program.[2]

Total real spending on cash assistance—including the EITC—rose to a peak in 1976, fell about 14 percent over the next eight years, and slowly returned to its old peak by the end of the 1980s. Contrary to a popular perception that welfare spending was soaring when President Reagan took office in 1981, real assistance outlays rose only one-fifth from 1971 to 1980 and actually fell 7 percent in the four years before 1981. Total spending for cash assistance rebounded slightly later in the 1980s, but in spite of surging poverty rates after the mid-1970s, by 1991 real spending barely exceeded the level in 1976.

In-kind benefits. In-kind assistance is provided in three main forms: as food (through food commodity distribution, subsidized school meals, and food stamps), housing (through public housing projects and other housing subsidy programs), and medical care (primarily through the federal-state Medicaid program). The history of in-kind assistance programs offers a marked contrast to that of cash programs. Real spending on means-tested in-kind programs has risen strongly and virtually without interruption since the mid-1960s, although the rate of increase fell off sharply during the first few years of the Reagan presidency (see Figure 3.2). The growth of Medicaid spending has, however, been much more sustained and dramatic than the rise in spending on food or housing assistance.

The fastest growth in food assistance programs occurred between 1969 and 1981, when federal spending jumped from $2 billion to $24 billion. Tighter eligibility limits and modest reductions in benefit generosity early in the Reagan administration reduced real spending on food and nutrition programs during the first half of the 1980s. But Food Stamp program enrollments and spending climbed sharply in the late 1980s and early 1990s as a result of surging unemployment in low-income families.

Housing assistance and energy aid grew more slowly than food assistance, but their climb persisted longer into the 1980s. Housing programs that involve new construction often require public funding commitments many years in advance. Once these commitments are made, the pace of public spending can only be changed with some delay. The Reagan administration slowed down the rate of commitment to new projects, but it did not dramatically change the pace of actual spending until the mid-1980s. Since reaching a peak in 1986, housing outlays for the poor have fallen moderately and then fluctuated within fairly narrow bounds.

The most striking expansion of means-tested assistance has occurred in the Medicaid program. Begun in 1965, it accounted for less than one-sixth of means-tested outlays in 1966, rose to one-third by 1981, and in the early 1990s approached one-half. Part of the rapid growth was due to the predictable expansion associated with any new program. The number of beneficiaries grew explosively as states initiated or extended their means-tested medical assistance programs. From the mid-1970s until the late 1980s the number of recipients stabilized at 22 million a year (U.S. House of Representatives, 1991, p. 1417), but inflation-adjusted outlays rose 80 percent. Spending increased both because medical costs have risen much faster than general inflation and because more resources have been devoted to providing medical care to each patient. The rapid increase was not the result of liberalized eligibility requirements: enrollment standards were effectively tightened for poor children and their parents as a result of tougher eligibility requirements for AFDC.[3] Overall enrollment in Medicaid remained flat even though the number of Americans living in poverty rose more than a quarter. In the late 1980s state and federal eligibility requirements for Medicaid began to be liberalized, especially for pregnant women and children. In addition, Congress required states to pay for a broader menu of services for some categories of beneficiaries. Spending once again began to soar—a staggering 45 percent in the three years after 1988. But even though the number of people eligible for Medicaid was pushed up by the 1990–91 recession, most of the rise in spending was due to medical inflation and program liberalization, not to a weak labor market. The sharp increase in Medicaid spending is unlikely to be reversed when the effects of the recession have passed.

Medicaid has almost certainly produced health improvements among the poor. But the value of the assistance to poor recipients is probably lower than the cost of providing it. If Medicaid recipients in 1990 had been given $72 billion in cash rather than the same amount of direct medical assistance, they would surely have spent far less than $72 billion on medical care. The same may be true for government assistance provided in the form of free or low-cost food, housing, and energy. Yet more than four dollars out of every ten in means-tested spending is for free medical care and three dollars for subsidized food, housing, and energy. Only three out of the ten dollars is transferred as cash. By contrast, in the early 1960s more than eight dollars out of ten was transferred as cash.

Whatever the preferences of assistance recipients, taxpayers and voters have demonstrated a strong partiality for transferring earmarked aid rather than cash. As total means-tested assistance rose from 1.3 percent of the gross national product in 1960 to 3.3 percent in 1989–1991, cash aid fell from 1.1 percent to slightly less than 1.0 percent.

This allocation of transfers might have occurred because many voters are less concerned about poverty in general than about specific types of deprivation—lack of food, decent housing, and essential medical care. Voters may be generally satisfied with the highly unequal rewards handed out in the economic race, at least as rewards are measured by money incomes. But they are unwilling to tolerate starvation, homelessness, and lack of access to needed medical help for those who fail. Income poverty is complacently tolerated. The lack of sufficient income to secure a minimally comfortable life is viewed as a just reward for economic failure.

Overall trends in means-tested spending. The fraction of national income distributed to the poor through means-tested programs has risen nearly 150 percent since 1960. Much of the increase occurred between 1965 and 1972, when spending measured as a percentage of GNP nearly doubled, rising to 2.5 percent of national income. Spending jumped another one-half percentage point between 1974 and 1976, primarily as a result of the severe 1973–75 recession, but then fell back modestly during the subsequent expansion. Spending rose again in the 1980 recession and then remained around 3 percent of GNP for the next decade. Outlays as a percentage of GNP did not rise appreciably in the 1981–82 recession, in spite of the large jump in poverty, primarily because of program cuts enacted during President Reagan's first term in office. Means-tested spending began to surge once again in 1990. Some of the extra spending was due to rising joblessness. But much of it was traceable to liberalization of the AFDC, SSI, and Medicaid programs. Between 1989 and 1992, outlays on income-conditioned transfers rose 0.9 percent of GNP, one of the fastest rates of rise on record. Spending will recede when the recession ends. But two-thirds of the rise is due to increased spending on means-tested medical care, and little of this increase is likely to disappear. After a decade and a half of relative stability in the share of GNP devoted to means-tested programs, the share has once again begun to climb.

Effectiveness in reducing poverty. How efficient have these programs been in reducing poverty? A high fraction of means-tested benefits is distributed to families whose pretransfer incomes are below the poverty line. Using detailed monthly and quarterly statistics covering April 1986, Daniel Weinberg (1991) has estimated that 84 percent of all means-tested transfers, including cash and in-kind benefits, is received by families with monthly pretransfer incomes below the poverty line. Sheldon Danziger and Weinberg, in Chapter 2, show that about two-thirds of means-tested benefits are received by families whose incomes, excluding means-tested benefits but including social insurance benefits, are below the poverty line. Virtually all of the remainder is received by families with incomes near the poverty line (see Table 2.6).

The target efficiency of means-tested transfers should hardly come as a surprise, because by definition, benefits are restricted to poor and near-poor families. The surprising fact is that they reduced poverty so little. Weinberg (1991) reports that only 34 percent of the April 1986 poverty gap was removed by income-conditioned transfers, including transfers received under both cash and noncash programs.[4] Given that the monthly poverty gap was slightly more than $9 billion and monthly outlays on income-conditioned transfers amounted to about $10.4 billion in fiscal year 1986, the amount of poverty reduction seems peculiarly small.

The modest impact of means-tested programs has a number of causes. Government outlays must cover both program administration and benefit payments, but only the payments directly reduce poverty. In addition, Census surveys are plagued by misreporting of income, especially means-tested income. Only 72 percent of AFDC benefits was reported or imputed on the 1988 Census survey that provides the main source of information about the prevalence of low family income in 1987 (U.S. Bureau of the Census, 1991d, p. 216). Underreporting thus reduces the measured impact of transfers. Finally, the institutionalized population, primarily in nursing homes, receives a sizable percentage of means-tested benefits, particularly Medicaid. In 1986, 43 percent of all Medicaid payments went for long-term care services (U.S. Department of Health and Human Services, HCFA, 1991, p. 3). Nursing home residents are excluded from most Census income surveys, even though their well-being is substantially improved by income-conditioned transfers. Indeed, without Medicaid benefits the elderly and disabled poor could hardly afford to be institutionalized.

In spite of ample evidence that the benefits are well targeted but nonetheless remain too small to eliminate poverty, many critics claim that they are shamefully wasted on the nonpoor. And statistics in support of this view are not difficult to find. The U.S. Office of Management and Budget (OMB) published figures in the early 1980s showing that benefits payments under means-tested programs far exceeded the size of the poverty gap but that only half the gap was filled by these payments. In 1982, for instance, the poverty gap was $54 billion while benefit payments reached almost $79 billion. Yet the gap was reduced by only $27 billion as a result of income-conditioned payments, which suggests that two-thirds of payments went to the nonpoor (Stockman, 1984, pp. 247, 295).

One might infer from these statistics that our society is generous to a fault in attempting to reduce poverty but unaccountably careless in permitting benefits to be siphoned off by the nonpoor. The OMB statistics, however, reflect a definition of the nonpoor different from the one used in Weinberg's 1991 analysis. Rather than computing the fraction of benefits going to the pretransfer poor, OMB calculated benefits received by the *prewelfare* poor. Thus the poverty gap is computed after taking account of the value of social insurance payments and the insurance value of Medicare benefits. Both the poverty gap and the number of poor are obviously much smaller under that definition. According to the OMB definition, society is wasting a large part of the Medicaid benefits that go to people whose well-being is brought near or slightly above the poverty line by Social Security and Medicare. I suspect that this view is shared by very few people with elderly or disabled relatives helped by the Medicaid program.

A very high fraction of all means-tested benefits goes to people whose incomes, without government help, would fall below the poverty line. Virtually all of the remainder goes to people with incomes close to the poverty threshold. But many people receiving means-tested transfers also receive government help in another form: social insurance. The combination of social insurance and means-tested transfers raises the well-being of some assisted families, particularly elderly families, comfortably above the poverty threshold, but it leaves the well-being of many others, especially single-parent and single-person families, below it. And 14 percent of the prewelfare poor do not receive any government benefits at all (see Chapter 2).

It would be simple to increase the target efficiency of means-tested transfers. Most if not all means-tested assistance could be combined into a single cash transfer with a confiscatory marginal tax rate both on earnings and on social insurance benefits. If the cash transfer were noncategorical, single-member households and other groups presently suffering serious poverty would receive more generous treatment than under the existing transfer system. Uniting separate programs into a single cash grant would eliminate the possibility that transfer recipients could receive multiple benefits whose combined value substantially exceeds the poverty level. The high tax rate would ensure that benefits would be paid only to the poor, not to the near-poor.

Although this kind of reform is single-minded and logical, it would be politically unpopular, because voters prefer to ensure access to minimal housing, nutrition, and medical care selectively rather than to guarantee everyone a minimum level of money income. And because voters (or their political representatives) also appear inclined toward imposing modest marginal tax rates in programs that offer subsidized medical care, housing, and food, means-tested programs are less efficient than they might be. Nonetheless, these transfers are the nation's least costly mechanism for reducing the gap between market-provided incomes and the resources required for a standard of living above the poverty level.

Social Insurance

Social Security, Medicare, workers' compensation, and unemployment insurance are the major social insurance programs available in the United States. Workers' compensation was the nation's first social insurance program. Established by state governments early in the century, the joint public-private program insures wage earners against earnings losses and medical bills caused by an injury on a job. Social Security Old-Age and Survivors Insurance and federal-state unemployment insurance were introduced in the New Deal, primarily to insure wage and salary workers in industry. The population covered by these programs has since been expanded repeatedly and now includes almost the entire work force.[5] Social Security Disability Insurance was added in 1956. Medicare—medical insurance for the aged and disabled—began in 1965 as an extension of the basic Social Security program.

None of the social insurance programs was specifically designed to eliminate poverty. The cash social insurance programs insure workers and their dependents against earnings losses occurring as a result of the retirement, death, disability, or temporary joblessness of a breadwinner. Medicare protects the elderly and disabled against extraordinary outlays for hospital and medical services. Obviously, social insurance programs offer protection against several important causes of poverty, but other sources of hardship were ignored in their design. A new labor market entrant or even an experienced worker who suffers a long bout of unemployment can expect to receive little help under the system, for example, because unemployment benefits are restricted to experienced workers and are usually available for only six months. Workers who are steadily employed but at low wage rates should also expect little aid for their families, at least until they reach age sixty-two, become disabled, or expire. Many poor people are thus excluded from receiving benefits.

By contrast, nearly all middle-class and affluent workers can expect to receive social insurance benefits sometime during their lives, and the level is often exceptionally generous. For current Social Security and Medicare beneficiaries, benefits received have far exceeded total taxes paid. Because Social Security benefit levels are scaled to the level of past wages, it is actually possible that the difference between benefits and past taxes is larger for affluent retirees than for poorer retirees (Hurd and Shoven, 1985). As the system matures and workers pay high social insurance taxes over a longer part of their careers, however, windfall gains for those with high lifetime incomes will become much less common.

Even though social insurance may provide income protection primarily for the middle class, the programs are far more important than means-tested transfers in lifting families out of poverty. In Chapter 2, Danziger and Weinberg estimate that more than a third of social insurance benefits were received by families with 1989 private money incomes below the poverty line (see Table 2.5). Among family units comprising members older than sixty-five, Social Security alone reduced pretransfer poverty by 72 percent in the mid-1980s, decreasing the poverty rate from 56 percent to 14 percent. Among Americans over sixty-five, social insurance reduced pretransfer poverty by nearly three-quarters. Social Security eliminated 85 percent of the pretransfer poverty gap for elderly families (U.S. House of Representatives, 1991, pp. 1171–72).

As suggested earlier, Social Security and Medicare are much less redistributive when viewed from the perspective of a lifetime. Because the beneficiaries include virtually everyone older than age sixty-five, most of the recipients had moderate or high incomes before they retired. In addition, the pretransfer poverty rate of the elderly overstates the hardship they would face in the absence of Social Security. If social insurance had never been invented, many of the elderly would have worked longer, would have accumulated more savings, or would have chosen to live in the households of more affluent relatives, especially their children. Although estimating the precise effect of Social Security and Medicare on the earnings, savings, and living arrangements of the elderly is impossible, it is likely that the total impact has been important (Danziger, Haveman, and Plotnick, 1981). The programs' effect can be seen in the very sharp declines in poverty among the aged that have occurred as real benefits have risen. In 1959 the income poverty rate of the elderly was 35 percent among the elderly but 22 percent for the remainder of the population. By 1990 the rate for the elderly had tumbled to 12 percent and for the nonelderly to 13.5 percent. If one takes account of in-kind income—including Medicare—the poverty rate for the elderly was less than 10 percent in 1990 (U.S. Bureau of the Census, 1991c, p. 14). A large share of this decline in poverty among the elderly has been due to the increase in Social Security and Medicare benefits since 1960.

Unemployment insurance is less effective as an antipoverty program. A higher proportion of benefits is received by families whose annual incomes would be above the poverty line in the absence of social insurance payments. To be insured under unemployment insurance, an unemployed worker must have had a recent and fairly stable work history. This criterion precludes benefits for important classes of the poor—the nonemployed, the erratically employed, and the chronically unemployed or underemployed. Still, the program is redistributive, and it appears even more so when evaluated according to a weekly or monthly accounting period rather than an annual period. Although only 18 percent of unemployment compensation recipients were below the poverty line before they became unemployed, 61 percent were in poverty once earnings ceased (Burtless, 1984, p. 126).

One of the main differences between unemployment insurance and Social Security is that, for most workers, unemployment is temporary while retirement and disability last indefinitely. Because unemployed workers typically find jobs after only brief spells of joblessness, their annual earnings may put them well above the poverty line. Retired and disabled workers usually do not engage in paid employment at all. Consequently, their annual earned incomes are well below the poverty line. But for both the temporarily unemployed and the retired and disabled, social insurance is vital for maintaining income when earnings cease.

The notion that unemployment insurance, Medicare, and especially Social Security are intended for the middle class is at once a political strength and an ideological weakness of the programs. Because benefits are broadly distributed and provide crucial support for millions of families, and because all taxpayers can reasonably expect to receive similar benefits at some future date, social insurance is by far the most popular vehicle of income redistribution (Cook, 1990). But the vast size of the recipient population prompts heated criticism from both the right and the left. If social insurance simply redistributes income from one phase of a worker's life to another, conservatives argue, why is government intervention needed at all? Workers and their employers could surely devise a redistribution scheme more efficient and satisfying than one imposed by the state. Conservatives are correct—for some workers. Far-sighted workers would make adequate provision against the risks of unemployment, disability, old age, and early death. But because many people are myopic about these risks, most voters favor forcing workers to insure themselves against the loss of earnings capacity. What is more, experience has shown that publicly provided insurance is financially more secure than the private alternatives. Social Security and Medicare have not been affected by financial market fluctuations, and benefits under the programs have never been in jeopardy because of competitive losses suffered by individual companies, industries, or regions. Nor have benefits been eroded by inflation. Given this track record, few voters can be persuaded that social insurance should be abandoned or significantly scaled back.

Critics on the left question the logic of social insurance as a method of redistribution. Why should poor wage earners be heavily taxed in order to pay for benefits received mostly by the middle class and affluent elderly? Writers in the popular press excoriate a system in which "18 million Americans earning less than $15,000 at full-time, year-round jobs 'contribute' their FICA dollars, [while] a CEO and spouse [can] retire and expect to receive more than $24,000 annually in tax-sheltered Social Security and Medicare benefits" (Howe and Longman, 1992, p. 94). This criticism rests on the assumption that social insurance is not redistributive enough: it ought to give less to the affluent or impose lighter burdens on the working poor. In reality, however, social insurance represents a better financial deal to most low-income workers than it does to workers who earn high wages. The pretransfer poor receive 35 percent of social insurance benefits (see Table 2.5). A large share of the remainder is paid out to families not far above the poverty line. Critics of Social Security sometimes forget something else: the supposedly secure middle-class status of a Social Security recipient does not mean that he or she would remain there long if Social Security or Medicare were drastically curtailed.

More fundamentally, the political popularity of social insurance rests to an important degree on the perceived tie between contributions and benefits. Payments made to the well-to-do elderly, like payments to the less affluent, are regarded as a right earned by virtue of prior tax contributions. The link between benefits and contributions makes the program more palatable to taxpayers and makes benefit payments acceptable as a form of government aid to recipients. Critics of social insurance who condemn the system because it dissipates so much of its resources on the nonpoor think that the aim of social welfare spending is to aid the needy. By and large, the public does not agree. The far more popular goal of social insurance is to protect ordinary workers and their dependents against earnings losses throughout their careers and against high medical bills in old age. It is doubtful that the immense amount of redistribution carried out through social insurance would continue for long if the link between contributions and benefits were severed.

Social insurance programs face growing public scrutiny, not because of their philosophical defects, but because of their budgetary and behavioral implications. The anxiety about retirement and disability insurance, jobless benefits, and third-party payment of medical bills is a natural consequence of their rapid growth over the past half-century and the anticipated cost explosion in the next century when the baby boom generation retires. From 1960 to 1975, real outlays on both social insurance and means-tested transfer programs grew at an unsustainable rate, increasing more than 9 percent a year. After 1975 spending growth slowed, but the growth in social insurance programs slowed less than the growth in means-tested transfers. Between 1975 and 1990, means-tested outlays rose at an annual rate of only 3.3 percent, while social insurance spending increased—on top of a much higher base—at a rate of 3.8 percent. Since the mid-1970s, annual spending on Social Security, Medicare, unemployment insurance, and black lung benefits has *increased* by an amount exceeding total outlays on all means-tested programs.

Real outlays in certain social insurance programs climbed even more rapidly (see Figure 3.3 and Table 3.1). Expenditures on Old-Age and Survivors Insurance (OASI) have quintupled since 1960. Outlays grew especially rapidly between 1968 and 1973, increasing at an annual rate of 10 percent. This rise occurred because of the maturation of the OASI program—new beneficiaries were receiving much higher benefits than older ones—and because of a 20 percent jump in real basic benefit levels implemented between 1970 and 1973. Since 1973 OASI outlays have grown more slowly, averaging about 5.1 percent a year between

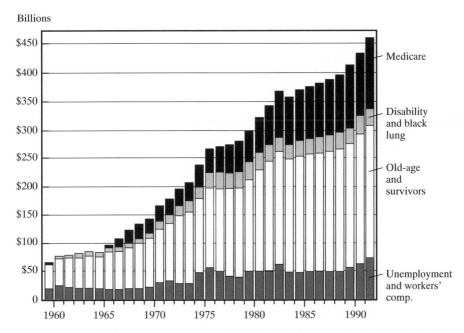

Figure 3.3   Social insurance spending, 1960–1992 (in billions of 1990 dollars). (Data sources: U.S. Office of Management and Budget, *Budget of the U.S. Government,* various years; U.S. House of Representatives, 1991, 1992.)

1973 and 1983 and just 1.5 percent a year since 1983. The growth in OASI spending is expected to remain low until 2010, when the baby boom generation will begin to retire. The sharply slower growth in old-age benefits derives partly from the elimination of unintended double indexing of benefits, effective in 1979, and from the delay in cost-of-living adjustments, voted in 1983.

Disability Insurance (DI) is a program that is particularly important for low-wage workers who are at risk of entering poverty should their earnings cease (Haveman, Wolfe, and Warlick, 1984, esp. pp. 79–85; Burkhauser, Haveman, and Wolfe, 1992). Outlays on the program have followed a peculiar course. Expenditures rose tenfold between 1960 and 1977 and fluctuated within fairly narrow bounds between 1977 and 1989. Outlays grew at a particularly fast rate between 1968 to 1977, in part because of the 20 percent Social Security benefit increase mentioned earlier, but mostly because the caseload doubled. The number of applications for benefits increased sharply in the period, and standards for eligibility were loosened. But the number of beneficiaries fell one-fifth between 1977 and 1983 as eligibility standards were tightened (U.S House of Representatives, 1991, p. 114). In 1989 enrollments and outlays once again began to climb, in this case because of a weak labor market, which tends to boost applications for disability benefits, and to some extent because of a more liberal administrative definition of disability.

Unlike spending on old-age and disability insurance, spending on Medicare rose strongly and without interruption since the program's inception in 1965. Though the rapid rise in Medicare in the late 1960s was predictable, the increased spending after 1973 was largely unexpected. Medicare expenditures measured in constant dollars more than quadrupled between 1973 and 1991, growing at a compound annual rate of more than 8 percent. The number of people enrolled in Medicare has risen by about one-quarter of that rate. Most of the rise in outlays has been due to rising utilization of medical services and to medical care inflation that has far outstripped general price inflation. Compared with the Medicare-covered population in the late 1960s and early 1970s, the covered population today is using more and far more costly medical services. As with Medicaid, the program has generated measurable health benefits for the elderly, but it is doubtful that the eligible population would be willing to pay for this much health care on its own if the program were converted to cash grants that cost taxpayers the same amount of money.

Workers' compensation and unemployment compensation are the only social insurance programs offering significant benefits to active workers, but the programs have enjoyed unequal fortunes in the past three decades. As a percentage of wage and salary income, workers' compensation payments have doubled since 1960, and now amount to 1.3 percent of total wages and salaries. By contrast, unemployment benefits have shrunk noticeably. Although unemployment insurance coverage was extended to new classes of workers in the decade and a half before 1976, the percentage of job losers actually collecting unemployment benefits began to slide in 1980 (Burtless, 1991a). Much of the decline was due to tighter restrictions on eligibility and sharp cutbacks in the after-tax value of benefits. Unemployment insurance, like OASI and DI, was liberalized in the decade ending in 1976 but was scaled back over the next decade, so that near the end of the 1980s fewer than one in three jobless workers received unemployment compensation. Spending on jobless benefits began to climb during the 1990–91 recession, but remained below the level that would have been attained under similar circumstances before the early 1980s. Contrary to a widespread view that middle-class entitlements were spared from the budget axe, spending on the *cash* social insurance programs was curbed in the late 1970s and 1980s.

Nonetheless, social insurance programs continue to be important in the struggle against poverty. Social insurance spending is much higher than spending on means-tested assistance, and insurance benefits keep far more low-income families out of poverty. The relative size of social insurance and means-tested programs would have been difficult to foresee forty-five years ago. In June 1950 more old people were receiving government aid under the Old-Age Assistance (OAA) program than under Old-Age Insurance (2.8 million as opposed to 2.1 million), and the average OAA payment in 1949 was 70 percent higher than the average primary insurance amount under OAI. Assistance rolls were expanding fast enough to remain comfortably ahead of the insurance rolls (Derthick, 1979, p. 273). Disability insurance and Medicare had not yet been invented. The disabled received cash aid under public assistance programs, and the aged and disabled received government help in paying medical bills through means-tested programs.

The development of Disability Insurance and Medicare, the maturation of the Old-Age Insurance program, legislated increases in real cash benefit levels, and the extension of Social Security, Medicare, and unemployment insurance coverage to nearly all classes of workers have dramatically increased the scope of social insurance. For low- and average-wage workers who become insured, social insurance frequently makes the difference between a life in want and a life of comfortable subsistence when a breadwinner is faced with unemployment, disability, or forced early retirement. But other groups still experience high poverty rates. More than a fifth of all children under eighteen and an even larger proportion of children under six live in families with money incomes below the poverty line (U.S. House of Representatives, 1991, pp. 1053–54). For the most part, families of these children are poor because of circumstances not covered by the nation's social insurance programs—divorce, illegitimacy, or long-term unemployment on the part of a parent. And means-tested assistance by itself is simply not generous enough to eliminate their poverty.

Investment in Education and Training

When the War on Poverty was launched in 1964, the Johnson administration believed that its antipoverty strategy would raise the earnings of the able-bodied poor rather than increase transfers. In outlining the administration's proposals, the 1964 *Economic Report of the President* conspicuously omitted any mention of cash aid to the nonelderly, nondisabled poor. "Americans want to *earn* the American standard of living by their own efforts and contributions," the report asserted. "It would be far better, even if more difficult, to equip and to permit the poor of the Nation to produce and to earn the . . . $11 billion [required to eliminate poverty]" (U.S. Council of Economic Advisers, 1964, p. 77). Among other elements, the report called for improved labor market exchange, expansion of educational opportunity, and added job counseling and training for poor teenagers and adults.

President Johnson's economic advisors had a powerful faith that "if children of poor families can be given skills and motivation, they will not become poor adults" (U.S. Council of Economic Advisers, 1964, p. 75). To be fair, this faith was widely shared at the time by social scientists and the public. It derived from the well-documented association between educational attainment, on the one hand, and social status and income, on the other. Because those at the top of the earnings distribution had more education than those on the bottom, it was believed that by raising the quality and amount of training received by workers on the bottom, inequality of income could be reduced. A scientific model to rationalize this faith was advanced in the early 1960s when the theory of human capital investment was first developed (Schultz, 1963; Becker, 1964).

Faith in education led to a variety of program initiatives. Space does not permit a review of all of the education and training programs introduced during or after the War on Poverty. Their number is too large, their target populations too numerous, their aims too diverse, and their funding levels too small to justify such a discussion. Figure 3.4 shows the trend in real federal outlays for targeted human capital programs since 1960. Outlays are divided into two categories. The first includes expenditures on education programs, primarily for economically disadvantaged students in nursery, elementary, and secondary schools and in college. Because it is unclear whether the guaranteed student loan (GSL) program strictly targets the poor, its outlays are shown separately. The second category includes federal expenditures for training, work experience, and public service employment (PSE). The PSE program did not always carefully target the low-income

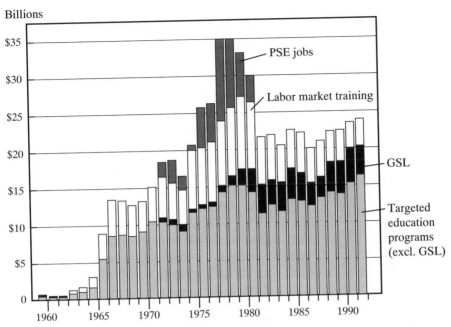

Figure 3.4 Spending on targeted human capital programs, 1960–1992 (in billions of 1990 dollars). (For data sources, see Figure 3.3.)

population, although most jobs went to the economically disadvantaged, especially during the late 1970s when the program achieved its largest scope. For this reason, PSE spending has been separately tabulated as well.

Federal spending on targeted education programs, particularly Head Start and Title I of the Education Act, rose dramatically: from $1.7 billion to $8.5 billion in constant 1990 dollars between 1965 and 1967. Spending on training programs tripled. Nevertheless, by 1968 federal spending on targeted education and training was only a quarter of the level of spending on means-tested assistance programs. Little of the rise in means-tested benefits during the Johnson administration was in the form of *cash* assistance, of course; most of the increase was in in-kind aid. Nonetheless, there was a wide disparity between actual trends in government spending and the President's 1964 promise to restrain assistance outlays while emphasizing investment in education and training.

Education and training spending rose much more slowly under President Nixon, about 7 percent a year from 1968 to 1975, even including outlays for the new GSL and PSE programs. The main focus was in means-tested spending, which grew nearly 12 percent a year (on a much higher base). During the Ford and early Carter administrations, however, spending on targeted education and training programs spurted once again, rising more than two-thirds between 1975 and 1978. Most of this rise was due to increased spending on PSE, which leaped from less than $1 billion to $11 billion, and on the GSL program, which rose from $0.6 billion to $1.1 billion.

Spending on the main targeted human capital programs trailed off in the latter part of the Carter administration and then dropped precipitously after President Reagan's election. Between 1978 and 1983 outlays for programs other than PSE and GSL fell by one-fifth; including the PSE and GSL reductions, outlays fell nearly two-fifths. After 1983 the decrease was much slower. Labor market training programs absorbed steadily smaller amounts of federal funds over the 1980s and early 1990s, but targeted education programs began to rebound after 1986. Growing public concern that the public school system was failing led to a modest bipartisan effort to boost federal spending on schools and early childhood development programs. Nonetheless, federal spending on targeted education and training programs remained sharply lower in the early 1990s than it had been in the late 1970s and early 1980s.

Federal programs to educate and train low-income children and adults represent the only important category of antipoverty programs in which spending patterns broadly conform to widely held perceptions about the history of social welfare outlays. The programs were inconsequential before the Kennedy administration, expanded very rapidly under Johnson's War on Poverty, grew more slowly during the administrations of Nixon, Ford, and Carter, and then shrank dramatically under Reagan. Meanwhile, total real spending on both means-tested and social insurance transfers has risen almost every year, no matter which party was in power. Presidents can exercise more budgetary control over grant-in-aid programs than over entitlement programs, particularly Social Security, Medicaid, and Food Stamps, which are indexed to inflation. When prices rise sharply, as they did during the terms of Presidents Nixon and Carter, or joblessness increases, as it did under Presidents Ford, Reagan, and Bush, spending on indexed entitlement programs will automatically increase. By contrast, there is no direct connection between prices or unemployment and federal spending on education and training. For that reason, outlays on targeted human capital programs provide a direct reflection of the incumbent president's views on the desirable size and composition of government spending for the poor.

Even if a president wishes to trim poverty spending, the amount devoted to education and training programs is simply too small for changes in outlays to have much effect on trends in total poverty spending. As a percentage of GNP, for instance, outlays for targeted human capital programs and PSE rose from virtually nothing to 0.85 percent in 1978 and since then have fallen to less than 0.45

percent, but the drop has been dwarfed by movements in means-tested transfers, which rose 0.4 percentage points of GNP between 1978 and 1983, and in social insurance, which rose 1.9 percentage points (Figure 3.5). Increases in Medicaid expenditures alone were enough to counterbalance the decline in human capital outlays.

Although the discussion has so far focused on federally funded human capital investment programs targeted on low-income children and adults, state and local governments also support these kinds of programs. Most of their investments, however, are centered on students in public schools or local colleges and universities, and only a small proportion targets the economically disadvantaged. This spending has been important, nevertheless, in increasing the economic and social mobility of the poor. Arguably, it represents the nation's most important and most costly public policy to reduce long-term poverty.

Effectiveness of education and training programs. Outlays for targeted education and training programs have been comparatively small, overall, but it is still

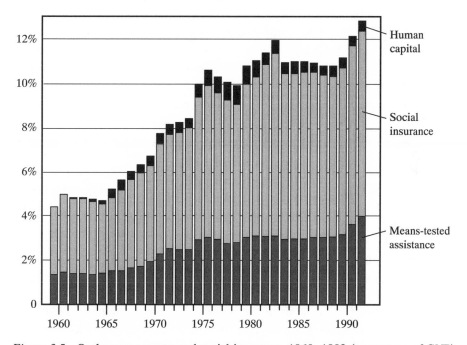

Figure 3.5 Outlays on poverty and social insurance, 1960–1992 (percentage of GNP). (Data sources: U.S. Office of Management and Budget, *Budget of the U.S. Government,* various years; *Social Security Bulletin, Annual Statistical Supplement* (January), various years; U.S. House of Representatives, 1991, 1992.)

important to evaluate their antipoverty effectiveness. Such an evaluation, however, requires more extensive analysis than can be given here. The literature on targeted education and training programs is enormous and its quality highly variable; it includes some studies showing no program effects, or even harmful effects, on cognition, achievement, and postprogram earnings. I concentrate here on training programs.

Training programs should be more immediately effective than education programs in reducing poverty: training is generally provided to teenagers about to enter the labor force and to adults of working age and is supposed to be directly relevant to employment. Education assistance, by contrast, is not specifically aimed at improving job skills and is provided to students who may be years away from earning a living. Most careful studies suggest that the main training programs have increased participants' average earnings, at least in the short run (Barnow, 1987). Public service jobs, when they were available, provided income directly to otherwise unemployed disadvantaged workers but apparently achieved only minor success in raising postprogram earnings.

On a microeconomic level the gains from some programs have been impressive. The Congressional Budget Office estimates that adult women in CETA-sponsored classroom training, on-the-job training, and work experience programs increased their annual real wages by $1,270 to $2,100 (in 1990 dollars), a gain of 25 to 75 percent of average earnings before enrollment (U.S. Congressional Budget Office and NCEP, 1982, pp. 19, A-42). The most recent evaluation of the JTPA training programs showed gains for adult men and women ranging between $585 and $625 a year (Bloom et al., 1993, p. 4). In view of the costs of these programs, the earnings gains by adults are large enough that taxpayers might reasonably prefer to spend money on training rather than on direct transfer payments. One dollar spent on training ultimately raises the incomes of participating adults by more than one dollar. Effective training thus not only redistributes slices of the economic pie from the nonpoor to the poor but increases the size of the pie.

We should not judge an antipoverty strategy solely by its successes, however. Many adults, and the great majority of teenagers, are not helped by most of the low-cost training strategies the United States has tried. Training remains a highly uncertain mechanism for raising the incomes of any *individual* breadwinner and is only modestly effective in raising the *aggregate* income of trainees—adult men and women or teenagers. I suspect that the effect on earnings of education programs targeted on younger students is even more tenuous. The lesson to be drawn, then, is not that targeted education and training programs are without value; they are modestly helpful. But unfortunately, they are unlikely to make a reliable or sizable difference in the lives of most people who participate in them.

Economic Limits to Poverty Spending

Social insurance and poverty-related expenditures have increased markedly in the past third of a century, both absolutely and as a percentage of national output (see Figure 3.5 and Table 3.1). Such spending climbed in the context of generally rising government budgets, but it has also become a much larger fraction of government spending. In the two decades after 1960, social insurance and poverty spending increased from 16 percent to 34 percent of government outlays and stayed near that percentage during the next decade. Between 1960 and 1990 overall government spending as a share of GNP rose almost 7 percentage points. Nearly all the increase was concentrated in the three categories of spending already discussed—means-tested transfers, social insurance, and targeted education and training programs. The expansion in other nondefense spending as a share of GNP was just about offset by the decrease in defense spending.

How much has the nation reduced poverty with these outlays? Disturbingly little. Census tabulations show that the percentage of all Americans in poverty was 22.4 percent in 1959, fell to 11.1 percent in 1973, and rose to 13.5 percent by 1990. Much of the reduction was concentrated among the elderly and disabled. Single women with children, aged widows, and other groups continue to suffer very high poverty rates.

Census statistics mask the full extent of poverty reduction, however, because they exclude the consumption gains resulting from in-kind transfers. The official poverty statistics count only cash incomes in measuring family resources, but the growth in means-tested transfers has been overwhelmingly concentrated in in-kind programs. The official series thus provides a defective yardstick for measuring long-term progress against poverty. The Census Bureau itself estimates that the number of poor in 1990 might have been overstated by 9 to 23 percent, depending on the way noncash assistance is valued (U.S. Bureau of Census, 1991b, p. 11). The overstatement of the poverty population was far smaller in 1960, when in-kind benefits were much lower. But even with in-kind transfers accounted for, the percentage of the population that is poor has expanded significantly since the 1970s and remains astonishingly high in view of the rise in national income during the 1980s (see Chapter 2).

A variety of attempts have been made to explain why poverty declined so little after the late 1960s even though transfers increased so much. As already noted, the goal of the most expensive transfer programs is not primarily to reduce income poverty. Social insurance programs protect family incomes when wages have been lost because of unemployment, retirement, disability, or death. Many in-kind assistance programs are designed to ensure the provision of particular merit goods—food, housing, and medical care. In addition to reducing the level of want among the pretransfer poor, social insurance and in-kind transfers also provide benefits to the nonpoor and to the pretransfer poor whose incomes have already been raised above the income poverty line by other transfers. In addition, despite the immense sums spent on transfers, some of the poor are not eligible for any cash aid and qualify for only nominal in-kind assistance.

Can the nation afford to increase the share of national income devoted to reducing poverty? Here we should distinguish between poverty spending that represents a claim on society's limited resources and spending that redistributes income among households. The former reduces the resources available for other worthwhile consumption and investment. The capital and labor used in education and training programs and in administering public transfer programs have other potential uses in both the public and the private sectors. By devoting real resources to aiding the poor, society is forgoing the opportunity to invest those resources in better roads, houses, or capital plant and equipment. (It is also, of course, passing up the opportunity to consume more yachts, video recorders, and trips to Disney World.) But an overwhelming fraction of poverty spending consists of transfers rather than direct government purchases of goods and services. Those transfers neither add to nor subtract from national income; they merely redistribute it among households.

As long as the nation is willing to impose the taxes necessary to finance spending to reduce poverty and as long as the taxes do not seriously impair incentives to work and save, there is no macroeconomic reason to limit outlays to current levels. For much of the postwar period the nation seemed willing to pay for added transfers through added taxes. Social insurance was financed with very visible earmarked taxes, and the taxes roughly kept pace with social insurance spending. Means-tested transfers and targeted education and training programs are another story. These programs are financed out of general revenues, the same source used to pay for nearly all other government activities. Since 1981 the federal government has been unwilling to finance its general obligations—including targeted transfers, education, and training—with tax revenues, relying instead on borrowing to pay for part of its current spending. In one respect this situation can hardly be considered unusual; all but one of the federal budgets after 1960 was in deficit (as the deficit is usually measured). What is unusual since the early 1980s is the size of the deficits and the expectation that large deficits will persist indefinitely.

The macroeconomic problems arising from deficits are not caused by how much is spent on poverty or indeed by how much is spent on any other particular category of government activity. They are instead caused by the tendency of the deficits to absorb domestic saving, thereby reducing domestic investment in capital formation. This problem has grown more acute since the mid-1980s, when private saving in the United States plummeted.

During the eight years of the Reagan administration the federal budget deficit acted as a brake on added poverty spending. The prospect of large and growing federal deficits put pressure on Congress and the President to hold down government spending. But this brake was essentially political rather than economic. Although federal deficits do indeed have important economic consequences, fear of those consequences did not deter Congress or the President from significantly increasing spending on national defense in the early 1980s, on biomedical research throughout the 1980s, or on deposit insurance for insolvent thrift institutions later in the decade. Nor did the deficit stop Congress or the President from permitting a significant liberalization in SSI and Medicaid benefits after 1988. Nor, for that matter, did the large deficits spur the government to take straightforward corrective measures, for example, by raising taxes. In the long run an economically defensible level of poverty spending must depend on how much society is willing to tax itself. If people are willing to tolerate heavier tax burdens, the budget deficit represents at most a temporary political check rather than a permanent economic limit to outlays on means-tested transfers and targeted education and training.

Assuming that poverty expenditures are financed by an appropriate level of government revenues, the main objection to increased spending is a microeconomic one. Both the taxes raised to support poverty spending and the spending itself induce distortions in economic behavior. These distortions may reduce national income and aggregate welfare even as the added poverty spending raises the income and increases the welfare of the poor. Arthur Okun (1975) likened public redistribution to a leaky bucket. With the best of intentions, the state compels families at the top of the income distribution to place money in a bucket that is carried to families on the bottom. In passing from families at the top to those on the bottom, some money leaks out of the redistributive bucket—either because of added inefficiency at the top or diminished incentives on the bottom. For his part, Okun was willing to accept a certain amount of leakage, possibly as much as 60 percent of the bucket's original contents. But he noted that other taxpayers were less tolerant; they would find even a one-percent leak unacceptable.

This analogy leads to a natural question: how big is the leak? Economists have focused on two kinds of leaks: reductions in labor supply and reductions in saving. Unfortunately, the size of these distortions is unknown. Some evidence on labor supply is suggestive, however. During the 1970s the federal government sponsored four negative income tax (NIT) experiments to determine how liberalization of cash assistance programs affected work incentives. Even though the plans tested were quite different from existing public assistance programs for the able-bodied poor, the responses of people enrolled in the plans did show the responses we might observe if welfare benefits were raised. On balance, the statistical studies of the experiments imply that means-tested transfers have a statistically significant, but comparatively small, effect on the labor supply of low-income men and women. An increase in basic assistance levels that raises the total incomes of poor families by 50 percent would reduce their average labor supply 3.5 percent to 8.5 percent (Burtless, 1987). Because wage earners in poor families have very low earned incomes to begin with, the effects of these labor supply reductions on economy-wide labor supply and earnings would be modest.[6]

Even if the overall work reduction is small, the earnings loss among poor breadwinners could represent a large fraction of the higher payments provided to low-income families. Earnings reductions would thus offset much of the income gain that higher benefits are supposed to achieve. To take an extreme illustration, tabulations for the Seattle and Denver NIT experiments show that taxpayers spent approximately $3.00 on additional transfer payments in order to raise the incomes of participating two-parent families by $1.00. Men and women in the experiments reduced their earnings in response to the NIT plans, thus lowering the net income gains they received while at the same time boosting the cost of the plans to taxpayers.[7] Even if the economy-wide earnings loss from liberalizing transfers is small, taxpayers might legitimately wonder whether it is worth raising taxes by $3.00 to raise the incomes of poor two-parent families by just $1.00.[8]

Admittedly the example is extreme. Other tabulations from the Seattle and Denver experiments show that it was less costly to raise the incomes of single-parent families by $1.00. Moreover, statistical evidence from the experiments and from nonexperimental sources can be used to devise transfer plans more efficient than the ones tested in Seattle and Denver. In estimating the cost of simple transfer schemes that would eliminate poverty among families with children, analysts have calculated that taxpayers would spend $1.29 to $1.89 to raise recipients' net incomes by $1.00.[9] To return to Okun's analogy of a leaky bucket, roughly a fifth to a half of the money placed in the redistributive bucket would be lost in transit. If this estimate is accurate, is it unacceptably large? One's answer ultimately depends on an ethical, not an economic, judgment.

This discussion of work incentive effects has concentrated on the effects of means-tested transfers. It is worthwhile to differentiate the impact of various kinds of programs. The effects of transfer programs should be clearly distinguished from those of wage subsidy and education and training programs. Transfers provide income support to families who might otherwise be forced to increase their incomes on their own. Some kinds of transfers—such as AFDC—impose high marginal tax rates on wage earnings and reduce even further the incentive to work. By contrast, wage subsidy programs and education and training programs attempt to *increase* the earnings of participants; if they succeed, these programs contribute to economic efficiency and growth.

There is also an equally important difference between social insurance benefits and means-tested transfers. Social insurance benefits are largely paid for by eventual recipients. Workers may expect that most of their current tax contributions will eventually be returned to them as unemployment or retirement benefits. Viewed in this light, social insurance is simply a form of delayed compensation and should cause no more labor supply distortion than private health insurance, pension benefits, or other forms of nonwage compensation. Hence there are good reasons to believe that social insurance taxes should cause less labor supply distortion than an equivalent amount of income or other taxes raised to pay means-tested benefits. In spite of this distinction between social insurance and means-tested transfers, nearly all informed analysts would agree that increasing present levels of either type of transfer would reduce the level of self-support among affected low-income breadwinners.

Another objection to transfers is that they distort the incentive to save and consequently reduce aggregate saving and investment. Martin Feldstein (1974) forcefully raised this objection in the case of Social Security. Although his original research was marred by a serious data error, the argument continues to be accepted by many economists. But his objection to transfers seems less serious than the claim that they reduce aggregate labor supply. Private saving showed no particular trend during the period in which Social Security benefits were liberalized (1949–1978). The recent decline in private saving occurred *after* Social Security payments were scaled back by legislation that became effective in 1979 and 1983. In addition, as Henry Aaron (1982, pp. 51–52) has observed, if an important object of policy is to increase net savings and investment, there are far more direct and reliable methods to accomplish this than by reducing transfers. For example, if the federal government ran budget surpluses rather than deficits, the amount of domestic savings available for investment would soar.

Analyses of incentives do not provide a clear message to the policymaker who is considering general increases in poverty spending. The efficiency costs of an overall increase may be large or small, depending on the microeconomic specialist consulted. The uncertainty is reduced once attention is focused on particular reforms or benefit increases, but even then the statistical evidence may be too imprecise or contradictory to support strong conclusions about losses in earnings or savings. In summarizing the literature on incentive effects in 1981, three economists concluded that "research findings are too varied, too uncertain, and themselves too colored with judgment to serve as more than a rough guide to policy choices" (Danziger, Haveman, and Plotnick, 1981, p. 1020). There is no reason to modify that conclusion today. An economist might reasonably suggest reforms to reduce poverty more cheaply or with fewer distortionary economic effects than present policies, but current knowledge does not permit an economist to predict reliably the total efficiency gains or losses that would arise from a particular policy. Although the direction of effect might be known with tolerable accuracy, the magnitude of change would remain uncertain.

Existing theory and evidence have only limited use in predicting the exact terms of the tradeoff between poverty spending and economic prosperity. Economists are a long way from being able to say what price is paid for marginal increases in overall spending and even further from knowing the total penalty paid by the United States for its current level of spending. Some international comparisons may be suggestive. The United States spends a smaller share of national income on redistribution than do most other advanced industrialized nations. Not surprisingly, by devoting fewer resources to redistribution the United States also accomplishes less redistribution, leaving a greater degree of income inequality than found in other countries.

Evidence that the United States spends less on public redistribution has been developed by the Organisation for Economic Co-operation and Development during the past decade (OECD, 1983, 1986; Saunders, 1984; Oxley and Martin, 1991). Table 3.2 shows statistics on social security and other transfers, per capita national income, and income growth in the seven largest OECD countries and Sweden. The first two columns show the percentage of gross domestic product (GDP) devoted to social security and transfers in 1979 and 1990. The OECD definition of social security and transfers includes public spending on health, pensions, and other income maintenance programs. Much of this spending is actually received by the nonpoor, of course, but the overall level of spending provides a rough index of the amount of public redistribution that is attempted in each country. Nations are ranked in order of their social welfare spending in 1990. The United States ranks near the bottom on this scale.

The third column shows per capita GDP in 1989, measured in each country's national currency and then converted to U.S. dollars using purchasing power parity exchange rates. The United States ranks at the top of the income scale, although the percentage gap with most other OECD countries is shrinking. The last two columns show annual growth rates in real per capita GDP in the periods 1960–1979 and 1979–1989. Japan, which devoted the smallest proportion of national income to social welfare spending in 1981, enjoyed by far the fastest income growth in the two periods. But the United States, which ranked second lowest in social welfare spending, also ranks at or near the bottom on the growth scale. Nations that devote substantially more income to redistribution have not suffered conspicuously slower income growth: nations that spent twice as much on social welfare grew at least as fast as the United States or faster.

These statistics do not prove that activist redistribution policy imposes *no* economic penalty. Many factors besides social welfare policy have affected income

Table 3.2   Social expenditure and economic growth in eight OECD countries

Country	Social security and other transfers as % of GDP[a]		GDP per capita[b]	Annual growth in GDP per capita (%)	
	1979	1990	1989	1960–1979	1979–1989
France	20.4	23.5	$15,500	3.7	1.7
Sweden	19.3[c]	21.2	16,300	2.8	1.8
West Germany	18.9	19.3	15,600	3.2	1.6
Italy	14.8[c]	18.9	14,600	4.1	2.2
United Kingdom	12.8	13.7	15,000	2.3	2.0
Canada	9.9	12.8	20,400	3.5	2.0
United States	10.2	11.5	21,600	2.2	1.7
Japan	10.3	11.2	16,500	6.5	3.4

Sources: Oxley and Martin (1991), pp. 158–160; and unpublished data from the U.S. Department of Labor, Bureau of Labor Statistics.

a. Social security and other transfers include government outlays on public pensions, health insurance, and other income maintenance.

b. Per capita gross domestic product (GDP) is measured in U.S. dollar prices converted using purchasing power parity exchange rates as calculated by the OECD.

c. 1980.

growth in the eight countries. The high levels of American output per worker in 1960 and 1979 probably made it much more difficult for the United States to sustain high growth rates. But the fact remains that redistributional policies more generous than those in the United States appear to be consistent with rates of long-term growth that are higher than the rate it has enjoyed over the past few decades.

Although it is not obvious whether the nation has enjoyed a growth dividend as a result of its comparatively frugal social welfare policy, the policy has imposed real hardship on Americans with low market incomes. Table 3.3 compares relative poverty rates in six of the eight countries listed in Table 3.2 plus Australia (poverty statistics for Italy and Japan are not available). Timothy Smeeding (1992) calculated these rates using census files from the Luxembourg Income Study, which contain comprehensive measures of money income and some in-kind benefits for households in a variety of countries. Persons in families receiving adjusted incomes less than 40 percent of a country's median income are

Table 3.3   Relative poverty rates among children, adults, and the elderly in seven
                industrialized countries

Country (year of survey)	Children	Working-age adults	Elderly	Overall
Sweden (1987)	1.6	6.6	0.7	4.3
West Germany (1984)	2.8	2.6	3.8	2.8
France (1984)	4.6	5.2	0.7	4.5
United Kingdom (1986)	7.4	5.3	1.0	5.2
Australia (1985)	9.0	6.1	4.0	6.7
Canada (1987)	9.3	7.0	2.2	7.0
United States (1986)	20.4	10.5	10.9	13.3

Source: Data from Smeeding (1992), reported in U.S. House of Representatives, Committee on Ways
and Means (1992), p. 1289.
Note: Income includes all forms of cash income and near-cash income, such as food stamps, minus
national income and payroll taxes. Income is adjusted for family size using the U.S. poverty line
equivalence scale. Persons defined as poor have incomes below 40 percent of the national median
income.

classified as poor. (Family income is adjusted to reflect family size using an
equivalence scale.)

Because the official U.S. poverty line is approximately 40 percent of U.S. median income, Smeeding's estimated poverty rates for the United States are close
to the official Census rates. Within every age group, the U.S. poverty rate is above
the comparable rate in other countries. Some of the differences are striking.
Among the elderly, the poverty rate in the United States is nearly four times
higher than it is, on average, in the other countries; among children, poverty is
more than twice as high. Although part of the difference between the United
States and other countries may be explained by greater inequality in U.S. market
incomes, most of the differences are due to the smaller size of government transfers in the United States. It is notable, for example, that the incidence of relative
poverty across countries has an almost perfect inverse correlation with the level
of social welfare spending, shown in Table 3.2.

A variety of factors keep poverty rates lower in northwestern Europe than they
are in the United States. Some countries, such as Sweden, have a more egalitarian
distribution of wages, permitting low-wage Swedish workers to earn comparatively high annual incomes. More commonly, western European countries offer
more generous transfer benefits to a wider range of low-income families. Unem-

ployment benefits, for example, usually last far longer than six months, their maximum duration in the United States. Children's allowances and generously subsidized child care centers raise the incomes of families with children. Old-age and disability programs typically provide higher basic benefits than comparable programs in the United States. Most countries in northwestern Europe have established institutions that guarantee public or private health insurance to nearly all if not all of their residents. Tens of millions of Americans, by contrast, including poor Americans, have no health insurance coverage (see Chapter 10).

The choice of redistribution policy rests ultimately on political rather than on purely economic considerations. The United States has not chosen modest redistribution and high rates of poverty primarily out of economic motivations. The country has not consciously limited redistribution because Americans are more responsive to the harmful effects of taxes and transfers than are Europeans (although they may be). Economists know next to nothing about the comparative economic efficiency of policies in different advanced nations and nothing at all about the relative responsiveness of different populations to identical tax-transfer policies. Even if economists possessed such knowledge, it could not be used, by itself, to determine the amount of national income that governments ought to divert to the poor. Of greater importance in deciding this issue would be society's stance on redistribution. Voters with a strong preference for equality may be willing to sacrifice two dollars in national output in order to divert one additional dollar to society's poorest member. Conversely, voters with a weak taste for equality may not wish to give up even one penny of their own income in order to raise the net incomes of the poor by one dollar.

Future Prospects

In the absence of good working knowledge about the terms of the tradeoff between national output and income equality, redistributional policies are determined by a political process that largely depends on voter tastes. I am referring here not just to an abstract taste for equality but also to voter preference or aversion for particular mechanisms of distribution. Americans might in theory possess a stronger preference than Europeans for strict equality in the distribution of political and judicial rights, but the taste for equality does not extend to the distribution of economic rewards. Greater economic equality in the United States would require that a highly prized distribution mechanism, the market, be supplemented or replaced by a more controversial one: government redistribution. The market enjoys greater prestige in the United States than in nearly any other country. The rewards it confers are therefore respected in a way that may be difficult to understand in less market-oriented societies. As long as legal remedies exist to ensure that the market race is fair, most Americans seem willing to believe the rich and the poor will get what they deserve.

In view of the slow growth and widening disparities in U.S. *market* incomes, it is hard to be optimistic that economic growth alone will dramatically reduce poverty soon. Voter resentment over the unfairness of government subsidization of illegitimacy, family desertion, and idleness makes it equally inconceivable that a massive new public aid program is just around the corner. Social welfare spending since the mid-1960s has substantially improved the living standards of many poor families, and these improvements ought not be forgotten. But much of the increased spending was concentrated on the lucky poor insured by our social insurance programs—the aged, the infirm, and the temporarily disabled. Most of the remainder was devoted to in-kind benefits that raised specific forms of consumption, but not the money incomes, of the poor. The problem of income poverty remains acute for important classes of Americans.

For economists and policymakers seriously interested in the fate of the poor, the main hope for future improvement lies in a rebound in economic growth or in an advance in the effectiveness of existing policies. While I doubt that there is much chance that slow economic growth or modest policy reform will dramatically reduce poverty, I am even more skeptical that we will witness a revolution in popular attitudes toward redistribution anytime soon. Yet if poverty in the United States is to fall to levels now common in other industrialized countries, such a revolution will be needed.

The Dynamics and Intergenerational Transmission of Poverty and Welfare Participation

PETER GOTTSCHALK, SARA MCLANAHAN,
AND GARY D. SANDEFUR

The traditional approach to the measurement of poverty (as in Chapter 2) has been to examine the size and composition of the poverty population by analyzing cross-sectional data on yearly income. Yet a good part of the poverty policy debate focuses on issues that cannot be addressed with data on yearly income. There is substantial interest, for example, in long-term poverty or the welfare dependence of a single generation and the links between the outcomes of parents and their children. Statistics on who is poor (or who receives welfare) during a single year provide no information on the total number of years that individuals and families are poor (or receiving welfare). Nor do they tell us if today's poor (or welfare recipients) grew up in households that were poor or received public assistance. Here we examine the recent empirical research on poverty and welfare dynamics and the emerging research on the links between generations.

The vision of a permanently dependent underclass, mired in poverty and dependency, gained considerable attention during the 1980s. Conservative analysts such as Charles Murray (1984) argued that a "welfare trap" robbed recipients of the will to better their lot. Welfare offered the opportunity to drop out of the labor market and to abandon the traditional family model by making it possible to raise children while unemployed and unmarried. Furthermore, the resulting debilitating effects of welfare were asserted to be passed on to successive generations. According to this view, welfare programs were a cause of the problem, rather than part of the solution to poverty. The way to save people from long-term poverty and dependence was to scale back the welfare system.

Ironically, the notion that people were trapped in long-term poverty was one of the motivations for the War on Poverty. Drawing on the work of Oscar Lewis (1961) and Michael Harrington (1962), liberals used the idea of an intergenerational poverty to galvanize public support for the creation of work and training programs for youth. These programs promised to reunite the poor with the rest of society. In effect, the War on Poverty was waged on behalf of the children of the poor, who were assumed to be trapped by poverty rather than by welfare. According to this view, welfare provided the transitional financial support necessary to allow the poor to gain the skills to become self-sufficient.

That the specter of a permanently poor class has been used to justify both the creation and the dismantling of social programs is indicative of the controversy surrounding these issues. Moreover, just as both liberals and conservatives have used the existence of the permanently poor to promote their policy agendas, both groups have also denied or downplayed the existence of permanent poverty at one point or another.

Two factors have contributed to the conservatives' emphasis at times on the transitory nature of poverty. The first is their belief in the openness of society. Sensitive to criticisms that markets lead to a rigid class division among social and economic classes, they have argued that there is considerable mobility across the income distribution and, hence, that for many families poverty is not a permanent status. Second is their belief that official measures of yearly poverty seriously exaggerate the amount of poverty. One of the primary defects of annual income as a measure of the distribution of well-being is that it ignores offsetting changes in incomes in other years.[1] Milton Friedman makes the case most forcefully by asking us to consider two societies that have the same distribution of annual income: "In one there is great mobility and change so that the position of particular families in the income hierarchy varies widely from year to year. In the other, there is great rigidity, each family stays in the same position year after year. Clearly, in any meaningful sense, the second one would be the more unequal society" (1962, p. 171). According to this view, we should be most concerned with the distribution of lifetime well-being. If many of the poor in one year are not poor in the following year, then the truly needy, or truly poor, are a small subset of the poor in a single year.[2]

Liberals have also at times downplayed the existence of permanent poverty, though for two somewhat different reasons. First, their belief that income is largely determined by factors outside the control of the individual, such as the health of the economy, leads them to stress the transitory nature of poverty and welfare recipiency. Families fall upon hard times. During these bleak periods the less fortunate fall into poverty and may need to participate in government programs. Outside conditions may change, however, leading to exits from both poverty and welfare.

Second, liberals are also reluctant to embrace the notion of an underclass because of their experience with the debate over the "culture of poverty" in the late 1960s. Although the concept of a dysfunctional culture was originally proposed as a critique of capitalism, the culture of poverty argument soon came to be viewed as "blaming the victims" for conditions beyond their control. According to this view, it was not "the system" but rather the poor's lack of will to avoid the "welfare trap" that caused long-term poverty.[3] As black clients became an increasing proportion of the welfare caseload, this argument became open to charges of racial bias. As a result, liberals backed off from any discussion of long-term or intergenerational poverty during the 1970s for fear of being labeled racist or unsympathetic to the poor.

That liberals and conservatives have such different views on intragenerational and intergenerational dynamics is due, in part, to their very different models of the causes of long-term poverty and the role of welfare in reducing or exacerbating poverty. The causal explanation, put forward by conservatives, is that welfare programs create dependency and, therefore, perpetuate poverty (Murray, 1984; Mead, 1986). The availability of welfare encourages women to bear children out of wedlock, encourages families to break up, and eliminates the need for absentee fathers to contribute to the economic and social requirements of their children, thereby encouraging long-term dependency. Furthermore, long-term dependency is assumed to be passed from one generation to the next.

For liberals, long-term poverty and welfare participation have generally been explained in terms of the lack of employment opportunities or the existence of jobs that do not provide earnings sufficient for a family to have a minimally adequate standard of living (Harrington, 1962; Wilson and Neckerman, 1986). If employment opportunities continue to be inadequate, then parents will not be able to earn enough to support their children. Poverty will continue, and in some cases, dependency on welfare will also result from the inadequate economic environment.

William Julius Wilson and Kathryn Neckerman (1986) have further broadened the focus to the connections between inadequate employment opportunities, family structure, and poverty. They argue that the lack of employment opportunities, especially for black men, has led to a lower rate of marriage and a higher rate of out-of-wedlock childbearing among black women. Inadequate employment opportunities thus produce poverty and welfare dependence indirectly through effects on family structure as well as directly through reduced income.

From this brief review, we can see that conservatives are likely to view long-term poverty as evidence of the dangers of welfare. At the same time they stress that American society is fairly open, so that many of the poor are only temporarily poor. Liberals are likely to point to the problems faced by the long-term poor as a way of marshaling sympathy for the poor and garnering support for government interventions to combat poverty, including policies to improve market opportunities and to expand programs. At the same time, liberals downplay any negative behavioral effects of long-term welfare participation.

Who is correct in this debate is still a highly contested issue. Part of the debate rests on logical arguments. Liberals argue that because welfare is freely chosen by recipients, it can hardly be called a "trap." Recipients obviously believe that welfare is the best of the bad options they face. There is no logical basis for arguing that the mother herself would freely choose welfare if it formed a "trap" that she wished to avoid. Welfare provides a steady, if meager, source of income, which must be preferred to the option of working and raising a family as a single parent or the option of marrying the father, who may not be able to support his children financially. Although it is possible to argue that the children or taxpayers are worse off when the mother accepts assistance, it is not consistent to argue that recipients make choices and that these choices make them worse off.

Similarly, conservatives argue that liberals deny the inevitable work and marriage disincentives inherent in the welfare system. By paying a mother more if she doesn't work and doesn't marry, the welfare system discourages mothers from following either of these socially desirable activities. Because both marriage and work lead to higher income, the welfare system creates long-term poverty and dependency. Therefore, according to conservatives, the logical outcome of a more generous welfare system is to form a trap that locks recipients into long-term poverty.

The relevant question, however, is not whether a trap exists or whether there are disincentives, for it is certainly true that some families receive welfare for protracted periods and that there are disincentives. The question is the quantitative magnitude of these factors. We approach this highly ideological debate by examining two central issues: the prevalence of long-term poverty and welfare participation and the disincentives caused by public assistance; and the relationship between poverty, income, and welfare use in one generation and the next.

Evidence on Intragenerational Mobility

Dynamic issues have received less attention than the static measures of poverty, in part because longitudinal data sets such as the Panel Study of Income Dynamics (PSID) and the National Longitudinal Survey of Youth (NLSY) have been widely available only since the late 1960s. These data sets only now have enough years of data to study both long-term poverty and welfare recipiency and to observe the outcomes over multiple generations.

Income and Poverty Dynamics

We begin by documenting the extent to which poverty is a permanent or transitory condition. Figure 4.1 presents data on the length of poverty spells. This figure, based on data from the Panel Study of Income Dynamics, counts the num-

a. All races

Proportion

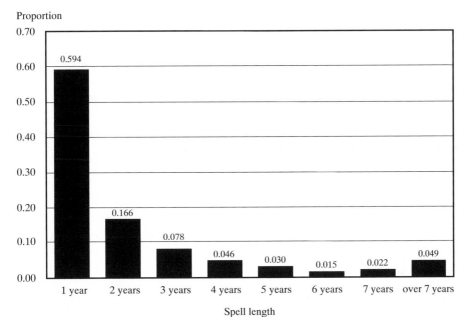

b. By race

Proportion

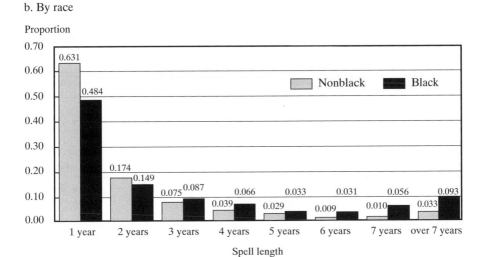

Figure 4.1 Annual poverty spell distribution. (Authors' tabulation of Panel Study of Income Dynamics, 1968–1987, distribution of first observed spell.)

ber of consecutive years that a person lived in a family with an annual income below the family's annual poverty line. It asks the question, "If you follow a group of people who have just started new poverty spells, how long will these poverty spells last?"

Figure 4.1a shows data for persons of all races. It shows that 59.4 percent of poverty spells last only one year.[4] An additional 16.6 percent last only two years. Thus nearly three-quarters of all poverty spells are shorter than two years. At the other extreme only 7.1 percent of the spells last seven or more years. Figure 4.1b shows the corresponding data for persons disaggregated by race. From this figure it is clear that blacks stay in poverty longer than nonblacks. Of the poverty spells of nonblacks, 63.1 percent last less than one year; the corresponding figure for blacks is only 48.4. Blacks also have considerably more long spells. Almost 15 percent of their poverty spells last seven or more years, while only 4.3 percent of the spells for nonblacks are this long.

These data classify a family as poor if the family's yearly income falls below its yearly poverty line. The implication of this measure is, therefore, that families can smooth income across the year. For example, if the family has a large income in the last two months of the calendar year, it is assumed that the family had sufficient savings to tide it through the lean months and, hence, take its members out of yearly poverty. Although it might be reasonable to assume that families can save enough to smooth their incomes over short periods, it may not be reasonable to expect that poor families can smooth their incomes through savings or borrowing over a full year. The monthly accounting period used in many transfer programs suggests that policymakers recognize that poor individuals may not be able to save or borrow over more than a one-month period. If this is the case, then the proper accounting period for measures of poverty is considerably shorter than a year.

Patricia Ruggles (1990) tabulated the distribution of consecutive months in which a family is poor.[5] She finds that over 80 percent of all persons whose incomes fell below their poverty lines in any one month had spells that lasted eight months or less. Only 11 percent failed to have a single month with income over the poverty line in a two-year period. If a monthly accounting period is used, there is thus even more movement in and out of poverty.[6]

If a person falls into poverty, how long will he or she remain poor before having at least one year out of poverty? The answer, found in Figure 4.1, is that most low-income people, including most blacks, will be poor for less than two years. Suppose we now ask a different question. If a person is currently poor, how long will this person have been poor by the time he or she finally escapes from poverty? This question differs from the question addressed by Figure 4.1.

An extreme case can clarify the difference between the length of *new spells* and the length of *spells in progress.* Suppose that there are 11 poverty spells in a ten-year period. A new one-year spell starts in each year and a ten-year spell starts every ten years. Therefore, in each year there is one person in the midst of a poverty spell that lasts one year and one person in the midst of a ten-year spell. The vast majority (10 out of 11) of the *new* spells turn out to be short. Now consider the length of spells *in progress* during any given year. Because in each year there is always one short and one long spell in progress, half the spells in progress are long while the other half are short. This is in sharp contrast to the fact that less than 10 percent of new spells are long. Both facts are correct, but these two measures have seemingly different implications.[7]

The focus on spells in progress has been used to bolster the case that poverty is a permanent state. For example, using the same data on which Figure 4.1 is based, we calculated the duration of poverty spells that were in progress in 1977 and found that over 20 percent lasted more than seven years. In contrast, Figure 4.1a shows that only 5 percent of new spells lasted longer than seven years. Although most bouts of poverty are relatively short, roughly a fifth of all poor people at any point in time are in the midst of a long spell. Viewed in this light, the problem of long-term poverty seems more severe.

The second argument used to bolster the case for the permanence of poverty is that those who do escape poverty do not make large gains but, rather, join the ranks of the "near poor." To explore this question we classify persons according to their family incomes, measured as a proportion of the family's poverty line (the income/needs ratio) in two adjacent years. An income/needs ratio of less than one indicates the family was poor in that year. Figure 4.2 shows the family income/needs ratios in 1987 for all persons classified as poor in 1986.[8] Two-thirds of all poor persons were also poor in the second year. Roughly 26 percent moved into the next income group, with incomes between 1.0 and 2.0 times the poverty lines. Approximately 91 percent of those who were poor in 1986, therefore, had incomes less than twice the poverty line in the following year. Mobility out of poverty does not represent movement into the middle class for the vast majority of people.

It has been documented extensively elsewhere that the United States experienced large swings in inequality and poverty during the 1980s.[9] Did the United States experience similar changes in income mobility? Figure 4.3 shows how three measures of mobility have changed between 1968 and 1987. The two bottom lines show the probability of staying poor in adjacent years and in adjacent three-year periods.[10] These measures indicate a slight upward trend starting in 1973.

This increase in the probability of a continuing poverty spell, however, results in part from the rise in the overall poverty rates during that period. As long as

Proportion

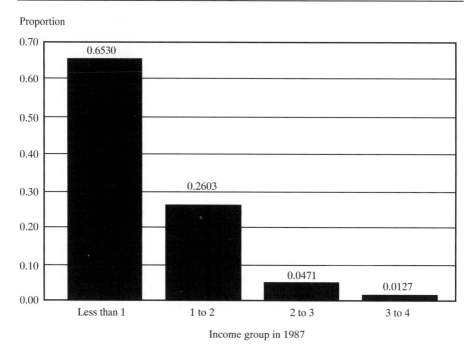

Income group in 1987

Figure 4.2 Distribution of poor persons in 1986 by income/needs in 1987. (Authors' tabulation of Panel Study of Income Dynamics, 1968–1987.)

poverty rates are rising, we would expect the poor as well as the nonpoor to have higher probabilities of being poor in the following year. This effect can be eliminated by focusing on people in the lowest 25 percent of the income distribution (the lowest quartile). This measure is independent of changes in the mean of the income distribution because 25 percent will always be in the lowest quartile, no matter what happens to average incomes. The top line of Figure 4.3 shows the probability that a person will stay in the lowest quartile of the income distribution in adjacent years. What is remarkable is the virtual stability in this measure of mobility.[11] Between any two years, roughly 80 percent of persons in the lowest quartile remained in the bottom of the distribution. Although the poverty rate has risen since 1973 and inequality of annual income grew substantially during the 1980s, income mobility remained relatively constant.

How does the United States compare with other countries? Greg Duncan and his colleagues (1991) present data for six industrialized countries. Table 4.1 indicates the proportion of families with children in these countries making transitions out of the bottom decile.[12] Column 2 shows the increase in income experienced by those families who made the jump out of the bottom decile.[13] These data show very similar patterns across countries with very different social systems. In the United States a family had a 22 percent probability of leaving the lowest decile. This puts the United States in the middle of this group of countries. Both France and the Netherlands have very similar probabilities. Somewhat higher, at 26 percent, are Canada and Ireland. The only country with a markedly lower probability that a person will exit the lowest decile is Sweden (16.2 percent).

Whether the United States has too much or too little mobility is a normative question. What we can say, however, is that mobility in the United States has been very constant and that it is quite typical of other industrialized countries.

Welfare Dynamics

The public debate during the 1980s over welfare reform was largely driven by the perception that a large number of welfare recipients were incapable of becoming self-sufficient without either a large carrot to persuade them off the program or a large stick to force them off. Conservatives charged that welfare recipients stayed on welfare for long periods, soaking up tax dollars and living in perpetual dependency. Liberals downplayed long-term dependency, acknowledging that a small proportion of the welfare population had long welfare spells but emphasizing that most recipients used welfare on a temporary basis.

Duration of single AFDC spells. We begin by answering the following ques-

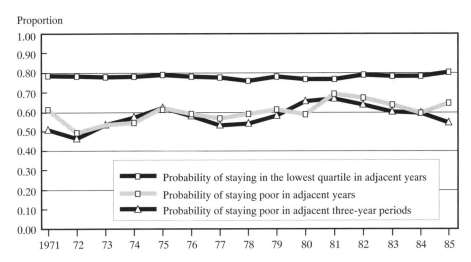

Figure 4.3   Changes in income mobility: Movement out of poverty and out of the lowest quartile of the income distribution. (Authors' tabulation of Panel Study of Income Dynamics, 1968–1987.)

Table 4.1 Transitions out of lowest decile for families with children, by country

Country	Percentage of lowest decile escaping lowest decile in following year	Percentage change in income for median family in lowest decile
Canada–Quebec		
All	26.0%	20.6%
Quebec	23.2	16.7
France	21.0	10.2
Ireland	26.7	21.5
The Netherlands	21.3	7.5
Sweden	16.2	8.5
United States	22.6	15.1

Source: Duncan et al. (1991), table 1.

tion. If all the Aid to Families with Dependent Children cases that opened in a given year were followed for their duration, how long would each spell last?[14] Figure 4.4 shows that most AFDC spells are short. For blacks, 33.7 percent of spells last only a year, and an additional 16.2 percent end in the second year.[15] For nonblacks, the corresponding figures are 44.0 and 22.8 percent.[16] By the end of two years, half of the welfare spells for blacks and two-thirds of the spells for nonblacks have ended.

These data provide evidence that most welfare entrants are not trapped in perpetual dependency.[17] But Figure 4.4 also shows that although most cases are not long, a substantial minority of cases remain open for protracted periods. At the end of seven years, 5.8 percent of the AFDC spells of nonblacks were still in progress and 25.4 percent of the AFDC spells of blacks were still in progress.

Recidivism and duration of multiple spells. Roughly half of the families leaving AFDC or Food Stamps will return to these programs at some future date. The duration of a single spell thus gives only a partial picture. To know whether recipients use AFDC for extensive parts of their child-rearing years, one must take account of recidivism and the combined length of multiple spells. Data on multiple spells, however, are limited.

An alternative measure of participation across multiple spells is to estimate the number of years a family receives AFDC, without regard to breaks in spells. Figure 4.5 shows our estimates of the number of years a woman who received welfare would receive AFDC in the first nine years after the birth of her first child.[18] These distributions are shown separately by race for all women who received AFDC (Figure 4.5a for blacks and 4.5b for nonblacks).[19]

Proportion

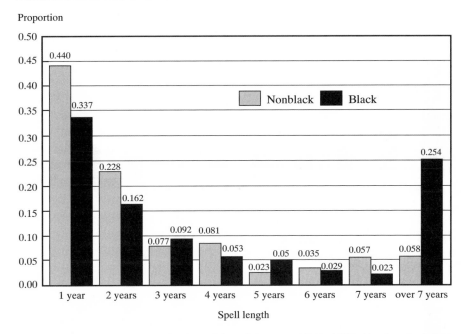

Figure 4.4 Distribution of AFDC spell length by race, 1974–1987. (Authors' tabulation of Panel Study of Income Dynamics, 1974–1987, distribution of first observed spell.)

As expected, the number of total years on welfare is substantially higher than the number of years on welfare in the first spell. Although roughly half the initial spells of blacks last two years or less, just 27.7 percent of black recipients received AFDC for only two of the ten years when multiple spells are taken into account.[20] For nonblacks the proportion of spells of two years or less drops from 66.8 to 41.3 when multiple spells are included. The short spells are partially replaced by spells of three to four years as people with short spells exit and return for short periods. Including multiple spells, however, also increases the proportion of long spells. The proportion of initial spells that lasted seven to ten years is 21.1 percent for blacks and 11.7 percent for nonblacks. When multiple spells are included, these figures increase to 34.4 and 18.0 percent.

Differences across time and across countries. With the recent attention on long-term welfare participation one might conclude that long-term dependency was worse in the United States than in other countries or that the situation was becoming worse. Neither of these conclusions would be warranted.

First, comparing welfare duration across countries indicates that the United States is not an outlier. Duncan and colleagues (1991) compare the duration on public assistance of single-parent families in the United States and in three other industrialized countries. They find that 36 percent of spells in the United States

a. All black recipients

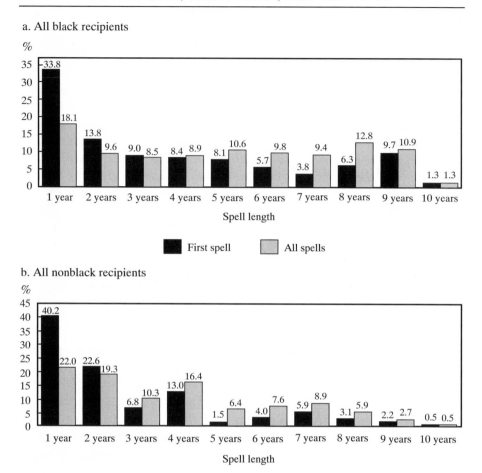

Figure 4.5 Estimated distribution of years a mother receives AFDC in the first ten years after conception of her first child. (Authors' calculations based on the Panel Study of Income Dynamics, 1974–1987.)

lasted three years or more. This is slightly more than the 26 percent in Germany (FRG), but less than the 58 percent in Canada and considerably less than the 84 percent in the United Kingdom.[21]

The second common assumption is that long-term welfare recipiency in the United States has gotten worse. To explore this hypothesis we constructed a measure of permanence that could be traced over time. Figure 4.6 shows the probability that a person who had received assistance in each of the last three years would receive assistance in all three of the subsequent years. This is a rough measure of whether a long-term recipient remains a long-term recipient.[22] The data in Figure

Proportion

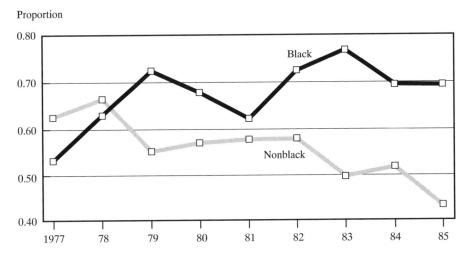

Figure 4.6 Probability of receiving AFDC for the next three years for persons who had received AFDC for the previous three years. (Authors' tabulations of Panel Study of Income Dynamics, 1974–1987.)

4.6 indicate that permanence has increased for blacks, but substantially declined for nonblacks.

Effects of welfare participation. Because the vast majority of people who become welfare recipients, or who become poor, have relatively short spells, there is substantial mobility out of both poverty and welfare. To view either as a trap from which there is no escape is clearly inconsistent with the facts. Roughly a third of black recipients and a fifth of nonblack recipients, however, receive assistance over protracted periods.

The central policy issue is whether there is a causal link between welfare and poverty. Does the opportunity to participate in welfare programs cause people to stay poor, by discouraging work and marriage and encouraging recipients to have larger families? Although answering this question is difficult, there is a substantial literature, reviewed by Robert Moffitt (1992), that has attempted to identify causal links.

To establish causality between public assistance and poverty, one would ideally like to have a controlled experiment in which welfare programs were changed, but all other factors were held constant. Unfortunately, this ideal is rarely met.[23] Instead researchers have largely had to rely on the considerable diversity in the generosity of welfare programs both across geographic areas and across time to see if higher benefits caused participants to change behavior.[24]

If welfare causes greater poverty, it must either lower a family's income or raise its poverty line. The former would occur if public assistance reduced hours worked or led to fewer earners in the family; the latter, if welfare led to increased childbearing, which would lead to larger families and higher poverty lines.

Studies of the effects of public assistance on work effort have universally found a reduction in work hours. Moffitt (1992) summarizes these studies by concluding that female heads reduce their earnings by about $.37 for every dollar of transfers. This means that family income increases by $.63 for every dollar transferred. Whether this is a large or small labor supply response is in the eye of the beholder.

Neither the experimental nor the econometric evidence, however, supports the prediction that AFDC raises poverty by lowering total income. Post-transfer income would decline only if increasing AFDC by $1 would lead to more than a $1 decrease in earnings, a response that is substantially larger than that found in the literature. The often-heard assertion that welfare raises poverty by lowering work effort thus does not have empirical support.

The other causal link between welfare and poverty is through family structure. If welfare induces families to break up or keeps families from forming, then the poverty-increasing impact of female headship could be ascribed to welfare. Welfare may also induce families to have more children, which would increase the family's poverty line. As a result families whose incomes fell below their new higher poverty lines would drop into poverty.

A plausible case can be made that increasing welfare benefits will increase family disruption and single parenthood. By reducing the costs of single parenthood, welfare makes it easier for women to raise children on their own. The issue is how large the effect is. If it is large, and if being raised in a single-parent household reduces children's life chances (an issue we will return to later), then conservatives may be correct in warning us about the long-term dangers of an overly generous welfare system. If the effect is small, their concern is misplaced, and liberals are correct in arguing that reducing or eliminating welfare benefits will do children more harm than good.

Numerous empirical studies, using different data and different methodologies, have attempted to answer the question of whether welfare causes family disruption. They have compared the rise in welfare benefits and divorce rates over time. They have also used cross-sectional data on cross-state variation in welfare benefits to see if states with high benefits have higher rates of family instability and single parenthood than states with low benefits. And finally, they have used micro-level data to determine if individuals living in high-benefit states are more likely to divorce or give birth out of wedlock than individuals living in low-benefit states.

An early review of the empirical research on welfare use and family instability

(Garfinkel and McLanahan, 1986) concluded that increases in welfare between 1960 and 1975 could account for no more than 15 percent of the growth in female-headed families during that same period (see also Chapter 8). More recently, after an extensive review of the literature, Moffitt reached a similar conclusion: "Although the studies of the 1980s show slightly stronger effects than the earlier studies, the effects are still generally small in magnitude. In particular, insofar as it is possible to determine, none of the studies finds effects sufficiently large to explain, for example, the increase in female headship in the late 1960s and early 1970s" (1992, p. 31).

We conclude that welfare does have disincentive effects. These effects are not large enough, however, to support assertions that increases in welfare benefits increase the number of families in poverty.

·   ·   ·

Welfare is not an inescapable trap that drags families into poverty and keeps them there for most of their lives. Most welfare and poverty spells are short. At most, the "culture of dependency" thesis is applicable to a small fraction of the poor. Yet a substantial minority of welfare spells are long. Given the low level of financial support, these families also remain poor during protracted periods. There is thus a case to be made for the need to confront long-term dependency, not only to reduce the burdens on the taxpayer but also to raise these families out of poverty.

Although more generous welfare benefits do lower labor supply and may lead to changes in family structure and living arrangements, the effects are not sufficiently large to cause poverty rates to rise. Lowering welfare benefits will, therefore, increase poverty rates and will not substantially shorten poverty spells. In the terms made popular by Okun (1975), the transfer system is like a leaky bucket. The incomes of the recipients do not go up by a dollar for each dollar put in the bucket because of the disincentives of the transfer system. The net transfer is, however, positive. A reformed and more generous welfare system could clearly reduce poverty (for a discussion, see Chapter 8).

Evidence on Intergenerational Dynamics

We now extend our analysis to poverty and welfare dynamics across generations. Again this issue has a political context. Liberals tend to focus on the intergenerational transmission of family background, income, and poverty. If low-income families have few resources to pass on to their children or to use to finance their children's education, then their children will be more likely to become poor adults themselves. Inasmuch as poverty leads to welfare participation, this will also lead to intergenerational welfare participation. According to this view, the intergenerational transmission of poverty causes the intergenerational correlation in welfare participation. Conservatives tend to argue the opposite. Welfare perpetuates poverty and dependence across generations by promoting out-of-wedlock childbearing, by breaking up families, and by eroding the work ethic. These early childhood experiences lower children's achievement and lead to poverty and welfare participation in the next generation.

Intergenerational Correlations in Poverty and Income

If successive generations have similar incomes, then parents and their children are likely to have similar probabilities of falling into poverty.[25] Although early studies of intergenerational income mobility tended to find relatively low correlations, recent evidence suggests the correlation is substantial.[26] For example, Donald Treiman and Robert Hauser (1977) estimated that the intergenerational correlation of income was between .24 and .36 for men aged 25 to 34; Jere Behrman and Paul Taubman (1990) and Gary Solon (1992) found correlations of father's and son's income of .58 and .40 respectively. Such a high intergenerational correlation in income implies relatively little mobility in incomes across generations.

What do these correlations imply for someone who is born in a low-income family? Solon (1992) estimates (assuming an intergenerational correlation in income of .40) that the probability that a son whose father was in the bottom quintile (20 percent) of the income distribution will remain in the bottom quintile of the income distribution as an adult is .42. Growing up at the bottom of the income distribution poses a significant disadvantage in American society.[27] Similarly, Mary Corcoran and her colleagues (1987) find that children growing up in families that experience long-term poverty have significantly lower education, wages, and incomes.

Intergenerational Correlations in Occupational Status over Time and across Countries

Although individuals can generally provide reliable information on the education and occupations of their parents, they are less likely to be able to report reliably on their parents' income. Sociologists thus prefer to use education and occupation as proxies for the economic well-being of successive generations. Focusing on occupations has the additional advantage of facilitating comparisons in mobility, both across time and across countries.

In *The American Occupational Structure*, Peter Blau and Otis Duncan (1967) developed a method that imputed the status of an occupation as a function of the education and earnings of people who held that occupation. Blau and Duncan found that the correlation between the occupational status score (later known as the Duncan Socio-Economic Index, or SEI) of sons and their fathers was .40, which is very similar to the recently estimated correlations between father's and son's incomes, wages, and earnings.

Has the correlation in SEI changed over time in the United States? Steve Rytina (1992) reports an intergenerational correlation of SEI of .34 for the period 1972–1985; Robert Hauser and John Allen Logan (1992) report an intergenerational correlation of SEI of .30 for the 1987–1990 period. If we accept comparisons across studies in intergenerational correlations in SEI over time, the results suggest that occupational status inheritance declined as reflected in a change in correlations from approximately .40 in 1962 to .30 in the 1987–1990 period.[28]

Researchers have also compared intergenerational occupational mobility in the United States with that in other countries.[29] Harry Ganzeboom, Donald Treiman, and Wout Ultee (1991) conclude that there is disagreement over the extent to which the patterns of intergenerational mobility vary across countries. Some studies find that the intergenerational mobility patterns do not differ much between countries (see, for example, Erikson and Goldthorpe, 1985); others find a good deal of variation (see, for example, Wong, 1990). There is agreement, however, on two issues. First, the level of relative mobility in the United States is at least as high as in other industrialized countries. Second, the level of relative mobility has increased in most countries in the years since World War II.

The Role of Family Background and Family Structure

The research on the intergenerational relationships in the experience of poverty can be viewed as part of a larger body of sociological research on the effects of family background on social and economic achievement in adulthood. The research shows that, in addition to income and father's occupation, family background characteristics, such as parents' education, whether or not parents remained married, and number of siblings, significantly affect children's achievement (Jencks et al., 1972; Featherman and Hauser, 1978).

The effects of family background factors as well as of family income are mediated by other variables, among the most important of which is an individual's education. In other words, background has a strong effect on education, which in turn has a strong effect on income.

Although family structure—whether or not a child grew up in a "broken family"—has long been included in status attainment models, interest in family instability as a possible mechanism for explaining the intergenerational transmission of poverty increased in the 1980s.[30] Today most of the background characteristics known to affect children's well-being have changed in ways that would be expected to benefit children. Parents are more educated than they were several decades ago; fathers' occupational status has risen; and the number of siblings in the family has declined. In contrast, family instability, which is believed to reduce children's well-being, has become increasingly common since 1950. Hence researchers have focused on the role of family structure in reproducing poverty across generations.

Does family instability harm children? If we ask whether growing up in a nonintact family is associated with being poor in adulthood, the answer is yes. Figure 4.7 shows the likelihood of experiencing several "high-risk" events—dropping out of school, having a child out of wedlock before age twenty, and being idle in late adolescence—for children who grow up in intact and nonintact families. Each of these events increases the risk of poverty and welfare dependence in adulthood, and each is a fairly good proxy for children's lifetime income.

Children from nonintact families are more than twice as likely to drop out of high school as children from intact families. Young women from nonintact families are between two and four times as likely to give birth out of wedlock as young women from intact families, and young men from nonintact families are about 1.5 times as likely to become idle as their peers from intact families. These effects are consistent across different race and ethnic groups (Figure 4.8) and for children from different class backgrounds (Figure 4.9). About half of the association between family instability and child well-being is due to difference in family income. Most of the rest is due to differences in parenting behavior (such as helping with school work and supervising social activities) and residential mobility.

Although family structure has a sizable impact, family disruption does not automatically relegate children to long-term poverty or welfare dependence. Most children finish high school, delay childbearing, and become attached to the labor force regardless of whether they live with one or both parents while growing up.

Is the family structure effect large enough to justify the present concern over the increased exposure of children to family instability and single parenthood? To put this effect into context it is useful to compare it with the effect of having parents who do not have a high school degree. Children whose parents do not finish high school are twice as likely to drop out of school as children whose parents graduate. Single parenthood thus has roughly as large an impact as the effect of having a parent who has not graduated from high school.

Have the effects of family structure changed over time? Given the increase in single parenthood during the 1970s and 1980s, one might expect that children from nonintact families would be doing better today than they were in the 1960s. The stigma associated with single parenthood should be lower and the institutional support for single mothers should be higher because single parenthood is more common and more socially acceptable.

a. High school dropout (males and females)

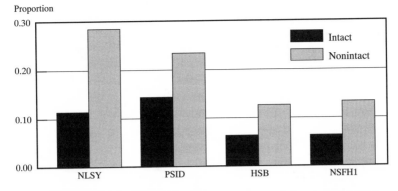

b. Teen premarital birth (females)

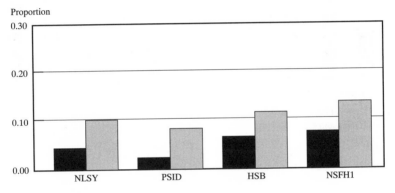

c. Idleness (males)

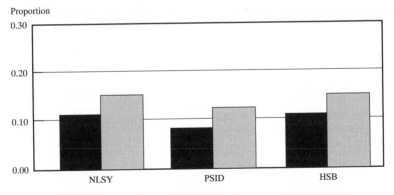

Figure 4.7 Family instability and children's attainment. (Estimates are based on four nationally representative surveys: the National Longitudinal Survey–Youth Cohort (NLSY), the Panel Study of Income Dymamics (PSID), the High School and Beyond Study (HSB), and the National Survey of Families and Households (NSFH). The bars represent "predicted values" based on models that control for race, parents' education, number of siblings, and region of residence at age sixteen.)

Proportion

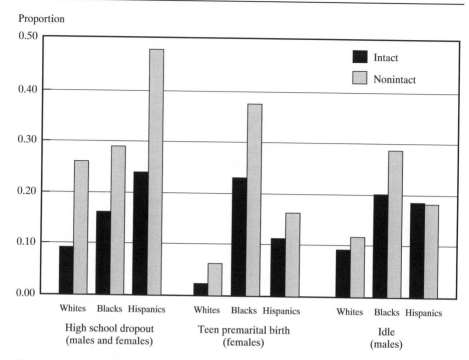

Figure 4.8   Race differences in the effects of family instability on children's attainment. (Estimates are based on the NLSY; on bars, see Figure 4.7.)

Insofar as there has been a change in the correlation between family instability and children's outcomes, the relationship has become stronger and more negative. In particular, the effect of family instability on teen premarital birth is about twice as large for women born after 1960 as it is for women born prior to 1960. In retrospect, these findings are not that surprising, given the change in the composition of single-mother families during the past several decades. Whereas during the 1940s and 1950s a substantial proportion of single mothers were widows, by the early 1970s an increasing proportion were divorced or never married. Single parenthood entered into voluntarily appears to be a more negative experience for children than single parenthood resulting from a parent's death (McLanahan, 1985).

Does family instability itself reduce the lifetime earnings of children or is it just a proxy for something else that causes both instability and children's lower achievement? We suspect that children from nonintact families might be less successful as adults than children from intact families even if their parents had stayed together. Couples that break up (or never marry) are different in many ways from couples that stay together, and these differences may well affect children's attainment regardless of whether the parents marry and stay together. The preexisting conditions most frequently mentioned by those who believe that family disruption has no independent effect on children's well-being are poverty, economic insecurity, and parental conflict.

Although finding good data on family characteristics prior to disruption is difficult, a number of studies have been able to control for at least some of the conditions that pre-date divorce and separation (Cherlin et al., 1991). These studies indicate that although the correlation between family structure and children's well-being is substantially reduced once preexisting differences are taken into account, it is not eliminated entirely. On the basis of our own research and our reading of the literature, we conclude that family structure has a moderate causal effect on children's lifetime income.

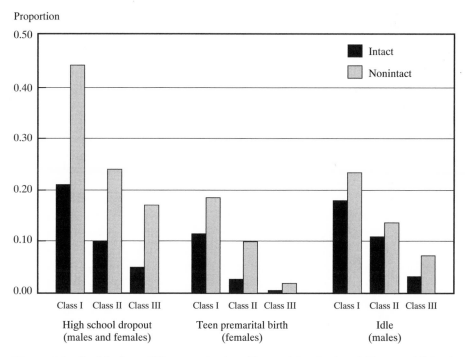

Figure 4.9 Social class differences in the effects of family instability on children's attainment. Class I is defined as having a mother who has less than a high school education, Class II is defined as having a mother who has only a high school education, and Class III is defined as having a mother who has attended or graduated from college. (Estimates are based on the NLSY; see Figure 4.7.)

In sum, welfare does not appear to be a very important link in the intergeneration transmission of poverty. Family structure appears to play some causal role in determining children's lifetime income, and welfare undoubtedly plays some role in the growth of female-headed families, but neither effect is large enough to account for the correlation between poverty in one generation and poverty in the next generation.

We began by asking whether individuals who experienced poverty as children were more likely to experience poverty as adults than individuals who were not poor as children. Longitudinal surveys do not yet contain enough years to observe both parents and their children over their full adult lives. The available research does indicate, however, that there is substantial persistence across generations in both occupational status and in family income. Individuals whose families were poor at some point during their childhood are therefore more likely to be poor as adults than individuals whose families were never poor. Nevertheless, the "inheritance" of poverty is by no means inevitable.

Intergenerational Correlations in Welfare Participation

The research on intergenerational welfare participation suggests common patterns across generations. Peter Gottschalk (1992) finds that although a substantial proportion of the daughters of welfare recipients do not receive welfare themselves as adults, their risk is substantially greater than the risk of daughters whose mothers did not receive welfare. The probability that a nonblack daughter has a child and receives welfare is .261 if the mother received welfare, whereas it is only .066 if the mother never received AFDC. The comparable figures for blacks are .486 and .136.[31] McLanahan (1988) finds that coming from a family that received 50 percent or more of its annual income from welfare while the daughter was between the ages of twelve and sixteen has the strongest effect among welfare indicators on AFDC participation for whites, while a simple measure of welfare receipt during the ages twelve to sixteen has the strongest effect for blacks.

Because of the lack of data on full welfare histories of both generations, few studies attempt to construct measures of long-term welfare use in both generations. Greg Duncan, Martha Hill, and Saul Hoffman (1988) measure welfare dependence as heavy use, defined as receiving welfare continuously for a three-year period. They find that 64 percent of the women whose families were highly dependent during their adolescence (defined as ages thirteen to fifteen) did not use welfare themselves between the ages of twenty-one and twenty-three. Only 20 percent were heavy welfare users themselves. When the analyses are adjusted for differences in the background of the individuals (income and family structure), the relationship between family of origin's welfare use and children's welfare use declines but remains positive.

Moffitt (1992) reviews these and other studies and concludes that there is consistent evidence of strong correlations between parental welfare receipt and daughter's welfare receipt, even though this preliminary research has not yet explained the causes of the strong intergenerational correlation. Because families receiving welfare are poor—indeed, poverty is a condition of welfare receipt—we would expect children from welfare families to have higher rates of poverty and welfare use as adults than children from nonpoor, nonwelfare families. Intergenerational correlation, therefore, does not necessarily indicate a causal relationship. Daughters and their mothers may simply share characteristics that increase the probability of their both receiving assistance.[32] For example, if both the mother and the daughter grow up in neighborhoods with poor-quality schools, both will be more likely to have lower earnings and, hence, a greater need for income assistance. In this case, taking the mother off of welfare will not lower the probability that the daughter will receive assistance. Changing the quality of the school the daughter attends, however, will raise her income and, in turn, lower the probability that she receives public assistance.

.   .   .

We have focused on two broad issues: (1) the extent to which individuals and families are poor for long periods of time or use welfare for extended periods; and (2) the extent to which the experiences of individuals as children are associated with their economic situation as adults or, more specifically, the extent to which poverty and welfare use are passed on across generations.

The results regarding the first issue suggest that a majority of the poor remain poor for short periods of time, and that a majority of welfare recipients receive welfare for only a few years. There is, however, a minority who experience long-term poverty or welfare dependence. By most accounts, nevertheless, temporary dips into poverty and short-term participation in welfare are much more common than long-term spells of poverty and dependence.

The results regarding the second issue—whether poverty and welfare dependence are passed along from generation to generation—also suggest that the media and some scholars have overstated the extent to which poverty and welfare are traps in which individuals and families are caught. The large majority of families and individuals who are poor or who use welfare are not trapped, and neither are their children. It is true that individuals who lived in poor families as children are more likely to experience poverty as adults, and it is true that individuals whose families participated in welfare programs when they were children are more likely to receive welfare as adults. But it is also true that as many as two-thirds of the children from these families manage to escape poverty and dependence when they grow up.

We know a great deal about the sizes of the intra- and intergenerational correlations in both incomes and welfare participation. What is more difficult to pin down is the extent to which these reflect causal links. Our review of the intragenerational literature suggests that increasing public assistance will lead to some offsetting decreases in earnings and may cause some increase in female headship. These behavioral feedbacks are certainly not large enough, however, to offset fully the increased income from welfare. In other words, public assistance reduces poverty, but not dollar for dollar.

We know less about the causal links between generations. Although we know that income is correlated across generations, for example, we do not know the extent to which raising the incomes of the parents will raise the incomes of their offspring. Similarly, we do not know whether helping a mother avoid having to receive welfare will lower the probability that her daughter will participate when she is an adult. There may be a causal link, but the observed correlation may reflect only the fact that parents and their children face similar circumstances that yield similar outcomes. If this is the case, then altering the outcomes of the parents without altering these circumstances will have no effect on the child.

Finally, our examination of single parenthood and its relationships to welfare and poverty suggests that there may be a causal link between family instability and children's future economic well-being. Our review suggests that children who grow up in single-parent families are more likely to drop out of high school, become idle, and become unmarried teen mothers than are children who grow up with both parents.

CHAPTER FIVE

The Underclass:
Concept, Controversy, and Evidence

RONALD B. MINCY

Today antipoverty policy is at a critical stage. Policies to promote upward mobility for poor and socially distressed people continue to be discussed. Many observers, however, question the need to maintain a unified social perspective by linking these policies in some way or by grouping the people targeted by these policies (Jencks, 1991). In the 1980s, by contrast, many felt the need for a unifying categorization. Journalists, who emphasized values, culture, and attitudes, stimulated much interest among the public and policymakers in the *underclass* (Aponte, 1988). Social scientists, who sought to inject some precision into the discussion, also became interested in the underclass. Their work wrestled with issues such as size, growth, and composition of the underclass; the effects of structural economic changes on black employment; declines in black marriage rates; and neighborhood effects on youths' choices in the areas of sex, crime, and schooling. What have we learned from the recent studies? What do the findings suggest about appropriate policy interventions? Here I review the underclass research literature from the perspective of an economist and policy analyst.

Poverty before the War on Poverty

Observers can interpret the underclass literature from two historical perspectives: first, as part of a long-standing tradition of seeking to distinguish the deserving from the undeserving poor; and second, as an attempt to restore balance and breadth to poverty research and policy analysis and to create an interdisciplinary framework for the study of poverty.

Michael Katz (1989) prefers the first interpretation. He argues that distinguishing two groups among the poor is a centuries-old tradition used to justify who will receive limited public and private charity. The yardsticks for distinguishing between the two groups vary with place and time. Under Elizabethan poor laws, for example, members of a community would provide for neighbors, but not for strangers. By another yardstick, communities would provide for their feeble, infirm, or mentally ill members, but not for the able-bodied. According to Katz, values and attitudes are modern yardsticks for distinguishing groups among the poor. In the 1980s Americans resolved to end support for members of a welfare culture that was believed to condone idleness and dependency. Katz argues, therefore, that "underclass" is merely a modern euphemism for the undeserving poor.

Restoring ideological balance and conceptual breadth to poverty research and policy analysis is the second historical perspective for interpreting the underclass literature. Today the conventional view of the ideal antipoverty program is one that places family income above some social minimum. Such a simple approach was not always prominent. Beginning in the late 1950s, anthropologists and sociologists such as Edward Banfield (1958), Michael Harrington (1962), and Oscar Lewis (1966) began to apply their work on rural poverty to urban sociology. There were important differences among these authors, but all emphasized the values, attitudes, and lifestyles of a "poverty class," including work patterns and family formation (Haveman, 1987). They also made similar assumptions about a "culture of poverty" that could influence individual choices. They argued that the cumulative effect of values and attitudes of the poverty class could affect the behavior of members of that class in ways likely to keep their incomes low. This analysis implied that, to be effective, antipoverty strategies would have to influence the values, attitudes, and culture of the members of the poverty class, so that they would make decisions that would alleviate income poverty.

Ironically, the literature surrounding the Moynihan Report (U.S. Department of Labor, 1965) comes closest to modern underclass literature, because it recognized the importance of constraints on individual choices and viewed those choices comprehensively. Daniel Patrick Moynihan, then assistant secretary of labor, based much of his analysis on the work of historians and urban sociologists, including black scholars such as E. Franklin Frazier (1939, 1962) and Kenneth Clark (1965), and recognized racism as a key constraint that shaped black choices leading to high black poverty rates. He argued that patterns of family formation, emerging from slavery, destroyed the capacity of blacks to sustain two-parent families. He also saw racism, operating through employment discrimination, as the cause of high black male unemployment rates. Finally, Moynihan emphasized that unemployment undermined the position of black males in their families and communities, which contributed to high delinquency rates among black youth.

Like the modern underclass literature, Moynihan viewed the problems of the black community as a whole, not in isolation. Borrowing a phrase from Kenneth Clark, Moynihan described these joint problems (including unemployment, drug use, delinquency, and especially out-of-wedlock childbearing) as a "tangle of pathologies." Journalists' accounts of Moynihan's work emphasized this culturally loaded interpretation of the social problems in the black community. They ignored the attention that Moynihan and others who rejected the culture of poverty thesis (for example, Gans, 1968; Valentine, 1968; Rainwater, 1968) paid to racism and unemployment. The Moynihan Report thus raised the ire of the civil rights community and of black scholars in particular. Drug use, delinquency, and out-of-wedlock childbearing among blacks became taboo subjects for liberal social scientists until the early 1980s (Wilson, 1987).

At the same time that liberal social scientists withdrew from discussions of multiple social problems among urban blacks, the War on Poverty led to an expansion in research on the economics of poverty (Haveman, 1987). Economists in the Johnson administration defined this war to be an economic one. The critical tasks for social scientists were to describe the composition of the poverty population and to determine how many people were poor so that analysts could assess the effectiveness of the War on Poverty.

The conceptual framework of the economist was much narrower than the complex conceptual framework of the sociologist and the anthropologist. First, economists focused on a single dimension, income poverty. Government analysts had already begun to use $3,000 as a measure of income poverty, and the Orshansky index, an income level based on household consumption and nutritional standards, was soon adopted as the official government poverty standard. Nevertheless, economists undertook extensive research on alternative ways of measuring economic well-being and inequality. Although these measures were conceptually complex, the data needed to compute them were more readily available than the data needed to measure the dimensions of poverty discussed in the sociological and anthropological literature.

Second, when economists thought about social policy intervention, they emphasized the agents and routes most natural to their discipline and, in their judgment, most easily manipulated by policymakers: individuals, not classes or communities. They also emphasized incentives more frequently than values, attitudes, and institutional constraints. The major strategies underlying the War on Poverty reflected these emphases. These strategies included economic growth to expand employment opportunities for the poor and improvements in the human capital of the poor adults and children, programs under the Manpower Development and Training Act, Head Start, Upward Bound, and Title I of the Elementary and Secondary Education Act, and so on. The Community Action Program, however, a third major part of the War on Poverty, attempted to provide the poor, especially minorities, improved access to the institutions that would promote upward social mobility.

Conservatives filled the void left by the economists and liberal social scientists who retreated from discussions of the nonincome dimensions of poverty (Wilson, 1987; Katz, 1989). In the early 1980s, conservative policy analysts built upon the culture of poverty thesis by arguing that Great Society programs actually increased poverty. These programs allegedly weakened incentives to work; undermined traditional American values among the inner-city poor; and encouraged drug abuse, indolence, delinquency, and promiscuity (Gilder, 1981; Murray, 1984).[1] Economists' studies of labor-supply responses, especially studies based on the negative income tax experiments, did not support the first assertion, and a flurry of studies quickly undermined assertions about the effects of changes in the value of government expenditures (Danziger and Gottschalk, 1985; Burtless, 1986; Pencavel, 1986). These reports, however, were not enough to overcome the influence of conservative policy analysts and journalists, whose writing on deteriorating inner-city conditions also emphasized cultural explanations. Together these analysts and members of the media fueled a growing uneasiness that there was something desperately wrong in America's inner cities and that Great Society programs, along with a developing welfare culture, were at fault (Aponte, 1988).

The Core Underclass Hypotheses

Research on the underclass emerged against this background, as several analysts proposed hypotheses that challenged the explanations offered by journalists and conservatives. William Julius Wilson (1987) developed the most comprehensive set of hypotheses, and his work has dominated the emerging research.[2]

Wilson's Theory of the Underclass

Wilson developed four related hypotheses to explain the growth of poverty and social problems in black urban ghettos. These hypotheses dealt with changing employment opportunities, declines in black marriage rates, selective out-migration from ghetto areas, and neighborhood (or contagion) effects. Together they offered an internally consistent theory that avoided arguments about racism, discrimination, and cultural pathologies and suggested changes in government policies.

Changing employment opportunities. Wilson's hypothesis concerning the role of changing employment opportunities involved three component hypotheses. These hypotheses emphasized demand-side forces that combined to increase joblessness among inner-city black workers. He gave first place to a hypothesis about structural changes, that is, changes in the industrial and occupational composition of urban employment, that reduced the demand for low-skilled labor.[3] These structural changes hurt low-skilled black men the most. Urban employment grew in white-collar and clerical occupations that tended to require some postsecondary schooling or specialized training, and the black inner-city work force lacked the skills to match the needs of a growing number of urban employers. Hence the term *skills mismatch*. *Spatial mismatch* and *slow economic growth* were the other demand-side hypotheses in Wilson's view of changing employment opportunities. Wilson hypothesized that employers of low-skilled workers, especially in manufacturing, were moving their operations away from the inner city. Employers were also paying wages that, net of transportation costs, discouraged blacks from commuting. Finally, Wilson hypothesized that low-skilled blacks were more often working in manufacturing industries that were most vulnerable to the high local unemployment rates that prevailed in many northern cities during most of the 1970s.[4]

Declines in black marriage rates. Next, Wilson hypothesized that joblessness and low wages among inner-city black men led to increased poverty and several other social problems. For example, black men who could not support themselves in mainstream jobs turned to hustling, including criminal activity and drug selling. Rising numbers of female-headed and welfare-dependent families were the other major social problems that Wilson hoped to explain. According to Charles Murray (1984), increases in the real value of benefits under Aid to Families with Dependent Children had caused the social problems. To counter this argument, Wilson and Kathryn Neckerman (1986) asserted that structural changes reduced the number of *marriageable (that is, employed) males* in inner-city neighborhoods. This decline lowered marriage rates and increased out-of-wedlock births and welfare dependency.

Selective out-migration. For Wilson, the most important policies linked to the underclass were not welfare but equal employment opportunity, affirmative action, and fair housing laws that disproportionately benefited working- and middle-class blacks. He hypothesized that increased income and greater access to suburban housing enabled working- and middle-class blacks to leave inner-city ghettos in the 1970s. This *selective out-migration* resulted in an increasing concentration of poverty and other social problems.

Neighborhood effects. Finally, Wilson hypothesized that selective out-migration had three important consequences for low-skilled blacks. First, a larger proportion of the families that remained in inner-city ghettos had poverty-level incomes and related social problems. Second, inner-city residents were isolated from upwardly mobile role models, neighborhood institutions, and social networks that could help them move into the mainstream. Third, inner-city residents were isolated from important sources of resistance to social problems such as crime, out-of-wedlock parenting, and dropping out of high school. Individuals, especially children, surrounded by poverty and social problems and removed from mainstreaming institutions, were more likely to make choices leading to their own poverty and social disadvantage. These *neighborhood (or contagion) effects* helped to explain the rapid growth of poverty and social problems.

Other Underclass Hypotheses

Although Wilson provided the most comprehensive theoretical framework to reinterpret cultural and public policy explanations for the underclass, there were other hypotheses. These hypotheses involved the availability of low-skilled employment, the causes of declining black marriage rates, and race.

Wilson portrayed low-skilled blacks as the victims of reduced demand for low-skilled labor. Lawrence Mead, by contrast, argued that low-skilled immigrants had maintained high employment levels despite the additional handicap of language (Wilson and Mead, 1987). The difference, Mead said, was that immigrants rarely relied on Great Society programs to sustain their incomes, even if they did not work. Blacks, who were raised in welfare-dependent families, were accustomed to receiving government support, with no corresponding social obligation (Mead, 1986, 1992). They therefore refused the unpleasant, low-paying jobs that were abundantly available.

Wilson also minimized the role of discrimination as a cause of the social problems evident among inner-city blacks. The major references to employment and housing discrimination were in regard to its reduction, at least for working- and middle-class blacks. Not only did Wilson minimize the role of discrimination, but he rejected race-conscious policies among potential solutions. These policies, he argued, had limited potential for political support and ignored the confluence of race and class that caused the underclass. Instead, Wilson recommended active government intervention to stimulate full employment and balanced economic growth. This universal approach would benefit inner-city blacks and others.

Other analysts argued that race-conscious policies were still needed. Douglas Massey (1990a) argued that blacks and many Puerto Ricans shared two attributes that increased poverty rates in their neighborhoods in the 1970s. The first attribute was skin color; many Puerto Ricans are black. The second attribute was geographic concentration in the northern and midwestern cities that experienced both structural change and high rates of segregation against blacks. The structural changes reduced incomes of low-skilled workers. Segregation, however, spatially concentrated these income declines in black and Puerto Rican neighborhoods. Continued efforts to reduce housing segregation were therefore needed to prevent future increases in the concentration of black and Puerto Rican poverty.

William Darity and Samuel Myers (1983) also argued that race-conscious policies were still critical. They were among the first to recognize that nonmarriage was the distinguishing feature of the increase in black female-headed families. They argued that changing demographic constraints—more than welfare or earnings trends—were the dominant explanations of nonmarriage among black women. The most important demographic constraints were increases in black male mortality and incarceration, which represented the long-term results of racism. These constraints reduced the ratio of males to females and hence marriage rates. Nearly a decade later, high rates of mortality, nonmarriage, and incarceration among black males are receiving increased attention by mainstream scholars (Sampson, 1987; Testa, 1991; Freeman, 1992).

Meanwhile, Darity and Myers have proposed an alternative to Wilson's structural thesis about underclass formation. Their thesis offers a more pessimistic interpretation of structural change, the rising mortality and institutionalization of black males, increasing numbers of black females who never marry, the growth of female-headed black families, and the role of the black middle class.

First, in contrast to Wilson's argument that macrostructural changes have inadvertently weakened the labor market status of low-skilled black males, Darity and Myers see a different process: "The structuralism we embrace is one wherein race is central; and where the changes in industrial society—from traditional capitalism towards a managerial age—by design eliminate the need for the very class of persons Wilson and others call the underclass" (Darity et al., 1990, p. 42). Black males (presumably, low-skilled black males) thus became a superfluous source of labor.

A provocative volume edited by Darity and colleagues (forthcoming) supports this view of the marginalization of black males. The authors' arguments include a review of historical evidence suggesting differential enforcement of criminal law, which has resulted in staggering incarceration rates among young black males. The authors also discuss the role of the military draft, which has exposed many young black males to military bases, where laws against the use, sale, and possession of drugs have not been adequately enforced. They even implicate the supply-side emphasis of U.S. drug policy, which has maintained high prices for illegal drugs that lure young black males into criminal activity.

Second, according to Wilson, selective out-migration isolated blacks in the underclass from working- and middle-class blacks. By inference, it would seem helpful if blacks in the underclass were reintegrated with blacks from other classes, perhaps by strengthening the institutions within the black community where such integration could take place. Darity and Myers, however, are more skeptical about the role of the black middle class. In their view,

Much of the middle-class has emerged as a component of the new managerial elite. And, it is the managerial class that is supervising the control and regulation of the unwanted surplus. Thus, in the case of crime and violence, Wilson sees the middle-class as helping to instill values and behaviors that curb individual pathologies. Darity-Myers see members of the middle-class as supporting the means for further control and institutionalization of the unwanted, superfluous inner-city residents, creating further marginalization of many young black males, and thereby increasing observed pathologies like crime and violence.   (Darity et al., 1990, p. 43)

Increases in public-sector employment among middle-class blacks have placed them in settings where they are service providers and custodians of the black underclass. These positions include prison guards, welfare caseworkers, probation officers, teachers in ghetto schools, and directors and staff of community development corporations and community-based service agencies. As recent arrivals in these institutional settings, members of the black middle class may be insecure and therefore likely to distance themselves from the black underclass and to respond to them in unsympathetic ways (Anderson, 1990; Farkas et al., 1990). Middle-class blacks, however, also operate civil rights and community-based service organizations committed to supporting lower-income blacks. In recent years, for example, the National Urban League has provided leadership in the youth service community to increase male responsibility programs targeting young black males from high-risk environments. The movement to develop Africentric Rites of Passage programs, targeting the same population, has been led by the National Association of Black Social Workers. And the National Center for Neighborhood Enterprise, a leader in the movement to empower low-income black communities, emerged out of the civil rights movement.

Although Darity and Myers do not detail the policy implications of their structural theses, one thing is clear. Policies that ignore the legacy of racism in this country have no hope of ameliorating the (black) underclass. The policy implications of class conflict within the black community may seem even more intractable, but they are a less immediate concern. The movement of blacks into the middle class and the managerial elite undoubtedly creates new class tensions within the black community, or exacerbates old tensions (Brown and Erie, 1981). It is probably too early to tell, however, whether the net effect of this development on the black underclass is positive or negative.

Wilson provided a consistent theoretical framework to explain why the underclass emerged. Although the empirical support for his arguments came from analyses of data that failed to control for other changes that could have accounted for the same phenomena, his work has stimulated a flood of more rigorous empirical tests of the underlying hypotheses.

Evidence Concerning Wilson's Theory of the Underclass

Since 1985 many quantitative studies have tested the four core hypotheses in Wilson's theory of the underclass. Analysts generally agree that changing employment opportunities have decreased black employment. Studies also offer qualified support for the hypotheses concerning selective out-migration and neighborhood effects, but little support for the hypothesis concerning black male joblessness and marriage.

Changing Labor Market Opportunities

Studies generally support the hypothesis that skills mismatches have hurt black male employment. In the 1970s and 1980s urban areas, especially in the Northeast and North-Central regions, lost jobs in industries that formerly paid high wages to low-skilled workers (Kasarda, 1989). Many service jobs were lost, as well. This loss in particular reduced the opportunities for black male youths to enter the labor market, because the first jobs most young people can get are service jobs; indeed, the most severe declines in labor market status occurred among black male youth (Johnson and Oliver, 1991).

The quantitative evidence also supports Wilson's theory concerning spatial mismatches. Low-skilled blacks remained in central-city areas; employers moved to the suburbs. Inner-city blacks thus lost access to employment to a greater degree than did whites and suburban blacks (Holzer, 1991). Studies have also found that black earnings and employment probabilities are hurt when blacks must commute long distances to work (see, for example, Ihlanfeldt and Sjoquist, 1989).

Even more important than skills and spatial mismatches has been the decline in the wages of low-skilled workers. Since the early 1970s wages of less-skilled workers have declined and, especially during the 1980s, employers increased pay differentials between workers with and without college training and between workers with more and less experience (Blackburn, Bloom, and Freeman, 1990; Katz and Murphy, 1990; Levy and Murnane, 1992). These trends are industry-wide. Further, wage reductions for workers with less skill, less education, and less experience account for most of the reduction in labor market participation among these workers since the early 1970s (Juhn, 1992).

Finally, the literature strongly supports the notion that local unemployment rates have increased black male joblessness. Black youths living in metropolitan areas with tight labor markets had higher earnings and lower unemployment rates than black youths living in metropolitan areas with slack labor markets (Bound and Freeman, 1990; Cain and Finnie, 1990; Freeman, 1991).

Declines in Black Marriage

Studies of marriage trends provide little support for the marriageable-male hypothesis. There has been a long-term decline in black marriages since the early 1950s, despite fluctuating black male employment throughout this period (Jencks, 1988; Ellwood and Crane, 1990). In addition, marriage rates have declined for high-skilled and employed black men as well as for the low-skilled and the jobless (Lerman, 1989; Ellwood and Crane, 1990). Studies also show that the declining labor market status of men can account for only a fraction of the secular decline in black (or white) marriage rates (Ellwood and Rodda, 1991; Mare and Winship, 1991; Hoffman, Duncan, and Mincy, 1991).

Out-Migration of Middle-Income Blacks

Most studies support the selective out-migration hypothesis, at least for large northern cities. Edward Gramlich and Deborah Laren (1991) examined the selective out-migration hypothesis directly.[5] They found that rich black families left poor black neighborhoods, and that some poor black families replaced them. The poverty rates therefore increased in poor black neighborhoods.

Other studies examined the selective out-migration hypothesis indirectly. Andrew Kavee and Michael White (1990) analyzed net migration from Chicago neighborhoods between 1970 and 1980. They found that the higher the percentage of blacks in a given neighborhood, the lower the percentage of blacks in that neighborhood with at least a high school diploma. Richard Greene (1991) examined trends in population and poverty rates in metropolitan areas and concluded that in large northern cities, population declined and poverty increased. This scenario is consistent with selective out-migration. Paul Jargowsky (1991) studied changes in black household income and changes in the sorting of black low- and high-income households across neighborhoods ("neighborhood sorting"). He concluded that, at least in the large northern cities, neighborhood sorting accounted for about half the increase in black ghetto poverty. He emphasized, however, that his study ignored the effects of racial segregation, without which "there would be no ghetto poverty" (p. 20).

Massey and colleagues have forcefully made this point. Massey accepted the role of spatial, structural, and macroeconomic changes in lowering black household income, but rejected the selective out-migration hypothesis. With colleagues, he presented three kinds of evidence against this hypothesis: (1) black segregation does not decline with black income and education; (2) interclass segregation among blacks is lower than interclass segregation among other minority groups; and (3) levels and changes in black poverty have no effect on black interclass segregation (Massey and Denton, 1988; Massey and Eggers, 1990). Massey

(1990a) illustrated the confluence of racial and class segregation using a careful simulation model. This model showed that rates of racial and class segregation helped to confine the effects of declining black incomes to black neighborhoods that were already poor in 1980. The result was rising concentrations of black poverty and of correlates such as crime, welfare dependency, and female-headed families.

Neighborhood Effects

Empirical research on neighborhood effects is at an early stage. Studies have mostly examined the effects that peers and neighbors have on the decisions of teenagers regarding crime, employment and earnings, educational attainment, and sexual behavior. There have been only a few studies, however, that include even minimal controls for family background characteristics when estimating the effects of peer and neighbor characteristics on these decisions. Such controls are important because community amenities, including the attributes of one's neighbors, are part of the bundle of goods and services that people purchase with housing. Those with higher incomes can more easily afford housing in neighborhoods in which most households have at least one employed person. Household income may also be positively correlated with the earnings of neighbors. If employment status and earnings are negatively correlated with the probability that one commits certain kinds of crimes (for example, burglary, drug selling, or drug-related acts of violence) and positively correlated with educational attainment, then studies without controls for family background characteristics will overestimate peer and neighbor effects.

The few studies with such controls provide selective and mixed support for peer and neighbor effects. Christopher Jencks and Susan Mayer (1990) found little evidence of peer or neighborhood effects on crime and drug use; Anne Case and Lawrence Katz (1990), however, reported that the number of crimes committed by neighboring youth and their use of alcohol and illegal drugs had significant and positive effects on similar choices by sample respondents. Jencks and Mayer also found that peers significantly affected academic achievement. Other researchers have noted that youths achieved greater academic success if they lived in neighborhoods or zip-code areas with lower proportions of blacks; unemployed males; lower-income, female-headed, or welfare-dependent families; or higher proportions of managerial or professional workers (Datcher, 1982; Corcoran et al., 1990; Brooks-Gunn et al., 1991; Crane, 1991; Clark and Wolf, 1992).

Studies of employment indicate that the higher the percentage of unemployed males and welfare recipients in a given neighborhood, the fewer hours a person in that neighborhood will tend to work. None of the neighborhood quality indices significantly affected wages or total earnings, however (Datcher, 1982; Corcoran et al., 1990). This finding is consistent with an interpretation of social isolation that Wilson (1991c) accepts: that inner-city youth find labor market entry difficult because they have few adult contacts who can provide information and referrals about job vacancies.

Peers and neighbors most strongly affect choices about childbearing. The more female students at a given school who have had (or thought they would have) a child out of wedlock, the more likely it is that a teenage girl who attends that school will become an unmarried mother (Abrahamse, Morrison, and Waite, 1988). The more male-headed or two-parent families, professional and managerial workers, and families with incomes exceeding thirty thousand dollars in a given neighborhood, the less likely it is that a teenage girl who lives in that neighborhood will become an unmarried mother (Case and Katz, 1990; Brooks-Gunn et al., 1991; Crane, 1991). The higher the proportion of families headed by women and receiving AFDC in a given neighborhood, the more likely it is that girls growing up in that neighborhood will remain single and receive AFDC by age twenty-five, although these results vary by race (Hoffman, Duncan, and Mincy, 1991). Finally, the higher the neighborhood poverty rate in a given neighborhood, the less likely it is that teenage girls in that neighborhood will use contraceptives and the more likely it is that they will become pregnant (Hogan and Kitagawa, 1985).

Ethnographic Evidence and Wilson's Theory of the Underclass

Quantitative studies have two important shortcomings for underclass research. First, they leave certain important issues about neighborhood (and other) effects unresolved, because they tell us little about the mechanisms through which these effects occur. Second, quantitative studies reveal little about illegal acts such as assaults, burglary, drug use, and drug selling. Even when outcomes do not involve illegal acts, individuals may be reluctant to report accurately acts that violate social norms (delaying childbirth until marriage, for example).[6] Survey data on several outcomes related to the underclass are therefore generally unavailable. Without these survey data, quantitative studies cannot test hypotheses about the underclass. The findings of recent ethnographic and small sample research, however, provide helpful insights about these outcomes and the mechanisms through which neighborhood effects operate.

Unlike quantitative researchers, ethnographers focus on groups in communities; it is natural for them to study multiple outcomes for a demographic group in particular community settings (for example, young males in ghettos). Much ethnographic research involves peer groups.

Ethnographic evidence supports Wilson's hypotheses about the underclass. Most ethnographers conclude that macrostructural changes are a leading cause of increasing joblessness, crime, violence, and drug selling among less-skilled males, a conclusion that is consistent with Wilson's hypothesis about changing employment opportunities. These changes, as well as declines in entry-level wages, prolong peer group association and gang participation among white, black, Chicano, and Puerto Rican teenage and young-adult males. Further, ethnographic studies find that young men "hustle" when high-paying employment is unavailable (Williams and Kornblum, 1985; Hagedorn, 1988; Taylor, 1989; Anderson, 1990; Jarret, 1990; Bourgois, 1991; Fagan, 1992). Hustling can mean being idle, working "off the books" for an otherwise legal firm, or selling books, clothing, jewelry, and artwork (sometimes hand crafted) on the street, but it also includes involvement in petty crime and drug selling at various levels. Another conclusion of ethnographic research is that joblessness reduces marriage rates. Elijah Anderson (1989, 1990) and Mercer Sullivan (1989), for example, argue that young minority males do not legitimate out-of-wedlock births through marriage when they lack jobs paying wages high enough to support a family. Families and communities, moreover, do not pressure young couples to marry under these circumstances and sometimes oppose marriage plans involving males who are poor prospects.

Ethnographers also conclude, like Wilson, that peer groups affect choices about health, education, sexuality, substance abuse, and criminal behavior, although parental supervision plays an important mediating role. Anderson (1990) describes the development of peer groups among black female teenagers in ghetto neighborhoods. Sex is a recurring theme in girls' peer group conversations, ranging from who is "going with" whom to who is having sex with whom to who is having a baby with whom. This environment orients peer group members to early sexual intercourse; they become the "fast" young girls that boys in the neighborhood prey upon (Anderson, 1989). Such a peer group is generally ignorant about contraception and the risks of early sexual intercourse, and early pregnancies are inevitable. Not all young girls in ghetto neighborhoods, however, face this outcome. Girls from more "decent" and stable ghetto families, like most girls in most communities, are prepared for marriage and family under the watchful eyes of their mothers, older female relatives, and older female friends (Anderson, 1989; Jarret, 1990).[7]

Ethnographic research provides important clues about the operation of neighborhood effects and the reasons some young residents of poor and underclass areas participate in crime. In seeking to explain these effects, many observers focus on the absence of middle-class adult role models in poor or underclass areas. The ethnographic literature, by contrast, suggests that peer groups may be the more important mechanism through which neighborhood effects operate, at least for youth. Even if young people are surrounded by adult high school dropouts, the commitment of their peers to schooling may play a bigger role in their academic performance and prospects of graduating. The conventional wisdom sees rigid boundaries between teenagers in school (or young adults working in low-wage jobs) and youth or young adults who are idle or involved in crime. The ethnographic literature, however, suggests that youth and young adults with slim prospects for stable, high-paying, mainstream jobs engage in a variety of activities to make money. Youth or young adults may be engaged in various sorts of hustling in the same month that they attend school, look for work, or work in an unstable, low-paying job. Studies relying on small-scale survey data also find that drug selling is a part-time activity for some youth and young adults otherwise engaged in mainstream activities such as attending school or working in low-wage employment (Brounstein et al., 1990; Reuter, McCoun, and Murphy, 1990).

Verifying the conclusions of ethnographic research through studies based on large sample surveys may be difficult, but its insights have important policy implications nonetheless. Policymakers may be unable, for example, to integrate communities so that the children of high school dropouts regularly interact with adults with more schooling. But policymakers can support educational enrichment programs targeting youth peer groups that, in turn, can encourage and support their members' efforts to increase academic achievement and attainment. If drug selling is just one of many forms of hustling, larger expenditures to increase stable, low-wage employment, accompanied by earnings subsidies, could reduce the rapidly increasing criminal justice expenditures associated with mandatory sentencing for selling small quantities of illegal drugs.

Although some reallocation of expenditures toward employment services, earnings subsidies, and other services is needed, so are expenditures to increase public safety. The ethnographic research suggests that the fear of crime and violence is high in poor and underclass neighborhoods (Hagedorn, 1988; Taylor, 1989; Anderson, 1990). This is consistent with Wilson's selective migration hypothesis and is supported by research based on small sample surveys (Case and Katz, 1990; Freeman, 1992). That some families cannot leave the underclass neighborhoods they live in reinforces the importance of viewing the underclass inclusively. That is, underclass policies need to target poor, "decent" people in addition to the irresponsible parents, fast young girls, and street hustlers who ruin the quality of life of everyone who lives in the neighborhood.

In Search of an Empirical Definition of the Underclass

The issue of targeting policy raises other questions about how to define and measure the underclass. After years of editorializing about the underclass, journalists have naturally been interested in how large this population is and whether it is growing. Policymakers have had similar questions, and they have also wanted to know the extent of overlap between the social problems associated with the underclass and other problems that fell within their administrative responsibilities. This information helps them target services to people or areas where they are most needed. The Central Virginia Health Planning Agency, for example, used measures of the local underclass area population to plan the location of health centers. The Enterprise Foundation used these data to think about where new housing developments might be located. The Presidential Commission on the Human Immunodeficiency Virus Epidemic considered testimony relating drug use to the spread of the AIDS epidemic. One finding was that AIDS morbidity and mortality involving women and children tended to be concentrated in underclass areas in New York City (Mincy and Hendrickson, 1988).

Although several researchers have attempted to measure the underclass, progress toward a consensus measure has been slow. There has been considerable disagreement over questions ranging from the basic characteristics of the population to estimates of its size, given an empirical definition. Consensus has been delayed not only by the complexity of the underclass concept and the limited data available but also by controversy involving the racial implications of measurement efforts and the reconciliation of perspectives from different disciplines.

Two key elements made the underclass concept complex: multiple social problems and social or spatial context. The first element restored the multidimensional perspective that was typical of poverty discussions before economists dominated the field (Glasgow, 1980; Auletta, 1982; Wilson, 1987).[8] Wilson included the following dimensions:

> Today's ghetto neighborhoods are populated almost exclusively by the most disadvantaged segments of the black urban community, that heterogeneous grouping of families and individuals who are outside the mainstream of the American occupational system. Included in this group are individuals who lack training and skills and either experience long-term unemployment or are not members of the labor force, individuals who are engaged in street crime and other forms of aberrant behavior, and families that experience long-term spells of poverty and/or welfare dependency. These are the populations to which I refer when I speak of the *underclass*. (Wilson, 1987, pp. 7–8)

The second element added the spatial or social context in which social problems occurred. Wilson described this context as follows:

> In my conception, the term *underclass* suggests that changes have taken place in ghetto neighborhoods and the groups that have been left behind are collectively different from those that lived in these neighborhoods in earlier years. It is true that

long-term welfare families and street criminals are distinct groups, but they live and interact in the same depressed community and they are part of the population that has, with the exodus of the more stable working- and middle-class segments, become increasingly isolated socially from mainstream patterns and norms of behavior.   (Wilson, 1987, p. 8)

Later, Wilson (1991a), concerned about the emphasis being placed on the spatial aspects of his concept, gave more attention to social isolation, particularly the lack of contact members of the underclass have with people connected to mainstream employment (Van Haitsma, 1989).

Although no empirical researcher could completely satisfy the data requirements created by these two elements, the elements provided an analytical framework that could be used to develop four methods of measuring the underclass (see Figure 5.1). This framework required investigators to identify the underclass using one or more dimensions of social disadvantage. Some researchers, including Wilson, chose poverty or persistent poverty. Like the government analysts and economists who tried to define poverty during the War on Poverty, these observers took advantage of the simplicity and wide availability of income data. Others chose the multiple dimensions Wilson highlighted, sometimes including

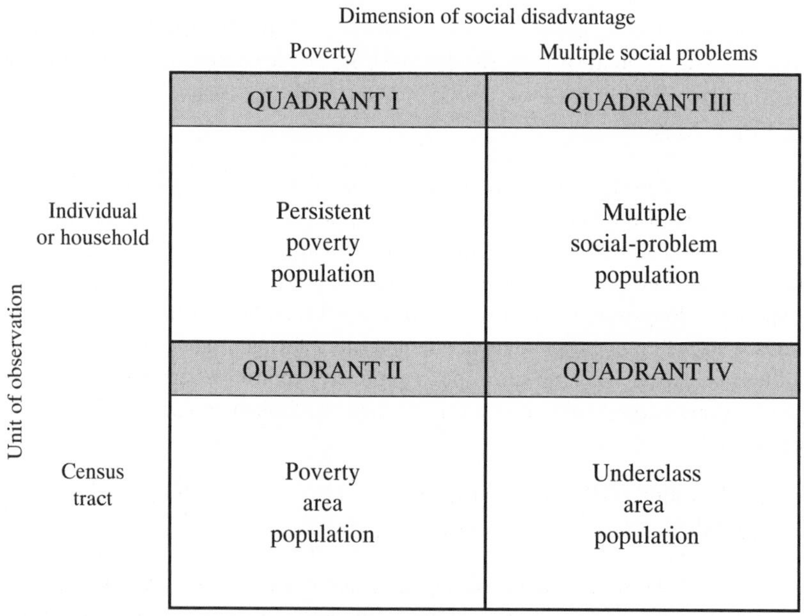

Dimension of social disadvantage

	Poverty	Multiple social problems
	QUADRANT I	**QUADRANT III**
Individual or household	Persistent poverty population	Multiple social-problem population
	QUADRANT II	**QUADRANT IV**
Census tract	Poverty area population	Underclass area population

Unit of observation

Figure 5.1   Framework for underclass measurement.

poverty, sometimes not. The framework also required researchers to choose a unit of observation. Some used census tract or network data to incorporate spatial or social context; others chose individual or household survey data after explicitly rejecting Wilson's spatial or social context.

Alternative combinations of dimensions of social disadvantage and unit of observation produced four approaches for measuring the underclass: (1) the persistently poor population; (2) the poverty area population; (3) the underclass area population; and (4) the multiple problem population. Estimates of the size of the underclass depended on the combination chosen. For a given unit of observation, estimates of the underclass using poverty as the only dimension of social disadvantage are larger than estimates using multiple dimensions of social disadvantage. The number of people who are poor exceeds the number of people who are poor and unemployed and on welfare. For given dimensions of social disadvantage, estimates of the underclass that incorporate spatial or social context are smaller than estimates that ignore these contexts. The poverty population in the United States exceeds the total population living in very poor areas.

Estimates of the size of the underclass also vary by the scope of the data used. Some researchers focused on large metropolitan areas or on metropolitan areas in which blacks represented significant portions of the total population. These were the areas Wilson emphasized. Other investigators included smaller metropolitan areas, or nonmetropolitan areas, because the forces allegedly responsible for the emergence of the underclass (especially industrial change and selective out-migration) might have affected these areas as well. Obviously, the broader the scope of the data, the larger the estimate of the size of the underclass.

Tables 5.1 and 5.2 compare estimates of the size and growth of the underclass using the four approaches of Figure 5.1.[9] Other reviews of the measurement literature may also be consulted (see Ruggles and Marton, 1986; Wiener, 1988; Mincy, Sawhill, and Wolf, 1990; Prosser, 1991).

The Persistently Poor Population

Before Wilson's work, many observers thought of the underclass as the poorest of the poor (Aponte, 1988). Thus studies of persistent poverty (Figure 5.1, quadrant I) focused on length of time in poverty as the dimension of social disadvantage that identified the underclass. These studies used data from the Panel Study of Income Dynamics (PSID), a nationally representative household survey, to identify households with poverty-level incomes for five or more years. Using this standard, estimates of the underclass ranged from 3 million to 20 million people (Ruggles and Marton, 1986). These studies included the elderly and disabled, who represented about half of the persistently poor population. Few observers,

Table 5.1 Size estimates and definitions of the underclass

Source	Operational definition of the underclass	Size (in millions)	Data set[1]	Geographic coverage[1]	Year
Bane and Jargowsky (1988)	All poor in extreme urban poverty areas	1.8	P Census	100 cities	1979
Gottschalk and Danziger (1986)	a. All persons living in extreme urban poverty areas	3.7	P Census	100 cities	1979
	b. Long-term AFDC recipients in extreme urban poverty areas	<1.0	P Census	100 cities	1984
Nathan (1986)	Black and Hispanic poor living in poverty areas	4.1	P Census	100 cities	1979
Littman (1991)	a. All persons in poverty areas[2]	41.1	CPS	U.S.	1980
	b. All poor persons in poverty areas	11.6	CPS	U.S.	1980
Ricketts and Sawhill (1988)	a. Residents of neighborhoods with high levels of female-headed households, high school dropouts, welfare dependency, and men not regularly part of the labor force	2.5	Census	U.S.	1979
	b. All persons in definition (a) neighborhoods in Hughes' (1989) cities	0.6		Eight SMSAs	1979
	c. All residents of extreme poverty areas[3]	5.6		U.S.	1979
	d. All poor residents of extreme poverty areas	2.5		U.S.	1979
	e. All poor residents of (a) underclass neighborhoods	1.1		U.S.	1979
Hughes (1989)	a. All persons in "deprivation" neighborhoods[4]	3.2	Census	Eight SMSAs	1979
	b. All persons in black majority urban tracts	3.6	Census	Eight SMSAs	1979
	c. All persons in black majority deprivation tracts[5]	~2.4	Census	Eight SMSAs	1979
	d. All persons in "underclass" neighborhoods[6]	0.9	Census	Eight SMSAs	1979

Study	Description				
Adams, Duncan, and Rodgers (1988)[7]	All persistently poor living in a household where head exhibited all of four underclass characteristics	0.8	56 cities	PSID	1980
Reischauer (1987)	a. Persons in families with persistently low income and a head with limited education who worked less than 3/4 of the year	8.1	U.S.	PSID	1982
	b. Persons in families with (a) traits and where head is a member of a minority, has dysfunctional attitudes, and antisocial behavior, and lives in neighborhoods with high levels of these characteristics	1.4	U.S.	PSID	1982
Kasarda (1992)	All households with multiple social problems	5.3	95 cities	PUMS	1980
O'Hare and Curry-White (1992)	All adults with multiple social problems	3.0	U.S.	CPS	1990

Source: Wiener (1988).

1. P Census refers to published data from U.S. Bureau of the Census (1985). CPS = Current Population Survey; PSID = Panel Study of Income Dynamics; PUMS = the U.S. Census Public Use Microdata Sample; SMSA = Standard Metropolitan Statistical Area.

2. Littman defines poverty areas as census tracts with poverty rates of 20 percent or more.

3. Extreme poverty areas are defined as census tracts with poverty rates of 40 percent or more.

4. A deprivation neighborhood is defined as having high levels of female headship, welfare dependency, and men not regularly part of the labor force.

5. This number is the result of multiplying 0.75 by the total population of the deprivation tracts in the eight SMSAs. See also Table 5.2, note 3.

6. "Underclass" is defined using the Ricketts and Sawhill (1988) methodology.

7. This study estimates that 31 percent of the persistent poor are members of the underclass and that the persistent poor consist of 5.2 percent of the U.S. urban population. The estimate derived for this table is the result of multiplying these two numbers by the number of people in families in central cities from CPS, P-60.

Table 5.2 Growth estimates and definitions of the underclass

| Source | Operational definition of the underclass | Size (in millions) | | Percent growth | Geographic coverage[2] | Data set[2] |
		1970	1980			
Bane and Jargowsky (1988)	All poor in extreme urban poverty areas[1]	0.98	1.62	66	50 cities	P Census
Gottschalk and Danziger (1986)	All persons living in extreme urban poverty areas	1.90	3.20	68	50 cities	P Census
Hughes (1989)	a. All persons in "deprivation" neighborhoods	1.09	3.19	192	Eight SMSAs	Census
	b. All persons in black majority urban tracts	3.16	3.61	14	Eight SMSAs	Census
	c. All persons in black majority "deprivation" tracts[3]	~0.82	~2.39	192	Eight SMSAs	Census
	d. All persons in "underclass" neighborhoods[4]	0.89	0.90	1	Eight SMSAs	Census
Ricketts and Mincy (1988)	a. All persons in underclass neighborhoods (1980 criteria)[5]	0.75	2.48	230	U.S.	Census
	b. All persons in underclass neighborhoods (1970 criteria)	2.54	5.17	104	U.S.	Census
	c. All persons in underclass neighborhoods (current year criteria)	2.54	2.48	–2	U.S.	Census
	d. All persons living in extreme poverty areas	3.78	5.57	48	U.S.	Census
	e. All poor persons living in extreme poverty areas	1.87	2.53	35	U.S.	Census

Source: Wiener (1988).

1. Extreme poverty area refers to census tracts with poverty rates of 40 percent or more.

2. P Census refers to published data from U.S. Bureau of the Census (1985). SMSA = Standard Metropolitan Statistical Area.

3. Hughes does not actually provide an empirical result for his "black majority deprivation" definition. He does state that "over three-fourths of the deprivation tracts in each metropolitan area are also black majority tracts" in 1980. The estimate for this table is the result of multiplying 0.75 by the total population of the deprivation tracts in the eight SMSAs for both 1970 and 1980.

4. Underclass is defined according to the methodology developed by Ricketts and Sawhill (1988).

5. Underclass neighborhoods are characterized by high levels of female headship, high school dropouts, welfare dependency, and men not regularly part of the labor force. Criteria refers to the year for which the standard deviation was used as a cutoff.

however, believed that these persistently poor people were members of the underclass.

The Poverty Area Population

The first direct efforts to measure Wilson's underclass concept extended his analysis of the poverty area population (Figure 5.1, quadrant II) in large cities (Gottschalk and Danziger, 1986; Nathan, 1986; Bane and Jargowsky, 1988). The usual range of the estimates in 1980 was from under 1 million to 5.57 million people, depending on the number of cities, the definition of poverty areas, and the types of people included in poverty areas (see Table 5.1).

These studies used the poverty rate as the dimension of social disadvantage and the census tract as the unit of observation. The earliest studies used census tracts with poverty rates of 20 percent or more (referred to as *poverty areas*), which yielded estimates of the poverty area population of between 3.7 to 4.1 million in large cities. Later studies used census tracts with poverty rates of 40 percent or more (termed *extreme poverty areas*) in large cities. These studies suggested a smaller extreme poverty area population of 1.8 million persons in large metropolitan areas. Estimates of growth of the poverty area population ranged from 66 percent to 192 percent (Table 5.2).

The variation in estimates of the poverty area population reflected reasonable efforts by empirical researchers to generalize from Wilson's study of Chicago and a few other large metropolitan areas. The earliest estimates used data for the 100 largest cities, which were available in published form and reflected Wilson's large metropolitan area focus. Estimates also depended on the types of people researchers included in their measure. Reflecting Wilson's focus on minorities, some researchers included only minorities (Nathan, 1986). Other investigators included only poor people, reflecting another focus of Wilson's work (Gottschalk and Danziger, 1986; Bane and Jargowsky, 1988).

Some observers criticized studies of the poverty area population because they focused only on large cities or metropolitan areas. This focus supported the perception that the poverty area population was a rapidly growing problem affecting urban blacks and Puerto Ricans exclusively and nationwide (Mincy, 1991). This finding would seem paradoxical if, as Wilson claimed, structural changes—not culture or discrimination—were the primary reason for the growth of the poverty area population. When Ricketts and Sawhill (1988) used all extreme poverty areas to estimate the extreme poverty area population, they found 2.5 million people. Other studies, focusing on all metropolitan areas, showed slower growth of the poverty area population (Table 5.2); considerable regional variation in rates of growth of this population; and more whites in the poverty area population in smaller metropolitan areas (Ricketts and Mincy, 1990; Jargowsky and Bane,

1991; Mincy, 1991). These studies also supported Massey's (1990a) explanation of growth of the black and Puerto Rican poverty area population. He argued that this growth was due to the concentration of these groups in highly segregated metropolitan areas in the North and Midwest, which experienced economic changes tending to increase minority poverty rates.[10]

Mark Littman (1991) argued that nonmetropolitan areas were also affected by structural changes. He estimated the poverty area population to be 11.6 million persons, using poverty areas in metropolitan and nonmetropolitan areas. In addition, he found that the poverty area population actually declined between 1970 and 1980 once he accounted for changes in metropolitan area boundaries.

The Underclass Area Population

Measures of the persistently poor or poverty area populations have often focused on income. In doing so they neglect the critical question, posed by journalists, policymakers, and many members of the public, of whether the underclass is a phenomenon distinct from poverty. Erol Ricketts and Isabel Sawhill (1988) have provided the most direct answer to this question. They used multiple social problems to identify the underclass and the census tract as the unit of observation.[11] In their view, underclass areas (Figure 5.1, quadrant III) were proxies for a heterogeneous group of families and individuals who exhibited distinct social problems, but lived and interacted in the same neighborhood (Wilson, 1987, p. 8). Their estimates showed an underclass area population of 2.5 million people in 1980 (Table 5.1), which had grown by 232 percent since 1970 (Table 5.2) (Ricketts and Mincy, 1990).

The Ricketts and Sawhill measure has been criticized for being sensitive to the way researchers weighted the components to form a composite index. The estimates of size and growth in Tables 5.1 and 5.2 reveal these variations, as well as variations produced by using large cities rather than all tracted areas in the United States.[12] Other critics argued that Ricketts and Sawhill's estimates were inadequate because data limitations determined the components of their composite index (Prosser, 1991). Crime, for example, is a social problem that many observers associate with the underclass. Because there were no crime data in the Decennial Census, however, crime could not be included in the Ricketts and Sawhill measure.

The Multiple Social Problem Population

Some critics of attempts to measure underclass area populations have argued that membership in a class should be based only on the characteristics of individuals (Aponte, 1988; Jencks, 1988, 1991).[13] Several studies, therefore, have provided estimates of a multiple social problem population, which did not account for spatial or social context (Figure 5.1, quadrant IV).

Robert Reischauer (1987) and Terry Adams, Greg Duncan, and Willard Rodgers (1988) produced estimates of the multiple social problem population that combined persistent poverty (or low income) with social problems. Resulting estimates ranged from less than 1 million to 6.1 million people, depending on the number of cities included (Table 5.1). More recently, John Kasarda (1992) and William O'Hare and Brenda Curry-White (1992) produced estimates of the multiple social problem population, excluding poverty or low income. Their estimates ranged from 333,000 to 3,000,000 adults, depending on the number of metropolitan areas and year. Kasarda, who focused only on the ninety-five largest metropolitan areas in 1980, found that 85 percent of adults with multiple social problems were black or Hispanic. Like others, this large-city study concluded that the underclass is a large-city, minority problem. O'Hare and Curry-White, however, who used a national sample including rural areas, showed that in 1990, 55 percent of the multiple problem adult population in rural areas were non-Hispanic whites.

Controversy and Measurements of the Underclass

In addition to disagreements about the use of poverty, social problems, or spatial context, controversies have also slowed consensus on underclass measurement. Several critics initially rejected claims of agnosticism by researchers who focused on social problems, other than poverty, which they described in normative terms. These critics claimed that such research drew attention away from Wilson's thesis that structural changes—not a cultural value system—were primarily responsible for underclass growth (Aponte, 1988; Wilson, 1988). Herbert Gans (1990) claimed that these studies were dangerous, because they supplied racists with evidence and a slippery code word, *underclass,* with which to victimize the black poor. Wilson (1991c) expressed skepticism about the social problem measures of the underclass. He cautioned, however, against the development of an atmosphere, reminiscent of the years immediately following the Moynihan Report, in which charges of racism might drive liberal social scientists away from the field.

Despite Wilson's warning, a cloud remains over the literature. Few researchers now use the term *underclass.* Those who do usually add disclaimers or apologies to ward off charges of "blaming the victim" and racism. Just as income poverty came to dominate the poverty literature after the Moynihan Report, the spatial concentration of poverty is beginning to dominate the "underclass" literature, under a new term, *ghetto poverty* (Wilson, 1988).

There are positive aspects to this trend. First, there is already consensus on the meaning of poverty, a one-dimensional measure of social disadvantage. When someone says "poverty," there is an official government standard to which everyone can turn. Although there is mounting criticism of this official standard, its familiarity to the public, journalists, and policymakers creates strong resistance to change (Ruggles, 1990). Second, the official poverty standard means that data on the characteristics of the poor, including their spatial concentration, are readily available. These data show correlations between poverty and social problems that are high enough to convince some observers that there is no need to focus on social problems.[14]

This trend may also have some undesirable aspects. If the study of the poverty area population really becomes the study of ghetto poverty, the focus will remain on inner-city blacks and Puerto Ricans. The research will continue to ignore the concentrations of poverty and social problems among whites in smaller metropolitan and nonmetropolitan areas. Poverty and social problems among low-skilled whites in smaller and nonmetropolitan areas could have the same qualitative origins as similar problems among the ghetto poor (Mincy, 1991; O'Hare and Curry-White, 1992). If so, ghetto poverty research will miss an opportunity to test hypotheses about the effects of changing employment opportunities. Also, by keeping their focus on blacks and Puerto Ricans, ghetto poverty researchers may fall victim to some of the same charges (of racism) that drove them away from studying the underclass.

Finally, in emphasizing poverty, researchers avoid questions about choices. Sociologists emphasize laws, market forces, and institutional constraints as the causes of poverty (Ellwood, 1989; Prosser, 1991). Poverty becomes a condition, not a choice (Mead, 1988). Economists ask limited questions about the schooling, work, marriage, and fertility choices that make some people poor. These choices are the result of the prices of goods and services that people face, including the price of labor services, and their values (or attitudes) and family background characteristics, as well as the constraints that sociologists emphasize. Economists, however, who substitute the word *preferences* for values, usually avoid other questions about choices. For example, economists rarely ask how peers, neighbors, co-workers, and family members affect preferences.[15] To guide policies on the underclass, researchers must reconcile these analytical approaches. This reconciliation will not be easy, but the results will be more useful to policymakers than theories that focus on only one approach and exclude others.

The Future

Closure of the discussion of empirical definitions of the underclass requires a judgment about the value of the concept, the appropriateness of the term used to identify the concept, and the best approach for measurement. The concept, term, and measurement strategy must (1) reflect the core idea of a nonelderly, nondisabled population, with marginal attachment to the labor force or with income from sources other than legal work, and (2) include the social context that inhibits labor force attachment.

Concept. I agree with Wilson that Martha Van Haitsma (1989) formulates the abstract concept of the underclass best. In Van Haitsma's formulation the defining characteristic of the underclass is labor force detachment and income derived from sources other than work in the formal economy (for example, AFDC or crime).[16] This formulation is more specific than Wilson's original formulation about the characteristics one might use to identify the underclass, which eliminates subjective ideas about deviance from mainstream norms or general social dysfunction. Like Wilson's original formulation, Van Haitsma's is complex, because the social context must be specified along with labor force detachment and nonwork income. This complexity will create measurement problems, but it is necessary to prevent stretching the concept too far. There are labor force nonparticipants and people with nonwork income who do not face social context barriers that prevent them from changing their status (for example, missionaries and college students).

Is this revised underclass concept useful? Yes, because it focuses on what may be a growing social policy challenge for which there are no well-known or agreed-upon solutions. To be sure, this social policy challenge overlaps with other policy concerns, such as income poverty. The underclass, however, is unique. For poor people who are not members of the underclass—the working poor, for example—more money represents an obvious and agreed-upon solution. Few observers oppose subsidizing the earnings of the working poor, although opinions vary on how to provide subsidies (Ellwood, 1988; Mincy, 1990; Horrigan and Mincy, 1993). Policy solutions for the underclass must overcome barriers to labor force nonparticipation before earnings subsidies or income supplements can take effect.

Terminology. What should we call the concept? Any term is appropriate as long as the term captures the idea of a population detached from the labor force and includes the population's social context. The term *underclass* is appealing because it relates to the same hierarchical earnings or occupational structures conveyed by the terms lower class, working class, middle class, and upper class. Webster's dictionary defines class as "a group of people considered as a unit according to economic, occupation, or social status; especially, a social rank or caste; as, the working class, the middle class." Members of the upper class are successful entrepreneurs, corporate and political leaders, and other professionals (such as doctors and lawyers). We group these people together because they all have prestigious occupations and most earn high incomes. If the doctor has a family, we usually think of her husband and children as members of the upper class, even if they earn lower incomes and have lower-status occupations. Members of the lower class are domestic workers, dishwashers, retail sales workers in fast food restaurants, and so on, if they have no family members with higher incomes and occupational status. We group these people together because they have low-status occupations, they earn low wages, and many are among the working poor.

If occupation and income were all that we implied by these terms, we could substitute the term *upper-income groups* for upper class and the term *lower-income groups* for lower class. But when we use the term *class,* we add ideas about the social contexts in which members of these occupation and income groups operate. These social contexts often maintain one's position (and the position of one's children) in a certain class. By extension, the term *underclass* denotes a group of people who have trouble entering and remaining in the labor force and who are in a social context that prevents such attachment.[17] If they have no family members who are attached to the labor force or who derive income from work, the dependents of members of this group are also members of the underclass. These are admittedly simple-minded notions of class that may not satisfy a sociologist, but this simplicity is sufficient for most policymakers, concerned voters, journalists, and economists.

Unfortunately, the term *underclass* does not appeal to everyone. The rhetoric and controversy of the 1980s make it impossible for some observers to focus on the concept's straightforward connection, through earnings and occupational structures, to terms like *middle class* and *lower class.* More important, individuals who do not participate in the labor force and other residents of communities that pose barriers to labor force attachment may also reject the term *underclass* as too pejorative. Such a response makes it more difficult for community leaders to use the results of underclass research in community-based solutions. Yet, most other terms that come to mind to describe this population will also be criticized. There is nothing particularly flattering about the term *ghetto poor,* for example.[18]

Measurement. How should we measure the concept? A variety of approaches are possible, and the choice depends upon the hypothesis scholars want to test, the problem policy analysts want to solve, and the available data.

Scholars must think carefully about how they use race, ethnicity, and metropolitan area to test hypotheses about the underclass. For example, scholars should test the hypothesis that race and ethnicity cause labor force detachment. The test should rely on race and ethnic variations in measures of labor force detachment, holding constant social context, economic context, and individual-level variables that could clarify the roles that race or ethnicity play in determining employment status. Even if scholars believe that the underclass is a black and Puerto Rican problem, what enables other race and ethnic groups to escape? Scholars cannot answer this critical question if they define the underclass to include only blacks and Puerto Ricans, or if they include only blacks and Puerto Ricans in their samples. Scholars should also test the hypothesis that residence in a particular type of area causes labor force detachment. The test would examine variations in labor force detachment across areas (suburban, exurban, central-city, and so on) and control for variables that would clarify why the type of area one resides in causes labor force detachment (segregation, industrial composition, local unemployment rate, and so on). Scholars who restrict their samples to large metropolitan areas or central cities cannot observe the required variations.

Unfortunately, the need to incorporate social context in underclass measures compromises these guidelines. Some theorists, for example, may legitimately speculate that a culture of poverty exists in certain distressed communities. Ethnographic studies tell us that youth in these communities scoff at their neighbors who work in low-wage jobs, but accept families on welfare and idolize successful drug dealers. Or local employers may discriminate against all residents of these communities or against all graduates of high schools located in these communities. Economists call this statistical discrimination. In either case, residence in such a distressed community is a barrier to labor force attachment and is therefore an appropriate measure of social context. Here, at least, the scholar can disentangle the hypothesis test from the social context by examining whether residents of distressed communities have lower rates of participation in the labor force than do similar residents of other communities.

Policy considerations should also affect underclass measurement. Analysts should ask whether policymakers need to define the underclass problem exclusively or inclusively. An exclusive definition would focus on labor force nonparticipants only. Suppose, for example, that policymakers want to assess the benefits of establishing an enterprise zone in a distressed community. An exclusive definition would lead analysts to consider only the increases in income that accrue to those who formerly did not participate in the labor force but who now get jobs in firms that open up in the enterprise zone. An inclusive definition would also focus on income and other welfare gains accruing to those who are already labor force participants and others who made up the social context. Previously employed residents of the distressed area may be able to reduce their commuting costs by resigning from their more distant jobs to take jobs located in the enterprise zone. Even if they continue to work at distant jobs, their children may be safer because there are now fewer idle young males committing crimes in the area.

Data limitations affect underclass measurement in policy analysis and hypothesis testing. Once researchers choose a measure of labor force detachment, they must choose some measure of social context. The characteristics of a person's friends, neighbors, relatives, and other associates that can ease or inhibit that person's labor force attachment are obvious ways to observe social context. But what is the appropriate unit for observing these characteristics? Most researchers have used census tracts, a proxy for neighborhoods, as the unit of observation. Census tract data have many limitations, including small time-series variation, because a new Decennial Census appears only once every ten years. To provide estimates of the size, growth, and composition of the underclass that will be useful to policymakers, however, analysts need many observations of people detached from the labor force and measures of their social context. To test hypotheses about the causes of the underclass, analysts need many observations of people attached and detached from the labor force, in a variety of social contexts, some harmful to the prospects for employment, others not. The cost of obtaining samples large enough for this work from surveys means that census tract data will continue to dominate the field.

Networks provide another unit for observing social context. To study networks, scholars examine the nature and quantity of relationships between a sample of survey respondents and other people or institutions. This approach allows a nonspatial interpretation of social context. Roberto Fernandez and David Harris (1992), for example, use network analysis to study Wilson's idea of social isolation. They examine the nature and quality of contacts involving nonpoor, working poor, and nonworking poor people who live in poverty areas or extreme poverty areas in Chicago. Fernandez and Harris thus use poverty status and work as the central defining characteristics of the underclass and note that work is related to Van Haitsma's formulation.

For our purposes, the most interesting of Fernandez and Harris's social context dimensions was percentage of "mainstream" friends, measured by the friends' employment, welfare, and educational status. These measures of social context thus also reflected labor force attachment or occupational status. Fernandez and Harris found that black men and women had fewer mainstream friends if they were nonworking poor.[19] Black residents of areas with higher poverty rates also had fewer mainstream friends, regardless of the residents' class (work/poverty status). Living in high-poverty areas, however, did not reduce contacts between nonworking poor blacks and mainstream friends. This finding suggests that for blacks, at least, any resident of a high-poverty area is likely to have fewer mainstream friends than a resident of a low-poverty area. But once one becomes a member of the nonworking poor, moving to a low-poverty area would not improve one's chances of making mainstream friends. Fernandez and Harris interpret this to mean that policies should be targeted at nonworking poor people, wherever they live. An alternative interpretation is that anyone (for example, the working poor and the nonpoor) who lives in a high-poverty area can benefit from policies that help to overcome the isolating effects of such areas.

As a policy analyst I continue to use the Ricketts and Sawhill (1988) measure of the underclass. Its four basic components measure, or predict, labor force detachment or income derived from sources other than work. With this measure policy analysts can think about services, incentives, regulations, and opportunities that help single mothers on welfare to become self-supporting; underemployed men to find full-time, full-year employment; and teenagers to avoid pregnancies and dropping out of high school. Individually tailored approaches will help most people achieve these goals; my reading of the qualitative and quantitative evidence, however, suggests that Wilson's original insight was powerful. When individuals and families who are detached from the labor force cluster together in the same communities, a social context emerges that puts them and their neighbors, especially youth, at risk. The Ricketts and Sawhill measure includes all residents of areas with high concentrations of people who are (or are likely to be) detached from the labor force or without earnings. The measure therefore focuses the attention of policymakers on welfare gains and losses experienced by those who are nonparticipants in the labor force and others. Such a focus helps to frame policy discussions inclusively.

Policy Implications

Unlike conservatives' proposals, Wilson's key policy recommendations involved not less government, but a redirection of government policy. Race-conscious policies had little effect on low-skilled blacks and could no longer find support among middle-class voters, who have seen their living standards fall since the mid-1970s. Wilson argued instead for universal policy goals, primarily balanced economic growth and skills enhancement. How have these recommendations influenced policy? How have growth and skills enhancement affected the underclass?

Evaluating Wilson's Policy Recommendations

The policy recommendations growing out of Wilson's core hypotheses have had little effect. His major recommendations were job training and sufficient macroeconomic stimulus to raise the fortunes of the inner-city underclass along with the fortunes of other Americans. Such stimulus would presumably have domino effects, from higher black male employment to higher black marriage rates to lower rates of female headship, welfare dependency, and crime among blacks. These policy recommendations left many practical questions unanswered. For example, although Wilson argued that changes in industrial and occupational structures hurt low-skilled, central-city blacks, he did not suggest how policymakers should respond to these structural changes. Nor did he suggest what policymakers should do to ensure that low-skilled workers would benefit from economic expansion in a way that they did not benefit from the expansion of the 1980s. To some extent, therefore, Wilson's recommendations seem vague and at odds with his theoretical emphasis on spatial and structural mismatch.

Economic growth and training in basic skills are widely supported policy goals that provide the necessary economic and political conditions for reducing the underclass. Without these, it is hard to see how to overcome the two fundamental barriers faced by people in the underclass: detachment from the labor force and from legal earnings. Growth and basic skills training are politically safe policies; virtually no one in America opposes them. If more members of the underclass worked in low-wage jobs, moreover, they would join the working poor and become beneficiaries of the growing demand to "make work pay."

Macroeconomic performance during the 1980s, however, suggests that policy goals with universal appeal are not enough to overcome the obstacles that non-participants in the labor force and others in distressed communities face. The 1980s witnessed a ninety-two-month economic expansion, and dropout rates among minorities declined. Nevertheless, large gaps remained between the achievement scores of blacks and whites. Labor force participation continued to decline among low-skilled minorities, especially black males, and the social problems linked to the underclass showed little sign of improvement. Low-skilled, minority workers in tight labor markets had better labor market outcomes than similar workers in slack labor markets. This experience suggests that policymakers could try to sustain the national unemployment rate at a level low enough to produce favorable results for all such workers. Such an effort, however, might conflict with other macroeconomic priorities (Freeman, 1991). In addition, policymakers have found balanced growth to be an elusive goal. Wilson did not specify whether the economic growth he preferred should exhibit balance across metropolitan areas (that is, cities and suburbs), regions, or skill and education groups, but in any case, none of this occurred.

Other Policy Recommendations

The underclass literature suggests both old and new policy initiatives and reforms. During the 1980s and early 1990s policies affecting the underclass were politically feasible, but ineffective. They relied too much on remediation and incarceration and ignored risks to successful adult transitions, fairness, opportunity, and race.

People begin the process leading to labor force detachment, hustling, and welfare dependence before they are adults, and therefore age is important when thinking about strategies to reduce the underclass. Policymakers can do more to help youth reared in underclass neighborhoods to overcome the risks their environment poses to their successful transition to adulthood. Reading, writing, and communication skills will help children compete when they enter the labor market in their teenage or young adult years. But until they overcome risks such as lack of parental supervision and exposure to violence and drug selling, they cannot achieve these basic competencies.

The current welfare system requiring taxpayers and single mothers to support children born out of wedlock is neither effective nor fair. Policymakers need to reform this system so that low-skilled and unemployed absent fathers can participate in an emerging social contract that requires fathers and mothers to support their children. Both single mothers and absent fathers must be able to get the additional or remedial training they need. If graduates of training programs cannot find private sector employment, then opportunities must be available in the public sector. And if wages for entry-level jobs remain low, trainees must become beneficiaries of expanded efforts to subsidize the working poor.

Race conscious policies, moreover, must acknowledge and break down pure and statistical discrimination in employment, housing, and credit markets; help low-skilled black workers to compete against low-skilled women and immigrants; and promote black business ownership and other community empowerment strategies.

Prevention. In addition to targeting nutrition and education programs at poor children in early childhood, policymakers need to intervene in the lives of early adolescents in underclass neighborhoods. In early adolescence, young people make critical choices about study time and other aspects of schooling, school completion, substance abuse, drug selling, and early sexual intercourse. These choices have important implications for adult employment and wages, health and disability, exposure to the criminal justice system, and fertility and parenting. Further, unless parents take extraordinary measures to restrict and control their children's associations, peer groups have substantial and negative effects on the choices of boys and girls in underclass neighborhoods.

Public policy must help parents in underclass neighborhoods meet the challenges of rearing early adolescents in high-risk environments. An inclusive approach is required, because the targets of intervention include youth who already show some signs of trouble (such as truancy, fighting, or substance abuse) and youth who are only at risk. Training in parenting skills will be needed, so that youth do not go unsupervised. But policy must also make possible new or rehabilitated institutions, to give youth in underclass neighborhoods safe havens from the streets, and supportive environments, to help them identify and build on their strengths. In these settings, programs must be available to develop and use positive peer pressure to influence critical choices. Finally, these interventions need to go beyond current approaches, which try to persuade youth to avoid specific delinquent behavior. Programs must provide genuine opportunities for youth development. Early adolescents need to be helped to

- master basic competencies;
- identify, practice, and master strategies for overcoming developmental challenges such as drug abuse, violence, teenage parenting, and so on;
- participate in activities that contribute to their families and communities; and thereby
- develop and maintain positive attitudes and relationships with their peers, families, and communities.[20]

This recommendation sounds expensive, but so are the alternatives. Young men and women from high-risk neighborhoods, especially blacks, account for a disproportionate share of welfare and criminal justice costs. Although welfare costs are small, and policymakers can further reduce them by lowering benefits and making eligibility more difficult, criminal justice costs already rank second among the fastest-growing components of state budgets, after Medicaid. Overcrowded penal systems have forced several states to turn to early release programs, intensive probation, house arrests, and other alternatives that put criminals back on the streets and threaten public security.

Fairness. Although the quantitative literature provides little support for Wilson's marriageable-male hypothesis, many low-skilled males father children out of wedlock. As Rebecca Blank points out in Chapter 7, in recent years employment and job training programs have focused on low-skilled and jobless women with children.[21] Although the programs do not increase wages, they are cost-effective, because they increase hours of work sufficiently to substitute earnings for welfare. Public policy should continue to support the transition from welfare to work for single mothers on AFDC, and should make that transition easier and more rewarding. With only a single source of income, however, most such families remain poor. Blank also points out that publicly provided employment and training services for low-skilled and jobless persons are limited and that these services have had very modest effects on the employment and earnings of men. As a result, the public policy mechanism for requiring and enabling low-skilled fathers to be responsible for their children lags far behind the corresponding mechanism in place for low-skilled mothers.

Changes in the Family Support Act create new pressures to address this lag. The act includes provisions that will increase collections of child support from employed-absent fathers and extend employment services to husbands in married-couple families on AFDC. These changes reveal a new principle in welfare policy, namely, to require and enable fathers to meet their parental responsibilities. Low-skilled and unemployed-absent fathers should not be exempt from this principle, especially because their partners and children remain poor when the mother is the only worker. Is this recommendation punitive and paternalistic? Not entirely. Some low-skilled and unemployed-absent fathers provide small and irregular child-support contributions, often in-kind (diapers, clothing, child care, and so on) (Sullivan, 1989). Extending employment services to these fathers could increase the size and regularity of the contributions they are already making and help reduce poverty in the custodial household. Nevertheless, this reform would be fully consistent with recent welfare-waiver programs that provide benefits only when participants fulfill social obligations relating to schooling or marriage, for example. But what good will training do if low-skilled fathers and mothers cannot find jobs or raise their wages?

Opportunity. Public service employment can play a larger role than Blank proposes. Blank generally opposes public service employment, except for teenagers, because the costs outweigh the benefits, especially for low-skilled men. She prefers to provide government-supported training that enables low-skilled men to find private sector jobs. This strategy assumes the cooperation and willingness of the private sector to hire workers they have resisted during the past. If these jobs do not materialize, the alternative for some people is hustling. When hustling involves criminal acts, the victims incur costs. Crime also exposes perpetrators to incarceration and long-term unemployment, both of which have significant individual and social costs. If we could account for these costs, it is not clear whether the costs of public service employment would appear less extreme.

Public service employment could also help prevent one of the foregoing recommendations from joining the list of social control mechanisms that Darity and Myers foresee. Recent demonstration programs, authorized by the Family Support Act, extend employment services to low-skilled, absent fathers, in return for paternity establishment and a long-term child support obligation. If participants cannot meet this obligation because they cannot find or keep private sector jobs, they can—and have been—incarcerated. If public sector employment were available for graduates of training programs, there would always be a way for fathers to meet their child support obligations. Fathers would therefore be more willing to establish paternity, take on long-term child support obligations, and participate in more extensive training to increase their lifetime earnings.[22]

Blank also sees no reason why noncustodial parents are ineligible for the Earned Income Tax Credit, a provision about which I have expressed skepticism elsewhere (Horrigan and Mincy, 1993). Extending EITC to noncustodial parents who work and pay child support could help to

- increase income in single-parent households that now depend on the custodial parent's earnings alone;
- overcome the public's reluctance to support employment services for the fathers;
- increase labor force participation among low-skilled men; and
- ensure a greater return on publicly funded employment services.

Race. The literature does not support Wilson's call to redirect government policies away from issues of race. Employment discrimination continues to bar low-skilled blacks and Puerto Ricans from already limited employment opportunities (Cross et al., 1990; Turner, Mikelsons, and Edwards, 1991). Declines in efforts to enforce equal opportunity laws may have caused increased discrimination (Bound and Freeman, 1990). Housing segregation concentrates the effects of declining opportunities in black and Puerto Rican neighborhoods. Housing discrimination also limits the housing choices of middle-class blacks to suburban ghettos, far from centers of employment growth. George Galster (1991) has suggested important feedback effects between poverty and housing segregation. Race-conscious policies may continue to be unpopular among middle-class white voters. Incidents such as the 1992 riot in Los Angeles that followed the acquittal of police officers accused of beating a black motorist, however, may convince these voters that the costs of existing racial inequities are too high.

Race-conscious policies must go beyond civil rights issues, however, especially in employment, because the growing diversity of the low-skilled labor force gives race, sex, and immigrant status increasing significance. Some employers of low-skilled workers regard black workers, especially males, as more devious, argumentative, intimidating, and uncooperative than women or immigrants (Kirschenman and Neckerman, 1991; Kirschenman, 1991; Tienda and Stier, 1991b). Black males may develop these postures in response to "street life" and their hostile relationships with whites in school, the workplace, and elsewhere (Anderson, 1990; Bourgois, 1991; Majors and Billson, 1992). Employers may rely on informal recruiting and transportation systems to avoid black workers. Besides reducing pure race discrimination, therefore, policies must help black workers, especially males, to compete against women and immigrants for low-skilled jobs. This could be accomplished if the youth development programs suggested earlier incorporated training in bicultural competence (that is, the ability to alternate between street culture and workplace culture, when required).

Although race-conscious policies are important, what happens to the black underclass will crucially depend on what blacks do for themselves. John Kasarda (1989), for example, compares blacks with Asian immigrants who, like blacks, are poorly educated and spatially concentrated in urban areas. According to Kasarda, Asian immigrants have overcome these and other obstacles, including discrimination, through business development. He argues that financial weakness and family disorganization within the black underclass make it unlikely that blacks can accomplish the same. This is a challenge that the black community must wholeheartedly accept.

Although lack of wealth is a significant obstacle to black entrepreneurship, human capital also plays a critical role. Many Asian businesses in the United States are begun not by poorly educated immigrants but by well-educated immigrants, with foreign degrees, who lack English-language skills (Bates and Dunham, 1992). These entrepreneurs begin in small retail businesses, which require relatively small amounts of capital and serve limited markets (for example, the Korean grocery or liquor store in an underclass neighborhood). As these entrepreneurs profit from their businesses, they accumulate wealth, which enables them to trade up to businesses reaching larger markets. They also acquire language skills that enable many to leave self-employment entirely. If business ownership is to aid in reducing the black underclass, it will thus most likely play a role among blacks with human and financial capital, namely, the middle class.

Family disorganization is another serious obstacle to self-employment among the underclass. But it is precisely cooperation in kinship networks within the black community that helps "decent" families overcome the risks of underclass neighborhoods and helps middle-class families pursue upward social mobility. The family disorganization that now threatens the black community from within is hardly more formidable than the external threats blacks have faced over the last thirty years.

Despite these external threats, blacks have made enormous progress toward the priorities of the civil rights movement: political freedom and educational opportunity. Black political power and sophistication have grown so strong in recent years that a backlash occurred in the 1992 presidential campaign. The candidate of the Democratic party, traditionally a champion of civil rights, was virtually silent on issues pertaining to race and urban decay.

Success in the sphere of education has also been noteworthy, but this may have reduced black entrepreneurship. Members of the black middle class have English-language skills and other credentials needed for professional employment. The opportunity costs of entrepreneurship are, therefore, higher for native-speaking and domestically educated blacks than for Asian immigrants (Bates and Dunham, 1992). A recent issue of *Ebony* magazine listed the one hundred most influential black Americans. This prestigious group included teachers, preachers, lawyers, and lawmakers. The article listed only six black leaders, however, whose influence stemmed from their ability to employ a black person.

Unlike Kasarda and Darity and Myers, I believe that it is premature to discount the black middle class. Today black middle-class liberals and conservatives are working vigorously on behalf of underclass neighborhoods. As policymakers and foundation officers, they have won approval for an unknown, but probably large, share of the grant proposals for research and community development projects focusing on underclass neighborhoods. Middle-class black liberals have stepped up their efforts to improve education, housing, health care, and prenatal care and to reduce violence, drug use, and so on. These community-based service efforts are not carried out for residents of underclass neighborhoods, but with them. Middle-class black conservatives have set their sights on self-help strategies. These begin by empowering residents of underclass neighborhoods through tenant management and ownership of low-income housing, and extend to community control of other aspects of community life, such as education and safety.

Although improved services and empowerment are needed, blacks are generally finding that at best these approaches help to maintain people in poverty. Liberal and conservative distinctions in the black community are thus beginning to blur as both emphasize the need for black business development.

Like most Americans, middle-class blacks were angered by the young blacks and Hispanics who burned Korean businesses in Los Angeles in 1992. But these scenes will not drown out the cries of black merchants and artisans who were looted and lynched during Reconstruction. This denial of black property rights crippled the nascent black entrepreneurship that followed slavery and left another legacy for blacks to overcome today. Both black liberals and black conservatives are therefore increasingly interested in improving access to credit markets, community development banks, and targeted job-tax credits within enterprise zones. These are the micro-policies needed to provide incentives for black-owned businesses, which are much more likely to employ black workers than are other firms (Moss and Tilly, 1991; Bates and Dunham, 1992).

Small-business development and wealth accumulation are the keys to successful black entrepreneurship, but these keys depend on a lower deficit and strong economic growth. Ironically, then, the major macro-policy issues of the presidential campaign—deficit reduction and an expanding economy—may bind the fortunes of the underclass to the fortunes of the black middle class, and to the rest of our society.

.   .   .

The early 1980s saw rising public frustration with the growth of idleness among men and welfare dependency among women and children in ghettos. Journalists pointed to a perverse set of ghetto values and attitudes. Conservatives blamed generous Great Society programs, which they claimed created a culture of dependency. Economists, preoccupied with inadequate income, were typically silent about these and other disturbing trends. Liberal social scientists from other fields had little to say, or were largely ignored, because these trends had become taboo subjects since the Moynihan Report.

The underclass literature emerged against this lopsided discourse about the causes of poverty when William Julius Wilson provided a comprehensive set of hypotheses to explain the emergence of the underclass. Since 1985, Wilson's work has drawn social scientists from many disciplines back into a broader debate about poverty. Studies attempted to test Wilson's hypotheses; to offer and test other hypotheses; and to measure the size, growth, and composition of the under-class. Substantial progress occurred on some core hypotheses, but disagreements and controversy slowed consensus on underclass measurement.

Tests of the core underclass hypotheses have supported or clarified much of Wilson's theoretical framework. Worsening employment opportunities, created especially by slack local labor markets, has helped to reduce black male employ-ment and earnings. Race-conscious decisions by employers about hiring and lo-cation, however, have barred low-skilled blacks from jobs open to immigrants and women. And labor market trends have explained only a fraction of the decline in black marriage rates. In larger northern cities, selective out-migration has in-creased poverty rates in black and Puerto Rican neighborhoods. Yet persistent housing segregation has probably been the larger constraint that concentrated the adverse effects of declining employment opportunities in poor black and Puerto Rican neighborhoods. Finally, even after controlling for family income and background, black youths are more likely to make choices leading to adult pov-erty and future social distress. That they have many poor and socially distressed neighbors and few high-income and socially advantaged neighbors explains some of this result. Neighbors have a greater effect on the choices of white youth, how-ever.

Given the complexity of the concept and the limitations of data, methodologi-cal disagreements have been inevitable. Still, four methods for measuring the un-derclass have indicated that the underclass constitutes between 1 and 10 percent of the U.S. population, with rapid growth in a few large metropolitan areas.

Controversy also slowed consensus. Most studies centered their measurement efforts on the ghetto poor. Critics charged that these studies supported the percep-tion that the underclass was almost exclusively a black and Puerto Rican problem. Other studies focused on concentrations of people with underclass social prob-lems, excluding poverty, whether these people lived in large-city ghetto areas or not. Critics charged that these studies diverted attention from changing opportu-nities and emphasized behavior originating from a perverse culture among poor minorities. Nevertheless, these social problem studies suggested that there was a white underclass, concentrated in smaller metropolitan and nonmetropolitan areas, that studies of ghetto poverty ignored.

The underclass literature has reestablished a broader debate about poverty and its causes. Social scientists have continued to study the nonincome dimensions of social disadvantage. Like the work of their predecessors before the Moynihan Report, their work is now attracting the attention of poverty analysts and policymakers. The underclass literature has found a useful way to consider how individual choices about sex, schooling, and employment are affected by the choices of peers, neighbors, and members of one's social network. This discussion is an important advancement beyond contentious debates about poverty and welfare cultures. And, most important, policy discussions now include declines in employment opportunities, continued housing segregation, and employment discrimination.

Wilson's universal policy goals, such as economic growth and skills enhancement, are the necessary, but not sufficient, conditions for reducing the underclass. Targeted policies are needed to promote prevention, fairness, and opportunity and to confront racial disparities squarely. Interventions should focus on early adolescents in underclass neighborhoods to help them overcome the risks their environments pose for their development and to prepare them to enter the labor market. Employment services need to target low-skilled mothers and fathers in order to reduce poverty in single-parent households. If private sector opportunities are unavailable or wages too low, public service jobs should be provided, along with wage subsidies to increase work and child support from custodial and noncustodial parents. Finally, race-conscious policies must be pursued for their effects on blacks in the underclass and middle class. Policies that promote access to employment and housing; proper workplace decorum; and basic reading, writing, and communication skills will have the most direct effect on blacks in the underclass. Policies that promote access to credit and small-business growth, however, including macro-policies for a declining deficit and an expanding economy, are also needed to increase employment opportunities for blacks in black-owned businesses.

CHAPTER SIX

Poverty in Relation to Macroeconomic Trends, Cycles, and Policies

JAMES TOBIN

Robert Lampman of the University of Wisconsin is the intellectual father of the War on Poverty, at least to the extent any economist can claim paternity. He was the principal author of Chapter 2 of the 1964 *Economic Report of the President,* where the economic rationale and strategy of the war were laid out. As an alumnus of the President's Council of Economic Advisers, called to Washington in December 1963 to help shepherd the annual report into print, I participated in editing the chapter. Walter Heller, the council's chairman, had proposed the antipoverty initiative to President Kennedy, whose sympathetic interest had been whetted by reading Michael Harrington's *The Other America* and John Kenneth Galbraith's *The Affluent Society.* President Johnson enthusiastically adopted the War on Poverty as an integral part of his Great Society and a corollary of the Civil Rights revolution, a cause he had also embraced.

In June 1967 I published an article in *The New Republic* entitled "It Can Be Done! Conquering Poverty in the U.S. by 1976." Sargent Shriver, the antipoverty "czar," had boldly, one could say recklessly, announced this ambitious Bicentennial goal. When I wrote the article, its title was not as outlandish as it sounds now. I was not relying solely or even principally on Shriver's direct programs. These, in Lampman's spirit, were measures to improve the earning capacities of individuals and communities by education of infants, children, youth, and adults; by improving public health and individual health in disadvantaged localities; by programs offering vocational training and job experience; by comprehensive neighborhood development initiatives. These programs could not be expected to work miracles in one decade. Over that short horizon, I put greater weight on the market magic of general prosperity and growth. My primary argument was that the poverty remaining after those two forces had done their work was within the feasible reach of means-tested transfers like the negative income tax. Those transfer programs were not enacted, of course, and in 1976 the economy was just recovering from a deep stagflationary recession. The promised land receded. We'll be lucky to reach it by 2026.

I am afraid that it's a mistake to declare wars against social and economic conditions or national crusades for societal reforms. The goals are elusive, the troops unruly, the enemies amorphous. Wars on poverty, energy dependence, and drugs have proved to be incapable of sustaining the degrees of commitment essential to their prosecution, even by the Presidents who declared them. William James longed for moral equivalents of war, but evidently Americans can't do better than football.

Macroeconomic Progress and Poverty Reduction

"Rising tides lift all boats" is an overused cliché. For our purpose, the proposition is that good macroeconomic performance reduces poverty. The idea is sometimes caricatured as "trickledown," but I think that label should be confined to proposals to better the lot of the poor by transfers or tax concessions to the rich. In any case the cliché sometimes serves as an excuse for doing nothing specific about poverty. Today the tides don't seem to rise as much, and leaks seem to consign some of the boats to the bottom.

Until about 1970, macroeconomic progress was an extremely powerful engine of poverty reduction. In the 1930s Franklin Roosevelt saw one-third of the nation ill fed, ill clothed, ill housed. Backward application of Molly Orshansky's absolute poverty income thresholds puts the figure closer to two-thirds.

The war against Germany and Japan was the most effective war against poverty in America's recorded experience; some of the war's achievements showed up in the subsequent decade. In the 1940s military and economic mobilization truly generated jobs for all. In 1944, when defense purchases accounted for two-fifths of GNP, the remainder available for civilian use was greater in real terms than the entire GNP of 1939.

During the 1940s and 1950s, shifts of labor from subsistence and other labor-intensive agriculture into jobs of higher value added in urban industry, often involving migration from South to North, were an important source of overall economic growth. Edward Denison (1974) credits such shifts with 19 percent of the growth in net national product per person employed in 1941–1948 and 14 percent in 1948–1954. This growth was especially important for reduction of poverty among migrants, both blacks and whites. Today the urban industries that gave them jobs have been moving away from big cities—to suburbs, to the South, overseas. Many jobs have been lost to global competition and new technology, and many of the remaining ones have moved away. The few jobs that replace them are generally by location and specification inaccessible to the populations left behind, especially the minority populations. The obstacles to migration and occupational shift are formidable.

Figure 6.1 compares for five decades, 1940 to 1990, the reduction of poverty in percentage points and the percentage growth of per capita real GNP. Figure 6.2 shows the progress against poverty over the fifty years since 1939 for blacks and whites separately, and also plots the reduction in the percentage shortfall of real personal income per capita from its 1989 value. The latter is a graphically convenient measure of overall economic progress, to which the decline in poverty can be compared.

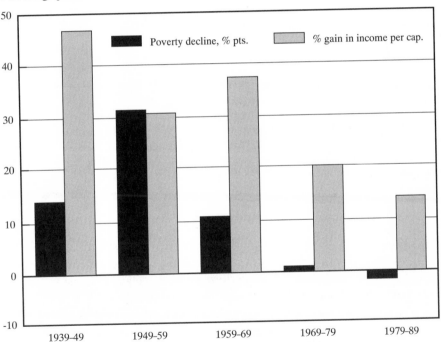

Percentage points

Figure 6.1   Progress against poverty, five decades. Ten-year decline in percentage points, national poverty rate of persons, compared to percentage gains in real income per person, 1939–1989. (Poverty rates prior to 1959 estimated by Reynolds Farley from Decennial Census data for *A Common Destiny*, report of the National Academy of Sciences Committee on the Status of Black Americans, 1988; subsequent poverty rates, official Census data; personal income, U.S. Department of Commerce, National Income and Product Accounts.)

Percentage points

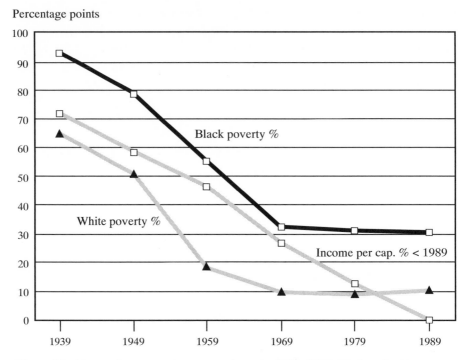

Figure 6.2 Poverty by race and aggregate income, 1939–1989. Black and white poverty at ends of six decades, compared to personal income shortfall. Poverty: percentage of persons living in poor households. Personal income shortfall: percentage shortfall of national personal income (per capita in 1990 dollars) below 1989. (For data sources, see Figure 6.1.)

Figure 6.3 plots 1959–1990 annual poverty rates against per capita real personal income (NIPA). In Figure 6.3 can be seen the episodic setbacks to progress against poverty, relative to macro performance, in cyclical recessions. The setback in the 1980s was the most serious.

It was to be expected—and it was expected, certainly, by Lampman—that there would be diminishing returns in poverty reduction to overall gains in per capita income, just because the densities of the income distribution would diminish as the poverty rate declined. When the Orshansky thresholds were near the mode of the distribution, a small proportionate rightward shift in the distribution, resulting from macroeconomic growth, could take many people out of poverty. The numbers would be much fewer in the thinner left tails of the distribution. Figure 6.4 illustrates this effect by expressing the 1990 family income distribution in terms of the ratio of income to mean income and assuming that the distribution thus transformed applied also in the past. Trends of overall economic growth take the form of leftward treks of the ratio of thresholds to mean or median income. Diminishing returns from this source were important before 1970, when the poverty threshold occurred at the high frequencies of the distribution, but they have not been of much significance since.

Disappointing Macroeconomic Performance since 1973

Clearly macroeconomic performance has been less successful in reducing poverty since 1973 than before. Both of the two obvious possible explanations, the weakness of the tide and the leakiness of the boats, apparently hold. Macroeconomic performance itself has been disappointing, and so has been the response of poverty numbers to the macroeconomic performance that did occur.

The growth of per capita real gross domestic product (GDP) slowed down. The

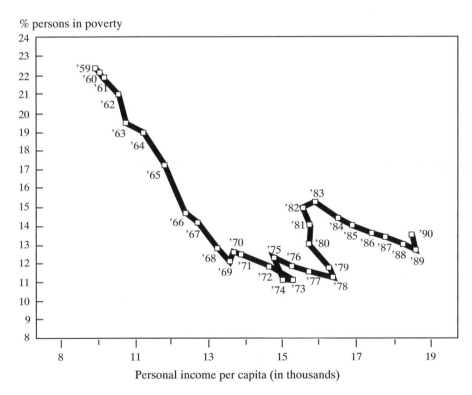

Figure 6.3 Poverty and income per person. National poverty percentage plotted against personal income per capita (1990), yearly, 1959–1990. (For data sources, see Figure 6.1.)

Frequency

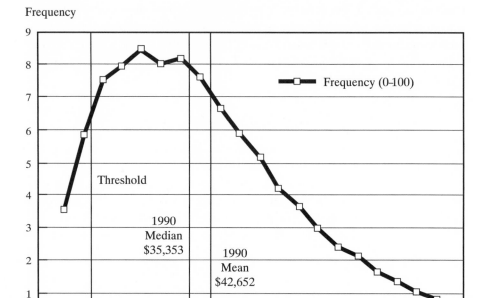

Income as % of mean income

Figure 6.4 Family money income, 1990: Frequency distribution, that is, percentage of families at indicated ratios of income to population mean income. Families in the income bracket corresponding to 11.7% of mean family income are about 3.5% of all families, for example. (Data source: U.S. Bureau of the Census, Current Population Reports, series P-60, nos. 180, 181.)

trend growth of productivity per person-hour in the business sector has been about two percentage points lower since 1973 (0.8 percent per year) than in the previous quarter-century (2.9 percent per year). Not only was the growth of potential output at full employment weaker, but potential was less frequently and fully realized. Cyclical recessions were more severe after 1973, and the unemployment rate averaged 2.2 points higher.

Figure 6.5 compares potential and actual GDP since 1973. Cyclical recessions and slowdowns generate increasing shortfalls of actual from potential, and it has taken long and slow recoveries to erase these gaps. Figure 6.6 shows how closely correlated these GDP gaps are with the unemployment rate. This correlation, known among economists as Okun's law, is one of the most important and reli-

Trillions

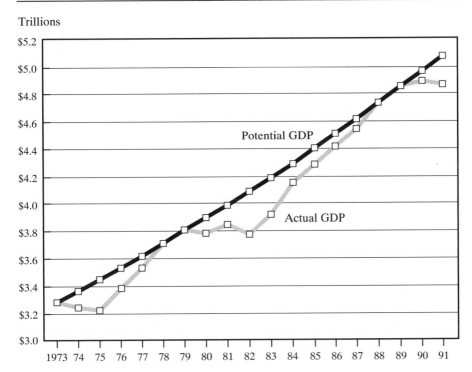

Figure 6.5 Actual and potential gross domestic product, in trillions of 1987 dollars, yearly, 1973–1991. (Data sources: actual GDP, U.S. Department of Commerce, National Income and Product Accounts; potential, author's estimates.)

able regularities in macroeconomics. Arthur Okun also pointed out that, as is evident in Figure 6.6, changes in the GDP gap are a multiple of the changes in unemployment rates. The same cyclical macroeconomic forces that move employment up and down move labor force participation, hours of work, and productivity in the same direction. The average 2.2 points of higher unemployment since 1973 translates into an average percentage GDP gap about 6 points higher.

Parts of the recent story of weaker macroeconomic performance are breaks in the relationships between broad measures—such as per capita real GDP, personal income per capita, and overall unemployment rates—and measures closer to the determination of poverty status. In particular, both David Cutler and Lawrence Katz (1991) and Rebecca Blank (1991) have called attention to changes in the structure of wages disadvantageous to the poor.

Real hourly and weekly earnings have been declining for twenty years. The growth of worker productivity has slowed down. Moreover, earnings have even

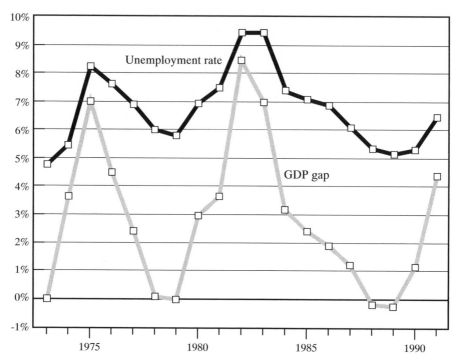

Figure 6.6 Output gap and unemployment rate. Gap between actual and potential GDP, as percentage of actual GDP, compared with yearly average national unemployment rate, 1973–1991. (Data sources: output gap and percentage shortfall of actual GDP from potential GDP shown in Figure 6.5; unemployment rate, U.S. Bureau of Labor Statistics.)

fallen behind productivity, an unusual phenomenon. As Cutler and Katz point out, however, the share of labor in business value added has stayed fairly constant. Compensation inclusive of fringe benefits has risen roughly in step with productivity. This is the labor cost that matters to employers. But the explosion of employment-related fringe benefits, largely for health insurance, has been of value mainly to long-term employees with high wages and salaries. It has meant little to workers and families at risk of poverty, for whom the relentless decline of take-home pay has been the grim reality.

Cutler and Katz point out that the rise in the wages of unskilled and less-educated workers relative to skilled and better-educated workers, a stylized fact of past business cycle recoveries, did not take place in the 1980s. Blank finds, using Current Population Survey (CPS) data of the Census Bureau, that the jobs taken by the working poor pay relatively less well than in the past. Likewise, James Medoff (1992) has found from CPS data that since 1979 the job openings that can be found by job losers are, relative to the universe of jobs, lower in pay and more frequently without pensions and health insurance.

Estimating Macroeconomic Effects on Poverty

Two macroeconomic outcomes of crucial importance for the prevalence of poverty are real wages and unemployment. As real wages rise throughout the economy, more and more workers are able to earn enough for themselves and their families to escape poverty. Decade to decade, it is the trend in real wages that matters. But the trend has not been constant; wage growth has slowed since about 1973.

The overall unemployment rate is a barometer indicative of opportunities to work. It would be expected to be an important determinant of poverty, even though most unemployed are not poor and most poor are not unemployed (according to the Census definition, which requires an individual to be both entirely jobless and looking for work).

Changes in poverty rates from year to year can, I have found, be fairly well explained by these two macroeconomic variables, specifically by regressions on changes in average real weekly earnings and in an unemployment rate. First differences of the dependent variable and these two explanatory variables are used to avoid spurious correlations and biased estimates due to serial persistence. A third independent variable is also both logical and empirically successful. It is the *level* of the ratio of the poverty threshold for four-person families (constant in real terms) to the previous year's median family income.

Several such regressions are reported in Table 6.1 for post-transfer poverty from 1961 to 1990 and pretransfer poverty from 1967 to 1988. In them the constant is constrained to be zero, so that no time trend in poverty is built in. Trends may improve fits, but when they have no convincing rationale they are statistical artifacts of little help in understanding, forecasting, and policymaking. The earnings variable is in constant 1982 dollars, because poverty thresholds are defined in real dollars. The unemployment variable is the rate for white male adults, chosen for its quality as a macroeconomic cyclical barometer rather than its direct relevance to persons at risk of poverty. The third variable serves as a proxy for the density of the income distribution in the neighborhood of the poverty line. As illustrated earlier in Figure 6.4 and now again in Figure 6.7, macroeconomic progress against poverty can be described as a downward trend in this ratio. Using its level in the year before as a regressor for the change in poverty is like using a nonlinear function of the previous level of the poverty rate itself, recognizing that the potential for reductions in poverty declines with the actual poverty rate.

The specifications of these equations are simple, straightforward, and parsimo-

Table 6.1 Time series regressions of annual changes in poverty rates

Sample years	Dependent variable	Constant	DE (1982$)	T/M (−1) (%)	DUWM (%)	Adjusted R^2
			Independent variables			
1. 1961–1983	DPP (% points)					0.59
Coefficients		0	−0.04	−0.0089	0.465	
(Standard errors)			(0.024)	(0.0033)	(0.168)	
Variable mean	−0.3		0.46	42.78	0.16	
Variable s.d.	0.92		7.01	5.08	1.00	
2. 1961–1990	DPP (% points)					0.58
Coefficients		0	−0.053	−0.0075	0.386	
(Standard errors)			(0.020)	(0.0026)	(0.125)	
Variable mean	−0.25		−0.07	41.3	0	
Variable s.d.	0.71		6.31	4.33	0.99	
3. 1961–1990	DFP (% points)					0.61
Coefficients		0	−0.038	−0.0073	0.382	
(Standard errors)			(0.018)	(0.0024)	(0.115)	
Variable mean	−0.25		−0.07	41.3	0	
Variable s.d.	0.71		6.31	4.33	0.99	
4. 1968–1983	DPPP (% points)					0.78
Coefficients		0	−0.039	0.001	0.555	
(Standard errors)			(0.019)	(0.003)	(0.132)	
Variable mean	0.3		−1.31	39.77	0.36	
Variable s.d.	0.9		7.52	1.53	1.07	
5. 1968–1983	DPPP < 65 (% points)					0.79
Coefficients		0	−0.038	0	0.633	
(Standard errors)			(0.019)	(0.003)	(0.137)	
Variable mean	0.29		−1.31	39.77	0.36	
Variable s.d.	0.97		7.52	1.53	1.07	

Notations of variables:

DPP	First difference, poverty rate (%) of all persons.
DFP	First difference, poverty rate (%) of families.
DPPP	First difference, pretransfer persons' poverty.
DPPP < 65	First difference, pretransfer poverty, persons aged less than 65.
DE	First difference, average weekly earnings in 1982 dollars.
T/M (−1)	Previous year's value, poverty threshold income for four-person family as percent of median family income.
DUWM	First difference, unemployment rate, white males aged 20 and older.

% persons in poverty

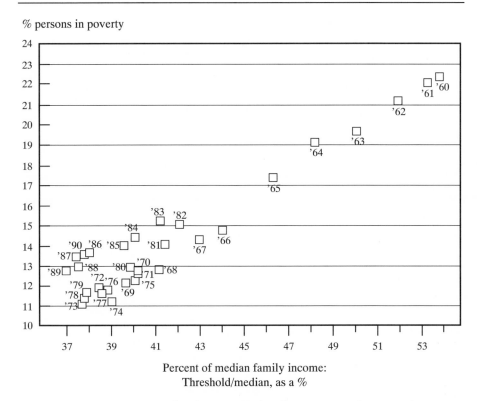

Percent of median family income:
Threshold/median, as a %

Figure 6.7 Poverty and median income. National percentage of persons in poverty, plotted against the ratio of family poverty threshold to median family income, yearly, 1960–1990. (For data sources, see Figure 6.4.)

nious. They implement a priori hypotheses, without trial-and-error "data mining." The results confirm expectations of the signs of the coefficients. Over half of the variance in year-to-year changes in poverty is explained. It is not surprising that other systematic and stochastic determinants are also at work.

Welfare benefits and other transfers would affect post-transfer poverty rates more than prepoverty rates; the better fits shown for the latter equations (Table 6.1, regressions 4 and 5) were to be expected. Likewise it is logical that unemployment has a bigger effect on pretransfer poverty. Regressions 1 and 2 in Table 6.1 provide some evidence that in the 1980s unemployment effects became smaller and wage effects larger than before. The slowdown in progress against poverty in the 1980s is evident in Figure 6.7; the poverty rate was higher in that decade relative to the ratio of the poverty threshold to median income.

Earnings and unemployment also explain variations in poverty rates among states. Table 6.2 reports results for single-year cross sections, for both official poverty rates and pretransfer rates. The table also shows a regression for cross sections of changes in official poverty by state between two years, 1979 and 1987. The fit of this regression is not significantly improved by adding the 1979 poverty rate as a third explanatory variable.

Table 6.2   Cross-section regressions of state poverty rates (fifty states and the District of Columbia)

Sample years	Dependent variable	Constant	Independent variables			Adjusted R^2
			DHE	DUR	PP 1979	
Changes between Two Years						
1A. 1979–1987	DPP (% points)					0.56
Coefficients		−0.069	−0.766	0.709		
(Standard errors)			(0.476)	(0.098)		
Variable mean		−0.71	0.238	−0.639		
Variable s.d.		2.23	0.455	2.217		
1B. 1979–1987	DPP (% points)					0.57
Coefficients		−0.087	−0.683	0.744	0.064	
(Standard errors)			(0.484)	(0.104)	(0.065)	
Variable mean		−0.71	0.238	−0.639	11.23	
Variable s.d.		2.23	0.455	2.217	3.5	
			HE	UR		
Levels, One Year						
2. 1986	PP (% points)					0.77
Coefficients		17.93	−1.737	1.806		
(Standard errors)			(0.279)	(0.145)		
Variable mean		13.82	9.6	6.96		
Variable s.d.		4.44	1.15	2.21		
3. 1985–1986	PPP (% points)					0.74
Coefficients		19.76	−1.725	1.673		
(Standard errors)			(0.281)	(0.146)		
Variable mean		14.85	9.6	6.96		
Variable s.d.		4.23	1.15	2.21		

Notations of variables:
PP	Poverty rate (%) of all persons.
DPP	Change in PP from 1979 to 1988, in percentage points.
PPP	Pretransfer poverty rate of all persons.
HE	Hourly earnings in current dollars.
DHE	Change in hourly earnings from 1979 to 1987, in 1979 dollars.
UR	Unemployment rate, all workers.
DUR	Change in UR from 1979 to 1987.

It is reassuring that all the cross-section regression coefficients on earnings and unemployment variables have the same signs as in the national time series regressions. In Table 6.2 equations 1A and 1B are similar to the time series regressions of Table 6.1, in that the change in the poverty rate is the dependent variable. In the state cross sections, however, "change" is for each state the difference between two years that are nine years apart, 1978 and 1987. Only the unemployment rate is significant by usual standards. The earnings coefficient passes the test only marginally, at a 10% significance level. That those coefficients are larger in absolute magnitude than their counterparts in Table 6.1 is to be expected. They reflect the associations of poverty with these two explanatory variables not only in economy-wide trends and cycles but also in the sharper swings in the fortunes of particular states and regions.

In the state cross-section regressions, 2 and 3, the dependent variable and the two basic explanatory variables are levels in a single year. The coefficients are larger than in the change regressions. They reflect persistent interstate differences in prosperity and affluence, in all their dimensions. A state with a chronically high unemployment rate or a chronically low wage rate is likely to suffer a high poverty rate. But gains in earnings and employment over one year or even nine years will not reduce a poor state's poverty to the level of states that have long been prosperous. Lasting differences among states in affluence will be reflected in the generosity of welfare benefits and other transfers. This may be the reason why here, unlike the national time series regressions of Table 6.1, the macroeconomic variables explain post- and pretransfer poverty about equally well.

There is some evidence that year-to-year poverty changes in recent years have been algebraically greater than equations fitted to observations through 1983 would predict. This is illustrated by Figure 6.8, for changes in official poverty for all persons, which exceeded such forecasts in every year from 1984 through 1990. (This was not a wholly new phenomenon; within the sample period most of the unexplained residuals were positive after 1976.) The errors of forecasts averaged 0.26 percentage points over 1984–1990 and reached 0.64 in 1990. Similar consistent overoptimism shows up in forecasts for 1984–1988 from 1967–1983 regressions for pretransfer poverty rates for all persons and for persons aged less than sixty-five.

These underpredictions of poverty since the mid-eighties are consistent with the findings of Cutler and Katz, Blank, and Medoff cited earlier. I can report two additional possibilities, related to each other. One concerns the relationship to the overall civilian unemployment rate of unemployment rates specific to age-sex-race populations vulnerable to poverty, as estimated by simple regression without trend or other explanatory variables. For black males, both teens and adults, unemployment rates since 1983 are higher than would be expected from equations

% change

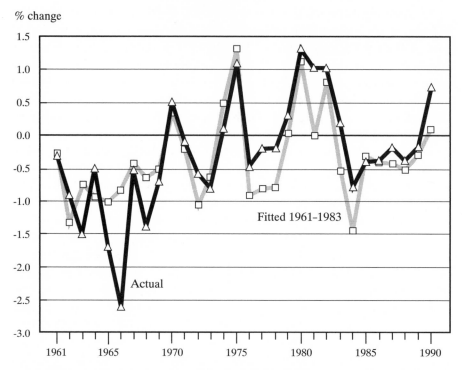

Figure 6.8 Yearly changes in poverty, 1961–1990. Changes in national percentage of persons in poverty, actual and as estimated from 1961–1983 regression on three macro variables: first difference of average real weekly earnings; first difference of an unemployment rate; the *level* of the ratio of the poverty threshold for four-person families (constant in real terms) to the previous year's median family income. (Earnings and unemployment data, Bureau of Labor Statistics; income and poverty data, see Figure 6.4; regression, see Table 6.1, no. 1.)

fit through 1983. For black adults these errors of forecast are as high as 2.3 percentage points and average 1.6 over 1983–1991; for black teens, they are as high as 5.2 points and average 3.6. In both cases 1959–1991 regressions with a multiplicative dummy variable, which turns out to increase the sensitivity of specific unemployment to general unemployment after 1982 by about 15 percent for black adults and 17 percent for black teens, fit well.

These effects do not apply to black females. Indeed the reverse appears to be true: their recent unemployment rates are lower in relation to the economy-wide rate than past relationships would predict.

The second findings reinforce the first. They concern the relationship of the labor force participation rate of a demographic group to its own unemployment rate and/or the general employment rate. Broadly speaking, regressions of this kind support the familiar "discouraged worker" effect: higher unemployment rates lead to withdrawal from the labor force. This effect appears to be stronger since 1983 for black males, especially teens and young adults. Their labor force participation has been less since 1983 than regressions on pre-1983 unemployment observations predicted. No such behavioral change has been evident for whites or for black females.

Together these results add up to disturbing declines in the employment/population ratios of potential workers and breadwinners in demographic groups vulnerable to poverty. Such declines are not easy to overcome by strong macroeconomic performance.

Some clues to these adverse developments are provided by Medoff (1992). He finds that aggregate job vacancies, as measured by the Help Wanted Index compiled by the Conference Board, a New York nonprofit business research institution, have been abnormally low in recent years relative to contemporaneous unemployment rates. Vacancies are what pull people from the category NILF (not in labor force) into LFP (labor force participation, employed or looking for work). As already noted, Medoff also finds that meaningful vacancies are for jobs inferior in pay and other terms.

All these findings are consistent with the view that, independent of overall macroeconomic performance, changes in the nature and location of jobs are adverse to persons and families at risk of poverty.

I confess I come to conclusions of this kind reluctantly. In the past I have been skeptical of periodic structural explanations of higher unemployment rates and higher poverty rates. I have thought that the American people are very mobile and adaptable and that the U.S. economy adjusts quickly to sectoral shocks, provided an overall macroeconomic climate of prosperity is maintained. Think of the country's smooth economic demobilization after World War II, which confounded the pessimists. Think of the fashionable structural explanations of high unemployment in 1960–61 and 1979–1982, both followed by recoveries that brought unemployment rates below what they had been at previous cyclical peaks. In my experience, structural hypotheses have usually been excuses for policymakers to do nothing to stimulate the economy.

This may be the case today too, although the current structural problems should lead to the opposite conclusion, namely, that more macroeconomic stimulus is needed and is safe. Because labor shortages are the sources of wage inflation, the scarcity of vacancies, even while unemployment rates are below rates at the troughs of previous business cycles, suggests that expansionary monetary and fiscal policies will be helpful and not inflationary.

Expansionary monetary policy, the province of the Federal Reserve, would consist mainly in further reduction in the discount rate at which the Fed lends to banks and in the money market rates the Fed controls by its open market operations. In addition the Fed, in cooperation with the Treasury, could enter government bond markets with a view to lowering long-term rates. Besides stimulating business investment and home building, these measures would have as a by-product a lower foreign exchange value of the dollar, making American goods more competitive in world markets and trimming the nation's trade deficit.

Expansionary fiscal policy would also be desirable, probably essential. This business cycle is the first in forty years in which no fiscal stimulus has been given to help recovery, by new expenditures or tax cuts or both. Fiscal stimulus to aggregate demand for goods and services and labor is necessarily deficit increasing, at least in the short run. At present, fiscal policy is paralyzed by the political fear of adding to the mammoth deficits inherited from the twelve years of the Reagan and Bush administrations.

Whether recovery comes about by deliberate policy or by good fortune, even when prosperity is restored the prospects for poverty-vulnerable workers are not promising. More of them are likely to be unemployed or not in labor force than was true before 1980.

The Unemployment-Inflation Tradeoff

An overall unemployment rate between 5 and 5.5 percent is very likely to be as low as we can hope and expect. The Federal Reserve, whose monetary and interest rate policies are the major macroeconomic controls on the economy, will probably not want to allow lower unemployment without convincing evidence that it would not trigger ever higher wage and price inflation. At present estimates of the inflation-safe national unemployment rate, unfortunately, the unemployment rates of black male teens and adults will be extremely high and, evidently, even higher than in the past. And many potential workers vulnerable to poverty, again more than in the past, will not even be in the labor force. Joblessness in these disadvantaged groups does virtually nothing to mitigate the wage and price inflation rates that concern the Federal Reserve.

Could the unemployment target of federal monetary and fiscal policy be moved below 5 percent? Policymakers may often exaggerate the social costs of inflation, but they will probably be unwilling to accept more inflation risk as long as the public also exaggerates those costs. But policymakers could respond to evidence that inflation is a lesser risk than in the past. In 1979–80 the Federal Reserve and most economists thought the inflation-safe unemployment rate was 6 percent or higher. Thanks to good wage and price behavior in the 1980s, the Fed kept the recovery going until unemployment fell below 5.5 percent.

Are there reasons to expect further improvement in the inflation-unemployment tradeoff? The scarcity of job vacancies is one reason. Moreover, both employers and employees, union and nonunion alike, are more sensitive than they formerly were to competitive threats to their markets and jobs. There is renewed interest in public and private programs to train and retrain workers and to assist conversions and adjustments of firms, industries, and localities.

These developments might somewhat enhance future contributions of macroeconomic performance to poverty reduction. But not by much. It would be wishful thinking to count on significant help from this source, especially over the short and medium run.

Macroeconomics and the Politics of Antipoverty Policy

Another avenue of transmission of macroeconomic performance to poverty is its effect on the adequacy and efficacy of antipoverty programs and transfers. As we know, the political climate of the 1970s and especially the 1980s was inclement. War on Poverty programs on which Robert Lampman, Sargent Shriver, and Lyndon Johnson pinned their hopes were stingily financed, even discontinued. Means-tested cash assistance fell sharply in purchasing power. Differences between prewelfare and post-transfer poverty percentages and poverty deficits narrowed during the 1980s. (I realize that causation cannot be surely inferred from these comparisons. Disciples of Charles Murray could doubtless contrive explanations based on extreme endogenous welfare dependency.) At the same time, government outlays for open-ended in-kind programs of benefit to the poor have greatly increased. One such program is Food Stamps, which has the political protection of agricultural interests. The most important, the most expensive, and the fastest growing is Medicaid, though not because poor patients are getting care of noticeably higher quality. Faced with exploding health care costs, federal and state politicians and voters feel they are doing their bit, or more, for the poor, and their hearts harden against cash assistance.

The general macroeconomic disappointments of the 1970s and 1980s have a great deal to do with the political unpopularity of means-tested cash assistance. Lyndon Johnson's instinct was that cutting pieces of the pie for the poor was easier when the pie was rapidly growing. The declining trend of real wages made the great middle class cynical of government, fed up with taxes, and skeptical that welfare beneficiaries deserved help.

Future Prospects

What can we expect in the future? According to the regressions of Table 6.1, return to an overall unemployment rate of 5 percent, with a corresponding adult white male rate of 3.6 percent, 0.7 points below the 1990 rate, could by itself lower poverty rates for persons, pre- and post-transfer, by 0.3 to 0.4 points. These reductions would be a one-time contribution of successful countercyclical macroeconomic policy. Yet the present disposition of our monetary and fiscal policymakers evidently means that so low an unemployment target is unrealistically ambitious.

Full recovery, to whatever target will appear inflation-safe to the Federal Reserve, seems likely to take several years. One reason, of which the weak Help Wanted numbers cited above are symptomatic, is the irreversible nature of many recent and prospective layoffs. Some of these eliminations of jobs are belated adaptations by American companies to the global competition assailing them ever since 1980. Others are permanent cutbacks of the armed services and of defense-related jobs all over the country, the clouds of which peace dividends are silver linings. Because the armed services have provided important opportunities for minority youth, their force reductions are particularly bad omens for progress against poverty. This cyclical recovery will depend in unusual degree on the creation of new jobs rather than the restoration of old ones. Permanent new jobs will require policies that generate and are expected to sustain adequate aggregate demand. Commitment to a sustained long-run program of public investment in infrastructure, education and training, and environmental protection would be a good way to promote recovery in the short run while meeting long-term social needs.

I am more optimistic about the trend of real wages. Productivity growth in manufacturing was a bright spot in the 1980s recovery. Companies whose structural adjustments are eliminating jobs are also becoming more efficient, leaner as well as meaner. Modest improvements in productivity growth should now show up in earnings as well as, indeed even more than, in compensation. In the years ahead fringe benefits are likely to fall relative to take-home pay. But the yields in poverty reduction will be small and slow. An increase of the real wage by 1 percent a year will reduce poverty by only about 0.13 points a year.

These unemployment and earnings effects together would lower poverty by a bit less than 2 points in one decade—nothing to write home about. We will need specific war-on-poverty measures—though not a new declaration of war—and more adequate and effective transfers to achieve speedier progress. As to the possibility that improved macroeconomic performance will soften the hearts of taxpayers and of politicians seeking their votes, it is hard to imagine conversions that will make additional budgetary resources available for new battles against poverty or for more adequate transfers.

The federal budgetary outlook is grim. After the defense share of GDP hit its 1980s peak in 1986 at 6.5 percent of GDP, the share fell to 5.4 percent of potential output in 1991. The Clinton budget will reduce it further to 3.2 percent or less in 1997, a decline in annual expenditures of more than $100 billion in 1991 dollars. But increases in other outlays are eating up these peace dividends. The principal villains are interest on the debt, the legacy of the profligate tax cuts and defense spending of the Reagan-Bush years, and health care, especially Medicare and Medicaid.

Although the Clinton economic and fiscal program for the five years 1993–1997 contemplates using a third of the gross budgetary resources resulting from tax increases and expenditure cuts, mainly defense savings, for new nondefense initiatives, these initiatives are largely for public investments in infrastructure and education. Little is budgeted for antipoverty programs beyond further liberalization of the refundable Earned Income Tax Credit against personal income taxes. Welfare reform is geared to reducing dependency more than to reducing poverty.

Whatever is done to reform health care will have major fiscal consequences. Without reform, Medicare and Medicaid will add 2 percent of GDP to the federal deficit between 1996 and 2002. The reforms are likely to help the poor, especially those uninsured or dependent on Medicaid. But they will reinforce the squeeze on other government programs.

Entitlements to non-needs-tested transfers, especially Social Security, are often the targets of deficit hawks who do not have to run for office. But the Social Security Trust Fund is running ever-growing annual surpluses, now about $70 billion. The Clinton tax plan would raise from 50 to 85 percent the fraction of benefits taxable to the affluent elderly. If Social Security benefits of future retirees are to be reduced, the natural corollary would be to reduce the Social Security taxes they contribute while active workers. If so, no deficit reduction would be achieved. Otherwise payroll contributions would become ordinary taxes, regressive ones at that, blatantly used for general federal purposes. Although it would be possible and defensible to reduce equally Social Security benefits and contributions and then to increase ordinary income taxes in order to reduce the deficit, this triple play would be politically dubious.

Unfortunately, the Reagan administration succeeded all too well and all too permanently in its objective of crippling civilian government by giving away tax revenues, creating a political taboo against raising taxes, and generating a deficit and debt to brandish against civilian expenditures. The victory may yet be sealed by a constitutional amendment requiring super-majorities in both houses of Congress either to adopt a deficit budget or to raise taxes.

Although chronic budget deficits of the magnitudes of the Reagan and Bush years are harmful, cures for them can easily turn out to be worse than the disease. The point of deficit reduction is to free savings absorbed by the deficit for the financing of productive investments by the private sector. This process, the reverse of "crowding out," requires reductions in interest rates to entice businesses and households to borrow money and build plants, buy equipment, introduce new technology, engage in research and development, and construct houses. The theory is that these capital investments will benefit future Americans, raising their productivity, wages, and living standards.

The process requires the active cooperation of the Federal Reserve to bring interest rates down and to overcome the immediate adverse effects of deficit reduction on business activity and jobs. Without the Fed's aggressive help, deficit reduction could arrest or reverse cyclical recovery and actually diminish private investment and other future-oriented uses of resources. Even in prosperous times, the effects of deficit reduction on the future well-being of the society depend on how it is done. If it occurs at the expense of consumption by present-day affluent taxpayers or of unnecessary and unproductive defense or nondefense expenditures, future generations come out ahead. If it comes at the expense of public investments in education, infrastructure, housing, inner-city development, improved health care, jobs programs, and welfare reform, the verdict is not so clear. Given the patent economic and social deficiencies of America today, my judgment is that those public investments, neglected as they have been since 1980, will serve future generations better than holding down the federal debt in order to channel more funds to private borrowers.

A Final Remark

Looking back to the optimistic expectations I had in the 1960s, I do not think I can account for the extent of their disappointment by macroeconomic factors or by any economic factors. My own city of New Haven is a miniature version of the web of urban pathologies of New York, Washington, D.C., Detroit, and Milwaukee, possibly also of Los Angeles. Manufacturing jobs have moved to the suburbs or more distant locations. Middle- and upper-class households, predominantly white, have moved out as well. Minority populations and poverty are concentrated in city neighborhoods. According to the 1990 Census, only 21 percent of the 49,000 New Haven households but 39 percent of the 255,000 suburban households (in New Haven County outside the city itself) have incomes over $50,000 a year. The median city household income is $22,000, the suburban median is $40,000. In the city are the major problems of poverty, troubled public schools, welfare, joblessness, homelessness, ill health, crime, drug trade, family instability, and fiscal crisis. Outside the city is the tax base, and there is no way to tap it to help the city. These urban problems reinforce each other. Together they constitute a socioeconomic system dynamically unstable downward—a vicious circle.

What unforeseen developments are the most obvious negative "shocks"—to use economists' jargon—to which the demoralization of inner-city neighborhoods can be attributed? They are drugs, guns, and AIDS, all obviously interrelated. Although they are outside my assigned topic, it is clear that understanding them and prescribing remedies are crucial if improving macroeconomic trends and policies are to have good effects inside as well as outside these neighborhoods.

CHAPTER SEVEN

The Employment Strategy:
Public Policies to Increase Work and Earnings

REBECCA M. BLANK

The majority of the Nation could simply tax themselves enough to provide the necessary income supplements to their less fortunate citizens . . . But this "solution" would leave untouched most of the roots of poverty. Americans want to *earn* the American standard of living by their own efforts and contributions. It will be far better, even if more difficult, to equip and permit the poor of the Nation to produce and earn the additional [money needed to raise them out of poverty].

Economic Report of the President, January 1964

There has been a continuing and strong emphasis in the United States on economic self-sufficiency as the primary goal of antipoverty policy for the able-bodied.[1] The *Economic Report of the President* (1964), which laid out the intellectual foundations for Lyndon Johnson's War on Poverty, makes this point unequivocally. Almost thirty years later, the public discussion continues to emphasize the "employment strategy" as the best cure for poverty, as opposed to the "income transfer strategy," which is seen as merely alleviating the symptoms of poverty without addressing its root causes. A successful employment strategy can lead to increased skills, more time in the labor market, decreased unemployment, and higher wages. From a social perspective, such policies promise reduced public assistance payments and increased productivity, thereby generating long-term benefits for both poor and nonpoor alike.

There are two different perspectives that underlie public efforts to increase employment among the poor. One perspective seeks increases in family income as the desired result. I will call this the *income goal.* Employment programs can achieve the income goal by increasing the hours of work and/or the wages of poor individuals sufficiently so that earnings gains are greater than any concomitant decline in public assistance income. From the income goal perspective, policies that decrease public assistance income and force families to replace it with labor market income are ineffective and even punitive if there is no net gain in a family's aggregate income.

The alternative perspective focuses on the value of earned income and work to family well-being, regardless of its effect on total income. I will call this the *work goal*. Proponents of the work goal want employment programs to increase the share of total income from earnings, even if this occurs through a dollar-for-dollar replacement of transfer income with work income. Proponents of the work goal argue that work plays an integrating role in people's lives; it gives them a sense of self-worth and fosters an awareness of their interconnections and responsibilities to society. Increased work thus benefits poor families even if their income does not rise.

American policies with regard to employment among the poor have constantly swung between those who have argued primarily for the income goal and those who have argued primarily for the work goal. The tensions between these perspectives were particularly acute during the 1980s, as Republican administrations argued for the work goal, while Democratic Congresses resisted unless the income goal was also met.

The last two decades have brought both substantial changes in public policy designed to increase the work effort of the poor and substantial changes in the labor market opportunities available to less-skilled workers. Recent major expansions of work-welfare programs and of tax supplements to work were politically possible because the policy community became convinced that these programs would satisfy both the work goal and the income goal. Other changes have been more controversial.

Changing Labor Market Opportunities in the Larger Economy

Programs designed to increase employment and earnings among less-skilled workers are highly affected by the overall demand for these workers and the starting wage levels available to them in the economy. Over the past decade, changes in labor market opportunities for less-skilled workers have affected both job availability and wages.

Lower Unemployment and Continuing Strong Employment Growth

After fifteen years of an upward trend in unemployment rates, capped in 1982–83 by the highest unemployment levels since the Great Depression (above 10 percent), unemployment fell through the rest of the 1980s. It reached a sixteen-year low in March 1989 at 5.0 percent, before increasing in the recession of the early 1990s to a peak of 7.8 percent in June 1992. Figure 7.1 presents the employ-

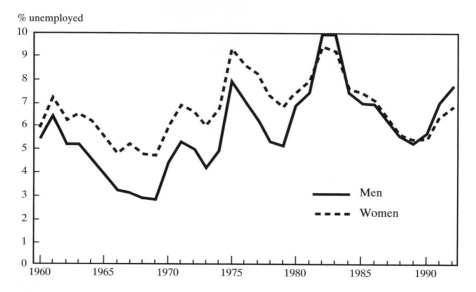

% unemployed

Figure 7.1   Unemployment rates by sex (civilians, age 16 and over). (Data source: U.S. Department of Labor, *Employment and Earnings,* various issues.)

ment rate for men and women between 1960 and 1992. Since 1980, women's unemployment rates have been as low or lower than men's.

Despite the recession of the early 1990s, unemployment has clearly moved downward over the past decade. Certain groups, however, continue to experience greater problems with unemployment. Table 7.1 presents unemployment rates among several groups in the population in 1992. Unemployment among black adults has been above 10 percent since the mid-1970s, about twice the rate of white unemployment. Teenage unemployment also stayed stubbornly high even as aggregate unemployment fell, particularly among teens from black or Hispanic families.

Along with the decline in unemployment during the 1980s came strong growth in employment. The number of workers over age sixteen grew by almost 19 percent between 1980 and 1990, while the population over age sixteen grew by only 12 percent. Strong employment growth has been a long-term characteristic of the U.S. economy. Employment has grown faster than population in every one of the last three decades.[2] Both the baby boom, whose members entered adulthood in the 1960s and 1970s, and women, who have entered the labor force in steadily increasing numbers, have found jobs. This long-term growth stands in substantial contrast to most western European economies, where unemployment rates remained stubbornly high over the 1980s and where employment levels have been

Table 7.1   1992 Unemployment rates by race, sex, and age (in percent)

	Men	Women
Total labor force	7.8	6.9
Adults (20 years and older)		
White	6.3	5.4
Black	13.4	11.7
Hispanic	10.4	10.1
Teens (ages 16–19)		
White	18.4	15.7
Black	42.1	37.2
Hispanic	28.1	26.5

Source: U.S. Department of Labor (1993), table 39, p. 218.

relatively stagnant. Between 1979 and 1990, for example, the unemployment rate in western Europe rose from 5.7 to 7.8 percent while U.S. unemployment fell (OECD, 1992, table 2.15).

One interpretation of these trends is that the simple availability of jobs has not been a major constraint for most less-skilled U.S. workers who seek employment, at least over the long run. (During the height of the recession of the early 1990s, of course, job shortages were more severe.) Although rising unemployment during the 1970s created concern about job shortages and was one of the reasons behind major efforts at the creation of public jobs through the Comprehensive Employment and Training Act, such concerns were not widely discussed in the 1980s. The public debate focused instead on worker skills and labor market preparation.

Aggregate employment has not been a major problem, but for certain groups job availability remains a key concern. The work of William Julius Wilson (1987) and others has focused attention on the problems of minority workers in inner-city locations, who may have experienced increasing isolation from jobs when employment opportunities in their communities declined and they were unable to relocate due to both limited income and housing discrimination. Young urban minority males have had particularly high rates of unemployment and nonparticipation in the labor force (at least in the mainstream economy).

Declining Real Wage Opportunities

Although aggregate employment has expanded, concern about the nature of the jobs being created has also increased. Some observers have claimed that a growing number of positions for less-skilled workers are "bad jobs"—paying low wages, offering few nonwage benefits, and providing few opportunities for training or long-term economic advancement (see, for example, Harrison and Blue-stone, 1988). If this is true, the opportunities for poor families to earn their way out of poverty may have diminished even though jobs are available.

There is widespread agreement within the research community that inflation-adjusted wages have fallen among less-skilled male workers. Employed white men between the ages of eighteen and sixty-five who had less than twelve years of education earned 15.8 percent less per week in 1989 than in 1979 (see Table 7.2). In contrast, white men with more than twelve years of education earned 11.7

Table 7.2 Average weekly earnings by years of school and sex, calculated among nonelderly adults who work (1989 dollars)

	Men			Women		
	1969	1979	1989	1969	1979	1989
I. White						
All workers	$550	$534	$565	$258	$268	$325
% change		−2.9	+5.8		+3.9	+21.3
Less than 12 years of education	$441	$411	$346	$210	$205	$202
% change		−6.8	−15.8		−2.3	−1.5
12 years of education	$531	$500	$485	$250	$250	$274
% change		−5.8	−3.0		+0.0	+9.6
More than 12 years of education	$696	$631	$705	$327	$320	$405
% change		−9.3	+11.7		−2.1	+26.6
II. Black						
All workers	$365	$404	$436	$214	$265	$326
% change		+10.7	+7.9		+23.8	+23.0
Less than 12 years of education	$316	$310	$333	$153	$186	$191
% change		−1.9	+7.4		+21.6	+2.7
12 years of education	$398	$407	$379	$237	$253	$289
% change		+2.3	−7.4		+6.8	+14.2
More than 12 years of education	$482	$509	$548	$339	$352	$415
% change		+5.6	+7.7		+3.8	+17.9

Source: Tabulations from U.S. Bureau of the Census Current Population Surveys, March 1970, 1980, and 1990, based on the civilian population aged 18–65. Inflation adjustments are based on the GDP deflator.

percent more per week in 1989 than in 1979. The evidence indicates that wage declines are largest among less-skilled young men just entering the labor force.[3] Less-skilled black men have not experienced as much wage decline as less-skilled white men, but more-skilled black men have not gained as much.

In the 1990s, young men who have a high school degree or less can generally expect to earn less than their fathers earned twenty years earlier. This wage decline is not the result of the shift of low-skill jobs from the manufacturing sector to the service sector. Real wages have declined for *both* manufacturing jobs and service sector jobs, so that even less-skilled workers who find jobs in manufacturing industries in the 1990s face reduced wage opportunities.

The reasons for these changes are much debated.[4] Fundamentally, the demand for less-skilled workers appears to be declining faster than the number of less-skilled workers, and their wages are therefore drawn downward. This trend is related to the increasing internationalization of the U.S. economy, which places less-skilled U.S. workers in competition with less-skilled (and typically lower-paid) foreign workers, and to technological changes that have accelerated the demand for more-skilled workers. Declining unionization, which is correlated with these trends, has also hurt the wages of less-skilled workers.

In contrast to men, women's wages do not show as rapid an increase in inequality. Overall, women's wages have risen faster than men's during the 1980s. Less-skilled women can expect to earn at least as much if not more than their mothers did twenty years ago. Table 7.2 indicates that the earnings of less-skilled women have been flat (for high school dropouts) or rising (for high school graduates or those with some post–high school training). Black and white women are largely at parity in their wages at all skill levels and have shown similar trends over the past decade. The primary reason less-skilled women's wages have not shown the same declines as men's is that less-skilled working women have been in occupations and industries that have not been as hard hit by wage declines. It is still worth noting, however, that although these wage trends have brought men's and women's wages closer together, women still earn substantially less. Women without high school degrees earn only 58 percent of what their equivalent male colleagues earn.

As a result of these trends, it has become harder for many low-income families to escape poverty through employment. The high poverty rates of the last decade are in fact closely related to wage changes among less-skilled workers (Blank, 1993). The result has been greater attention to the income goal and an increased search for policies that will "make work pay."[5] In turn, this effort has given impetus to calls for educational reform and school-to-work transition programs, aimed at helping disadvantaged young workers prepare for the more skill-demanding labor market of the twenty-first century.

Demographic Changes among the Poor

The earnings opportunities of the poor are affected not only by the job options available in the economy but also by the household composition of their families. Changes in household composition over the past several decades have made it more difficult for many poor families to take advantage of job opportunities.

The share of poor families that are headed by a woman, with no husband present, has increased from 24 percent in 1960 to 54 percent in 1991. Among poor families with children under age eighteen, currently more than 60 percent are headed by single women. This increase in female-headed families has three negative effects on the earning opportunities of poor families. First, because there are typically fewer adults in female-headed families, the probability decreases that such families might have more than one earner. Second, such families are more likely to have to pay for child care outside the home, increasing their work-related expenses. Third, because women in general have lower earnings than men, female family heads typically earn substantially less than male family heads, even when they work an equivalent number of hours. In 1991, women working year-round, full-time earned only 74 percent of that earned by year-round, full-time male workers.

These changes in household composition—which are occurring at all income levels—have increased the number of smaller, poorer families. Programs aimed at improving the labor market opportunities of poor families have had to deal more and more with the particular problems of families in which the mother operates as both the primary earner and the primary parent. This has prompted greater attention to the links between employment opportunities and the availability of subsidiary services, including child care and health insurance.

Major Employment and Income Trends

These changes in labor market opportunities and in household composition have produced changes in employment patterns among the poor. Changes in employment, changes in wage levels, and changes in household composition combine to produce changes in family earnings and income. Table 7.3 presents the general trends in work behavior, in the share of family income that comes from earnings, and in family income levels among nonelderly adults in low-income families. ("Family" in Table 7.3 includes unrelated individuals as one-person families.) I have tabulated these numbers for 1969, 1979, and 1989 for nonelderly men and women who live in families whose total income falls into the bottom 20 percent of the family income distribution in each year.[6] I show these data for all men and women who are single or married, and who live with or without other children or relatives in the household.

Table 7.3 Labor market participation and income sources among nonelderly adults in families in the bottom 20 percent of the income distribution, by sex and family type

		Single		Married	
		Children or other relatives in the household?		Children or other relatives in the household?	
	All persons	No	Yes	No	Yes
A. Men					
Percentage of sample					
1989	40.7	24.3	3.5	5.6	7.3
Percentage working					
1969	74.8	73.2	66.8	70.4	82.9
1979	66.8	68.9	53.7	52.7	77.1
1989	65.0	68.7	51.3	44.1	75.0
Own earnings/family income					
1969	58.4	59.5	29.5	52.4	68.8
1979	51.7	58.1	29.0	35.1	57.1
1989	52.4	60.2	32.7	28.7	54.4
Family income					
1989	$7,187	$6,760	$7,049	$7,799	$8,212
Change in family income (%)					
1969–1979	−10.5	−4.8	−15.1	−7.5	−12.2
1979–1989	−2.3	−2.4	−5.0	+0.6	+1.4
B. Women					
Percentage of sample					
1989	59.3	25.0	19.8	7.0	7.4
Percentage working					
1969	47.3	62.7	52.0	30.9	30.2
1979	48.8	61.3	48.7	27.7	34.0
1989	51.0	62.4	48.3	29.8	39.9
Own earnings/family income					
1969	31.1	53.9	30.2	11.8	9.6
1979	34.2	51.4	32.4	11.4	12.1
1989	37.0	53.6	33.3	13.6	15.3
Family income					
1989	$6,833	$6,508	$6,327	$7,922	$8,257
Change in family income (%)					
1969–1979	−8.9	+0.8	−13.5	−5.8	−12.6
1979–1989	−3.6	−4.1	−4.1	−1.4	+1.8

Source: See Table 7.2. "Family" includes unrelated individuals as one-person families, as well as multiperson families composed of all related persons who live together.

The rows labeled "percent working" in Table 7.3 show the percentage of each group who work at least one week during the indicated year. Two particular trends in labor force participation stand out. First, work has declined for all groups of men in low-income families over these two decades, although more of this decline occurred during the 1970s; declines in male employment over the 1980s have been relatively small. Other research also documents substantial declines in labor market participation among low-income men over the past several decades (Juhn, 1992). These trends are strongest among black men, particularly unmarried black men. Sixty-five percent of all low-income, nonelderly men reported working in 1989. The corresponding rates for nonwhite and white men were 56 and 68 percent, respectively.[7]

This decline in labor market participation among nonelderly low-income men has been the subject of substantial concern. The decline in part reflects a shorter work life due to increased schooling and earlier retirement, but it may also reflect an increase in time spent in off-the-books employment. Research has indicated that the declining wages available to large groups of predominantly less-skilled men can explain most of the decline in labor market participation among white men since the mid-1970s and about half the decline among black men (Juhn, 1992). But the long-term decline in male labor supply is not fully explained by the more recent decline in wage rates. For instance, although wages for less-skilled workers are lower than they were in the 1970s, they are higher than they were in the 1950s, when male labor force participation was much higher. This comparison suggests that labor supply trends are affected by relative wage comparisons and wage expectations as well as absolute wage levels.[8]

Second, in contrast to men, women's labor market involvement in low-income families has not declined. As Table 7.3 indicates, married women in low-income families, living with children or other relatives, are working more. Among low-income single women, with and without children, work effort has been relatively constant. Over the 1970s, there were declines in the probability of work among low-income black women, both married and single; in the aggregate data these were more than offset by increases in white women's employment. In 1969 low-income black women were much more likely to work than low-income white women; by 1989 the reverse was true.

It may seem surprising that these data do not show sharp increases in labor market participation among single low-income women, given the increase in aggregate female labor force participation over these years. But even among women at all income levels, there is actually no increase in the percentage working among those who are single and living with children and other relatives, and only a small increase among those who are single and living alone. The big increases in female labor force participation over these decades all occur among married women. Nonetheless, single women still work much more than married women, as Table 7.3 indicates; much of the increase in aggregate female labor market participation has occurred because women are spending more time as single adults.[9]

Several rows in Table 7.3 indicate how much individuals are contributing to family income through their own earnings. For instance, column 1, row 7, indicates that the earnings of nonelderly men in low-income households accounted for 52 percent of their family's total income in 1989. Among married men, there has been a steep decline in their contribution to total family income, which reflects their decline in labor market participation as well as recent declines in male earnings. Married women show a simultaneous increase in the extent to which earnings contribute to family income. Among single men and women, the role of their own earnings in total family income has stayed largely constant over the past two decades.

Table 7.3 also indicates family income levels and changes in family income experienced by these low-income adults over the last two decades. Almost every low-income group experienced substantial declines in their family income over the 1970s and smaller declines over the 1980s. Tabulations by Gary Burtless suggest that over the decade 1969–1979, family income was most heavily affected by changes in labor market involvement. But over the decade 1979–1989, the decline in wage rates drove most of the decline in family income.[10] This result emphasizes again the negative impact of recent declines in real wages on poor families.

In summary, work effort over the past several decades has fallen among low-income men, has been relatively constant among low-income single women, and has increased among low-income married women. The trends for nonwhites are somewhat different from the trends for whites, and show larger declines in work. But most of these changes occurred in the 1970s. Changes in labor supply were not the primary determinant of declining real incomes among low-income families over the 1980s. In that decade, steady declines in real wages for less-skilled men eroded the earning power of many poor families and were one of the primary causes behind declines in male labor force participation and in family income at the bottom of the income distribution. In 1990, over 60 percent of poor families contained at least one worker and over 20 percent contained a full-time year-round worker, yet still remained poor.

On the one hand, a growing number of poor families face lower earnings opportunities because they are single-parent families, headed by women. On the other hand, among those poor families headed by men or married couples, the men are facing declining earnings opportunities in an economy whose demand for less-skilled workers is falling. As a result, it is now probably more difficult to implement an "employment strategy" as a way to reduce poverty than it has been at any time in the recent past.

In the debate between the income goal and the work goal in employment policy, these trends have also worked against those who want to focus primarily on employment rather than on income. As wages among many less-skilled workers fall, it is hard to provide employment incentives without somehow addressing the problem of declining real wages. In addition, as increasing numbers of poor families are headed by single parents, it is less clear that more time in the labor market is always to the advantage of the family, particularly if affordable, effective child care is not readily available.[11]

Recent Employment Policies

The discussion of employment and work-incentive programs among policymakers and analysts has been extensive over the 1980s and early 1990s. This focus has been due in part to the influence of several Republican administrations that have emphasized "economic empowerment" rather than the expansion of transfer programs. The discussion has also been prompted by concern over employment options for the poor, which have been increasingly limited by the demographic and economic trends already outlined. As a result, major changes have occurred in the work incentives faced by low-income families. In general, the policies designed to expand employment opportunities can be separated into three general categories: (1) policies designed to structure transfer programs so that they reward work effort; (2) policies designed to provide services that directly improve their recipients' work opportunities, including education, job training, and job search assistance; and (3) policies designed to structure the tax system or other nonwelfare programs so that work effort is rewarded.

Work and the Structure of Welfare

The Aid to Families with Dependent Children program was enacted as part of the Social Security Act of 1935, with the explicit goal of providing support to deserving widows so they would not have to leave their children and go to work. With increases in labor market participation among married women and in the number of single mothers who are divorced or never-married rather than widowed, the AFDC program has become increasingly controversial. One major criticism of AFDC is that it creates work disincentives and encourages women to collect welfare rather than to find a job.

Given labor market trends, it is interesting that the controversy over employment incentives has focused on single women with children, a group whose work behavior has not deteriorated in recent decades. Indeed, one might expect a much stronger policy discussion about the need for employment programs aimed at low-income men. But work incentives for low-income women have generated so much more interest for at least two reasons. First, single women with children are the primary nonelderly group in the population who have been eligible for substantial amounts of public assistance.[12] Both federal and state officials hope for lower public assistance expenditures if this group can be moved into greater employment. Second, as more and more women at all income levels enter the labor market, many people are increasingly uncomfortable with the idea of public transfers that pay welfare recipients to stay home with their children.

Benefit levels and eligibility requirements for AFDC are largely set at the state level, while the federal government shares the cost of the program and regulates the payment of benefits. AFDC has traditionally been available only to single-parent families who meet strict income and asset eligibility tests. Until 1990, married-couple families were eligible for AFDC only in some states. Since 1990, all states have been required to make AFDC benefits available to married-couple households. The eligibility rules for two-parent households are stricter, however, and over 90 percent of the AFDC caseload is still composed of single mothers and their children.

Declining Benefit Levels

Because states set benefit levels, they vary enormously around the country. For a family of four, maximum benefit payments in 1992 varied from $144 in Mississippi to $1,027 in Alaska, a variation that is far greater than any difference in cost of living between states. Because benefit levels are only infrequently changed by state legislatures, AFDC benefits have been seriously eroded by inflation. Figure 7.2 graphs the change in inflation-adjusted maximum benefit levels for a family of four from 1970 through 1992 for the median state in each year. In 1992 dollars, median benefits were at a high of $761 per month in 1970 and fell to a low of $435 per month by 1992, a decline of 43 percent.

Women who receive AFDC are also eligible to receive food stamps, a federally run program that provides vouchers that can be used to purchase food. Most evidence indicates that, particularly among women with children, food stamps are the equivalent of a cash grant, because most women spend as much or more on food than food stamps provide. Food stamps are financed by the federal government and have uniform eligibility rules across the country. They somewhat offset the inequities of AFDC payments, therefore, because women in states with lower AFDC benefit levels receive more in food stamps. Food stamps have been inflation-indexed over most of the past two decades, and thus have not suffered

AFDC + food stamps

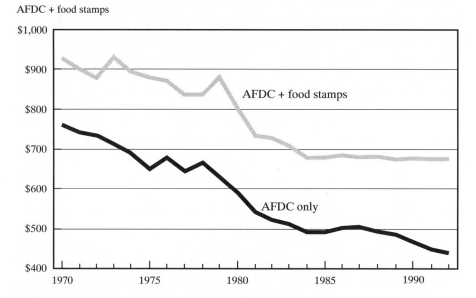

Figure 7.2   Median state AFDC and Food Stamp monthly benefits (for family of four, 1992 dollars). (Data source: U.S. Department of Health and Human Services/U.S. Department of Health, Education and Welfare, various publications.)

from the same decline in real value as AFDC. As plotted in Figure 7.2, food stamps add significantly to AFDC benefits, but because food stamps are largely unchanged in real terms, the downward trend in AFDC income still dominates the combined benefit line.[13]

This decline in public assistance benefits has meant increased work incentives for low-income female-headed families. As the transfer income available from AFDC falls, work is relatively more attractive and fewer families are eligible for AFDC. Indeed, the share of female-headed families receiving AFDC fell over the 1980s, in part because of these benefit changes and in part because of other eligibility changes legislated in the early 1980s. Such changes in work incentives may satisfy the employment goal but, depending on the extent to which families can make up for lost AFDC income, may not meet the income goal.

Changes in Benefit Reduction Rates and Eligibility Rules

The AFDC program provides a guaranteed benefit level that is reduced as earnings increase. This design ensures that as family income rises, the welfare subsidy declines. But it also creates work incentive problems. For welfare recipients, a dollar earned in the labor market results in less than a dollar of income because benefits are lost at the same time. The higher the benefit reduction rate, the lower the rewards of working for welfare clients.

In 1967, in a major reform of the AFDC program that was designed to encourage work, the federal government mandated that states allow women to earn up to $30 a month without penalty to their AFDC benefits. When earnings rose above $30 a month, AFDC benefits would be reduced by $.67 for every $1 earned, a two-thirds benefit reduction rate. (Although today $30 a month seems an extremely small work incentive, this amount, if it had been inflation indexed, would be the equivalent of $120 a month in 1992 dollars.) This structure remained in place until 1981.

The structural problems embedded in the AFDC program have been characterized as the "iron triangle" of welfare reform. Essentially, if one is concerned about the well-being of those who cannot work, the benefit level can be raised—but higher benefits for nonworkers cause work disincentives. If one is concerned about work disincentives, the benefit reduction rate can be lowered, allowing workers to keep a higher share of their earnings and reducing the welfare benefit more slowly as earnings rise—but this puts more people on the program and raises program costs. If one is concerned about program costs and participation, one can either cut benefits (hurting the well-being of those who can't work) or raise tax rates (hurting work incentives). Any proposal for welfare reform must make compromises in responding to these three concerns.

Before 1981 a great deal of policy discussion focused on the question of how to set benefit levels and benefit reduction rates in the face of these contradictory goals. This discussion culminated in President Carter's 1977 welfare reform proposal, the Program for Better Jobs and Income, in which he proposed a nationalized welfare system with different benefit levels and different benefit reduction rates for families with work-eligible and non-work-eligible adults. This proposal, however, became entangled with other problems during Carter's presidency and never came close to passage.

The 1967 reforms also encouraged states to provide job placement assistance to job-ready AFDC recipients in a program known as the Work Incentive Program (WIN). Although a number of states ran small AFDC job-placement and work programs throughout the 1970s, in 1981 President Reagan proposed a different solution to the problem of work incentives through a major expansion in these programs. Rather than trying to induce recipients to work through some combination of benefit levels and tax rates, he proposed mandating that nonworking AFDC recipients who were ruled "work eligible" spend a certain number of hours in an assigned public sector job as a condition of receiving benefits. In addition, for those recipients who found paid employment, Reagan proposed that after four months the benefit reduction rate rise from two-thirds to 100 percent (a

$1 decline in benefits for every $1 earned) and that the $30 earnings disregard be eliminated. Such revisions, he claimed, would reduce the caseload, reduce AFDC costs, and have no effect on work effort if implemented together with work mandates (Doolittle, 1986). This proposal was only partly enacted in the Omnibus Budget Reconciliation Act of 1981 (OBRA). Congress accepted Reagan's proposed changes in the structure of benefits for earners, but it refused to mandate work in return for AFDC benefits. OBRA did, however, allow states the option of running various mandated work programs should they choose.

The 100 percent benefit reduction after four months for women who find work while they are on AFDC essentially eliminates all incentives to work for this group. Each dollar in earnings results in a dollar's reduction in AFDC benefits, leaving a woman economically no better off if she is employed, unless her earnings are larger than the maximum AFDC grant (in which case she would be ineligible for AFDC).

Researchers have studied the effects of this change by comparing the work behavior of AFDC recipients before and after the legislative change (Hutchens, 1986). Surprisingly, these studies showed almost no decrease in work effort among continuing AFDC recipients after the new rules were implemented. It has been suggested that these studies stopped too soon, and that it took several years for women to adjust their behavior. For instance, before these program changes, approximately 16 percent of AFDC recipients said they worked and also collected some benefits. Three years after these program changes, only 5 percent of AFDC recipients said they were working (Moffitt, 1992). But because the most work-eligible AFDC recipients lost eligibility in the 1981 legislative changes, these percentages may reflect the changing selectivity of those on AFDC rather than the effect of changes in program rules. At this point, although most researchers believe that these rules altered work behavior, there is no good measure of the magnitude of this effect. At best, most observers conclude from these and other research results that the effects of tax changes on work incentives are not large for the AFDC population.

The women who lost AFDC eligibility entirely as a result of the 1981 program changes worked more than they had previously. Yet although they worked more hours than before, there was little gain in their total income; their wages were low enough that the additional work income barely replaced the lost AFDC income (Hutchens, 1986). There is no evidence that former AFDC recipients found jobs that paid enough to make them substantially better off. On the contrary, because they were working more (which means less time for parenting or other home-based activities) and had little or no increase in income, many researchers concluded that these women and their families had become worse off.[14] This conclusion implicitly emphasized the income goal in employment policy, and was sharply disputed by those who emphasized the employment goal and who believed these changes to be beneficial.

Efforts to reinstate a lower benefit reduction rate in AFDC have been unsuccessful, although some minor eligibility changes have been reversed and the $30/month earnings disregard has been reinstated for the first twelve months of welfare receipt. These efforts have waned as the focus of concern over work incentives for AFDC recipients has shifted in the 1980s from program parameters to mandated work programs. In recent years, the policy discussion at the federal level regarding work incentives and welfare has been almost entirely about the effectiveness of work-welfare programs and not about the structure of AFDC benefit payments.

During the recession of the early 1990s, AFDC caseloads rose very rapidly. Some public officials have suggested that this was the result of AFDC work disincentives, pulling women out of the labor market and into reliance on welfare. This explanation makes little sense. AFDC is a less-attractive option for single parents now than it was ten or twenty years ago; benefit levels are lower and any attempt to supplement AFDC income with earnings produces little net income gain. Although there are currently no good studies of recent caseload changes, it is likely that these changes reflect the recession-induced rise in unemployment, combined with the ongoing decline in earnings for many less-skilled workers.

One effect of the early 1990s recession has been the reemergence of proposals designed to discourage AFDC participation by changing AFDC program parameters. This discussion has occurred not at the federal level but at the state level. Pressed by serious budget problems, many states have targeted AFDC programs as a source of budget savings. Proposed reforms are typically designed to limit AFDC benefits or eligibility among certain groups, although the focus is less on encouraging work than on discouraging other types of behaviors (Center on Budget and Policy Priorities, 1991).[15]

The changing impact of AFDC program structure on work incentives over the past two decades can be summarized in three points. First, a steady decline in the purchasing power of AFDC benefits has raised work incentives among the low-income population and made AFDC an increasingly less attractive option. Second, legislative changes in eligibility rules and benefit reduction rates have also reduced AFDC eligibility and increased work among those families affected by these changes. Third, for those who continue to utilize AFDC, work incentives have declined, largely because of high benefit reduction rates. Fewer AFDC recipients found it attractive to work while collecting welfare in the 1980s.[16]

Direct Employment Service Programs

Programs that directly offer education, training, and job search assistance to disadvantaged workers provide a very different way to encourage employment. Rather than relying on employment incentives, through tax or transfer programs, these programs try to remedy the labor market problems of the poor. Programs vary in their definition of these problems: some have emphasized education and skill training to improve worker productivity and wages; others have focused entirely on job search, assuming that the problem is lack of information about the labor market; still other programs have stressed job creation, either through the public sector or through subsidizing private sector employers to hire disadvantaged workers. I will discuss direct employment service programs aimed at AFDC recipients separately from those aimed at other disadvantaged workers.

Work-Welfare Programs: The Latest Wave of Reform

Concern about the work behavior of welfare recipients is not new. Since 1967 states have required certain AFDC recipients to register with state employment offices as a condition of their payments. As discussed above, although Congress did not pass President Reagan's proposed mandatory work-for-your-benefits program in 1981, it did allow states (at their option) to mandate job training, job search, and work-for-benefits programs. A number of states immediately implemented narrowly focused work-requirement programs, and by the mid-1980s some states became interested in running more extensive work programs for AFDC recipients, providing expanded job search and employment assistance and making efforts to include more recipients in the program.

These programs, which came to be called *new style workfare* or *work-welfare*, generated a great deal of public attention. Initial opposition to the programs came from various groups who feared that the programs would be punitive, used to drop people from AFDC without providing any serious job skills or training. This opposition faded only after initial evaluations indicated that most AFDC recipients supported the programs and that clear employment gains occurred.

Many work-welfare programs followed a similar structure. First, AFDC recipients were screened to determine if they were "work-eligible." Clients with disabilities, clients who were needed at home to care for disabled relatives, and clients with preschoolers were typically excused from the program. Second, recipients were required to participate in a work-preparedness program. In most cases this involved some form of job search training. In a few states limited skills training or education was also included. Third, after completing the training component, clients were assisted in job search efforts. Clients who did not make an acceptable effort to participate in these activities could be "sanctioned"—have their AFDC benefits reduced or eliminated. Clients who failed to find a job through these efforts would either continue in the process or could be assigned to a more traditional work-for-your-benefits program.

The underlying philosophy behind these programs became known as *mutual obligations:* women who request assistance from the state in the form of AFDC payments must in turn be willing to take advantage of opportunities provided by the state to move off public assistance and toward economic self-sufficiency. If the state has an obligation to support poor women and their children, these women have an obligation to the state to accept assistance that will prepare them to leave AFDC and enter the work force. What differentiated these efforts from work-for-your-benefits programs is that they provided some labor market preparation and attempted to help women find private sector employment rather than mandating employment in an assigned public sector job as a precondition for receiving benefits.

There were other differences as well in these experimental work-welfare programs. One element of their success was their recognition of the importance of subsidiary services in making job training and search efforts possible. Programs subsidized the cost of child care, for example, for mothers who needed it, and frequently paid transportation expenses to child-care facilities and to job training seminars or job interviews.[17] For many women, leaving welfare meant losing health insurance, because AFDC recipients are automatically eligible for Medicaid but few of the low-wage jobs available to less-skilled women provide health insurance.[18] Several states therefore tried to make Medicaid insurance available to women for some period after they left AFDC.

In addition, many states recognized the importance of a coordinated program structure.[19] Program implementation included consolidating and centralizing services for clients, so that caseworkers became case managers, dealing with the entire range of services necessary to bring their clients through the AFDC–work training program. The 1981 legislative changes allowed states to give AFDC offices direct oversight of their work-training programs, rather than leaving them under the control of state labor departments.

The states that began to design more complex work-welfare programs needed permission to waive certain AFDC program rules. One of the conditions of the federal waivers was that each state evaluate the effects of its program through an approved research design. The Manpower Demonstration Research Corporation (MDRC), a research organization specializing in the evaluation of employment programs, played a key role in helping many states design and evaluate their work-welfare programs. MDRC was a strong proponent of random assignment evaluation, a technique by which one group of participants is randomly assigned to a "control group" and given no special services beyond what they would normally get as AFDC clients. The remaining participants are assigned to an "experimental group" and given the full range of program services. If the random assignment is done correctly, the control and the experimental groups should have similar characteristics, except that the experimental group receives program services. Any difference in outcome between the two groups—differences in welfare use, in labor market participation, or in wages—can then be ascribed to the effect of the program.[20]

MDRC evaluated a number of state work-welfare programs using a random assignment experimental design. The results showed clear positive results in terms of employment gains for program participants. The cost-benefit evaluations indicated that states more than covered the cost of the programs through lower AFDC costs. These results were considered extremely believable by other researchers because of the use of random assignment in the evaluation.

The results from these evaluations are complex and vary somewhat from state to state.[21] At least three main findings emerge, however. First, even rather minimal efforts at job search assistance seemed to produce employment and income gains among female AFDC recipients. These effects persisted and even grew over the three years after the program. In Arkansas, for instance, by the end of the third year after the program, the employment rate among work-welfare program participants was 6.2 percentage points higher than the 18.3 percent employment rate among nonparticipants; participants' earnings were 31 percent ($337) higher (Gueron and Pauly, 1991, table 1.1, app. table B).

Second, the benefit-cost evaluations indicated that the returns from the programs were greater than the costs from a government budget perspective. Because these programs only provided limited services, the costs per participant were relatively low, ranging from $102 to $953 (Gueron and Pauly, 1991, app. table A-1). These costs were typically recouped through reductions in AFDC and other transfer payments.

Third, although the results indicate a clear return to running these programs, average income gains are relatively low in absolute terms. The increase in earnings for program participants was significant, but it was on the order of $150 to $600 per year in most states. Almost all of these gains occurred because of increases in work hours rather than in wage rates. This is perhaps not surprising, given that few of these programs provided extensive additional training and education. (A few programs that did were much more expensive. For some groups, these more extensive programs produced gains that appeared to result from real increases in skills and wages.) Thus none of these programs provided a solution to poverty and need among female-headed households. They improved women's labor market involvement, decreased women's reliance on welfare, and created small increases in total family income. There is no evidence that these programs moved many families out of poverty.

The positive evaluations of these experiments changed the discussion of work incentives by policymakers and analysts. Both those who wanted to pursue the income goal and those who wanted to pursue the employment goal were persuaded that work-welfare programs would be beneficial. Opposition to mandated work programs declined. In 1988 the Congress passed the Family Support Act (FSA), which required that all states establish mandatory work-welfare programs, to be called Job Opportunities and Basic Skills Training (JOBS).[22] All programs were to have certain common elements, but states had substantial leeway in program design. In comparison with the state-run programs of the 1980s, which were largely job search assistance programs, JOBS requirements placed much more emphasis on training and education. JOBS also required states to provide child care subsidies and Medicaid eligibility to women for a year after they left AFDC for employment.

A nationally funded evaluation of JOBS programs is under way, but little information on the effectiveness of this federal mandate is yet available.[23] Evaluation of California's GAIN program, which started before the JOBS mandates but is very similar in design, has found overall increases in employment and earnings and decreases in welfare spending among participants; these gains have continued for two years after program participation (Riccio and Friedlander, 1992; Friedlander, Riccio, and Freedman, 1993). Because GAIN was initiated prior to the passage of the Family Support Act, however, there are several reasons to believe that state programs put in place to meet the JOBS requirements may be somewhat less effective than GAIN or other work-welfare programs run in the 1980s. First, states that ran work-welfare programs on their own initiative in the 1980s may have been particularly committed to them and worked harder at effective implementation. States with little enthusiasm for the federal mandate may implement it far less effectively.

Second, JOBS programs began just as the economy entered a prolonged recession. State budgets were hit particularly hard in the early 1990s, and many states scaled back their original JOBS design and ran quite limited programs. In addition, implementing effective job placement programs for less-skilled workers is difficult when unemployment is rising. By 1993 many states were behind on their performance goals for JOBS and were requesting permission to delay implementation of the requirements.

The discussion of work incentives for welfare recipients has changed remarkably since the early seventies. As more and more women work, providing welfare for women who remain at home has become increasingly unacceptable. With this altered perspective and the perceived success of the states' 1980s experiments with work-welfare programs, the discussion has changed from a focus on incentives, through varying benefit levels, program parameters, and eligibility rules, to a focus on direct services and mandated participation in mutual obligation programs. Between 1990 and 1995 all states must provide an increasing share of their work-eligible AFDC recipients with some form of education, job training, and/or job search activity. Although this law has not yet been fully transformed into policy at the local level, in part because of the recession of the early 1990s, it has set the direction for future efforts.

Given that social and economic changes are continuing to move more women into the labor market, policy efforts designed to supplement and support that trend may be more successful than efforts expended on men, whose labor force participation has steadily fallen. Certainly the trends of the last two decades indicate that low-income women with children who seek public income support will continue to face increasing demands to prepare and search for employment as a condition of assistance.

Employment Service Programs for the Nonwelfare Population

AFDC recipients have been the target of the most policy concern in recent years. Yet a substantial number of families not eligible for AFDC also face problems in the labor market. The steady decline in the labor market participation and wages of less-skilled men indicates the need to consider serious job training and skill enhancement efforts aimed at all disadvantaged adult workers. As of the first year of the Clinton administration, however, general job training and job search assistance programs for the non-AFDC population remained quite limited. This deficiency stems at least in part from our striking lack of knowledge about how to run such programs effectively.

The first major training program enacted in the post–World War II era was the Manpower Development Training Act (MDTA), which began in 1962 as a classroom training program aimed initially at unemployed skilled workers (Ginzberg, 1980). MDTA quickly evolved into a program focused on less-skilled and minority workers and also came to include programs aimed at disadvantaged youth. MDTA was replaced by the Comprehensive Employment and Training Act in 1973. CETA was designed to provide on-the-job training for less-skilled workers. It also funded temporary public sector jobs, in the hope that workers would use these as a springboard to private sector employment. At its height in 1977–78, CETA placed over 1 million people in public sector jobs and provided some form of training assistance to another 1.3 million disadvantaged workers.

CETA was terminated in 1982 and replaced with the Job Training Partnership Act. Like CETA, JTPA is designed to offer job training and search assistance to disadvantaged workers, but has less funding and fewer placements. JTPA programs differ from those of CETA in at least two major ways. First, JTPA provides no funds for public sector job creation. It places participants in private sector jobs, on the theory that these jobs offer better opportunities for long-term labor market involvement. Second, JTPA is run not by local governments but by local "private industry councils" (PICs). These councils, composed of representatives from the local private sector, determine what type of training and job placement would be most beneficial to participants and local employers alike. Because PICs have a great deal of discretion in the structure of their program, JTPA programs can be quite different across locations.

By the late 1980s, JTPA programs served a little over 700,000 clients per year, of whom almost half were teenagers. When states began experimenting with expanded work-welfare programs, most states relied on the local JTPA organization to provide training and placement for their work-welfare participants.

After thirty years of job placement and training programs for disadvantaged workers, there is astonishingly little reliable evidence on the effects of these programs, outside that already cited for the AFDC population. This problem exists largely because early evaluation techniques have become discredited with further research. Provisions were made to evaluate the effectiveness of CETA programs on a regular basis. Evaluation results varied somewhat between different years and different sample populations; most studies found small earnings gains on the order of $200 to $600 per year, with larger effects for women than for men (Bassi and Ashenfelter, 1986; Barnow, 1987). There also appeared to be substantial problems in some locations with displacement of other workers by CETA-funded workers in the public sector employment program. None of these studies used random assignment evaluation techniques, however, and the results depended on a variety of assumptions about the appropriate control group and/or model of the effect of training. A special panel established by the U.S. Department of Labor to review the research evidence on CETA concluded, "the estimates of net impact of CETA are not reliable and . . . the true net impacts of CETA are still open to question" (JTLSR Advisory Panel, 1985).

One job training program run in the late 1970s and aimed explicitly at extremely disadvantaged workers was the National Supported Work Demonstration. Supported Work took ex-drug addicts, long-term AFDC recipients, ex-convicts, and disadvantaged youth and provided them with group counseling and job placement into structured work settings that typically included job training. These programs were evaluated using a random assignment experimental methodology. The results indicated significant gains to the AFDC recipients, some small gains to ex-drug addicts, but zero or insignificant gains to other groups (Hollister, Kemper, and Maynard, 1984). Given the high level of assistance provided to participants in this program, these findings were particularly discouraging. Still, the population served by this program was explicitly chosen to be the least work-ready, and those who participated were more disadvantaged than the average CETA or JTPA participant.

As a result of the problems with the CETA evaluations, the federal government funded a large random assignment evaluation study of JTPA in the mid-1980s. The initial results of this evaluation indicate that JTPA has generally positive and significant effects on the earnings and employment of adult men and women, increasing earnings by about $500 per year and increasing employment by 2 to 3 percentage points (Bloom et al., 1993). The results for out-of-school youth are more disappointing. There is no evidence that this population gained from its participation in JTPA programs. These results are based on earnings and employment levels eighteen months after the start of JTPA training.

Evaluations of a few more limited job training efforts are also available. The Minority Single Female Parent Demonstration provided intensive employment assistance services to its targeted group in four different locations around the country (including AFDC and non-AFDC recipients). The results from a two-and-a-half year follow-up are mixed: participants in two sites show few gains, in one site show gains in employment but not in earnings, and in another site show significant gains in both employment and earnings (Burghardt et al., 1992). Similarly mixed results are emerging from an evaluation of a youth training program known as JOBSTART, run in thirteen different locations around the country. JOBSTART attempted to increase the employment, earnings, and education of seventeen- to twenty-one-year-old high school dropouts. The program successfully increased training and education levels, but four years after the beginning of the program the earnings gains among participants were largely insignificant. There is some indication of increasing gains over time, however, and there was a decrease in AFDC usage among many of the young women (Cave et al., 1993).

Although the evidence is somewhat scattered, at least two conclusions are apparent with regard to job training programs for disadvantaged workers. First, job training programs can produce small and positive effects in people's lives in terms of increased employment and increased income. These findings are most consistent for adult women, but the results of the JTPA evaluation for adult men are encouraging. Data from California's GAIN program are consistent with this JTPA evaluation, showing similar gains for both men and women who participate in job placement and training. Nevertheless, although current research results indicate that ongoing efforts at effective job training programs can promise positive results, no evidence exists that major expansions in job training programs will provide large declines in poverty or substantial increases in employment.

Second, there is still a great deal we don't know about how to run effective job training programs for disadvantaged workers, particularly for men and youth. Current research indicates that the benefits of job training efforts for these populations are at best uncertain. There seems to be a great deal of variance in the effectiveness of programs across localities, for example, which indicates that effectiveness is crucially affected by the quality of local staff members and their implementation procedures. At a minimum, there is a need for more extensive experimentation and evaluation of different training approaches. Despite almost ten years of funding public sector employment in the 1970s, our information on the effectiveness of these and other efforts is seriously flawed.

Particularly in a period when less-skilled adult male workers are experiencing significant wage declines and related declines in labor market participation, the lack of a job training program for disadvantaged male workers that makes a large difference in their labor market participation or earnings levels is discouraging. Certainly the lack of documented success in this area is one reason that policymakers have been reluctant to fund major expansions of job training programs aimed broadly at the disadvantaged population. Efforts to encourage states, localities, and the private sector to experiment with and seriously evaluate a variety of alternative job training efforts for the non-AFDC population might greatly increase the confidence of policymakers that effective job training efforts can be designed.

Tax Policy and Work

Transfer programs and job training and placement programs affect work effort by affecting the amount of total income—either from the labor market or from the government—that is potentially available to a family. Tax policy affects work effort by altering how much of that income a family actually gets to keep and spend on its own needs. The 1980s witnessed two major tax reforms, in 1981 and 1986, ongoing increases in Social Security taxes, and, in the early 1990s, a major expansion in the Earned Income Tax Credit, designed to increase work incentives for low-wage workers.[24] All of these changes might be expected to influence the returns from work available to less-skilled workers and to affect their employment effort. The net effect of the changes to be discussed was to eliminate federal tax payments for a substantial number of poor families. In 1986, at the point of major tax reform, a family of four whose earnings were at the poverty level lost over 10 percent of its income to federal income and Social Security taxes. By 1992 a family of four whose earnings were at the poverty level paid no federal taxes (U.S. House of Representatives, 1992, p. 1482).

Federal Income Tax Parameter Changes
The lack of inflation indexing in the federal tax system produced "bracket creep" that steadily increased the income tax burden on poor families through the mid-1980s (Blank and Blinder, 1986): family incomes (but not their purchasing

power) generally rose with inflation; because the standard deduction and personal exemption did not increase with inflation, many families were pushed into higher tax brackets. The 1986 tax reform substantially raised the standard deduction and the personal exemption, reducing the number of poor families that owed federal income taxes. Both tax parameters are now indexed to inflation, to ensure that their value will not erode in the future.

Social Security Tax Changes

Offsetting the legislated increase in the standard deduction and the personal exemption has been the steady rise of Social Security taxes, which are levied on all earned income up to a maximum well above the median income. In 1992 a low-income worker paid 7.65 percent of his or her earnings into Social Security, up from 6.13 percent in 1980.

Low-income individuals and families without children benefited from the income tax reforms, but they have ended up paying about the same share of earned income to the federal government as they did before the reforms because Social Security tax increases have offset the federal income tax changes. For families with children, the tax gains have been more substantial, largely because of the expansion in the EITC.

Earned Income Tax Credit

The most dramatic changes in tax liability for low-income families have occurred because of the expansion of the EITC, first enacted in 1975. For low-income families with children, the EITC provides a supplement to earnings, through either a tax reduction or (for those who owe no taxes) a refundable tax credit.[25] In 1993 a family with a child under age eighteen and total earnings under $7,520 received from the government an additional $.176 for every $1 earned, which thus supplemented wages to low-income families through the tax system. When earnings reached $7,520, the family received a supplement of $1,324 (.176 multiplied by $7,520). The family continued to receive a constant supplement of $1,324 until its earnings reached $11,840. After $11,840, the supplement was reduced at a rate of $.1257 for every $1 earned. The break-even point, when the supplement went to zero, occurred at $22,370 of earned income.

Major legislative expansions in 1993 brought even bigger changes, phased in through 1996, when low-wage earners with two or more children are scheduled to receive a supplement equal to 40 percent of the first $8,425 in earnings, for a maximum supplement of $3,370; for those with one child, that supplement is 34 percent of the first $6,000. Some credit is available for families with two or more children until earnings reach $27,000. As of 1994, low-wage nonelderly adults without children also have access to EITC subsidies (Leonard and Greenstein, 1993). This revision substantially expands the cost of the EITC and the number of lower-middle income earners who are eligible to receive it, but it also produces a major expansion in the rewards to working.

Like the work-welfare programs of the 1980s, the EITC has been popular in Congress in part because it promises to meet both the income goal and the employment goal. For those out of the labor market or working very little, the EITC encourages greater work effort by increasing the returns to work. Because these wage gains accrue entirely to the family (there is no offsetting reduction of other benefits), there is a real increase in income, as well. Although no actual data are currently available, simulations indicate that about 10 percent of those poor families eligible for the EITC escape poverty because of the EITC supplement (Scholz, 1990).

Supporters of the EITC often stress that it encourages work effort by increasing the effective wage rate received by workers whose earnings are low. A careful look at the structure of the EITC, however, reveals that this claim is only partially accurate (Hoffman and Seidman, 1990). For those who are out of the labor market entirely or who have very low earnings the EITC presents a clear incentive to increase work hours, because the tax credit raises the effective wage that a person is receiving. For persons who are earning enough to receive a constant supplement or for those whose supplement is being slowly taxed away as their earnings increase, the effect of the EITC on work effort may be negative. The question of whether the EITC increases or decreases work effort thus depends on how many individuals are in which part of the earnings distribution. When the EITC is expanded to groups higher in the income distribution, the number of people who are in the constant or declining part of the supplement increases, which will not increase work effort. There are no existing studies of the impact of EITC on work effort.[26] Current recipients may be persons who would work even in the absence of the EITC.

One reason the EITC may have only small effects on labor supply is lack of information about the program. Some eligible workers may not know about the EITC and hence not receive it. Others may not find out how much they will receive until they have filed their tax returns. In addition, the somewhat complex structure of subsidies under the EITC may make the incentives within the program difficult for even its recipients to understand. And because the program is run through the tax system and is entirely unrelated to other job training and income transfer programs, which are run out of local welfare and employment offices, the government officials whom most poor people are in contact with (caseworkers) are not well informed about the EITC. This lack of knowledge may further reduce the extent to which recipients understand this program. It is thus quite possible that the EITC, though providing more spendable income for low-income families, may have only a small effect on their labor market behavior.

The EITC is often not viewed as a major budget item because it does not require direct expenditures (except for those persons receiving refundable credits) and only involves the noncollection of certain tax revenues. Yet the amount of tax income forgone plus refunds paid through the EITC is estimated at $10.7 billion in 1992, a substantial amount (U.S. House of Representatives, 1992, p. 1019). This cost is as real to the federal budget as the cost of paying out AFDC dollars to women with children. The lack of good evaluation research on a program as large as the EITC is extremely unfortunate.

For families with children, the effect of the EITC on tax burdens has been substantial. The federal income tax threshold—the income level at which a family first begins to pay taxes—for low-income families with children is at a post–World War II high. Because of the federal income tax changes, including the expansion of the EITC, a family of four did not pay federal income taxes in 1992 until its income had passed 129 percent of the poverty line. Ten years earlier, in 1982, the tax threshold occurred at 88 percent of the poverty line (U.S. House of Representatives, 1992, p. 1480). The result is a clear reduction in tax burden and enhanced returns from work, which should result in greater work effort.

The EITC is particularly effective when interacted with the minimum wage. The minimum wage in 1991 rose to $4.25 per hour, up from $3.35 in the 1980s; at this rate a full-time worker would earn $8,500, below the poverty line for a family of two or more. Compared with earlier levels, the minimum wage is currently relatively low; adjusted for inflation, it is at a lower level than in the 1950s, 1960s, or 1970s. Raising the minimum wage would increase earnings among less-skilled workers, but this strategy is problematic. First, the minimum wage is badly targeted as an antipoverty device. The majority of minimum wage workers are second or third earners in middle-income households. Minimum wage expansions are therefore not very redistributive in their impacts (Horrigan and Mincy, 1993). Second, there are disemployment effects to the minimum wage; as wages for less-skilled workers rise, employers hire fewer of them. This problem may be less serious, however. Disemployment is largest among teenagers, who are the group of minimum wage workers least likely to come from poor households and about whose unemployment there may be less policy concern. In addition, recent studies indicate these disemployment effects to be small or nonexistent, at least in the short run and at current levels of the minimum wage (Card, 1992a, b; Katz and Krueger, 1992).

By itself, the minimum wage is not high enough to guarantee a worker escape from poverty, but the minimum wage makes it easier for the EITC to move poor families toward the poverty line. At a lower minimum wage, the EITC would have to be much larger in order to raise workers to the poverty line. The "phase-out" of the EITC would have to be much steeper, or eligibility for the EITC would be at a much higher point in the income distribution. Either of these program changes would increase the work disincentive effects of the EITC at higher income levels. The combination of the EITC and the minimum wage together thus provide a more effective antipoverty policy than either one alone.

Other Tax Incentives for Employment

At least two other tax programs assist employment. The Dependent Care Credit is available as a deduction from federal taxes of up to $4,800 in child care expenses for low-income families ($2,400 for one-child families). This credit is not refundable, however. Most poor families with children therefore do not benefit from it, because few of them owe tax liabilities.[27]

The Targeted Jobs Tax Credit (TJTC) is available to employers who hire low-wage workers from certain target groups. Employers' taxes can be reduced by up to $2,400 per worker, essentially subsidizing the wages paid to these workers and theoretically making it more attractive for employers to hire them. Many employers who could collect on the TJTC do not, and there is evidence that eligibility for such programs stigmatizes workers in the labor market rather than helping them (Burtless, 1985). There is little research evidence that the TJTC has stimulated increases in the employment of disadvantaged workers.

.   .   .

To summarize the effect of tax changes on work effort among low-income families is difficult. Few good studies directly relate tax changes to labor market changes. Gary Burtless (1991b) and Barry Bosworth and Burtless (1992) conclude that the tax changes of the 1980s had, at best, a small positive effect on the labor supply of low-income persons. The rate changes and the parameter changes in the income tax system that benefited the poor have been largely offset by expanding Social Security rates. The EITC, although it has expanded substantially in the past five years, may have mixed effects on labor supply. It may also be so complex and so poorly understood that few people have adjusted their work efforts in response to it.

Developing an Effective Employment Strategy

What primary issues must be faced by any program that is designed both to increase labor market opportunities and to reduce poverty among its clients? The role of the economic environment, the importance of employment-related services, the mix of private sector and public sector responsibilities, and the politics and budgeting of employment programs must all be considered. Some of these factors involve direct employment services; others operate through the parameters of the welfare and tax systems.

The Role of the Economic Environment

Employment service programs and work incentives are crucially dependent upon job availability. A strategy that moves people into the labor market will only work if jobs are available. In the course of business cycles, therefore, there will always be times when employment strategies are less effective because of high unemployment rates. For this reason alone, employment and work enhancement programs can never be complete antipoverty strategies in themselves.

As already mentioned, the U.S. economy has shown long-term strength in job creation. At an aggregate level, the simple availability of jobs is not likely to be a restriction after the economy recovers from the recession of the early 1990s. In certain local areas, however, job availability may continue to cause serious problems. Job training programs or work incentive enhancements may have much smaller benefits in rural areas, where fewer jobs are available. In areas where public and private transportation options are limited, such as very poor urban ghetto neighborhoods, lack of access to available jobs may similarly limit employment (Kasarda, 1988). Although major job creation efforts, such as a national public sector job creation program, are probably not needed, more limited and targeted job creation programs may be useful for certain areas (particularly inner city or rural areas) or populations.[28]

Of much greater importance in the current economic environment is the question of what types of jobs are available and whether these jobs pay enough to allow a full-time worker's family to escape from poverty. The relatively small earnings gains among women in even the most successful work-welfare programs are an indication of the low earnings opportunities available to many less-skilled women. The declining wages available to less-skilled men imply that even in families headed by men low wages may limit the success of public efforts to promote work.

The declining demand for less-skilled workers is driving the decline in wages. The similarity of this trend to economic changes that are occurring in Canada as well as in a number of western European economies suggests that U.S. policy can probably do little to reverse it.[29] At least in the foreseeable future, less-skilled workers cannot expect substantial improvements in their real market earnings opportunities, and some (especially men) may even see further declines.

If current wage trends cannot be readily reversed (and I see no evidence that this can be done), then the role of policy must be either to upgrade the skills of the work force or to cushion the effects of these changes through policies that supplement low wages and "make work pay" for less-skilled workers. One implication of this is that an "employment strategy," aimed at simply getting people into jobs, may be increasingly incomplete as an antipoverty policy. Some combination of job placement assistance and earnings supplements, such as the EITC or child care subsidies, may be necessary to raise families above the poverty line.

The Importance of Employment-Related Services

Many poor families face multiple problems when considering entry into the labor market. They may need acceptable and affordable child care, there may be family members with health problems, or they may lack adequate transportation to job locations. The extent to which a work program needs to deal with these issues as well as the more traditional questions of job placement and job training is an open question. On the one hand, the EITC supplements earnings with additional dollars on the presumption that when work is attractive enough, people will resolve these other problems. On the other hand, the design of the JOBS program assumes that AFDC recipients need assistance with both job placement and related services such as child care.

For some groups, the nonwage aspects of employment are crucial. Particularly if the number of poor single-parent families continues to grow, attention to subsidiary employment services will remain important for policymakers. Four specific types of "related services" will be particularly crucial.

1. It is possible that major reforms in the availability of health insurance to all persons, particularly low-wage workers, might change work behavior. At present, the lack of health insurance in many low-wage jobs makes work a less-desirable option than public assistance (which provides medical coverage through the Medicaid program) for families that face sizable medical costs.

2. Major subsidies to either the purchasers or providers of child care for low-income families could make work look far more attractive to low-income women with young children.

3. Changes in the location of low-income or subsidized housing, such as an increase in housing vouchers, could improve the job availability and job contacts of low-income (and particularly minority) families. Research has indicated that AFDC recipients who are relocated from public housing to middle-income suburban locations do better in terms of future employment and income than those who are relocated to poorer city locations (Rosenbaum and Popkin, 1991).

4. Attention to public transportation systems, both in routing and in cost structure, could improve access to employment and raise the returns from employment for some families.

Some work-welfare programs have tried to coordinate services in these areas. States are mandated to provide assistance with child care, health care, and transportation expenses for JOBS program participants. Any woman who gets a job and leaves AFDC must, by federal mandate, be guaranteed an extra year of eligibility for Medicaid benefits and child care assistance. But even initiatives that address these issues separately (such as health care reform) without tying them directly to employment programs may well strengthen people's willingness and ability to pursue employment.

Public Sector and Private Sector Responsibilities

Because most employment occurs in the private sector, analysts debate how responsibilities for employment and work-incentive programs should be shared between the government and the private sector. In job training and job search programs, for example, the private sector has a strong interest in ensuring that workers are trained for jobs that the private sector needs filled. But even in other work-incentive programs, there are questions about sectoral responsibility.

On the one hand, private sector involvement is crucial in the design of effective training and job search programs. On the other hand, the private sector can never be solely responsible for the job training of disadvantaged workers. First, the private sector is typically unwilling to invest in the training of high-risk workers. Government subsidies to induce private sector participation are often necessary. Second, the private sector, because of its need to show an economic return, often is not willing to conduct evaluations of government-sponsored training programs, to coordinate programs, or to provide any of the subsidiary services that low-income families may need. The government has a clear role here in the coordination and evaluation of programs and the provision of affiliated services. Third, the private sector may be less able and willing to maintain programs during recessionary periods. Only the federal government is equipped to provide counter-cyclical funding to ensure that employment and training programs continue in difficult economic times.[30]

The ideal is to create programs that rely upon the strengths of each sector. The government sector may be best at redistributing funds, generating political support, and coordinating and evaluating overall programs; the private sector may best understand the near-term market demand for labor and be best able to choose the types of training, skills, and jobs toward which less-skilled workers should be steered. In a time of declining demand for these workers, the public sector faces a challenge in providing sufficient incentive to motivate the private sector to participate in employment and training programs for this group.

The Politics and Budgeting of Employment Programs

Work-incentive programs cost money up-front, but only return that money over time and in a somewhat diffuse fashion. Job training programs require funding for participants at an early stage. If the program successfully generates more work effort, the returns accrue through increased taxes, decreased transfer expenditures, and higher economic productivity. But these returns are received by many agencies and groups; the costs are often paid by only a few.

The cost structure of employment programs poses two problems. First, cost sharing among the parties that benefit is crucial because of the large initial costs involved and because the benefits of effective employment programs are spread broadly across the public and private sectors. Those programs that are funded out of general revenues, such as AFDC or the EITC, share costs through the tax system. But equitable cost sharing in direct service programs is difficult to arrange. The specifics of cost-matching provisions between the federal and the state governments for the JOBS program, for example, are crucial in determining the types of programs states operate.

Second, because employment programs require substantial advance investment before they show returns, they appear to be a risky investment. Some amount of political "selling" may be required in order to persuade the private sector and state and local governments to take the risks inherent in making the initial investment in employment programs. In either case, there is a major role for the federal government to play in encouraging and supporting employment programs. Its broader taxing authority and potentially greater ability to consider long-run returns make its involvement crucial.

Policy Recommendations

There have been a number of substantial changes over the last two decades in the policies designed to expand work opportunities and move poor families toward economic self-sufficiency. What follow are explicit policy recommendations for the near future and a few cautions as well.

1. Continued attention to a strong underlying macro-economy. Any employment strategy depends heavily upon a strong demand for new workers. It benefits no one to run employment programs that simply displace current workers with subsidized workers from government employment programs. Spending dollars to encourage work will produce little in the way of results in the midst of recession or in areas where jobs are disappearing. A healthy macro-economy with long-term expanding employment is probably necessary for an effective employment strategy to work.

Inevitably, there will be times when the business cycle turns down. When this occurs, the private sector will have little incentive to provide training or jobs to disadvantaged workers. In these periods public sector spending on employment programs should perhaps be designed countercyclically. Job creation programs in the public or private sector, for example, will be more useful in economic down-turns. Such programs could be limited to a few target populations in boom times, but be designed to expand when the unemployment rate goes above a certain level.

2. Educational reform, aimed at improving the skills of today's children, to prevent future problems of less-skilled workers whose wages are inadequate to provide self-sufficiency. The best program to attack the root cause of low wages among less-skilled workers is one that decreases the number of less-skilled work-ers in the economy. The share of workers with low levels of education has been steadily declining, but close to 40 percent of nonelderly adults in the bottom 20 percent of the income distribution are still without a high school degree. Too many public schools—particularly in urban areas—provide inadequate education and inadequate job market preparation to their students. I leave the discussion of effective educational reform to Richard Murnane in Chapter 11. But the best long-term response to the declining demand for less-skilled workers is policy that promotes skill training and effective schooling for today's children.

3. Serious efforts to ensure the broad and effective implementation of JOBS, expansion of JTPA, and experimentation with job training programs for youth and adult men. Programs known to be effective should be strongly supported. There is good research evidence that education, job training, and job placement programs aimed at AFDC recipients can make a modest but significant difference in their labor market attachment. The effective implementation of additional such programs is needed as soon as possible. The recession of the early 1990s has slowed down the implementation of JOBS and forced many states to scale back their original plans. The federal government should consider providing additional financial incentives for states to run more extensive programs, as the economy begins to recover.

Similarly, the evidence now indicates that the JTPA program is also producing employment and earnings gains for its adult participants. Given the problems fac-ing less-skilled men in this economy, the expansion of JTPA should be consid-ered. There is little reliable evidence on the effectiveness of different types of training programs for non-AFDC recipients. But the federal government could provide financial incentives for states, localities, and private sector firms to experiment with a range of demonstration training programs for less-skilled workers, particularly youth and less-skilled adult men. Localities could be allowed waivers that would permit them to run alternative types of training programs in place of JTPA; such endeavors could be undertaken with federal oversight in a process similar to that used to allow states to run experimental work-welfare programs in the 1980s. It is crucial that any such experiments be subject to rigorous evaluation.

4. Create stronger work incentives for those on AFDC. Because of funding limitations and implementation problems, many AFDC recipients will continue to lack access to substantive job training and employment programs. It seems foolish to continue to confront these clients with a one-to-one reduction in benefits should they go to work. Two options are possible: either the earnings disregard of $30/month should be raised ($120/month, the inflation-adjusted value of the $30 disregard established in 1967, might be a reasonable level) and/or the benefit reduction rate should be lowered back near its previous rate of 67 percent. Either change would at least provide an incentive for women who are unable to work full-time to still work part-time while receiving some AFDC assistance. For those women who can work full-time and leave AFDC, this increase in the benefit reduction rate should not retard their movement into full-time work if JOBS programs are implemented effectively.

5. Maintain the current level of EITC benefits; do better advertising and outreach for the EITC; fund serious evaluation of the effects of the EITC. Given the problem of declining wages among less-skilled workers, a wage supplement like the EITC provides better work incentives than many other programs for those who are out of the labor market. It is not clear that many families understand the real advantages of the EITC, because the program is so complex. The IRS should work through local welfare agencies, employment offices, and housing authorities to advertise the advantages of the EITC more effectively. The subsidy provided by the government for every dollar of work among low-wage workers will only stimulate more work effort if these workers understand the incentive.

Although it is true that the EITC may have negative effects on work effort among workers who are at the declining part of the subsidy, I would rank this as a less-important effect than the initial incentive the EITC provides to enter the labor market and receive some earnings. Getting those who are entirely out of the labor force into some contact with jobs and employment is worthwhile, even if the cost is slight decreases in hours among those who are already working a substantial number of hours.

6. Expand a variety of employment-related services, not only because of their direct benefits, but also because of their effects on work behavior. Among the list of reforms that should be considered are expanding and making refundable the

Dependent Care Tax Credit,[31] altering housing subsidy programs in order to encourage locational choice outside of urban ghetto areas, and paying attention to the routing and pricing of public transportation systems so that areas where less-skilled workers live are linked to areas where low-skill jobs are available. Major reform in the health insurance system of this country, so that all persons have access to health insurance, is on the agenda of the Clinton administration. All of these programs obviously need to be evaluated on a variety of bases other than their impact on work incentives, but their work-behavior effects should be seen as part of the justification for considering such efforts.

7. *Target special programs on young workers in high unemployment areas, particularly inner-city and rural areas.* Special measures may be needed to address the extremely high unemployment rates among out-of-school youth, especially minority youth in ghetto areas. Among the programs that should be considered are public sector job and job training programs, aimed at providing work experience and training to young workers who may have difficulty finding private sector jobs due to discrimination or lack of work skills; apprenticeship programs that link youth in isolated inner-city areas with jobs and job mentors in nearby suburban or downtown areas where jobs are more available; and school-to-work transition programs, for high school students who are not college bound, that link employers and students through internship and job placement programs. In its first year the Clinton administration spoke about several of these programs in a preliminary way. A national youth service program, providing work experience and giving participants credit toward future educational expenses, was started in the summer of 1993. If this program expands, it should be explicitly designed to recruit participants among low-income and inner-city youth.

Several other policies deserve a brief mention. *Increases in the minimum wage* are often proposed to raise the earnings of less-skilled workers and provide a floor for further EITC increases. The current minimum wage of $4.25 is comparatively low when adjusted for inflation, relative to historical levels. Small increases in the minimum wage, to perhaps $4.75 or $5.00 an hour, may be useful and may have few negative side effects. But this policy change should receive lower priority than those already discussed. The majority of minimum wage workers do not come from poor households. Given that only a limited amount of political energy and capital is available to enact new programs, analysts and lawmakers need to focus on policies that are targeting the poor more efficiently. Moreover, because the declining demand for less-skilled workers is driving down wages in many less-skilled jobs, major increases in the minimum wage could produce much larger disemployment effects than those measured so far.

The Clinton administration is also discussing *time limits or restrictions on long-term AFDC eligibility,* forcing people off dependence on transfer dollars. If "time-limited welfare" means decreasing AFDC benefits and eligibility after a certain period, there is little evidence that such a strategy will benefit the families involved or produce increases in overall income (the eligibility cuts following OBRA did not). The experience of work-welfare programs indicates that the wages and job options available to less-skilled women are extremely limited; increased hours of work do not produce large economic returns. Female heads of households, in particular, face complex child care issues, and the welfare of their children could be seriously harmed by further declines in AFDC benefits and any arbitrary termination of welfare support. Terminating AFDC may meet the work goal, but there is little evidence that it would meet the income goal or improve economic well-being among families.

If "time-limited welfare" means an AFDC program that significantly increases its efforts to involve participants in job search and employment training after they have been recipients for a certain period of time, however, such an effort could well produce positive results. The program might, for example, involve increasing JOBS services to AFDC recipients after one year on AFDC. This definition of time-limited welfare is one that requires real inputs of money and services to longer-term AFDC recipients; additional budget dollars will be needed.

It should be obvious, indeed, that the overall agenda just proposed would require substantial resources. Expanded AFDC tax incentives, expansions of the EITC to persons without children, serious reform of the public schools, and more extensive implementation of JOBS are all programs requiring more tax dollars. The hope is that investing dollars in these programs will produce a return—greater work hours among the low-income population, which in the long run will reduce transfer payments and increase tax revenues. Evidence already indicates that the set of programs recommended here can produce benefits that can outweigh their costs if they are effectively implemented. The problem is providing the initial political impetus to spend the money before the benefits are visible.

The "employment strategy" is a crucial one for U.S. antipoverty policy. The strategy resonates with the cultural values of the country, and it is also an approach that for some groups will produce long-term reductions in poverty and economic need by permanently moving them into greater labor market involvement. Employment incentives have been substantially increased in several major programs over the past decade, through the JOBS programs, through the expanded EITC credits for those entering the labor force, and through the ongoing reduction in the real purchasing value of AFDC benefits.

Yet "employment strategies," though an important component of any antipoverty program, are not going to be the solution to poverty. There is probably little we can do to reverse the trend of declining real wages for many less-skilled workers; this trend may dominate any policy effort to increase work incentives. The effects of serious job training and employment programs have also been discouragingly small for most workers. Even the women on AFDC who clearly benefit from these programs do not show large income gains.

At best, employment programs can serve as one piece of a larger overall strategy to fight poverty. In an economy where many poor families have difficulty reaching economic self-sufficiency even after entering the labor market, more and more poor individuals may choose to exist outside of the legitimate labor market. In this sense, ongoing attention to work effort and the work goal may be crucially important in the years ahead. But in order to decrease economic need and meet the income goal, it may be necessary to accept that the best policy is a mix of programs that ensures adequate income through a combination of public assistance and earnings.

No "magic wand" exists that can be waved over people whose skills are limited, whose schooling may have been inadequate, and who have experienced past failures in the labor market. The best effort we can make is to prevent the children of today and tomorrow from finding themselves in this position when they are adults. But our inability to solve poverty through work and employment programs does not mean that these programs should not be run. We have ample evidence that these programs can make improvements in people's lives, encouraging them to work more, earn more, and become more integrated into the economic mainstream.

Single-Mother Families, Economic Insecurity, and Government Policy

IRWIN GARFINKEL AND SARA MCLANAHAN

The conditions under which most single-mother families subsist in the United States and the challenge these families pose for policymakers are topics of great importance to the nation's future.[1] More than half of the current generation of children will live with a single mother before reaching age eighteen, and many of these children will spend their entire childhood with a mother who is single. Most mother-only families will experience heavy doses of economic and social insecurity, which are known to be harmful to children's future well-being. Given that so many children are affected and given that the effects are so important, society has a strong interest in reducing the insecurity of single mothers and their children.

Government can reduce economic insecurity, but doing so will increase dependence on government. It will also increase the prevalence of mother-only families, by lowering the costs of family dissolution. Whether to give priority to reducing economic insecurity or to reducing dependence and prevalence is a major policy dilemma.

The choice between priorities involves conflicts among values fundamental to American culture: community, compassion, self-reliance, and self-interest. Values of compassion and community tell us that we should make single parenthood more secure. Values of self-reliance and short-term self-interest suggest that we should make it more austere, thereby discouraging dependence and prevalence while minimizing costs. "Long-term" self-interest, however, may point in the direction of reducing economic insecurity. Reducing insecurity would be called for if the relationship between insecurity and children's future well-being turned out to be strong, while the relationship between government support and prevalence and dependence turned out to be weak. The choice also depends upon answers to factual questions, such as, What is the extent of insecurity? How serious are the ill effects on children? How effective are government measures in reducing insecurity? To what extent do government benefits lead to increases in dependence and prevalence? We seek to reconcile the debate over values and choices by answering these questions and by proposing alternative policies that minimize the trade-off between reducing insecurity and reducing dependence and prevalence.

Economic and Social Insecurity

First we address three questions: How widespread and severe is the social and economic insecurity of single mothers and their children? What are the proximate causes of economic insecurity? Can government do a better job of reducing insecurity than it is currently doing?

Insecurity Is Widespread and Severe

Children who live in mother-only families are exposed to high levels of economic and social insecurity. About half of these children live in families with incomes below the poverty level, and nearly three-quarters live in families with incomes less than 1.75 times the poverty line (U.S. Bureau of the Census, 1991a). Low income is only the most extreme form of economic insecurity. Income instability is another. Most single mothers who have been divorced experience a large drop in income, even if they do not fall below the poverty line. Researchers have found that on average the postdivorce income of a single mother is about 60 percent of her predivorce income (Duncan and Hoffman, 1985; Holden and Smock, 1991). Divorce introduces other forms of insecurity as well. When a marriage breaks up, women and children undergo changes that involve the loss of social status as well as of family members and friends. Changes in residence are perhaps the most common form of social instability in newly formed mother-only families. One study showed that about 38 percent of divorced mothers and their children change residence during the first year after a divorce (McLanahan, 1983). This change not only requires adjustment to a new neighborhood and living conditions but may also mean the loss of important social networks and support.

Changes in employment are common for women who are recently divorced. In an effort to reestablish her predivorce standard of living, a divorced mother may enter the labor force for the first time or increase the number of hours she works outside the home. Greg Duncan and Saul Hoffman (1985) have shown that the proportion of mothers who worked one thousand or more hours per year increased from 51 percent before divorce to 73 percent afterward. Changes in employment are stressful for mothers as well as children. If the children are young, new child care arrangements must be made, and both mother and child are likely to experience uncertainty about the situation.

Economic and social insecurity has direct implications for the mental health of mothers and children. Research on stressful life events indicates that changes in social roles or status may lead to increases in psychological distress and anxiety and to a sense of helplessness and hopelessness. Undesirable and involuntary changes are thought to be the most stressful, particularly when they involve the disruption of social networks and support systems. Not surprisingly, epidemiological surveys show that single mothers report substantially higher rates of anxiety and depression than do married women and men, and facility utilization statistics show that mother-only families with children consume a disproportionate share of community mental health services (Guttentag, Salassin, and Belle, 1980). A good deal of the variation in psychological distress appears to be caused by economic insecurity.

Perhaps the most far-reaching consequence of family disruption is its effect on children's well-being. Numerous studies conducted during the past decade show that children who grow up in mother-only families—whether headed by divorced or never-married mothers—are disadvantaged in a number of ways in comparison with children who grow up with both parents (McLanahan and Booth, 1989; McLanahan and Sandefur, 1994). The former are less likely to graduate from high school, are more likely to have a child while still in their teens and to give birth out of wedlock, and are less likely to become attached to the labor force. Although some of these disadvantages are due to differences in family characteristics or individual traits that predate divorce or out-of-wedlock birth, at least part of them are a consequence of single parenthood itself (Manski et al., 1992). In particular, the income drop associated with marital disruption accounts for a substantial part of the difference in educational attainment between children from intact and nonintact families.

Proximate Causes of Economic Insecurity

Economic insecurity in mother-only families has three proximate causes: (1) low earning capacity and absence of economies of scale, (2) inadequate and irregular child support payments from nonresident fathers, and (3) low levels of public support.

Mother-only families experience more economic insecurity than two-parent families in part because they lack economies of scale (two adults can live more cheaply together than apart) and in part because they have a lower earning capacity (one potential worker and child care provider rather than two). These two structural sources of inequality are exacerbated because the single parent in this case is a woman rather than a man. Although the wage gap among full-time workers narrowed during the 1980s, women still earn only 69 percent as much as men (U.S. Bureau of the Census, 1991d).

A second factor contributing to the economic insecurity of single mothers is the absence of child support from nonresident fathers. Only six of ten mothers potentially eligible for child support actually have such an award. Of those who have an award, only half receive the full amount to which they are entitled, and over a quarter receive nothing. The proportion of single mothers with an award varies, depending on marital status. Divorced mothers are those most likely to have an award—eight of ten—whereas never-married mothers are those least likely—three in ten. The failure to establish paternity continues to be a major stumbling block in obtaining a child support award for mothers who were not married to the father of their children. Despite dramatic improvements over the last decade, only 30 percent of children born out of wedlock have paternity established, and without paternity there can be no child support obligation (Nichols-Casebolt and Garfinkel, 1991).

Many observers argue that nonresident fathers do not pay child support because they are poor. Poverty is only part of the problem, however. Many fathers who are delinquent are not poor. Moreover, the argument that fathers cannot afford to pay child support ignores the fact that single mothers are also poor. The issue is not whether fathers can afford to pay; rather, it is what the father's *fair share* is of child-rearing costs and whether he is paying that share. Although no consensus exists on this issue, analyses based on the two most widely used standards indicate that nonresident fathers are contributing less than one-third of their fair share of child support (Garfinkel and Oellerich, 1989). It is difficult to avoid the judgment that a major part of the problem lies with the traditional child support enforcement system, which is run by the local judiciary in a highly discretionary manner (Garfinkel, 1992).

The third proximate cause of economic insecurity in mother-only families is the relatively meager support provided by the government to such families (see Chapters 2 and 3). Most single mothers must be poor in order to qualify for government benefits. Aid to Families with Dependent Children, Food Stamps, Medicaid, and public housing are all income-tested programs. Widows, who account for only 7 percent of single mothers, are an exception. Most widowed mothers are covered by Survivors Insurance (SI), regardless of whether or not they are poor. By drastically reducing public benefits as earnings increase, income-tested programs replace rather than supplement earnings. Welfare programs have been called a "poverty trap" for single mothers because they discourage work (by imposing a high tax rate on earnings) and yet provide insufficient income for a family to live above the poverty line. In effect, single mothers with low earning capacity are forced to choose between (1) working full time, living at or near the poverty line, possibly going without medical care, and having no time for their children; and (2) not working, living below the poverty line, having Medicaid, and having time with their children.

International Perspectives

Single-mother families in the United States are much worse off, relative to the average family, than are single-mother families in other Western industrialized nations. The first column in Table 8.1 shows that 53 percent of mother-only families in the United States have incomes less than 50 percent of median family income. Comparable figures for Canada, France, Germany, the Netherlands, Sweden, and the United Kingdom are 45 percent, 16 percent, 25 percent, 7 percent, 6 percent, and 18 percent.

Although there are differences in the earning capacity and child support receipts of single mothers in the United States compared with those of single mothers in other countries, a larger difference lies in the effectiveness of government transfers in reducing poverty (McLanahan and Garfinkel, 1991; Wong, Garfinkel, and McLanahan, 1993). The second column in Table 8.1 shows that the U.S. in-

Table 8.1 Poverty, effectiveness of government transfers, dependence, and prevalence of single-mother families in seven wealthy nations

Country	Percentage poor (below half of median income)	Percentage reduction in pretransfer poverty by government benefits	Percentage of single mothers dependent on government benefits for half or more of income	Percentage of families with children headed by single mothers
Canada	45	19	39	13
France	16	59	25	12
Germany	25	34	39	11
Netherlands	7	89	75	12
Sweden	6	81	33	12
United Kingdom	18	75	71	13
United States	53	5	38	22

Source: Columns 1–3, Smeeding and Rainwater (1991); column 4, figures for Canada, France, Sweden, and the United States from McLanahan and Garfinkel (1991), for Germany, the Netherlands, and the United Kingdom from Ermisch (1990).

come transfer system reduces pretransfer poverty by only 5 percent.[2] In contrast, other countries do much more for single mothers. Canada reduces pretransfer poverty by 19 percent, France by 59 percent, Germany by 34 percent, Sweden by 81 percent, the Netherlands by 89 percent, and the United Kingdom by 75 percent. Mother-only families fare much better in the Netherlands and Sweden, and to a lesser extent in France and the United Kingdom, than in the United States because the governments of those countries bear a much greater share of child-rearing costs.

The United States is the only industrialized nation in the world that does not provide cash allowances for all children. Instead, the United States grants a deduction of about $2,300 per child for the purposes of calculating federal income tax liability. The deduction is worth about $300 per year to taxpayers in the lowest bracket, about $700 to taxpayers in the top bracket, and is worth nothing to families whose incomes are so low that they owe no taxes. Similarly, although every other nation has some form of national health insurance, thus far the major United States health care program for families with children, Medicaid, limits nearly all of its benefits to families headed by single mothers receiving AFDC benefits (see Chapter 10). Finally, as we will discuss in a later section, the United States spends much less on day care than other industrialized nations, especially France and Sweden, and this too has important implications for earning capacity.

The Prevalence and Dependence of Mother-Only Families

We now examine the prevalence and economic dependence of single mothers and the role of government in encouraging both.

Prevalence

The proportion of families headed by single mothers rose gradually during the 1950s and sharply after 1960. Whereas in 1960 about 8 percent of all families with children were headed by single mothers, by 1990 the figure was nearly 25 percent. The proportion of children who will ever live in a mother-only family is even larger: demographers estimate that about half of all children born in the 1980s will do so before reaching age eighteen—45 percent of white, non-Hispanic Americans and 85 percent of African Americans (Bumpass, 1984). The median length of time spent in a mother-only family is about six years. For children born to unmarried mothers, it is over ten years.

The composition of mother-only families has also changed dramatically during the past three decades. In 1960 a majority of single mothers were divorced and separated, a substantial proportion were widowed, and only a small proportion were never married. Today divorced mothers still account for the majority of single mothers, but widows account for a negligible proportion, and nearly 40 percent of single mothers have never been married (U.S. House of Representatives, 1991). The shift in composition has implications for children's economic well-being. As noted earlier, children who live with divorced mothers are more likely to have a child support award than children who live with never-married mothers, and children who live with widowed mothers receive much more generous public benefits than do children whose fathers are still alive. Thus the economic vulnerability of single mothers has been growing at the same time that their numbers have been increasing.

Several explanations have been advanced to account for the increase in mother-only families. The four most common are the increase in women's employment opportunities, the decrease in men's employment opportunities, the increase in government assistance, and changing social values. The explanation most relevant to our discussion is the role of government.

Both economic theory and common sense suggest that increasing the economic security of single-parent families will lead to increases in single parenthood. Higher benefits increase the ability of a poor single woman with a child to live independently and to be selective about a new mate. Neither theory nor common sense, however, suggest how large the effect will be.

Compared with increases in employment opportunities for women, decreases for men, and changing social values, government benefits account for a very small portion of the growth of mother-only families.[3] Garfinkel and McLanahan's (1986) review of empirical research in the United States concluded that government transfers reduced remarriage, but appeared to have only a minor effect on divorce and on out-of-wedlock births. The expansion of public assistance and increase in benefits that occurred between 1960 and 1975 accounted for no more than 15 percent of the overall growth in female headship and no more than 30 percent of its increase among the low-income population. Furthermore, although welfare benefits have declined since 1975, female headship has continued to grow. The most recent review of the literature comes to the same conclusion: welfare has had very little effect on female headship (Moffitt, 1992).

This conclusion is consistent with cross-national comparisons of the prevalence of single mothers and the generosity of government benefits. As shown in Table 8.1, the proportions of single-mother families in Canada, France, Germany, the Netherlands, Sweden, and the United Kingdom are all considerably lower than those in the United States,[4] yet these other countries provide more generous government benefits to all families, including those headed by single mothers, than does the United States. The effects on prevalence of differences in generosity of benefits across countries are clearly outweighed by the effects of other differences. These international comparisons undermine the argument that the high prevalence of single parenthood in the United States is attributable to overly generous public aid. The comparisons suggest, rather, that even large increases in the generosity of provision for all families may have only small effects on the prevalence of single parenthood.

Welfare Dependence

Along with changes in family structure, welfare dependence has become a more common experience for children. Because this topic is treated in more detail elsewhere in this volume (see Chapter 4), we provide only a brief summary of relevant points.

Over the years a large proportion of families headed by single mothers have been dependent on the government—37 percent in 1967, 62 percent in 1975, and 42 percent in 1987 (Moffitt, 1992). During the months that a family receives welfare, most of its income comes from the government. Single mothers who receive welfare can thus be said to be highly dependent, at least while they are receiving aid. As already noted above, income-tested programs such as AFDC encourage dependence by imposing a high tax rate on any earnings that a woman receives while she is on welfare. Single mothers who receive welfare are thus unlikely to work in the legitimate labor market, because working does not improve their standard of living (Edin and Jencks, 1992).

How long do single mothers stay on welfare? Are they dependent for a short or a long time? Are their children likely to be dependent when they grow up? The answer to the first question is that about a third of the families who ever go on AFDC are dependent for eight years or more; another third are dependent for less than three years; and the remaining third are dependent for three to eight years (Ellwood, 1988). It is the first group that policymakers usually refer to when they express concern about long-term dependence. Although this group represents only one-third of the families that ever rely on welfare, it represents two-thirds of the welfare caseload at any point in time.

The answer to the second question is that children who grow up in families that are dependent on welfare are more likely to become welfare recipients themselves than children who grow up in families that do not rely on welfare. This does not mean, however, that welfare dependence in one generation causes dependence in the next generation. As discussed in Chapter 4, intergenerational correlations in poverty, family income, and fathers' occupation are quite high, and therefore we would expect the correlation in welfare to be high as well. If the children of poor parents are more likely to be poor when they grow up, we would expect to find them overrepresented among welfare recipients. This finding would simply indicate that the welfare system was helping those it was intended to help. As for the question of whether parents' welfare use *causes* children's welfare use, the answer is that no one knows. This is a thorny analytical problem, and the data needed to answer the question are not available. The most thorough review of the literature to date concludes that while there may be some causal effect, it is small (Moffitt, 1992).

Why is dependence of single mothers viewed as a problem by so many people? The blind, the disabled, and the poor elderly receive public assistance, and many of them are entirely dependent on government benefits, yet we hear little public discussion about the dependence of these groups. Why are single mothers different? What does this tell us about the dilemma?

Dependence is politically problematic when adults who are expected to work derive the greater part of their income from government benefits for a long period of time. When AFDC was established in 1935, most married mothers did not work outside the home. Thus AFDC was designed to allow poor single mothers, mostly widows, to imitate the child-rearing practices of middle-class married mothers: to stay at home and raise their children.[5] In the 1960s the situation changed dramatically. Married mothers, including mothers with small children, began entering the labor force in ever greater numbers, and conservatives and liberals alike came to believe that single mothers should be encouraged to imitate the behavior of married women once again. In 1962, at the behest of President Kennedy, Congress passed legislation to provide social services to welfare mothers so that they could leave welfare and become independent. In 1967 the federal government tried to induce AFDC mothers to work by creating work incentives within AFDC. When this failed to have much impact, Congress began in 1972 to legislate work requirements for mothers with children over age six. In the early 1980s the Reagan administration rejected the approach of creating work incentives within the AFDC program. Instead, it sought to cut benefits to working mothers and to force nonworking mothers to work in exchange for their benefits. The Family Support Act of 1988 tightened work requirements for mothers with children over age three and provided increased federal funding for services such as job training and day care. Mothers who became employed were offered free child care and free health care for up to one year after leaving welfare.

In sum, the concern over the dependence of welfare mothers is largely due to changes in social norms about women's roles and child-rearing practices. As married mothers increased their labor force participation, public expectations regarding the appropriate behavior of poor single mothers changed as well. Moreover, for the welfare system to discourage work at a time when middle-class mothers were choosing to work outside the home seemed unwise and inefficient.

Can Government Reduce Insecurity and Dependence at the Same Time?

In the United States, the dilemma of whether to minimize economic insecurity or dependence on government aid has generally been resolved in favor of reducing dependence. In order to minimize costs and discourage dependence on the government, the United States restricts eligibility for most benefit programs—AFDC, Food Stamps, Medicaid—to single mothers who are poor, and provides very low levels of assistance to those who qualify. As a result, about half of single mothers get no help at all from the government; the other half receives help, but not enough to lift them over the poverty line.

Between 1950 and the mid-1970s priorities shifted, and cash and in-kind benefits were raised substantially. Poverty rates for families headed by single mothers declined, and welfare caseloads soared. Between the mid-1970s and 1992, however, welfare benefits were either reduced or allowed to erode, and poverty rates increased while dependency declined. As long as the United States relies so heavily on income-tested benefits, it will find it impossible to escape this tradeoff between poverty and dependence.

A key question facing U.S. policymakers in the 1990s is whether a better system for aiding single mothers can be devised—a system that does a better job of reducing poverty and economic insecurity without encouraging dependence.

We can learn a good deal from examining the policies of other countries. The western European countries and Canada spend a greater proportion of their child welfare budget on non-income-tested programs than on income-tested programs. In terms of cash benefits assistance alone, income-tested benefits account for 70 percent of U.S. transfers to families headed by single mothers, compared with 53 percent in Canada, 55 percent in France, 34 percent in Germany, 63 percent in the Netherlands, 45 percent in Sweden, and 51 percent in the United Kingdom (Wong, Garfinkel, and McLanahan, 1993).[6] In addition, all of the other countries have universal health care coverage, while the United States has Medicaid. Universal programs make all mothers a little dependent on government, whereas income-tested programs make a large minority of single mothers 100 percent dependent.

In addition to income testing, the *level* of benefits and the *degree to which they are complementary to work* also affect the extent to which public benefits encourage dependence. The third column in Table 8.1 shows the percentage of single-mother families that receive more than half their income from government benefits. Considering the first and third columns together, it is obvious that reducing poverty does not invariably lead to high levels of dependence. France and Sweden do a much better job than the United States in reducing poverty, but they do not have higher rates of dependence. This is because they invest heavily in day care, which encourages work and discourages dependence. As a consequence most single mothers in these two countries work outside the home and contribute to their own economic support.

Also of interest is the fact that Canada and Germany have dependency rates that are very similar to those in the United States, and yet they do a better job of reducing economic insecurity. Note that the United Kingdom and the Netherlands also do a much better job of reducing insecurity but have higher rates of dependence. Again, the latter two countries rely heavily on income-tested programs but have substantially higher benefits than the United States.

Income Security Policy

Now that many married women work, the American society is no longer willing to support single mothers to stay at home and raise their children. Even as cash and in-kind welfare benefits were raised to unprecedented levels during the 1960s, the nation began enacting legislation to reduce long-term dependence upon welfare.

Yet society has also been unwilling to provide the government supports that are necessary to allow poor single mothers to earn enough to support their families through paid employment. Recently there has been movement toward changing policy so that single mothers are both less dependent and more economically secure. This new movement addresses two of the three proximate causes of low income for single mothers: low earning capacity and inadequate private child support. As of 1993, investments in raising the earning capacity of poor single mothers through work and training programs and facilitating the utilization of earning capacity through child care have been small. Major progress has been achieved in compensating for low earning capacity by means of the Earned Income Tax Credit and in strengthening child support.

Earning Capacity

Efforts to expand employment and training opportunities within the last decade have focused on the welfare system.[7] The Family Support Act of 1988 tightened work requirements for mothers with children over age three and provided increased federal funding for services such as job training and day care. Mothers who become employed are offered free child care and free health care for up to one year after leaving welfare. Although evaluations of work-welfare programs indicate that their benefits exceed their costs, the overall effects on welfare caseloads are modest. The effects on poverty are even smaller (Gueron and Pauly, 1991).

Even these modest gains are unlikely to be realized in the absence of substantial public investments. States must bear 50 percent of the costs of services, and so far have not provided much new funding. Senator Daniel Patrick Moynihan has proposed increasing the federal appropriations for job services within AFDC from $1 billion to $5 billion.

Some have proposed going even further and limiting the time that families can receive cash welfare benefits; after that time, the government would offer work relief jobs rather than cash assistance (Garfinkel and McLanahan, 1986; Ellwood, 1988; National Commission on Children, 1991). Although the Clinton administration had not yet unveiled its welfare reform proposal by late 1993, the President seemed to be leaning in this direction. While campaigning and in his first year of office, he spoke repeatedly of ending welfare as we know it. Work relief has two limitations. First, as Gary Burtless argues in Chapter 3: "For the majority of America's long-term dependent poor to escape poverty, employment programs must be combined with some form of earnings supplement." In the absence of additional supplements to earnings, such as refundable tax credits for children and assured child support benefits, work relief could easily worsen the economic plight of families headed by poor single mothers.

Second, because work relief is more expensive than cash relief per family assisted, it will increase public costs, at least initially. Work relief will be cheaper if it is instituted in an environment where work in the private sector is made more attractive by public benefits that supplement earnings, so that fewer families will find work relief preferable to employment opportunities in the private sector. In short, work relief can only make a positive contribution to both reducing insecurity and dependence simultaneously if it is accompanied by a substantial increase in public investment.

The United States has done more during the past decade to compensate for low earning capacity than it has done to increase it. The major instrument for supplementing earnings is the Earned Income Tax Credit (EITC), a refundable tax credit available to all families with earnings below a certain level. Begun in the 1970s as a means of increasing the earnings of low-wage workers, it was originally viewed as a way of offsetting payroll (Social Security) taxes for poor families. Expanded in 1986 and again in 1990, the credit in 1994 represents a substantial income supplement to families with incomes under $20,000. As part of his long-term budget package, President Clinton proposed and the Congress in 1993 adopted a major expansion of the EITC for families with two or more children (see Chapter 7).

The EITC is attractive, compared with welfare, because of its simplicity and its anonymity. Because it is administered through the income tax system, there is only one form to fill out and families that receive benefits are not stigmatized.

(Even this form, however, and the administration of the EITC have been criticized for being overly complicated.) Moreover, the EITC is popular with the general population because it appears to reward work. A mother with no earnings receives no subsidy. The more a mother earns, up to a certain amount, the more she receives. Expansion of the EITC requires additional expenditures of public funds.

A third way of dealing with the problem of low earning capacity is to subsidize the cost of child care, which is expensive and represents a substantial portion (about 17 percent) of the budgets of the 80 percent of single mothers who pay for child care. Child care represents an even higher portion of the budgets of poor single mothers who pay for it—approximately 23 percent (McLanahan, Garfinkel, and Watson, 1987).

Although the federal government provides several subsidies for child care expenditures, the subsidies encourage a bifurcated system, ignoring the poor while providing the largest subsidy to middle- and upper-middle income families in the form of the dependent care tax credit in the federal income tax. Under this non-refundable tax credit, families can subtract from their tax liability between 20 percent and 30 percent of child care expenditures up to a maximum of $720 for one child and $1,440 for two or more children. For families whose earnings are so low that they owe no taxes, the credit is worth nothing. In 1992 this program accounted for about $2.7 billion of the $5.5 billion in federal expenditures on child care. The next biggest expenditure was $1.9 billion for Head Start, which targets poor children. The Family Support Act of 1988 provides child care support for single mothers who are participating in work and training programs. Under this law, mothers who get a job will receive child care benefits for up to one year after they leave welfare. About $0.5 billion has been allocated to this program. In addition, 1990 legislation provides for federal grants amounting to about $750 million annually to states for child care. A host of other programs also contain minor child care subsidies.

In France and Sweden excellent institutional child care is available to parents of all income levels, and most of its cost is paid from taxes. The costs are quite high. The Swedish child care subsidy for each child is twice as large as the combined value of the Swedish child allowance, housing allowance, and advanced maintenance payment (Garfinkel and Sørensen, 1982). Free child care increases the net (after expenses) wage rate of mothers both by eliminating a major employment expense and by increasing the demand for female labor. By increasing work and wages, the generous provision of child care transcends the dilemma of whether to reduce poverty or dependence. Because child care subsidies complement rather than substitute for earnings, generous government support in France and Sweden does not lead to high levels of dependence on the government. Mothers who make the greatest use of the subsidy have an independent source of income.

Some have proposed increasing the value of the child care credit and making it refundable, meaning payable if the credit amount exceeds taxes owed (Robins, 1990a). Others have recommended giving schools the responsibility for child care for children above age three and enacting paid parental leave programs to ensure care by parents during the first year of life (Zigler, 1989; Kamerman, 1991). Each of these proposals has merit. All can be justified on the grounds that they may increase children's cognitive development. All but the last can be justified on the grounds that they promote gender equity and increase the labor supply of poor women. The point to be stressed, however, is that providing quality child care will require a substantial increase in government expenditure.

Child Support

The most notable advances toward increasing the economic security of single mothers have been in the area of child support. Before 1975 child support was almost exclusively a state and local matter. State laws established the duty of nonresident parents to pay child support but left all the details up to local courts (see Cassetty, 1978; Chambers, 1979). Judges decided whether any child support should be paid, and if so, how much. They also had full authority over what could be done if the nonresident parent failed to pay.

In 1975 the federal Office of Child Support Enforcement was established, as were offices at the state and county levels. Additional legislation at intervals thereafter strengthened enforcement. In 1984 a major piece of child support legislation, passed unanimously by Congress, required the states to adopt numerical child support guidelines for the purposes of determining child support awards and to withhold child support obligations from the wages of parents who had become more than one month delinquent in their payments of child support.

The Family Support Act of 1988 went even further. The guidelines required of the states in 1984 were made presumptive, meaning that judges could depart from them only if they submitted written justification for doing so. The 1988 legislation also required that by 1994 the child support obligation be withheld from wages and other sources of income from the outset, rather than waiting until delinquency occurs. The act set performance standards for states in the establishment of paternity, required states to obtain the social security numbers of both parents at birth, and authorized federal payment for 90 percent of the costs of blood tests used to establish paternity. In addition, Wisconsin and New York were given authority to use federal funds that would otherwise have been devoted to AFDC to experiment with a government-guaranteed minimum child support benefit, to be discussed in greater detail shortly.

If the private child support enforcement system were perfected—awards established in all cases, all awards updated annually to the amounts called for in current child support guidelines, and 100 percent payment of obligations—about one quarter of the poverty gap for families headed by single mothers would be eliminated. That would be a notable achievement, but perfection is not likely. And even perfection would leave three quarters of the poverty problem unsolved. Child support enforcement can make an important contribution, but it cannot eliminate the need for substantial public contributions.

Two Proposals for Increasing Public Support for Children

Improving single mothers' earning capacity and strengthening fathers' child support obligations will reduce poverty and economic insecurity in single-mother families. Still missing, however, is the public obligation. Caring for children is the responsibility not only of individual parents but also of the public. Because children constitute the nation's future labor force, they are the nation's most valuable asset. Increasing their economic security and reducing their families' dependence on welfare resembles an investment.

Either additional benefits can target only the poorest children who live with single mothers, or, at the other extreme, they can be made available to all children. In general, the less targeted the benefits, the more helpful they will be in preventing poverty and reducing dependence upon cash welfare assistance. Providing benefits to all families as opposed to only single-parent families will also minimize the incentive to become or remain a single-parent family. Limiting benefits to poor single-parent families requires the lowest expenditure of public funds; making benefits available to all families requires the greatest expenditure.

Programs that provide benefits to rich and poor alike—Social Security, public education, national health insurance, child allowances, and to a lesser extent refundable tax credits—are like a public park: they are part of the landscape or environment that all families experience. In the American culture, welfare programs are for economic failures. According to one of the country's dominant myths, symbolized by Horatio Alger, anyone can make it, if only he or she works hard enough. This myth remains a carrot offered to the millions of people who want, and have the wherewithal, to succeed. But it has been, and remains, an emotionally threatening stick for those who do not have the opportunity, talent, or luck to make it economically. Although a large number of families receive welfare benefits from Food Stamps, Medicaid, AFDC, and the Supplementary Security Income program, the evidence suggests that millions of people who are eligible for welfare benefits do not claim them (Rainwater, 1982; Moffitt, 1987; Robins, 1990b). Many overcome their initial hesitation to apply for help, but many do not. In contrast, except in very rare cases, no such hesitation to apply for social security benefits exists. For this reason a society that wishes to underwrite and encourage its poorer members rather than scold and discourage will rely more upon social security programs than upon welfare programs.

Two reforms would provide substantial additional benefits to children irrespective of income: a refundable tax credit for all children and a child support assurance system for children with a nonresident parent.[8] Both would substantially reduce poverty and dependence on welfare. Both have been endorsed by the National Commission on Children, a bipartisan commission appointed by President Reagan and the Congress and chaired by Senator Jay Rockefeller. The first is expensive because it is universal; the second is cheap because it is targeted.

A refundable child tax credit. All industrialized countries except for the United States have a child allowance. There is some evidence that the United States is moving in this direction, notably the proposal put forth by the National Commission on Children for a refundable child tax credit of $1,000 per child, and even more important, the embodiment of a version of this proposal in the program advocated by Bill Clinton during his 1992 presidential campaign. This credit would replace the child exemption in the income tax.

In economic terms, a refundable tax credit is equivalent to a child allowance for all children. The administration of the programs differ. Whereas child allowances are mailed to all families on a weekly or monthly basis, families with a worker would receive the credit during the year in the form of an offset to taxes withheld. Families with no wage earners would be required to apply for the refundable credit.

The arguments for a refundable tax credit for children are succinctly stated by the National Commission:

> Because it would assist all families with children, the refundable child tax credit would not be a relief payment, nor would it categorize children according to their "welfare" or "nonwelfare" status. In addition, because it would not be lost when parents enter the work force, as welfare benefits are, the refundable child tax credit could provide a bridge for families striving to enter the economic mainstream. It would substantially benefit hard-pressed single and married parents raising children. It could also help middle-income, employed parents struggling to afford high-quality child care. Moreover, because it is neutral toward family structure and mother' employment, it would not discourage the formation of two-parent families or of single-earner families in which one parent chooses to stay at home and care for the children. (National Commission on Children, 1991, p. 28)

On the one hand, it is politically noteworthy that despite the $40 billion cost of the $1,000 refundable tax credit, the recommendation received the unanimous support of the commission.[9] On the other hand, it appears that the high cost of refundable credits prompted President Clinton, as opposed to presidential candidate Clinton, to abandon his advocacy of them.

Child support assurance. The proposed Child Support Assurance System (CSAS) is conceived of by its authors as a new social security program (Garfinkel and Melli, 1982; Garfinkel, 1992). Under it, all nonresident parents are required to share their income with their children. The sharing rate is a proportion of the nonresident parent's gross income and is determined by legislation. The resulting child support obligation is routinely withheld from income, just as income and payroll taxes are withheld. The child receives either the full amount owed or a minimum benefit set by legislation and provided by the government, whichever is higher. Like Survivors Insurance, which is part of the current social security system, Child Support Assurance aids children of all income classes who suffer an income loss owing to the absence of a parent. The cause of the absence differs, of course. Survivors Insurance compensates for the loss of income arising from widowhood; Child Support Assurance compensates for the loss arising from divorce, separation, or nonmarriage. The percentage-of-income standard, in conjunction with routine income withholding, makes most of the financing of Child Support Assurance similar to a proportional payroll tax, which is used to finance all of our social insurance programs. In the Child Support Assurance case, however, the "tax" applies only to those who are legally liable for child support. The assured-benefit component of Child Support Assurance makes the benefit structure of the system like all other social insurance programs in that it provides greater benefits to low-income families than would be justified on the basis of the family's contributions or taxes.

Both the National Commission on Children (1991) and the National Commission on Interstate Child Support Enforcement (1992) recommend that the federal government fund state demonstrations of a CSAS. The report of the former succinctly states the arguments in favor of such a system:

It would rapidly and significantly reduce childhood poverty because the amount of the cash payment, in combination with earnings, additional tax benefits from a refundable child tax credit, and the expanded Earned Income Tax Credit, would enable most low-income, single parent families to escape poverty, provided there is at least one full-time worker earning at least the minimum wage. In addition, we believe it would encourage work and reduce welfare dependency because the insured benefit (unlike welfare) would not be reduced dollar-for-dollar by the custodial parent's earnings. It would give custodial parents a strong incentive to cooperate in establishing paternity and locating the absent parents of their children and perhaps eventually help reduce the incidence of out-of-wedlock childbearing. (National Commission on Children, 1991, p. 103)

The United States has already taken giant strides toward a CSAS on the collection side. But the task has not been completed. Despite the adoption of guidelines, the courts are still heavily involved in determining child support obligations. Few states have yet implemented universal routine withholding of child support obligations, and all states are a long way from universal establishment of paternity. Crossing state lines remains a very effective way to avoid a child support obligation. Finally, neither the federal government nor any state has adopted an assured child support benefit. Although Wisconsin applied for and received a federal waiver to use federal AFDC funds to help finance an assured benefit, the initiative was stalled by a change in state administration. New York State began testing a restricted version of an assured benefit in 1989, limited to low-income families who qualified for AFDC. In his 1993 State of the Union message, President Clinton made it clear that he would propose legislation to strengthen child support enforcement. Whether an assured benefit would be included in the package or even what the nature of the collection-side reform proposals might be was not known.

Although the assured benefit is much less costly than a refundable tax credit, both national commissions recommended demonstrations rather than a full-fledged implementation, because some commission members feared that a guaranteed minimum child support benefit, being limited to families with a living absent parent, would increase the number of such families. It is true that benefits restricted to families with absent parents are more likely to increase such families than are benefits provided to all families, but it does not follow that such benefits should be avoided altogether. Single-parent families are poorer than two-parent families and therefore require more help. The good that is done by providing extra benefits to single-parent families must be weighed against the harm that is done by increasing their numbers. We have already seen that the effects of AFDC and other public benefits on female headship have not been large. Thus an alternative, reasonably conservative position is that we should institute a low federal assured child support benefit and finance state experiments with higher benefit levels.

Effects on family income. Table 8.2 illustrates the effects of a refundable tax credit and child support assurance on the incomes of poor single mother families who face a choice between welfare and working at the minimum wage. In all cases the hypothetical family is headed by a single mother who can earn the minimum wage, has two children, and receives $50 per month in child support. Because welfare benefits vary dramatically by state, we illustrate the effects for families living in states with low benefits (Texas), median benefits (Illinois), and high benefits (New York). The major contrast is between the unemployed welfare-dependent mother and the poor mother who works full time at the minimum wage.

The top panel of Table 8.2 displays the effects of the existing tax-transfer struc-

Table 8.2 Effects of Child Support Assurance (CSA) and a Refundable Tax Credit for Children (RTCC) on income of a single parent with two children

	Texas		Illinois		New York	
	No work	Full-time work	No work	Full-time work	No work	Full-time work
Actual Situation in 1991						
Earnings	$0	$8,500	$0	$8,500	$0	$8,500
Child support	600	600	600	600	600	600
Tax credit	0	0	0	0	0	0
AFDC	2,208	0	4,404	0	6,924	0
Food stamps	3,241	1,864	2,582	1,864	1,826	1,864
Tax	0	(650)	0	(650)	0	(650)
EITC	0	1,235	0	1,235	0	1,235
Total	$6,049	$11,549	$7,586	$11,549	$9,350	$11,549
1991 Situation with CSA and RTCC						
Earnings	$0	$8,500	$0	$8,500	$0	$8,500
Child support	3,000	3,000	3,000	3,000	3,000	3,000
Tax credit	2,000	2,000	2,000	2,000	2,000	2,000
AFDC	0	0	4	0	2,524	0
Food stamps	2,584	544	2,582	544	1,826	544
Tax	0	(1,390)	0	(1,390)	0	(1,390)
EITC	0	1,235	0	1,235	0	1,235
Total	$7,584	$13,889	$7,586	$13,889	$9,350	$13,889

Note: The assumptions are that the parent receives $50 per month in private child support and has an earning ability equal to the minimum wage. Earnings are calculated at $4.25 per hour for 2,000 hours. AFDC is calculated allowing the $90 earnings disregard. Private child support up to $50 is disregarded. Texas is a low-AFDC-benefit state; New York is a high-benefit state; the Illinois AFDC benefit was exactly the national median in 1991. The RTCC and AFDC are subtracted dollar for dollar. If the gross monthly income is below the eligibility level of $1,144 per month, food stamps are calculated beginning with a maximum monthly benefit of $277 per month for three persons in 1991, and then subtracting 30 percent of counted income. Counted income is 80 percent of earned income, child support payments, RTCC and AFDC less $116 per month standard deduction, and a $95 per month shelter expense. EITC is calculated at 17.3 percent of $7,140 of earnings. Tax includes both income tax and FICA. CSA is taxable. AFDC = Aid to Families with Dependent Children; EITC = Earned Income Tax Credit.

ture on family incomes. The bottom panel displays the effects of adding refundable child credits and child support assurance to the existing system. The effects of adding these new programs depend importantly upon how the new and old programs are integrated with each other. The examples in the bottom panel assume that policy decisions are made to reduce AFDC and Food Stamp benefits by $1 for each $1 dollar in benefits from child credits and child support assurance. Two aspects of the top panel are notable. First, welfare families in low-benefit states have abysmally low benefits. Because of differences in the cost of living across states, the numbers in the table overstate true differences among states. Second, the rewards to work for poor mothers in high-benefit states are meager. In this case, the numbers understate the problem because they ignore the loss of Medicaid when the mother goes to work.

Refundable tax credits and the assured child support benefit lead to a slight increase in the incomes of families dependent on welfare in low-benefit states and no increase in the incomes of families dependent on welfare in states with average and above average welfare benefit levels. But these programs increase the incomes of families headed by mothers who work at the minimum wage by 20 percent. In the median benefit state, full-time work at the minimum wage leads to an income more than double that on welfare. Even in the high-benefit state, a minimum wage worker can earn 150 percent more than the welfare benefit. These numbers demonstrate that if we so choose we can reduce both poverty and dependence.

The EITC figures in both panels of Table 8.2 reflect the law as of 1991 and therefore include neither the effects of the scheduled increases in existing law nor the effects of President Clinton's proposed increases. Existing law will increase the EITC and the total income of full-time workers by about $700. The President's proposed expansion of the EITC would increase these figures by about $2,100. Combining an expanded EITC with refundable tax credits for children and child support assurance would lead to even further reductions in both poverty and dependence.

·   ·   ·

One of two American children will spend part of his or her childhood in a family headed by a single mother. These children are exposed to heavy and harmful doses of economic and social insecurity. The government can reduce the economic insecurity of these families. Although doing so may increase the dependence of single mothers on the government, such an outcome is not inevitable. Targeting benefits on poor single mothers enlarges the proportion of single mothers who become heavily dependent on the government, but providing benefits to all single mothers—rich and poor alike—reduces heavy dependence. Similarly, providing generous child care benefits increases work and thereby simultaneously promotes security and independence. Promoting both economic security and independence requires a much greater commitment of public funds, however, than does the sole objective of promoting security.

Even though increasing security makes single parenthood more attractive and may thereby increase the prevalence of such families, the empirical evidence indicates that the effects are small. For any given level of benefit, moreover, the effects will be smaller if the benefit is available to both one- and two-parent families. Thus promoting security while minimizing the prevalence of single-parent families also requires a much larger commitment of public funds than does the objective of promoting security among single-parent families.

To promote both economic security and independence while minimizing prevalence will require a much greater commitment of public funds than Americans have heretofore been willing to make. In income security policy, as in most of life, we get what we pay for.

CHAPTER NINE

Updating Urban Policy

JEFFREY S. LEHMAN

In the 1990s, urban policy is once again at the forefront of antipoverty discussions. Early in the decade, escalating economic and racial polarization in and around America's largest cities facilitated outbursts of violence against and by poor minority groups. During the 1992 presidential campaign, the three major candidates all emphasized the need to develop policy elixirs that might restore a sense of urban health.

Other chapters in this volume discuss general antipoverty policies. Given the high concentration of poverty in the cities, those policies are inseparable from any serious discussion of urban policy. Indeed, a strong case can be made that the best urban policy is not limited to cities but is, rather, a "nonurban urban policy" (Kaplan, 1990).

This chapter's mandate is to consider the most prominent urban policy proposals that are not discussed in other chapters. Two such proposals stand out. "Enterprise zones" are (primarily) an *urban* urban policy, designed to stimulate economic activity in depressed neighborhoods. "Guaranteed public jobs" are a *nonurban* urban policy, many of whose beneficiaries would be residents of the country's most depressed cities.

How should one evaluate such proposals? One fruitful source of ideas is history: one can review the knowledge gained from our nation's experience with similar programs in the past. A second source is theory: one can attempt to measure such programs according to how well they promote whatever societal aspirations one thinks most relevant. In the domain of urban policy, for example, such aspirations might include the commitment to give each citizen a fair opportunity for geographic and social mobility through employment. This chapter aims to synthesize historical and theoretical arguments, in order to frame an agenda for updating urban policy.

The "Underclass" and Employment in the Formal Economy

In Chapter 5, Ronald Mincy reviews the substantial research literature on the "urban underclass." He documents the fact that average incomes in some urban neighborhoods have declined sharply since 1970. And individuals living in those neighborhoods have suffered in ways that are not fully captured by the Census Bureau's measure of income poverty. Significantly, the great majority of citizens who are living in America's most deprived urban neighborhoods are black.

The "underclass" literature has explored a range of significant social phenomena, including education, crime, and nonmarital childbearing. But one concern dominates: the extent to which the residents of some neighborhoods lack employment in the formal economy. Joblessness is not merely a source of ultimate concern; it also enters into many models of neighborhood decline as an intermediate cause of other forms of social distress. William Julius Wilson (1987) sees lack of employment as a cause of nonmarital childbearing. For William Sabol (forthcoming), unemployment is linked directly to crime. Martha Van Haitsma (1989) calls weak attachment to the formal labor market "the thread that ties the various indicators together." Lawrence Mead (1992) declares "nonwork" to be the "most fundamental" problem "afflicting the racial ghetto and the long-term poor." To the extent that some neighborhoods seem to have slipped into downward spirals of mutually reinforcing self-destructive behaviors, all these commentators see employment in the formal economy as the best way to break that spiral.

Yet the specific policy responses advocated by different observers have varied widely. Wilson has argued for a comprehensive program of economic and social reform, highlighting macroeconomic policies to promote growth and tight labor markets, child support assurance, child care support, and family allowances. David Ellwood (1988) has stressed an expanded Earned Income Tax Credit, transitional support, universal health insurance, child support assurance, and a guaranteed minimum-wage public sector job as a last resort. Mickey Kaus (1992) would modify Ellwood's plan by replacing the children's allowance with "day care . . . integrated into the larger system of child care for other American families" and by paying a subminimum wage in the public sector jobs. Mead (1992) would impose "a more authoritative work policy" until "at least the lion's share of today's nonworkers accept that some opportunity exists for them, . . . take and hold available jobs, and get on with their lives." And a broad spectrum of political leaders have advocated the creation of federal "enterprise zones."

What is the best way to increase employment in underclass neighborhoods? In Chapter 7, Rebecca Blank suggests that aggregate data for the national economy over the past three decades are consistent with the perspective "that the simple availability of jobs has not been a major constraint for most less-skilled U.S.

workers who seek employment, at least over the long run." The country as a whole seems capable of sustaining an adequate supply of jobs—an adequate demand for workers. That observation might seem to support the view that policymakers should rivet their attention on the supply of labor, stressing either human capital investment or Mead-style authoritarianism.

But as important as concern with the nature of the work force may be, it should not be the end of the story. For one thing, there are important social costs to insisting that all workers be willing to relocate to whatever corner of the country promises the most plentiful supply of jobs. Moreover, even if all workers were always willing to move, the underclass literature provides suggestive (albeit not conclusive) evidence that traditional human capital investment programs may not suffice to bring some communities fully back into the general job market.

Consider the following social dynamic disclosed in interviews conducted as part of the Urban Poverty and Family Structure Project in Chicago. Many young black male employees distrust white employers, grounding that distrust in centuries of American racial oppression. That distrust can, in and of itself, make them less valuable as potential employees. In one anecdote, a black employee views a request that he take on extra responsibility as the continuation of a legacy of exploitation. He resists. But by resisting he makes himself less valuable to the employer than a Mexican American who sees the request as benign (Taub, 1991; see also Kirschenman and Neckerman, 1991).

The distrust problem exemplifies a more general concern with job accessibility. A job that is outside of commuting distance may be inaccessible to a worker who appears formally capable of doing the tasks involved. Similarly, a job controlled by an employer who is distrusted may be inaccessible to a worker who appears formally capable of doing what is required. The job may be inaccessible because the worker refuses to take the position. Or it may be inaccessible because the worker's defensiveness makes him less productive for the employer.

Some public policies must respond to the sense of potential employers that certain workers are unqualified. But other public policies may be needed to respond fully to the fact that for some potential workers, certain jobs are inaccessible. Enterprise zones and guaranteed public sector employment are each potential initiatives to respond to the problem of job inaccessibility.

Enterprise Zones and the Problem of Spatial Targeting

Enterprise zones are a simple idea. Troubled neighborhoods are first identified as targets for redevelopment. Entrepreneurs who subsequently initiate new ventures in those neighborhoods benefit in a variety of ways, ranging from relaxed zoning regulation to direct governmental grants (see generally Boeck, 1984). The redevelopment offers a cluster of different benefits to the community, but it is often said that "job creation is the goal of enterprise zones" (Pitts, 1992).

Although the United States has, at various times, endorsed the use of federal incentives to encourage economic development in "underdeveloped" regions such as Appalachia, the notion of a generalized program of "enterprise zones" that could help cities as well as rural areas did not attract widespread attention until the late 1970s. The concept had been popular in Asia, and then in England. In the United States the phrase was introduced by the Heritage Foundation in early 1979, was advanced in Congress by Representatives Jack Kemp (R–N.Y.) and Robert Garcia (D–N.Y.) (H.R. 7240, 96th Cong., 2d sess., 1980), and was then popularized in a book by Stuart Butler (1981). But notwithstanding the endorsement of the concept by President Reagan in his 1982 State of the Union message, no full-fledged enterprise zone proposal emerged from Congress during the 1980s.[1]

Yet despite the absence of federal legislation, thirty-seven states and the District of Columbia established enterprise zone programs, offering a grab bag of small incentives (Bird, 1989; Rubin and Wilder, 1989; Levitan and Miller, 1992). Some emphasized investment incentives. Others furnished subsidies for employment and employee training.

Enterprise zones are nonuniversal programs, since they draw clear distinctions among communities. To be sure, *no* social welfare program is truly "universal" (offering benefits to every living human being); what distinguishes different social welfare programs from one another is the *way* in which they define their particular "targets." What makes enterprise zones particularly intriguing is that they are *spatially* targeted programs.

Most social welfare programs are targeted on the basis of nonfinancial personal characteristics of recipients, such as age, disability, or family structure. In addition, "means-tested" programs are targeted on the basis of the financial characteristics of a family or household. Spatially targeted programs are distinctive because, in addition to whatever nonspatial target restrictions they may impose, they show a special concern for one or more plots of land. Some such programs, like the Tennessee Valley Authority, act directly upon the land. Most, however, like enterprise zones, address spatial needs indirectly; they provide benefits to individual human beings who demonstrate some *link* to the favored area.

Spatial targeting is not a binary condition. Just as income-targeted programs can use a low or high eligibility cutoff, programs can be more or less spatially targeted by aiming at a larger or smaller region. And whereas some programs are spatially targeted by design from the beginning (as in the case of programs aimed exclusively at "blighted neighborhoods"), others become spatially targeted by default (as in the case of a large public housing project that could have been situated anywhere, but is ultimately built on a specific site).

One need not rely on spatially targeted programs in order to concentrate benefits on the residents of distressed neighborhoods. For example, a nationwide subminimum wage public jobs program would provide no benefit to a neighborhood where everyone is already employed at an average wage; such a program could, however, provide substantial benefits to residents of a neighborhood where most of the residents are looking for work. A program that is relatively universal in form may thus, in practice, distribute its benefits in a spatially targeted manner.

At least three equity-based concerns should make policymakers somewhat nervous about spatial targeting. The first relates to potential arbitrariness in who benefits from the program and who must bear its costs. A spatially targeted program benefits some people who are characterized by deprivation x at the same time that it fails to benefit other people who are just as fully characterized by x. The assumption that those chosen to benefit from the program are worse off because there is more of x in the immediate environment is an empirical assumption, not a universal fact. Similarly, a spatially targeted program may impose its costs unequally across the community. The dollar costs of a program to subsidize the construction of a new factory in a depressed neighborhood may well be allocated broadly; but the burdens of increased pollution and traffic are likely to be concentrated on residents of the targeted area.

The second, related concern has to do with the artificiality of geographic boundaries. Metropolitan areas, neighborhoods, and communities are more sociological than geographic. Two people living on opposite sides of a census tract boundary may have more in common with each other than either one does with various neighbors who are fellow census tract co-residents. In the same way, next-door neighbors may have entirely different sets of links to social and employment networks, or to sources of transportation and child care. The policy relevance of geography is not automatic.

Whereas the first two concerns were static, the third is dynamic, relating to the danger of creating new restraints on mobility. A person who receives spatially targeted benefits may well forfeit those benefits if he or she moves out of the relevant area. That risk may not be a significant deterrent to movement for some recipients, but it could be for others. To the extent that a spatially targeted program deters beneficiaries from taking advantage of opportunities that present themselves, it might exacerbate rather than alleviate the problem it is intended to address.

Yet those three concerns are just that: concerns. None of them is necessarily dispositive. The following four examples suggest situations in which one might well want to define the beneficiaries of a social welfare program on the basis of geography:

1. Geographic markers might reflect, or even define, a community where the harms to bystanders ("negative externalities") of individual or collec-

tive conduct interact in such a way that the cumulative effect is intensified. (Imagine a neighborhood where employment levels were so low that children grew up believing that no matter what they did, they would not be able to get jobs.) In the underclass literature, this possibility is commonly addressed under the rubrics of "neighborhood effects" and "concentration effects."

2. Geographic markers might reflect, or even define, a community where cooperation will leave everyone better off than if everyone pursues an individualistic strategy. (Imagine a neighborhood where high-income families have fled because they feared that all the other high-income families were about to flee.) In the underclass literature, this variant of a prisoner's dilemma is sometimes discussed as a problem of "tipping," of "vicious cycles," or of "downward spirals."

3. Geographic markers might be the best available proxies for non-geographic features that one cannot or does not wish to measure. (Imagine a wealthy community giving money to everyone who lived in a particular "poor neighborhood" because it did not want the invasion of privacy associated with determining the incomes of individual families in that neighborhood.) In the underclass literature, one frequently encounters arguments about whether the identification of particular neighborhoods as the locus of a particular kind of suffering or misconduct reflects reliance on a "good proxy" or merely on a "bad stereotype."

4. Geographic markers might define a political community that feels enough mutual identification and solidarity that it wishes to undertake wealth redistribution *within* its borders. (Imagine a mixed-income community in which the wealthy residents banded together and paid to establish a public library that would provide equal benefits to all residents, rich or poor.) In the underclass literature, this possibility is usually discussed only indirectly, when the boundaries to such political communities are challenged through, for example, proposals to finance public schools on a metropolitan or statewide basis.

In Chapter 5, Mincy effectively makes the case that, in *some* cities, with regard to *some* neighborhoods, one or more of the foregoing justifications may apply with enough force to warrant experimentation with spatially targeted responses. But when thinking about a proposal such as enterprise zones, one must analyze the details of the proposal and the specific context in which it is to be implemented.

I shall discuss in some detail the enterprise zone program (estimated to cost $2.5 billion over five years) that was adopted by Congress and signed by President Clinton in August 1993 (U.S. Congress, 1993). That program authorized the creation of six urban "empowerment zones" and sixty-five urban "enterprise communities." (It also provided comparable programs for rural areas and for Indian reservations.)

The urban empowerment zones and enterprise communities are designated by the Secretary of Housing and Urban Development after having been nominated by the relevant state and local governments. To be nominated, zones and communities must satisfy specific criteria with regard to size and must have a condition of pervasive poverty, unemployment, and general economic distress.[2] In addition, the relevant state and local governments must have committed themselves to a "strategic plan" that includes direct public investments in the nominated area and indirect support for private for-profit and nonprofit institutions to do likewise. (The strategic plan can "generally" not include any support for companies that merely relocate existing businesses from outside the nominated area to inside the nominated area.)

Once an area is designated an enterprise community or an empowerment zone, "enterprise zone businesses" are eligible for a package of tax incentives. (To oversimplify, "enterprise zone businesses" must carry out substantially all their operations within the zone, and at least 35 percent of their employees must be zone residents.) In connection with the handful of areas designated as empowerment zones (but *not* in connection with enterprise communities), two additional benefits are provided:

- enterprise zone businesses are eligible for some special accelerated depreciation deductions with regard to new investments in property used in the zone, and

- any employer (whether or not it is an enterprise zone business eligible for other tax benefits) is eligible for a nonrefundable tax credit equal to 20 percent of the first $15,000 in wages paid to any employee who is a zone resident and who works in the zone.

Several features of this program should be emphasized. Note first the requirement that other governmental entities nominate the zone and commit themselves to a "strategic plan" with regard to the zone. One theoretical justification for spatially targeted programs is that they can catalyze cooperation in an environment where cooperation can yield significant social dividends. (In practice, it is not always clear how significant those social dividends will be in any given neighborhood.) Yet the notorious failure of the most visible federal effort at "comprehensive" mobilization of resources in poor neighborhoods, the "Community Action" programs of the late 1960s, demonstrated that federal funds cannot by themselves catalyze cooperation. Indeed, they can have the opposite effect if they promote political competition for control over scarce funds (Moynihan, 1969; Morris, 1980, pp. 61–67; Lemann, 1991, pp. 129–202).

The "nomination" and "strategic plan" requirements use the prospect of federal subsidies to encourage advance bargaining by those constituencies whose cooperation is desired. Moreover, the criteria to be used in designating enterprise zones include the extent to which private entities are committed to participate in the joint effort and the extent to which the overall course of action is enforceable. Ideally, such advance commitments should increase the *likelihood* that such a program will yield whatever social dividends are possible. Standing alone, however, they cannot ensure that such social dividends are in fact possible.

Second, note the eligibility requirements for investment incentives: (a) the business must be conducted within the zone, and (b) more than one-third of the employees must be zone residents. The requirement that business be conducted within the zone suggests a belief that the mere physical location of new businesses within the zones will be beneficial. That assumption is not implausible, especially where effects unrelated to employment are concerned. The flow of workers to an active business can increase a neighborhood's sense of vitality and make it less attractive to criminals. At a minimum, new business can provide another voice calling for attention from the police. A retail business, for example, can also provide new consumer opportunities for local resident. But there is little evidence that a bare requirement that a business locate in a neighborhood will significantly improve the employment prospects of residents (Pitts, 1992).

The burden of improving resident employment prospects is intended to be borne by the second of the two eligibility requirements: that more than one-third of employees be zone residents. Yet not even that requirement will ensure that a new business will increase resident employment. The new businesses can still hire residents who were previously employed elsewhere. Those residents will presumably be willing to switch jobs only if they believe that the new jobs will be better for them. But if the goal is to increase total employment rates for zone residents, there is no guarantee that even one-third of the new jobs will have contributed toward that goal.

Even worse, the 1993 program allows an employer to qualify for tax incentives by moving an existing business that already relied on zone residents for one-third of its work force into the zone from outside. To be sure, the "strategic plan" requirements prohibit state and local governments from helping businesses that simply move. But nothing in the program prevents such businesses from claiming the *federal* investment incentive benefits.

The experience of limited state-based enterprise zone programs to date gives one reason to be cautious when predicting the net employment gains from a federal enterprise zone program. Some evaluations have found positive benefits to regional employment from certain programs (Papke, 1991; Rubin and Trawinski, 1991). But others have found the incentives inadequate to stimulate much new enterprise in the zones (U.S. General Accounting Office, 1988; Birdsong, 1989; James, 1991). Moreover, to the extent that the state-based programs have had any effect, it appears at most to have been "locational" (affecting where within a given market a business locates) rather than "generative" (affecting the aggregate amount of employment or business activity for the economy as a whole) (Birdsong, 1989; Levitan and Miller, 1992). These results mimic those obtained by researchers who have studied the effects of state and local tax incentives more generally (Dewar, 1990). The magnitude of the incentives under a federal enterprise zone program would, to be sure, be far greater than under any existing state program. But the case remains to be made that any amount of simple investment incentives tied to the location of a business will generate higher levels of employment in that area.

Third, consider the feature of the program that might seem to hold more promise in that regard—the 20 percent credit for employers who hire zone residents to work *in* one of the handful of "empowerment zones" (even if other of the same employer's employees do their work outside the zone). The new credit resembles the Targeted Jobs Tax Credit (TJTC), without the TJTC's usual requirement that a worker live in an economically disadvantaged family, but with two spatial constraints: worker residence and work situs. The policy question posed by the work situs restriction is the same one already discussed with regard to the investment incentive provisions: what benefits might flow from having a given worker do his or her job inside a zone rather than outside it? If the work situs restriction were discarded, one would then simply be left with the question whether tax credits like the TJTC are good programs overall and, in particular, good in ways that might sensibly lead to the inclusion of "zone residents" as a new target group.

Evaluations of the TJTC, which has been available since 1978, express disappointment with the program. It has been described as "perhaps the most outstanding example of an entitlement program with extremely low participation rates despite a very generous subsidy offer" (Bishop and Kang, 1991). Moreover, those employers who have claimed the credit have tended to do so with regard to employees whom they would have hired even in the absence of the credit (deHaven-Smith, 1983; Levitan and Gallo, 1987; Bishop and Kang, 1991). For many employers, membership in a targeted group stigmatized a prospective employee in a way that reduced the employer's expectations of the employee's productivity more than the credit would have reduced the employer's expected wage costs (see Burtless, 1985). For others, the information costs of determining whether a prospective candidate was in fact a member of a targeted group were too high

(Bishop and Kang, 1991). Indeed, problems associated with implementing the target requirements seem little different from the problems often associated with implementing programs that deliver services directly through the public sector (deHaven-Smith, 1983).

Presumably the information costs associated with determining whether a job candidate lives in an empowerment zone are lower than the costs of determining whether he or she is a member of a TJTC-targeted group.[3] But there is little reason to believe that the stigma associated with being an empowerment zone resident is any lower. Overall, given the experience with the TJTC and the restrictive work situs requirement, one should not be wildly optimistic about the potential employment gains from the employment credit features of the 1993 empowerment zone program.

To be sure, the lesson of this analysis is not that we should give up on any program that might be labeled an "enterprise zone" proposal. Rather, it is that the effects of such a proposal are likely to turn on small details of its structure. Some enterprise zone proposals are not likely to have much effect at all. Others might make it marginally more likely that an investor will be able to turn a profit from a venture that he or she might well have undertaken in any event. Some might make it easier for neighborhood residents to buy retail goods. Still others might significantly enhance the employment opportunities available to neighborhood residents. However, if our *primary* aim is the last one—to expand substantially the number of jobs available to the urban poor—it seems that we need a different enterprise zone plan from the one that was adopted in 1993.

Guaranteed Public Sector Jobs

A more direct approach to increasing employment among the ghetto poor is to have government agencies hire people. David Ellwood has argued that welfare should be replaced by a form of "transitional assistance" and that governments should "offer a limited number of minimum-wage jobs to those who had exhausted their transitional assistance" (1988, p. 124). Ellwood expects that this program would be small and temporary, because few people will find such jobs attractive once they can do better in the private sector (1988, p. 125).

Philip Harvey has made the case for a more expansive "employment assurance program," suggesting that guaranteed public sector jobs be provided at "market wages." Harvey defines "market wages" to mean "wages equivalent to those normally offered for similar work in the regular labor market . . . Indeed, the program could simply adopt existing government wage schedules for comparable jobs" (1989, p. 31). He argues that a large, permanent program would come at a surprisingly low net cost, and that taxpayers would gladly pay that cost in exchange for full employment security. In response to concerns about productivity, he suggests that the range of salaries available to different kinds of public sector jobs (ranging down to purely routine casual labor paid per day or on a piecework basis), combined with the possibility of being fired from any particular job, would be enough to maintain appropriate worker incentives. In response to concerns about competition with the private sector, he offers a list of areas where the private sector currently maintains only a minimal presence and where the social benefits of a public presence would be appreciated.

Mickey Kaus has taken the idea in the opposite direction, arguing for a more restricted form of transitional assistance and a different kind of guaranteed public job. Whereas Ellwood envisions minimum wage public jobs (supplemented by a greatly expanded Earned Income Tax Credit), Kaus prefers "a useful public job at a wage slightly *below* the minimum wage for private sector work" (supplemented by an even more greatly expanded EITC) (Kaus, 1992, p. 125). And whereas Ellwood describes his public sector jobs as available only to those who have exhausted transitional assistance, Kaus would make the jobs "available to everybody, men as well as women, single or married, mothers and fathers alike . . . [i]t wouldn't even be necessary to limit the public jobs to the poor" (Kaus, 1992, p. 125). By having his jobs pay less than the minimum wage (before the EITC is taken into account), Kaus would ensure that participants would always have an incentive to prefer work in the private sector.

Guaranteed public sector jobs programs have traditionally been analyzed under the heading "public service employment" (PSE). PSE proposals must contend with at least four types of criticism:

1. The jobs will be "bad jobs." PSE positions might not be worthwhile in some absolute sense—because from the worker's perspective the jobs might not be "fulfilling," because from society's perspective the jobs might not be "socially valuable," and/or because they might not provide workers with skills that are transferable to the private sector.

2. The jobs will "substitute" for jobs that would otherwise exist. PSE positions might simply replace jobs that are already being performed, so that there will be no net increase in employment opportunities. Some relatively high-paying jobs might even be eliminated in favor of PSE jobs. The net result would be a kind of back-door federal subsidy of the costs of local government operations.

3. The jobs will go to the non-needy because of "creaming" or patronage abuses. PSE positions might be allocated to the most capable workers—workers who are the most likely to have "gotten by" without them—in order to create a deceptive appearance of success. Or they might be allocated to workers solely to enhance their loyalty to a particular local politician.

4. The jobs will be more expensive than they are "worth." PSE positions might have *some* value and might create *some* net new employment opportunities, but not enough to justify the overall cost.[4]

Some sense of the weight to be given these objections can be gained from the most recent federally funded PSE programs. After the large-scale Works Progress Administration projects of the 1930s, the most substantial experience with public service employment in the United States came during the 1970s, in the form of the Emergency Employment Act of 1971 and its successor, the Comprehensive Employment and Training Act of 1973. CETA supplemented traditional employment and training programs with PSE for victims of both "structural" and "cyclical" unemployment.[5] CETA was administered in the form of federal grants to local government "prime sponsors" (or state governments, in the case of rural areas), which in turn established the PSE positions. In response to complaints of "overcentralization" in prior education and training programs, most authority for planning and managing the programs was delegated to state and local elected officials (Mucciaroni, 1992, p. 153).

In its early implementation, CETA received all four types of PSE criticism. Just as significantly, the program's reputation was badly damaged when the national press published a series of stories describing some of the more outlandish local projects, such as the infamous "nude sculpting workshop" (Baumer and Van Horn, 1985; Mucciaroni, 1992). Accordingly, when CETA was reauthorized in 1978, it was amended in significant ways. Advisory groups, known as "private industry councils," were established to increase the role of the private sector and thereby improve placement rates. Wages were lowered to minimize the likelihood of creaming. The duration of PSE positions was limited so as to minimize fiscal substitution. And strict new penalties were combined with heavier-handed centralized administration control to combat fraud, waste, and abuse.

CETA was not subjected to experimental, random-assignment evaluation, and the econometric evaluations yielded varying conclusions. Nonetheless, the evaluation literature suggests that even before the 1978 amendments, PSE was providing significant long-term earnings increases for white and minority women participants, although not for men (Bassi, 1983; Bassi and Ashenfelter, 1986; Barnow, 1987). Rough efforts to undertake more comprehensive cost-benefit analyses were also encouraging (Franklin and Ripley, 1984, p. 198). Moreover, the 1978 reforms provided effective responses to the most concrete criticisms just outlined (Mirengoff, 1980, 1982; Baumer and Van Horn, 1984). With regard to creaming, for example, by 1980 as many as 92 percent of new PSE enrollees were low-income workers.

Unfortunately, those same 1978 amendments helped to undercut the program's political support. More intrusive bureaucratic fraud-prevention efforts meant heavier administrative burdens for local governments. Furthermore, stricter targeting and lower wages meant that the jobs were more likely to be "bad jobs" in two senses—they were less likely to produce genuine value for the local government agencies and they were less likely to yield a worker who could make an easy transition to the private sector (Franklin and Ripley, 1984; Baumer and Van Horn, 1984; Mucciaroni, 1992). And the earlier scandals had forever tainted the program in the public mind. After Ronald Reagan was elected on a platform dedicated to shrinking the size of the federal budget, it was only a matter of time before the program was eliminated and replaced by the Job Training Partnership Act, which explicitly precludes the use of its funds to pay for public service jobs.

CETA left a legacy of skittishness about public service employment. On the one hand, it appears feasible to run a decentralized PSE program that is popular with local officials, provides a form of revenue sharing, and (in part by creaming the pool of eligibles) produces alumni who can make a successful transition to the private sector. On the other hand, such a program would not in any way respond to the concerns that motivate the underclass literature.

More ambitious guaranteed public job proposals along the lines suggested by Ellwood, Harvey, or Kaus would respond more directly to those concerns. All propose relatively universal programs where creaming would be impossible. Among the three, Harvey's plan offers the most latitude for structuring genuine worker incentives within the PSE ranks, but also runs the greatest risk of creating a separate worker pool with little movement to the private sector. Harvey's plan also promises the most significant changes in the overall structure of the economy. Kaus's plan would cause the least disruption in the private sector and maintain the most mobility, but also poses the greatest administrative challenges for the managers responsible for running the projects.

Far more difficult, however, is a serious political problem noted by Harvey that all three proposals must confront. Americans have deep ideological concerns about the size and scope of government. Although they may endorse guaranteed job proposals when responding to surveys, in practice the logic of limited government has trumped the logic of the work ethic and economic opportunity.

Designing a Policy Response: Mobility Enhancement and "Access-to-Enterprise Zones"

The primary concern raised by spatially targeted programs, such as enterprise zones, is a concern about mobility—in space and in society. To the extent that mobility is a simple descriptive fact about the existing world, to the extent that people are free and able to move easily across geographic boundaries, there is great force to the equity concerns identified earlier in this chapter. Although those concerns may be outweighed by the benefits of spatial targeting, we must worry about arbitrariness and artificiality in the designation of program beneficiaries.

Yet in the United States, mobility is not merely a descriptive property; it is also an aspiration. Our conceptions of equal opportunity require that citizens have a fair chance at competing for jobs for which their talents qualify them. Those conceptions are threatened if some citizens are forced to compete in a labor market that is significantly "smaller" than the market that others compete in, whether because they lack the same access to transportation or because they are impermissibly penalized by certain employers for traits that should be treated as irrelevant.

Thus, at a minimum, urban employment policy should work to ensure that no group of citizens is forced to compete in an artificially constricted labor market. A labor market can be constricted in at least two ways: *directly,* if employers discriminate in choosing employees, or *indirectly,* if there is discrimination in residential markets and if one's employment opportunities are influenced by where one lives.

Race-Based Employment Discrimination

The "underclass" described in Chapter 5 includes the residents of the most heavily depressed urban black ghettos. There continues to be strong evidence that labor markets for blacks are constricted "directly" because employers discriminate on the basis of race. Before exploring potential policy responses, it is useful to distinguish among three different types of discriminatory behavior:

- actions that are *contrary* to the actor's monetary self-interest, but nonetheless indulge his or her personal animus or ignorance (actors who pay to satisfy a "taste" for discrimination, sometimes called "pure" discrimination by economists),

- actions that *promote* the actor's monetary self-interest (at least in the short run) because they indulge the prejudices of other people the actor engages with, such as customers, suppliers, other employees, or lenders (actors who make money by "catering" to the discriminatory tastes of others), and

- actions that *promote* the actor's monetary self-interest (again, at least in the short run) by exploiting generalizations that are true on average even though they are false in a substantial percentage of specific cases, where it is expensive to identify the specific cases (actors who make money through "statistical" discrimination).

Although some of these forms of discrimination could be predicted to disappear eventually if they occurred in isolation in a perfectly competitive market (Becker, 1957; Arrow, 1971), in contemporary America many if not all of them are likely to prove quite durable for a long period of time (Brest, 1976; Akerlof, 1985; Donohue, 1986; Strauss, 1991).

Moreover, these durable forms of discrimination are all morally objectionable. Some writers appear to take the position that statistical discrimination is perfectly acceptable because the actor wants "only" to make profits and has no *active* desire to harm others in the process (Epstein, 1992). But such a view is quite out of synch with our ordinary sense of morally acceptable behavior.

Charles Lawrence (1987) and Mark Kelman (1991) have argued that tacitly transmitted cultural stereotypes about racial minorities inflict pervasive harms on all members of the group by shaping the larger society's unconscious and habitual patterns of perception. Even if one ignores those generalized harms, however, a strong case can be made that statistical discrimination is socially unacceptable. In his overview of the subject, David Strauss (1991) identifies three costs of statistical discrimination:

- It can lead members of the group that is discriminated against to under-invest in human capital in a way that is inefficient for society as a whole.
- It can perpetuate the harms that flow from past wrongs.
- It can entrench demoralizing racial stratification.

Strauss thus argues that statistical discrimination is objectionable, not because of its effect on the "individual victim of discrimination," but rather because of the "aggregate effects of statistical discrimination on the minority population" (1991, p. 1648).

I would go even further and suggest that statistical discrimination will often be objectionable even when one restricts one's attention to the individual victim. Focus for a moment on a person who does *not* match the stereotype being deployed. She in fact has a competence the employer desires. Yet the employer has concluded that she lacks that competence merely because she has an immutable trait that in earlier times was the basis for socially accepted violence. The pain she experiences seems qualitatively different from the disappointment any job applicant feels when an employer underestimates her competence.

The statistical discriminator might try to excuse the discrimination by protesting that many of the group members being discriminated against—maybe even a majority—will not have their competence underestimated because, by hypothesis, they will match the stereotype. Yet in other contexts we do not normally find such an excuse for self-interested behavior satisfactory. In civil society, we use informal norms and legal rules to lead people to "take into account" the interests of others. That means considering the number of individuals who could be harmed, the likelihood that each of them will be harmed, and the extent of harm they could suffer. We fault people who press ahead with behavior that they know carries a significant risk of seriously harming innocent victims.[6] When one considers both the frequency with which individuals do not fit racial stereotypes and the extent of harm inflicted on such individuals by statistical discrimination in employment, the practice seems morally intolerable.

The most obvious response to employment discrimination is antidiscrimination legislation. Since 1964, federal law has generally prohibited employers from engaging in any of these forms of durable discrimination. The evidence suggests that such laws have had a substantial impact in reducing the incidence of discriminatory behavior (Jaynes and Williams, 1989). At the same time, however, it is clear that the legal prohibition has fallen far short of eliminating the behavior (Aleinikoff, 1992). In the early 1990s several studies confirmed that racial discrimination remains a significant feature of American society. In the area of direct discrimination by employers against employees, studies using "testers" by both the U.S. General Accounting Office (1990) and the Urban Institute (Cross et al., 1990; Turner, 1991) documented significant levels of discrimination against blacks and Hispanics. And Joleen Kirschenman and Kathryn Neckerman (1991) documented an extraordinary willingness of employers to articulate racial generalizations about potential workers in face-to-face interviews with the researchers.

The Civil Rights Act of 1991 made several significant changes that should make it easier for victims of racial discrimination to recover damages, and that should therefore strengthen the legal deterrent to such discrimination. If a black job applicant can show that race per se played a role in an employer's decision not to hire him, the act provides that the employer cannot attempt to justify the decision by asserting that the applicant would not have been hired in any event. And to combat the possibility that employers might find ways to rely on other factors as subterfuge proxies for race, the act provides that employers whose hiring policies have a disparate impact on black workers must bear the burden of showing that those policies are justified by business necessity.

Surely a national urban policy agenda must seek to enhance mobility by responding to racial discrimination in employment. And yet, given the limited power of legal regulation to alter rationally self-interested behavior, policymakers should realize that antidiscrimination legislation is unlikely to trigger radical growth in the labor market opportunities of black adults. Accordingly, this aspect of the agenda requires other components as well. The federal government should draw on the tools of public education and advertising to educate citizens about the phenomenon of statistical discrimination and its moral objectionability. Moreover, to the extent that those efforts remain inadequate, the public sector may need to develop other ways to compensate for the artificial restrictions imposed on some workers' employment opportunities.

Indirect Constriction of the Labor Market

Even if direct constriction of the labor market opportunities of black workers were eliminated, one would still be concerned about the possibility that employment opportunities for some urban black adults are constricted indirectly, via residential segregation. Douglas Massey (1990a, 1993) has argued that a great deal of the increase in concentrated disadvantage known as the "underclass" is due to the interaction between a general nationwide increase in the poverty rate and high levels of residential segregation by race. And it is an undisputed fact that American housing markets are profoundly segregated on the basis of race (Farley and Allen, 1987; Jaynes and Williams, 1989; Farley, 1991).

Given the extent of residential segregation, the so-called spatial mismatch hypothesis describes another social phenomenon that might constrict the employment options available to some black adults. In general form, the "spatial mismatch" hypothesis suggests simply that ghetto residents have fewer earnings opportunities than they would have if they lived in the suburbs. To the extent the hypothesis is accurate, one can address urban employment problems by helping ghetto residents to overcome the barriers of space. Until quite recently the federal government spent substantial amounts of money to directly support residential segregation (Judd, 1988; Schill, 1990), so the argument that the federal government owes such assistance to ghetto residents seems morally compelling.

Social scientists have attempted to measure the importance of spatial mismatch ever since John Kain articulated the hypothesis in 1968. Several recent reviews have reached differing conclusions. Keith Ihlanfeldt and David Sjoquist (1989), John Kasarda (1989, 1990), Harry Holzer (1991), and Michael Schill (1992a) have all been persuaded that spatial mismatch is at least a "significant factor" in explaining poverty among urban blacks. In contrast, David Ellwood (1986b), Christopher Jencks and Susan Mayer (1990), and Phillip Moss and Christopher Tilly (1991) are largely unconvinced.

Even if spatial mismatch is important, however, the policy implications depend on the mechanism through which the spatial mismatch arises. It may arise simply because the cost in money and time deters potential employees from taking jobs that they are aware of and that are available to them. In that case, substantial gains can be made by extending urban public transportation networks to link all parts of metropolitan areas efficiently and by distributing transportation vouchers to citizens who could not otherwise afford to get to work. One might even make such gains by subsidizing the purchase of cars.

But any spatial mismatch might also have arisen for other reasons. For example, space can be a proxy for social, rather than geographic, isolation. It can indicate isolation from information about when jobs become available. Or it can indicate isolation from the personal acquaintanceships and informal networks that can enable one applicant to gain a job ahead of an otherwise indistinguishable competitor (Pedder, 1991).

Information isolation can be partially remedied through the creation of computerized job banks and information centers of the sort advocated by Kasarda (1988) and Wilson (1991a). Isolation from personal acquaintanceship, however, is a much tougher problem. It calls for strategies to reduce the extent of residential segregation. Such strategies could include increased enforcement of laws against residential racial discrimination, structural efforts to reduce the extent of residential economic segregation, and increased use of housing vouchers to improve the purchasing power of low-income blacks.

The choice among these strategies depends on the causes of residential segregation. Such segregation reflects the interaction of several different factors. The most important are (1) overt racial discrimination by landlords, homesellers, realtors, and lenders; (2) "race neutral" socioeconomic residential segregation; and (3) the preferences of tenants and homebuyers to live with neighbors of their own race ("self-steering") (Schelling, 1972; Yinger, 1976, 1979; Galster, 1986; Jaynes and Williams, 1989).

Even if one puts to the side the almost intractable issue of self-steering, the housing market continues to be permeated by overt racial discrimination (Galster, 1986; Darden, 1987; Massey and Gross, 1991; Turner, 1992). An extensive study using testers found high rates of discrimination by sellers and landlords against black and Hispanic homebuyers and renters (Turner, Struyk, and Yinger, 1991). An econometric analysis of lending practices in California and New York found widespread discrimination against racial minorities (Schafer and Ladd, 1981). Moreover, preliminary 1991 data on national lending practices offered little reason to believe that much had changed in the succeeding decade (Wienk, 1992; LaWare, 1992). Finally, although the tester study concluded that, on average, realtors are not "steering" black clients to neighborhoods that are *significantly* different from the ones they steer white clients to, nonetheless, "blacks were steered to substantially less white neighborhoods in 8 percent of the audits, to substantially lower income neighborhoods in 5 percent of the audits, and to substantially lower value neighborhoods in 12 percent of the audits," and "neighborhoods that are [a higher percentage] black or Hispanic are less likely to be advertised, recommended, or shown, all other things being equal" (Turner, Struyk, and Yinger, 1991, pp. 28, 32).

As in the case of employment discrimination, it thus seems that antidiscrimination law enforcement is a necessary but imperfect tool of public policy. On the one hand, it has been suggested that the legal prohibition of overt discrimination stretched the geographic boundaries of the ghetto in ways that, though not producing integration for most blacks, have "permitted the filtering process to work to eliminate much of the completely unacceptable housing stock and to upgrade the quality of housing for minority families" (Orfield, 1986, p. 24). On the other hand, the Fair Housing Act received remarkably little administrative and judicial enforcement during the first twenty years after its enactment (Kushner, 1988).

In 1988 Congress amended the Fair Housing Act to make both public and private enforcement much more feasible. A preliminary review of the effects of those amendments finds that enforcement through both public and private litigation has grown significantly, but that efforts at increased administrative enforcement have been handicapped by inadequate administrative capacity (Kushner, 1992). Drawing on his own work and the work of others, Anthony Downs (1992) has offered a catalog of ways to reduce residential discrimination. He assigns highest priority to six kinds of direct action:

1. Expanding HUD's enforcement staff,
2. Establishing metropolitan-area-wide antidiscrimination agencies,
3. Increasing HUD support for state and local agencies,
4. Expanding HUD-sponsored tester-based activities,
5. Requiring state agencies to abolish caps on the amount of damages that victims can recover, and
6. Conditioning the availability of Community Development Block Grant funds on the use of certain minimal antidiscrimination enforcement tools.

The Downs suggestions would respond to some of the most overt forms of residential segregation. And yet not even stepped-up antidiscrimination enforcement will counteract the segregating effects of socioeconomic differentials and of self-steering by both black and white consumers. One possible response to the effects of socioeconomic differentials would be to challenge suburban zoning practices that preclude the production of inexpensive housing in some suburban towns. In 1991, the President's Advisory Commission on Regulatory Barriers to Affordable Housing called for the limitation of federal subsidies to states that do not take action to minimize such practices (Downs, 1991; U.S. Advisory Commission, 1991). Michael Schill (1992b) has argued that such initiatives, though legally feasible, are unlikely to make much political headway unless the suburbs are coopted with a significant payment of federal funds.

A more likely possibility would be to greatly increase the availability of housing vouchers or allowances that permit low-income households to leave the ghetto if they wish to. During the 1970s, Congress spent approximately $150 million to conduct an enormous social experiment known as the Experimental Housing Allowance Program (EHAP) (Bradbury and Downs, 1981; Struyk and Bendick, 1981; J. Friedman and Weinberg, 1982; Lowry, 1983). Although the experiment examined the effects of housing allowances on household demand and government administration, the biggest component had to do with the degree to which housing allowances would affect housing supply. EHAP offered housing allowances for up to ten years to all low-income renters and homeowners in metropolitan Green Bay, Wisconsin, and metropolitan South Bend, Indiana (Lowry, 1983).

Before the experiment, empirical disputes had given rise to a stalemate between advocates of supply-oriented programs (programs designed to increase the total number of housing units available) and advocates of demand-oriented programs (programs designed to give poor people more money with which to bid for existing housing units). Advocates of demand-oriented programs observed that they were likely to be more efficient than supply-oriented programs, because they enhanced the freedom of tenants to make utility-maximizing choices. Critics of demand-oriented programs observed that in tight housing markets where race- and class-based discrimination restricts options, a demand-oriented subsidy could easily lead to a bidding up of rents without any increase in quality—at least in the short run. An increase in rents would shift the benefits of the program from participants to landlords. Moreover, unless the demand-oriented subsidy were provided as a universal entitlement for *all* low-income households, a generalized bidding-up of rents could actually *harm* nonparticipating low-income households (Hartman, 1964; but see Stegman, 1972).

The debate over the choice between demand-oriented and supply-oriented subsidy strategies recapitulates several other longstanding debates in the housing policy community. One concerns the efficacy of the "filtering" or "trickle-down" process as a source of housing supply for low-income households. That process has always been, and remains, the principal source of low-income housing in the United States (Downs, 1990, pp. 88–92). New housing units of very high quality that are added to the stock can only be afforded by upper-income households. Those households leave slightly older, slightly deteriorated houses, which drop in value as the demand for them falls, and are then taken over by middle-income households. Those households, in turn, vacate still-older housing, and the process continues, so that each income class upgrades its living conditions without an enormous increase in cost. Old units, still in serviceable condition, trickle down to expand the supply of housing available to low-income groups.

Over time, supporters of supply-oriented housing policies have engaged in substantial internal debates over *where* in the filtering process new housing units should be added. Tax incentives for homeownership and other tax incentives for new residential construction have long been viewed as useful mechanisms for adding new units at the top of the process. "Shallow" subsidies (providing a small amount of money per beneficiary) for moderate-income families add new units into the middle of the process. "Deep" subsidies (providing a substantial amount of money per beneficiary) for low- and very low income families add new units at the bottom.

Supporters of heavy reliance on filtering have argued that the higher one looks to add units in the trickle-down chain, the less expensive the subsidy that is required "per unit." In theory, the cost savings permit policymakers to "loosen" the housing market through low-cost supply-side policies while simultaneously expanding a demand-side policy of voucher assistance for the poor. Critics of heavy reliance on filtering have objected that large old houses designed for high-income families may require such high ongoing maintenance expenditures that they deteriorate more and more rapidly as they near the bottom of the filtering chain. Such houses can quickly deteriorate beyond serviceability, so that they are abandoned without adding to the supply of decent quality housing for the poor. Critics have also objected that the process can be slow and uneven—dependent on aggregate levels of housing supply and demand in a given area, and subject to disruption by market imperfections such as racially segregated housing markets.

The findings of the different EHAP experiments were, in broad outline, quite consistent. They indicated that recipients of housing allowances ended up with decent quality housing and used almost all of the allowance to reduce the burdens of rent on their overall budget. Moreover, additional housing consumption did not stimulate rent inflation, at least in markets with a vacancy rate of at least 5 percent. In markets with such a vacancy rate, suppliers redistributed vacancies and made improvements to existing dwellings (see also Weicher, 1990). These findings were consisting with the results of an Urban Institute simulation in the late 1970s (Struyk, Marshall, and Ozanne, 1978). The Urban Institute study argued that local market conditions have a strong impact on the effectiveness of various housing programs and that over the long term local conditions should determine the optimal mix between supply- and demand-oriented programs.

Since EHAP, the most extensive study of the effects of housing vouchers on the employment opportunities of ghetto residents has been undertaken in connection with the Gautreaux Assisted Housing Program. The Gautreaux program was created through a consent decree in the aftermath of a judicial finding of widespread discrimination in Chicago's public housing program (E. Warren, 1988). It gives applicants for public housing a choice among up to three homes in either the city or the suburbs (Schill, 1992a).

A research team has undertaken a series of studies comparing those households that took advantage of the Gautreaux program to leave Chicago with those that remained in the city (Rosenbaum, Kulieke, and Rubinowitz, 1988; Rosenbaum, 1991; Rosenbaum and Popkin, 1991). Gautreaux participants who moved to the suburbs were 14 percent more likely to have a job than those who remained in the city, even though there was no difference in the average hourly wage obtained by workers in the two groups (Rosenbaum and Popkin, 1991). Although the magnitude of the effect is not enormous, it is substantial enough to justify continued support for the use of housing vouchers as an employment enhancement program. Moreover, other studies seem to find even greater effects along other dimensions, such as the level of children's school achievement and overall "neighborhood satisfaction" (Rosenbaum, 1991; Schill, 1992a).

In sum, a national urban policy agenda should address indirect restrictions on employment opportunities—restrictions that flow from residential segregation. This aspect of the agenda should have several components. It should include improvements in public transportation and job information networks. It should incorporate Downs's proposals to improve enforcement of antidiscrimination laws. And it should expand the availability of Gautreaux-style housing vouchers, in order to improve families' ability to compete in the housing market (subsidizing increased construction where necessary to maintain adequate vacancy rates).

Beyond Mobility: Access-to-Enterprise Zones

Policymakers must be aware that even the most aggressive pro-mobility strategy will inevitably be incomplete. Even if people are given broader opportunities to move out into the labor market, they may not choose to take advantage of them. Movement almost always involves costs. Old friendships and sources of informal support suffer; it takes effort to establish new ones. For some people, those costs may prove more important than the new opportunities that moving might bring.

Undoubtedly some observers will be tempted to say that no further public action is required once everyone has been offered a meaningful opportunity to move. But such a response is too glib. The justification for public action is not merely the need for compensatory justice for certain individuals; rather, it is that, by hypothesis, certain neighborhoods are the scenes of interacting externalities whose synergistic harms to the community as a whole exceed the sum of their harms to individual citizens.

What approach should policymakers take to intervening in underclass neighborhoods? I would recommend that we begin by devoting federal dollars to experimenting with what can be termed "access-to-enterprise zones" (AEZs)—neighborhoods whose residents are singled out for the intensive provision of job opportunities through work subsidies and guaranteed public jobs.

Return to the possibility posed at the beginning of this chapter—that young adults in a neighborhood share an overwhelming distrust for the formal job market. Suppose that their environment offers them few examples of adults who have held down jobs that pay a wage adequate to keep them out of poverty. Suppose further that out of frustration and boredom they become actively engaged in predatory crime within their neighborhood. The increased crime drives away the retail businesses that help to make neighborhoods attractive and drives away neighbors with the financial ability to support neighborhood institutions. A downward spiral ensues. (See Myrdal, 1957; Wilson, 1987; Blakely, 1989.)

What is called for is a set of policy interventions designed to break the downward spiral. More effective police services might help. But it also seems essential to provide young adults with reason to believe that they can achieve an acceptable level of material prosperity through lawful work. To reverse the spiral, one needs to combine lower crime rates with higher neighborhood income, to enable the restoration of commercial and social anchors that act as stabilizing forces for a community.

Unfortunately, there are no sure-fire policy interventions guaranteed to accomplish those goals. We are still experimenting, groping for policy configurations that work. It is in that spirit that I would propose experimentation with the AEZ hybrid. AEZs would blend ideas from earlier enterprise zone and guaranteed jobs proposals. The overall AEZ program would emphasize two kinds of employment stimulus: a private sector AEZ tax credit and an AEZ guaranteed jobs program.

The AEZ tax credit would give any private sector employer who hired an AEZ resident a nonrefundable tax credit equal to 40 percent of the first $15,000 of the worker's wages each year. A similar credit was made part of the 1993 empowerment zone program. Unlike that program, however, the AEZ tax credit would not require that the worker carry out job activities within the AEZ. The AEZ tax credit would be twice as generous as the 1993 empowerment zone program: 40 percent of the first $15,000 worth of wages instead of 20 percent. Moreover, because the justification for AEZ intervention is the assumption that individuals sometimes benefit when they have a neighbor in the work force, regardless of that neighbor's family income, the AEZ tax credit would not carry the TJTC's usual requirement that a worker live in an economically disadvantaged family.

In the first section of this chapter, I discussed the low participation rates associated with the TJTC. That phenomenon suggests that an AEZ tax credit alone might well not be enough to trigger a surge in AEZ employment. Accordingly, I would supplement it with a public sector guaranteed jobs program for AEZ residents—a more limited and slightly modified version of Harvey's proposal.

The AEZ guaranteed jobs program would carry out tasks identified in consultation with the local government AEZ sponsor. The CETA experience gives reason to be concerned about the risk that local political priorities might overwhelm and distort the program. To minimize that risk, the AEZ guaranteed jobs program would be federally funded *and* administered, along the lines of the Works Progress Administration of the New Deal.

Perhaps the trickiest problem associated with designing a guaranteed jobs program involves choosing what wage to pay program participants. Flat wage proposals such as Kaus's and Ellwood's would seem to offer workers little reason not to shirk on the job. But Harvey's "market wage" proposal could lead some workers to forgo private sector opportunities, thereby increasing program costs and passing up options that, at least in American society, might provide a better stepping stone to long-term employment. Accordingly, I would propose experimentation with a "compressed wage scale" for participants in the AEZ guaranteed jobs program. The scale would start at the minimum wage and go up, but would be designed with the goal of maintaining a genuine incentive for participants to seek out and accept private sector opportunities for which they have the appropriate skills.

To avoid the perverse effect of undermining the mobility of AEZ residents, it would be necessary to maintain "transitional" eligibility for AEZ "benefits." Consider a hypothetical worker who takes an AEZ guaranteed job and then moves to a private sector job, thanks in part to the private sector AEZ credit. Suppose she is able to save enough money to move to a safer neighborhood in the city, and that she would like to do so. In order to permit her to carry out her plan, the AEZ program would provide that, for one full year after moving, she would retain full eligibility to participate in the guaranteed jobs program and to qualify an employer for the private sector tax credit. The employer tax credit would be phased out during the succeeding two years.

Access-to-enterprise zones would be designated by the Department of Housing and Urban Development, based on applications received from the relevant state and local governments. The research literature discussed in Chapter 5 indicates that the most serious urban problems are concentrated in a relatively small number of metropolitan areas. These areas should be the targets of the AEZ experiment.

It is important that each AEZ application include a local commitment to a "strategic plan" to revitalize the AEZ, similar to the commitment required in the 1993 law. Priority would be given to applications from local governments that had obtained referendum approval from zone residents. The primary criterion for designating which zones would be eligible to participate in the experiment would be the unemployment rate within the zone.

The theme of social mobility discussed earlier reinforces the importance of the local "strategic plan" commitment. Mincy's discussion in Chapter 5 documents the relationship between "socialization effects" and youth opportunities for social mobility, including wages, total earnings, and hours worked. Thus, to enhance social mobility, the "strategic plan" should concentrate on developing responses to those socialization effects. Such responses might involve reorienting police services toward community policing models (Belknap, Thorash, and Trajanowicz, 1987; Green and Mastrofski, 1988; Skolnick and Bayley, 1988; Clairmont, 1991; Leighton, 1991). Or they might involve commitments to support nonprofit groups that are engaged in economic development, training, or mentorship activities within the AEZ (Mayer, 1984; Ross and Usher, 1986; Ferguson, 1990; Mincy and Wiener, 1990; Caftel, 1992; Lehman and Lento, 1992).

Anecdotal evidence, moreover, suggests that sometimes programs designed by community-based organizations are able to accomplish more than centrally designed programs. Local design may enable more supple responses to relevant variations in the socioeconomic context in which the program functions (Taub, 1988). Participation in a program's design may induce volunteers to cooperate more enthusiastically in its implementation. The "strategic plan" requirement could facilitate community-based experiments with new ways to counteract socialization-effect obstacles to social mobility (Schramm, 1987).

Past experience with CETA and the Model Cities program suggests a potential political trap associated with the AEZ proposal. The trap would be set if the proposal's design were substantially altered in order to obtain political approval. For example, one type of alteration would make the program touch a greater number of electoral districts, but with much less intensity. The trap would be sprung if that alteration led to a program that would be too small to catalyze change *anywhere* and would therefore be adjudged a complete failure (Sundquist and Davis, 1969; Warren, Rose, and Bergunder, 1974; Frieden and Kaplan, 1975).

A different kind of alteration would maintain the intensity of programmatic intervention, but raise the total cost by addressing it to many more electoral districts. Note that such an alteration need not, in and of itself, be a problem. The budget constraint facing social welfare programs is not entirely exogenous to the policymaking process. Programs about which people are genuinely excited can increase the overall amount available to be spent on human needs.

But the trap that would lie dormant in this type of alteration is that, while the program might well bring about valuable improvements in some areas, substantial amounts of money would also be spent in areas in which spatial targeting was never theoretically justified to begin with. The trap would be sprung when someone decided to criticize the program as "target inefficient." Or, even worse, the inescapable consequences of political compromises in the design phase might be characterized as scandalous examples of "waste" in the implementation phase (Mucciaroni, 1992).

These sorts of political traps may not be avoidable. Much depends on the extent to which political leaders are persuaded that our large cities face distinctive problems that are of truly national concern. If the leadership is persuaded, a targeted AEZ experiment may be a useful source of insight into other questions. Is the phenomenon of distrust such a significant feature in urban racial landscapes that it affects job opportunities? Would the availability of guaranteed public jobs really make much of a difference in the extent of that distrust? To what extent do other, more locally driven, aspects of urban policy determine the effectiveness of federal programs like AEZs? At this point, we do not know enough to speak with confidence.

·   ·   ·

In the early 1990s, concerns about the plight of the black urban poor have led to increasing interest in devoting substantial public resources to enterprise zones and guaranteed public jobs programs. I have reviewed those proposals and discussed the technical and political objections they have faced, and I have proposed an alternative approach to updating our national urban policy, organized around the theme of social and spatial mobility.

I have suggested that long-term and short-term policy responses to inner-city unemployment should proceed simultaneously on three fronts. The first front involves direct mobility constrictions that take the form of racial discrimination in employment. As part of the long-term response to those constrictions, policymakers and citizens generally need to be educated about the ongoing role played by direct racial discrimination in employment—particularly the variant known as "statistical discrimination." It will also be important to monitor how the changes made by the Civil Rights Act of 1991 are implemented.

The second front involves indirect mobility constrictions that may flow from residential segregation. Here the long-term response should include both improvements in public transportation and job information networks and intensified enforcement of laws against discrimination in housing. Perhaps most important, it should include expansion of the provision of housing vouchers to low-income families living in depressed urban neighborhoods.

The third front involves policies addressed to the needs of people who cannot or will not move. The access-to-enterprise zone proposal is an idea for providing a short-term response to the lack of meaningful employment opportunity in depressed neighborhoods. The proposal combines three elements: private sector tax credits, guaranteed public jobs, and a commitment from local governments to interventions that address other contributors to neighborhood distress.

Any discussion of an urban policy agenda should conclude with a note of caution. Action along the three fronts I have described cannot, standing alone, do much to respond to the broad array of problems confronting the urban poor. National policies described in other chapters in this volume—policies of macroeconomic stimulation, human capital development, health care, and income support—remain far more significant. But even after all these other policies are in place and fine tuned, more can be done to address the needs of America's black urban poor. The three fronts I have identified here are likely places to begin.

Reform of Health Care
for the Nonelderly Poor

BARBARA L. WOLFE

Health care reform was one of President Clinton's most important policy foci in his first year in office. The two central problems of the existing health care system are the increasing cost of medical care generally and the access to care of certain disadvantaged populations, particularly the poor. The growing number of Americans who are without medical insurance to cover the cost of care is the primary problem of access, but the lack of nearby doctors or clinics in many areas is also a problem. Costs and access are, of course, related. If more people have access, utilization and costs will increase; if the rate of increase in medical care expenditures is not stemmed, it will be difficult to increase access.

A Brief Background

The United States spends more per capita on health care than any other country. In 1990, total expenditures for health care were $666.2 billion.[1] Table 10.1 presents an overview of the total costs, per capita costs, and share of the gross national product spent on medical care over the last three decades. It documents the substantial increase in resources devoted to health care over these thirty years—from $631 per person in 1960 to $2,566 per person in 1990 (both in 1990 dollars), an annual rate of growth in real terms of 5.06 percent—as well as the substantial increase in the share of GNP devoted to health care. In the late 1980s the share of GNP spent on health care went up by one percentage point every forty months. It was 12.2 percent in 1990. This rate seems to be accelerating and was projected to reach 14.3 percent of GNP, or $898 billion, in 1993.[2] Even if the rate of increase remained at the lower pre-1990 rate, by the year 2000 we would be spending at least 15 percent of GNP on health care.[3]

Medical care is financed by several sources. About 23 percent is financed

Table 10.1   National health expenditures, 1960–1990

	1960	1970	1980	1990
National health expenditures (amount in billions)[a]	$120.0	$250.5	$396.7	$666.2
Per capita amount[a]	$631	$1,166	$1,686	$2,566
Share of personal health care expenditures covered by private insurance	21.0%	23.4%	29.7%	31.8%
Share of personal health care expenditures covered by public insurance	21.4%	34.6%	39.7%	41.3%
Share of personal health care expenditures covered by out-of-pocket dollars	55.9%	39.5%	27.1%	23.3%
Health care spending as a share of GNP	5.3%	7.3%	9.2%	12.2%
Percentage of population uninsured			14.6%[b]	15.7%

Source: U.S. House of Representatives (1992), pp. 287–291, 318.
a. Constant 1990 dollars adjusted using CPI-U.
b. 1979 data.

by private sources (the consumer directly); 26 percent by private health insurance plus 10 percent by private health insurance in the form of federal and state tax subsidies toward the purchase of insurance; and 41 percent by direct public spending, including 17 percent by Medicare and 14 percent by Medicaid (Steuerle, 1991).

The dominant form of health insurance is private insurance. Approximately three-quarters of the population is covered by private plans, two-thirds through plans offered at their (or a family member's) place of employment—so-called employer-based plans. The tax system encourages this arrangement, because the contribution of employers to health insurance is not counted as part of an employee's taxable income. As of 1987 these employer contributions were 5.1 percent of wages and salaries.[4] Since the value of this subsidy varies by marginal tax rate, it provides virtually no benefit to the poor; the estimated 1992 value of the federal tax subsidies was $270 for households in the lowest income quintile and $525 for those in the next quintile, compared with $1,560 for those in the highest quintile (Steuerle, 1991). Not surprisingly, given the small subsidy to the poor, a far smaller percentage of them are covered through employer-based private insurance; indeed, in 1989 only 2.7 percent of persons below 50 percent of the poverty line obtained health insurance at their place of employment, as did 6.2 percent of those between 50 and 100 percent of the poverty line and 13 percent of the near-poor (100 to 150 percent of the poverty line); in comparison, 41 percent of those at 250 percent of the poverty line were insured through their employer. Including family members, the percentages covered by employer-sponsored insurance in each of these income groups were 13.3, 23.1, 45.5, and 86.9 percent, respectively.

Nearly 10 percent of the population is covered by Medicaid, a joint federal-state public program that pays for the health care of some of the low-income and disabled populations. As of 1990, approximately 18 percent of all children and about 61 percent of poor children were covered by Medicaid (U.S. House of Representatives, 1992). The largest public program that provides health insurance is Medicare, a federal program providing coverage to those aged sixty-five and over and to those who are disabled and who qualify to receive Social Security benefits based on their disability.[5]

For businesses, the cost of health care is escalating rapidly, more rapidly than the combination of increases in productivity and overall inflation. This limits firms' ability to shift the increase in premium costs to employees.[6] In response, firms are cutting back their coverage, both by reducing the generosity of the coverage (by increasing deductibles and/or the coinsurance rate) and, more important, by reducing coverage of workers' dependents.[7] Coverage for part-time employees has been cut, as have benefits for temporary employees.[8]

Public spending on health care is also increasing rapidly. Medicaid continues to grow as a share of state budgets, reflecting price increases, increased eligibility due to the high unemployment rates of the 1980s, and increases in benefits and eligibility mandated by the federal government. Similarly, health care spending is the second-fastest growing component of the federal budget (outpaced only by the growth in the public debt). At both levels of government, health care spending accounts for at least 14 percent of total expenditures.[9]

The other major aspect of the health care dilemma is the increasing number of people without health insurance. Between thirty-three million and thirty-seven million U.S. citizens do not have any health insurance coverage at a point in time, including perhaps twenty to twenty-five million who were uninsured throughout the year. Another twenty million have too little health insurance to protect them from the financial burdens of a major illness.[10]

According to Current Population Survey data, the percentage of the nonaged population who were uninsured as of March of each year increased from 14.6 percent in 1979 (the first year such data were collected) to 17.5 percent by 1986. This occurred as firms reduced private coverage, as persons became unemployed, as increasing numbers worked in industries that tend not to provide coverage (such as the service sector),[11] as premiums for private coverage rose, and as states attempted to reduce their Medicaid expenditures by restricting eligibility for Medicaid (and welfare).[12]

The probability of being uninsured is far greater among persons who live in families with incomes below the poverty line or just above it than among those who live in families with higher incomes. About 60 percent of those without insurance live in families with incomes below 200 percent of the poverty line, and nearly 30 percent live in families with incomes below the poverty line.[13] Persons with lower incomes are less likely to leave the rolls of the uninsured within the first few months of noncoverage than are those with higher incomes. According to Katherine Swartz and Timothy McBride (1990), nearly 29 percent of those in families with incomes less than half the poverty line at the beginning of their spell of being uninsured have spells lasting at least thirteen months, compared with 25 to 26 percent for those above 150 percent of the poverty line.[14] Young persons are much more likely to be uninsured than older persons, those with lower incomes more likely than those with higher incomes, and Hispanics more than whites, with blacks intermediate between these two groups. Those living in single-parent households are less likely to be protected than childless couples. Table 10.2 pre-

Table 10.2 Who are the uninsured?

	Incidence (% uninsured all year)	Composition (% of uninsured all year)
Age		
< 6	9.7	9.9
6–18	11.6	21.4
19–24	20.3	19.0
25–54	10.4	41.9
55–64	8.6	7.9
All ages < 65	11.4	100.0
By Income Needs		
< Poverty line (PL)	27.5	33.0
PL to 1.25 × PL	26.6	9.5
1.25 × PL to 2 × PL	19.5	22.3
2 × P1 to 4 × PL	8.1	24.7
> 4 × PL	3.5	10.6
Ethnic/Racial Group		
White	8.8	58.3
Black	16.2	17.6
Hispanic	25.3	19.2

Source: P. Short (1990), tables 1–3. Calculations use data from the National Medical Expenditure Survey.

sents the incidence of lack of insurance by age, race, and income group as well as the distribution of the uninsured across these groups.

There is evidence of a link between insurance coverage and the utilization of medical care. Those with insurance use more care (controlling for health, age, and location) than those without coverage; those with more extensive coverage use more care (at least outpatient care) than those with less coverage. For example, one study found that low-income persons without insurance had on average half the number of physician contacts than those insured had in 1986 (Freeman et al., 1990). A Kaiser/Commonwealth survey in 1992 found that 19 percent of the uninsured had been refused care over the prior twelve months because they did not have insurance or could not pay (M. Smith et al., 1992). The Pepper Commission Report (1990) cites evidence that among persons with serious illnesses, the uninsured saw physicians only half as often as the insured (p. 34), and that cancer treatments differed for persons with and without insurance. The uninsured are also less likely to have a regular source of care. In addition to delayed and forgone medical care,[15] the lack of coverage causes financial insecurity, inequitable burdens across communities, and increased costs for businesses due to the shifting of the costs of care for uninsured and underinsured persons; it also increases participation in welfare programs such as Aid to Families with Dependent Children.

Health and the Poverty Population

Poor health and poverty are correlated. To some extent poor health may cause poverty by restricting the hours one can work and the kinds of work one can perform, as well as by necessitating costly medical care and special equipment or services. In turn, limited resources, including lack of health insurance, the limited ability to pay for the indirect and direct costs of medical care, and the inadequate housing and living conditions associated with poverty, may cause health problems.

Evidence of the association seems clear. The National Center for Health Statistics (1991) reported that limitation of activity and self-reports of poor and fair health are higher among the low-income population than among those with middle or higher incomes. In 1989, 23.2 percent of those with family incomes less than $14,000 reported some limitation of activity, while 14.8 percent of those in families with incomes between $14,000 and $25,000, and 8.4 percent of those in families with more than $50,000, reported such limitations. Similarly, nearly 20 percent of those in this lowest income group reported fair or poor health, compared with 10 percent and less than 4 percent of those in the middle- and higher-income groups.[16]

Probably the starkest tie between poverty and health is among those who are severely mentally ill and homeless. Approximately 1 percent of the population is believed to be severely and chronically disabled through mental illness, with schizophrenia and major mood disorders being the most common diagnoses for this group. Most of these persons are poor, uninsured, and unemployed. The chronically mentally ill rarely work (the employment rate is estimated to be 25 percent) and as of 1989, their average income was $4,200 a year (Task Force on Homelessness and Severe Mental Illness, 1992, p. 10). About half of this group receives public transfer funds such as Social Security Disability Income and Supplemental Security Income; others receive no publicly provided income. About one-third of the homeless are believed to be severely mentally ill, and about 5 percent of the severely mentally ill are believed to be homeless at any point in time (ibid.). (See Appendix A for a more detailed discussion of the homeless and health.)

The homeless suffer particularly poor health. Ill health may be the cause of homelessness if illness or disability leads to loss of income and housing. Homelessness itself can lead to malnutrition and exposure to infectious disease. But what may contribute most to the ill health of the homeless is the problems that being homeless pose for successful treatment. Without a permanent residence it is difficult for the homeless to be followed up or contacted; living on the street or in a shelter is not conducive to rest and recuperation; and sticking to a medication regimen may be almost impossible when there is nowhere to store the medication.

Other health problems that low-income persons are more likely to develop include high blood pressure, obesity, cancer, and infectious diseases such as tuberculosis; they are also more likely to be victims of violent crime, with resulting higher rates of mortality and injury. Low-income persons have a risk of death from heart disease that is 25 percent higher than that of the average-income person.

Low-income children are more likely to be exposed to lead, which leaves them vulnerable to impaired development; to have higher levels of iron deficiency (U.S. Department of Health and Human Services, 1991, pp. 29–31); and to contract AIDS, due primarily to exposure at birth or through breastfeeding (Children's Defense Fund, 1989, p. 37; see Appendix B for more detail). They are also two to five times more likely to die of cancer, heart disease, congenital anomalies, and pneumonia/influenza than are children in higher-income families (Nelson, 1992).

A greater proportion of blacks than nonblacks are poor. The net result appears to be an additional set of health problems concentrated among blacks.[17] These problems include high blood pressure; coronary heart disease; diabetes and its complications such as blindness, kidney failure, stroke, and heart disease; and sudden infant death syndrome. The higher rate of teen out-of-wedlock births among blacks increases the risk of infant mortality and low-birth-weight infants—and may produce a continuing relationship between poverty and poor health.

Table 10.3 illustrates another link between health and income. The adult population is divided into income deciles using "equivalent" income—income adjusted for family size and composition. Then, using the 1980 National Medical Care Utilization and Expenditure Survey, the distribution of two measures of poor health are calculated. The first measure is those persons with a health condition (or conditions) that are associated with a limitation; the second measure is those who self-report that they have poor health. Both distributions indicate that poor health is concentrated among those with low incomes. This is particularly the case for those reporting poor health.

There is also evidence that poor health limits earnings. Peter Ries (1990) reported that in the mid-1980s the percentage of currently employed persons who reported fair or poor health was relatively low (3.8 percent among eighteen- to forty-four-year-olds); the percentage among those not in the labor force was much higher (12.6 percent). Other studies (Luft, 1975; Lee, 1982; Haveman et al., 1993) have also demonstrated a link between health and labor force participation and earnings, particularly among men.

Wolfe and Steven Hill (1993) find that women aged eighteen to sixty living in lower-income households, older women, women with less schooling, single mothers, and other not-married women are all more likely to report greater health problems than other women. Working women tend to have better health than

Table 10.3   Distribution of health status of adults by income needs

Income/needs decile	Health limitations	Poor health
1	21.4%	30.7%
2	16.2	19.0
3	12.5	11.9
4	10.3	10.4
5	8.6	9.3
6	6.8	4.9
7	6.4	4.4
8	5.3	2.3
9	5.7	4.3
10	6.6	2.9
Total	100.0	100.0

Source: Gottschalk and Wolfe (1992). Calculations use data from the 1980 National Medical Care Utilization and Expenditure Survey.

women who do not work, and poor health negatively influences one's ability to earn enough to move the family above the poverty line, at least among single mothers. Having a disabled child also reduces the mother's earning capacity.

Turning to the link between poverty and poor health, we note again that at any point in time, the poor and near-poor are less likely to have health insurance than the rest of the population. Most of those who have coverage are covered by Medicaid, the state-federal entitlement program, but it covers less than one-half of the poor. Those not covered include single persons and childless couples who are not generally eligible for Medicaid. Many older children and nonpregnant women, men in single-parent households, and couples in families with an unemployed head of household, however, are also not eligible for Medicaid in a number of states because of the state financial standards for coverage.

In general, the poor have more difficulty obtaining medical care than the rest of the population. This is the case even though, on average, low-income persons use more medical care than higher-income persons because they are in poorer health (S. Mayer, 1991; Gottschalk and Wolfe, 1992). Their greater difficulty in obtaining care reflects several phenomena. First, they are less likely to have insurance and therefore they visit the doctor less often. According to a 1986 study, of those in families with incomes less than $15,000, those with insurance had an average of 7.5 physician visits a year, while those without coverage had 3.5 visits per year. Hospital days vary as well, but by less than physician visits.[18]

Second, many of those with Medicaid find that restrictions on Medicaid limit the amount of care they can receive; moreover, many physicians refuse to treat Medicaid patients because of the program's low reimbursement amounts.[19]

Third, access problems are likely to get worse. States are further restricting Medicaid for the nonelderly in order to finance the increasing and high cost of the elderly and disabled populations covered under Medicaid as well as the federally mandated coverage of pregnant women and of children born after September 30, 1983. In addition, the federal government now requires states to pay Medicare premiums and out-of-pocket costs for persons with incomes below the poverty line.[20] Moreover, institutions (hospitals and clinics) that once provided a safety net—medical care for those without insurance and the financial means to pay for care—are facing increased pressure and have less ability to provide charity care (see Feder, Hadley, and Mullner, 1984). These pressures come from the greater demands of the increased numbers of uninsured, the AIDS epidemic, continuing drug use by drug abusers, and changes in reimbursement formulas of public and private insurers.[21]

Fourth, areas with heavy concentrations of poor residents, whether inner-city or rural, have difficulty attracting physicians. This shortage reflects the financial differences between a practice in an area in which most people have private insurance or Medicare versus an area with Medicaid coverage and large numbers who are uninsured, as well as the perceived differences in working conditions such as greater crime in poor urban areas (see Kindig et al., 1987). The shortage in rural areas is expected to become worse with the retirement of physicians there, the reductions in the federal program designed to increase the supply of physicians to rural areas (National Health Service Corps), and financial pressures on community and migrant health centers.

Fifth, the total cost of care and the location of care are significant barriers to the receipt of care by the poor. Many poor people do not have cars and must rely on public transportation. A combination of residential location and health problems may require a cab ride to obtain care. For those living in rural areas, particularly areas with very low population densities, the problem is even more acute because the number of providers is low and declining.[22]

As a result of these problems and a host of others, less preventive medical care is delivered to the poor. The rate of immunizations in large urban areas, for example, is far lower than in other areas. As of 1985, the rate of measles vaccination was 55.5 percent in central cities and 63.3 percent in the outlying areas; for rubella it was 53.9 percent, compared with 61 percent; for polio, 47.1 percent compared with 58.4 percent. Poor children aged five to eleven were three times less likely to see a dentist in 1986 than a child in a high-income family and nearly four times more likely to have never seen a dentist (Children's Defense Fund, 1989, p. 61). Among children under age eighteen, more than one-fifth (22 percent) of poor children had no contact with a physician in 1986, compared with 14 percent of children in higher-income families. In 1987, a far lower percentage of low-income women over forty had ever had a mammogram and clinical breast exam than other women—22 compared with 36 percent (U.S. Department of Health and Human Services, Public Health Service, 1990).

Overall, once health is taken into account, the poor do not use more care than the nonpoor. Two recent studies (S. Mayer, 1991; Gottschalk and Wolfe, 1992) suggest that greater use by the poor is due to the health and age of the poor and that after adjusting for such differences there appears to be an equal distribution of medical care dollars across the income distribution.[23] It is those without insurance, not the insured poor, who use less care.

For certain diseases, less access and later contact with the medical profession leads to poorer health. One indicator of this pattern is the lower five-year cancer survival rates of blacks versus whites. For example, the 1981–1988 male survival rate was 47.2 percent for whites compared with 33.4 percent for blacks; for women the rates were 57.4 percent and 44 percent, respectively. For breast cancer the rates were 67.5 percent versus 57.4 percent; for prostate cancer, 75.6 percent versus 63 percent. With few exceptions the pattern for cancer survival persists.

Are the greater health problems of the poor due to poverty, lack of insurance, or a low level of information regarding the value of, or inclinations to attend to, preventive health care, broadly defined? Recent work suggests that individual behavior—for instance, smoking, alcohol and drug use, nutrition, exercise, inoculations, and medical care—differs between the poor and nonpoor. Poor people seem to place a lower weight on future health status than do the nonpoor. One implication of this finding is that the provision of health insurance alone may have less influence on the health of the poor than one would expect.

Poverty itself plays an important role in these behavior patterns. A number of health problems as well as substance abuse (smoking and drug abuse) are associated with low education, which suggests that some behaviors are related to a lack of information. If more information on the harmful effects of drug abuse and cigarette smoking were provided in an appropriate forum, a reduction in such behaviors would follow. Such information could be provided in clinics, in special targeted programs, and in schools. An example regarding low-birth-weight infants is presented in some detail below.

Persons living in areas of concentrated poverty, and the poor in general, may also face far higher *indirect* costs of receiving medical care than those with more resources. These costs include the loss of hourly wages, the cost of transportation, the increased probability of losing one's job, the cost of learning where care can be obtained—all weighted by the high value of income for those with very low incomes.[24] Such costs are likely to limit the use of care by the poor, including care for their children, where the indirect costs are multiplied. When this is combined with limited hours when care is available—for most, prime work hours—many poor persons may forgo preventive care and seek care only for serious health problems. Public intervention can influence this behavior by making medical care more available in the community and by expanding the hours during which medical care is offered.

In addition, many of the poor may fail to place as high a weight on the future as those with more resources. Those living in poverty may be overwhelmed by today's problems and not have the energy to cope with planning for the future. The poor have a higher probability of premature mortality and must struggle to provide a safe environment for themselves and their children. Under these conditions, it is not surprising to find a lower weight placed on "health investments" such as preventive doctor visits, reductions in smoking, and so forth. Poverty creates a different opportunity set, which in turn creates a different set of choices. Reduce poverty and the choices are likely to change. The following two examples of poverty and poor health outcomes illustrate these issues.

The United States has high rates of infant mortality and low birth weight relative to those of other developed countries. These rates are particularly high for blacks and Hispanics. Over the 1970s the rates declined rapidly; they then were relatively stable, but increased somewhat after the mid-1980s. Increased pregnancies among unmarried teens, a reduction in available abortions, increased use of drugs, and a lack of prenatal care contribute to these phenomena. Of the known risk factors, only a reduction in smoking has reduced these rates in recent years. One newer explanation of the increasing rates of low-birth-weight infants is the increased use of drugs, particularly cocaine and crack, among pregnant women. According to Arden Handler and colleagues (1991), the exposure of infants *in utero* to cocaine is associated with a threefold increase in the risk of low-birth-weight births.[25] Low birth weight is in turn associated with long-term increased probabilities of disability, particularly neurodevelopmental handicaps[26]—as well as a far greater risk of infant mortality.[27] Medical care costs are also much higher—on the order of $12,000 per low-weight baby in 1991 dollars for infant care alone for those born in New York City.[28]

How prevalent is the use of drugs during pregnancy? We lack accurate statistics, but according to one study (Phibbs, Bateman, and Schwartz, 1991), about 11 percent of newborns in one hospital in New York City were exposed prenatally to cocaine or crack. Theodore Joyce, Andrew Racine, and Naci Mocan (1992) estimate that between 30 and 80 percent of the two-percentage-point increase in black low-birth-weight births in New York City (from 11.0 to 13.1 percent) over the years 1984–1989 was due to increased use of cocaine; among Hispanics, they suggest, drug use is far less important. Chronic alcohol use can also create health risks for infants; infants of alcoholic mothers may be at a greater risk of congenital heart defects—another expensive malady that persists over many years (Phibbs, 1991).

Another risk factor for low-birth-weight infants is smoking. A study of white married women, aged twenty to thirty-four, found that the probability of having a low-birth-weight baby increased by 26 percent for every five cigarettes smoked per day; based on this the authors estimate that the elimination of smoking would reduce the incidence of low birth weight by 19 percent (Kleinman and Madans, 1985).[29] Little is known about antismoking programs for pregnant women. However, a small recent randomized trial of smoking cessation (the Maternal Smoking and Infant Birth Weight trial) found that cigarette consumption was cut in half by an intervention program—with no significant differences by maternal characteristics (Hebel, Nowicki, and Sexton, 1985). The cessation of smoking reduced low birth weights, especially among women at greatest risk of having a low-birth-weight infant. These results have policy implications; they suggest that prenatal care, information about the dangers of cigarette smoking, and a program to eliminate smoking among pregnant women could reduce the incidence of low-birth-weight infants.[30]

Another intervention that seems promising in reducing low-birth-weight babies is enhanced prenatal care. Enhanced prenatal care generally uses case management to provide nutrition counseling, health education, psychosocial counseling, and home visitation, as appropriate. Early evidence from North Carolina and Kentucky suggests that a sizable reduction in low-birth-weight infants is possible through enhanced clinic-based care for Medicaid-eligible women (Guyer, 1990).

Another health-related problem among the poor is the growing number of young children who are not vaccinated against common childhood diseases. New epidemics of diseases that are easily preventable can result. For example, the number of reported cases of measles went from a low of about two thousand cases in 1982–83 to twenty-five thousand in 1990. This tremendous increase was attributed to the lack of immunization and, in particular, to the lack of immunization of poor minority children living in urban areas. According to the Centers for Disease Control (1991), Hispanic and black preschool children living in urban areas are seven to nine times more likely to contract measles than white children are.

The National Vaccine Advisory Committee has attempted to discover why children are not being vaccinated. Many of their explanations focus on the role of the medical care profession. Adequate records may not be available or a child's immunization status may not be assessed when care is received in a clinic—the site of care for many low-income children, including perhaps half of all black and Hispanic children. There is also little coordination among public assistance agencies. Many children who are not vaccinated are enrolled in Medicaid and the Special Supplemental Food Program for Women, Infants, and Children (WIC), which indicates that Medicaid coverage itself does not ensure that vaccinations will take place. Moreover, the health care delivery system may require separate appointments to be made in advance, a physical done prior to immunization, a referral, and administrative fees to be paid.[31] A further reason for limited vaccinations involves the limited hours that clinics are open and providers are in their offices. A lack of communication due to language barriers also contributes to the lack of care received. The current system is failing at this important activity and the results are all too evident. The "causes" seem to rest primarily not with problem behaviors of parents but, rather, with the "high costs" imposed through the medical and welfare systems.

Overall, reported health problems are greater for the poor than the nonpoor, whether the measure is self-reported rating of health as excellent to poor, bed disability days, percentage with a chronic condition, or number of acute conditions per year. These factors lead to a greater need by the poor for medical care. At the same time, lack of insurance reduces the use of medical care among the poor. Other factors also limit use, particularly of preventive care, and these include the indirect costs of utilization, hours of service by providers, and limited numbers of private providers in low-income areas.

Public Programs

The situation facing poor persons with regard to medical care was far worse prior to the introduction of a federal-state program designed to allay the problem—the Medicaid program. Most poor persons were without the financial resources to pay for medical care, and many went without care: in 1963, a few years before the introduction of Medicaid, 54 percent of the poor did not see a physician, and in 1964 children under age fifteen in families with high incomes saw physicians 67 percent more often than children in low-income families (Davis, 1975, pp. 42–43). The introduction of the Medicaid program clearly improved access to health care among the poor. By 1971, children in families with high incomes saw physicians only 20 percent more often than children in low-income families (Davis, 1975).

Medicaid

The primary public program providing health care coverage to the low-income, nonelderly population is the Medicaid program, first established under Title XIX of the Social Security Act of 1965. The program is a combined federal-state program in which the federal government pays between 50 percent and nearly 80 percent (depending on the state's average per capita income) of the cost of services, and sets up some requirements. The states have substantial leeway, however, in determining who is eligible, what care is covered, and reimbursement formulas and amounts. Traditionally, for the nonelderly population, those eligible for Aid to Families with Dependent Children must be covered, as well as those on Supplementary Security Income, a program for the blind and those severely disabled with low incomes. Across all states, as of 1990, only 45.2 percent of the poor were covered by Medicaid, including about 70 percent of those younger than age six, a bit more than 50 percent of older children up to age eighteen, but only about a third of poor adults aged nineteen to sixty-four. Thus the majority of the nonelderly poor are not covered by Medicaid. This is even more the case for the near-poor—those with incomes between 100 and 133 percent of the poverty line. Less than 20 percent of this population is covered by Medicaid.

As of 1990, 25.3 million persons were covered by Medicaid, including 11.2 million children and 6.0 million adults in AFDC families; total expenditures were $64.9 billion, including $17.7 billion spent on the AFDC-eligible population (U.S. Department of Health and Human Services, Social Security Administration, 1991). Since 1972, AFDC children have accounted for approximately a constant percentage of all Medicaid recipients—about 44 percent. AFDC adults have increased as a proportion of those eligible—from about 18 percent to 24 percent. The AFDC-eligible population has accounted for a decreasing proportion of Medicaid expenditures, however, going from a third in 1972 to a quarter in 1989. Over this period, the big increases in Medicaid expenditures have been for disabled persons, blind persons, and those aged sixty-five and over.

Populations newly covered as of 1992 are all pregnant women and all children born after September 30, 1983, whose family income is below the poverty line, whether or not they receive welfare. States may, at their discretion, provide coverage to individuals who meet the categorical requirements of AFDC or SSI, whose incomes are above the eligibility line, but whose medical care expenses reduce their net income to below the eligibility limit. These persons are called the "medically needy." (Appendix C provides detail on eligibility as of 1992.) AFDC recipients have far lower Medicaid expenditures per capita than other persons covered by Medicaid. In 1990 Medicaid payments averaged $811 per child and $1,429 per adult in an AFDC family, compared with $2,568 for all recipients (U.S. House of Representatives, 1992, p. 1662).

There are five major problems with the way Medicaid operates. The first is its "all or nothing" character (Moffitt and Wolfe, 1992). Most low-income persons are either eligible for Medicaid or they are not. If their income goes up by one dollar and this moves them off of AFDC, they lose their Medicaid eligibility. This "notch effect" creates an incentive to become eligible for and stay on AFDC and hence Medicaid. The less likely these women are to receive private insurance at their place of employment, should they work, the stronger the effect is. Robert Moffitt and Wolfe (1992) find that Medicaid does keep some women on AFDC and out of the labor force. The impact is large, however, only for women whose families have high expected medical care expenditures. The "notch" problem has been reduced somewhat by mandating the coverage of poor pregnant women and young children below the poverty line and thus reducing the link between AFDC and Medicaid. The link is also reduced, to a limited extent, by the Family Support Act of 1988, which allows Medicaid to continue for a year beyond the time a family leaves the AFDC rolls.

A second problem is that coverage varies substantially by state. The eligibility income level—the so-called monthly need standard (the income cutoff for AFDC and hence for Medicaid)—ranged, in 1992 for a family of three, from $324 in New Mexico to $1,112 in Vermont. The poverty line in that year was $940 on a monthly basis. For the medically needy, in states with such a program, the protected (net) income level for a family of three in 1989 varied from $250 in Tennessee to $934 in California.[32] States also differ in the service limitations they have imposed; for example, as of 1989, thirteen states had limits on the number of inpatient days covered; twelve states required a second opinion for certain surgery; thirty-one had limits on the quantity of any prescription; and five states had a limit on the number of physician office visits (U.S. Department of Health and Human Services, 1991, pp. 71, 75). Thus a poor single mother with an income that is 75 percent of the poverty line may receive no coverage in one state, full coverage with few constraints in a second, and have limited benefits and difficulty in finding a provider in a third state. Average expenditures per AFDC child and adult reflect these differences: as of 1989, average expenditures for AFDC children varied from $384 in Alabama to $927 in New York to $1,650 in Alaska.

A third problem is that many people with low incomes are not covered by Medicaid, just as two-parent families, couples, and single persons are generally not covered. With the mandated extension of AFDC to families with an unemployed head of household, benefits were expanded, but even for such families, the low-income standards in some states leave a large number of the working poor without coverage.

A fourth problem is that low reimbursement rates in some states have led some providers to refuse Medicaid patients. Physicians are more likely to treat Medicaid patients when reimbursement is relatively high than when Medicaid fees are low (Mitchell, 1991).

Finally, our current medical welfare system (Medicaid, general assistance, other public medical service delivery programs, and charity care) functions as a substitute for private health insurance. This structure forces consumers to face an "either-or" situation; either rely completely on the medical welfare system, or rely completely on privately purchased medical care and health insurance. There is little incentive for low-income consumers to contribute partially toward the cost of their coverage. For many, the additional benefit from private health insurance is less than its cost, given the availability of the medical welfare system.

Consideration of the effects of the medical welfare system helps explain why the probability of being uninsured is lowest at high-income levels and rises steadily as we move toward lower-income levels, and it suggests that the current structure may increase the size of the uninsured population.

Medicare

The primary public program that provides health care coverage to the aged population is the Medicare program. The low-income elderly are covered by both Medicare and Medicaid. Aged and disabled persons with incomes below the poverty line (who meet an asset test as well) are eligible (as qualified Medicare beneficiaries) to have Medicaid pay the Medicare premiums, copayments, and deductibles for them. The Medicare program is described in Appendix D.

Sources of Care for the Uninsured Poor

What sources of care exist for the uninsured poor? There are both federal grant programs and state programs that provide some access to care for those without other means. These include federal block grants to the states for Maternal and Child Health Services, which provide care to low-income women and children; Community Health Centers, which provide primary care on a sliding fee schedule to low-income populations (and coverage to others as well in underserved areas); Migrant Health Centers, which provide care to seasonal and migrant workers; the Indian Health Service, which provides care to Native Americans; remaining obligations to provide care to indigents under the Hill-Burton Act, which funded the building of many hospitals; and a variety of other specially targeted programs. Most counties or states provide general assistance that provides limited access to health care services to very low income persons not otherwise covered, although recently some states have discontinued or reduced such programs. And hospitals provide care to the poor—some $3.0 billion dollars worth in 1988, according to the American Hospital Association ("uncompensated care"). Most of these programs face declining resources, however, and may have to withhold services. Hospitals, moreover, are under pressure not to shift the cost of uncompensated care to private and public insurers.

The Current System and Proposals for Reform

Why do we look to the public sector for intervention in the medical care sector? One strong motivation is the lack of sufficient information about health care that individuals face in a number of ways. For many conditions, individuals do not have the knowledge to judge what care would most benefit them, and even after receiving care do not know if they would have been better off with no care, with alternative care, or with the care they received. This may be particularly true for those with limited educations. Rapid changes in technology exacerbate this problem, so that even for chronic or repeated ailments, a consumer finds it difficult to understand the options for care. In addition, the price is rarely known—or at least fully known—before care is received.

We also look to the public sector because except for preventive care, and care for certain conditions, much of the need for future care is unknown: illnesses and accidents are difficult to predict. This creates financial uncertainty, given that much of medical care can be very expensive. There are also several types of externalities in health care that suggest public sector involvement. For a contagious disease, one's own health is influenced by the health of those with whom one comes in contact. Persons living in poor sanitary conditions and in areas with low levels of immunizations may be particularly vulnerable. And some health conditions influence the well-being of others—those in the community at large may feel pained if someone who is visibly ill does not receive medical attention, particularly if the reason is lack of financial resources.

The private responses to these problems cause additional difficulties in terms of the access the poor have to health care. The inadequacy of information, for example, has led to the establishment of licensing of medical care providers. Beneficial though this is, such restrictions limit those that can practice—and may reduce the care that is available, particularly in low-income and rural areas, and increase prices.

Physicians act as their patients' agents, making the decisions that patients would make were they able to judge appropriate care themselves. However, under a system in which providers are reimbursed (paid) for each service—the so-called fee-for-service system—physicians are placed in a position of potential conflict of interest: doing more for a patient can increase their income.[33] If reimbursement is very low or uncertain, providers may be reluctant to provide care to the poor when the opportunity cost is providing care to those paying higher fees.

The fear of a large financial loss because of expensive medical care leads to the demand for health insurance—insurance that will pay for medical bills should the need for care arise. Yet having insurance—or being eligible for, or nearly eligible for, public insurance—leads persons to behave as though the price of medical care is far lower than its true cost. The result is a greater demand for medical care than would be the case without such subsidies for the purchase of medical care.[34] And this greater demand increases the price of medical care and makes it more expensive for the poor than in a market without such insurance.

The presence of such externalities has led to the direct provision of some medical care—public health centers and community health centers in low-income areas—as well as to tax subsidies toward health insurance.

Five Alternatives

All of the "imperfections" in the medical care market influence its performance and suggest a variety of reforms. Many economists, policy analysts, and politicians have proposed alternative health care plans. These plans can be classified into five categories. The first is the employer mandate or the so-called pay or play plan. These plans require employers to provide some minimum level of coverage to all employees and their dependents. Employers would either provide insurance to employees directly, following set specifications both on the breadth and depth of insurance coverage and on the "proportion of the premium paid for by the employer,"[35] or they would pay a fixed percentage of their payroll (or a fixed percentage up to a maximum per employee) into a pool, which would then offer coverage to these employees and their dependents. The insurance pool would be organized by (but not necessarily run by) the public sector and would also offer insurance to those not otherwise covered.[36] Individuals insured through this arrangement, at least the nonpoor, are likely to pay a significant portion of the cost. Firms that have few workers may be exempted from this mandate.

An example of this type of plan that is generous to the poor is that of the Pepper Commission. Under this plan, any firm with more than twenty-five employees must eventually participate. Covered firms must provide certain minimum benefits. Medicaid would become a federal program, operating uniformly across all states, and open to those not otherwise covered—the self-employed, those working for small firms, those working for firms that decide to pay, and those who are unemployed. The poor would be covered without required premiums; the near-poor would pay a premium of no more than 3 percent of their income.

Employer mandates do not generate any government budgetary costs (but do lead to tax expenditures—forgone taxes—under the current tax subsidies to insurance). They are thus seen as more politically attractive than plans that increase government spending. There is a crucial tradeoff, however; to the extent that the pay component—the special payroll tax—covers the full cost of premiums for employees and contributes to the coverage of the low-income uninsured in general, the payroll taxes required will be substantial. If the special payroll taxes are low (and hence more politically acceptable), employers now providing insurance might stop and instead join the plan—giving the public sector a far larger role and creating the need for raising additional revenues as well.

The second set of reform plans expands the current public programs, Medicaid and Medicare (or only one of these), by expanding eligibility and/or by allowing those without insurance to buy into these plans under an income-conditioned payment scheme. People could "buy into" Medicaid, for example, with the price of the buy-in set inversely to family income (K. Davis, 1989). Such a plan would eliminate Medicaid's categorical eligibility requirements and vastly increase the number of participants. Medicaid would be a mechanism to distribute an income-related subsidy for the purpose of purchasing the covered services. More modest versions would restrict the extensions to particular groups: all pregnant women, infants, and young children; those with incomes less than twice the poverty line; disabled persons; adults under age sixty-five with family incomes below the poverty line; and/or those who retire before age sixty-five (the current age for eligibility for Medicare).[37] There are drawbacks in relying on the expansion of Medicaid as it is presently structured to solve the uninsured problem: it provides extensive benefits and hence may be more expensive than necessary; it is horizontally inequitable if applied only to certain targeted groups; and, as noted in the previous section, it may contribute to the size of the uninsured population at the same time that it attempts to reduce it. (See section on Medicaid, above.) Extending a Medicaid buy-in to the seriously disabled population with special needs would represent an efficient as well as equitable arrangement, however, for special chronic care benefits are covered under Medicaid, but not under usual health insurance contracts.[38] Private firms may be reluctant to hire the disabled if they are to be included in the firms' own health policies, and private insurance often does not cover more specialized health-related expenses. Offering the disabled the option of buying into Medicaid would increase their employability and might also encourage firms to offer other employees coverage.[39]

A third set of plans modify the tax incentives currently in place regarding health insurance by reducing and/or modifying federal tax subsidies.[40] The current subsidies are worth more to higher-income persons, because they increase with one's marginal tax bracket. Proposed modifications would provide refundable tax credits to low-income families,[41] permit tax-free accounts for health insurance and health care expenditures (Pauly et al., 1991), and/or set a maximum on the amount of the employer-based premium that can be excluded from the employee's tax base.[42] This maximum could be based on an actuarial cost of a basic insurance plan for families of specified sizes and ages (with an adjustment for disability).[43]

The fourth set of policies being discussed involve some form of nationalized health insurance, ranging from the expansion of current public programs to full-blown "single-payer" systems like those of Germany or Canada (see Appendix E). Providers remain private, but the financing is public. These plans seek to eliminate the high cost of "overhead" caused by the duplication of forms, administration, and other requirements of multiple payers.[44] Another advantage is uniformity of benefits across all persons, regardless of income.[45] A national plan like that of Germany covers most people through their place of employment using nonprofit insurers, called sickness funds. These sickness funds are heavily regulated: they must offer a minimum plan; employees and the self-employed (except those with high incomes) must enroll in a plan; dependents must be covered; unemployed and retired persons and their dependents must be covered by the sickness fund that covered the individual while employed; no deductibles are permitted; and there is cost sharing only for hospital care and prescription drugs. Persons with low incomes are protected from cost sharing. Financing is via mandatory payroll contributions that cover most of the costs.[46]

Canada's plan offers another option: everyone is insured, and the central government finances a fixed part of the cost. Each province sets its own terms for additional financing, fee schedules, regulations, and other requirements. Most providers are paid according to a fee schedule, and patients cannot be charged directly—there are no copayments. There are restrictions on the number of practitioners allowed to practice (in a number of the provinces), and hospitals operate on an annual budget.

A third option is a nationalized health care system in which providers work for the government, as in Great Britain. The budget allocated to medical care is determined at the national level, along with decisions on all other public programs such as defense, transportation, and so on. Each person registers with a family doctor, paid on a per capita basis. Patients see a specialist or go to the hospital with a referral from their family doctor (except in an emergency). Hospitals have a global budget. There is limited cost-sharing, which is waived for those with low incomes and those who are pregnant.[47]

A fifth set of policies focuses on the role of competition in reducing health care expenditure increases; these are so-called managed competition plans that are favored by the Clinton administration. These plans would "empower the demand side" by facilitating the formation of health care alliances, also called health insurance purchasing cooperatives. These organizations would bargain with provider groups to obtain a specified set of services for its members. The groups' market power would come from the purchasers enrolled (the administration proposes to include employees of all firms up to a specified size, such as 5,000 employees). In the administration's version the average premium cost in the region for the specified package of benefits offered by health care plans would be subsidized via the tax system (see the third set of policies, above); any additional premium would be paid with after-tax dollars. The use of a specified and uniform benefit plan, the tax subsidy limit, and information on providers to be gathered by the health care alliance will promote competition by improving the opportunities or choices consumers have. In most versions, mandated community rating also decreases the cost of coverage for those currently uninsured (those in small firms, part-time workers, and those unaffiliated with the labor market), and makes it easier to compare plans. Large firms can take advantage of these requirements in their bargaining, though they may be harmed by the switch to community rating. (For a summary of President Clinton's plan as submitted to Congress, see Appendix F.)

Why Is Change Difficult?

It is unlikely that President Clinton's health care reform policy will be quickly legislated. Why is this the case?

It is unlikely that the United States will move to provide comprehensive insurance coverage for all of the poor and near-poor, unless or until the growth in expenditures on health care has been, or is anticipated to be, slowed. This is due to the general assumption (and fear) that covering the uninsured will substantially increase total costs. At the same time, it is very difficult to enact *major* changes that will substantially reduce expenditure growth. Some changes may be enacted that leave implementation to the state or local level; tax incentives may be altered to subsidize the cost of buying insurance for those not insured at their place of employment; managed competition or coordinated care may be fostered; Medicare fee schedules (DRGs, RBRVs) may be used by more payers; but little in the way of major *national* change that reduces health care expenditures can be expected to be implemented in the near term, for several reasons.

First, entrenched interest groups wish to avoid any change that might penalize them. The private insurance sector, including its employees, for example, would fight against the shift to public provision of health coverage, or mandated private coverage of high-risk persons, especially if funded via a payroll tax. Private health providers (depending on the proposed plan) may fear reduced compensation and further regulation of their services. Suppliers of medical equipment also fear loss of business. Employees and their dependents who currently have broad coverage provided by their employers with little cost sharing required of them also prefer the status quo, as do employees of firms that do not offer coverage but who are covered by the policy of other family members. Employers in firms that do not offer insurance or offer only limited coverage may fear the increase in costs, as do high-salaried workers. And the value that some low-income earners place on health insurance may be less than the cost of proposed plans.

Parties who might gain tend to be more diffuse and may not coalesce to lobby for a proposed change. These groups include employers who now provide extensive coverage; providers who primarily serve low-income populations, especially those who are uninsured; individuals who are not covered because they are high risk and/or who are not covered at their job; employees who see their wages eroding as the cost of insurance coverage takes a larger and larger share of total compensation; employees who wish to change jobs but do not for fear that they will lose coverage, at least for preexisting conditions; and finally, employees who fear the loss of coverage either because they anticipate reductions in breadth of coverage or because they anticipate losing their job.

Second, mandating coverage may increase unemployment, particularly among low-skilled workers, and may force some small businesses into bankruptcy; this is a problem primarily for employer-mandated plans.[48]

Third, many citizens (employers, employees, and others with private income) fear that these plans will lead to higher taxes. On the surface, most of the new plans appear more costly to employees than the current system, because few employees fully understand that they are now paying (albeit with pretax dollars) for most of their health insurance. Furthermore, employees would not be likely, at least immediately, to gain the full value of their current contribution to health insurance (this refers to the component now known as the employer's contribution) in their paychecks if coverage were to be removed from their place of employment.[49] And it is likely, under any scenario, that some people will lose (pay more, get less coverage) and others gain (obtain coverage, pay less). But it is difficult to predict accurately what sort of redistribution of costs and benefits will occur.

Fourth, there is little willingness to provide the highest-quality care to those publicly insured (for example, to those on Medicaid or those currently unin- sured), but there is also an unwillingness to "bite the bullet" and establish explicit rationing or to set up clearly defined dual standards of care. Discussions of gener- ous specified benefit plans in order to avoid dual quality of care are examples of this difficulty.

Fifth, there is also a reluctance to hold down the rate of improvement in tech- nology or to move away from the so-called technological imperative (to do all that is technologically possible to help a patient). Although it is assumed that people want every possible treatment to maintain their lives, the rapid spread of living wills demonstrates that individuals sometimes choose to limit major life- saving efforts when there is little chance for long-term survival or for a high- quality life. The state of Oregon has also tried to move away from the goal of providing all possible health services to a limited number of Medicaid recipients. It provides coverage to a greater number of persons through the use of a list of medical priorities and the allocation of a specified level of dollars according to that priority list. Other care is not provided under the Oregon Medicaid plan.[50]

What Can Be Done? A Suggestion for Reform

What all of this suggests is that major change will be difficult over the next few years, but that realistic attitudes toward medical care could increase the probabil- ity of change. One area of concern is the need for more accurate information. If people had an accurate picture of the likely cost of covering the uninsured and of how much they are now paying—and for what—they could better assess pro- posed changes. The general assumption that covering the uninsured will substan- tially increase the costs of medical care may not, in fact, be true. About half of those uninsured at any point in time will have coverage within about eight months, and their utilization of the system is unlikely to increase substantially if they have coverage all of the time rather than intermittently. In addition, most people without insurance now receive care when they are seriously ill. These costs are already included in medical care expenditures. Some increase in expen- ditures can be expected, at least in the initial period in which coverage is ex- tended, but the total cost may be small—and smaller than is publicly perceived.

If the full Clinton reform plan is not passed, steps can be taken to repair the current health care system and improve the position of those in poverty. I propose covering *all* children under the age of nineteen for a specific set of services. Such a "Healthy-Kid" program would provide primary care in community care centers.

Further medical care would be referred to other private providers, but the community care center would remain the manager of care for all children who lived in the area.[51] Certain basic care would be provided to all children and pregnant women without charge; specific additional care would require copayments which would be income-conditioned and rise with family income.

I propose copayments so that consumers will not purchase or use too much care, as they are now encouraged to do under many existing plans.[52] The use of copayments, particularly coinsurance, improves efficiency incentives in this regard. With coinsurance, consumers pay a part of the cost of their medical care and hence are expected to act more like consumers of traditional retail goods and services; that is, they are expected to "shop" for medical care selectively, not buying more than they need, and looking for a good value. Small, required copayments, however, may create substantial financial hardship among the poor and a much greater response among low- than among higher-income persons. To prevent this, copayments would be income-conditioned: smaller copayments or a lower percentage for children and pregnant women of low-income families, and greater copayments (or a higher percentage) for children and pregnant women of higher-income families.

The plan would be operated through the Health Care Financing Administration (HCFA), which now runs Medicare. The payments to the community providers would be in the form of a prepayment for all specified services, similar to payments to a health maintenance organization (HMO), except for required copayments. The payments to providers would depend not on the income of the child's family but only on geographic location (and perhaps on the child's underlying health status, for those with a chronic condition).[53] The (group of) community providers would be responsible for paying all of the additional costs of care for children in its jurisdiction; HCFA would provide reinsurance above a set limit.

Why a capitation system? Prospective payment pays a provider a set amount to cover a specified set of services for a designated period of time. The provider would not be paid more to provide more care—and, in fact, would be at risk to pay for the cost of care for the individual over the set time period. The result could be too little care rather than too much care, hence the addition of reinsurance to avoid creating an incentive for providers not to care for the most seriously ill among children and pregnant women.[54] Salaries could be used as an alternative way to reimburse providers. Salaries are likely to be the most neutral form of reimbursement in terms of the amount of care delivered—the physician does not gain financially by providing more care or lose financially from the provision of more care. The physician who is responsible for many children and pregnant women, however, would be paid the same as one responsible for far fewer. Prospective payment compensates for overall differences in workload and allows differential compensation for more seriously ill patients, and for pregnant women relative to children.

A final alternative, that of a fee schedule, is also less attractive than prospective payment. A fee schedule such as that used for Medicare reimbursement under Part B of the program (Supplementary Medical Insurance)—either for a list of services provided, such as a relative value scale,[55] or a less complex list—fixes the price of each type of care. It may, however, be an incentive to provide too many services—or to provide too many of a more highly reimbursed service.[56] Hence a prospective reimbursement scheme is recommended for Healthy-Kid.

Such a plan would go a long way toward increasing immunizations among all children, especially those in low-income areas, and would thus be consistent with the revised vaccination proposal of the Clinton administration. It would provide a place to go for continuing care, a place that would be known to teens, particularly those at risk, so that early prenatal care should be increased. It would eliminate the need for a number of programs that provide either limited services or services to a limited set of persons and so would potentially create savings in, for example, EPSDT (Early and Periodic Screening, Diagnosis and Treatment), Title V Maternal and Child Health Block Grant programs, and state health plans for low income children such as the Children's Health Insurance Plan of New York State. A rough estimate of the cost of such a program is $40–$45 billion, based on a current Medicaid average expenditure per child of approximately $800 per participant and netting out the cost of Medicaid for children and pregnant women currently covered.[57]

Children are relatively inexpensive to cover: including all of them in one program would avoid a dual-quality system, ensure access to basic preventive services such as immunizations, and provide access to family planning and prenatal care for teens. Providing coverage for children would reduce the cost of employer-based and other private coverage, therefore increasing the probability of greater private coverage for adults.[58] Locating programs in communities would encourage appropriate utilization and reduce the use of emergency rooms and other expensive and inefficient forms of care. Providing coverage for pregnant women in their communities should encourage the early use of prenatal care, facilitate provision of information, and hence decrease the need for high-cost care such as intensive care for infants with low birth weights.

I would also cap the tax subsidy on employer-based health insurance. This could be done at a level that reflected the actuarial cost of insurance *without the cost of children or pregnant women,* since they would be covered separately. These savings in lost federal tax revenue, which are likely to be in the $25–$36 billion range (see Employee Benefit Research Institute, 1992, table 5), could be used to finance Healthy-Kid. In addition, such a cap might induce a redesign of policies to provide protection for major health problems—rather than first-dollar coverage.[59] Insurance companies would have an incentive to design policies that provide full coverage for care that is cost-effective (immunizations, certain screening programs), but require significant copayments for other care. Insurers would face a new incentive—to provide coverage such that the premium is not much beyond the cap—and this would be an incentive to redesign policies in order to reduce the costs of the plan. Employees would have a greater concern with the cost of their insurance, because they would directly pay any amount over the cap with post-tax dollars. And new copayments should increase consumers' concern about the cost of medical care.

These changes would leave some of the poverty population without coverage, particularly single persons, childless couples, and parents in two-parent families. Three options seem possible: do nothing at this time, extend refundable tax credits, or expand the community health center network. My first choice would be to expand the community health centers for these persons. The centers would use a sliding scale, as many already currently do. The federal government would forgive or pay off 10 percent of medical students' medical school loans (or a fixed dollar amount) for each year they worked in these centers, while paying them a salary equal to that of a median worker in that urban area or state. The additional financing of each center would come from Medicaid (Medicare) to cover the costs of services provided to Medicaid (Medicare)–covered persons; private insurance to cover the cost of services rendered to its consumers; and general revenue to cover any remaining gaps, which should be small. To improve access in underserved rural areas I would use a similar arrangement to encourage providers to locate in these areas. The disadvantage of this proposal is that it is likely to lead to dual-quality care, because primarily low-income residents would use the community health care system.

The other "do something" alternative is to extend refundable tax credits—really a voucher—to those with incomes below the poverty line, to allow them to buy a basic plan that covers nonelective hospital care and physician care. Families with incomes up to twice the poverty line could receive a reduced credit along a graduated schedule. The credit would only be available to those who did not receive other subsidies—Medicaid, Medicare, or tax subsidies through the tax system.[60] States would be mandated to require insurance companies operating in the state to join a pool that offered such basic coverage to all who desired such a package.[61] The disadvantage of this approach is the high tax rate associated with it.

A cap on the tax subsidy for health insurance, a refundable tax credit to the poor and near-poor, or a loan-forgiveness approach to the expansion of community health care centers and the introduction of Healthy-Kid is a combination of the tax incentive and a limited form of nationalized health insurance. The plan contains useful first steps in improving, as well as learning about, the current U.S. health care system. First, it would provide uniform coverage and improved access for all low-income children and pregnant women. Second, it should lead to increased cost-consciousness of consumers—and hence to insurance packages with improved incentives to reduce the rate of increase in medical care expenditures. It should be able to do this without the need for expensive regulation such as rate regulation or required approval for large capital expenditures. Third, it creates a link between the Healthy-Kid program and the limit on tax subsidies, which may make the latter easier to pass politically. Fourth, it provides a way to grant some coverage to all of the poor—and to reduce the inequitable burden placed on communities and states with large numbers of poor and uninsured persons. Fifth, it reduces the disincentive effect of Medicaid on recipients' willingness to increase their labor force participation. And six, it does not have large negative employment effects. Finally, it contains a set of alternative delivery systems and financing systems—a program for children, a refundable tax credit, and a modification of incentives in the tax subsidy—that could lead to larger-scale improvements in the longer run.

Who Are the Homeless?

Why are those with severe mental health problems among the homeless? Who are the homeless? One explanation for the presence of the severely mentally ill among the homeless relates to the allocation of resources within the mental health care delivery system (National Institute of Mental Health, 1991). Over the past thirty years, there has been a push for deinstitutionalization of the mentally ill. It is argued that treatment in the community is more humane and can be as successful as treatment in the mental institution. As a result, community mental health centers (CMHCs) were established, and the number of state mental hospital beds declined by almost 70 percent from 1969 to 1983 (National Institute of Mental Health, 1987). But resources did not follow patients—state mental hospitals still consume a disproportionate share of state mental health budgets (about 63 percent).

Deinstitutionalization, then, has not been accompanied by adequate services for the mentally ill in many communities and, in most cases, existing services are not coordinated and require considerable effort to obtain. The decline of the availability of marginal housing—single-room occupancy hotels, rooming houses—has also contributed to the growth of the homeless population. These factors have led to the rise in the number of homeless mentally ill persons.

Homelessness is not a problem unique to the mentally ill. The number of homeless individuals has been increasing over the past decade; during 1990, 300,000 to 400,000 individuals were estimated to be homeless at any point in time, although one group claims that as many as two million were homeless at some point during the year (Alliance Housing Council, 1988). Most who become homeless remain so for only a few weeks or months at a time, although a considerable portion may remain homeless for extended periods.

The homeless are most often single males in their twenties or thirties, and are likely to be members of racial minorities; one of the fastest-growing subgroups of the homeless population, however, is families with young children, whose members may make up one-sixth of the homeless population. These families are often characterized by multigenerational welfare dependence, low maternal educational attainment, and very young mothers (Vladeck, 1990).

The homeless are, for the most part, uninsured. In addition, the homeless often resist contact with the "system," are often regarded as undesirable patients by health care providers, may have multiple diseases, and are usually difficult to keep in the outpatient health care system. At the same time, it is difficult for most providers to discharge a recovering patient from the hospital when he has no-where to go. Facilities caring for the recovering or chronically ill homeless are few in number.

APPENDIX   B

AIDS and the Poor

Another special health care problem to be mentioned is Acquired Immunodefi-ciency Syndrome (AIDS). Many of those at high risk of AIDS are also at high risk of being uninsured. The incidence of HIV infection—the precursor to AIDS—is increasing among intravenous drug users, their sexual partners, and children. This group is likely to be young, unemployed, have low incomes, and be members of minorities—the same characteristics associated with being uninsured. AIDS pa-tients are also likely to lack insurance because of loss of employment (and em-ployer-sponsored insurance benefits) due to their illness and because of screening or preexisting condition clauses of private insurers. A number of them become homeless as a result of these losses.

Although AIDS affects people in all income groups and is ultimately fatal, women of childbearing years are of particular concern because there is a high rate of transmission to their infants; 30 to 40 percent of infants born to HIV-infected mothers develop AIDS, and most of them die within five years. Women who die of AIDS leave children who must be cared for by others. AIDS is now one of the ten leading causes of death among women of this age group, and the infection occurs at much higher rates among minorities living in inner cities. According to data reported in J. Wiener and Engel (1991), as of 1988, the death rate of black women was nine times that of similarly aged white women.

The lifetime medical costs of treating a patient with AIDS have been very high—approximately $60,000 on average (1992 dollars). This cost has been shift-ing to the public sector. A recent study of hospitalized AIDS patients in New York City, San Francisco, and Los Angeles found a significant shift in financing from the private sector to the public sector over the 1983–1987 period. The aver-age percentage of hospitalizations paid for by private insurance decreased from a bit over 70 percent in 1983 to about 42 percent in 1987 (Green and Arno, 1990). The resulting burden falls primarily on the public sector and the patient.[62]

Medicaid Eligibility Rules and Service Provision

Medicaid is designed to provide health insurance to three groups of persons: low-income families with children, the low-income elderly, and those with disabilities. Because Medicaid is a joint federal-state program, states have significant leeway in determining eligibility. Here is only a broad outline of those covered (as of early 1992).

Eligibility

1. *Categorical eligibility.* States are required to provide benefits to persons receiving cash assistance under federally supported welfare programs. These include Aid to Families with Dependent Children and Supplemental Security Income.

2. *Additional coverage for children and pregnant women.* Since 1990, states have been required to extend Medicaid coverage to pregnant women, infants, and children under six with family incomes less than 133 percent of the poverty line. This can be extended at a state's discretion to those with incomes below 185 percent of the poverty line. Since July 1991, states have been required to cover all children born after September 30, 1983, to age eighteen, if they live in families with incomes below the poverty line.

3. *Optional medically needy.* States may provide Medicaid coverage to families with children (and to the elderly and those with disabilities) who have very high medical care costs relative to their income. Their income less their medical costs (net income) must be below a limit set by the state. This limit may be no greater than one-third higher than the state's maximum benefit level for AFDC.

4. *Additional coverage for the elderly.* States are required to provide certain Medicaid benefits for the elderly with incomes below the poverty line. This program (known as the Qualified Medicare Beneficiary Program) covers Medicare premiums, deductibles, and other costs partly covered by Medicare. States have the option of extending to this group full Medicaid benefits as well.

Services

There are ten categories of services that must be covered and thirty more that may be covered. One that must be covered is the Medicaid Early and Periodic Screening, Diagnosis, and Treatment Program (EPSDT). This provides routine screening visits and follow-up treatment for the health problems of children below the age of twenty-one. Others include inpatient and outpatient hospital services; laboratory and x-ray services; skilled nursing home services (SNF) for those over twenty-one; home health care services for those entitled to SNF care; family planning services and supplies; physicians' services; and nurse midwife services. Optional services include drugs, intermediate care services, dental care, physical and occupational therapies, eyeglasses, and inpatient psychiatric care for those less than twenty-one and over sixty-five. States can also establish limits on required services, such as days covered, although certain services to children may not be capped.

Expenditures

The estimated cost of the Medicaid program for 1992 is $104.4 billion, of which 57.4 percent is paid for by the federal government. Only about 25 percent of these expenditures go to the low-income, nonelderly, nondisabled population, although this population accounts for about 68 percent of all those covered. In 1990, 24 million individuals were served, of whom 10.7 million were dependent children under the age of twenty-one, and 5.6 million were adults in families with dependent children. The average expenditure for low-income, nonelderly, nondisabled individuals is far below the Medicaid average: per child it was $811; per AFDC adult it was $1,429, compared with an overall average of $2,568 as of 1990. The amount spent on children varied substantially by state, from 6.5 percent in New Hampshire to 31.3 percent in Alaska (in 1990). (See I. Shapiro et al., 1991; U.S. House of Representatives, 1992).

A P P E N D I X   D

Medicare

The primary public program that provides health care coverage to the aged population is the Medicare program, first established under Title XVII of the Social Security Act of 1965 and substantially expanded by the 1972 Amendments to the Social Security Act to cover those receiving Social Security under the disability program[63] as well as those with end-stage renal disease. Medicare is a federal program with a common set of benefits across the nation. The program has two parts: Part A, or hospital insurance, which is automatically provided to those sixty-five and over who qualify for Social Security; and Part B, or Supplementary

Medical Insurance, covering physicians and related services, which is voluntary and requires a premium to be paid monthly. Anyone sixty-five or older not eligible for Part A can pay a premium to enroll, but must then enroll in Part B as well. The premium for Part A is set at the actuarial value. In 1990, 33.0 million persons were covered, 32.9 million under Part B. Total Medicare expenditures were $116.7 billion, of which slightly less than 60 percent were for Part A, nearly all of which went for inpatient short-term hospital stays. Medicare covers limited nursing home and home health care for short periods under strict regulations.

Medicare requires substantial cost sharing: for Part A, the patient pays an initial deductible (set equal to the average per diem cost nationwide of a hospital day) in a benefit period (a period that begins with the day a patient is hospitalized if he has not been hospitalized during the prior sixty days); a copayment of one-fourth of the deductible for every day hospitalized from the sixty-first to ninetieth days in a benefit period; and a copayment of one-half of the deductible for a one-time lifetime reserve of sixty additional days. Beyond this, the patient is fully responsible for all hospital costs.[64] For care in a skilled nursing home, if the patient meets certain requirements for any coverage, no copayments are required for the first twenty days; for the next eighty days, a copayment equal to one-eighth the hospital per diem cost is required; and beyond one hundred days the patient is responsible for all charges. For hospice care, no copayments are required, but a patient must be certified as terminally ill with a prognosis of no more than six months to live and he must waive standard Medicare Part A benefits for services related to his terminal illness. For Part B, the patient pays a deductible each year before Medicare begins to share the costs of care. After this, Medicare pays 80 percent of the allowed charge, and the patient pays the remainder of the bill. If the provider accepts assignment (the allowable charge), the patient pays 20 percent; if not, the patient pays the difference between the 80 percent of the allowable charge and the actual charge. On average, in 1986, aged beneficiaries paid nearly a third of physician charges (U.S. Department of Health and Human Services, 1991, p. 53). The actual charges are now capped at a fixed percentage of the allowable charge, and a new system to establish allowable charges—a relative value scale—is being phased in. This scale assigns weights to medical services on the basis of resource inputs.

The majority of Medicare recipients who are not covered by Medicaid (73.5 percent of all elderly or 78 percent of those without Medicaid coverage) have additional private insurance ("Medigap"), which covers the deductibles and copayments of services approved by Medicare. They generally do not cover additional hospital days or long-term care, but do provide some coverage for drugs. More than a fifth of the elderly in families with incomes below $14,000 have only Medicare coverage and remain vulnerable to high medical care costs.

Problems with Medicare from the consumer's perspective include the cap on inpatient coverage, leaving the elderly vulnerable to large medical expenditures; the limited coverage of nursing home care; the large copayments; and little or no coverage of pharmaceuticals. From the perspective of the public sector, the growing number of elderly, the high and growing medical bills per person due to the aging of the population, and improvements in technology create pressures as expenditures on Medicare continue to increase rapidly.

A P P E N D I X   E

Three Nationalized Systems

Germany

The German system of medical care resembles the U.S. system in some ways: ambulatory care is provided by private practitioners who are paid on a fee-for-service basis and who provide care to patients who choose to receive care from them; hospital care, however, is provided by doctors who work for the hospital and are paid by salary. (The fee-for-service payment to a physician is based on a negotiated fee schedule,[65] while the hospital payment is based on a negotiated per diem rate.[66]) Most people receive insurance through their place of employment (many plans are based on occupation), and health insurance is offered by numerous insurers. Unlike in the United States, 90 percent of these insurers are nonprofit or quasi public and are known as sickness funds. Sickness funds must offer a minimum plan, but additional benefits can be offered. Employees and the self-employed (except those with high incomes) must enroll in a plan; white-collar employees can choose a substitute or national fund rather than their employer's fund. Persons with low incomes are protected from cost-sharing requirements. Financing is via mandatory payroll contributions of 8–16 percent of wages, subject to a ceiling. The government contributes toward the coverage of the retired, the unemployed, and students. Payments to providers are all based on scales, but reimbursement is higher for substitute funds and private insurance.

Canada

The Canadian plan combines private fee-for-service practitioners with hospitals that operate on a budget that is set annually. Providers are paid according to a fee schedule, and patients cannot be charged directly—there are no copayments. All citizens of Canada are covered; the central government covers a share of the cost of the plan; the provinces, the rest. Each province has its own plan in terms of sources of additional financing, fee schedules, and regulations. Compared with the United States, there is far more restriction on the number of practitioners allowed to practice (in a number of the provinces); there is far less investment in new capital and diffusion of new technology; there is more queuing, more denial of care, but greater contact with physicians; and there is far less concern with financial insecurity over the uncertainty of the costs of future medical care and insurance coverage.

Great Britain

Great Britain has a nationalized health care system under which providers work for the government. The budget allocated to medical care is determined at the national level along with decisions on all other public programs, including defense. Each person is signed up with a family doctor. The doctors are paid on a per capita basis and their office costs are covered directly by the government. Patients see a specialist or go to the hospital with a referral from their family doctor (except in an emergency). Hospitals have a global budget; there is some attempt at equalizing availability of hospital beds by building hospitals or adding capacity in regions with few beds relative to the population. Inequality in available hospital facilities continues to exist. There is only very limited cost-sharing, and this is waived for those with low incomes and those who are pregnant. Along with the national health system, which covers all citizens, is a small but growing private-sector insurance industry. The private insurance is primarily used for elective procedures, for which a wait would be involved in the national system.[67] Persons with higher incomes tend to be privately insured, although unions have recently begun bargaining to gain private coverage for their members. Among developed countries, Britain spends relatively little on medical care under this nationalized system. Utilization of care remains somewhat unequal; those in higher-prestige occupations receive more care for a given illness than those in lower-prestige occupations. The reason for this is likely to be related to education—those with more education raise more questions and push the system harder. They also find out about opportunities to avoid the queue in other regions, while those with less education seem more willing to accept the advice of their family doctor. Thus this system has some inequality in the utilization of care, but financial insecurity is avoided across all income classes.

·   ·   ·

For a description of a number of other systems, including those in France, Denmark, Italy, the Netherlands, Portugal, Spain, Switzerland, and the United Kingdom, see van Doorslaer, Wagstaff, and Rutten (1993).

Managed Competition and the Nonelderly Poor

The 1993 Clinton administration health reform proposal, the Health Security Act, centers on reforming the U.S. health care system via managed competition. This approach has several implications for the nonelderly poor.

The main ingredients of managed competition are as follows. Providers (hospitals and physicians) are to be organized into health plans or "accountable health partnerships" (AHPs) that will contract to provide a specified set of services for a per capita rate. They will contract both with very large employers and with publicly created health alliances (HAs). The HAs will contract only with AHPs, not with individual providers. The HAs are to act as "purchasing agents," seeking bids to provide a specified set of benefits, gathering information related to the quality of care, collecting premiums and paying the premiums (not fees) out to the contracting AHPs. Consumers will select a package based on the premiums and on information about quality. The standardization of the package of benefits and quality information should enhance consumer choice. These ingredients will then stimulate bidding or price competition by the AHPs. The price competition will focus on the premium. The consumer is expected to pay 20 percent of the average regional premium plus any additional difference between the average premium of the AHPs and higher premiums, hence motivating the providers in an AHP to bid a low price to secure patients.

Only a standard benefit package is likely to be permitted, but supplemental coverage will be allowed, with the consumer paying the full price. Consumers will not have to pay additionally if they are part of a high-risk group. The HAs are to make such adjustment in the premiums paid to AHPs, which will not be permitted to exclude care for preexisting conditions or to turn down anyone wishing to enroll in their plan as offered to the health alliance.

Because this program may not decrease the rate of expenditure increase, the program is to be combined with a form of global budget or cap on premium increases. This is not likely to apply to consumer out-of-pocket expenditures on health care. The form of ceiling focuses on maximums by state or geographic area for the premium rate for the specified benefit package, and may include mandated use of fee schedules such as those being used by Medicare to pay providers (DRGs for hospitals and RBRVs for physicians).

The acute care portion of Medicaid that now covers some low-income people is to be folded into the plan via enrollment in the HAs. Under this approach, these individuals would be provided the specified benefit package and would move into the overall pool of consumers. Those on AFDC or SSI would be covered via Medicaid payments to the HA set at 95 percent of current average AFDC expenditures in the region. Those not on AFDC or SSI would be directly folded into the HA. Other low-income persons would also be included in the HAs, with a public subsidy toward the purchase of the standard options up to the regional average. The subsidy would depend on family income and would taper off as income increased. (One option is full subsidy to 100 percent of the poverty line; then a specified percentage payment of family income until the premium is fully paid, which will occur at 150 percent of the poverty line.) Payments to the health plans would not differ by Medicaid, low income, or other status.

From the perspective of low-income persons, how will they fare? The advantages to this population of the plan, assuming coverage is extended to all under the subsidy noted, are:

1. Increased coverage of the low-income population. Many are not covered; they would be covered under the new program or at least be offered a subsidy.

2. By joining the general population and hence no longer having a separate plan, they should be more attractive to providers. Compensation to providers will not be lower than that for other consumers; access should increase.

3. By breaking the link between health insurance coverage and welfare, welfare participation may decrease and labor force participation increase.

What are the disadvantages?

1. For those now covered under Medicaid, the benefits provided may decrease. The standard package is likely to be less generous than most state Medicaid plans in operation today. This is particularly an issue for those not on cash assistance (AFDC or SSI) who will lose Medicaid coverage and not be eligible for additional ("wrap-around") benefits.

2. If payments are the same (or are only adjusted for major chronic conditions), but some low-income persons have additional problems, providers may still seek to avoid providing care to this population. A standard capitation means providers will want to locate and attract the healthiest members of society.

3. Limited access in terms of providers' locations will not be dealt with adequately in this plan. Those in undeserved areas are likely to have to

travel for care, and there is no incentive to provide additional hours of care that may be especially important for access for low-income wage earners and their children.

4. Depending on the type of quality information to be collected, there may be incentives created to avoid the most seriously ill or those with multiple problems such as the homeless, the chronically ill, and those with a variety of problems such as poor housing, sanitation, and so on. The availability of such information to providers may intensify the problems of access of the poor, especially those with poor health.

5. If, as part of the bargain to gain the cooperation of the medical profession, malpractice reforms are accomplished that weaken the policing role of malpractice, quality of care may fall, especially among providers practicing in areas with many persons who have a low level of education.

6. If the experience in the United Kingdom is suggestive, a uniform system leaves in place many inequalities in utilization of care. Those who understand the system and push receive more care than those who do not.

7. Permitting the purchase of supplementary packages means those with more income will have greater coverage than the low-income population; and one expects that utilization differences will follow. This arrangement may thus institutionalize dual quality care.

This discussion assumes that coverage would be adequately subsidized for all poor and near-poor people. If this is not the case and instead a number of persons face high copayments that they cannot cover, or some remain without coverage, those with limited or no coverage could be worse off than they are currently. To the extent that managed competition works to reduce expenditures, there would be less "slack" to cover the cost of uncompensated or reduced-price care to the uninsured poor.

Finally, to the extent that the low-income population incurs above-average health expenditures, including them in the regional pool will increase the average premium for all members of the pool. This may cause a negative change in attitude toward this population, an increase in the polarization of regions, or pressure to modify (increase) the premium paid on behalf of this population.

CHAPTER ELEVEN

Education and the Well-Being
of the Next Generation

RICHARD J. MURNANE

Once again, the performance of the American educational system has become a serious public concern. Both private and public reports have sounded the alarm that the nation is at risk because of the inadequacies of the education it provides its children. These studies, in turn, have prompted observers to conclude that deterioration in America's schools has been a significant cause of the drop in the real wages of young workers over the past twenty years.

That conclusion is almost certainly not true. The wage decline stems primarily from the stagnation in productivity (output per worker). After increasing at a rate of more than 2 percent per year in the years from 1948 to 1973, productivity abruptly stopped growing in 1973, remained stagnant through the rest of the decade, and grew only very slowly during the 1980s. The rapid decline in the rate of productivity growth was too precipitous to blame on relatively slow-moving changes such as a possible reduction in the quality of the work force. Moreover, it was not only the real wages of young workers that fell, but the wages of older workers, who had completed their schooling before test scores declined during the 1970s (Blackburn, Bloom, and Freeman, 1990). The rate of labor productivity growth since 1973 has also fallen in other countries, including France, Germany, Britain, and Japan (Baily and Chakrabarti, 1988). It is not sensible to conclude that changes in the quality of U.S. education played a large role in the productivity decline that affected many countries and workers of all ages. The critical question concerning American education relates not to its economic effects in the past but, rather, to linkages among education, productivity, and wages in the future.

Education in Perspective

Raising workers' productivity and hence their wages should not be the only goal of American education. There are many other important objectives, including fostering creativity and appreciation of the arts and teaching students the rights and obligations of citizenship in a democratic and pluralistic society. At the same time, the stability of American democracy may depend on the nation's success in allowing minority groups and today's poor children to share more fully in the country's economic progress. In this sense the enhancement of productivity growth is firmly linked to social values.

Linkages between education and economic performance run in both directions. The quality of education has economic effects, and the operation of the economy influences the effectiveness of the educational system. In particular, the incentives for minority youth living in inner cities and for poor children in general to work hard in school are greatly diminished when there are few well-paying jobs available to them when they graduate (Wilson, 1987). This reality underscores the need to find ways of providing good jobs—jobs paying enough to support children—for all of the nation's workers.

Home Experiences Influence the Acquisition of Skills

Although the United States has looked primarily to the schools to solve a variety of social problems, including the low skill levels of many labor force entrants, it has long been known that family background is a stronger predictor of cognitive skill levels than are variables depicting school quality (Coleman et al., 1966). Said differently, family stresses and the lack of learning resources that accompany poverty reduce children's cognitive skills and the likelihood that children complete high school (McLanahan, 1985; Schorr, 1988). These effects are particularly severe for children who live in areas of concentrated poverty, where they encounter few, if any, successful role models (Wilson, 1987). Moreover, the effectiveness of schooling depends on the quality of the home environment, and this condition becomes more important as children grow older (Snow et al., 1991).

Accordingly, the United States cannot rely solely on improvements in formal education to increase the quality of its future work force. If we are to improve the skills and attitudes of future generations of workers, we must also focus attention and resources on the quality of the lives children lead outside of school. This concern is all the more critical today, when one child in five is poor (Duncan and Rodgers, 1991).

Many Factors Influence Labor Productivity

The productivity of the labor force, defined as the output produced by each hour of work, does not depend solely on the skill levels of workers. Many other factors contribute, including the quantity and quality of capital equipment, the pace and character of technical change, and the way that labor is organized in the production process (Denison, 1985).

The importance of workplace organization is illustrated by the General Motors–Toyota NUMMI joint venture. The Toyota management system was introduced to a GM plant that had been closed, in part because of low productivity. Eighty percent of the labor force used in the joint venture consisted of workers previously laid off by GM. Within two years, productivity in the plant rose close to levels achieved by Toyota plants in Japan. The introduction of the Toyota management system dramatically increased labor productivity, using essentially the same work force that GM had labeled as seriously deficient (Krafcik, 1986; Brown and Reich, 1988).

This example demonstrates that productivity depends critically not only on the skills that workers acquire at home and at school, but on how workers are used. Although this notion plays a role in many theoretical treatments of labor productivity (Nelson and Phelps, 1966; Welch, 1970), it is missing from most empirical investigations and from documents such as *A Nation at Risk,* which criticizes the quality of American education (National Commission on Excellence in Education, 1983). It is important, therefore, that policymakers concerned with increasing productivity pay as much attention to promoting the effective use of existing labor force skills as they do to improving the skills that workers bring to their jobs.

Education, Skills, and Wages

Even though improvements in education by themselves will not have a marked effect on productivity, [education does foster economic growth and influence the wages and employment options of workers.] Understanding the effects of educational attainment and skill on wages and employment provides clues for devising an educational strategy to enhance the earnings potential of poor children.

Educational Attainments

Although the 1970s and 1980s were not prosperous decades for most Americans, the burdens of stagnant productivity and a changing economy have not been equally shared. Particularly hard hit have been workers with relatively low education levels. Since 1973 the wages (net of inflation) of male high school dropouts and high school graduates have fallen steadily. In 1991 the average wage for male dropouts was 26 percent lower than in 1973. For male high school graduates, the decline was 21 percent. For females, whose average wage at every point in time has been lower than that of comparably educated males, the declines were smaller, but still meant significant declines in living standards. The average wage of female high school dropouts in 1991 was 11 percent lower than in 1973, and for female high school graduates the comparable decline was 6 percent (Mishel and Bernstein, 1992).

The wages of college graduates were also lower in 1991 than in 1973, but this group fared considerably better than less-educated workers. Male college graduates experienced a 12 percent decline in average wages—less than half the decline of male high school dropouts—and the 1991 average wage of female college graduates was within 1 percent of its 1973 level (Mishel and Bernstein, 1992). As a result, the gap between the average wages of college graduates and high school graduates has increased markedly. In 1973, the average wage of male college graduates was 41 percent greater than the average for high school graduates. In 1991, the differential was 56 percent. For females, the comparable figures are 48 percent in 1973 and 56 percent in 1991. These wage trends, which to a large extent reflect long-term changes in the structure of the economy, are likely to continue. High school dropouts and high school graduates will thus continue to fare poorly relative to workers with more education.[1]

But what about the absolute incomes of high school graduates and, consequently, their standard of living? Their standard of living will depend to a large extent on their ability to find stable employment—something that has proved difficult for many young Americans. In 1988, 32 percent of male high school graduates aged twenty-nine to thirty-one had held their current job for less than one year. For male dropouts, the comparable figure is 49 percent. The figures for women who did not leave the labor force to raise families are similar (Osterman, 1991).

Employment instability is costly. Male high school graduates aged twenty-nine to thirty-one who held the same job for three years or more earned an average hourly wage of $11.15; it was $6.68 for those with less than one year on the job (Osterman, 1991). Among the reasons for the differential is that workers with short spells of employment often receive less training from their employers than do long-term workers, and workers with more training tend to be paid higher wages.

[Young people from minority groups who lack a college education have particular difficulty finding employment.]Just 29 percent of black high school dropouts aged sixteen to twenty-four were employed in 1990, compared with 57 percent of white dropouts. For high school graduates not enrolled in school, 56 percent of blacks and 79 percent of whites held jobs (Osterman, 1991).

Provision of good jobs to high school graduates will depend on the number of firms that follow the example of NUMMI and invest heavily in training and in reorganizing production—activities that promote the problem-solving behavior that leads to high productivity and higher wages. A critical public policy question is how to stimulate firms to make these investments in training and reorganization. To date there is little hard evidence on this issue. One hypothesis, supported by limited data, is that the quality of available workers may influence firms' decisions about whether to invest in worker training and the reorganization of production that lead to high-skill, high-wage jobs (Kenney and Florida, 1992). This leads to the question of what skills employers who pay high wages seek in new employees.

Required Skills

Reliability is at the top of employers' lists of the attributes they want in new employees. In addition to coming to work on time every day, employers want workers who follow directions and get along with their co-workers (Committee for Economic Development, 1991).

How important are cognitive skills in enabling workers to obtain and keep high-paying jobs? Increasingly, the ability to comprehend technical manuals and to use arithmetic to formulate and solve problems is important. For example, John Willett, Frank Levy, and I examined the extent to which high school seniors' scores on a test assessing skills in using arithmetic to solve simple problems predicted their wages (in 1988 constant dollars) six years later. For 1972 male graduates, the difference between weak knowledge of elementary mathematics and mastery was associated with a predicted wage differential at age twenty-four of 46 cents per hour. For males graduating in 1980, the same differential in math score was associated with a larger differential at age twenty-four, $1.15 per hour. The same pattern is present for females, with the test score differential corresponding to a predicted wage differential at age twenty-four of 74 cents per hour for 1972 high school graduates and $1.42 per hour for 1980 graduates.[2]

This research suggests that mastery of reading and math skills taught no later than junior high school is increasingly significant in determining access to relatively high paying jobs for high school graduates. The evidence does not concern statistics or calculus or physics, subjects taught to a minority of students in the last years of high school. I emphasize this because many American schools have found it easier to offer excellent instruction in advanced material to a subset of motivated students preparing for elite colleges than to help all students acquire threshold levels of literacy and mathematical problem-solving skills. The evidence supports the importance of this latter goal.

Another reason to be careful about the link between skills and productivity concerns the way skills are measured. Many skills, including the ability to communicate clearly, write well, and work with other people, are primary determinants of productivity in many jobs (Secretary's Commission on Achieving Necessary Skills, 1991). It is important that our schools teach, and that our children learn all of these skills. Currently, however, authentic ways to measure most of these skills are lacking. Student skills are typically measured by scores on multiple-choice tests. Yet scores on such tests often do not provide valid measures of competence. Sylvia Scribner (1986), for example, has shown that experienced workers routinely perform computation tasks on their jobs that they cannot do on written tests similar to those administered in most schools. One implication is that encouraging schools to maximize students' test scores is not a sensible policy. As long as multiple-choice tests are used to measure student achievement, the goal should be defined in terms of helping *all* students to achieve *threshold* levels of competency—such as mastery of fractions and decimals. A second implication is that developing assessment strategies that provide valid and reliable measures of students' abilities to perform real world tasks must be a part of school reform.

Trends in the Educational Attainments and Cognitive Skills of U.S. Students

One quarter of American young people leave school without a high school diploma (Finn, 1987).[3] Among young Latinos, the most rapidly growing demographic group, the dropout rate is close to 40 percent (National Council of La Raza, 1990). These students will find it extremely difficult to earn enough to support a family. Moreover, most dropouts are excluded from attending college, which is increasingly the path to a middle-class job.

In 1986 the National Assessment of Educational Progress (NAEP) examined the literacy skills of twenty-one- to twenty-five-year-olds (Kirsch and Jungeblut, 1986) and found that more than 90 percent could follow simple directions, solve single-step problems, and make inferences when all of the necessary information appeared in a single sentence. More than 30 percent, however, had difficulty gathering information from several sentences and "analyzing non-routine or multi-step problems" (Venezky, Kaestle, and Sum, 1987). Analysis of the item scores indicated that the problem lay in the subjects' ability to use reading to solve problems.

The 1986 NAEP literacy assessment of young adults also provided information on the average literacy skills of young adults with different amounts of education. Not surprisingly, the number of years of school completed was a strong predictor of literacy skills. But these favorable results concerning length of schooling do not mean that students graduating from high school have the literacy skills needed to function productively in the workplace. Although graduates have higher average skills than high school dropouts, a disturbingly high proportion of graduates are weak in literacy skills. The same pattern is present for mathematics skills. The

1990 National Assessment of Educational Progress reported that only 56 percent of seventeen-year-olds could "compute with decimals, fractions, and percents; and use moderately complex reasoning" (Mullis et al., 1991, p. 6).

The NAEP literacy and mathematics assessments show strong relationships between family background and children's skills. For example, parents' educational attainments are strong predictors of their children's literacy and mathematical skills (Dossey et al., 1988). Several factors seem responsible for this correlation; parents' educational attainments are strongly associated with the availability of literacy materials in the home, the probability that children will choose a college-preparatory curriculum in high school, and children's educational attainments.

The recent national assessments also indicate that minority group members have much lower skills on average than do whites. Although part of the reason is found in differences in educational attainment, minority group members still have much lower average literacy and problem-solving skills than do their white counterparts with the same amount of formal education—a pattern related to the higher incidence of poverty among minority group families.

A significant proportion of young adults thus lack threshold levels of problem-solving skills—skills that are crucial in adapting to new technology and in learning the skills needed in new jobs. Particularly distressing is the evidence that members of minority groups and those from poor families are especially likely to lack these skills.

On the surface, it may seem that the key to improving the level of critical skills is to make teachers and students work harder. Current efforts in this direction include increased use of standardized tests to monitor students' performance, with poor performance jeopardizing school administrators' job security and students' promotion and graduation. This approach, however, creates incentives for teachers to focus instruction on the arithmetic computation skills and word recognition skills that are emphasized on standardized tests to the neglect of more difficult to assess problem-solving and literacy skills. The National Science Board attributes improvements in U.S. students' performance on routine computations between 1978 and 1986, as well as the decline in their mathematical problem-solving skills, to such a focus by teachers (National Science Board, 1987). Similarly, an analysis of the NAEP literacy assessment concluded that "[attention to multiple text features and the integration of information over many sentences] are skills that are rarely taught except in relation to narrative tests, and rarely tested with forms, charts, and other non-prose texts" (Venezky, Kaestle, and Sum, 1987).

In short, state testing programs influence what is emphasized in the classroom (the de facto curriculum) and what students learn. Accordingly, in designing policies to improve skill levels, the educational system must work smarter rather than just working harder.

The Changing Demographics of American Students and New Labor Force Entrants

Students and new labor force entrants will increasingly be individuals with characteristics that historically have been associated with low literacy and mathematics skills. One such group is children living in poverty. In 1991, 21 percent of children lived in families classified as poor, an increase from 16 percent in 1969.[4] Moreover, poverty is an enduring condition for many children. Mary Jo Bane and David Ellwood estimate, for example, that "the average poor black child today appears to be in the midst of a poverty spell which will last for almost two decades" (Bane and Ellwood, 1986).

Children who grow up in poverty typically do poorly in school and encounter difficulties in the labor market (Venezky, Kaestle, and Sum, 1987; Snow et al., 1991). Contributing reasons are the lack of educational resources in the home, the stresses within families associated with low income, and the lack of access to high-quality schools.

A second group whose representation in the school-age population is increasing rapidly consists of minority group members, especially Latino children. As the recent NAEP literacy and mathematics assessments document, children from minority groups historically have had lower achievement levels on average than have white children. One compelling reason is the greater incidence of poverty among minority group families. In 1989, 44 percent of black children and 38 percent of Latino children lived in poverty, compared with 15 percent of white, non-Latino children (National Council of La Raza, 1990).

The poor lifetime job prospects of children from minority groups and among poor children raise important issues of equity. In the years ahead, these concerns about equity will be joined with concerns about the productivity of the economy. As the proportion of new labor force entrants coming from minority group families and poor families grows, the productivity of the work force will increasingly depend on the productivity of workers from these backgrounds.

An important challenge facing the nation is to improve the skill levels of new entrants to the labor force, especially those who bring to the schools and later to the labor force characteristics that have historically been associated with low achievement. The policy recommendations discussed later in this chapter should help meet this challenge. But it is important to keep in mind that the roots of the low achievement of many American children lie in the circumstances of poverty in which they live. Consequently, educational policy changes not accompanied by policies that significantly reduce the poverty that dominates many children's lives will have only a modest influence on their academic achievement.

A Role for Federal Education Policy

In the United States, responsibility for elementary and secondary education has traditionally been left primarily to the states, which in turn delegate an extraordinary amount of authority to 15,000 local school districts. As a result, the governance structure for education is extremely decentralized, and the federal role is limited. At no time in the nation's history has federal policy exerted a strong influence on how teachers and students spend their time in school.

There have been important changes, however, in the nature of the federal role. In particular, Supreme Court decisions and federal legislation have significantly influenced children's educational opportunities. Of particular importance are the 1954 Supreme Court decision in *Brown v. Board of Education,* which ruled segregated education to be inherently unequal; the Elementary and Secondary Education Act of 1965, which provided the first significant federal funds for the education of disadvantaged children; and the 1975 Education for All Handicapped Children Act (PL94-142), which guaranteed all handicapped children a free and appropriate public education. These federal initiatives resulted in increases in federal funding for education, reaching a high point in 1979, when federal expenditures accounted for 9.8 percent of total expenditures on public elementary and secondary education (National Center for Education Statistics [NCES], 1991a).

During the 1980s the federal role in funding public education contracted, so that in 1989, federal expenditures accounted for only 6.2 percent of total expenditures (NCES, 1991a). This contraction is unfortunate, especially during a period when slow economic growth and declining earnings for high school–educated workers have become national problems. Improving the skills of the labor force contributes to solving these problems. Improving the quality of elementary and secondary education should be a national goal, and the federal government should be willing to increase taxes to pursue this goal.

Given the structure of educational governance in the United States, the federal government can exert the most leverage by supporting the promising initiatives of local schools and states. Two quite different types of initiatives, school-based reforms and systemic reforms, are currently being developed, and federal government policies can influence their effectiveness, especially their impact on poor children.

School-based reforms attempt to change the way teachers and students in individual schools interact. Led by James Comer (1980), Henry Levin (1988), Theodore Sizer (1992), Robert Slavin (Slavin, Karweit, and Madden, 1989), and others, these efforts include the development of a set of principles to guide practice and the formation of partnerships with the faculties of specific schools interested in changing dramatically how teachers interact with each other and with students.

Despite the lack of rigorous evaluations verifying their effectiveness, school-based reform efforts are appealing because they attempt to improve the quality of the daily school experience of children attending a particular school, especially children from poor families. Indeed, many of the initiatives are taking place in schools serving high concentrations of such children. For this reason, federal education policies should support school-based reforms.

A number of states, including California, Kentucky, and South Carolina, are implementing systemic reforms aimed at changing in fundamental ways the rules under which all schools operate. Elements of systemic reform include creating standards for the skills students should master and new ways of assessing whether students meet these standards, designing curriculum tied to new standards, attracting talented teachers, improving teacher training, and increasing incentives for students to devote more time and energy to schoolwork. The logic underlying systemic reform is that while no single policy change will improve education dramatically, the simultaneous implementation of all of these changes can alter the daily experiences of students and teachers in ways that will improve the quality of education.[5]

It is too soon to know the effects of systemic reform efforts, but one concern is that poor students will not benefit, because they come to school less prepared to learn than do more affluent children and because they are less likely to receive the quality and quantity of instruction needed to meet new learning standards. Federal education policy should aim to ameliorate these conditions.

Suggestions for Federal Education Policies

Two types of policy suggestions can contribute to the quality of education provided to disadvantaged children. In one category are proposals that the federal government should not encourage. In the other are affirmative measures the federal government can and should take.

Policies to Avoid

Educational vouchers for families and merit pay for teachers have been advocated in recent years as educational reform strategies. Both are attempts to deal with critical issues: the need to increase accountability and the need to improve incentives for high-quality performance. Unfortunately, the evidence indicates that neither proposal holds much promise for improving the quality of education, especially that provided to poor children.

Educational vouchers. Some analysts argue that the key to improving American education is the introduction of a tax-funded voucher system that would allow parents to purchase education at any public or private school (Chubb and Moe, 1990a). In my judgment, the case for vouchers is weak. The potential gains are small, and there is substantial risk that a politically acceptable voucher plan would increase current educational inequalities. Greater parental choice within the public school system would be a step forward; it would improve accountability and might improve student achievement. But the evidence does not support spending public monies on private schools.

Those who support vouchers argue that private schools, freed from public bureaucracies, do a far superior job of raising student achievement. The data do not support this point. It is possible to compare the current achievement test scores of students in public schools and those in private schools. These comparisons indicate that even the largest estimates of differences in achievement are small relative to the goal of providing all students with strong basic skills. Scores from the 1990 NAEP mathematics assessment, for example, show that even though private school students tend to come from better-educated families than public school students (and parental education is a strong predictor of student achievement), their average achievement is only marginally better. Among students in the twelfth grade, 55 percent of those in public schools, 46 percent in Catholic schools, and 49 percent in other private schools had not mastered "reasoning and problem solving involving fractions, decimals, percents, elementary geometry and simple algebra," content that had been introduced by the seventh grade (NCES, 1991b). Approximately half the students attending each type of school graduate without basic mathematics skills. Simply increasing the number of students attending private schools would do little to improve mathematics achievement.

Further evidence on the impact of a voucher system is presented in Chapter 12. Charles Manski uses a simulation model to explore the consequences of promoting competition between public and private schools. In his model, all students receive a voucher that can be used either to pay for public schooling or to contribute to the cost of private schooling. He finds that the type of voucher system he models would not equalize educational opportunity across income groups. Whatever the value level of the voucher, young people living in wealthy communities receive higher-quality schooling than do those living in poor communities. Moreover, high-income youth in a given community receive higher-quality schooling on average than do low-income youth.

Would it be possible to design a voucher system that provided high-quality education to all children, including those disadvantaged by poverty or special needs? We do not know; it has never been tried. Twenty-five years ago, however, the federal government tried to find a community willing to experiment with a system that provided vouchers with higher values for disadvantaged children, mandated that no participating school could charge families more than the value of the voucher, and required schools facing excess demand to allocate half the available places by a lottery. No community wanted to try such a regulated system (Cohen and Farrar, 1977). But such regulations are essential to protect the educational options of disadvantaged children. Thus a system of vouchers that protected the interests of disadvantaged children does not appear to have a significant constituency, and it is only such a system that would have the potential to improve the education provided to poor children.

Merit pay. Plans that tie teachers' compensation to supervisors' evaluations of their performance have a long history. Thousands of school districts have adopted such schemes over the last seventy years. The vast majority of districts dropped merit pay within five years, however, and did so well before teachers' unions gained their present power. Although the reasons vary, a common theme is that the plans were expensive to administer, did not increase effort levels by individual teachers, and worked against the teamwork that is a critical component of effective schooling. Indeed, there is no evidence that any urban school district has improved its educational performance by adopting a merit pay plan. The few districts that have had long-lived merit pay plans are those that add merit pay to exceptionally high uniform salary scales, that serve middle-class student populations, and that tend to award merit pay more for extra work than for superior teaching performance (Murnane and Cohen, 1986).

New and Renewed Policy Initiatives

Fortunately, a number of policies promise significant improvement in educational quality. Some, such as preschool programs for disadvantaged children and compensatory education efforts, are already in place, but on the basis of past performance warrant amendment, expansion, and additional resources. Others grow naturally out of the foregoing diagnosis of the current problems in the American educational system.

Preschool programs for disadvantaged children. Over the last twenty-five years, several experimental programs have provided three- to five-year-olds from disadvantaged families with education, health, and nutrition services, combined with social services for participants' families. Many of these programs, including the well-known Perry Preschool program, had significant long-term benefits for their intended beneficiaries: lower rates of school dropouts, placement in special education classes, teenage pregnancy, unemployment, and criminal involvement. In addition, these programs enhanced college attendance and participation in post–high school training programs (Berrueta-Clement et al., 1984; Schorr, 1988;

Barnett, 1992). Most important, the dollar value of these benefits outweighed their costs. Moreover, the evidence suggests that 80 percent of the benefits of the Perry Preschool program accrued not to participants themselves but to society in general in the form of higher tax payments, lower transfer payments, and reduced crime (Gramlich, 1986). Preschool programs for disadvantaged children are clearly an important target of opportunity for federal educational policy.

Since the mid-1960s, the federal government has funded preschool services under the Head Start program. In 1992, 600,000 three- and four-year-old children participated in Head Start at a cost of $2.2 billion. Many evaluations of Head Start have been conducted, and the results are encouraging. The evidence on short-term effects is strong: children who participate in Head Start are more ready for school than comparable children who do not participate. The evidence on me-dium-term effects is also quite encouraging: Head Start participants have less need for special education classes and are less likely to be retained in grade than nonparticipants (Barnett, 1992).

No careful evaluation of the long-term effects of Head Start has yet been con-ducted.[6] The case that Head Start may have long-term positive effects rests on the success of Perry Preschool and other intensive preschool intervention programs that provide full-time, year-round services by highly trained staff.[7] Most Head Start programs, however, are extremely modest interventions, providing children with three to four hours of services for eight months per year, often with inade-quately trained staff.

Funding for Head Start should be dramatically increased, for four reasons. First, as recommended in a recent report of the National Head Start Association (1989), the quality of the programs at many sites should be improved. Common needs are increased staff training, better compensation for staff, and upgraded facilities. Second, the length of the program day should be extended to five or six hours, to make Head Start more like the programs that are known to have made long-term differences in the lives of disadvantaged children. Third, the program day should be combined with child care lasting ten hours, in order to make Head Start useful to families in which all adults have full-time jobs. This is especially important in light of the provision in the Family Support Act of 1988 mandating that all mothers receiving welfare payments either work or participate in educa-tion or training. Fourth, the program should include "two generation approaches," aimed not only at helping the child but also at helping parents to develop the skills to help their children. Finally, funding is needed to make high-quality Head Start programs available to the more than one million eligible children currently not being served.

Compensatory education. The instrument used by the federal government to improve the schooling of the nation's disadvantaged children is Title I of the Elementary and Secondary Education Act of 1965, subsequently renamed Chapter 1 in the 1981 reauthorization. Chapter 1 paid for services to five million children in 51,000 schools at a cost of $6.1 billion for fiscal year 1991 (Office of Technology Assessment, 1992).[8]

Quantitative evaluations of Chapter 1 indicate that it is not as effective as Head Start. Many analysts question the reliability of these evaluations, however (Kaestle and Smith, 1982). No analyses of the long-term effects of Chapter 1 on schooling or postschooling outcomes have been conducted, and because virtually all school districts in the country receive Chapter 1 funds, it would be difficult to design a high-quality evaluation of the program's long-term effects. As a result, evaluations of Chapter 1 programs are typically conducted by comparing the achievement within the same school of children who do and do not participate. This approach is flawed, because even those children who do not participate in a Chapter 1 program in fact receive additional attention when their class size is reduced by the pullouts of Chapter 1 children. Thus the achievement of the "control group" children may rise as a result of the indirect influence of Chapter 1.

The evaluations of Chapter 1 are also inconsistent with the findings of the National Assessment of Educational Progress, which indicate that the gaps between the average reading and mathematics skills of nine-year-old black children and white children have closed over time, as have the gaps between the skill levels of children from low-income and more affluent families. Although the narrowing of these differentials cannot definitively be attributed to Chapter 1, no compelling alternative explanation has been suggested. In fact, one explanation for the relative improvement in the reading achievement of low-income and minority group children over the 1980s is that Chapter 1 stimulated awareness of the needs of disadvantaged children and increased the attention paid to them in school (Kaestle and Smith, 1982). Chapter 1 has also funded a core of professionals who act as advocates for the program (Peterson, Rabe, and Wong, 1986). In sum, Chapter 1 merits continued support. At the same time it is important to experiment with strategies to make the program more effective in enhancing the skill levels of disadvantaged children.

Designing regulations for the use of Chapter 1 funds has always been difficult. The goal is to use the money to improve the education of disadvantaged children, and therefore the regulations prevent districts from treating the funds as general aid. Most school districts found that they could comply most easily by hiring special Chapter 1 teachers to instruct eligible children outside the regular classroom during the school day.[9] Thus one type of instruction replaced another, but the time devoted to learning was not increased. Moreover, Chapter 1 instruction typically focused on developing the initial reading and computation skills emphasized on the standardized tests used to evaluate program effectiveness. The instruction thus neglected aspects of problem solving that are critical to using mathematical skills in the work place.

The legislation reauthorizing Chapter 1 in 1988 made changes to address these problems. It allowed schools in which at least 75 percent of the students were eligible for Chapter 1 assistance to spend the money on schoolwide improvement programs. It also introduced criteria for accountability by individual schools and required those that did not meet state-established standards for achievement to be identified for program improvement. Although the accountability procedures do focus attention on improving students' achievement, they also discourage use of Chapter 1 funds for kindergarten and first grade classes because the procedures mandate that achievement gains be measured from the end of the first grade. The higher students score on this initial test, the more difficult it is to show subsequent gains. The procedures also inadvertently create incentives to retain students in the same grade for more than one year (Slavin and Madden, 1991).

Four reforms are needed in Chapter 1. First, a larger portion of the $6.1 billion currently spent on Chapter 1 should be devoted to reaching the most educationally disadvantaged students, who are disproportionately concentrated in high-poverty schools.[10] In addition, funding should be increased to $8 billion, with the increase allocated to schools serving high concentrations of eligible children. Second, Congress should encourage the development of schoolwide reforms by permitting them in schools in which at least 50 percent (instead of 75 percent) of the students are eligible for Chapter 1. Third, local education authorities should be permitted to negotiate accountability agreements with individual schools under which schools would be given several years to demonstrate progress. The achievements could be measured by scores on tests that measure mastery of curricula tied to new achievement standards. Finally, funds should be set aside for the development of the entire faculty, for solving attendance problems, and for teaching parents how to help their children learn more effectively. All these recommendations are aimed at using Chapter 1 to make improved schooling for disadvantaged children a crucial part of systemic reform.[11]

Preparation for work. The difficulties that many high school graduates, especially minority group members, experience in making the transition from school to work is a critical national problem. The federal policies that have the greatest impact on job opportunities for youth are those that affect the overall unemployment rate. Teenagers, especially those from minority groups, tend to be the last workers hired and the first fired. Consequently, even a small reduction in the overall unemployment rate results in a dramatic increase in the demand for young workers, as their employment rate is especially sensitive to macroeconomic conditions.

Inadequate reading and math skills and unawareness of the importance of regular attendance, punctuality, and reliability also contribute to the difficulties young workers experience in obtaining jobs with futures. Several principles of integration should guide attacks on these problems. The first is the importance of integrating vocational training with instruction in traditional academic subjects such as language arts and mathematics. The value of this approach stems from research in cognitive science showing that many students learn academic material most successfully when it is taught in the context of preparation for real jobs (Resnick, 1987). The second principle is that school-based learning should be integrated with experience in real workplaces. This too helps many students to master academic skills. It also aids students in understanding the importance of regular attendance and punctuality that employers demand. The third principle is that high school education should be integrated with postsecondary education. Jobs that pay enough to support a family increasingly require some postsecondary education, and it is critical that students see their high school work as leading to the postsecondary educational credentials that employers value.

Although these three types of integration are commonly accepted as principles on which to build programs for improving young people's work readiness, putting these principles into practice has proved difficult. The integration of vocational and academic education requires new curricula. It also requires teachers who understand both academic subject matter and industrial applications, and who have the skills and the commitment to integrate the two types of instruction. Integrating schoolwork with workplace experience requires large numbers of employers to offer meaningful work experience to students. This necessitates a change in the practices of most American firms, which tend to underinvest in training, even for their own regular employees (Kochan and Osterman, 1994). Integrating high school curricula with curricula in postsecondary educational institutions requires coordination between institutions with different norms and operating procedures.

The traditional federal approach to improving services to a target population is to identify a group of providers and supply them with funds along with regulations governing their use. This model characterizes both Head Start and Chapter 1. In the case of improving work readiness for adolescents and young adults, the problem is more complex, because no single set of institutions—high schools, employers, or community colleges—can provide highly effective programs without coordinating its efforts with those of the other types of institutions. One role for federal policy is to facilitate such coordination and to promote the three types of integration discussed here.

In recent years there have been various promising federal initiatives. The 1990 Perkins Act mandates that vocational education programs integrate academic and occupational training. Although it is not yet clear how much integration is actually taking place, the idea is becoming central to discussions among vocational educators concerning how to improve practice. One model eligible for Perkins Act funding that seems worthwhile is the career academy, an idea that stems from a program for disadvantaged youth begun in Philadelphia in 1969. Each academy is organized as a school within a school and has a particular theme, for example, business, or health occupations. Curricula are designed to blend academics and vocational material to capture students' interests. Local employers provide mentoring for students and internships in the academy's industrial field (T. Bailey and Merritt, 1992).

The Perkins Act also provides $64 million in funding for the development of Tech Prep or Two plus Two programs, which coordinate the curriculum of the last two years of high school and two years of community college, preparing students to work in a cluster of related occupations. One advantage of Tech Prep programs is that they provide students with an entree to postsecondary education. Doing so may facilitate upward mobility by making it easier for participants to invest in further education. At the same time such a program could mitigate a danger inherent in the development of school-to-work transition programs, namely, that low-income students and those from minority groups may be counseled into these programs instead of urged to prepare for four-year college programs that provide access to high-salaried occupations.

Youth apprenticeships are another area of initiative. The federal government has provided funding for the development of apprenticeship programs that provide participants with a combination of work-based mentoring and academic instruction.

All of these initiatives hold promise in that they incorporate elements of the three types of integration. There is very little evidence at this point, however, concerning the success of alternative approaches to preparing adolescents and young adults for work that pays enough to support them and their children. Until such evidence is available, prudent policy is a mixture of support for integration, such as that embodied in the 1990 Perkins Act, and experimentation with alternative ways to stimulate coordination among schools, community colleges, and employers.

To encourage creative approaches to integration, the federal government should fund demonstration programs of sufficient duration to allow information to be gathered about the potential of alternative approaches. Requests for proposals should specify particular interest in projects that serve disadvantaged students and that offer creative approaches to one or more of the integration principles. Projects might, for example, offer new ways of stimulating vocational faculty and academic faculty to work together, new strategies for obtaining employers' involvement in work-based learning programs, or new incentives to community colleges and high schools to join forces in developing Two plus Two programs. The design of the demonstration programs should include provision for evaluations assessing the effectiveness of alternative approaches.

One other federal government initiative that might promote the development of youth training programs is the coordination of labor laws and regulations. Some analysts argue that ambiguous regulations and conflicts between state and federal statutes dealing with child labor, fair labor standards, and health and safety deter employers from participating in training programs. The federal government could clarify its own regulations and, by developing model legislation as the Bureau of Standards does in the area of weights and measurements, encourage states to adopt common labor laws and regulations.[12]

Teachers for urban schools. The years from now to 2010 are likely to be a time of increasing shortages of skilled teachers as teachers hired in the baby boom years of the 1950s and 1960s retire and student enrollments (the children of the large baby boom generation) rise once again. Two dimensions of the potential teacher shortage problem are particularly relevant to the education of disadvantaged children. The first is that urban school districts serving large percentages of poor and minority group students typically find it more difficult to staff their schools with qualified teachers than do suburban school districts. Second, the percentage of minority teachers is declining, a disturbing trend given the increasing percentage of students who are minority group members (Murnane et al., 1991).

The federal government should offer incentives to increase the number of skilled teachers working in urban school districts and the number of talented minority-group college graduates working in the nation's schools. Several approaches have already been tried, including loan forgiveness for college graduates who become teachers. A more effective strategy appears to be providing grants for college expenses to academically able college students and demanding in return a number of years of teaching service in urban school districts (Arfin, 1986). Places could be reserved in such a program for academically able minority group members and for students with training in subject fields in which there are particular shortages, including mathematics, physics, and bilingual education. The U.S. experience with the Teacher Corps, a Great Society program that from 1966 to 1975 focused on recruiting teachers for service in poverty areas, provides several lessons for the design of a new federal initiative in this area (Bosco and Harring, 1973; Freibert, 1981).

Monitoring the quality of education provided to poor children. State-initiated systemic reform programs that specify new standards for the skills students should master—including the ability to think and write clearly and to solve problems—have the potential to improve the education provided to American children, including those from poor families. But this improvement will occur only if students receive high-quality instruction in the skills emphasized in the new standards. For many students from poor families this has not happened. The schools they attend often lack the facilities for hands-on science and the materials that facilitate the teaching of mathematical problem solving. Too often instruction in these schools emphasizes drill and practice, rather than problem-solving and the development of thinking skills (Oakes, 1990). Unless instruction improves dramatically in the schools poor children attend, systemic reforms will exacerbate the disadvantages these children face.

An important federal responsibility is to monitor the quality of instruction received by children in the nation's schools, with special attention to whether children from poor families receive instruction in the skills embodied in new learning standards. The federal government should fund the creation and maintenance of this monitoring system.[13] The development and operation of the system should be carried out by a private organization protected from political whims, however. One promising strategy is to make the system part of the National Assessment of Educational Progress.

·   ·   ·

Several key lessons emerge from a review of U.S. educational policy, particularly as it relates to the prospects for children from poor families.

- The cognitive skills of American workers are only one of many factors influencing their productivity. Attempts to improve the productivity of the labor force and the earnings of workers should also focus on other contributing factors, including the systems of management under which workers are utilized.

- Educational reform measures alone can have only modest success in raising the educational achievements of children from low-income families. The problems of poverty must be attacked directly.

- A critical challenge for federal educational policymakers is to ameliorate the disadvantages that children from poor families face. Taken together, several policies—Head Start, Chapter 1, preparation for work, and teacher recruitment—offer promise for improving the education of poor children.

CHAPTER TWELVE

Systemic Educational Reform and Social Mobility: The School *Choice* Controversy

CHARLES F. MANSKI

Education as an Instrument of Social Mobility

Today, as in the past, education policy is seen as an appealing instrument for enhancing social mobility. The appeal arises from the conjunction of institutional and empirical facts.

The essential institutional fact is that schooling is the main point of contact between government and children. Almost all children in the United States are subject to compulsory schooling laws in effect throughout the nation, and the great majority obtain their education in public schools.

The empirical basis is the association between schooling and life outcomes, both within a generation and from one generation to the next. A strong positive association exists between a person's education and his or her subsequent socioeconomic status (see, for example, Murphy and Welch, 1989). There is also a strong positive association between a person's education and that of his or her children (see, for example, Manski et al., 1992).

The empirical association between education and life outcomes suggests that education policy can influence mobility both within and across generations. A child growing up in a low-income family is, if educated, more likely to become a high-income adult. And an educated child is more likely, as an adult, to see that his or her children are well educated.

The use of education to increase social mobility presumes that two conditions hold. First, the empirical association between education and outcomes must be structural; that is, the observed associations must persist if education policy is changed. Second, policies must be capable of influencing educational attainment.

Belief that education truly does affect social mobility is widespread and will not be questioned here. This chapter is concerned with the effect of policy on the education of disadvantaged youth.

Targeted Programs and Systemic Reform

The present American system of elementary and secondary education took shape in the 1800s, when the states enacted compulsory schooling laws and established locally controlled districts providing free public schooling from kindergarten through grade twelve. In this century the structure of education has remained basically unchanged, except for the elimination of de jure racial segregation in the 1950s.

With the general features of American education fixed, policy has sought to influence social mobility through numerous programs targeted at disadvantaged youth. Current federal programs, discussed in Chapter 11, range from the Chapter 1 grants to school districts with high rates of enrollment of low-income students, to the Head Start program for preschoolers, to the Pell Grant scholarships for low-income college students. States have long subsidized school districts with low tax bases and some have recently enacted "learnfare" programs, which withhold welfare payments from families whose children fail to meet attendance requirements. Local school districts, which bear most of the responsibility for elementary and secondary education, undertake a host of classroom, extracurricular, and social service activities aimed at disadvantaged youth. Private groups sponsor an eclectic array of programs.

Recent events call into question whether the American education system will continue to maintain its historical form. Increasingly, educators and public officials bemoan the perceived inadequacy of America's schools and call for "systemic reform," "restructuring the schools," and the like. In his April 1991 speech unveiling his *America 2000* education strategy, for example, President Bush declared: "For the sake of the future, of our children and of the nation's, we must transform America's schools. The days of the status quo are over." He went on to say, "there will be no renaissance without revolution" (U.S. Department of Education, 1991, pp. 2, 3).

Criticism of the organization of public school systems has become especially prominent. It is widely held that decision making is too concentrated in school district administrations, that teachers and principals lack the incentives and the authority to perform their jobs effectively. Agreement on the existence of a problem does not, however, imply consensus on its solution. Some advocate transfer of decision-making power from central administrations to school principals; others recommend transfer of power from administrators and principals to classroom teachers or to parents. Some see the need for a greater concentration of decision making rather than less, through the establishment of a national curriculum and/or a national student-testing system.

The disparate calls to restructure American education may fade, but there is a real possibility that major changes will occur. These changes could affect the educational prospects of disadvantaged youth far more than any plausible change in existing targeted programs. It is thus important to understand the potential consequences of systemic reform.

What Would Choice Do?

Among the proposals for systemic educational reform, the Bush administration's call for school *choice* in *America 2000* sought the most radical change in the existing system and has generated the greatest controversy. The term "choice" has sometimes been used to describe various modest ideas: open enrollment plans within existing public school systems and targeted programs offering private school scholarships to low-income youth. But *choice,* as defined by *America 2000,* would drastically change the U.S. system of school finance by subsidizing enrollment at secular private schools and, courts permitting, at religiously affiliated schools as well.

Implementation of such a systemic school *choice* program might substantially affect the education of disadvantaged youth, whether for good or for bad. As of this writing, there is no imminent prospect that *choice* programs will be enacted by the states in anything like the form advocated in *America 2000.* Opposition to public subsidization of private schools is strong, and the inertia of the established education system makes radical change hard to bring about. But because the *choice* idea has rhetorical support and intellectual appeal, it must be considered seriously. The recent push for *choice* may have failed, but other proposals will undoubtedly surface in the future.

Unfortunately, consideration of *choice* to date has been anything but serious. The policy debate has been long on advocacy and short on analysis. We know very little about the educational consequences, for disadvantaged youths and for others, of adopting a systemic *choice* proposal. To move the debate away from advocacy and toward analysis, this chapter examines systemic *choice* and its implications for social mobility.

Theoretical and Empirical Arguments for Choice

Educational Alternatives in the Established System

The present American educational system offers substantial choice among educational alternatives. First, families choose public school districts when they select residences. Second, compulsory schooling laws do not require attendance in a public school in the district of residence. A child may enroll in a private school or, in some areas, in an out-of-district public school, or be educated at home. In 1988 about 12 percent of American students in elementary and secondary education were enrolled in private schools (National Center for Education Statistics, 1991a, table 2).

Third, a range of schooling alternatives is typically available within each public school district. Some districts permit attendance in any high school in the district, conditional on meeting school-specific academic requirements and, possibly, racial integration criteria. Within high schools, students routinely select among curricular tracks and choose among elective courses within each track. The range of formal options is typically more limited at the elementary and middle school levels, where neighborhood schools prevail and where elective courses are less common. But elementary schools often informally permit parents to request specific teachers for their children. And some districts operate districtwide "magnet schools" as well as neighborhood schools.

Fourth, and perhaps most important in the long run, institutional barriers do not usually discourage the creation of new educational alternatives. The states, which provide the legal foundation for schooling, typically permit local public school districts to reconfigure their systems as they deem appropriate. And the states do not make it overly difficult to establish new private schools or to shut down old ones. In the language of industrial organization, the private school industry is characterized by relatively free entry and exit.

School Finance and Classical Economics

Although the U.S. educational system offers many alternatives and is open to the creation of new ones, proponents of systemic *choice* argue that school finance policy effectively limits the available options and impedes the development of superior alternatives. Government support of public schools, they say, should be replaced by educational vouchers permitting students to choose among any public or private school meeting specified standards.

The voucher idea has a long history. Tom Paine proposed a voucher plan in 1792, in *The Rights of Man* (see the discussion in West [1967]). The awakening of modern interest is usually credited to Milton Friedman (1955, 1962), followed by Christopher Jencks (1966), Henry Levin (1968), John Coons and Stephen Sugarman (1978), and others. Eventually, advocacy of vouchers was recast as a broader call for educational *choice*.

The theoretical argument for *choice* is a straightforward application of elementary principles of classical economics. Tax support of public schools distorts the incentives faced by both the consumers and the producers of schooling. Consumer incentives are distorted because the residents of a given school district are encouraged to enroll their children in that district's public schools rather than in private schools or out-of-district public schools, where they may have to pay substantial fees. Producer incentives are distorted because the price differential between a district's public schools and other educational alternatives gives the public schools local monopoly power over district residents; hence, the public schools can attract students even if they do not provide the type and quality of education that families want.

The textbook solution to these problems is to eliminate the distortion of incentives. Assuming that society wishes to fund schooling at all, the replacement of public school support with a voucher system would achieve this solution. The argument for vouchers applies in principle to all settings, but the proponents of *choice* maintain that it holds especially forcefully when applied to school districts with high poverty rates. Under the present system, the poor are particularly limited in their educational options, because private school enrollment or change of residence to another public school district is not financially feasible. Hence public schools in poor districts have especially great monopoly power and, consequently, the least incentive to respect consumer preferences. The *America 2000 Sourcebook* states: "Rich parents, white and non-white, already have school choice. They can move, or pay for private schooling. The biggest beneficiaries of new choice policies will be those who now have no alternatives. With choice they can find a better school for their children or use that leverage to improve the school their children now attend" (U.S. Department of Education, 1991, p. 41).

Empirical Evidence

To some, the theoretical argument for vouchers is sufficiently compelling to make empirical evidence unnecessary. But not everyone views classical economics as a sufficient basis for radical revision of school finance. So recent proponents of *choice* have sought to bring to bear empirical evidence as well.

The absence of data makes impossible a direct empirical comparison of *choice* and the current system of public school finance. An experimental voucher plan was designed in the late 1960s by the U.S. Office of Economic Opportunity but was not carried out in the form intended (see Center for the Study of Public Policy [1970] for the original design, and Witte [1990a] for a discussion of the implementation). In 1989 the state of Minnesota initiated a program subsidizing the enrollment of at-risk youth in out-of-district public schools, and in 1990 the city of Milwaukee began an experiment with vouchers usable by low-income youth at private schools. These efforts have not been in place long enough for conclusions to be drawn. More important, they are too small in scale and restricted in scope to yield significant lessons about the operation of a systemic *choice* policy.

Lacking direct empirical evidence, *choice* proponents have argued indirectly, from empirical studies comparing the achievement of students in public and private schools. During the 1980s, a series of studies, from Coleman, Hoffer, and Kilgore (1982) through Coleman and Hoffer (1987) and Chubb and Moe (1990a), have interpreted available achievement data as showing that private schools, especially Catholic ones, do a better job of educating students than do public schools. The validity of this interpretation has certainly not been accepted universally (see, for example, Cain and Goldberger [1983] and Witte [1990b]). Nevertheless, *choice* proponents have accepted it as fact and have concluded from it that a voucher system would improve educational outcomes by inducing more students to enroll in private schools.

The Rhetoric of Choice

To proponents of *choice,* the foregoing theoretical and empirical arguments lead to definitive policy conclusions. President Bush, in his *America 2000* speech, stated: "The concept of choice draws its fundamental strength from the principle at the very heart of the democratic idea. Every adult American has the right to vote, the right to decide where to work, where to live. It's time parents were free to choose the schools that their children attend." A president may, perhaps, be excused for hyperbole, even if he appears to consider public school finance a form of enslavement. But what of the political scientists John Chubb and Terry Moe, who, in an article titled "Choice *Is* a Panacea," wrote, "of all the reforms that attract attention, only choice can address the basic institutional problems plaguing America's schools" (1990b, p. 7). Such is the present rhetoric of *choice.*

The Economics of *Choice* Reconsidered: How Relevant
Is Classical Thinking?

During the past thirty years the basic intellectual argument for systemic *choice* has not notably advanced beyond the classical economic ideas sketched by Friedman (1955, 1962). If anything, recent advocacy of *choice* views the matter more simplistically than did Friedman. It seems enough today to declare that *choice* promotes "consumer sovereignty" and "competition."

It may be that recent *choice* advocacy reflects conservative values more than concern with economic distortion. Nevertheless, the economic merits of *choice* warrant careful consideration. The first question is whether classical economics provides a reasonable basis for the formation of education policy. After all, classical economics does not say that markets always optimize social welfare. It says only that a market system can achieve a social optimum if production technologies, consumer preferences, social objectives, and the information available to the relevant economic actors satisfy certain conditions. We must therefore ask whether education is adequately approximated by these classical conditions. At a qualitative level, it is easy to raise doubts about the fit between classical economics and education.

Informational Issues

A market for schooling cannot be expected to perform as promised by advocates of *choice* unless society and families are adequately informed about the education provided by schools. If collection and transmission of such information is costly, then the superiority of a market system relative to public provision of schooling is not clear-cut. Two separate but related potential problems are described here. (For further discussion of these informational questions, see Levin [1991].)

Public monitoring of the social interest in schooling. Advocates of *choice* must agree with proponents of public school finance that society's interest in education goes beyond the interest felt by individuals. For suppose that society felt no need for education beyond that which individuals were willing to purchase; that is, suppose that the social returns to education were the same as the private returns. Then there would be no reason for government to fund education at all, whether through vouchers or through public schools.

Classical economics argues that an effective way for society to express its interests is for the government to subsidize the price of education that is socially desired but would not be purchased by families in the absence of subsidies. Given such subsidies (that is, vouchers), the market will produce socially optimal educational outcomes. There is no need for the government to produce education itself through public schools.

But the classical prescription presumes that society can costlessly monitor the use of its price subsidies. This assumption does not seem realistic when applied to schooling, whose content may be rather difficult to monitor from a distance. If public monitoring of schooling is costly, then a voucher system is not obviously superior to public school finance. Should society implement a voucher system and not monitor the use of its subsidies, then students and schools could subvert social objectives by using the subsidies to further their own private interests. Should society pay the cost of monitoring, then it must ask whether these costs exceed whatever benefits private schooling offers relative to direct public production of education, through the public schools. The social choice between vouchers and public school finance depends on the magnitude of monitoring costs and on the efficiency of private schools relative to public schools in producing education.

Some *choice* advocates believe that government does not need to monitor educational content because parents and students, acting in their own self-interest, will make appropriate schooling decisions. Chubb and Moe (1990b), for example, argue: "The state will not hold the schools accountable for student achievement or other dimensions that call for the assessment of the quality of school performance. When it comes to performance, schools will be held accountable from below, by parents and students who directly experience their services and are free to choose" (p. 11). This statement, which denies the presence of any deviation between the public and private interest in schooling, is inconsistent with advocacy of *choice.* As noted earlier, there is no economic argument for subsidizing schooling if public and private interests coincide. (There may, however, still be an economic argument for the government to offer student loans if the private capital market does not operate efficiently.)

Consumers' knowledge of the educational content of schooling. The classical argument for market allocation of goods supposes that consumers and firms have full information about the product in question. Modern economic theory extends the argument to situations in which consumers and firms have incomplete but identical product information. The merits of markets relative to other allocation mechanisms are not clear-cut if consumers have less information than do firms. Then competition does not ensure that firms produce the goods that consumers want.

But consumers of schooling do not have the same information as producers. Asymmetric information seems inherent to education in general and to schooling in particular. The traditional economic prescription for dealing with asymmetric information is for the government to provide consumers with the information they lack and let the market do the rest. This is what *choice* proponents recommend; for example, Chubb and Moe (1990b) propose the establishment of "Parent Information Centers." I have pointed out, however, that public monitoring of the content of schooling is likely to be costly. It is also costly for the government to transmit its accumulated information to children and their families. Hence public provision of information in a market for schooling may or may not be preferable to public production of schooling.

Critics of *choice* see the transmission of schooling information to disadvantaged youth as particularly problematic. The concern is that less-educated parents may not be able to interpret information on schooling alternatives properly. If so, their children would themselves tend to make poor schooling choices. (See the discussion in Levin [1991].)

Student Interactions in the Production of Education

Classical economics assumes that individual consumers interact through their joint determination of market-clearing prices but are otherwise unconnected. Consider, however, how schools produce education.

The prevailing technology places a teacher in a class of students who may interact strongly with one another through their participation in classroom activities and through their relationships outside of the classroom. Even if the students in a class do not interact directly, they interact indirectly whenever the teacher takes the composition of the class into account in making instructional decisions. These intra-classroom interactions among students are enhanced by further direct and indirect interactions at the school level. For example, the course offerings at a given school and the quality of the teachers who choose to work there may depend in part on the composition of the student body. Interactions among students thus pervade the production of education.

The study of student interactions forms an important focus for research in the sociology of education and in educational psychology (see, for example, Reuman, 1989, and Gamoran, 1992). From the perspective of economics, student interactions generate "external" effects; that is, they make the social returns to schooling differ from the private returns.

Students pursue their private interests and cannot be expected to make schooling decisions that take into account the effects of their behavior on others. Society's problem is to design an educational system that recognizes these external effects. The present system of public school finance provides society a means, albeit imperfect, of internalizing the external effects produced by student interactions. By funding public schooling, society gives students an incentive to enroll in public schools rather than in private alternatives where they would have to pay tuition. Students who accept society's offer of free public schooling in return give society some control over their placement in specific classes and schools. Society then uses this control to promote student interactions thought to be socially beneficial, from ability tracking to mainstreaming disabled students to racial and socioeconomic integration.

The reason that the public school system is only an imperfect mechanism for promoting beneficial student interactions is, ironically enough, that society permits young people and their families to choose other alternatives. If a public school district adopts policies that a given family perceives as insufficiently in line with their private interests, then the family chooses not to accept the offer of free schooling and instead moves to another district or enrolls its children in a private school.

Could society promote socially beneficial student interactions through a voucher system? It might in principle be possible to establish a system that provided incentives for students to interact voluntarily in a socially desired manner. But this system could not simply grant all students a uniform voucher. Society would have to set up a voucher schedule in which the grants students received varied with the composition of the school in which they enrolled and the classes they attended. Moreover, this voucher schedule might have to vary across students, depending on the manner in which they interacted with others.

Quantitative Analysis of School Finance Policy

The Need for Quantitative Analysis

Qualitative analysis of a matter as complex as the design of our educational system does not carry one very far. *Choice* advocates can argue that a voucher system is inherently superior, on economic grounds, to public school finance only if they presume that education approximately fits the assumptions of classical economics. Once this assumption is questioned, possible advantages for public school finance emerge and we are in the messy real world of tradeoffs.

In the world of tradeoffs, qualitative analysis does not suffice. We need to pin down magnitudes. How difficult is it for the public to monitor educational content at a distance? What information can students and families be expected to possess about the characteristics of their educational alternatives? How do students interact in the production of education? How do families decide among the educational options presently available and how would they decide under a voucher system? How efficiently do public and private schools now produce education and how would the move from public school finance to vouchers affect the efficiency of production?

It is disappointing and frustrating that serious attention has not been given to such questions of magnitudes during the thirty years in which *choice* has been actively debated. We have no means of forecasting the new educational equilibrium that would follow the introduction of a voucher system. In the absence of quantitative analysis, rhetoric reigns.

There are two complementary ways to learn what choice would really do. One is to experiment with voucher systems and observe the outcomes. Such experiments would have to be carried out on something like the scale of contemplated operational systems. *Choice* proponents argue that voucher finance would provide public schools with the incentive to operate more efficiently. *Choice* opponents argue that vouchers would exacerbate the racial and socioeconomic segregation of our schools. These claims cannot be evaluated in small-scale experiments, which provide schools with little incentive to change their behavior and which can have at most minor impacts on enrollment patterns. (See Garfinkel, Manski, and Michalopolous [1992] for a discussion of the general problem of using small-scale experiments to learn the full-scale effects of social policies.)

The second approach is to develop plausible models of the behavior of the relevant actors, namely, students and schools. This done, one may simulate alternative school finance policies and forecast their impacts on school enrollments and productivity. Simulations cannot, of course, be definitive, but they can suggest the direction and magnitude of the impacts to be expected from policy changes. Moreover, the development and application of formal models has value; models force one to come to grips with issues that may be only vaguely perceived in qualitative policy discussions.

In an effort to gain a better understanding of school *choice,* I have developed a model of the market for schooling and used the model to simulate the operation of alternative school finance policies. I hope most readers will feel that the specified models and school finance options are sufficiently realistic to allow them to learn something from the policy simulations. At the same time, I anticipate that many readers may wish to know what happens under behavioral and institutional assumptions different from those imposed here. I cannot report here all the simulations that may potentially be of interest. But I can help readers to perform their own simulations. The documented computer program (Manski and Shen, 1992) developed for this study is available for general use. The program, which may be obtained through the Institute for Research on Poverty, can be applied to simulate the market for schooling in communities of different socioeconomic compositions under a range of behavioral assumptions and school finance policies.

Main Features of a Model of the Market for Schooling

The model assumes that schooling outcomes are determined by the interaction of three sets of actors: students, private schools, and public schools. (For details, see Manski [1992].)

Students. I suppose that a community comprises a population of heterogeneous students, each of whom must choose between public schooling and private schooling. In reality, various public and private schooling options may be available; if so, a student may be interpreted as choosing between the best option of each type. Although I refer to the student as the decision maker, the reader may think of parents as making the choices. It does not matter who makes the choices, as long as the family acts as a unit.

Each student has three background attributes: family income, academic motivation, and private school preference. The last attribute measures the strength of a student's preference for private school relative to public school enrollment, holding fixed the tuition costs and the achievement levels associated with enrollment in the two sectors.

Students interact in the production of education, as already discussed. In particular, the achievement of a student enrolled in a given school sector increases with the fraction of highly motivated students in that sector. Achievement also increases with the amount per student that a school sector spends on instruction.

Each student evaluates the two sectors and chooses the better option. The value (or utility) that a student associates with a given sector depends on the tuition cost, the achievement attainable in the sector, and the student's intrinsic preference for the sector. The importance that a given student attaches to achievement depends on his or her own motivation; students with high motivation are more concerned with achievement than are those with low motivation. The importance of cost varies with family income; students from low-income families are more concerned with cost than are those from high-income families.

I assume that students correctly perceive the characteristics of their schooling options. The model neglects the informational issues discussed above because they are too complex to address adequately here.

Private schools. The private school sector chooses its tuition and its instructional expenditures per student. I assume that the private sector is free to set any tuition it wishes. This is the current situation, and it would persist under any voucher system permitting private schools to supplement their voucher revenues with tuition revenue.

Because entry into and exit from the private school industry is not very costly, I assume that the private sector acts competitively. This implies that private schools must, in equilibrium, use all their revenues (that is, tuition plus vouchers) for instructional purposes valued by students rather than for other purposes not valued by students. Moreover, competition drives tuition to a level that maximizes private sector enrollments.

Public schools. The revenue available to the public school sector is a predetermined government subsidy per enrolled student; public schools are constrained by law to charge no tuition. In contrast to private schools, public schools are not competitive and so need not spend all their revenue on instruction valued by students. Public schools choose how much revenue to spend on instruction and how much to spend for other purposes not valued by students.

How do public schools actually spend their revenues? This is a central question in the *choice* debate. As I interpret them, *choice* advocates argue that public schools choose to maximize the surplus they have available for furthering noninstructional objectives. *Choice* proponents claim that the public sector surplus is "bureaucratic waste," but there is no compelling evidence that this assertion is true. The public schools can use their surplus to achieve goals that are socially desired even if not valued by individual students.

The bureaucratic waste hypothesis makes the strongest possible case for *choice*. In contrast, the *choice* argument is weakest if the public sector spends all its revenues for instructional purposes, as would a competitive firm. Because I do not want to take a stand on the controversial question of public school behavior, I report policy simulations under both assumptions.

Market equilibrium. The market for schooling is in equilibrium if the schooling choices made by students, the tuition level chosen by private schools, and the instructional expenditures chosen by public schools are such that no actor wishes to change his or her behavior.

Table 12.1   Simulated effects of alternative school finance policies: Poor community

	Public schools maximize surplus			Public schools act competitively		
	Size of voucher to private school			Size of voucher to private school		
	0	2	4	0	2	4
School Attributes						
Private school tuition	5	1	0	8	5	1
Instructional expenditures valued by students						
Public school	2	2	3	4	4	4
Private school	5	3	4	8	7	5
Proportion of highly motivated students						
Public school	.36	.26	.08	.46	.44	.38
Private school	.80	.64	.56	.90	.84	.68
Family income distribution						
Students in public school						
Low (0–21)	.44	.55	.32	.33	.35	.44
Lower middle (21–32)	.35	.25	.32	.33	.35	.28
Middle (32–44)	.14	.12	.17	.21	.19	.15
Upper middle (44–63)	.04	.05	.09	.08	.07	.06
High (63–100)	.02	.04	.09	.05	.04	.06
Students in private school						
Low (0–21)	.00	.14	.30	.00	.00	.10
Lower middle (21–32)	.19	.33	.30	.00	.03	.32
Middle (32–44)	.32	.25	.20	.04	.23	.27
Upper middle (44–63)	.22	.13	.10	.29	.29	.15
High (63–100)	.27	.14	.10	.67	.45	.16
Proportion of Youth Enrolled in Public School						
All youth	.68	.38	.13	.92	.85	.59

Policy Simulations

I discuss here the findings from simulations of alternative school finance policies applied to three typical communities with varying income distributions and public school funding levels. These communities are designated poor, average, and wealthy.

I am concerned with systemic *choice* systems, in which the same voucher is available to all students in a community. The simulations vary the government subsidy of private school enrollment from zero to $2,000 per student to $4,000 per student. The lower end of this range expresses current school finance policy. The upper end considers a voucher larger than those enacted in recent experiments. The voucher offered by Milwaukee in 1992, for example, was $2,500.

Table 12.1   (continued)

	Public schools maximize surplus			Public schools act competitively		
	Size of voucher to private school			Size of voucher to private school		
	0	2	4	0	2	4
By family income						
Low (0–21)	1.00	.71	.14	1.00	1.00	.87
Lower middle (21–32)	.80	.32	.14	1.00	.98	.56
Middle (32–44)	.49	.22	.11	.99	.83	.45
Upper middle (44–63)	.31	.19	.12	.77	.57	.38
High (63–100)	.13	.14	.12	.47	.34	.34
Average Instructional Expenditures Valued by Students						
All youth	2.96	2.62	3.87	4.31	4.44	4.41
By family income						
Low (0–21)	2.00	2.29	3.86	4.00	4.00	4.13
Lower middle (21–32)	2.60	2.68	3.86	4.00	4.05	4.44
Middle (32–44)	3.53	2.78	3.89	4.06	4.52	4.55
Upper middle (44–63)	4.09	2.82	3.88	4.90	5.28	4.62
High (63–100)	4.63	2.86	3.88	6.10	5.98	4.66
Average Schooling Cost						
Paid by government	2.72	2.77	4.00	3.69	3.70	4.00
Paid by families	1.60	0.62	0.00	0.62	0.74	0.41

Note: A "poor" community provides a public school subsidy of $4,000 per student and has the following income distribution: low 30%, lower-middle 30%, middle 20%, upper-middle 10%, high 10%. All monetary figures are in thousands of 1988 dollars. For a full explanation of the table, see Manski (1992).

Tables 12.1, 12.2, and 12.3 report two versions of each simulation. In one version, the public school sector maximizes its surplus (the difference between revenues and instructional expenditures). In the other version, the public school sector spends all of its revenues on instruction valued by students. Table 12.1 presents results in a typical poor community, 12.2 in an average one, and 12.3 in a wealthy community.

In each simulation, I report the actions chosen by students and schools: the fraction of students enrolled in public schools, the tuition set by private schools, and the instructional expenditures chosen by public schools. Also reported are statistics describing the equilibrium composition of the public and private schools: the fraction of highly motivated students in each sector and the income

Table 12.2   Simulated effects of alternative school finance policies: Average community

	Public schools maximize surplus			Public schools act competitively		
	Size of voucher to private school			Size of voucher to private school		
	0	2	4	0	2	4
School Attributes						
Private school tuition	7	3	2	10	8	5
Instructional expenditures valued by students						
Public school	3	3	4	6	6	6
Private school	7	5	6	10	10	9
Proportion of highly motivated students						
Public school	.38	.34	.34	.48	.46	.44
Private school	.80	.72	.68	.94	.90	.82
Family income distribution						
Students in public school						
Low (0–21)	.27	.35	.37	.21	.22	.24
Lower middle (21–32)	.27	.27	.24	.21	.22	.24
Middle (32–44)	.23	.19	.17	.21	.22	.22
Upper middle (44–63)	.15	.12	.12	.21	.20	.18
High (63–100)	.08	.08	.09	.16	.14	.13
Students in private school						
Low (0–21)	.00	.01	.01	.00	.00	.00
Lower middle (21–32)	.00	.11	.15	.00	.00	.00
Middle (32–44)	.13	.22	.23	.00	.00	.09
Upper middle (44–63)	.34	.30	.29	.03	.16	.32
High (63–100)	.53	.36	.32	.97	.84	.59
Proportion of Youth Enrolled in Public School						
All youth	.73	.57	.53	.96	.92	.84

distribution of the enrollment in each sector. Finally, I report two measures of spending per student, averaged over public and private sector enrollments: instructional expenditures per student and total schooling costs per student.

Persistent Outcome Patterns

The following persistent patterns are noteworthy.

- Instructional expenditures valued by students are almost always higher in the private schools than in the public schools. The difference lies between $1,000 and $6,000 in every simulation except one. The one exceptional

Table 12.2 (continued)

	Public schools maximize surplus			Public schools act competitively		
	Size of voucher to private school			Size of voucher to private school		
	0	2	4	0	2	4
By family income						
Low (0–21)	1.00	.99	.97	1.00	1.00	1.00
Lower middle (21–32)	1.00	.76	.64	1.00	1.00	1.00
Middle (32–44)	.83	.53	.46	1.00	1.00	.93
Upper middle (44–63)	.54	.34	.32	.99	.94	.75
High (63–100)	.30	.22	.25	.79	.66	.53
Average Instructional Expenditures Valued by Students						
All youth	4.07	3.86	4.94	6.18	6.32	6.48
By family income						
Low (0–21)	3.00	3.03	4.06	6.00	6.00	6.00
Lower middle (21–32)	3.02	3.48	4.73	6.00	6.00	6.01
Middle (32–44)	3.68	3.93	5.08	6.00	6.00	6.22
Upper middle (44–63)	4.83	4.31	5.35	6.03	6.25	6.76
High (63–100)	5.80	4.56	5.50	6.86	7.36	7.40
Average Schooling Cost						
Paid by government	4.40	4.27	5.06	5.73	5.68	5.68
Paid by families	1.87	1.29	0.94	0.44	0.64	0.79

Note: An "average" community provides a public school subsidy of $6,000 per student and has the following income distribution: low 20%, lower-middle 20%, middle 20%, upper-middle 20%, high 20%. All monetary figures are in thousands of 1988 dollars. For a full explanation of the table, see Manski (1992).

case occurs in the wealthy community (Table 12.3) when the public schools are assumed to behave competitively and the voucher level is zero. This simulation shows that less than 0.5 percent of all students enroll in private schools. Here the public schools are so attractive that a private school sector is essentially not viable. (Those few students who do enroll in private school are ones whose private school preference is so strong that they prefer private schooling even though the public schools are less costly and spend more for purposes valued by students.)

- The proportion of highly motivated students in the private sector is always well above that in the public sector. This finding is related to the finding

Table 12.3   Simulated effects of alternative school finance policies: Wealthy community

	Public schools maximize surplus			Public schools act competitively		
	Size of voucher to private school			Size of voucher to private school		
	0	2	4	0	2	4
School Attributes						
Private school tuition	10	7	6	9	12	10
Instructional expenditures valued by students						
Public school	4	5	6	10	10	10
Private school	10	9	10	9	14	14
Highly motivated students						
Public school	.34	.38	.36	.48	.46	.46
Private school	.90	.86	.84	1.00	1.00	.98
Family income distribution						
Students in public school						
Low (0–21)	.13	.13	.14	.10	.10	.10
Lower middle (21–32)	.13	.13	.14	.10	.10	.10
Middle (32–44)	.26	.25	.26	.20	.20	.20
Upper middle (44–63)	.30	.30	.29	.30	.30	.31
High (63–100)	.17	.18	.18	.30	.29	.28
Students in private school						
Low (0–21)	.00	.00	.00	.00	.00	.00
Lower middle (21–32)	.00	.00	.00	.00	.00	.00
Middle (32–44)	.01	.02	.05	.00	.00	.00
Upper middle (44–63)	.30	.30	.32	.00	.00	.02
High (63–100)	.69	.68	.64	1.00	1.00	.98
Proportion of Youth Enrolled in Public School						
All youth	.75	.77	.74	1.00	.99	.98

that instructional expenditures are greater in the private sector. Among students with the same family income and a preference for private schools, those with high motivation are more willing to pay private school tuition in return for the benefit of larger instructional expenditures. The private schools thus attract more highly motivated students than do the public schools.

- Within each community, the proportion of students enrolling in public school almost always decreases as family income rises. The only exceptional case is a corner solution. Consider the poor community with a surplus-maximizing public sector and the voucher set at $4,000. The equilib-

Table 12.3 (continued)

	Public schools maximize surplus			Public schools act competitively		
	Size of voucher to private school			Size of voucher to private school		
	0	2	4	0	2	4
By family income						
Low (0–21)	1.00	1.00	1.00	1.00	1.00	1.00
Lower middle (21–32)	1.00	1.00	1.00	1.00	1.00	1.00
Middle (32–44)	.99	.97	.94	1.00	1.00	1.00
Upper middle (44–63)	.75	.77	.72	1.00	1.00	1.00
High (63–100)	.43	.47	.44	1.00	.96	.93
Average Instructional Expenditures Valued by Students						
All youth	5.48	5.93	7.06	10.00	10.04	10.09
By family income						
Low (0–21)	4.00	5.00	6.00	10.00	10.00	10.00
Lower middle (21–32)	4.00	5.00	6.00	10.00	10.00	10.00
Middle (32–44)	4.05	5.11	6.25	10.00	10.00	10.00
Upper middle (44–63)	5.48	5.92	7.12	10.00	10.00	10.01
High (63–100)	7.41	7.12	8.25	10.00	10.15	10.30
Average Schooling Cost						
Paid by government	7.54	8.13	8.41	9.99	9.91	9.86
Paid by families	2.46	1.63	1.59	0.00	0.13	0.23

Note: A "wealthy" community provides a public school subsidy of $10,000 per student and has the following income distribution: low 10%, lower-middle 10%, middle 20%, upper-middle 30%, high 30%. All monetary figures are in thousands of 1988 dollars. For a full explanation of the table, see Manski (1992).

rium private school tuition is zero, so the public sector enrollment rate does not vary with income.

- Students perceive that the quality of schooling, both public and private, is generally lowest in the poor community and highest in the wealthy community. In our model, the quality of schooling is synonymous with student achievement. The achievement of students enrolled in a given school sector increases with instructional expenditures and with the proportion of highly motivated students. The simulations show that the values of these variables are generally lowest in the poor community and highest in the wealthy one.

- The government consistently pays the largest share of schooling costs. In these simulations, the proportion of schooling costs paid by the government ranges from 63 percent to 100 percent. Students pay the remainder.

COMMUNITYWIDE EFFECTS OF SCHOOL FINANCE POLICY

- Suppose, as do *choice* advocates, that the public school sector maximizes surplus. Then, as *choice* advocates predict, increasing the voucher level induces the public school sector to increase the amount that it expends for instructional purposes valued by students. As the voucher increases from zero to $4,000, public school expenditures valued by students increase from $2,000 to $3,000 in the poor community, from $3,000 to $4,000 in the average one, and from $4,000 to $6,000 in the wealthy community.

- The equilibrium private school tuition almost always falls as the voucher level increases. If the public sector maximizes surplus, then as the voucher increases from zero to $4,000, private school tuition falls from $5,000 to zero in the poor community, from $7,000 to $2,000 in the average one, and from $10,000 to $6,000 in the wealthy community. If the public sector behaves competitively, tuition falls from $8,000 to $1,000 in the poor community and from $10,000 to $5,000 in the average one. The one exception to the general monotone relationship occurs in the wealthy community, where tuition rises slightly, from $9,000 to $10,000.

    Observe that, in some of the simulations, private school tuition falls even faster than the voucher rises. In these cases, introducing vouchers induces the private school sector to lower the amount it expends on instructional purposes.

- The proportion of students enrolled in public school falls as the voucher level increases. The effect is most pronounced in the poor community, where public school enrollment falls from .68 to .13 or from .92 to .59, depending on the assumption made about public school behavior. There is a less substantial but still sizable drop in the average community, from .73 to .53 or from .96 to .84. The effect is negligible in the wealthy community, where public school enrollment falls from .75 to .74 or from 1.00 to .98.

    The pattern of decreasing public school enrollment usually holds within each income group. There are, however, some simulations in which increasing the voucher generates a slight increase in public school enrollments among upper-middle- or high-income students. This result is theoretically possible. Increasing the voucher can lead private and public schools to change their behavior in a way that diminishes the quality advantage enjoyed by private schools.

- As the voucher level increases, the proportion of highly motivated students typically falls in *both* school sectors. The reason for this seemingly paradoxical result is that the students who move from public to private school have higher average motivation than those who remain in the public sector but lower average motivation than those students already enrolled in private school. This effect is largest in the poor community, where the enrollment shift is most pronounced, and is negligible in the wealthy community, with its small enrollment shift.

- As the voucher level increases, the average schooling cost per student paid by government rises by about $1,000 if the public school sector maximizes surplus and changes negligibly if the public school sector behaves competitively. In principle, the introduction of a voucher program could either decrease or increase total government spending on schooling. Each student who transfers from the public to the private schools saves the government money as long as the voucher level is less than the subsidy that the government provides the public schools per enrolled student. At the same time, however, a voucher program commits the government to pay for part of the schooling of existing private school students, who presently receive no government support. In the simulations reported here, the latter effect always turns out to be as large or larger than the former one.

EFFECTS OF SCHOOL FINANCE POLICY ON LOW-INCOME STUDENTS

- As the voucher level increases, the average amount that schools expend for instructional purposes increases if the public school sector maximizes surplus. This amount remains constant, but at a higher level, if the public school sector behaves competitively.

  Suppose that the public school sector maximizes surplus. Then increasing the private school voucher from zero to $4,000 implies that the average amount schools expend for purposes valued by low-income students increases by between $1,000 to $2,000. This occurs in part because the public school sector increases its instructional expenditures and in part because some low-income students shift their enrollment to the private sector, which expends more on instruction.

  Now suppose that the public school sector behaves competitively. Then increasing the private school voucher has negligible effect on the average amount schools expend for instructional purposes. Under the competitive-behavior assumption, public schools always spend all their revenue on purposes valued by students, and very few low-income students transfer from public to private schools.

- The average amount that schools expend on instructional purposes varies with community type more than it does with voucher level. If the public school sector maximizes surplus, expenditure per low-income student within a community increases by between $1,000 and $2,000 as the voucher rises from zero to $4,000 but, holding the voucher level fixed, increases by between $2,000 and $3,000 as one moves from the poor to the wealthy community. If the public school sector behaves competitively, the expenditure per low-income student within a community does not change as the voucher rises but, holding the voucher level fixed, increases by almost $6,000 as one moves from the poor to the wealthy community.

· The effect of voucher level on income segregation in the schools varies across communities and with the assumption made about public school behavior. Suppose that the public school sector maximizes surplus. Then we find the following as the voucher level increases from zero to $4,000. In the poor community, the predominance of low-income students in the public schools falls from .44 of enrollment to .32, and the representation of low-income students in the private schools increases from zero to .30. In the average community, the low-income proportion of public school enrollment increases from .27 to .37, while the representation of low-income students in the private schools remains minuscule, changing from zero to .01 of enrollment. In the wealthy community, the income distributions of the public and private schools do not change at all; the distribution of income in the public schools is always a bit skewed toward the low end, relative to the community's income distribution, and the private school sector is always an enclave of the two highest income groups.

Now suppose that the public school sector behaves competitively. Then we find the following: In the poor community, the low-income proportion of public school enrollment increases from .33 to .44 and the low-income proportion of private school enrollment increases from zero to .10. (Both fractions increase because, as the voucher level rises, more students in the three middle-income groups transfer from public to private school than do students in the low-income group.) In the average community, the low-income proportion of public school enrollment increases from .21 to .24 and the representation of low-income students in the private schools remains zero. In the wealthy community, the income distributions of the public and private schools essentially do not change at all.

·   ·   ·

The reader may draw several lessons from this critique of the *choice* debate and analysis of alternative school-finance policies.

The immediate lesson is that qualitative reasoning cannot determine the merits of alternative school-finance policies. Qualitatively plausible arguments can be made both for public school finance and for voucher systems. So magnitudes matter. To make progress in pinning down magnitudes one can experiment with various policies in various environments and observe the results. Or one can use plausible models of the behavior of students and schools to simulate the operation of the market for schooling.

Whether one experiments or simulates, outcomes are likely to vary with the specifics of the policy under consideration and of the community in which it is implemented. The findings just presented demonstrate this well. The simulation outcomes vary with the size of the voucher, with the income distribution of the community, and with the assumption made about public school behavior. If other aspects of the scenario had been varied, further variation in outcomes would have been observed.

Some readers may feel uncomfortable that outcomes are sensitive to the specifics of the scenario. Life would be simpler if Chubb and Moe were correct in stating that *choice* is a panacea. But no such sweeping conclusion can be drawn. The analysis of this chapter suffices to show that the educational effects of systemic *choice* on low-income students are neither uniformly positive nor uniformly negative.

Can a reader learn more from the simulations than that some advocates of *choice* are naive? One can learn more if one feels that the assumptions underlying the simulations reasonably approximate the conditions of actual American communities. In this case, one can conclude that a system of uniform vouchers would not, even in the most favorable case, come close to equalizing educational opportunity across income groups. In every scenario considered, we have found that the high-income students in a given community receive higher-quality schooling, on average, than do the low-income students. Moreover, students living in wealthy communities receive higher-quality schooling than do students living in poor communities.

Poverty and Immigration
in Policy Perspective

MARTA TIENDA AND ZAI LIANG

The 1980s were the best of times and the worst of times for U.S. immigrants. These years were the best of times because the volume of immigration to the United States during the 1980s—7.4 million—approached the peak recorded at the turn of the century; because amnesty was extended to some 3 million undocumented immigrants;[1] and because refugee admissions reached an all-time high. Also to the benefit of prospective political migrants were the adoption of United Nations guidelines for identifying refugees, the creation of the Office of Refugee Resettlement, and the authorization of federal monies for resettlement assistance.

Yet the 1980s were also the worst of times, because employment opportunities for unskilled workers contracted appreciably after the 1982 recession (Blackburn, Bloom, and Freeman, 1990; Freeman and Holzer, 1991), because trends in inequality worsened during the 1980s (Tienda and Jensen, 1988; Blank, 1991), and because unemployment was high for most of the decade. The 1980s were bad times for prospective immigrants because the number of aliens apprehended reached an unprecedented high—11.9 million—exceeding the number of expulsions during the prior decade by over 3 million (Immigration and Naturalization Service [INS], 1991, table 57). Despite this sweet and sour message, the demand for U.S. visas has not abated.[2]

If the early 1980s were a time to debate the social and economic significance of immigration, the latter 1980s were a time of action. The Immigration Reform and Control Act of 1986 (IRCA) sought to "regain control of the borders" by increasing enforcement at ports of entry and imposing sanctions on employers who knowingly hired undocumented workers. Four years later, the 1990 Immigration Act, which regulated the admission of legal immigrants, was signed into law. Although the current admission criteria are relatively more responsive to social and humanitarian considerations, economic issues—jobs, income, and potential economic dependence—dominate policy discussions. At the same time, questions of cultural pluralism and the ability of society to manage, if not absorb, ethnic and racial diversity have become increasingly important as well.

Immigration research has burgeoned since the late 1960s, yet no consensus has emerged on the economic costs and benefits of immigration. Studies of the influence of immigration on poverty and welfare dependence are unusually rare and uneven. Here we survey and evaluate basic facts about the income, employment, and poverty status of immigrants that undergird the debate about the social and economic consequences of immigration. We identify points of tension between competing social and economic goals, and discuss the interface of immigration, employment, and antipoverty policy to address whether poverty and related issues should be considered in future revisions of admission guidelines. We also question whether the practice of admitting to a social democracy citizens of other countries is underwritten by any "social contract," and if not, whether this is feasible.

Immigration Policy and the "Social Contract"

> The bosom of America is open to receive not only the opulent and respectable stranger but the oppressed and persecuted of all nations and religions; whom we shall welcome to a participation of all our rights and privileges, if by decency and propriety of conduct they appear to merit the enjoyment. George Washington (INS, 1991, p. 13)

George Washington's view of immigration was humanitarian in principle and democratic in ideology, but it has not been fulfilled for countless immigrants. For many newcomers over the years, admission to the United States has meant conditional acceptance and limited social participation. The problem lies not in these general philosophical principles; the problem has been and continues to be the specification of a coherent set of admission guidelines that simultaneously protect the rights of U.S. citizens while allowing immigrants equal footing upon arrival. Whether it is possible to craft an immigration policy that simultaneously addresses political, socioeconomic, and humanitarian goals in a manner consistent with democratic ideology is highly debatable (see Abrams and Abrams, 1975; Teitelbaum, 1980). It is reasonable, however, to expect consistency in the stated goals of immigration policy and the legislative instruments used to achieve them.

Immigration and Poverty Policy in a Nutshell

Even before official records of U.S. immigrants were kept, the practice of admitting foreigners generated public protest. During the colonial and early post-Independence period, concerns about pauperism and poverty among immigrants

Table 13.1 Overview of major U.S. immigration legislation

Year	Legislation	Provisions
1875	Immigration Act	Bars criminals and prostitutes.
1882	Immigration Act	Prohibits immigration of convicts, "lunatics," "idiots," and persons "likely to become public charges."
1882	Chinese Exclusion Act	Bars entry of Chinese laborers.
1885	Contract Labor Law	Bars importation of contract labor.
1888	First Deportation Law	Deports contract laborers.
1891	Immigration Act	Increases the list of those inadmissible; deportation of illegal aliens.
1907	Immigration Act	Further increases the list of those inadmissable, including unaccompanied children under 16.
1907	Gentlemen's Agreement	Restricts Japanese immigration.
1917	Immigration Act	Bars immigration from most Asian countries.
1921	First Quota Law	Limits immigration of each nationality to 3 percent of the number of foreign-born persons of that nationality living in the U.S. in 1910.
1924	National Origins Act	Limits immigration of each nationality to 2 percent of the number of persons of that nationality as determined in 1890 census and sets a minimum of 100 for each country.
1929	National Quota Law	Annual quotas of 1924 for each country apportioned according to each nationality's percentage in 1920 census.
1940	Immigration Act	Transfers INS from the Department of Labor to the Department of Justice as a measure of national security.
1943	Bracero Program[a]	Provides for the importation of temporary agricultural laborers from North, South, and Central America. This program was later extended through 1947, then served as the legal basis for the Mexican Bracero program, which lasted through 1964.
1943	Act of December 17	Repeals Chinese exclusion laws.
1946	War Brides Act	Facilitates immigration of foreign-born spouses and children of U.S. military personnel.
1948	Displaced Persons Act	Enables refugees from Poland, Germany, Latvia, the USSR, Lithuania, and Yugoslavia to enter the U.S.

Table 13.1 (continued)

Year	Legislation	Provisions
1950	Internal Security Act	Increases grounds for exclusion; all aliens are required to report their addresses annually.
1952	Immigration and Nationality Act	Reaffirms national origins system; establishes preferences system; limits immigration from Eastern Hemisphere to about 150,000 (leaves immigration from Western Hemisphere unrestricted); eliminates all racial and gender bars to naturalization.
1953	Refugee Relief Act	Authorizes nonquota visas allowing 214,000 aliens to become permanent residents.
1962	Migration and Refugee Assistance Act	Begins federal program providing cash, medical, and educational assistance to refugees.
1965	Immigration and Nationality Act Amendments	Abolishes the national origins system; establishes an annual ceiling of 170,000 for the Eastern Hemisphere with 20,000 per country limit; distributes immigration visas according to a seven-category preference system; establishes annual ceiling for Western Hemisphere with no per country limit.
1966	Cuban Refugee Act	Authorizes the attorney general to adjust the status of Cuban refugees to that of permanent resident aliens, chargeable to the 120,000 annual limit for the Western Hemisphere.
1975	Indochina Migration and Refugee Assistance Act	Establishes a program of domestic resettlement assistance for refugees who have fled Cambodia and Vietnam.
1976	Immigration and Nationality Act Amendments	Extends per country limit and preference system to Western Hemisphere.
1977	Indochinese Refugee Act	Admits 174,988 refugees from Vietnam, Laos, and Cambodia.
1978	Immigration and Nationality Act Amendments	Brings both Eastern and Western Hemispheres under single worldwide ceiling of 290,000.
1980	Refugee Act	Removes refugees as the seventh preference category (607,805 refugees from Vietnam, Laos, Cambodia, and USSR entered); reduces the worldwide limit for immigrants from 290,000 to 270,000 to reflect removal of seventh preference category from the total.

Table 13.1 (continued)

Year	Legislation	Provisions
1986	Immigration Reform and Control Act	Grants certain undocumented aliens permanent resident status; imposes employer sanctions; reenforces border patrol; includes provision that allows admission of 33,636 refugees from Cuba and Haiti.
1990	Immigration Act	Increases total immigration under an overall flexible cap of 675,000 immigrants beginning in fiscal year 1995, preceded by a level of 700,000 during fiscal years 1992–1994. The 675,000 level to consist of: 480,000 family-sponsored immigrants; 140,000 employment-based immigrants; and 55,000 "diversity immigrants."

Source: Immigration and Naturalization Service (1991), appendix, pp. A.1–21; Jasso and Rosenzweig (1990), pp. 28–29, 340. We identified several discrepancies in the dates and content of specific acts among our sources. In these instances we used the 1990 Statistical Yearbook of INS (INS, 1991) as the definitive source.

Note: Between 1819, when Congress first mandated enumeration of immigrants admitted, and 1990, 127 separate legislative acts were passed to govern immigration. This table focuses on those acts that have direct or indirect implications for understanding linkages between immigration and inequality.

a. Bilateral agreement with Mexico, British Honduras, Barbados, and Jamaica over importation of temporary foreign agricultural labor to work in the U.S. It was initiated in 1942 under auspices of Department of Labor. It was formalized in 1943 by the Department of Justice.

dominated public discourse, as did fears about cultural diversity. Pauperism was more serious a threat than poverty because it entailed dependence on the state or private charity, whereas poverty was seen as a temporary condition to be overcome (Jensen, 1989). Concerns about pauperism were not totally unfounded; several countries purged their relief rolls by sponsoring emigration to the United States, and countless immigrants entered as indentured servants (Jensen, 1989). Consequently, early legislation sought to restrict immigration of the poor and to absolve the state (and thus taxpayers) of responsibility for immigrant paupers. Three themes have undergirded legislation governing foreign admissions since 1820:[3] (1) exclusions on the basis of race, usually justified on the grounds that cultural diversity posed irremediable social problems; (2) exclusion on the basis of social considerations, including general moral character and potential pauperism; and (3) exclusion for economic reasons, usually on the grounds that immigrants adversely affected the welfare of U.S. natives.

Table 13.1 summarizes the major pieces of immigration legislation since the passage of the Immigration Act in 1875, the first major federal legislation restricting entry of immigrants on the basis of their moral desirability.[4] To the criminals and prostitutes excluded by the 1875 legislation, the 1882 Immigration Act added those deemed to be "idiots," or "lunatic" and those "likely to become public charges." Two aspects of the early restrictionist legislation speak about linkages between immigration and poverty. First, racial considerations were an explicit criterion for exclusion, especially when employment conditions were suboptimal for native workers. Second, concerns about foreigners becoming public charges were explicit in the guidelines used to admit immigrants. Modern concerns with diversity and pauperism are highly reminiscent of the early post-Colonial period.

Since before 1900, immigration policy has been linked to the well-being of domestic workers, but not consistently. Chinese were the first targets of nativist protectionism, but the move to restrict Asian immigration more generally is evident in various acts passed during the early 1900s. The Immigration Act of 1917, for example, responded to the racism against Asians exacerbated by World War I. The First Quota Law, passed in 1921, marked an important turning point because it cemented and broadened the racist foundations of admission criteria. These quotas remained official doctrine until the mid-1960s. More important, the 1921 law set the stage for the 1924 National Origins Act, which limited the immigration of each nationality to 2 percent of the population of each nationality in the United States based on the census of 1890.[5] Because the foreign-born population derived primarily from northern and western Europe at the time of the First Quota Law, this region was favored as a source of future immigration (Thernstrom, 1980; Jensen, 1989; INS, 1991). A primary reason for restricting immigration from southern and eastern Europe relative to western Europe was the fear that recent newcomers (whose looks as well as languages were different from those of Anglo-Saxon origin) were less able to assimilate into the mainstream (Jensen, 1989).

The transfer of the Immigration and Naturalization Service (INS) from the Department of Labor to the Department of Justice in 1940 signaled a change in social philosophy toward immigration and the political goals it was to serve. After the Great Depression and amid the social isolationist ideology that dominated international relations, foreign workers were no longer deemed a necessary source of cheap labor. Thousands of immigrants (and countless native-born workers) were forcibly repatriated to protect the economic interests of domestic workers. And although restrictionist policies had clearly been evident prior to this time (Jasso and Rosenzweig, 1990, table 1.1), the administrative transfer of INS to the Justice Department reinforced a shift in priority from economic to political goals.

Until 1980, the most well known and well analyzed changes in immigration policy in the post–World War II period were the public laws that established the Bracero Program as an emergency labor source during World War II and extended it through and beyond the Korean conflict;[6] the Immigration and Nationality Act of 1952, also called the McCarren-Walter Act; and the 1965 and 1976 amendments to this act. These acts and amendments are the cornerstones on which the contemporary debate about immigration has been based. The Displaced Persons Act of 1948 has implications for debates about poverty and immigration in the 1990s because it is the precursor of the current posture toward refugees. Presented as a humanitarian gesture, refugee admissions were by definition political categories that could be redefined as international requirements demanded. In contrast to what is now official policy, however, the 1948 act did not accept an official federal role in ensuring the well-being of persons displaced by the war. In other words, the "social contract" provided by the 1948 act was minimal in comparison with what followed.

Although the Immigration and Nationality Act of 1952 basically reaffirmed the 1924 national origins system for admitting immigrants, its significance today stems from four provisions. First, it established a preference system as the basis for prioritizing admissions; second, it restricted immigration from the Eastern Hemisphere while permitting unrestricted migration from the Western Hemisphere; third, it removed naturalization restrictions on the basis of gender, race, and national origin; and fourth, it elevated to felony status unauthorized entry to the United States but exempted employers of undocumented migrants from criminal status. Concerns over "loss of control" of the borders—the dominant theme of the debate during the 1980s—was also evident in the institution of the alien address reporting system, which could be used by security and enforcement agencies.[7]

Few would quibble with the idea that nations have a sovereign right to control their borders through various means and to specify the criteria used to admit immigrants, but the contradictory purposes of the 1952 legislation were the subject of much criticism. Nowhere was the use of immigration policy for national self-interest to the detriment of immigrants more egregious than in this legislation, which on the one hand encouraged the use of undocumented foreign workers and on the other hand punished workers (but not employers) who were caught. Amid the social consciousness of the 1960s, the racist underpinnings of the national origins system for admitting immigrants became increasingly untenable. They were removed through the 1965 amendments to the Immigration and Nationality Act. The restrictionist drive evident in the 1952 act was advanced further, however, by including the Western Hemisphere in the annual ceiling. Yet the preferential treatment of the Western Hemisphere persisted, because the 20,000 visa limit per country was imposed only on the Eastern Hemisphere—at least until the 1976 amendments were passed.[8]

Of great significance for the debate over undocumented immigration, the glaring contradiction in U.S. admission guidelines, which made it a felony to be an illegal immigrant but not to hire one, was *not* eliminated by the 1965 or the 1976 amendments to the McCarren-Walter Act. This anomaly provided political grist for supporters of the amnesty provisions of the 1986 Immigration Reform and Control Act. The 1965 amendments, which gave priority to family reunification as the basis of admission, formally stipulated that labor visas would not be issued to immigrants whose presence would replace or adversely affect the wages and working conditions of similarly employed domestic workers. But this qualification basically applied to the third and sixth preference categories, the only ones that required labor certification. Relative to the total numbers admitted, these categories are tiny. No comparable restrictions were placed on visas authorized under the family reunification provisions and the various exclusions for primary family members. The implicit welfare implication of this neglect is that families, rather than the state, were responsible for their foreign-born relatives.

Additional legislation created a legal distinction between refugees and labor migrants.[9] The Refugee Relief Act of 1953 admitted over 200,000 persons fleeing Communist regimes in Eastern Europe, but did not include any formal mechanisms to support resettlement activities (Goza, 1987). Between 1958 and 1963 an additional 200,000 plus Cubans were granted asylum, but they were not formally designated as refugees until 1966.[10] The Cuban exodus marked an important turning point in the federal government's treatment of refugees, however, in that their admission was accompanied by resettlement assistance. In other words, the legal distinction between economic migrants and refugees also implied two distinct social contracts, one with and one without guarantees to state-administered social supports. The initial commitment to provide social and economic assistance to refugees was informal until authorized by Congress, but it evolved into a well-defined, congressionally sanctioned program.

The Migration and Refugee Assistance Act of 1962 formalized the link between immigration policy and antipoverty policy—at least for refugees—as it marked the first long-term federal program providing cash, medical, and educational assistance to refugees.[11] Prior to this point, the federal government merely devised guidelines for refugee admission and indicated which countries qualified for refugee status. Assistance rendered to refugees was organized primarily by private organizations (Goza, 1987). Significantly, the INS does not identify the Migration and Refugee Assistance Act as part of immigration legislative history, because the Justice Department does not administer the resettlement assistance program. Social welfare policy and immigration policy thus have remained formally disarticulated, despite the new federal responsibility for the social welfare of political immigrants. Until the mid-1970s, the 1962 act was the reigning domestic refugee assistance program, primarily earmarked for Cubans. By the time the 1966 Cuban Refugee Act was passed by Congress, over 290,000 émigrés were residing in the United States (Portes and Bach, 1985, table 12).

The 1970s witnessed a spate of congressional acts admitting refugees, but with the benefit of resettlement assistance tied directly to the admission decision. The influx of 130,000 refugees from Southeast Asia (mainly Vietnam) after the fall of U.S.-backed governments in the region led to the Indochina Migration and Refugee Assistance Act of 1975. This act established a program of domestic resettlement assistance for refugees from Cambodia and Vietnam. The exodus of refugees from Indochina and from Communist countries in Eastern Europe led to the Refugee Act of 1980.[12]

Several provisions of the 1980 act are pertinent to our concerns with immigration and poverty. First, the act provided the first systematic criteria for admitting and resettling refugees of special humanitarian concern to the U.S. government. Second, the term "refugee" was defined in conformance with United Nations guidelines, and refugees were distinguished from asylees. Refugees were eliminated as a category within the preference system, and Congress was entrusted with decisions about annual refugee admissions. Third, the act established a comprehensive domestic program for the resettlement of refugees. Leaving the annual figure of authorized refugee admissions to be determined by the President in consultation with Congress allows great discretion in the number and the countries of origin of refugees. Nonetheless, the 1975 and 1980 Refugee acts represent a major change in the social contract between the federal government and political immigrants.

Interest in immigration flows remained high throughout the 1970s and 1980s because of the belief that the United States was losing control of its borders.[13] As issues surrounding refugees became more routinized, attention shifted to undocumented migrants.[14] Yet concerns over the economic and social consequences of immigration persisted. The retrenchment in social programs that occurred during the early 1980s also touched immigrants. Economic migrants, unlike refugees, were never the direct beneficiaries of resettlement assistance, but a 1981 act severely restricted the eligibility of immigrants to various publicly funded social welfare programs—AFDC and subsidized housing assistance in particular.

The Immigration Reform and Control Act of 1986 was enacted largely to remedy the problem of undocumented immigration. Two of its three major provisions sought to curtail the flow by focusing on both demand factors (the employer sanctions provision) and supply factors (the enhanced border control allocations).[15] In an effort to compensate for past failures of admission policies, the 1986 act authorized the largest amnesty program in U.S. history. Two groups of undocumented immigrants were eligible for amnesty: international migrants who had lived continuously in the United States since before January 1, 1982, and foreigners who had worked in agricultural industries for at least ninety days during 1986 (Bean, Vernez, and Keely, 1989; Espenshade et al., 1990).

IRCA refocused the policy debates from the need for immigration reform to an assessment of the key provisions of the legislation (Borjas and Tienda, 1993). But most studies have focused on the effectiveness of the border enforcement and employer sanctions provisions, to the virtual neglect of the adjustment experiences of legalized migrants.[16] Of interest for our exploration of linkages between immigration and poverty, IRCA included a restriction on access to means-tested income benefits for a period of five years after temporary resident status had been granted. Further, the admission of having received welfare benefits of any kind as an undocumented immigrant was grounds for exclusion from the amnesty program.

The Immigration Act of 1990, which was motivated by concern over the disarticulation of immigration and labor policy after 1965, strengthened labor certification and nonimmigrant visas as admission criteria. A second provision of the 1990 act was an allowance of 55,000 "diversity" visas to be allocated to countries underrepresented in recent flows—predominantly Western European nations. This provision represents a continuing interest in "whitening" the immigrant stream, but the instrument to achieve it has changed. During the nineteenth and early twentieth centuries, restrictionist measures were sufficient to keep out people of color, along with other "undesirables." In 1990, however, "diversity" visas were needed to ensure greater representation of whites among a largely "colored" stream. It is also noteworthy that the 1990 Act did not redefine the terms of the social contract for economic migrants; restrictions on their access to public assistance and housing assistance were retained. The different social contracts for political and for economic migrants thus remain distinct and intact.

Reflections on U.S. Immigration Legislation

George Washington's vision of immigration still hovers in the background, but it bears little resemblance to the country's succession of acts and decrees governing the admission of foreigners. U.S. immigration policy has been fraught with contradictions that defy easy explanation, much less prediction. The antipoverty component of immigration policy can be characterized as at best a story of benign neglect and at worst a story of systematic racial exclusion. But in part, the contradictions in U.S. admission policies stem from their historical separation from social welfare policy coupled with their weakened linkages with employment policy after 1965. Nowhere is this more evident than in the differential treatment of political and economic migrants and, in particular, in the extension of social welfare benefits and resettlement assistance to the former and not to the latter. By design or default, the immigrant category "refugee" has become a loophole for special interests that derive not from labor shortages, but from political interests.

In marked contrast to eligibility for domestic assistance programs, some refugee assistance benefits are extended to all political migrants, irrespective of class background (Pedraza-Bailey, 1985; Goza, 1987). If it can be shown that providing resettlement assistance to refugees reduces the likelihood of dependence over the long run, large social expenditures to facilitate the economic integration of the foreign born might find political support. The looming question is whether there is compelling evidence that resettlement assistance promotes self-sufficiency. But another equally challenging question is whether, in times of economic retrenchment and economic dislocation of low-income groups, politicians can avoid scapegoating immigrants for the failures of economic policy.

What Do We Know? Synthesis of Findings and Lessons from Experience

> Foreign immigration which in the past has added so much to the wealth, resources, and increase of power to this nation—the asylum of the oppressed of all nations—should be fostered and encouraged by a liberal and just policy.
>
> Republican Party Platform, 1864 (INS, 1991, p. 18)

> We heartily approve all legitimate efforts to prevent the United States from being used as the dumping ground for the known criminals and professional paupers of Europe, and we demand the rigid enforcement of the laws against Chinese immigration or the importation of foreign labor, to degrade American labor and lessen its wages; but we condemn and denounce any and all attempts to restrict the immigration of the industrious and worthy of foreign lands.
>
> Republican Party Platform, 1892 (Simon, 1985, p. 18)

The concerns represented in these statements, made over a century ago, are reminiscent of questions raised in the current debate. Are current immigrants more likely to be poor than earlier arrivals and, consequently, more likely to drain the public coffers? Do immigrants make natives and earlier arrivals poor by depriving them of employment opportunities and driving down their wages? Do wage and employment effects offset or reinforce one another, and who wins in this competition? More generally, is the net economic impact of immigrants positive or negative?

Leif Jensen (1989, p. 33) has pointed out that although many immigrants who arrived between 1860 and 1930 (the so-called Second Wave) were poor initially, there is no conclusive evidence about whether they were more destitute than earlier arrivals (the so-called First Wave), whether the labor market conditions prevailing during both periods were equally conducive to the integration of immigrants, and whether hardships experienced by the later wave were more enduring than those experienced by earlier arrivals. Similar questions comparing early and later arrivals can be levied about current immigrants.

Trends in Immigration: Cohort Sizes and Social Characteristics

Questions about the size and diversity of the flows have driven countless overviews of U.S. immigration history (Massey, 1981; Bouvier and Gardner, 1986; INS, 1991). Few studies, however, have focused on trends in poverty and economic well-being of the immigrants (Jensen, 1989; Simon, 1989; Borjas, 1990). Figure 13.1, which plots the size of immigrant cohorts by decade since 1900, confirms the well-known acceleration in the rate of immigration after 1960. Although the number of immigrants admitted during the 1980s approached the historical high recorded at the turn of the century, when nearly 9 million immigrants were admitted, the 1980s figure may actually exceed the historical maximum if

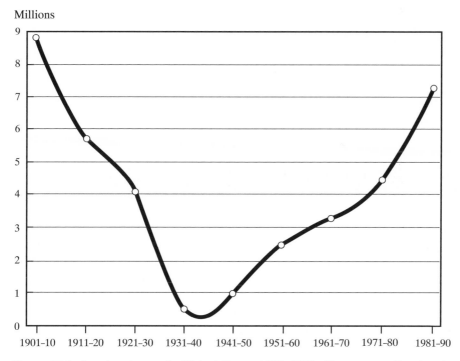

Figure 13.1   Immigration to the United States, 1901–1990. (Data source: Immigration and Naturalization Service, 1991.)

undocumented migrants are included. As a result of increased immigration, the foreign-born share of the U.S. population increased from just under 5 percent in 1970 to approximately 7 percent in 1990 (Borjas and Tienda, 1987, table 1; Bach, 1991, p. 1). This current proportion of foreign-born represents half the share registered at the turn of the century, which surpassed 14 percent (Borjas and Tienda, 1987, table 1).

The rise in immigration after 1960 is due to changes in admission policies following the 1965 reforms, which shifted the entry criteria away from economic and toward humanitarian and social considerations. Unplanned refugee flows from Cuba and Indochina, however, have also contributed to the growth and diversity of the foreign-born since 1960. Compared with immigrants who arrived before 1960, recent immigrants are more diverse with respect to national origins and skill levels. Table 13.2 highlights this diversity along regional lines. During the 1940s and 1950s well over half of all U.S. immigrants came from European countries, while the Americas and Asia accounted for less than 40 and 5 percent, respectively. By contrast, during the 1970s, immigrants from Asia and the Americas accounted for 80 percent of all immigrants, and this share rose to 87 percent during the 1980s.

The shift in regional origins was accompanied by substantial diversification in the socioeconomic origins of the immigrants (Massey, 1981; Borjas, 1990; Jasso and Rosenzweig, 1990). Although some immigrants—notably those from Asian nations—were relatively well equipped to enter the U.S. labor market, others—predominantly those from the Americas—came with limited labor market skills and low levels of education (Bouvier and Gardner, 1986; Bach and Tienda, 1984). The virtual exclusion of immigrants from Asia until after the 1965 amendments limited their access through family reunification, and made occupational preferences the main gateway to the United States (Keely, 1974). This meant that lower-skill migrants from Asia did not fit the priority categories for rationing visas.

Another post-1960 trend is the growth of undocumented immigration, with Mexicans making up the lion's share of the unauthorized flow (Passel and Woodrow, 1984; Warren and Passel, 1987; Tienda et al., 1991).[17] The exact number of undocumented immigrants and their flow patterns may never be known, but several reasonable estimates of the 1980 population currently exist. The most widely cited estimate is 2–3 million (Warren and Passel, 1987). This rough figure is reasonably consistent with the number of Mexicans who petitioned to adjust their lawful status under the provisions of the 1986 amnesty program—1.2 million, or 70 percent of the total who applied under the general amnesty program.[18]

The final major trend is the dramatic growth of refugee populations after 1960. As indicated in Table 13.2, approximately 214,000 refugees were admitted dur-

Table 13.2   Immigrants admitted to the United States by region of origin, 1941–1990

Region	Total immigrants (in thousands)	Regional share (%)	Total refugees (in thousands)	Regional share (%)
Europe				
1941–50	621	60.3	212[a]	99.4
1951–60	1,326	52.7	456	92.6
1961–70	1,123	33.8	55	26.0
1971–80	800	17.8	72	13.3
1981–90	762	10.4	156	15.3
Asia				
1941–50	37	3.6	1[a]	0.5
1951–60	153	6.1	33	6.8
1961–70	428	12.9	20	9.3
1971–80	1,588	35.4	211	39.1
1981–90	2,738	37.3	712	70.3
Americas				
1941–50	355	34.4	0[a]	0.1
1951–60	997	39.6	1	0.2
1961–70	1,716	51.7	132	62.1
1971–80	1,983	44.1	254	47.1
1981–90	3,615	49.3	124	12.2
Other[b]				
1941–50	22	2.1	0[a]	0.0
1951–60	40	0.9	2	0.4
1961–70	54	1.6	6	2.6
1971–80	122	2.7	3	0.6
1981–90	223	3.0	22	2.2

Source: Immigration and Naturalization Service (1991).
a. For refugees, the first period is 1946–1950 rather than 1941–1950.
b. Includes Africa, Oceania, and other unspecified areas.

ing the 1960s, with over 60 percent from the Americas (that is, Cuba) and an additional 26 percent from Europe. The 1970s witnessed a 2.5-fold increase in that number, to 540,000. Of these, approximately half were from the Americas and most of the remainder were from Indochina (39 percent) and Europe (13 percent). During the 1980s refugee admissions reached an all-time high, exceeding one million. Roughly 75 percent of refugees admitted during the 1980s were from Asia, compared with under 12 percent from the Americas.

Although the distinction between political migrants (refugees) and economic (labor) migrants has been overdrawn (see Portes and Bach, 1985; Goza, 1987), two aspects of refugee flows sharpen comparisons of economic well-being with voluntary immigrants. First, except for worldwide quotas negotiated on strictly humanitarian grounds, refugee flows are less predictable than regulated flows, and receiving nations may have limited control over their size and diversity. Second, and precisely because refugee flows are tied to political events, the reception for refugees has been vastly different from that for labor migrants, particularly after 1960. That is, even if refugee flows were similar in socioeconomic composition to voluntary migrant flows, by virtue of the two groups' differential treatment upon arrival, their pathways to economic integration could differ appreciably. Unfortunately, there is very little direct evidence bearing on this basic question.[19]

There is much speculation—but little consensus—about how changes in the demographic characteristics and social origins of immigrants and refugees have influenced recent trends in poverty and inequality. Given that various classes of immigrants enter the race for integration at grossly unequal starting lines, it is small wonder that rates of economic assimilation differ by regional origin, type of admission, and a host of other characteristics.

Immigrants' Employment, Poverty, and Welfare Participation

Are the foreign-born a net financial gain or loss to the United States?[20] A growing body of empirical research has addressed this question for three categories of immigrants: legal, undocumented, and refugees.

LEGAL IMMIGRANTS

Most of the recent controversy about immigration has centered on its impact on the labor market, but a second major focus of the literature on the economic impact of immigrants concerns the rates of economic assimilation of distinct groups of immigrants.[21] In the former domain, two issues dominate: one is the substitution (or displacement) effect of native workers by immigrants; a second is the effect of immigrants on the wages of native workers, particularly minorities and less-skilled workers (Greenwood and McDowell, 1986). A third possibility is that immigrant enterprises, as revealed by the high rates of self-employment among the foreign-born, stimulate economic growth.[22] In the latter domain, the dominant concern is whether recent newcomers can be assimilated economically.

Will immigrants catch up to natives? In an important study, Barry Chiswick (1978) showed that the annual earnings of recent immigrants in 1970 were 15 percent below those of native-born men. However, he estimated that the nativity wage gap would be closed after approximately fourteen years. Furthermore, he argued that after thirty years, immigrant men "overtake" by about 10 percent the earnings of statistically identical native-born men.[23] The implications of this result for poverty are clear: the foreign-born, even if poor initially after arrival, will not remain so forever. This understanding squares with general assessments of the immigrant experience throughout the nineteenth and early twentieth centuries (Lieberson, 1980).

George Borjas (1985, 1987) challenged Chiswick's conclusions by pointing out that in a single cross-section, the aging (assimilation) and cohort effects cannot be separated. Using two cross-sections from census data and employing a synthetic cohort approach, Borjas concluded that assimilation effects were nowhere as positive as Chiswick had suggested, and that recent cohorts performed more poorly in the labor market than did earlier cohorts. In contrast to Chiswick's claims, this result implies that poor immigrants probably will remain poor (Borjas, 1990).

That Borjas neglected to consider changes in the structure of employment that altered labor demand has been one source of criticism, particularly as evidence about the increase in wage inequality during the 1980s has unfolded (R. Freeman and Holzer, 1991). Period economic conditions have important implications for the labor market performance of immigrants. Borjas's findings concerning "declining immigrant quality" may reflect changes in the structure of employment opportunity, for there is general consensus that wage inequality has risen in recent years (Levy, 1987; Juhn, Murphy, and Pierce, 1989; R. Freeman and Holzer, 1991). Furthermore, Borjas was unable to monitor the selective effects of emigration in producing slower rates of earnings growth for more recent cohorts.[24] During the Depression and the following decade, perceived employment problems were solved by severely restricting immigration, frequently by targeting specific groups (see Table 13.1). Although the 1970s and 1980s have witnessed high rates of unemployment accompanied by massive changes in the structure of employment opportunities, immigration has continued to increase (Bach and Brill, 1991). This represents a significant departure from the past.

Robert LaLonde and Robert Topel (1990) reconsidered the issue of declining immigrant quality using a synthetic cohort approach to model assimilation.[25] Unlike Borjas, they considered how changes in wage inequality influenced rates of economic progress among immigrants. Like Chiswick, they show strong evidence of assimilation for most immigrant groups. LaLonde and Topel maintain that Borjas is correct in pointing to a decline in the average skill *composition* of recent immigrant cohorts, but that there is no evidence that returns to skill have declined *within* skill levels. This distinction is an important one both because the average decline in skill levels during the recent period was driven by changes in the regional origin composition of recent flows, and because this period was characterized by demand-driven changes in the structure of wages.

Although as yet unsettled, the Borjas-Chiswick debate emphasizes three link-ages between immigration and poverty: (1) initial human capital endowments; (2) returns to skill and U.S. labor market experience; and (3) changes in opportunities to work at jobs that pay family wages. In the absence of longitudinal data to trace the employment experiences of *actual* cohort wage growth, however, it is not possible to settle this debate conclusively.

Do immigrants adversely affect native workers? A second highly contested issue regarding the economic consequences of immigration revolves around the labor market impact on domestic workers. Borjas and others (Borjas, 1986; De-Freitas and Marshall, 1984; Muller and Espenshade, 1985; see also Borjas and Tienda, 1987, table 2) concluded that there is weak evidence that foreign workers displace native workers.[26] David Card (1990) presented convincing evidence that the massive influx of unskilled and semi-skilled Cuban workers had no discern-ible employment effects on Miami workers of any race or skill level. Joseph Al-tonji and Card (1991) also concluded that the presence of large numbers of immi-grants does not result in massive displacement of native workers, even low-skill workers. Given the rise in wage inequality during the 1980s, coupled with un-abated immigration of all types, it is conceivable that analyses of the 1990 census will produce different results.

George Borjas, Richard Freeman, and Lawrence Katz (1991) examined the ef-fects of immigration and trade on the wages of less-skilled native workers and obtained results at variance with previous work, including their own. They esti-mate that between 30 and 50 percent of the (9 point log) decline in the relative weekly wage of native high school dropouts during the 1980s can be attributed to the trade and immigration flows. Several explanations can be invoked to explain these discrepant findings: (1) earnings inequities worsened during the 1980s be-cause of the well-documented trends in wage inequality (Levy, 1987; R. Freeman and Holzer, 1991); (2) the comparison groups used in the early and later studies differ; (3) the results reflect an explicit consideration of changes in demand fac-tors; (4) certain assumptions and procedures used to generate the estimates can be questioned.[27]

Although questions about the employment effects on native workers of immi-gration have not been resolved, the early econometric studies may have been un-able to detect labor market impacts for several reasons: the cumulative effects of international migration had not yet fully emerged by 1980; the labor displacing effects of industrial restructuring had not yet run their full course; internal migra-tion served as an equilibrating mechanism for domestic workers (Card, 1990); or cross-city comparisons conceal intra-market dynamics between natives and im-migrants. In the words of Robert Bach and Howard Brill (1991, p. 6): "By aver-aging the economic conditions of immigrants and their impact across the national labor market, they [analysts who employ the production function methodology] systematically ignore the variability of experiences and circumstances in local and regional labor markets, among various firms or sectors of the economy, and among groups of new immigrants and native born workers."

Research focused on local labor markets or self-employment provides a quite different picture of the nature of labor market competition and complementarity between immigrants and native minorities. Alejandro Portes and Min Zhou (1991), for example, illustrate how immigrant industries not only provide strategies for the socioeconomic integration of Asians but also generate employment opportunities for inner-city blacks. Kevin McCarthy and Robert Valdez (1986) have argued that Mexican immigrants stimulated employment in California by providing a pool of low-wage labor essential for stimulating manufacturing growth.[28] Roger Waldinger's (1985) analysis of the uses of immigrant labor in New York City's garment industry is another illustration of how "ethnically organized communities can shape the *demand* for new immigrants workers, influence the recruitment of these workers, and provide jobs for them immediately upon entry to the U.S." (Bach and Brill, 1991, p. 5, emphasis added).

But there is also growing evidence that immigrants compete with domestic workers. Recent findings from the Chicago Urban Poverty and Family Life Study reveal that Mexican immigrants residing in high-poverty neighborhoods have higher employment rates than do similarly situated native blacks, whites, and Puerto Ricans (Tienda and Stier, 1991a; Van Haitsma, 1991). This evidence is particularly germane because Chicago's Mexican immigrants have lower levels of education, on average, than do blacks, whites, and Puerto Ricans who live in its impoverished neighborhoods. William Julius Wilson (1991a) attributes the differences in employment rates between Mexican immigrants and inner-city blacks to their unequal involvement in social networks and to harsh discrimination by employers (see also Kirschenman and Neckerman, 1991). It is unclear, however, what, if any, general conclusions about the labor market effects of immigration can be drawn from the study of poor Chicago neighborhoods unless these results can be replicated elsewhere.

Do immigrants become dependent on welfare? A third major issue concerns rates of poverty and welfare utilization among the foreign-born. Several recent studies have directly addressed these issues (Portes and Stepick, 1985; Jensen, 1988, 1989; Simon, 1989; Borjas, 1990). Jensen's (1988, 1989) analyses of nativity differentials in poverty between 1960 and 1980 provided substantial evidence that "poverty among immigrants increased as the new immigration unfolded" (1988, p. 133). His work uncovered several distinct trends. First, absolute poverty declined nationally between 1960 and 1980, but declines were less steep among families with immigrant as compared with native-born heads. Second, the inci-

Table 13.3   Immigration, poverty, and welfare participation, 1979

Country of birth	Poverty rate in U.S.	Welfare participation rate
Europe	8.8	6.7
Austria	7.8	7.1
Czechoslovakia	8.3	5.2
Denmark	7.3	3.8
France	10.0	6.5
Germany	8.2	4.6
Greece	10.4	6.4
Hungary	8.7	6.1
Ireland	7.8	6.5
Italy	8.2	7.1
Netherlands	7.1	4.7
Norway	8.5	6.8
Poland	8.1	6.3
Portugal	8.2	7.9
Romania	10.2	6.7
Spain	11.2	15.7
Sweden	7.9	5.8
Switzerland	8.2	4.4
United Kingdom	7.2	5.3
USSR	14.8	9.6
Yugoslavia	7.8	6.6
Asia and Africa	16.2	8.3
China	12.5	8.4
Egypt	9.8	5.0
India	6.0	2.8

dence of poverty among recent immigrants (i.e., those arriving during the previous five years) increased from 17 percent in 1960 to 28 percent in 1980, with virtually all the increase during the 1970s (Jensen, 1988, table 1). Third, he determined that all race and ethnic groups contributed to the rise in poverty among immigrants.[29] Thus the secular rise in aggregate poverty rates among recent immigrants derives from higher poverty rates among new cohorts combined with changes in the relative shares of poor immigrants.

In Table 13.3 we report 1979 poverty and welfare participation rates for forty-two countries that send immigrants to the United States. The most striking feature is the great dispersion in poverty rates within and between regions. Asian immigrants, for example, contrary to their image of greater success, have an average poverty rate similar to that of Latin American immigrants. Among European immigrants, the highest poverty rates correspond to immigrants from the former Soviet Union (nearly 15 percent), but no European nationality group exhibits a

Table 13.3   (continued)

Country of birth	Poverty rate in U.S.	Welfare participation rate
Iran	31.1	2.0
Israel	17.5	5.0
Japan	13.0	5.7
Korea	13.5	6.3
Philippines	5.8	10.3
Vietnam	37.0	29.4
Americas	*16.8*	*11.1*
Argentina	11.2	7.1
Brazil	11.3	5.5
Canada	7.7	6.2
Colombia	13.6	9.5
Cuba	12.2	17.3
Dominican Republic	33.7	25.9
Ecuador	16.9	11.9
Guatemala	18.3	9.6
Haiti	21.7	10.0
Jamaica	14.4	7.4
Mexico	26.0	12.7
Panama	16.7	11.8
Trinidad and Tobago	15.7	10.1

Source: Appendix Table A.7 from *Friends or Strangers: The Impact of Immigrants on the U.S. Economy* by George J. Borjas. Copyright © 1990, 1991 by Basic Books, Inc. Reprinted by permission of Basic Books, a division of HarperCollins Publishers, Inc.

poverty rate approaching or exceeding 33 percent, as observed among Iranian, Vietnamese, Dominican, and Mexican immigrants.[30]

Aggregate rates of immigrant poverty probably would be higher were it not for the high rates of labor force participation among the foreign-born (Bean and Tienda, 1987; Borjas, 1990). Low wages and high unemployment, however, undermine the effectiveness of work efforts in preventing poverty. Jensen (1989) shows that multiple-earner households were more prevalent among immigrant populations, and that this income-generation strategy was used more effectively by immigrant families than native families as a strategy to increase household income. One might speculate that this finding is a direct consequence of the more restricted access immigrants have to public assistance income, but it is also plausible that labor migrants are less inclined to accept transfer payments of any kind, other things equal.[31]

Several studies have undertaken comparisons among "statistically equivalent" native- and foreign-born family heads and have concluded that welfare participation rates of immigrants are lower than those of native heads (Blau, 1984;

J. Simon, 1984; Tienda and Jensen, 1986; Jensen, 1989). Aggregate rates of welfare participation are marginally higher because immigrants' characteristics increase their eligibility for benefits (that is, they are more likely to be poor). Because conclusions based on a single cross-section cannot address questions about changes in behavior, Borjas and Stephen Trejo (1991) estimated the impact of duration of U.S. residence (the so-called assimilation effect) on welfare utilization. Consistent with Borjas's claims about the declining "quality" of recent immigrants, they estimated that recent immigrant cohorts did exhibit higher welfare participation rates than previous cohorts. In addition, they found that longer exposure to U.S. social institutions increased the likelihood of welfare participation, and that the changing national origin mix of recent immigrants increased welfare participation among successive cohorts.[32]

A strong advocate of high levels of immigration, Julian Simon (1989), challenges arguments that the foreign-born represent a net drain on social entitlement programs. Simon maintains that immigrants' contributions to the tax system, associated with their high rates of labor force participation, may offset their use of transfer income. McCarthy and Valdez (1986), for example, concluded that in California immigrants' tax contributions exceeded the cost of public services consumed, with the notable exception of public education. Furthermore, high rates of emigration may result in uncollected social security taxes contributed over the course of working lives. This issue remains the subject of considerable speculation in the absence of reliable data.

UNDOCUMENTED AND LEGALIZED IMMIGRANTS

The significance of undocumented immigration for understanding trends in poverty and inequality depends on the employment status of these migrants as well as their access to and use of means-tested income benefits. Tienda and her associates (1991) analyzed an administrative file of amnesty applicants and concluded that immigrants legalized under IRCA differ from the foreign-born population enumerated in the Current Population Survey in four important respects: (1) a younger age structure; (2) a less-balanced gender composition; (3) a greater representation of Latin Americans; and (4) fewer years of U.S. residence (Tienda et al., 1991). These differences have important implications for the labor market status of recent versus earlier immigrants.

Can undocumented immigrants be assimilated economically? Recently legalized immigrants are predominantly wage laborers. Tienda and her colleagues (Tienda et al., 1991; Borjas and Tienda, 1993) have reported exceptionally high rates of labor force participation among these legalized immigrants. These rates exceed those of the total foreign-born population by 5 and 16 percent for men and women, respectively. The occupational profile of recently legalized immigrants mirrors the bifurcation pattern produced by legalized immigrants admitted after 1965, with Latin Americans disproportionately engaged in lower blue-collar service and operative jobs, and immigrants from Asia and Europe destined disproportionately for white-collar jobs (Keely, 1974; Jasso and Rosenzweig, 1990). Wage differentials among legalized immigrants are similar to those of immigrants generally, in that earlier arrivals earn higher wages than do later arrivals; women earn less than men in similar occupational categories; and incumbents of higher-status jobs earn less than individuals engaged in lower-status jobs.

Analyzing employment histories of a representative sample of legalized immigrants, Tienda and Audrey Singer (1992) challenged conventional wisdom about declining skill quality among undocumented immigrants. They showed that the average education levels of Mexicans, who make up over 70 percent of the legalized population, actually *increased* over time, from an average of less than 6 years for the pre-1975 arrival cohort to an average of 7.6 years for the post-1980 arrival cohort. Undocumented migrants from other parts of Latin America became more negatively selected over time, however, with education levels dropping approximately one grade among successive cohorts—from an average of 10.3 years for pre-1975 arrivals to 9 years for those who arrived during the 1980s. Undocumented migrants from other regions exhibit yet a third pattern of skill differentiation: a slight increase in average years of school completed during the 1970s (from 13.7 to 14.2 years) followed by a modest drop (to 13.5 years) during the 1980s.

Tienda and Singer (1992) also showed positive growth in real wages for cohorts that arrived after 1975 coupled with real wage declines for those who arrived before 1975. In other words, earlier arrivals experienced wage deterioration which paralleled that experienced by unskilled native workers. Finally, in response to the question of whether undocumented immigrants can be economically assimilated, Tienda and Singer demonstrated positive real wage returns to U.S. experience in an undocumented status for all regional origin groups. Because of the retrospective nature of their job history data, they were unable to consider whether or how changes in legal status per se influenced the labor market behavior and economic mobility of undocumented immigrants.

Although several analysts have attempted to estimate the labor market impact of undocumented immigrants, the available empirical evidence is inconclusive. Conclusions differ widely and appear to be sensitive to assumptions, data, and methodology (see Borjas, 1986; Bean, Lowell, and Taylor, 1988; Bach and Brill, 1991; Donato, Durand, and Massey, 1992). Similarly, speculation by various researchers that a change in lawful status would dramatically alter labor force behavior by discouraging work and encouraging economic dependence has not been empirically substantiated.

Do undocumented immigrants use welfare? If past behavior is an indicator of future behavior, welfare participation rates of undocumented immigrants will remain well below those of the native-born population. Table 13.4 reports rates of participation in various income transfer and in-kind programs by immigrants during the year before they applied for amnesty. Rates for undocumented immigrants refer to welfare participation during an entire twelve-month period; rates for the native population refer to a fixed month (December). This leads to greatly inflated rates for immigrants as compared with natives, but serves the purpose of generating highly conservative estimates.

The most striking feature is that for all programs, welfare participation rates of undocumented immigrants were well below those of the total U.S. population. Approximately 2 percent of undocumented immigrants from Mexico and from Latin America benefited from Medicaid assistance compared with approximately 9.5 percent of the U.S. population. That undocumented immigrant Medicare beneficiaries were virtually nonexistent can be traced to the young age structure

Table 13.4   Social service utilization by legalized immigrants in 1988 and total U.S. population in 1989 (participation rates during previous year or month)

Program	Mexican	Other Latin Americans	Others	U.S. total
Medicaid	2.08	1.80	0.31	9.45
Medicare				
Persons 65+	0.00	0.00	6.90	20.58
All persons	0.20	0.13	0.31	2.69
AFDC	1.91	1.58	0.31	4.49
SSI	0.27	0.48	0.00	1.85
UI	0.27	0.04	0.00	.74
SS	0.41	0.48	0.00	15.74
Food Stamps	4.50	2.51	0.51	7.60
(N)[a]	(2,936)	(2,275)	(981)	(248,762)

Source: Usage by legalized immigrants computed by authors from 1989 *Legalized Population Survey* by Westat, Inc. Usage rates for the U.S. population based on 1991 *Statistical Abstract of the United States* (table nos. 13, 148, 588, 593, and 615) and U.S. House of Representatives (1990), table 8.

Note: Participation rates for immigrants refer to previous year; participation rates for U.S. population refer to month of December. AFDC = Aid to Families with Dependent Children; SSI = Supplementary Security Income; UI = Unemployment Insurance; SS = Social Security.

a. Numbers in columns 1–3 are numbers of persons in samples; last column is total U.S. population, in thousands.

of this population (Tienda et al., 1991). Similar reasoning can be used to explain the low participation of undocumented immigrants in the Social Security program, relative to the U.S. population.

AFDC is the most controversial of the income transfer programs, although Food Stamp participation also has received increased criticism by opponents of generous benefits to the poor. Undocumented immigrants are eligible to receive benefits from either program if they bear a child in the United States, and hence claims of their categorical ineligibility for these programs must be qualified. ⌊However, levels of participation in AFDC and Food Stamps by undocumented immigrants are well below those of the U.S. population.⌋ Less than 2 percent of undocumented Mexicans reported receipt of AFDC benefits during an entire twelve-month period (circa 1989); this compares to 4.5 percent of all U.S. residents who received benefits during any given month in 1989. Similar differentials obtain for rates of participation in the Food Stamp program.

Although Table 13.4 provides evidence that undocumented immigrants do participate in entitlement programs, the extent of their participation is small by any standard. These data do not, however, address questions about the chronicity of welfare use by undocumented immigrants, which is another key issue that troubles policymakers.

REFUGEES

The relative economic success of Cuban and Southeast Asian refugees compared with recent labor migrants (especially from the Americas) raises the possibility that distinct modes of incorporation affect socioeconomic prospects long after the event of migration. Mode of incorporation refers both to the circumstances of departure, that is, the voluntary versus involuntary nature of the move and its sudden versus planned character, and to reception factors in the host community, that is, tacit acceptance versus active support (Portes and Rumbaut, 1990). Franklin Goza (1987) has called attention to the distinction between "anticipatory" and "acute" refugees as an important aspect of premigration experiences that influence long-term integration experiences. Briefly, anticipatory refugees depart prior to or during the early stages of a mass exodus, which implies that planning often permits them to move as intact families and to transport some of their financial resources. Because the first cohorts to depart from countries experiencing political upheaval are often from the more advantaged segments of society, the term "first-wave supremacy" has been used to recognize their above-average education and financial resources.[33] Acute refugees depart under conditions of emotional and economic strain, and their flight usually precludes taking any material possessions. As a group, acute refugees are more heterogeneous in terms of their social and economic backgrounds than anticipatory refugees.

Does refugee status influence adjustment experiences? From the standpoint of refugees' economic adjustment experiences (including their patterns of welfare utilization), the distinction between anticipatory and acute refugees implies that the former will assimilate more quickly than the latter, but it is not obvious how the adjustment experiences of refugees will differ from those of labor migrants, other things equal. On the one hand, because of their sudden and dramatic loss of status, and their presumed motivation to recover this loss, acute refugees may fare as well if not better than voluntary labor migrants. On the other hand, because of the unplanned and spontaneous character of their flight, acute refugees may be more disadvantaged in the new labor market than economic migrants, whose decisions to leave their homelands were voluntary and planned. Presumably labor migrants have greater discretion in selecting their destination than do political migrants, and the residential and employment options labor migrants confront are often facilitated by kinship ties at their destination (Massey et al., 1987).

Neither the circumstances of departure nor the reception factors confronting political and economic migrants are equal, however. As several scholars have noted with respect to both the Cuban and the Indochinese refugee flows, the distinction between anticipatory and acute refugees has as much to do with differential selectivity as with the circumstances characterizing their flight. Similarly, the distinction between voluntary (economic) and involuntary (political) migrants implies distinct contexts of reception at destination, and not merely different incentives and motivations to "make it in America" (Portes and Bach, 1985; Goza, 1987; Portes and Rumbaut, 1990).

Unfortunately very few studies systematically compare labor migrants with refugees. Goza's (1987) study, which examined differences between labor migrants and refugees in terms of postmigration social and economic characteristics, is a notable exception. He noted that "significant differences exist in the socioeconomic backgrounds and outcomes of refugees and labor migrants, and . . . these differences remain after extended periods of time" (p. 254). Specifically, refugee householders had nearly four fewer years of education, and they were more likely to receive public assistance than nonrefugee heads from the same country in Southeast Asia. Given the short period over which economic progress was assessed (five years) it is unclear whether the differentials Goza detected were transitory phenomena or unintended effects of the refugee resettlement assistance programs extended to Southeast Asian refugees.

The idea of providing refugees with resettlement assistance has been driven by the singular goal of promoting the economic self-sufficiency of political migrants (Bach and Aguiros, 1991). For Cubans, the first beneficiaries of resettlement assistance, programs established to promote economic integration were "vast in scope and imagination" (Pedraza-Bailey, 1985). Although the early programs were not legislated by law, they were impressive for their scope of coverage and the amount of private and public sector cooperation required to administer them. The Cuban Refugee Emergency Center was founded by President Eisenhower in 1960 with a discretionary grant of $1 million "to provide initial relief (food, clothing, health care), to help the refugees find jobs, and to initiate a resettlement program for employable refugees that would distribute them to other areas" (Pedraza-Bailey, 1985, p. 40). In 1961 the Kennedy administration allocated $4 million in discretionary funds to establish a Cuban Refugee Program within the Department of Health, Education and Welfare.

A hallmark of the Cuban Refugee Program was its cooperative links among several state and local governmental agencies, including the schools, the health department, and most important, the Employment Service of the U.S. Department of Labor.[34] Silvia Pedraza-Bailey (1985) reports that over 70 percent of all Cuban exiles participated in one or more of the multifaceted assistance programs. During its thirteen years of existence (from 1961 to 1974), over $950 million was spent on its various programs. Of this, over half ($496 million) was appropriated for direct welfare assistance, including health services (Pedraza-Bailey, 1985, table 2). Whether and how much the availability of resettlement assistance was directly or indirectly responsible for the impressive economic achievements of Cubans who arrived prior to 1980 is unknown. There has been no systematic evaluation of the integration experiences of Cuban émigrés who did and did not receive assistance.

Domestic resettlement assistance for refugees was fully institutionalized by the 1980 Refugee Act, which also created the Office of Refugee Resettlement (ORR). The 1980 act and its 1982 and 1986 amendments clearly stipulate that employment and economic self-sufficiency are the major objectives of resettlement (Bach and Aguiros, 1991; Bach, 1988). Like the Cuban Refugee Program that preceded it, the Domestic Resettlement Program authorized by the 1980 Refugee Act is comprehensive in the scope of services provided. Among its key provisions are: (1) cash and medical assistance to eligible refugees, aid to refugee children, social services, and program administration paybacks ($390 million in 1990); (2) formula grants to states for funding English-language and employment-related services ($60 million in 1990); (3) targeted assistance to supplement available services in areas with large concentrations of refugees ($43.9 million in 1990); and (4) a voluntary agency matching grant to agencies that provide assistance and services to refugees ($54.9 million in 1990) (Office of Refugee Resettlement [ORR], 1991).[35]

Robert Bach (1988, p. 39) estimated that during the first decade following the formalization of the Refugee Resettlement Program, the federal government spent over $4 billion on refugee programs, with public assistance accounting for about one-third of the total. Table 13.5 shows that in constant dollars, the federal appropriation for refugee resettlement programs has exceeded $5 billion, with nearly 65 percent earmarked for cash and medical assistance, support for unaccompanied minors, Supplemental Security Income, and the costs of administering these income transfer programs.

As generous as these appropriations may seem, particularly in comparison with the scale of the Cuban Refugee Program, funding for refugee assistance programs has been curtailed significantly. Figure 13.2, which charts ORR appropriations and obligations for resettlement assistance from 1980 to 1991 (in constant dollars), illustrates the declining federal commitment to refugees. These cuts affect all aspects of program administration and essentially shift the burden of support to the states. During the early 1980s, for example, states were reimbursed for up to thirty-six months of AFDC payments made to refugees; in 1990, only twelve

Table 13.5 Office of Refugee Resettlement appropriations of refugee assistance funds, 1980–1991 (constant 1982–1984 dollars, in thousands)

Year	A[a]	B[b]	C[c]	D[d]	Total
1980	394,875	112,401	28,659	7,702	628,034
1981	507,407	101,531	10,431	7,180	737,549
1982	504,183	66,882	7,892	7,229	665,286
1983	399,936	63,028	3,838	6,049	586,755
1984	343,199	64,360	3,844	8,072	520,763
1985	248,292	57,207	3,712	7,794	440,876
1986	196,873	51,486	3,474	7,275	373,040
1987	193,593	48,821	5,129	7,074	295,288
1988	197,342	46,105	6,480	4,941	293,400
1989	211,289	42,505	12,757	4,656	307,048
1990	160,860	45,960	42,081	4,420	298,434
1991	171,210	48,839	28,535	4,116	300,032

Source: Refugee Resettlement Program, *Annual Report, 1980–1991*, Office of Refugee Resettlement, U.S. Department of Health and Human Services.

a. This category includes cash assistance, medical assistance, unaccompanied minors, SSI, and state administration.

b. Social services.

c. Voluntary agency matching grant program.

d. Preventive health: screening and health services.

Millions

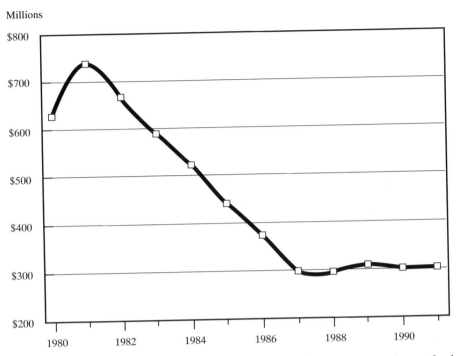

Figure 13.2 Office of Refugee Resettlement appropriations of refugee assistance funds (1982–1984 constant dollars). (For data sources, see Table 13.5.)

months of refugee's AFDC payments were reimbursed with federal monies. Although refugee cash and medical assistance is provided for individuals who do not qualify for AFDC and Medicaid, as the budget of ORR is slashed, the burden of AFDC payments to refugees has been gradually shifted to the states (personal communication, director, ORR Publicity Office). Furthermore, the policies of ORR have placed a growing emphasis on private resettlement projects with federal incentives.

Does assistance help refugees become self-sufficient, or does it promote dependency? Assessments of the refugees' progress toward economic self-sufficiency are mixed (Caplan, Whitmore, and Bui, 1985; ORR, 1991).[36] Robert Bach and Rita Aguiros (1991), for example, reported that within five years after arrival, the labor force participation rate of refugees approached that of the native-born population. That many labor force participants are among the poor precludes cash assistance. Hence hardships encountered in the labor market do not preclude poverty (Bach, 1988). Likewise, Nathan Caplan and his associates concluded that by many indicators (that is, poverty, dependency, and unemployment), Southeast

Asian refugees show steady economic progress. Bach and Aguiros (1991), however, report that California refugees experience longer waiting times to enter the labor force compared with those residing in other states.

The high rates of welfare participation among refugees (Caplan, Whitmore, and Bui, 1985; Goza, 1987; Borjas, 1990) raise important questions about the prevalence of chronic dependence on cash assistance and the reasons for chronic dependence. There are two views on this question. Caplan and his associates acknowledge that welfare participation was virtually universal among new arrivals from Southeast Asia, and they suggest that welfare participation was not a choice, but a circumstance of being a refugee. Alternatively, Bach and Aguiros (1991) claim that receipt of cash assistance is not universal among refugees, even upon first arrival. Their life table estimates of welfare exits suggest that while chronic dependence is not the norm for refugee households, there is evidence of duration dependence for a subset of the population. These authors estimated that 41 percent of all refugee households that reported receipt of public assistance were financially independent within two years. Within five years nearly 60 percent of refugee households that received assistance were off the rolls (1991, p. 331).

Welfare exit rates for the national population conceal appreciable differences in the probability of leaving the rolls among refugees living in California versus those living in other states. Five years after beginning a spell of public assistance, only 25 percent of refugees residing in California had exited the welfare rolls compared with 75 percent of refugees residing in other states.[37] On the basis of this assessment it appears that economic dependence *is* part of the California resettlement experience, but it is unclear whether persistence on the rolls reflects higher benefit levels relative to other states, better employment opportunities in areas where refugees are not residentially concentrated, or positive selection of refugees who do not live on the West Coast. Similar assessments of welfare participation should be made available for the Haitian and Cuban refugees (technically, "entrants") admitted during the 1980s. A Miami-based survey indicated that welfare participation and joblessness were significant problems confronting these "unwanted immigrants," although no estimates of chronicity of welfare use were provided (Portes and Stepick, 1985).

Despite the relatively generous funding of the Refugee Resettlement Program and the availability of a nationally representative survey to monitor the economic progress of migrants admitted as refugees, it is still unclear whether and how much receipt of resettlement assistance, including public assistance, improves the rate at which refugees adapt to the host society or, more generally, whether the economic returns on this massive investment exceed its costs. Like discussions about general welfare policy, the rationale for state intervention in refugee resettlement has been divided between the "front-end loading" and "labor market immersion" camps. The former strategy "emphasizes access to services and training, with cash assistance payments underwriting the cost of retraining during the early period of adjustment" (Bach, 1988, p. 39). The rationale for "front-end loading" is that retrained refugees will be better equipped to compete for good jobs. Fearing that the availability of cash assistance will generate dependency, employment-driven resettlement programs focus on placement, providing language and skill training only as resources permit. Whether one approach is more effective than the other in promoting the goals of self-sufficiency, and which is more cost-effective, are not well documented.

Although assessments of the economic progress of refugees are encouraging, there are signals that rates of progress have been slowed by changes in the general state of the economy (ORR, 1991) and by the reduction of funds to support the resettlement activities of new arrivals (personal communication, director, ORR Publicity Office). Several critical questions thus remain. How much of the economic progress of refugees derives from their access to state-supported resettlement assistance? To what extent does the generalized access to refugee assistance encourage long-term reliance on transfers and to what extent must one look to employment opportunities at various skill levels as an explanation for the different rates of progress of various subgroups? Finally, to what extent do the programs generate inequality among the populations they serve (Bach, 1988)? Given the massive federal investment in resettlement assistance for refugees, it seems reasonable to expect answers to these questions in future research.

Poverty and Immigration: Philosophy, Practice, and Policy

> [I]f we emphasize the economic role of immigration and admit more skilled workers, we sacrifice the goal of reuniting families; if we stress (as is now the case) the admission of relatives, we lose control of the effect of immigration on our labor markets. If we admit highly skilled immigrants, we may be hurting their home countries and our own less privileged citizens; if we fail to admit the highly skilled applicants, we deprive our country of their badly needed talents.   Elliot Abrams and Franklin Abrams (1975, p. 28)

By the mid-1970s, it was clear that the sweeping reforms undertaken within the framework of the civil rights movement had profoundly altered the forces driving international migration flows. In short, it appeared that immigration was exacerbating, if not directly generating, inequality. According to Bach, during the 1970s and 1980s, "immigration brought a new diversity to America that blurred distinctions between and created differences within racially and ethnically defined groups" (1991, p. 6). Perhaps as much as fears about the rise in immigrant poverty, concern about the diversity fostered by recent immigrant cohorts has kept immigration on the political agenda. Whether immigration occupies an equally high place on the social agenda, however, is questionable.

Our review suggests three possible mechanisms through which immigration increases inequality: (1) changes in the skill composition of recent immigrants directly contribute to the link between immigration and poverty because new arrivals are more likely to be poor; (2) the influx of large numbers of unskilled workers produce indirect effects on domestic poverty by increasing competition (that is, displacing workers or undercutting wages) with native (especially low-skill) workers; and (3) the policy of providing unequal access to state-supported resettlement assistance gives political migrants an unfair advantage over economic migrants. These mechanisms are highly reminiscent of those articulated at the turn of the century.

Because the current debate about immigration and poverty draws on old themes, it is fair to ask whether the issues and evidence used to frame the contemporary debates have changed and, more important, whether our understanding of immigration as a process of social stratification has improved. Despite the plethora of research devoted to documenting the first and second mechanisms linking immigration to poverty and social inequality, studies remain inconclusive about the net economic consequences of immigration for various reasons. Some reasons are methodological and center on the level of aggregation used to pursue questions; others derive from data limitations, notably the difficulties of drawing inferences about social processes from cross-sectional data about outcomes; still others stem from the analytic myopia that results from portraying the economic consequences of international migration in terms of individual adaptation and neglecting how immigration transforms local communities; and finally, others reflect the continually evolving character of social relations as the economic and political climate changes.

In general, the third mechanism through which immigration generates and maintains inequality, the differential federal treatment of political and economic migrants, has received less empirical scrutiny (except see Bach, 1988, 1991), yet it is the most critical for linking immigration and income maintenance programs. But it is overly simplistic to propose that the role of government intervention in shaping distinct economic trajectories for political and economic migrants can be uniquely isolated. The special interests of employers, the class backgrounds of specific nationality groups, the auspices of admission (that is, family reunification or labor certification), and the defining characteristics of receiving communities all play a part in shaping and reshaping the fortunes of recent arrivals (Portes and Rumbaut, 1990; Bach and Brill, 1991; Bach, 1991).[38] Stated differently, the social and economic reverberations of immigration result from a complex interplay of individual, contextual, and policy circumstances that defy simple generalization.

Alejandro Portes and Ruben Rumbaut (1990) have provided a useful conceptual framework for deciphering the ways government policy generates inequality within and between different classes of immigrants. Since the institutionalization of a federal role in immigrant settlement during the 1960s, government policy toward immigrants and their access to publicly funded programs can be characterized as one of either passive acceptance or active support. For refugees, the links between immigration and antipoverty policy have been made explicit and have been institutionalized through a comprehensive program of assistance and services authorized by an act of Congress (Caplan, Whitmore, and Bui, 1985). No comparable guarantees are extended to individuals admitted to the United States under the various quota and nonquota admission categories. Instead, Congress has deliberately restricted the access of recent immigrants to various entitlement programs (INS, 1991, p. A-18). Not only are legal immigrants precluded access to public assistance for three years subsequent to their admission, but the 1986 Immigration Reform and Control Act placed a five-year moratorium on access to welfare benefits to legalized immigrants. In other words, for immigrants granted amnesty in 1986, legal status implied conditional acceptance—the freedom to work above ground with very limited economic and social guarantees.

Thus the income maintenance of current immigration policy can at best be characterized as ranging from deliberate exclusion to benign neglect (or "passive acceptance") for most legal immigrants, versus the "active support" given to refugees who qualify for any of the comprehensive resettlement services authorized by the 1980 act. The implicit social contract to be drawn from current practices is that the families and relatives of labor migrants bear most of their direct welfare costs. A similar social contract was implicit in the Mexican Bracero program, except that the particulars differed. The contract labor program was a bilateral agreement between the Mexican and U.S. governments which provided assurances, at least in writing, that the welfare needs of the laborers would be included as part of the arrangement. In practice, however, the provision of housing and other forms of assistance required by workers was left to the discretion of employers, labor contractors, and local church groups (Bach, 1991).

The IRCA legislation, which on the one hand offered a change in legal status and on the other hand denied full access to the social benefits to which citizens were entitled, forces the issue of the significance of legal status as a condition for access to public entitlements. That the social and economic distinctions among immigrant groups are less meaningful than the legal distinctions between political and economic immigrants raises questions about whether the overriding goal of income maintenance policy is to eliminate dependency, to promote the economic well-being of the target populations, or to fulfill other implicit political goals (Bach and Aguiros, 1991). In any case, the justification for excluding some classes of immigrants from the benefits of resettlement assistance defy the humanitarian principles that presumably inspired current admission practices.

From a policy perspective it is reasonable to ask why the federal posture toward

economic refugees and political refugees is so markedly different. A more fundamental and rarely asked question is whether as a nation we have ever had a coherent vision about how to craft a social contract for the foreign-born. Bluntly stated,
why admit immigrants who will be placed at unequal starting lines in the race for
economic rewards? Our review of legislation governing foreign admissions reveals not only how immigration policy serves diverse political and economic interests but also how the "social contract" was qualified for those who entered
during times of fiscal retrenchment. We submit that both changes in the social
contract and in the opportunities to earn a living have contributed to a closer association between immigration and poverty during the recent past. In the aftermath of retrenchment during the 1980s, it appears that the political will to promote the principles of equity endorsed during the 1960s have all but disappeared.

- Accordingly, we recommend that the distinct social contracts among various classes of immigrants be eliminated, and that all immigrants admitted
  have access to the same benefits and privileges upon legal admission. This
  requires eliminating all moratoriums on access to benefits available to U.S.
  citizens.

· · ·

To understand how unskilled immigrants are able to survive and prosper economically even in the absence of active support from the U.S. government, it is fruitful to consider the role of organized ethnic communities in generating income
opportunities for new arrivals. Ethnic communities often provide employment
opportunities for recent arrivals, and they are also the source of the income supports that the federal government offers to refugees. That is, in various ways,
ethnic communities serve as economic and social safety nets for groups such as
Mexicans, Jamaicans, and other nonwhite immigrants who become the easy targets of discrimination when economic growth slows. Furthermore, a growing
number of studies have documented the role of entrepreneurship as a path of economic mobility for some groups of immigrants. In an economy stymied by slug-
gish growth and insufficient job creation, the allocation of funds to stimulate ethnic enterprise in the United States should be encouraged.

- Accordingly, we recommend that small business grants currently available
  to minority groups be extended upon arrival to all immigrants with demonstrated business experience in their origin countries. Further, special tax incentives should be offered for location in inner-city environments and for
  hiring disadvantaged inner city workers.

· · ·

The high rates of labor force participation among immigrants combined with high
rates of poverty suggests that working poverty may be more pervasive than non-

working poverty.[39] Congress and students of policy should be advised that attempts to strengthen the link between immigration and income maintenance policies must be rooted in discussions of working poverty. Employment is the critical step toward self-sufficiency, but it is not a sufficient condition to prevent poverty. In advocating for government investments to enhance the job skills of the foreign-born, it is appropriate to seek guidance in the experiences of the programs offered under the auspices of refugee resettlement assistance. Given projected shortages of skilled workers, and given the volume of unskilled immigrants admitted over the last decade, the long-term economic costs of not providing training to immigrants will probably exceed the short-run costs of adapting successful programs to the needs of immigrants.

Two prime sources of low incomes are inadequate skills, which imply a need for retraining programs, and low wages, which require federal intervention in reducing wage inequities. This can take several forms, such as direct subsidies to employers, raising the minimum wage, and providing income guarantees to full-time year-round workers. Against the backdrop of increased wage inequality among skill groups during the 1980s, an expanded employment and training program to provide unskilled immigrants the human capital resources needed to compete effectively in an industrialized service economy seems warranted.

- Accordingly, we recommend that JTPA be amended to target unskilled immigrants who enter under family reunification provisions for programs that include language instruction, apprenticeships, internships, and employment placement services.

· · ·

Assuming that there would be limited support for increasing the federal role in resettlement policies by extending various forms of cash assistance and in-kind programs to economic migrants, a focus on income maintenance and among the working poor seems justified as well.[40] One attractive income maintenance program that builds on the high rates of labor force participation among the foreign-born is the Earned Income Tax Credit. This program is designed for poor families with earnings, in recognition of the fact that the plight of the working poor is a great barrier to the elimination of poverty.

- Accordingly, we recommend expansion of the Earned Income Tax Credit to all immigrant families whose poverty status results from low wages.

· · ·

Finally, we wish to underscore the importance of investing resources to improve the data systems used to study the social and economic consequences of immigration. The existing immigration statistics data bases are woefully inadequate to answer questions about admission policies whose influences are not yet well understood (Jasso and Rosenzweig, 1990, p. 427). Since the Select Commission on Immigration and Refugee Policy issued its report in 1981, the call for a longitudinal survey of immigrants has been endorsed by researchers and by many policy analysts from various federal agencies. A longitudinal survey of immigrants promises to advance our understanding of assimilation and integration as social processes that transform not only the life chances of international migrants but also the communities in which they settle.

- Accordingly, we recommend that an inter-agency task force be constituted to design a longitudinal survey of immigrants and that funds be earmarked to follow a cohort of foreign-born individuals for a period of no less than 10 years.

.   .   .

We conclude by making explicit our general position on immigration policy. The President, the U.S. Congress, policymakers, and policy analysts must come to terms with the social underpinnings of international migration. "Despite all the uncertainties about the effects of immigration, experts in this field are in agreement on one point, that it will continue to grow" (Portes, 1992). Immigration's continuing growth is evident both in the failure of IRCA to stem the flow of undocumented immigrants and in the special provisions of the 1990 legislation to regulate legal migration. We know how to fight poverty and to promote refugee resettlement, but often lack the political will to translate knowledge into practices that are consistent with democratic philosophy. The remaining policy challenge is thus one of implementing immigration policies that promote fairness, nondiscrimination, and humanitarian principles while reflecting our constitutional freedoms. Political will cannot be legislated.

CHAPTER FOURTEEN

Antipoverty Policy, Affirmative Action, and Racial Attitudes

LAWRENCE BOBO AND RYAN A. SMITH

The 1980s and early 1990s have witnessed a sharp intensification of the debates over antipoverty policy and over how to fulfill the nation's commitment to racial equality. Commentators, scholars, and elected officials at all levels of government have increasingly staked out positions on matters of welfare reform and affirmative action. Indeed, discourse on these questions has taken on an urgent tone as a result of the deadly upheaval in Los Angeles in 1992 after a Simi Valley jury acquitted the Los Angeles police officers involved in the brutal beating of a black motorist of almost all the charges against them. These trends and events underscore the nation's failure to arrive at an effective consensus on how to address the interactive ills that flow from the enormous gaps in the quality of life between the economic haves and have-nots.

Is an "effective consensus" on antipoverty policy and on efforts to eliminate racial inequality possible in the United States? Can liberals and conservatives, Democrats and Republicans, and those on different racial and ethnic backgrounds, reach agreement on what measures should be taken to ameliorate poverty and racial inequity? We can only partially answer these simply put but terribly complicated questions here. Unlike the other essays in this volume, this chapter is not directly concerned with the objective dimensions of either poverty or racial inequality. Nor do we attempt to assess the successes or failures, or the tangible merits or shortcomings, of specific intervention strategies. Instead, our goal is to review what studies of public opinion and public opinion processes tell us about the levels of popular support for different social policies, whether aimed at attacking broad economic or race-specific inequalities.

This task is an important one. It can lead to developing a better understanding of the larger process of how and why some policies are adopted and others are not. It can point to those types of new reforms and initiatives that are likely to strike a responsive chord in the American electorate. Public opinion may have both direct and indirect effects on legislation. Political actors routinely attempt, albeit imperfectly, to anticipate and monitor public opinion (Monroe, 1983). Several studies point to an important connection between trends in public opinion and major policy change (Burstein, 1979; Page and Shapiro, 1983). There are occasions when public sentiment can be directly translated into policy. California's historic Proposition 13, for example, altered the resource base for a wide range of social programs. Detailed analyses have shown that a number of broad social attitudes and values, including explicitly antiblack attitudes (in addition to objective considerations such as home ownership), were potent determinants of support for Proposition 13 (Sears and Citrin, 1985).[1]

Furthermore, once enacted, public opinion can influence the likely success of social policy (Burstein, 1985). As the long, contentious struggles over school busing and affirmative action indicate, policies that are unpopular may founder when faced with mobilized public opposition.[2] In addition, advocates of various policy positions frequently invoke public opinion, American values, or other claims about the state of mind and preferences of the American public as reasons to support or oppose various policies (for example, Mead, 1992). Similarly, media commentators frequently characterize the public mood in explaining the apparent success or failure of a piece of legislation or a political candidate. In such a context, it is useful to have a reasonably objective assessment of the contours of the relevant aspects of public opinion.

None of this suggests that popular attitudes, beliefs, and values are the single or principal determinant of antipoverty or race-related social policies. Rather, it indicates that public opinion makes a genuine and consequential input to the policymaking process and the larger social discourse on these issues, as well as, in turn, being affected by them.[3] Consistent with this position is the increasingly explicit concern with aspects of public opinion now exhibited by policy analysts at both ends of the political spectrum. Liberal analysts (Wilson, 1987; Ellwood, 1988; Skocpol, 1991) as well as conservatives (Murray, 1984; Mead, 1986; Glazer, 1975) have invoked American values and beliefs in their advocacy of particular policy reform agendas.

Here we examine trends in public opinion with regard to antipoverty and race-based social policies. Has there been an antiwelfare or antiminority backlash in the policy preferences of the American mass public? We also examine the sources of individual's policy preferences. Key questions concern the role played by core American values in shaping policy preferences; how strongly connected policy values are to a person's socioeconomic status; and the possible roles of race and racism in policy preferences.

Trends in Social Policy Preferences

The Welfare State

The American public generally wants to help the poor and disadvantaged better help themselves, to provide for health care and old-age insurance (social security), and to invest more in education. All of this suggests, as Hugh Heclo (1986a, p. 327) has noted, that Americans do not have a "principled objection to national government actions on behalf of the poor." Programs aimed at income maintenance, however, encounter substantial ambivalence, if not outright opposition.

In a comprehensive review of trend data on public attitudes toward the welfare state, Robert Shapiro and J. T. Young (1989) emphasized that:

1. Support for welfare state policies has been "solid and stable from the 1970s to the early 1980s, despite some sizable increases in opposition to income maintenance and related 'welfare' activities" (pp. 60–61);

2. U.S. public opinion suggested a rank order of social programs, with Social Security, old-age pensions, medical care, and increasingly education enjoying a privileged status of high popular support, followed by somewhat lower levels of support for employment and, to a lesser degree, housing-related programs. Housing programs, in turn, were followed by income maintenance programs, which stood at the bottom of public preference;

3. Socioeconomic status and race were most consistently found to influence attitudes toward social programs—with blacks and those of lower economic status more supportive of social programs;

4. Contrary to some images conveyed by the media, younger cohorts are more supportive of the welfare state than their seniors; and

5. Compared with other Western nations, "the U.S. is consistently at the bottom in its support for different kinds of social welfare benefits" (p. 69). The American commitment to support for education was the only area where comparable cross-national data placed the United States ahead in terms of social policy support.

Although the United States tends to rank at the bottom of many cross-national comparisons of support for social programs, there are nonetheless a number of strong continuities across industrial nations in orientations toward the welfare state. Richard Coughlin (1979) performed a wide-ranging comparison of public opinion data from eight industrialized nations (the United States, Canada, Great Britain, West Germany, Denmark, Sweden, Australia, and France). He found a broad convergence of patterns in public opinion. For example, there was a nearly uniform rank order of preferred social programs. At the top stood old-age pensions and insurance, closely followed by health care. At the bottom were public assistance programs and other direct income transfer efforts, with the latter eliciting strong ambivalence and skepticism about potential abuses.

Coughlin's multination comparison also noted a general pattern of support for social guarantees. "A mass of survey evidence," he wrote, "gathered under diverse circumstances over the past thirty years or so indicates a strongly favorable attitude in all eight nations toward minimum social standards guaranteed by government. Although there is variance in the wording and structure of questions put to samples in the eight nations, the conclusion that there exists everywhere a strong collectivist component in majority attitudes is inescapable" (1979, p. 8). To be sure, the United States lagged behind other industrial countries. But even in the United States there was fairly robust support for health and work guarantees and a decent, if minimal, standard of living.

In all eight nations there was also a general commitment to freedom and mobility. That is, the collectivist impulses already discussed coexisted with varying degrees of concern for individual responsibility, achievement, initiative and hard work. Americans were distinct in the premium they placed on the values of individualism and self-reliance as well as the desire for social mobility. What is more, individualistic ideas and values seemed to be at the root of doubts about the merits of public assistance and income transfer programs. In the United States, Great Britain, and Canada there was a pattern of concern about potential welfare abuse and the risk that "deadbeats" would exploit the public dole. Such concern was not altogether absent in other countries (Denmark, for example), but typically was a less acute source of ambivalence about welfare policies.

The data presented in Figures 14.1, 14.2, and 14.3 update and exemplify the patterns identified in earlier reviews by Shapiro and Young (1989) and by Coughlin (1979).[4] Figure 14.1 indicates U.S. national trends in support for various social policy commitments based on responses to the following questions:

Help poor. Some people think that the government in Washington should do everything possible to improve the standard of living of all poor Americans; they are at point 1. Other people think it is not the government's responsibility, and that each person should take care of himself; they are at point 5. Where would you place yourself on this scale, or haven't you made up your mind on this?

Help sick. In general, some people think that it is the responsibility of the government in Washington to see to it that people have help in paying for doctors' and hospital bills (point 1). Others think that these matters are not the responsibility of the federal government and that people should take care of these things themselves

% favoring govt. commitment

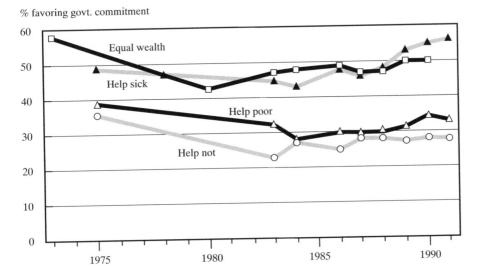

Figure 14.1 Support for social policy commitments. (Data source: General Social Survey, 1973–1991.)

(point 5). Where would you place yourself on this scale, or haven't you made up your mind on this?

Help not. Some people think that the government in Washington is trying to do too many things that should be left to individuals and private businesses (point 1). Others disagree and think that the government should do even more to solve our country's problems (point 5). Still others have opinions somewhere in between. Where would you place yourself on this scale, or haven't you made up your mind on this?

Equal wealth. Some people think that the government in Washington ought to reduce the income differences between the rich and the poor, perhaps by raising the taxes of wealthy families or by giving income assistance to the poor (point 1). Others think the government should not concern itself with reducing income differences between the rich and the poor (point 7). What score between 1 and 7 comes closest to the way you feel?

Figure 14.2 charts national trends for a series of questions that ask whether we are spending "too much," "too little," or "about the right amount" of money on various social issues. The list of issues includes: improving and protecting the nation's health, improving the nation's education system, Social Security, assistance to the poor, solving the problems of the big cities, welfare, and improving the conditions of blacks. The questions on spending on "Social Security" and

% saying too little is spent

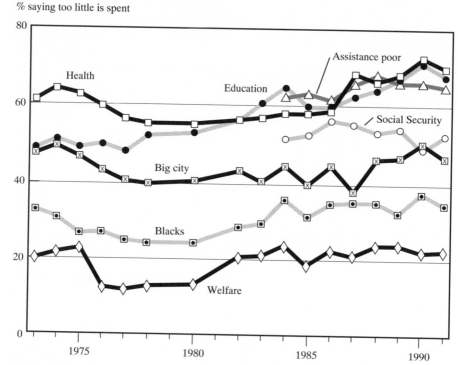

Figure 14.2 Trends in support for social spending. (Data source: General Social Survey, 1973–1991.)

"assistance to the poor" were added to the General Social Surveys only in the 1980s.

These data immediately confirm patterns identified in previous research. There is general stability and almost no sign of abrupt change. There is, moreover, no indication whatsoever of a general tilt away from commitment to social welfare policies.

In addition, as expected, the highest levels of support obtain for Social Security, health/medical care–related issues, and education. For example, support for increased spending on Social Security varies between 49 percent and 55 percent during the span of years from 1984 to 1991. Although not shown in Figure 14.2, a very low percentage of the public, usually under 10 percent, believes too much money is spent on Social Security.

Not only does health care receive the highest absolute levels of support for both types of policy attitude questions ("help sick" in Figure 14.1 and "health" in Figure 14.2), but both figures show a clear trend upward, with larger proportions of the population calling for increased government spending on health care. Support for increased spending on health care (Figure 14.2) rose from 57 percent in 1983 to just under 70 percent in 1991, an increase of 12 percentage points.[5] The depth of public concern over health care is not fully conveyed by the trend data alone. For example, a 1991 *Time*/CNN poll found that two-thirds of adults in a nationwide survey felt that health care should "be a right guaranteed by the government" as opposed to a need that individuals should pay for themselves (*The Polling Report,* January 13, 1992, p. 1). Issues of access to health care and the quality of the care provided do not seem to drive the public concern in this area. The steadily increasing cost of health care and the increasing burden placed on individuals, rather than employers, to cover these costs have fueled the growing support for a national health care program. Thus a 1991 Gallup survey found that more than one in four Americans said that in the previous twelve-month period they had been unable to pay for health care. According to Frank Newport and Jennifer Leonard: "When asked to identify the single biggest problem facing U.S. health care today, three in four named cost related issues—reinforcing the fact that it is the cost, not quality or accessibility which worries the average American" (*The Polling Report,* August 12, 1991, p. 6).

These concerns contribute to a growing consensus on the need for some form of national health insurance program. A number of different national and statewide polls have shown support for a national health insurance program to fall in the 60–70 percent range (Blendon and Donelan, 1991, p. 5). Alternatively, even higher margins support a mixed program of employer mandated coverage for those in the labor force and government-supported programs for the poor and unemployed (Blendon and Donelan, 1991). Careful investigations of the amount of additional taxes Americans would be willing to pay for more comprehensive health care coverage has yet to be conducted. Support for national insurance drops as the magnitude of tax increases to finance it rises. According to Robert Blendon and Karen Donelan, Americans back national health insurance if it entails only a modest increase in their tax burden (1991, p. 6).

There has also been a steady rise in support for additional spending to improve the nation's education system. Figure 14.2 shows that the proportion of adults nationwide who said that "too little" was spent on education averaged 51 percent during the 1973 to 1982 time span; in 1991, support for increased spending rose to 67 percent. For 1988–1991, the average level of support for increased spending on education was 68 percent.

Least popular in terms of levels of support for increased social spending is "welfare" (Figure 14.2). It is worth noting that the level of support for increased welfare spending was stable during the 1976 to 1980 period. These years, however, saw a rise in the proportion who felt that "too much" was being spent on welfare, which quickly rose from 43 percent in 1975 to 60 percent in 1977, where it stayed until roughly 1979. In the post-1980 period, there was a small but real rise in support for increased welfare spending. Many have interpreted this as a reaction against Reagan-era efforts to cut welfare programs (Shapiro and Young, 1989).

Reactions to the label "welfare" should not be taken as the definitive assessment of public support for helping the poor. The term "welfare" has become a red flag, apparently signaling waste, fraud, and abuse to many Americans. Nonetheless, Americans clearly want to help those in need (Heclo, 1986a; Lowi, 1986; Ellwood, 1988). Direct evidence on this point comes from experiments conducted in the 1984 and 1985 General Social Surveys. The "welfare" spending question was experimentally pitted against the "assistance to the poor" item. Only 19 percent of the national sample said "too little" money was being spent on welfare. Fully 65 percent, however, said "too little" was being spent on assistance to the poor (T. Smith, 1987). This consequential effect of different wording is evident in Figure 14.2, where the "assistance to the poor" question consistently exceeds "social security" in levels of support for increased social spending. It should be noted here that typically fewer than 10 percent in any given year express the opinion that "too much" is spent on assistance to the poor.

These sharply different levels of support for similar questions illuminate a point of some considerable importance.[6] These data suggest that Americans want government to help the poor, but insist that the role be limited and not replace an individual's obligation to pursue self-reliance. One sign of this notion of limited government involvement is evident in Figure 14.1 in response to the "help not" question. The low overall levels of support for this item show a clear reluctance to see government take on more or new duties relative to those it already has.

It is instructive, given the popular notion that "welfare" is a code word for blacks (Edsall and Edsall, 1991b), that support for increased spending on blacks is consistently higher than support for spending on welfare. Indeed, rates of perception that "too much" is spent on blacks tend to be half that for the welfare item, with the former averaging only 20 percent. In addition, as with the welfare question, there is a slight upward trend in the post-1980 period. Whatever the reactions to government spending on welfare and on blacks have in common, the term "welfare" adds something more that many Americans find disagreeable.

The trends themselves mask a number of underlying complexities to public opinion on social welfare issues. We have no reliable trend data that specifically call for ranking social priorities. Few, if any, surveys have carefully explored the costs or tradeoffs, such as increased taxes, that the American public might be willing to endure in order to enhance or enact a specific policy. In addition to the notion of a limited role for government, however, there are two other important constraints on support for social welfare programs.

One constraint on social policy support, whatever the nature of the specific program, is popular discontent over current tax burdens. For example, 43 percent of respondents to a 1979 national survey felt that they paid more than their fair share in taxes; 57 percent felt they paid a fair share. More important, when respondents were asked specifically about the amount of sales, property, social security, and federal income taxes they paid, they reported the greatest feeling of being taxed too much for the federal income tax (66 percent of respondents; Lau and Sears, 1981, p. 210). Given these patterns, it is not surprising that a 1991 ABC News/*Washington Post* poll indicated that 62 percent of adults nationwide favored a cut in the federal income tax (*The Polling Report,* November 11, 1991, p. 1).

Broad trends in the level of discontent with the federal income tax burden are shown in Figure 14.3. Discontent reached a high point in 1982, when 69 percent of adults felt that their federal income tax payment was "too high." This response reflected an increase from several years earlier. Increasing resentment of the federal income tax burden may be attributable to the tax reduction rhetoric of the Reagan administration around this time. Over the twelve-year period from 1961 to 1973, an average of about 55 percent of Americans felt that the federal income

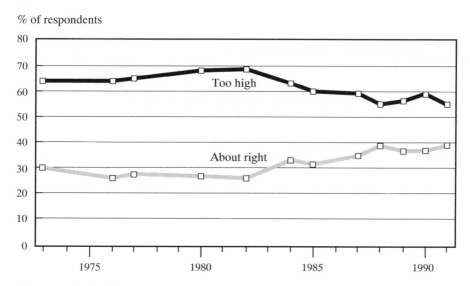

Figure 14.3 Opinion on federal income tax. (Data source: General Social Survey, 1973–1991.)

tax burden was too high (see Niemi, Mueller, and Smith, 1989, p. 76). Indeed, in the post-1982 period, levels of discontent ebbed, falling back to only 55 percent in 1991 for an overall drop of 14 percentage points. Virtually all of this change reflects movement into the "about the right amount" response category. Not surprisingly, fewer than 5 percent of Americans report feeling that the taxes they pay are "too low."

Despite discontent with taxes, Americans would support having more of their tax dollars go to support social services. The same poll that showed nearly two-thirds of Americans favoring a cut in the federal income tax also showed that 77 percent favored increased social spending. Indeed, 57 percent of Americans rated increased social spending as more important than cutting taxes. Similar results were found in a 1991 NBC News/*Wall Street Journal* poll, which showed that a plurality of Americans, 45 percent, preferred to see a peace dividend from the end of the Cold War be directed toward increased "spending on health and education." In contrast, only 14 percent thought these potential savings should go toward reducing taxes. The remainder divided between responses of "reduce the federal deficit" (35 percent) and "not sure" (6 percent).

Absent new and compelling justification, most Americans would not welcome a tax increase to fund more social service spending. Levels of discontent with taxes and whatever remains of the "tax revolt," however, do not extend to supporting efforts to downsize the current level of domestic social spending. Just the opposite is the case, as a number of national surveys point to a clear desire to see an increase in the proportion of federal tax dollars that go to social programs.

A second constraint on public support for antipoverty policies stems from enduring belief patterns about the causes of poverty and economic inequality. Table 14.1 reports national trends for four questions concerning explanations of poverty. Two questions speak to personal or individual causes of poverty, two questions speak to institutional or structural causes of poverty. Several patterns stand out. First, from 1969 to 1990, there has been a drop in the belief in both types of individualistic factors—"morals" and "effort"—as "very important" causes of poverty. For example, the percentage of Americans rating "loose morals and drunkenness" as "very important" causes of poverty fell by 11 points from 1969 to 1990, with most of this shift going into the "not important" category.

Second, there has been a slight increase in the attribution of poverty to institutional and structural causes. Table 14.1 shows a trend toward the belief that a lack of jobs and poor performance by the nation's schools are "important" or "very important" causes of poverty. This growth in the level of structural thinking about the causes of poverty is clearest for the item concerning limited job opportunities. The proportion of Americans who would deny altogether that limited job opportunities are an important cause of poverty fell from one of three adults in 1969 to

Table 14.1 Trends in explanations for the causes of poverty

Reasons	Year of survey			Difference
	1969	1980	1990	
Morals: Loose morals and drunkenness				
Very important	50%	44%	39%	−11%
Somewhat important	32	30	35	+3
Not important	18	27	26	+8
Effort: Lack of effort by the poor themselves				
Very important	57	53	46	−11
Somewhat important	34	39	45	+11
Not important	9	8	9	0
Schools: Failure of society to provide good schools for many Americans				
Very important	38	46	36	−2
Somewhat important	26	29	39	+13
Not important	36	26	24	−12
No Jobs: Failure of industry to provide enough jobs				
Very important	29	35	36	+7
Somewhat important	38	39	43	+5
Not important	33	28	21	−12

Sources: Kluegel and Smith (1986); J. Davis and Smith (1990).

Note: The introduction to the question read: Now I will read a list of reasons some people give to explain why there are poor people in this country. Please tell whether you feel each of these is very important, somewhat important, or not important in explaining why there are poor people in this country.

roughly one in five adults by 1990. Third, most respondents view poverty as having both individual and structural sources.

Fourth, despite the decline in individualistic explanations and the increase in structural perceptions of the causes of poverty, Americans remain strongly inclined to view the individual as responsible for his or her own economic conditions. The reason most often rated as a "very" or "somewhat" important cause of poverty at each of the three time points is a "lack of effort by the poor themselves." Fewer than one in ten people rate individual effort as not important across the 1969 to 1990 time span. Furthermore, if the responses of "very" and "somewhat" important are combined, then 91 percent of American adults in 1990 rated lack of effort as an important cause of poverty. None of the other potential causes receives such unequivocal endorsement, and this combined figure is essentially constant over the time period in question.

We have found four primary patterns in terms of levels of public support for a broad range of policies that capture most of what is intended by the phrase the "welfare state." First, there is no sign whatever of a strong ideological turn rightward against the welfare state. Some analysts conclude that there was a short-lived reaction against welfare from the late 1960s to the early 1970s (Kluegel, 1987, 1988; Shapiro and Young, 1989). This period of negative change, however, corresponds neither to the Reagan electoral victory in 1980 nor to broader macroeconomic trends and conditions (Kluegel, 1987, 1988). Second, American public opinion exhibits a relatively clear and stable hierarchy of social program support. At the top of this hierarchy, obtaining the highest levels of popular support, are health care, education, and social security programs. Surprisingly, a quite general item concerned with the level of spending on assistance to the poor also ranks in this top tier. At the bottom of this hierarchy are means-tested, income transfer programs colloquially described as "welfare." Falling between these extremes are jobs and housing-related programs. Third, from the late 1980s to the present there has been a significant increase in support for spending on health and medical care programs and a rise in support for spending on education. Fourth, relative to most other industrialized nations public opinion in the United States, much like U.S. public policy, reflects a weaker commitment to social programs.

Racial Attitudes and Race-Based Policies

Research on racial attitudes paints an increasingly complicated picture. On the one hand, former widespread support among whites for segregation and open discrimination as principles that should guide black-white relations have yielded to increasing support over the past fifty years for principles of equality (Lipset and Schneider, 1978; Kluegel and Smith, 1986; Schuman, Steeh, and Bobo, 1988; Jaynes and Williams, 1989). For example, national surveys show a sweeping increase in support for the broad goal of integrated schooling. Whereas only 42 percent of white Americans supported integrated schooling in 1942, 95 percent did so in 1983. Similar patterns obtain when one asks about public accommodations, mass transportation, the principle of integrated residential areas, and so on. This general decline in old-fashioned or Jim Crow racism, with its demand for strict segregation and open preference for white over black, continues to the present, reflecting both cohort replacement effects (older, more conservative people being replaced by younger, more liberal people) and individual change effects (K. Smith, 1985; Firebaugh and Davis, 1988). Indeed, Charlotte Steeh and Howard Schuman (1992) have shown that members of the younger generation, putatively an important contributor to current renewed signs of racial tension, remain more liberal than their predecessors and show no distinct signs of backward movement.

The decline of Jim Crow racism, however, has not been matched by support for governmental efforts to promote greater integration, to fight discrimination, or to move blacks into the higher education system and onto higher rungs of the occupational distribution more aggressively. Overwhelming majorities of whites oppose special government economic assistance to blacks. For example, Figure 14.4 indicates trends among white Americans in answering two questions on economic assistance for blacks:

Help blacks. Some people think that blacks have been discriminated against for so long that the government has a special obligation to help improve their living standard (point 1). Others believe that the government should not be giving special treatment to blacks (point 5). Where would you place yourself on this scale, or haven't you made up your mind on this?

Minority assistance. Some people feel that the government in Washington should make every possible effort to improve the social and economic position of blacks and other minority groups (point 1). Others feel that the government should not make any special effort to help minorities because they should help themselves (point 7). Where would you place yourself on this scale, or haven't you thought much about this?

Support for the idea of a government obligation to help blacks economically is relatively low, never reaching 30 percent in favorable responses, and both questions show a small decline over time.

% favoring govt. aid

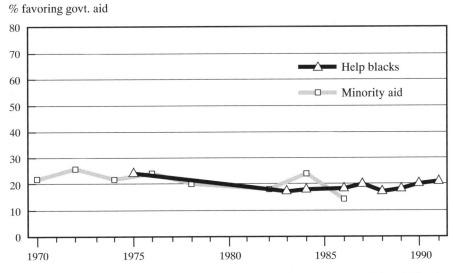

Figure 14.4 Support for government aid to blacks. (Data source: National Election Study, 1970–1986; General Social Survey, 1975–1991.)

In addition, support for racial policy questions typically exhibits weaker associations with respondent education, age, and region among whites than do questions focusing on Jim Crow racism. This lack of relation between the racial policy questions and background factors, especially level of education and age, leave little ground for anticipating substantially increased support in the future.

The support from a majority of blacks for government intervention to prevent discrimination and to facilitate integration of schools and communities and for the notion of a societal obligation to improve the economic condition of blacks is often matched by opposition from a clear majority of whites. Figure 14.5 provides perhaps the most extreme example of such a pattern, using the spending to "improve the conditions of blacks" question included in Figure 14.2. There is an enormous disparity, with over 80 percent of blacks supporting increased spending in this area compared with less than 40 percent of whites. (Below we examine the role that differences in social class background and other attitudinal factors may play in producing such large racial differentials.)

We do not yet have extensive trend data for questions that deal expressly with issues of affirmative action. Nonetheless, enough different questions have been asked to provide a fair bit of information on the distribution of opinion on the subject. To be sure, the term "affirmative action" is itself complex, covering a wide range of race-based policies. The level of support for affirmative action

% saying too little is spent

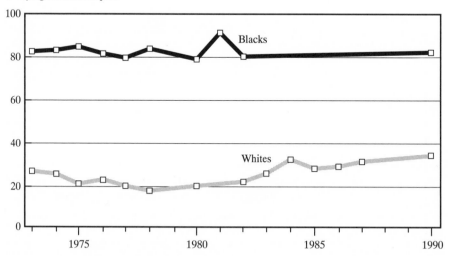

Figure 14.5 Support for spending on blacks. (Data source: General Social Survey, 1973–1991.)

hinges to a large degree on the precise type of program one asks about. For example, Seymour Martin Lipset and William Schneider (1978) emphasize that most white Americans support "compensatory" affirmative action policies. Such programs included race-targeted job training, special education, and even special recruitment effort programs. "Preferential" race policies, such as job hiring or college admission quotas, however, tended to elicit overwhelming opposition from white Americans. James Kluegel and Eliot Smith (1986) reported a similar pattern for their 1980 national data. Donald Kinder and Lynn Sanders (1987) found similar patterns using data from the 1986 American National Election Study (NES) survey. There is also some indication that compensatory policies in education are less objectionable than those dealing with employment. Black opinion tends to exhibit a similar difference in levels of support for compensatory versus openly preferential policies. Important race differences often remain, nevertheless, even for questions dealing with quotas and racial preferences.

The National Election Study surveys now regularly monitor opinion on affirmative action. Results for three key questions, and their wording, are given in Table 14.2. Nearly two-thirds of Americans object to special admission quotas for blacks at colleges and universities. Three-quarters or more object to giving blacks "preferences in hiring and promotion." In both instances, however, there is a modest trend toward decreasing opposition to affirmative action between 1986 and 1990.

These figures mask substantial racial differentials. Whereas 69.1 percent (strongly against and against categories combined) of whites from the 1990 NES opposed affirmative action in higher education for blacks, only 26.6 percent of blacks opposed it (see Tables 14.3 and 14.4). An equally large gap in black and white views emerged for the question of affirmative action in employment. Whereas 82.5 percent of whites opposed giving preference to blacks in hiring and promotion, only 37.4 percent of blacks adopted a similar position in 1990.

The Sources of Social Policy Preferences

The Impact of Economic Self-Interest

A large and growing number of studies have found that measures of socioeconomic status, especially income, influence attitudes toward welfare state policies (McClosky and Zaller, 1984; Kluegel and Smith, 1986; Knoke, Raffalovich, and Erskine, 1987; Hasenfeld and Rafferty, 1989; Bobo, 1991). Those individuals with lower incomes tend to favor a more generous welfare state and more redistributive taxation policies than do individuals with higher incomes. More surprising than the presence of such effects, however, is their relative smallness. For example, using data from a survey in Indianapolis, D. Knoke, L. E. Raffalovich,

Table 14.2   Changes in racial attitudes and affirmative action questions

NES racial policy questions	1986	1988	1990	Difference
On Affirmative Action in Education				
Strongly against	44.4%	46.2%	40.1%	−4.3%
Against	23.4	17.7	22.4	−1.0
For	16.1	16.2	22.4	1.0
Strongly for	16.2	19.9	17.1	1.0
Strongly for	16.2	19.9	20.4	4.2
On Affirmative Action in Jobs				
Strongly against	59.4	63.5	54.5	−4.9
Against	22.0	16.7	20.3	−1.7
For	6.9	7.7	9.5	2.6
Strongly for	11.7	12.1	15.7	4.0
Should Overcome Prejudice				
Agree strongly	30.8	40.6	27.2	−3.6
Agree somewhat	32.4	31.6	38.2	5.8
Neither	12.4	10.1	12.6	−0.2
Disagree somewhat	16.8	13.4	15.1	−1.7
Disagree strongly	7.6	4.3	6.9	−0.7

Source: Miller (1991).

Note: The questions of the National Election Study were worded as follows:

Affirmative action in education. Some people say that because of past discrimination it is sometimes necessary for colleges and universities to reserve openings for black students. Others oppose quotas because they say quotas give blacks advantages they haven't earned. What about your opinion—are you for or against quotas to admit black students? Responses: 1 = Against–strongly; 2 = Against–not strongly; 3 = For–not strongly; 4 = For–strongly.

Affirmative action in jobs. Some people say that because of past discrimination, blacks should be given preference in hiring and promotion. Others say that such preferences in hiring and promotions of blacks is wrong because it gives blacks advantages they haven't earned. What about your opinion—are you for or against preferential hiring and promotion of blacks? Responses: 1 = Against–strongly; 2 = Against–not strongly; 3 = For–not strongly; 4 = For–strongly.

Should overcome prejudice. Irish, Italians, Jewish and many other minorities overcame prejudice and worked their way up. Blacks should do the same without any special favors. Responses: 1 = Agree strongly; 2 = Agree somewhat; 3 = Neither agree nor disagree; 4 = Disagree somewhat; 5 = Disagree strongly.

and W. Erskine (1987) attempted to compare neo-Marxian and Weberian status group theories of the determinants of attitudes toward the welfare state. They found few, inconsistent, and minor effects of social class categories on support for specific welfare state policies, on support for broad economic management by government, or on racial and public assistance policies. More consistent effects were found for more continuous status factors, such as income. Even in this case, however, the overall amount of variance explained remained small. Similarly weak and inconsistent effects for income and other class variables were reported by William Form and Claudia Hanson (1985) in their analysis of a 1979 Illinois sample. Using national data, Jerome Himmelstein and James McRae (1988) examined the effects of income and Marxist class variables on economic and noneconomic issue attitudes. They too found a small tendency for income to increase conservatism on economic policy, but class exhibited "no coherent pattern at all" (Himmelstein and McRae, 1988, p. 506).

Since the research of Knoke and colleagues confirmed findings from several less carefully designed studies, they reached doubtful conclusions about the importance of self-interest (as gauged by objective status indicators) to welfare state attitudes. "The modest relation of the multiple stratification indicators to preferred governmental economic policy," they wrote, "challenges theorists who argue that stratification plays a central role in shaping political attitudes" (Knoke, Raffalovich, and Erskine, 1987, p. 155). These results do not surprise some political psychologists, who question the validity of using socioeconomic status measures such as self-interest measures and who see other psychological factors as far more consequential in shaping specific policy views (Citrin and Green, 1990; Sears and Funk, 1991).

Table 14.3   Changes in racial attitudes and affirmative action questions, whites

NES racial policy questions	1986	1988	1990	Difference
On Affirmative Action in Education				
Strongly against	50.4%	51.5%	44.8%	−5.6%
Against	25.5	20.0	24.3	−1.2
For	16.7	16.1	17.7	1.0
Strongly for	7.4	12.5	13.2	5.8
On Affirmative Action in Jobs				
Strongly against	66.8	69.6	61.4	−5.4
Against	22.5	17.2	21.1	−1.4
For	6.2	7.2	9.2	3.0
Strongly for	4.5	5.9	8.3	3.8
Should Overcome Prejudice				
Agree strongly	32.9	42.5	29.3	−3.6
Agree somewhat	33.7	33.0	40.2	6.5
Neither	12.4	9.5	12.7	0.3
Disagree somewhat	16.2	12.5	13.9	−3.7
Disagree strongly	4.7	2.3	3.9	−0.8

Source: Miller (1991).

Note: For question wording, see Table 14.2.

Table 14.4   Changes in racial attitudes and affirmative action questions, blacks

NES racial policy questions	1986	1988	1990	Difference
On Affirmative Action in Education				
Strongly against	12.3%	13.2%	14.1%	1.8%
Against	12.9	4.2	12.5	−0.4
For	12.9	13.7	10.2	−2.7
Strongly for	61.9	68.9	63.3	1.4
On Affirmative Action in Jobs				
Strongly against	19.7	21.2	11.4	−8.3
Against	19.0	13.8	13.8	−5.3
For	10.9	9.0	11.4	0.5
Strongly for	50.3	56.1	63.4	13.1
Should Overcome Prejudice				
Agree strongly	17.3	28.1	13.7	−3.6
Agree somewhat	25.6	24.8	23.7	−1.9
Neither	12.8	14.8	11.5	−1.3
Disagree somewhat	19.2	13.8	25.2	6.0
Disagree strongly	25.0	18.6	26.0	1.0

Source: Miller (1991).

Note: For question wording, see Table 14.2.

The Impact of Core American Values and Beliefs

Two types of psychological variables typically play an important role in shaping attitudes toward antipoverty and race-based social policies. These correspond to core American values of individualism and egalitarianism.[7] Individualistic beliefs cohere around the idea that opportunities in life are widely available and are largely unconstrained by the background attributes of individuals. Any resulting inequality is thus seen as fair, because individual effort and ability meet with appropriate rewards (Huber and Form, 1973; Kluegel and Smith, 1986). People holding these beliefs stress self-reliance and the fairness of the existing distribution of rewards. Indeed, this pattern of individualistic beliefs about inequality reflects deeper and longstanding American values of freedom and a complex of commitments embodied in the notion of Protestantism (McClosky and Zaller, 1984). As such, they constitute the "dominant" stratification ideology in the United States.

Individualism does appear to play an important role in shaping policy views. Studies of racial attitudes suggest that individualistic beliefs contribute to resistance to equal opportunity policies. People whose attitudes blend antiblack feelings and a belief that blacks violate values such as the work ethic and self-reliance are more likely to oppose affirmative antidiscrimination policies, affirmative action, and even black candidates for political office (Kinder and Sears, 1981; Kinder and Sanders, 1987). Whites whose explanation of black-white economic inequality faults the individual dispositions of blacks (for example, "they don't try hard enough") are among those most hostile to policies to help blacks (Apostle et al., 1983; Bobo, 1988; Kluegel, 1990). Media treatment of the affirmative action and poverty issues also tend to play on themes of individualism and self-reliance (Gamson and Modigliani, 1987; Iyengar, 1987, 1990). Many studies point to individualistic beliefs about the causes of poverty as central to the public's negative response to welfare programs (that is, income maintenance) and to recipients of welfare (Feagin, 1972, 1975; Williamson, 1974; Coughlin, 1979; Kluegel and Smith, 1986; Shapiro and Young, 1989).

Yet, American political culture has long emphasized values of democracy and equality (Tocqueville, 1969; Lipset, 1979; Feldman, 1984; McClosky and Zaller, 1984). Both in-depth interview (Hochschild, 1981) and sample-survey results (Hamilton, 1972; Shapiro and Young, 1989) reveal that a concern with limiting inequality and meeting basic human needs are potent strands of U.S. stratification ideology. As indicated earlier, Coughlin's (1979) comparative review found a general pattern of commitment in the United States and other industrialized nations to the idea that the government should provide a basic minimum standard of living.

Issue Frames, the Media, and Public Opinion on Poverty and Affirmative Action

The tendency among Americans to provide individualistic explanations for the causes of poverty rather than more structural or institutional explanations may be a function of the way the political and cultural elites and the media "frame" or "package" the issue of poverty (Gamson and Lasch, 1983; Gamson and Modigliani, 1987; Iyengar, 1987, 1989, 1990; Kinder and Sanders, 1990). Shanto Iyengar (1987, 1989, 1990) has shown that when the media directs the viewer's attention to national outcomes, explanations for poverty become predominantly systemic, that is, directed toward the government or the economy in general. When the media points to particular instances of poor people, in contrast, explanations for poverty become predominantly dispositional, that is, the individual is seen as having inadequate motivation, poor education, or inadequate skills (Iyengar, 1987).

Media packaging does not extinguish the likelihood that the personal characteristics (which include race, gender, level of education, religion, age, political party, and socioeconomic status) of those receiving the media message will have an impact on whether they will attribute poverty to individual or to structural causes. For example, nonwhites, females, Catholics, Democrats, Independents, and the "have-nots" were more likely to offer structural/systemic causes of poverty; college graduates, Protestants, professionals, the elderly, Republicans, and the more affluent were comparatively more likely to cite individual/dispositional causes of poverty (Iyengar, 1987, 1990).

The demographic, religious, and political characteristics of individuals are not the only factors that affect the way respondents assign causal explanations for poverty. The race, sex, age, and marital status of the individuals and families perceived to be in poverty also play an important role. Iyengar (1990) found that, when making causal attributions about poverty, his sample of white middle-class respondents placed a high premium on the race of the person perceived to be in poverty. Most notably, single black females with babies elicited the most powerful response; these mothers were viewed as particularly culpable and much less deserving of governmental support than their white counterparts (Iyengar, 1990). Iyengar observed, "when the poor person was white, causal and treatment responsibility for poverty were predominantly societal; when the poor person was black, causal and treatment responsibility were more individual" (1990, p. 35). These results led Iyengar to conclude that "framing welfare policy in terms of particular beneficiary groups will weaken rather than strengthen public support for welfare" (1990, p. 36). An important message of the Iyengar studies is that how an individual comes to assign responsibility for poverty is a function of his or her background characteristics, on the one hand, combined with the way the media frames the issue, on the other.

The importance of framing effects has also been demonstrated with survey questions seeking public opinion on affirmative action (Kinder and Sanders, 1990). Drawing on the work of William Gamson and his associates (1983, 1987) and using data from the National Election Study, Donald Kinder and Lynn Sanders (1990) set out to "mimic political debate with survey questions." They examined whether changes in public opinion on affirmative action could be induced with alterations in question wording. Random halves of a sample of whites were asked to think of affirmative action (in the domains of hiring and promotion, and college admissions) in one of two opposing frames: affirmative action framed either as "unfair advantage" or as "reverse discrimination." Regardless of how the question was framed, the majority of whites were strongly opposed to affirmative action, whether in the domain of hiring and promotion or in the domain of college admissions. With regard to hiring and promotion, 67.3 percent of whites were strongly opposed to affirmative action under the "reverse discrimination" frame; 62.5 percent expressed strong opposition under the "unfair advantage" frame. Affirmative action within the domain of college admissions yielded similar results, with 53.9 percent of whites strongly opposing affirmative action under the "reverse discrimination" frame, and 52.9 percent expressing strong opposition under the "unfair advantage" frame. These overall percentage differences between frames were statistically indistinguishable.

Although the average level of support for affirmative action was not changed by the "framing" experiment, the correlates of support for affirmative action differed dramatically between the two frames. Specifically, when affirmative action was presented in an "unfair advantage" frame, whites were more apt to express indignation, anger, and disgust as compared with when affirmative action was presented in a "reverse discrimination" frame. In addition, implicit race policies, such as federal spending on cities, jobs, and welfare, were all found to be correlated with opinions on affirmative action under the "unfair advantage" frame, but not under the reverse discrimination frame (Kinder and Sanders, 1990). Differences in political ideology further highlighted the importance of the "unfair advantage" over the "reverse discrimination" frame in promoting opposition to affirmative action. For example, Republicans and conservatives were more likely to oppose affirmative action than were Democrats and liberals, but only when the issue of affirmative action was framed in terms of "unfair advantage"—not when it was framed as "reverse discrimination." These findings suggest that the "unfair advantage" frame evokes a highly racialized and emotion-laden package of ideas and feelings that also have a powerful partisan and ideological overlay.

Although the prominence of the "unfair advantage" frame as a "central organizing idea" (Gamson and Modigliani, 1987) by which some whites come to understand affirmative action is borne out by Kinder and Sanders, the "reverse discrimination" frame finds particular resonance among whites who fear affirmative action on the basis of perceived threats to individual self-interest or group interest. Kinder and Sanders report: "When invited to think of affirmative action as discrimination against whites, Americans believed that affirmative action might set back the education of their own children, and especially those who were convinced that affirmative action was hurting whites in general, were noticeably more likely to oppose the policy" (1990, p. 88).

At the core of investigations of the effects of issue "frames" and "packages" on public opinion on affirmative action and poverty is the contention that elites in the United States play an important role in framing policy issue debates and hence in determining the content of public opinion. Performing a content analysis of Supreme Court opinions, political speeches, and articles in news magazines, William Gamson and Andre Modigliani (1987) examined changes in the language and symbolism on affirmative action held by U.S. elites. They identified three broad issue frames/packages on affirmative action that dominated the media, at one time or another, from 1969 to 1984: a *remedial action frame* (RA), where "the issue is whether race consciousness programs should be used to redress the continuing effects of a history of racial discrimination"; a *delicate balance frame* (DB), where "the core issue is how to maintain the proper balance, helping old victims of discrimination without creating new ones"; and a *no preferential treat-*

ment frame (NPT), where policies based on race or ethnic origin are viewed as antithetical to American ideals of self reliance and individualism. Four other "subpackages" fall under the NPT frame, the most noteworthy of which is the *reverse discrimination frame,* where the primary "issue is whether we are going to sacrifice individual rights in order to advance the well-being of some ethnic or racial groups" (pp. 148–149). Gamson and Modigliani note that Nathan Glazer's characterization of affirmative action as a "form of benign Nuremberg laws" (Glazer, 1978) and his assertion that the "first principle of a liberal society [is] that the individual and the individual's interest and good and welfare are the test of a good society" (Glazer, 1975) summarize the reverse discrimination frame (Gamson and Modigliani, 1987, p. 146). They found that the "remedial action" frame dominated the media in 1978. By 1984, however, it was overtaken by the "no preferential treatment" frame. At the time of the *Bakke* decision, the "delicate balance" frame briefly emerged but subsequently vanished, never reaching prominence again. Finally, Gamson and Modigliani report how opposition to affirmative action has recently changed from an "undeserving advantage" frame accompanied by "overt racist symbolism" to a "reverse discrimination" frame. They examine the reasons that the reverse discrimination frame has recently become dominant:

> Reverse discrimination had well-organized and articulate sponsors who actively promoted it. It met the news needs of working journalists for balance and dramatic form. Finally, it had strong positive resonances with larger cultural themes of self-reliance and individualism, and used antiracist and equality symbolism to neutralize the favorable resonances of its major competitor. No other alternative to remedial action had such a full array in its favor.   (Gamson and Modigliani, 1987, p. 170)

Gamson and Kathryn Lasch (1983) earlier laid the foundations for identifying the core themes and tracing the political culture of social welfare issues in the media. In particular, the "political culture of social welfare policy" was examined, and four dominant "packages" depicting the way people come to frame welfare policy and, in turn, welfare recipients, were identified: the "welfare freeloaders" package view welfare recipients as engaging in "welfare fraud or welfare recipients driving cadillacs," and phrases such as "workfare, not welfare" dominate the discourse; the "working poor" package views the poor as individuals who "welcome the ability to earn more through work but are discouraged in doing so by disincentives"; the "poverty trap" package is noted for its emphasis on the structural causes of poverty—individuals, under this package, are not blamed for their poverty; and the "regulating the poor" package suggests that the welfare system should function in the dual role of regulating "and maintaining a labor reserve . . . and relief functions to ameliorate discontent and assure quiescence and dependency in the 'surplus population,'" (Gamson and Lasch, 1983, pp. 402–408). It was through the identification of such core frames that Gamson and his associates were later able to measure the prominence of their usage in the media, and to trace the changes in their prominence over time.

This line of research, focusing on the role that framing plays in affecting the opinions people form on policy issues such as affirmative action and welfare (Gamson and Lasch, 1983; Gamson and Modigliani, 1987; Iyengar, 1987, 1989, 1990; Kinder and Sanders, 1990) draws a connection between the way elites debate and frame issues on the one hand, and the way policies come to be viewed by the mass public, on the other. According to Kinder and Sanders, "public opinion depends in a systematic and intelligible way on how issues are framed. By promoting rival frames, elites may alter how issues are understood and, as a consequence, affect what opinion turns out to be" (1990, p. 74). Perhaps the most obvious implication of this statement is the notion that controversial policies such as affirmative action and welfare would have a chance of being widely accepted if only they were framed or packaged by elites in a way amenable to the public. Yet the dynamics governing the careers of issue frames scarcely take place within a political vacuum in which political elites (that is, issue sponsors) engage in an ongoing struggle attempting to promote their own ideological orientations. On the contrary, the career of a given issue frame (or package) depends largely on the complex interaction of three broad forces: (1) the type of discourse among political elites on a given policy issue; (2) the type and frequency of media presentations of such discourse; and (3) how such discourse resonates with the mass public—with the last being composed of two constituent elements: the background characteristics of the individuals and groups who are targeted to benefit from the social policy in question; and the background characteristics of the individuals and groups who are not targeted to benefit from the social policy. It is the simultaneous interaction of these forces that shapes reaction to social policy proposals. Future research will have to specify clearly the connection between these interacting factors.

The Impact of Race

Are positions on social policy issues sharply polarized by race? That is, do blacks and whites exhibit clearly different levels of support for social policies? These questions take on special urgency given the mounting evidence that racial issues play an increasingly central role in American politics (Carmines and Stimson, 1989; Edsall and Edsall, 1991b). Significant black-white differences of opinion emerge for virtually all of the social policy items we have discussed thus far. Using data from the 1990 General Social Survey, Table 14.5 indicates the percentage of whites and blacks supporting various social policies. This group of

Table 14.5   Race and social policy support, 1990 General Social Survey

Policy questions	Whites	Blacks	Difference
Race-Neutral			
Social Security	50%	63%	+13%*
Equal wealth	49	68	+19**
Implicitly Racial			
Help poor	31	55	+24***
Welfare	20	43	+23***
Expressly Racial			
Blacks	34	82	+48***
Help blacks	16	55	+39***

* $p < .05$.   ** $p < .01$.   *** $p < .001$.

Source: J. Davis and Smith (1990).

Note: The base *N*s for whites range from a low of 517 to a high of 1,108. The base *N*s for blacks range from a low of 72 to a high of 158.

policies was selected to reflect those presumably race-neutral in character ("Social Security" and "equal wealth"), those with a large but implicit racial component ("help poor" and "welfare"), and those of an expressly racial nature ("blacks" and "help blacks"). Blacks are significantly more liberal in their views on each of these policies. The magnitude of the difference, however, corresponds directly to the racial explicitness of the policy. The more explicit the racial component, the larger the black-white gap in support. Thus the black-white gap in support for more spending on Social Security is only 13 percentage points, whereas the gap is 48 percentage points when the question refers explicitly to blacks.

These black-white differences may reflect average differences in socioeconomic standing and other background characteristics; differences in general values, beliefs, and ideology that may grow out of the different class and race-based social positions the two groups occupy; differences in racial attitudes; or different perceptions of collective group interests. Given the small number of black respondents in the 1990 GSS and the limitations in the scope of this chapter, it is not possible to provide a definitive answer to the question of which of these factors is most important. We can gain some leverage, however, by examining the magnitude of the black-white difference after controlling for indicators of each of the different factors that may have produced the apparent race-based differences in policy views.[8]

In general, differences in socioeconomic status and other background factors do not explain the black-white difference in social policy support. For the race-neutral policies, black-white differences in the level of support are attributable to black-white differences in general values, beliefs, and ideology. To a degree, this is also true of the implicitly racial policies. Where expressly racial policies are at issue, however, neither socioeconomic status, other background factors, general values, beliefs, ideology, nor racial attitudes fully account for the black-white gap. This suggests that for race-based policies an important element of perceived group or collective interests underlies the black-white polarization on these questions (see Bobo, 1988; Bobo and Kluegel, 1993).

Table 14.6 provides the basis for these conclusions. It shows the impact of race on social policy views under four different conditions using ordinary least squares regression. The first column reports the zero-order or bivariate relation of race on each policy support measure in the form of a standardized regression

Table 14.6 Summary of ordinary least squares analysis of race differences in social policy support, 1990 General Social Survey

Dependent variable	(1) Zero-order	(2) Demographics	(3) Values, beliefs, ideology	(4) Racial attitudes
Race-Neutral				
Social Security	.09**	.07**	.03 n.s.	.05 n.s.
Equal wealth	.12**	.11**	.01 n.s.	.02 n.s.
Implicitly Racial				
Help poor	.17***	.18***	.09*	.09 ($p = .05$)
Welfare	.13**	.13**	.04	.03
Expressly Racial				
Blacks	.27***	.30***	.20***	.16**
Help blacks	.31***	.34***	.26***	.17***

* $p < .05$.   ** $p < .01$.   *** $p < .001$.

Source: J. Davis and Smith (1990).

Note: Cell entries are standardized partial regression (beta) coefficients for the effect of race on social policy support.

Column 1: The OLS model includes a dummy coded variable for race (whites = 0, blacks = 1).

Column 2 shows the race effect after adding respondents' age, sex, education, family income, occupational prestige, and region of residence (South vs. non-South) to the model.

Column 3 shows the race effect after adding measures of structural explanations of poverty, individualistic explanations of poverty, equity norms, and political ideology to the model.

Column 4 shows the race effect after adding measures of perceived discrimination, antiblack stereotyping, and individualistic explanations of black-white economic inequality to the model.

coefficient. Column two shows the coefficient after adding socioeconomic and other background control variables to the equation. Column three shows the coefficient after adding measures of several key general value, belief, and ideology measures. Column four shows the coefficient after adding several measures of racial attitudes to the model. If the magnitude and statistical significance of the race coefficient decline as one moves across the rows, then the added variables "explain" some portion (or all) of the race difference in opinion.

White Racism and Social Welfare Policy Support

Having dealt with the overall pattern, magnitude, and sources of black-white differences in support for social policies, we can now pose an even more pointed question: Does racism undermine whites' support for the American welfare state? That is, setting aside average differences in levels of support by race, are the levels of whites' support for social policy driven by what they think and feel about blacks? Also, does the impact of racism on policy views among whites hinge on the specifics of the policy in question? Returning to data from the 1990 General Social Survey we have attempted to illustrate the impact of racial attitudes on social policy preferences. Table 14.7 shows the correlation between support for several social policy issues reviewed in the earlier section on trends and three different dimensions of racial attitudes. The social policy questions shown again

Table 14.7 The impact of racial attitudes on whites' support for social policy, 1990 General Social Survey

	Pearson's correlations			Variance explained		
	Stereo-typing	Black motivation	Racial discrimination	Base-line	Values, beliefs, ideology	Racial attitudes
Race-Neutral						
Social Security	.08	.07	−.05	.046	.065+	.065
Equal wealth	−.04	−.08	.06	.027	.140+	.144
Implicitly Racial						
Help poor	−.06	−.16***	.07	.053	.125+	.134+
Welfare	−.08	−.19**	.12**	.019	.099+	.113+
Expressly Racial						
Blacks	−.26***	−.35***	.25***	.058	.183+	.261+
Help blacks	−.29***	−.29***	.29***	.052	.153+	.243+

* p < .05.   ** p < .01.   *** p < .001.

Source: J. Davis and Smith (1990).

Note: Plus sign (+) indicates a significant increment to variance explained for each block of variables.

cover policies widely regarded as race-neutral, those regarded as having a large but implicit racial component, and those expressly targeted to assist blacks. The racial attitude dimensions are antiblack stereotyping, attribution of the black-white economic gap to a lack of motivation on the part of blacks, and attribution of the black-white economic gap to racial discrimination. In general, the correlation between racial attitudes and support for the race-neutral social policies is small, no higher than .08 and often smaller. The picture of no relation begins to change for the implicitly racial policies. Three of the six possible correlations between racial attitudes and social policy attitudes in this set are highly significant and of at least modest absolute value. Finally, each of the racial attitude measures has noteworthy correlations with the two expressly racial social policy attitudes.

To gain greater knowledge of the relative strength of racial attitudes as determinants of social policy views, the last three columns of Table 14.7 show the contribution to variance explained for several different models. The first or baseline model includes only demographic variables as predictors of support for each social policy measure.[9] The second model adds measures of crucial general value, belief, and ideology.[10] The third model then adds the three measures of racial attitudes in order to formulate a discerning test of whether and when racial attitudes contribute, above and beyond social status and general social outlook, to social policy support.

The results show that racial attitudes make no significant contribution to explaining support for either of the two race-neutral social policy measures. Given the breadth of the racial attitude measures involved, this is strong confirmation of the claim that levels of support for some types of social policies are genuinely untainted by racism. Racial attitudes do, however, make a significant contribution to levels of support for both of the implicitly racial social policies. This is particularly true for the question on support for spending on "welfare," where the racial attitude measures bring an increase of nearly 2 percentage points in the amount of variance explained. Although a larger range of questions needs to be analyzed before reaching a firm conclusion, this result tends to confirm the suspicion that the term "welfare" and its negative connotations stem from an implicit link to how one feels about blacks and the problem of racial discrimination.

Martin Gilens (1991) reviewed data showing that Americans tend to believe that most of the poor are black. Kluegel and Smith (1986) found that white Americans also tend to think that most blacks are poor. More to the point, Gilens (1991) has shown that the correlation between, on the one hand, beliefs faulting a poor work ethic among blacks for racial inequality and, on the other hand, social welfare policy attitudes grows substantially stronger as one moves from programs concerned with the elderly and public education to issues of unemployment and food stamps. There may be a historical basis for this connection. Because of the civil rights and black power protests of the era, Lyndon Johnson's Great Society programs increased the perceived association between race and the welfare state (see Skocpol, 1991).

Yet the case for the influence of racial attitudes should not be pressed too far. The lion's share of the variance in support for welfare spending remains unexplained, and most of what is explained is attributable not to racial attitudes but to the measures of general values, beliefs, and ideology.

The potency of racial attitudes is strongest for the two expressly race-based policies. In both cases the racial attitudes add substantially to the variance explained in support, even after having controlled for socioeconomic status and a host of general value, belief, and ideology measures. This finding might not be surprising save for the sometimes strident claims that opposition to race-based policies has nothing whatever to do with racism and instead reflects the so-called basic values and common sense of the American people (Roth, 1990; Weissberg, 1991).

Race-Targeting and the Bar of Public Opinion

Given the role that negative racial attitudes play in decreasing support for policies with implicit racial content, and the substantial part they play in determining support for expressly race-targeted policies, it is fair to ask whether it is possible to fashion race-targeted policies capable of eliciting a broad base of support in the general populace. A recent large-scale survey-based experiment was directed at addressing this question (see Bobo and Kluegel, 1993). Random halves of the 1990 GSS respondents were asked questions that differed only in whether they were targeted by race or targeted by income. Three questions dealing with business enterprise zones, special funding for school programs, and college scholarship funds were asked. Table 14.8 shows the results for these questions. In each case the broader of the two policies, the one targeted by income, received greater support among whites. On average, 22 percent more support was given for income-targeted policies than for race-targeted policies. (There was no difference among blacks in level of support based on income or race targeting.)

It is important to note, however, that both the special school funds question and the college scholarship question receive a greater than 60 percent favorable endorsement among whites. Furthermore, relative to many of the race-targeted policy questions discussed earlier, these questions have a comparatively weak connection to antiblack stereotyping and other expressly antiblack attitudes. Support for these policies also does not appear to violate notions of equity—reward based on merit—whereas the more outcome-oriented race-targeted measures clearly do.

This pattern of results suggests that race-targeted social policies could be developed that would not automatically arouse prejudice-based rejection among

Table 14.8 Survey-based experiment on whites' support for income-targeted or race-targeted
social policies, 1990 General Social Survey

| | Percentage of whites in favor of | | |
	Income-based targeting	Race-based targeting	Difference
Enterprise zones	71%	43%	−28%
Special school funds	86	68	−18
College scholarships	91	70	−21

Note: The *enterprise zone* question asked whether the respondent favored giving business and industry
special tax breaks for locating in (poor and high unemployment/largely black areas).

The *special school funds* question asked whether the respondent favored spending more money on the
schools in (poor neighborhoods/black neighborhoods), especially for preschool and early education
programs.

The *college scholarships* question asked whether the respondent favored providing special college
scholarships for (children from economically disadvantaged backgrounds/black children) who maintain
good grades.

whites or instantly be perceived as challenging the values of individualism and
the work ethic. Race-based policies that are clearly tilted toward enhancing opportunities or the ability to take advantage of opportunities appear to have a sufficiently broad base of support in white public opinion that they could be pursued
without immediately provoking controversy and conflict (see Bobo and Kluegel,
1993).

·   ·   ·

At the outset we posed the question of whether or not it would be possible to
achieve an effective national consensus on antipoverty policy and efforts to eliminate racial inequality. Although there is no definitive answer to this ambitious
question, we would respond as follows. First and foremost, most features of the
American welfare state enjoy a substantial degree of popular endorsement. Efforts to curtail spending, in fact, elicited an increased desire for social spending.
Second, public opinion appears to be clamoring for an expansion of support for
some aspects of the welfare state, most notably health care and medical coverage
and education. The trends here are both steady and clear. They are also borne out
by other data that indicate an increasing concern over the escalating and sometime catastrophic costs associated with health care.

Third, contrary to the views of many commentators and discussions in the
media, the American discontent with the federal tax burden does not translate into
a desire for cutting back on social programs. The opposite is true: it would appear

that a clear plurality of Americans favor shifting more resources toward social programs.

Fourth, income transfer programs, or welfare, does arouse considerable ambivalence and opposition. But under no circumstances does this skepticism amount to a preparedness to eliminate the social safety net. Instead, Americans seem to be calling for help for the poor that paves their way back into a state of self-reliance as quickly as possible.

Fifth, race and racism do play a considerable role in social welfare attitudes. Indeed, there are some policies that are implicitly racial in nature (such as welfare). This implicit racial coding undermines support for these programs. There is far from a tight identity, however, between "welfare" and programs that assist African Americans.

Sixth, programs targeted on the basis of race vary greatly in the reception they receive from white Americans. Programs directed at making up for disadvantages by enhancing the human capital resources of blacks and oth.*. minorities typically elicit high levels of support. Policies that involve preferential selection or quotas confront a solid wall of opposition.[11] Negative racial attitudes and perceptions of group interests as well as general values and beliefs about inequality contribute to these policy views.

Public opinion is not fixed and immutable; nor is it reducible to a single master motive or overarching theoretical principle. A complex and often policy-specific array of background and status factors, values, and ideological leanings as well as racial and intergroup attitudes and perceived interests undergird responses to social policy proposals. Such a complex set of considerations applies even in the case of race-targeted policies, where the exact policy objective—opportunity enhancement or equal outcomes—can shape the overall levels and likely wellsprings of popular support or opposition in important ways (Bobo and Kluegel, 1993). Indeed, even the precise language used to describe a policy ("assistance to the poor" versus "welfare," or "unfair advantage" versus "reverse discrimination") can influence who and how many people favor or oppose a given proposal.

Three critical ingredients are involved in the process of linking public opinion to policymaking and outcomes. First, the debates and exchanges that take place among contending elites over the shape that policy ought to take define the very language, symbols, assumptions, and meanings that an issue or policy proposal takes on. Second, subsequent media coverage and packaging of the issue for the public at large plays a crucial role in determining the outcome of the contest among elites for the mass public. Third, contextual considerations, such as sharply rising health care costs and a shift in who bears the burdens of such costs or upheavals such as the civil uprising in Los Angeles, also add to the mix. As a result, there is a measure of indeterminacy in how new or reform proposals will fare in the court of public opinion, a number of important continuities in American public opinion notwithstanding.

It would be a mistake to assume that the American public is largely conservative or liberal in its disposition toward social welfare and affirmative action policies. To be sure, some ideas or premises for social policy have broader, more immediate cultural resonance (for example, individualism, self-reliance) than others (for example, the structural/institutional causes of poverty). Similarly, policies of broader scope and potential constituency, all else being equal, are likely to have more immediate appeal than policies targeted to assist class- or race-based subgroups. Yet the implications of much of the research on media frames and effects, however, is that the vigor, inventiveness, and persistence of advocacy in favor of a particular policy objective and ways of "framing" an issue can significantly influence public support for a policy. The assumption that public opinion is known or fixed in a certain direction is probably more constraining than is public opinion itself. Reformers of the left or the right who take the contours of public opinion for granted or who assume that there is little need to promote actively particular issue frames and reinforce the values, assumptions, symbols, and catch phrases that lend meaning to questions of public policy are likely to falter before the bar of public opinion.

CHAPTER FIFTEEN

Poverty Politics

HUGH HECLO

Despite their syntax, social scientists are much like other people. Behind the often bloodless analysis of poverty statistics usually lies a core of prescientific personal commitments. Poverty, after all, is not a subject whose study confers great intellectual status or aesthetic pleasure. It is generally a messy, frustrating topic where uncontested answers are few and intellectual breakthroughs do not seem to exist. Fundamentally, I suspect, "poverty experts" get involved in reading and writing on the subject because at some personal level they are disturbed about the condition of disadvantaged people.

And because observers care, they wonder why it is that we do not do better. Reformism pervades poverty studies. Some would transfer more income, provide better services. Others would liberate the poor from the perverse effects of government intervention. Still others would recast programs to set behavioral standards for re-integrating the poor to the larger society. We do too much; we do too little; we do the wrong things and leave undone the right things. "Why don't we do better?" asks Reform. "What is, is what can be," answers Praxis. For reformers, the shadow that always seems to fall between the thought and the action is named politics.

Hence there is a strong temptation to read the politics as we want them to be, as a story where current failings are identified, new efforts undertaken, and the possible merged with the desirable. The political story we instinctively want to tell ourselves is the old one of repentance, revelation, and redemption. In what follows I have tried, perhaps unsuccessfully, to resist reading such personal preferences into the political calculus of antipoverty policy. After beginning with some obvious but important facts about the political context, the chapter examines long-standing American attitudes toward poverty policy. We will see how inevitable tensions between the desire to help the needy and expectations of work and self-support recurred in the 1980s, as well as why public preferences for employment rather than income maintenance for the able-bodied were not very well reflected in federal welfare programs before the 1988 Family Support Act.

The chapter then raises doubts about the most recent round of promises to cure welfare dependency through politically attractive "tough love" proposals. It goes on to suggest how a preoccupation with this narrow segment of poor Americans and stale, setpiece arguments between political camps inhibit serious consideration of the nation's broader poverty problems. The final section examines changes since the War on Poverty and the political poverty that seems to prevent us from creating and sustaining serious efforts to assist the official and "unofficial" poor.

Three Fundamentals

At least three basic facts shape everything else that might be said about the politics of poverty policy.

The first is that poor people do not have much power. They do not form political action committees or make major contributions to politicians. Poor people pay disproportionately less attention to and participate less in politics than other people, particularly in comparison with those toward the top of the income distribution. In the organized way through which power is exercised in modern American society, poor people do not matter very much.

This situation is unlikely to change. Efforts have occasionally been made in past years to give political expression to the one power resource poor people do have, their numbers. But these voter registration and other mobilization drives have generally proved disappointing. Similarly trade unions—which at certain times, on a few issues, championed the cause of the working poor—are a small and diminishing presence on today's political scene.

The conclusion to be drawn is obvious, but foundational. Antipoverty policies are less a matter of demands poor people make in the political process and more a function of what other people decide to do to and for them.

Second, America's poverty agenda is now inseparable from its racial debate. For most of our history, concerns about the poor made no pretense of considering racial inequality (Jones, 1992). Implicitly, of course, race has always played a powerful role in poverty policy. It has done so by shaping divisions among the disadvantaged and the politics for exploiting those divisions. In 1960 Lyndon Johnson explained to an aide what generations of white politicians had done:

> I'll tell you what's at the bottom of it. If you can convince the lowest white man that he's better than the best colored man, he won't notice you picking his pocket. Hell, give him somebody to look down on, and he'll empty his pockets for you. (Dallek, 1991, p. 584)

For over a century such racial politics helped entrench southern and conservative interests hostile to liberal social policies.[1]

Today, as always, it remains politically easier to engender resentment against the weak than against the powerful. Since the 1960s, however, the country has for the first time openly confronted and legitimized demands for racial equality. Those demands for the creation of a multiracial society are unlikely to disappear. At the same time demographic trends are accelerating the reality of such a society. Census data indicate that the racial composition of our population changed more dramatically from 1980 to 1990 than at any other time in the twentieth century, with the nonwhite population itself becoming more racially diverse (U.S. General Accounting Office, 1991b; Passel and Edmonston, 1992). Any antipoverty policy through which the haves address the have-nots faces the simultaneous and enormous challenge of speaking across deeply troubled racial barriers. And it will have to do so in a political context where both political parties feel an electoral need to win over white middle-class voters in the suburbs.

Finally, antipoverty efforts are bound up with the state of the economy, though not in any one-dimensional way when it comes to politics. In economic good times it is politically easier to feel generous, and poverty may seem a more incongruous condition demanding attention. But the poor can also appear more aberrant, and fewer people may identify with their situation. In economic hard times more people may feel their economic situation precarious, and political opportunities for more encompassing antipoverty coalitions grow. But antipoverty efforts also become harder to pay for, and the scramble for survival may do more to divide than to unite people. Economic conditions offer no simple shortcut through the politics of poverty.

Public Predispositions and Policy Legacies

Consider the following vignette:

> After years of argument, a rough consensus emerged among reformers. Despite its humanitarian motives, the welfare system was creating a dependency that hurt its clients and contradicted mainstream values. For those able to work, cash assistance should be at most a temporary form of emergency support. Instead of prolonged income support, help for those able to work should be through education, job training, work, and medical and child care to return the dependent poor to the social mainstream.

> Putting this new consensus into policy practice, however, was a different matter. Adequate public funds to implement the reforms were not forthcoming. Rather than spending more on better services to the poor, politicians frequently used the reforms

to cut the welfare rolls and produce short-term savings. Coordination of educational, employment, and other services proved difficult; implementation varied from place to place. Soon it became apparent that the reformers themselves were more divided than the earlier consensus rhetoric had made it seem. Some were willing to take tougher measures, withholding aid from those who failed to follow behavioral norms; others were more concerned by what they saw as the suffering caused by a punitive approach.

The most interesting point to be made about this story is that it could be extracted and retold again and again over the last two hundred years. The story recurs whenever Americans have sought to reform their prevailing programs for poor people.[2]

In the early nineteenth century, the reform movement that established poorhouses and other specialized institutions hoped both to cure the able-bodied from welfare dependency and restore them to independence, as well as to provide more humane treatment for the young, sick, and disabled who could not work (M. Katz, 1986). In the last third of the nineteenth century, the scientific charity reformers sought to abolish permissive cash assistance (outdoor relief) and to create specialized public services and private assistance tailored to the particular needs of those in distress. In the midst of the Depression in the 1930s, Franklin Roosevelt argued that to dole out relief was "to administer a narcotic, a subtle destroyer of the human spirit," and declared that the federal government "must and shall quit this business of relief" (Patterson, 1986, p. 59). Unemployable people would have their particular needs met by the states and localities; the federal government would put needy but employable people to work. In the 1960s, the Great Society's attack on poverty repeated the message of "a hand up, not a handout." Today welfare reformers around the country are urging replacement of the able-bodied's dependence on welfare with norms of work and personal responsibility.

In each instance, the status quo was condemned as inadequate for those in need and debilitating for those who could be returned to self-support. In each case, the new consensus aimed to help those in genuine need without fostering a dependency that would hurt those it was meant to help. And in each case the reforms as implemented fell far short of their original aspirations.

Historic Premises

The reason for drawing these comparisons is not to stigmatize current welfare reform efforts as little more than a reversion to the nineteenth-century poor law. There are huge differences in the times and conditions. The point is to highlight certain continuities, indeed constant predispositions, that underpin American attempts to deal with antipoverty policy. The Family Support Act signed into law by President Reagan in 1988 and the welfare reforms proposed early in the Clinton administration expressed these same ancient themes. Basically, there are three.

First, Americans have generally agreed that there is a public, governmental responsibility to assist those who are regarded as lacking the necessities of life. Contrary voices have argued for over a hundred years that charity is a purely private duty, that public aid distorts incentives and corrupts recipients, that "social justice" is a mirage excusing the expropriation of one person's property to favor another person (Hayek, 1976; Sumner, 1982 [1883]; Murray, 1984). These are powerful arguments, but they no more carried the day in the 1980s than they did in the 1880s.

Second, people should strive to be self-supporting, because full standing as a citizen depends on the independence that comes from work and personal earnings. According to Judith Shklar, both critics and defenders of welfare in the 1980s were "caught up in the Jacksonian web of ideas" (Shklar, 1991, p. 96). Every side in the political debate has always agreed that the policy aim should be to replace welfare dependency with the independence that comes from having a job. And Americans at all income levels and from all ethnic backgrounds continue to display a remarkable consensus on the value of hard work and the ability of individual effort to ensure success (Ladd, 1991, 1992). It is worth noting that this ethos is addressed not simply to the private hardship and loss of self-esteem that may accompany unemployment or dependence on welfare. The harshest judgments are reserved precisely for the able-bodied who feel *no* loss of esteem or remorse for depending on taxpayers. Public respect and standing that are at stake in the expectation of self-support.

Third, public spending should attempt to prevent and cure problems of poverty and welfare dependence. This is not egalitarianism. American antipoverty efforts have historically shunned any redistributive rationale that would justify taking money from some people so that others might live better. The words of Josephine Shaw Lowell's 1883 attack on public outdoor relief could just as well have been uttered by modern advocates of "human capital" investments: "To cure paupers and make them self-supporting, however costly the process, must always be economical as compared with a smaller but constantly increasing and continual outlay for their maintenance" (Abbott, 1937, p. 161).

These three predispositions reappear continually throughout the fifty-year period for which we have reliable survey data on mass public opinion. Thus surveys from the 1930s through the 1980s have consistently shown that anywhere from 65 percent to 96 percent of Americans (depending on question wording) believe that government should help the needy ("provide for all people who have no other means of obtaining a living," "help people who are unable to support themselves," "take responsibility for seeing to it that the poor are taken care of," and so on) (Page and Shapiro, 1992, p. 124).

Similarly, polls have always shown that while Americans want government to help those who cannot help themselves, they also expect the able-bodied to help themselves. And it is here that questions specifically about "welfare" (rather than the "poor" or "needy") tap a raw nerve. Surveys have consistently revealed that most Americans think that many welfare recipients could work, that fraud is widespread, and that recipients could often get along without the benefits if they wanted to. Opinion polls in 1972, 1976, 1977, 1979, and 1985 found most people in favor of requiring welfare recipients to go to work (Mead, 1986, pp. 233–240; Page and Shapiro, 1992, p. 125).

The public's preference for combining work and welfare is not simply a punitive instinct but part of a more general commitment to self-supporting employment. Since 1935 opinion polls have usually shown that two-thirds or more of Americans favor government action to ensure that jobs are available for everyone who wants to work (Page and Shapiro, 1992, p. 121; Weir, 1992, p. 52). Far from being imposed from above, these pro-work attitudes are shared among most of the poor and welfare recipients themselves (Goodwin, 1983; Gueron, 1987; Coalition on Human Needs, n.d.). By contrast extensive redistribution to reduce income inequalities has never commanded much public support, even in Depression-era polls. Nor have various proposals for minimum income guarantees, negative income tax schemes, government guarantees of jobs or a good standard of living ever appealed to many Americans. In general, the public's commitment is to ensuring would-be workers an opportunity, not a result.

These enduring predispositions are not so much a monolithic consensus as an enduring set of tensions within which people navigate the ambivalent claims of individualistic values and collective social responsibility (Heclo, 1986b; Bobo, 1991). Thus in one sense it is true to say that antipoverty policy—understood as the alleviation of income gaps for those at the bottom of the economic distribution—has never been a core commitment of American society (Marmor, Mashaw, and Harvey, 1990). "Income poverty" was created the official measure of poverty in 1964 for administrative and political convenience and has now become the dominant policy concept. But Americans have never expressed much interest in closing income gaps as such. However, Americans have always demonstrated a profound desire to fight "poverty," understood as a condition of immiserization, dependence, and hopelessness (Lehman, 1991). Poverty in this sense has been seen as thoroughly un-American. Against it have sounded all the familiar refrains of social reformers over the decades—help for self-help, aid for the deserving but no reward for vice and folly, a hand up rather than a handout.

These premises of public opinion require that poverty programs be carefully crafted and explained to Americans. But there is nothing inherently contradictory in such public views. Wanting very much to help the needy while giving the shiftless a cold shoulder is no more irrational than the desire for a legal system that protects the innocent while punishing the guilty. But the policy techniques to achieve these ends are imperfect, and the public and its representatives are always left with the choice of preferring to err on the one side or the other.

The New Consensus of Old

Political rhetoric notwithstanding, there was little change in Americans' social welfare ideas in the 1980s. In all important respects the so-called new consensus on antipoverty policy reflected in the 1988 Family Support Act was an updated version of the old consensus just sketched. Those in need should be helped; those who can work should be obliged to do so; welfare dependency should be prevented and cured, not underwritten by reshuffling money from rich to poor. In the words of the 1988 act, public welfare recipients would be "encouraged, assisted, and required to fulfill their responsibilities to support their children by preparing for, accepting, and retaining such employment as they are capable of performing."

Public attitudes in the 1980s showed little sign of a conservative conversion toward what commentators called the "Reagan Revolution." In fact the opposite was more the case. Major studies of poll results have found a strong swing in the public's "mood" in a conservative policy direction after the early 1970s, peaking around the time of Ronald Reagan's election in 1980 and then consistently moving toward more liberal preferences throughout the 1980s (Stimson, 1991; W. Mayer, 1992).[3] Judging from such an overall measure of "mood liberalism," the 1990s offer greater opportunities for new social policy initiatives than any time since the early 1960s and the launching of the New Frontier and Great Society programs. There is certainly more at work in American politics than such general public preferences, however.

A more detailed study of public attitudes in 1986, the high noon of Reagan popularity, indicates the strong elements of stability in public thinking about social welfare programs. It is worth noting that in this survey respondents were not asked about welfare or help for the poor but about specific programs (Medicare, Social Security, Supplemental Security Income, Medicaid, AFDC, Food Stamps, and unemployment insurance). The vast majority of people (ranging from 76 percent for the least popular program, Food Stamps, to 87 percent for Medicare) wished to see spending on these programs maintained or increased (Cook and Barrett, 1992). Other questions were asked to probe the depth of support for AFDC, Medicaid, and Social Security. As might be expected, supporters of Social Security were the most numerous and determined in backing the program, and Medicaid fared only slightly worse. AFDC showed the weakest profile of support versus opposition. Even so, at the high point of the Reagan years, the picture is not one of overwhelming hostility to this centerpiece of the much disparaged "welfare" system. One-third of Americans said they wanted to see spending on AFDC increased, 16 percent preferred cuts, and 52 percent wanted spending maintained as it was. Almost two-thirds said they were satisfied to pay taxes for AFDC; and to avoid cuts in the program, 25 percent of respondents said they would be willing to pay more taxes, write a letter, or sign a petition. By contrast only 19 percent said they would be willing to write a letter or sign a petition to oppose AFDC spending increases. Even if these answers exaggerate what people might actually do, these are not the responses of a public undergoing a conservative revolt against the welfare state or turning its back on the poor.

More interesting is the way the public calibrates its preferences depending on the kinds of needs different people are thought to have and the type of program in question. Cash assistance is seen as particularly appropriate for poor or disabled elderly persons and poor children, but not appropriate for able-bodied, working-age adults. Much the same priorities are applied to food assistance. By contrast, with programs of an educational nature the public gives highest priority to job training for poor adults and special education and rehabilitation programs for disabled persons. For catastrophic health insurance coverage, children in general are ranked highest, with the elderly slightly behind. As rough as these judgments necessarily are in such a survey, the results do not show a public that automatically favors one age group over another. Instead, people differentiate their judgments about who should be helped with what kind of assistance.

At the same time there is no mistaking the consistently vulnerable position of any program providing cash or its equivalent (increasingly true of food stamps) to able-bodied adults. Although the public's view of AFDC is not as overwhelmingly negative as portrayed by politicians and the media, a majority of people surveyed in 1986 doubted that AFDC clients used their benefits wisely and a third or more doubted that recipients really needed the benefits or wanted independence. And while two-thirds of the public did not want to see AFDC cut, 30 percent thought that half or more of AFDC recipients cheated the system. Results such as these for 1986 merge easily with a constant stream of findings over the years showing that most Americans feel too many people on welfare could be working, that they are getting money they are not entitled to, and that there is more concern for the "welfare bum" than for the hard worker (Page and Shapiro, 1992). In general it is fraud and lack of work effort that the public finds objectionable in the cash welfare system.

Thus policies targeting cash assistance on working-age adults are not only suspect to the public in a way that social insurance programs are not. They are also suspect in a way that education and job training targeted on working-age adults or cash assistance targeted on the elderly are not. Even social insurance is not immune from public suspicion when it comes to supporting able-bodied workers. Few in the public would abolish unemployment insurance, but that program ranks about the same as AFDC in terms of the distribution of public support for increasing, maintaining, or cutting spending.

In most regards the scale of the country's social welfare programs closely follows these basic contours of public preferences. We have a system dominated by programs that help prevent poverty among those who have met the prevailing sense of work obligation (Marmor, Mashaw, and Harvey, 1990, table 2.2). The employment-linked social insurance system thus accounted for 71 percent of all government spending on social welfare benefits in 1986. These social insurance benefits did far more to minimize officially measured poverty than did noncontributory means-tested programs. A welfare state following public preferences would certainly be wary of cash payments for able-bodied adults and concerned to tailor noncash assistance to particular kinds of need. This is roughly what we find in the 29 percent of spending on social welfare benefits flowing to people who have to demonstrate need. Within these means-tested programs almost three-fourths of the spending in 1986 was devoted to in-kind benefits (medical services, housing, educational assistance, and so on). This left about 8 percent of total spending allocated to means-tested cash assistance. But of this amount about half was going to impoverished aged, blind, and disabled persons (SSI); needy veterans; and working poor persons (under the Earned Income Tax Credit).

This left about 4 percent of social welfare funds spent on the two programs that Americans typically equate with "welfare"—AFDC and state-run General Assistance. Approximately 70 percent of AFDC recipients are children, however, and state efforts to terminate "employable" persons from General Assistance have applied to a little under half the GA caseload (Center on Social Welfare Policy and Law, 1992a). Thus a rough estimate would be that well under 2 percent of total social welfare spending went to the activity Americans are most wary about—giving money to able-bodied working-age people. (Treating Food Stamps as the equivalent of cash, rather than as an in-kind benefit, would put the share around 3 percent.)

Stepping back from these details, it is not difficult to see how the "new" consensus behind the 1988 Family Support Act fit easily with long-standing tenets of public opinion. The act promises work obligations for able-bodied adults, education and job training for those who need it to work, medical and child care services for needy people making the transition into the work force, and stricter expectations that people will take responsibility for themselves—hardly alien notions. Moreover, priority in the mandatory work, training, and education programs has to be given to those most likely to become long-term AFDC dependents (unmarried teen mothers, those with no work experience or high school diploma, and those already on AFDC for extended periods). The reform's main sponsor, Senator Daniel Patrick Moynihan, commented: "Conservatives have persuaded liberals that there is nothing wrong with obligating able-bodied adults to work. Liberals have persuaded conservatives that most adults want to work and need some help to do so" (Mead, 1992).

Even though passage of the 1988 act was sometimes in doubt, the important point is that policymakers generally agreed on the fundamental need to bring able-bodied recipients into the work force (Wiseman, 1991). There had been no such agreement during unsuccessful welfare reform efforts under Nixon and Carter. And this raises two related puzzles. First, if the "normal" state of public preferences is as I have described it, what really needs explaining is not the 1980s consensus on work requirements, personal responsibility, and so on. The odd thing is the permissive income maintenance approach of the 1960s and 1970s, which the newly discovered consensus of the 1980s saw itself as having to counteract. Second, in a country where welfare dependency has been anathema and rescuing people from its grip has been an enduring goal, why has the United States put such a meager effort into what our foreign competitors call labor market policy (job training, relocation aid, apprenticeship programs, and other employment-related services)? Why are we just now developing such programs for people dependent on welfare checks?

Manpower Policy Legacies

Some might say the answer to the second puzzle is obvious. Americans expect able-bodied adults to look after themselves in the labor market—to take care of their own health insurance, job search, retraining problems, and the like. And the government does help many working people indirectly through tax breaks for employer-based health insurance, home mortgages, and so on. However, tax-subsidized rugged individualism is too easy an answer. Political contests have occurred that could well have produced different outcomes more favorable to average working people. In the battles over these historical turns, some interests have won and others have lost, while the poor themselves have almost never had the political resources to even be in the fight.

For example, in the 1920s an emerging national system of well-baby clinics and public health services open to all women with children was cut short and abolished (Skocpol, 1992). Health care for poor families today would probably look vastly different had public health nurses, women's groups, and "pro-paternalist" politicians not lost out to organizations of private physicians, states' rights advocates, and other politicians who, by the late 1920s, had learned that the

Nineteenth Amendment would not produce a unified and politically threatening women's vote. After that, liberals campaigned to establish national health insurance for all citizens, encountered stiff opposition from doctors' organizations and conservative politicians, and were defeated by mid-century. The remnants of that battle—a Truman administration plan for hospital insurance for only the aged, Republican and AMA counterproposals for voluntary doctor's insurance, and means-tested health care for the destitute—were eventually cobbled together in 1965 to produce the current Medicare/Medicaid system (Marmor, 1973). It is too simple to think that American individualism and norms of self-support for working-age adults simply foreordained these results.

By the same token there is a largely forgotten historical legacy that accounts for the meager, often jerry-built employment policies available today. And this in turn helps explain the drift into an income maintenance rather than an employment-based approach to welfare in the 1970s. Business opposition and trade union indifference undercut the development of federal employment services at various points throughout this century (Mucciaroni, 1992; Weir, 1992). Rivalries among state-level retraining, unemployment insurance, and labor exchange bureaucracies added to the post–World War II fragmentation of effort. In the early 1960s, the Kennedy administration initiated labor market policies to deal with structural economic changes affecting the general adult work force. But these efforts were not sustained in Lyndon Johnson's administration, and manpower programs soon were transformed into racially focused adjuncts of Johnson's War on Poverty. Thus what began under Kennedy as an attack on shortages of skilled labor, worker displacement through automation, and depressed areas became part of a more narrow social program oversold by an increasingly unpopular president. Employment programs became especially vulnerable when white support waned for what were seen as programs for minorities, and when civil rights leaders made court-sanctioned affirmative action their preferred strategy for addressing employment issues.

Meanwhile, efforts by George Schultz and others to revive a comprehensive "manpower policy" early in the Nixon administration ran afoul of partisan conflict between the White House and Congress. As their New Deal coalition weakened under the strain of racial, cultural, and foreign policy tensions, congressional Democrats pushed temporary jobs programs as a way to win back political support and outflank Nixon. The resulting Comprehensive Employment and Training Act produced tens of thousands of short-term public service jobs in hundreds of locally managed sites during the mid-1970s. But CETA produced few successful transitions to private sector jobs and little apparent net gain in employment. Soon there were criticisms of ineffectiveness and waste as the public's worries shifted from unemployment to inflation. By the 1980s CETA was abandoned. For all of the 1960s' promises of computerized job banks, improved vocational education, and other employment services, there were few lasting results produced by the manpower policy initiatives over the years. Perhaps the most important by-product was the 1974 creation of the Manpower Demonstration Research Corporation (MDRC), a semipublic research organization whose evaluations of state welfare and work programs would provide most of the intellectual groundwork for the 1988 Family Support Act.

This brief review of labor market policies to help workers adjust to the changing demands of the economy represents a sorry chronicle of half-hearted, poorly administered, and politically orphaned gestures. Isolated from the unmet needs of the larger work force and without a strong administrative capacity for manpower policy in Washington, work and training programs for welfare recipients have languished in their own virtual policy ghetto.

Although manpower policy faded after the mid-1960s, we are still left with the first puzzle. Given the public predispositions described earlier, how did cash support for working-age people become the dominant image that today's welfare reformers feel they must combat? Again the history is informative. But to see what happened we should look beyond political sound-bites that would blame the plight of poor people on Great Society programs.

The Not-So-Great Society

The truth is that in the 1960s the War on Poverty and Great Society programs did not advocate permissive, income maintenance approaches for the poor. Apart from Medicare and other programs for the elderly, the emphasis was on creating economic opportunities and enhancing individuals' capacities to take advantage of those opportunities. None of the programs—from Head Start, education grants, job training, and child nutrition to community action agencies, Foster Grandparents, rural development, and Model Cities projects—aimed merely at providing income support. In this sense, the Great Society's War on Poverty stood foursquare with traditional norms of advancing individual opportunity and self-help, or what in the 1990s is labeled "empowerment."

Implementing these ideas was another matter. Many of the same obstacles will face new antipoverty policies in the 1990s, and the lessons are worth remembering. First, using education, job training, and other services to change people's lives was a slow and uncertain process. Indeed, it was a more complex type of social engineering than national policymakers had ever undertaken. And yet to gain political credit and easy legislative victories, the Johnson White House made vastly inflated promises about the results to be expected. When quick fixes to deep-seated social ills were not forthcoming, many politicians, group advocates, and policy experts lost patience (Aaron, 1978). Programs that developed a widespread, locally rooted constituency of participants and providers—Head Start being a prime example—were better positioned for long-term survival, despite their inability to show the immense short-term results that were foolishly promised (Zigler and Muenchow, 1992).

Second, implementing these economic opportunity programs was far more difficult than anyone had foreseen. This is usually to be expected, because in the United States the political system bureaucrats who will be charged with carrying out the new laws rarely participate in the top policymaking circles that design the programs. In one area after another—urban planning, community economic development, job training, and so on—Washington policymakers embarked on activities where there were meager administrative capacities to carry out and coordinate the work effectively. Bureaucratic capacities in the Departments of Labor or Health, Education and Welfare (the areas most relevant to antipoverty policies) had been allowed to go to seed since the New Deal. Federalism added to the complexity. Local agencies and nonprofit organizations were overwhelmed by the proliferation of uncoordinated federal programs and by the rules trying to control their operation second-hand from Washington. Congress's normal mode of reflecting federalism also helped undermine effective administration. As a price of passage, new domestic legislation invariably requires accommodations to congressmen's alliances with local constituencies. And these alliances are naturally always interested in claiming a share of both federal funds and administrative power. Thus the Model Cities proposal, the Great Society's *only* concentrated attack on ghetto poverty, was administratively fragmented and quickly broadened by Congress to include most congressional districts (Haar, 1975). The net result was to interlace barriers to the establishment of priorities and effective management into the very fabric of new social programs.

Third, as noted earlier, federal antipoverty policy and the Democratic domestic agenda more generally became caught up in the growing turmoil over civil rights. Never before (except perhaps for the brief interlude of Reconstruction after the Civil War) had federal domestic policies been developed in the context of an official stand for racial equality. One can recognize that questions of poverty and racial justice are intertwined and still acknowledge the immense political difficulty that can result from trying to address both problems simultaneously. Social programs originally justified in terms of advancing individual opportunity soon were perceived to be, and in part became, means of group advancement for blacks. Before any War on Poverty programs were in place (much less had time to affect the ghetto poor adversely, as would be claimed in the 1990s) the Watts riot of August 1965 had begun the process of alienating white support from antipoverty efforts. White backlash grew in and outside the Democratic party (Edsall and Edsall, 1991a). Perhaps equally important, heightened racial sensitivities also made it extremely difficult to talk about traditional concerns in welfare policy without opening oneself to charges of racism. In the public conversation about fighting poverty, problems of illegitimacy, family stability, and work expectations became virtually forbidden territory, especially for liberals who saw the importance of these issues (Rainwater and Yancey, 1967; Wilson, 1987; Moynihan, 1992). Hence the racist abuses of the past in welfare programs came to haunt present thinking about antipoverty policy.

Finally, a familiar dilemma of presidential leadership repeated itself. For the fourth time in fifty years the social reform agenda of a Democratic president was contaminated by the domestic fallout of foreign wars. For Woodrow Wilson and the Progressives it had been the reaction to the Versailles Treaty and the Red Scare; for FDR and loyal New Dealers it was the need to maintain business and other domestic support in the build-up to and conduct of World War II. Truman's Fair Deal agenda ran afoul of a new Red Scare and dissipated with the Korean War. For Lyndon Johnson it was Vietnam that weakened support for social reforms with growing presidential unpopularity.

The story needs to be told honestly. Antipoverty programs of the 1960s did not lose support because they contradicted basic American values. They lost support because politicians taught the people to expect quick fixes, because programs could not be effectively administered, because they became part of a racial imbroglio, and because their chief political sponsor lied to the people in fighting a dubious foreign war.

Slouching toward Income Maintenance, and Back

In this political quagmire, AFDC and other programs, insofar as they moved toward an income maintenance approach, did so more by default than by design. This was true on several fronts.

Once economists in 1964 defined an officially measured poverty line, policy thinking became dominated by what could be measured. This facilitated evaluations of policy and proposals in terms of how far they managed to close the rather arbitrary income gap of those below the poverty line. Such a view was reflected in the failed plans of the Nixon and Carter administrations to reform welfare with something resembling an income guarantee for closing the poverty gap.

Advocates of a more liberal income maintenance approach had greater success in the courts than they did in Congress. In this respect the Great Society did contribute to an ethos of entitlement, as lawyers and other Community Action employees from the new Office of Economic Opportunity challenged state laws restricting welfare eligibility. During the 1960s and 1970s, a complex series of court decisions struck down many state eligibility restrictions and moved cash assistance somewhat in the direction of a solely need-based entitlement (Melnick,

1991). As welfare administrators eased their screening process and "welfare rights" advocates pushed their claims, the rate of eligible female-headed families actually receiving AFDC benefits jumped from 60 percent in 1967 to 90 percent by 1971 (Michel, 1980).

Partly in response to growing claims of entitlement, the Democratic Congress in 1967 enacted welfare amendments imposing the first modest work and training requirements and freezing federal funds at existing levels for AFDC cases caused by illegitimate births or desertion. Then-professor Daniel Patrick Moynihan declared the restrictions "the first purposively punitive welfare legislation in the history of American national government" (Melnick, 1991, p. 217). But these work and training requirements were only marginally enforced, and the funding freeze on illegitimacy and desertion cases was repealed in 1969. These Work Incentive (WIN) amendments did, however, serve notice that, with the growing tendency for nonwelfare mothers to enter the work force, expectations for welfare mothers were changing as well. After World War II AFDC had increasingly become a program supporting single mothers (rather than the widowed mothers of the earlier Mother's Pensions and young AFDC program), but there was an inertial carryover of the early twentieth-century view that the mother's place was in the home (Howard, 1992). Gradually, from the 1960s onward, the growth of women's employment outside the home helped change this assumption about welfare mothers.

The drift toward welfare entitlements based purely on low income certainly did not proceed unopposed. Under Russell Long's leadership (D-La.) the Senate Finance Committee produced a steady stream of counterproposals to roll back the work of welfare rights advocacy groups and the courts. In 1971 the Talmadge amendment required parents with children over six years of age to register with the WIN program, and in 1973–74 the first significant federal measures to enforce child support payments from absent fathers were passed. Around the same time, Governor Ronald Reagan of California battled in the courts to maintain his more traditional, work-oriented welfare reform program.

These were only skirmishes, however. In the 1980s, with a growing anti-government mood and the arrival of the Reagan administration in Washington, a sustained attack on permissive "Great Society" approaches was under way. AFDC bills attached to budget legislation did not produce large savings, nor were they intended to. But they did slow much of the previous court-sanctioned momentum toward needs-based income entitlements. Many state eligibility requirements overturned by the courts were statutorily reintroduced by Congress. The "work incentive" exclusion of earned income from calculations of claimants' available income was restricted, thereby removing some 400,000 cases of mainly working poor persons from the AFDC rolls (U.S. House of Representatives,

Committee on Ways and Means, 1991, p. 657). Support obligations for men living with the family were now reinstated. But perhaps as a sign of changing social mores, there was no congressional interest in reviving the old custom in some states (overturned by the Supreme Court in 1968) of treating any sexual partner as a substitute parent, hence disqualifying the children in the family from AFDC.

The 1980s also witnessed a reassertion of the older, pre-1960s tradition of state variation in welfare assistance. The Nixon and Carter welfare reform proposals, as well as most court decisions in the 1960s and 1970s, favored greater national uniformity in AFDC benefits and administration. Then it was conservatives who argued for giving states more discretionary control over the programs. With the advent of the Reagan administration the stances were reversed, and in 1981 it was Democrats who fought conservatives' efforts to impose mandatory federal work and other requirements on state-administered welfare programs. The result was a compromise that allowed increased state experimentation, which in turn culminated in the lessons behind the 1988 Family Support Act. In passing that act, again it was Republicans who insisted on mandatory federal standards requiring states to achieve given levels of participation in work and training programs for employable AFDC recipients. The final compromise requires states, on a monthly basis, to have one-fifth of employable recipients in work programs by fiscal year 1995. How states do that is largely their business.

Thus by the early 1990s, much of the politics of poverty policy had reverted to the subnational level and revolved around the old federalism idea of the states as policy laboratories, each trying to see what works in welfare reform. The declining political concern with nationally uniform standards is reflected in the "welfare magnets" debate. In the mid-1980s poverty researchers began to revisit the old question of whether differences in public assistance benefit levels were attracting people from low-benefit to higher-benefit states (Peterson and Rom, 1990). Traditionally, the purpose behind such research was to make the case for more national standards in AFDC payments. By the 1990s, however, use of such research findings had switched to a more immediately appealing issue in statehouse politics: how to restrict benefits for immigrants from lower benefit states.[4] This magnet fear, plus the exit threat from businesses and others objecting to higher taxes, means that the states are not so much running independent experiments as jockeying for a comparative advantage in holding down both welfare benefits and the taxes needed to pay for such services. And this jockeying among states can cumulate in rather negative ways for the poor. This is an old problem of federalism that was long used to justify a more national welfare policy. But in recent years the fact that people in similar circumstance will be treated quite differently in various parts of the country has been of little concern. Instead, something else has surprised the latest generation of welfare reformers who crafted the 1988 Family Support Act.

Nonsupport for Family Support

Translated into practice and the play of partisan politics, there was less to the policy consensus of 1988 than met the eye. The Family Support Act (FSA) did not produce the comprehensive attack on welfare dependency that was intended. What has happened is more complex than middle-class politicians taking cheap shots at welfare stereotypes, though that is part of the story.

That the Family Support Act had to be implemented in the midst of a sustained economic downturn certainly did not help smooth the way for a constructive political approach. In the years 1989–1992 the U.S. economy faltered through a recession and anemic recovery. The result, together with years of cuts in federal spending to aid states and cities, was an unexpected and powerful squeeze on state budgets and antipoverty efforts.

At the same time that state revenue growth decreased, pressures on state spending increased. In part this was because the economic downturn helped increase welfare caseloads under AFDC (funded 20 to 50 percent by the states) and General Assistance (fully funded by the states). After remaining in the 3.6 to 3.8 million range since 1976, the number of AFDC families increased steadily from 3.8 million in late 1989 to 4.7 million families by the end of 1992. But this was hardly the major driving force behind state budget woes. As a percentage of 1992 state spending from general funds, AFDC formed only about 3 percent and General Assistance about 1 percent in 1992. Much more important were federally mandated increases in state spending, particularly for Medicaid, which increased from 3 percent of state budgets in 1970 to 13 percent in 1990. In addition to health spending, the other major source of state budget stress came from that symbolic by-product of America's festering social problems, growing prison costs.

Even assuming the best of intentions toward the poor, the result has been a cascading set of restraints on other programs. Federally mandated spending has put pressure on AFDC, where the federal government picks up only some of the costs, and this in turn puts even more pressure on General Assistance, where states have no federal mandates and pay all of the costs. In 1991 states accounting for one-third of the AFDC caseload cut the absolute level of benefits; states with 4 percent of the caseload increased benefits; and the rest made no change, effectively reducing the real value by the 5.4 percent inflation rate (Center on Social Welfare Policy and Law, 1992b). In that same year nineteen states cut benefits or otherwise scaled back their General Assistance programs and only four states raised benefit levels.

In this situation, states were reluctant to spend more of their own funds to match federal funds for the Family Support Act. Of the one billion federal dollars available for operating the Family Support Act's JOBS program (involving employment, education, and training for welfare recipients), financially strapped states used only 60 percent and only eleven states used their full allotment of federal funds (U.S. House of Representatives, Committee on Ways and Means, 1992, p. 620).

Tough Love

Budget problems, however, were only a part of the story. The Family Support Act had been crafted within a fairly self-contained fraternity of poverty experts and politicians specializing in the subject. Few in the general public were educated about the long-term commitment, money, and patience that would be required to show results. Likewise the mundane work of carrying through the various education and work programs of the act aroused scarcely any outside political or public interest (Johnson, 1992).

Meanwhile, the "welfare problem" proved an irresistible target for other politicians, especially at a time when many Americans were feeling economic hardship. Compared with the Family Support Act's rather solicitous approach to work requirements, social services, and personal responsibilities, the new proposals coming from various states were more demanding and at times punitive in requiring "proper" behavior from welfare recipients.

In general there have been four types of initiatives.

First, *benefit cuts* are the changes most clearly related to the states' budget problems. In the early 1990s, reductions in AFDC and/or General Assistance benefits were adopted or under serious consideration in at least twelve states. The remaining three types of proposals were less concerned with saving money (although that hope always lingers) and more focused on producing certain forms of approved conduct as related to work, education, and family (Burke, 1992).

Second, many *work proposals* have sought to strengthen mandatory work and training requirements that already exist under the FSA. Some plans would add further work and training obligations; others would allow additional earnings without loss of welfare benefits. A similar rationale underlies efforts currently proposed in eight states to lower or eliminate the cash benefit after a recipient has been on the rolls for a given period of time.

Third, initiatives have focused on *education*. Under the 1988 act, certain requirements for participating in educational programs are imposed on younger welfare recipients who lack a high school diploma or its equivalent. States can also require participation in JOBS programs, which may include educational courses for any recipient over fifteen who is not in full-time secondary or vocational school. Six states have enacted or are considering "Learnfare" proposals that would enlarge these requirements for teen parents, reducing and/or offering bonuses in welfare checks depending on cooperation with the stay-in-school rules. In several states adult parents' welfare benefits will be cut if their children fail to attend school regularly. These efforts to encourage responsible parenting shade into the final category.

The fourth sort of initiative may be termed an advocacy of certain *family values*. Efforts are being made to use welfare rules to promote what is regarded as desirable family behavior and/or to punish its opposite. The FSA moved in this direction by allowing states to require that never-married parents under eighteen live with their parents (or other adults under certain circumstances) as a condition of receiving AFDC benefits. Five states are now pursuing this option. Other "Wedfare" proposals aim to encourage welfare mothers to marry, using a variety of incentives such as disregarding a step-parent's income in assessing family need or offering a monetary bonus for marriage when followed by an absence from the welfare rolls for a certain period of time. In the name of encouraging responsible parenthood, plans are under way in at least six states to cut or deny benefits for additional children conceived or born while the mother is on welfare.

This movement occurring across the grassroots of American federalism has been dubbed the "New Paternalism" by some, "tough love" by others. The possibilities for reaping political credit were quickly recognized by national politicians who had taken little interest in the Family Support Act and its rather undramatic provisions about work, education, and family responsibility. In the House of Representatives, conservative Republicans proposed a "tough love" approach as a "first step to replace the welfare state" (*Washington Times*, April 29, 1992), an approach quickly endorsed by many GOP congressional candidates. Recipients of public assistance would be required to work or enroll in educational programs after one year on the rolls; benefits would cease after four years and could be retained by an AFDC recipient who married. In the Senate, Republicans and a few Democrats lined up behind Senator Alfonse D'Amato's proposals to prohibit welfare recipients who move to a state with higher benefits from receiving aid for one year and to require work programs for able-bodied recipients of General Assistance.

Further, state efforts in these directions were encouraged in the 1991 State of the Union address, when President Bush invited states to seek exclusion from federal welfare regulations so as "to replace the assumptions of the welfare state and help reform the welfare system." A well-publicized presidential waiver for Wisconsin's carrots and stick approach to reducing welfare dependency added to the momentum.[5] Thus the state experimentation that blossomed after 1981 and had seemed to culminate in the "new consensus" of the 1988 act developed into an even more diverse welfare system in the early 1990s through a kind of New Federalism-by-waiver.

The Allure of Posturing

The political dynamics at work in these "welfare reform" proposals are not difficult to fathom. The slow, often underfunded, understaffed, and undramatic work of implementing the FSA has been almost politically invisible to the public, while headline-grabbing "tough love" proposals attract media and political attention. California is a good example of how the glitz of political promises can easily overshadow the grit of chipping away at welfare poverty. Begun in 1985, California's GAIN program (Greater Avenues for Independence) served as the leading model for the Family Support Act's combination of education, job training, and other services combined with graduated work requirements. Underfunded, with long waiting lists for entering its supposedly mandatory program, GAIN yielded some of its first and most positive MDRC evaluations in the spring of 1992. These showed modest success, as participants earned 17 percent more and received 5 percent less from AFDC than the control group during the same period. But such results paled into public insignificance compared with the concurrent political and media attention given to Governor Pete Wilson's proposed Government Accountability and Taxpayer Protection Act. While spending on GAIN remained frozen, Californians debated a public referendum for an immediate cut of 10 percent in AFDC benefits (from among the highest levels in the nation). The plan would require another 15 percent cut in benefits for any family with an able-bodied adult after six months on the rolls. AFDC teen mothers would be required to live with their parents and receive a $50 bonus on their welfare checks for staying in high school. Other features would deny AFDC benefits to children born while a mother is on welfare, and new California residents would be limited for one year to the benefit levels prevailing in their former state of residence.

Although the consensus of the 1980s on work and personal responsibility helped legitimate the New Paternalism of the early 1990s, leading sponsors of the Family Support Act found the developments surveyed here contrary to the act's intended direction and spirit. In February 1992 hearings to find out what had gone awry, Senator Moynihan concluded, "I'm afraid all this originates with David Duke. He started talking about the 'threat' of people on welfare, and it struck a nerve" (*Washington Post,* Feb. 4, 1992, p. A13). Whether or not that diagnosis is true, the fact remains that political exploitation of public anxieties is a normal, predictable part of our democratic process.

This truth may help explain a coincidence: the most sweeping "tough love" proposals appeared in states where tax-raising governors faced tough reelection prospects in 1992. Conventional politics also helps explain why the social facts are irrelevant to some of the proposed forays into behavior modification. In general, the effect of the welfare system on a female family head's work effort or on her family arrangements is much too small to expect that major changes in her life will be produced by tightening this or that requirement in the AFDC program (Moffitt, 1992). Bonuses for marriage seem dubious when marriage is already the major way spells on AFDC are ended (Long, 1990). Eliminating benefits for additional children born to welfare mothers may make some taxpayers feel better, but it is an odd priority for the 1990s, after the percentage of AFDC cases with more than two children has fallen almost steadily for the past twenty years (from 50 percent in 1969 to 27 percent in 1990 [U.S. House of Representatives, Committee on Ways and Means, 1992, p. 669]). And it is surely odd for U.S. Senators to spend time debating work requirements for able-bodied persons in General Assistance programs when all but seven states already have such requirements and only one state (Alaska) provides any general assistance to the able-bodied. Will bad parents who do not monitor their children's school attendance and inoculations schedule become significantly better parents by threatened cuts to their welfare benefits? It seems unlikely. Perhaps some inner-city girls who become pregnant foreseeing hopeless prospects in life will stop getting pregnant by foreseeing the future loss of the new baby's welfare payment. Perhaps not.

The political exploitation is regrettable, but the public anxiety is real and both are so intertwined that it is probably impossible to prevent the former from feeding on the latter. Even before the 1992 Los Angeles riots over the acquittal on most charges of the officers involved in the brutal beating of a black motorist, Rodney King, Attorney General William Barr presented the annual crime report, showing a 5 percent national increase in violent crime, and concluded: "What we are seeing in the inner city [is] essentially the grim harvest of the Great Society . . . because we are seeing the breakdown of the family structure, largely contributed to by welfare policies" (*Washington Times,* April 27, 1992). Virtually identical comments from the Bush White House after the riots in South-Central Los Angeles produced a more critical backlash. But there is no mistaking the depth of public concern over what appears to be social disintegration in certain urban areas. It is a black Democratic assemblyman who has designed New Jersey's version of the New Paternalism in an attempt to deal with the breakdown of inner-city families and welfare dependency. In addition to the usual cuts for additional children and the removal of financial disincentives for fathers and stepfathers to stay with mothers, the New Jersey plan envisions a package of education, counseling, job training, child care, and other services tailored to each welfare family's full range of needs. Participation in these services is mandatory for continued receipt of cash assistance. Unlike the California referendum proposal, this type of welfare reform would cost more than the existing welfare system. Whether funding to sustain such an effort will be forthcoming is another matter.

So far, most of the New Paternalism initiatives remain merely proposals. As usual in our politics, the ink is hardly dry on the last round of plans to fix the "welfare mess" before the next round of tinkering has begun. Tough love initiatives were under way before most programs under the 1988 Family Support Act had even gotten off the ground. These FSA efforts in turn superseded a number of experimental state programs established under the 1981 regime of greater flexibility. But that regime was seen as a corrective to the preceding permissive income maintenance approach . . . which developed in response to impatience with Great Society opportunity schemes and weaknesses in the 1967 work incentive amendments. But then, too, the latter were reactions against the failed promises of the 1962 Public Welfare Amendments to provide intensive social services that would cure welfare dependency. Lest we forget, those 1962 amendments sought, in the words of their advocates in the Kennedy administration, to reverse "the whole approach to welfare from a straight cash handout operation to one in which the emphasis is on rehabilitation of those on relief and prevention ahead of time" (Patterson, 1986, p. 13). And this law, in turn, was reacting to local initiatives that sound strangely familiar. It was in 1960 that Louisiana cut off aid to families in which the mother since receiving AFDC benefits had given birth to another child. And it was in 1961 that the city government in Newburgh, New York, created a national stir by adopting policies that, among other things, cut benefits to unwed mothers who had another child, limited welfare for the able-bodied to three months, and required work from able-bodied adult males. Such are the cycles of our illusory policy commitments.

One might think there is something pathological in a political system that keeps promising itself to do what it manifestly does not do, namely, cure welfare dependency. In fact it is quite comprehensible, given the cramped view of political rationality that prevails. Politicians derive political rewards for proposing, not implementing, welfare reforms. The most attractive changes are those that promise to save taxpayers' money, offer prospects of dramatic change, and cater to the prevailing stereotypes.

In this regard social science does not help very much, despite its touching faith that knowing more facts will lead to more constructive change. Social science does not help mainly because it does not tell people what they want to hear. The general social science message, after decades of careful research, is that overcoming the employment and other problems of *long-term* welfare recipients is a costly and slow process that yields only modest increases in earnings and the very opposite of immediate budgetary savings (Michel and Levy, 1986; Gueron and Pauly, 1991). Strategies for social engineering to improve family behavior are even more uncertain and long-term, especially for those families with the most serious, compounded problems. These results are not the counsel of despair, but they do point to reforms that will be costly, slow, and modest in effect. In competing for support in the political arena, the odds of survival against promises that are cheap, splashy and short-term are not good.

But to attribute everything to the allure of political posturing is too cynical a reading of the evidence. We also keep making dubious promises to ourselves because unrelinquishable core commitments conflict with each other. As noted earlier, Americans want people to support themselves and to take personal responsibility for their dependents. That would be an easier aim to pursue if we did not also believe that there is a collective obligation to help the needy. But we do, and so the tension arises—anything we give to or do for people (needy or otherwise) interferes with what they would have done otherwise. And yet in real life, politicians who might advocate doing nothing for needy people so as to let the "natural" forces of scratching for survival operate would themselves not survive at the ballot box. Neither would politicians who preached that taxpayers owed another group of people a living. Of course in practice we often allow both circumstances—the survival of the fittest and the free ride—to occur. But these are not things Americans publicly endorse or design policies to promote. And so we keep making the promises.

Putting "Welfare" in Perspective

A more authentic politics of poverty policy would educate voters to face up to the fact that long-term "welfare dependency" is only a small part of the larger issues of poverty in and outside the nation's cities, within and across the races. Current "tough love" proposals are only the most recent manifestation of Americans' fixation on a small part of the poverty picture. One might think of four successively higher settings for looking at that picture.

First, at the center of the political debate on antipoverty policy is what might be called ghetto or "counter-culture" poverty. It is an image of able-bodied persons with virtually permanent dependence on cash welfare, people especially seen as unmarried minority women bearing children with a succession of minority men who are, at best, on the fringes of criminal activity. Refusing to talk about these perceptions for fear of raising the specter of racism does no one any good. In reality counter-culture poverty is only a small, but extremely intense, form of overall poverty conditions in the United States today. In 1989, as the New Paternalism was gathering strength, approximately 1.3 million families on AFDC were headed by minority, unmarried women—about one-third of the total number of families on AFDC, 23 percent of all poor families with children, and 38 percent of all poor female-headed families with children (U.S. House of Representatives, Committee on Ways and Means, 1991, pp. 629, 1145, 1147). Even these figures exaggerate the stereotypes Americans seem to worry about, because many persons are on AFDC for short, transitional periods (over time, about one-third of all AFDC recipients are on welfare for two years or less [Ellwood, 1986a]) and because at least a few are working full or part-time (the case for 8 percent of all unmarried mothers on AFDC in 1989). Many unmarried welfare mothers have also been found eager to participate in serious work and training programs when those are available (Gueron, 1987).

Another estimate of counter-culture poverty comes from studies of the "underclass"—people with very weak or nonexistent attachments to the labor market living in highly concentrated poverty areas of inner cities. In these ghettos, one finds the too familiar combination: meager employment opportunities, crime, dysfunctional families, welfare as a way of life. But again, if this is our political conception of the "welfare" problem or poverty, we are looking through the wrong end of the telescope. Different estimates of the size of the underclass abound, but a reasonable set of central estimates seems to fall in the range of 1 to 3 million people (see Chapter 5; Sawhill, 1988; Jencks and Peterson, 1991). Most of the increases in the population of these ghetto areas appear in a small number of major cities, particularly in the so-called Rust Belt. There is every reason to take the plight of these people seriously and to try to do something about it. But it is remarkable that this condition of 1 percent of Americans should dominate the public conversation about the 91 percent of all poor people, the 86 percent of poor Hispanics, the 79 percent of poor blacks who do not live in these unfortunate areas.

Second, overlapping and extending beyond the counter-culture poor are the "welfare poor"—a larger range of people distinguished by the fact that they are recipients of cash or cash equivalent payments from AFDC, General Assistance, and Food Stamp programs. This now amounts to upwards of 25 million Americans. These people, too, agitate the political debate and cause resentments, although not perhaps with the same intensity as the first set of underclass stereotypes. Some people, we can tell ourselves, are just down on their luck. But, again, the wariness of paying money to able-bodied adults prevents too much sympathy. We seem to make more allowances for the "welfare services" poor, the images of people using health services such as Medicaid or infant nutrition programs and educational services such as Head Start or JOBS programs. But by now we are entering areas of poverty that often do not register in public attention or serious political debates on poverty policy.

Third, pushing on beyond programmatic concerns, we come to the "income poor," those falling below the officially established poverty line of post-transfer, pretax income. Although this measure dominates expert policy analysis, it is safe to say that few other Americans think about the poor in terms of an income line that is set at three times the 1955 minimum food budget for families of different sizes, updated for price changes since then. Instead, hearing of an official poverty rate of 12 or 13 percent (about 31 million Americans in 1989), most ordinary people probably simply register a rough impression of the proportion of the population assumed to have inadequate levels of consumption. Over the last thirty years this official measuring line, which is fixed in absolute terms, has tended to fall relative to the median income of "mainstream" Americans (Ruggles, 1990). This has probably helped politically to isolate the official "income poor" as an aberrant group.

Equally important, "the line" has rendered more invisible the millions of people beyond official poverty who lead lives on the margins of economic distress and insecurity. These Americans, whom I will call the "unofficial poor," may live beyond the official line most of the time, but they share the diverse insecurity of people without much education, with jobs that do not pay very well or lead very far. They, like others, find their lives buffeted this way and that by joblessness, underemployment in a changing economy, illness that is uninsured or underinsured, day care that is a pastiche of unaffordable costs and improvisations, and any number of other problems. They need not cross a line to feel and be poor.

Methods for estimating the size of the unofficial poor population have used housing surveys, studies of public opinion regarding the minimum income needed to get along, construction of minimum economy budgets, and various techniques for updating the official 1955 poverty measure to take account of current standards of food expenditures in family budgets. The results converge on a threshold of self-sufficiency in the range of 140 to 170 percent of the official poverty line. Taking the midpoint (155 percent) yields a rough picture of a zone where millions of marginalized Americans live ($20,660 for a family of four in 1990). At this income level there is barely enough for the lowest-cost necessities such as food, housing, clothing, transportation, and medical care, and nothing at all for what better-off Americans take for granted—meals out, vacations, child care, lessons or allowances for children, haircuts, and so on. Below this level in 1989 were six million full-time workers and five and a half million part-time workers whose families totaled 30 million people (Schwarz and Volgy, 1992). But again this is just another "line," and lines must exclude as well as include, necessarily failing to capture something of who we are and how we live.

Fourth, a still larger picture would take account of the fastest-growing category of workers—part-time, temporary, or subcontracted employees, workers whose economic fortunes fluctuate from one year to the next with minimum employer fringe benefits. Although a few of these people are well-off consultants and the like, a good case can be made for calling most of this group the "contingent poor." Most such workers are women and minorities in low-wage jobs with few if any employer health or pension benefits and meager career prospects. Many are also vulnerable to employer cost-cutting strategies that close off access to public support programs. The Internal Revenue Service has estimated that over one-third of employers deliberately misclassify employees as "independent contractors" to avoid paying unemployment compensation and Social Security taxes as well as workers' compensation (duRivage, 1992). Such unpredictable, contingent employment outside the career currents of the mainstream labor market is now estimated to embrace 27 million to 37 million workers, or about one-third of the total U.S. work force (ibid.). The 1980s and 1990s have presented clear signs of economic insecurity creeping through not only the working classes but the middle classes as well.

The Welfare Fixation

Poverty politics is generally like an inverted pyramid leveraged from its narrowest point. What is politically salient varies inversely with the size of the poverty population in question. We construct the political metaphors of poverty from the two or three million in the tip of the base and barely notice the tens of millions beyond that who are struggling in quiet desperation. Any explanation for the fixation on counter-culture and welfare poor clearly does not lie in the number or audibility of the voices involved, for few of the diverse poor are heard in our normal political process, though advocacy groups try. The explanation stems from the visibility, acceptability, and affordability of counter-culture poverty.

Counter-culture poverty is the most visible form of poverty both in the social reality mediated through television and in the imagery of our mind's eye. The concentrated human problems here provide more than their share of the dramatic events and social horrors that are deemed newsworthy. It is an imagery of destitution, violence, and Otherness that slips nicely into our stereotypes of what poverty is supposed to look like. And because two-thirds of those in urban areas of concentrated poverty are black, it has a face many Americans expect to see, despite the fact that only approximately 6 percent of all blacks are among the ghetto poor, or that two-thirds of poor blacks in metropolitan areas live outside the worst areas of concentrated poverty (Jencks and Peterson, 1991, p. 464).

Counter-culture and welfare poverty are also the most threatening, because the former is associated with crime and social disorganization and the latter conjures a specter of long-term dependence on welfare checks that contradicts our most deeply held and widely shared norms about work and personal responsibility. This is not what Americans are supposed to be like, and it nags at us.

Despite the fixation, we do not pour resources into dealing with the problem.

This relates to a third reason it is politically convenient to be preoccupied with this part of poverty: it seems a tidy and even inexpensive way to think about poverty. The attractiveness of talking about this sliver of the poverty spectrum is especially enhanced from a New Paternalism perspective. Since decreeing behavioral standards is not costly, and since welfare spending is said to foster dependency, family breakup, and other ills, serendipity strikes. It seems we can do more good by spending less money, demean the poor less by demanding more from them. In truth, serious attacks on underclass behavior would require expensive forms of bureaucratic oversight that could easily prove more costly than welfare checks. Hence new paternalism proposals often do not go beyond political window dressing.

There are others who contend that the problems of ghetto poverty are so serious, so life-threatening from one generation to the next, that overwhelming attention to this aspect of poverty is well justified. They argue, with good evidence I think, that what exists in such urban areas is not this or that problem but a complex of interconnected problems—inferior schools, unstable families, joblessness, crime, discrimination, and so on—that compound to the point of extinguishing any real hope of a better life for young people (Jencks, 1992). Dealing in any realistic way with this socioeconomic catastrophe is going to be costly and will demand a long-term commitment to people whom many Americans would not want as neighbors. This is the dirty little secret buried in the shelves of social science poverty studies.

The Paradox of Fixated Inaction

This kind of social realism, however, immediately encounters certain problems of Realpolitik. The first is that inner cities have increasingly become minority enclaves that appear more distant from "mainstream" white America. Although this has increased the opportunity for blacks to hold public office, it has not helped to increase cities' economic resources or their political clout in national politics. On the contrary, cities that once were essential building blocks in coalitions capable of delivering votes are now more or less minority voices pleading for funds and delivering a smaller and smaller share of the votes that decide national elections. The brute fact is that both Republican leaders and Democratic strategists shaken by the loss of white Reagan Democrats can calculate, respectively, that inner-city votes may be dismissed or taken for granted. Both parties know that winning in national politics today depends on appealing, not to the South-Central Los Angeles, but to the Simi Valleys of America.

Second, for a variety of reasons, including the need to maintain law and order, political interest in inner cities and welfare reform often peaks when budgets are tight. The feeling that "we need to do something about these people" comes along just when serious efforts—which do require serious money—will appear too costly. It becomes easier to tell ourselves we have the will but not the wallet, forgetting that it takes an act of will to find and open the wallet. Politically speaking, overselling short-term fixes for long-term welfare dependency works better.

There is a third area where social and political reality collide. Any realistic, comprehensive effort to attack concentrated poverty entails a package of education, employment, medical, and early childhood development services that would be light years beyond what tens of millions of non–ghetto poor have available. Economic logic says that many of the official, unofficial, and contingent poor would then have an "incentive" to enter this welfare system. By contrast political logic says a more likely result would be to intensify class and racial resentment against the ghetto poor. How will the training, job placement, family support, and all the other services for those on welfare look to those many millions of other Americans who are not on welfare but need the same services? In a country where most people already feel that "there is more concern for the welfare bum than the hard worker," the political logic of resentment would seem the stronger force.

It would be difficult to exaggerate the politically corrosive effects of the Welfare Fixation for poverty politics. In essence, it undermines the possibility of a cross-race, cross-class coalition for antipoverty policy. And it does so from *both* sides of the racial divide. Whites, including poor whites, can use the "welfare dependency problem" (the polite term) to build and reenforce racial stereotypes. And many blacks, although they will among themselves criticize behavior associated with counter-culture poverty, find it very difficult to engage in the public conversation about the problem for fear of feeding prejudice and breaking minority solidarity in a white world. As a result the political systems' very ability to think about poverty turns in on itself. The larger picture and the swath of hardship cutting across the races virtually disappear from view.

The growing movement to cut AFDC benefits to the "after-born" (additional children born to mothers once they are on welfare) aptly illustrates the perversity of the situation. As noted earlier, the political priority being given to this reform does not stem from the size of the problem (given the twenty-year trend toward fewer children for AFDC mothers, never mind the new incentive the proposal offers for abortion). Rather it touches a nerve because of popular images of reckless taxpayer-subsidized procreation among poor minority women. The argument used in support of the plan, first by black New Jersey Assemblyman Wayne R. Bryant and then by other less well intended persons, sounds as if it is putting the welfare poor in a larger social policy framework of mainstream expectations. But it is actually doing the opposite and it *has* to do the opposite so long as our attention is confined to the narrow slice of the problem called "welfare dependency." The argument goes like this:

disallowing increased AFDC benefits to adult recipients who have additional children is [also] about responsibility. It suggests that individuals on welfare can make responsible decisions. Life is about decisions, and decisions often revolve around the family. A middle-class wage earner does not go to his boss to say, "I'm having another child, so I'm entitled to a raise." (U.S. Senate, Subcommittee on Social Security and Family Policy, 1992)

Of course this statement is reasonable, as far as it goes. But it is precisely because wages are not adjusted to take account of the number of children dependent on the workers' wage that social reformers over fifty years ago urged the creation of children's allowances. Although the United States is one of the few developed nations without such general cash allowances, the basic argument dismissed by the assemblyman does explain why U.S. taxpayers who have another child are entitled to a tax-subsidized increase in take-home pay (through dependents' deductions). It explains why low income earners are entitled to a larger Earned Income Tax Credit if they have two children rather than one and why additional dependents' benefits are paid under social insurance programs. The point is not that AFDC mothers should be supported with reckless abandon (they aren't), but that our preoccupation with a "welfare" image blinds us to a larger view of child support across a much larger spectrum of the population.

Stylized Arguments

The Welfare Fixation is the leading but not the only stylized argument that enervates poverty politics. Other generally unconstructive debates have to do with universalism, racial reparations, and paternalism.

Universal or Targeted?

Should social programs be open to all or target those in greatest need? At issue here is the problem of assembling a political constituency that can sustain solid support—that is, cross-class and cross-race support—for serious antipoverty commitments.

Advocates of universalism argue that focusing narrowly on the poor cannot generate the broad constituency that is needed (Skocpol, 1991). To supply financial resources and political protection, social programs must have something to offer the middle class. The negative fixation on financially starved and unpopular AFDC and General Assistance programs, together with the continued political invulnerability of broad social insurance programs, is used as prime evidence for the universalist case.

By contrast, advocates of targeted measures claim that it makes more sense, particularly in an era of tight budgets and huge deficits, to concentrate resources on those most in need. Moreover, unless they are to provide indiscriminate hand-outs, universal programs must be based on some form of earned entitlement. Those most in need may never get to the point of earning such benefits or may not have much chance of doing so without programs of intensive support focused on their needs (Greenstein, 1991).

Good counterarguments can be made on each side, depending on how one views the politics of the situation. Universalists contend that although budgets are tight, fiscal constraints will be eased and taxpayers more willing to pay for pro-grams if they themselves can see they are deriving benefits from the programs. Targeters answer that higher payroll taxes associated with universal social insur-ance programs are already crowding out public tolerance for the general revenues needed to finance programs concentrating on the poor. Universalists can show that the Social Security system does more to reduce the number of people in pov-erty than do the targeted, means-tested programs combined (thinking here of in-come poverty). Targeters can show that providing limited benefits to many people may be politically popular but that it is wholly ineffective in addressing the prob-lems of the most seriously disadvantaged (thinking here of counter-culture and welfare poverty).

Race-Neutral or Race-Specific?

What might seem a rather abstract academic debate has acquired a sharp edge in recent years on the equivalent matter of racial targeting in social programs. Should programs become more focused on deprived minorities or more race-neutral? Mirroring an old argument within the black community between integra-tionist and segregationist approaches, the two sides differ fundamentally over po-litical strategy. Thus some believe that policies targeted on racial minorities are needed to confront racism directly by appealing both to the decency of the larger society to honor the American Dream and to the self-interest of that society in avoiding the costs associated with minority underclass conditions. Equally thoughtful people on the other side would shift the emphasis to programs that are more clearly race-neutral. They argue that broader approaches are needed to con-front problems of economic inequality that affect many groups and that would still oppress blacks even if racism disappeared. Moreover, the growing economic problems facing working and middle-class whites reduce the likelihood that moral appeals or cost/benefit calculations will make majorities give up shrinking resources to help minorities. Such spreading problems do, however, increase the chances of winning wider support for social programs that encompass the majority's growing economic anxieties (Tollet, 1991; Wilson, 1991b).

Experience offers no unambiguous proof for any of these positions, and in practice there may be less difference between them than meets the eye. Universal

social insurance approaches with an earned entitlement have certainly proved politically popular, though support can slip if doubts creep in that people who could
work are inappropriately claiming benefits (for example, disability and unemployment insurance). Advocates recognize that targeting can occur within universalism, as it does in the Social Security formulae tilted toward low income workers. So the real question is often a practical political judgment as to how far to go
in nudging such systems to give disproportionate help to those at the bottom without antagonizing those toward the top of the benefit structure. Comprehensive
programs selectively applied make most sense where a broadly shared need can
also be especially intense for some people. This seems to be the direction we are
moving in with regard to child support enforcement/assurance for all single parents with child support awards.

Likewise, most advocates of targeting recognize the importance of a critical
mass of potential beneficiaries who are regarded as deserving of aid. But as we
have seen, aid must be widely deemed by the public as appropriate for their particular situation. AFDC—seen as cash assistance for often able-bodied, nonworking parents—has a very difficult time fitting that requirement. By contrast the
Earned Income Tax Credit, which is really a wage subsidy for working parents
with children, does not. Not surprisingly, spending for EITC in the first five years
of the 1990s is slated to be four times the amount set aside for a five-year period
of implementing the AFDC-based Family Support Act reforms.

It would make no sense, in the name of political constituency building, to fritter
away resources on a comprehensive program for, say, reading enhancement when
it is people suffering from illiteracy who really need the help. But conversely,
where a form of aid is seen as appropriate to a more widely shared need, it makes
little political sense to continue focusing help on only the narrowest band of the
poor, people who may indeed have some characteristics that are not attractive to
middle America. The viable approach is to orient programs to the kind of need,
not a narrow category of people. A prime example of an area where constituencies could be targeted but broadened is labor market policy, which does offer the
kind of assistance Americans consider appropriate for able-bodied, needy adults.
Enhanced vocational education, job training, and employment services would
likely gain political support by moving beyond the current focus on AFDC recipients to incorporate the unofficial and contingent poor (non–college-bound
youths, single mothers not on welfare, and so on). With today's racial minorities
destined to be over one-quarter of America's work force in another twelve years
and with even moderate income people threatened by structural economic
changes, it is surely time to revisit the discussion of manpower policy that was cut
short in the 1960s (U.S. General Accounting Office, 1991b).

On the question of racial targeting or race-sensitive policies, the evidence is fairly clear. Except where directly linked as remedies for past acts of discrimination, race-specific social policy is unlikely to command widespread support. This is certainly true of conventional "social welfare" programs outside the realm of affirmative action, court-ordered busing and antidiscrimination lawsuits. As we have seen, the public draws distinctions of deservedness and appropriate services for different kinds of need along a number of different scales. But politically speaking, minority racial status is not considered ipso facto a category of deservedness for special assistance.

For some thoughtful people this seems excruciatingly unfair, given the long course of our history when race understood as blackness has been used pervasively and automatically to ascribe undeservedness in all walks of life. Justice is seen to demand reparation. However that may be, there seems no realistic political prospect for building antipoverty policy on white guilt for racism. Before many Americans worried about racism, redistributive claims by ethnic whites never made much headway. Asked at the beginning of this century how he liked living in America, a Slavic immigrant replied, "My people do not live in America. They live underneath America" (Wiebe, 1967, p. 9). If whites in America have never been able to sustain a claim on the dominant white population for a major redistribution of resources, expecting a different reaction toward poor blacks is fanciful.

Of course it is possible for social welfare programs to appear racially targeted in a de facto sense simply because the poorest residents in areas of concentrated poverty are overwhelmingly members of minorities. Some of their needs can be linked to the growing employment problems of others with limited education and weak job skills. And where possible this linkage should be made, on grounds of both political strategy and American aspirations for an inclusive citizenship. But full-scale attacks on ghetto poverty will inevitably mean targeting resources disproportionately on minorities. Whether such efforts are seen as pro-black preferences or an act of solidarity with the country's children and its future will depend heavily on how political leaders help to educate the public.

Paternalistic or Permissive?

A final mode of stylized debate surrounds what some see as a "new politics of poverty," a politics based on a more assertive stance toward using public policy to direct the lives of the poor (Mead, 1992). According to this view, there is movement toward a new paternalism in which conservatives and Republicans once wary of government are increasingly willing to use federal power to make "tough love" demands on poor people to live up to mainstream values of work and personal responsibility. The traditional New Deal face-off between the political left and right is said to have been a conflict over meat and potato economic demands for government to do more or less. Providing opportunity was thought to be the key. The new politics is said to supplant this traditional economic battle of left and right with a new conflict dividing "soft" liberals, who are solicitous in expecting little from helpless people, and "hard" conservatives, who are willing to enforce demands that the poor meet the normal social expectations that everyone else in America does. Rather than simply expanding opportunities, "government must motivate poor adults to seize the opportunities that exist" (Mead, 1989, p. 22).

The other side of this set-piece debate scoffs that any such idea of a new politics is the old power of privilege dressed up in new clothes, a device for abandoning people in need. These observers argue that behavioral problems of the poor are embedded in a larger system of economic and social disadvantage that ultimately destroys motivation for a better life. Priority should be given, not to insisting on certain forms of behavior, but to changing the environment so that decent education, jobs, and other realistic opportunities are opened up to people in otherwise hopeless surroundings. Until that is done, assumptions of the poor's competence in a hostile environment are equivalent to the defense argument that Rodney King was always in control of what was happening to him.

And so the debate goes on. Welfare with a smile, or a scowl? New paternalists of the new politics can argue that liberals have a professional and bureaucratic stake in keeping the poor dependent and in telling minorities what they want to hear about victimization and helplessness. Opponents can counter that conservatives make a virtue of indifference and have a convenient way of discovering that the only effective approaches are ones that do not cost much. Why is it, they ask, that the "hard" perspective on obligation and personal responsibility falls so readily on the poor but that S&L looters, the well-heeled shiftless and other privileged people always seem to fall outside the purview of paternalists' moral policing?

Clearly this debate risks repeating the dead-end argument that has gone on for decades between cultural versus structural interpretations of poverty. Any impartial observer is likely to want to interrupt with the immortal words of the Certs commercial: "Stop, you're both right." Obviously there is something terribly wrong when approximately half of all persons on welfare are dependent for four or more years (Ellwood, 1986a). These are precisely the kind of people targeted for the working and training experiences in the Family Support Act. But it is also true that in 1990, of the 2 million married couples with children living below the official poverty line, 63 percent of the adults were working at least some of the year, and over a third had work levels approaching the equivalent of full-time work all year. Likewise, half of the 3.7 million poor single mothers with children worked some of the year, and almost a fifth were in, or close to, full-time, full-year employment (U.S. House of Representatives, Committee on Ways and

Means, 1992, p. 1283). If anything, the adults in such poor families with children were working more in 1990 than in 1975. To define the poverty problem as simply a matter of unmotivated, nonfunctional people who need government's tough love to make them seize the opportunities surrounding them is absurd. But the debate between pro- and anti-paternalists is unlikely to disappear, if only because there are powerful ideological agendas and political constituencies behind different sides of this stylized argument.

In reality, not much about the "new politics" is particularly new. As we have seen, in the long history of the poor law and poverty policy, there has always been a combination of positive and punitive measures, of insisting that poor people behave in certain ways and of trying to change the conditions that inhibit their ability to behave in those ways. What has changed in recent years is that the paternalist position, which traditionally was a dominant element in the local administration of welfare, has found voice at the national level. This is not so much due to any profound changes in liberalism and conservatism, as to the fact that in the last twenty-five years the national government has been given the major role in framing welfare rules that once were mainly a local concern.

As we have seen, this role shift has occurred in a somewhat back-handed way. Since the late 1960s, the courts have interpreted the law to mean that states are allowed to set only those eligibility rules that Congress authorizes (rather than the pre-1960s position of allowing states to set any rules Congress had not specifically prohibited). Rather than trying to reverse this general interpretive stance of the courts, Congress and the White House have proceeded to issue individual eligibility directives. Whether or not one calls it a new politics, putting the issue of welfare eligibility standards on the congressional agenda naturally causes partisan debate and difficult compromises. The result is evident in the hybrid quality of the Family Support Act as a semipermissive, semipaternalistic type of legislation, as well as in the new prominence of the federal rule-waiver process as a political tool.

Going beyond these stylized debates to find common ground requires holding not one but several ideas in mind at the same time. It is appropriate and necessary in a healthy political society to demand that welfare recipients—and others—play by the rules of work effort, lawfulness, and family responsibility. But the chief victims of those members of the underclass who do not play by the rules do not live in the suburbs. The primary victims are the many decent and disadvantaged people in inner cities who have to live with the miscreants in their midst. But enforcing behavior rules on unmotivated people leaves untouched the bulk of the "welfare" and the even more widespread "poverty" problems in which tens of millions of Americans are entangled. Is our politics up to finding such common ground?

The Poverty of Politics

Whether policymaking moves beyond stylized debates depends largely on political leadership. Politics, perhaps everywhere but certainly in our modern media-saturated society, is a struggle for control of the narrative, the stories that are told by which we understand ourselves. Whatever the set-piece arguments on "welfare," targeting, or the new paternalism, the hardship and suffering of poor people are real, and so too are the dangers of doing too much, doing too little, or doing foolish, self-defeating things in antipoverty policy. The task of political leadership is to help us see these dangers, to weigh them with realism, but not be paralyzed by them. On something as deeply divisive as race and class, the leadership obviously has to come from many quarters, not just from a voice from Washington. But such constructive engagement can certainly be inspired or devalued at the level of national political leadership.

According to one view, people get the leaders they deserve. Why don't the politicians and government really do something about the impoverishment and growing social cleavages? Perhaps because they are our representatives and know we prefer living as we do. Yet that is only a half-truth. Politicians not only represent us. They also represent us to ourselves. To a large extent society sees and makes itself through the stories politicians weave.

Perhaps most of the time democratic political leaders can be expected to do what they do best: follow. But they do have a choice. Inherent in leadership is the choice to awaken the slumbering potential that always exists for either divisiveness or inclusion, to exploit or to heal. More damaging than any welfare dependency in recent decades has been a political dependency on hidden race politics—one side using a coded language of family values and law and order while the other side uses a politics of denial to avoid talking about the self-destructive behavior of a minority within minority constituencies. An educating leadership that at least tries to live in truth will tell us that antipoverty policy requires a significant investment of tax dollars and private effort, part of it going to help people whom some Americans despise. It will risk teaching patience and realistic expectations and determined hope. But what about the political context that now facilitates or inhibits such leadership?

A Deteriorating Political Setting

After twenty-five years urban poverty, which in the meantime aroused little political attention, has come back on the national agenda. It has done so not in the genteel way that policy experts and politicians "discovered" poverty in the 1960s, but with the wrenching experience of watching human beings prey on each other. Each group—black, white, Hispanic, Asian—now has a public iconography of videotaped victimization: the black man beaten into the ground by a circle of police; the white and Hispanic motorists dragged out and beaten by young black men; the sobbing Asians overrun by Hispanic and black looters; the black girl shot from behind by the Asian storekeeper. In all of this there is both an invitation to tribalism and the opportunity for a better healing, and in this there is nothing new. Alfred North Whitehead observed that little separates catharsis from self-destruction: "The major advances in civilization are processes which all but wreck the society in which they occur."

The political context for antipoverty policy has changed dramatically since the 1960s. Some changes are obvious, others less so. To survey this changed context is to sense how much the politics of poverty is bound up with the poverty of our politics.

The most obvious transformation in the setting for antipoverty efforts in the 1990s compared with the 1960s is the immense inertial weight of federal budget deficits. An annual deficit that was around 1 percent or less of GNP for the first eight years of the 1960s is now four to five times in relative size. As a percentage of our national economic resources, we are currently spending more on unproductive interest payments on the national debt than we spent on *all* human resource programs (AFDC, Food Stamps, health care, education, job training, social services, and so on, but excluding Social Security) at the height of the Great Society in the 1960s (U.S. Office of Management and Budget, 1988, tables 3.1, 3.2).

Confidence in continued economic prosperity was high in the 1960s, a fact that no doubt made many Americans feel they could afford to be relatively generous toward the poor. Today a widespread worry prevails that there are more fundamental problems in the U.S. economy and its competitiveness in the world than will be cured by the next economic recovery. But as I suggested at the outset, these differences are not wholly negative for antipoverty policy. Potentially at least, a more general recognition of a shared economic vulnerability may broaden our perspective on poverty. Moreover, the aura of affluence made it possible, with a brief burst of unlocked energy in 1964–65, to enact legislative victories for antipoverty policy "on the cheap," so to speak. Since nothing else seemed to need be given up in return, poverty policy did not have to build any particularly deep political commitments to what was being done. Today there will have to be a much greater struggle over tradeoffs, more debate and delays; but that also offers a possibility for gradual political education on the subject to occur. The ground is harder to work, but if we can bring ourselves to do something the roots may go deeper than they did in the 1960s.

And now the Cold War has ended. Might this free up the resources needed for new policy initiatives? That remains to be seen. One favorable result is that liberal reformers now have less to fear from the old Red Scare, soft-on-communism tactics once used against them. But this cuts the other way too in the sense that closing ranks as a nation has always had greater appeal when facing some foreign foe. Early in this century arguments about "national efficiency" were frequently used to justify social reform measures that could be claimed to improve the manpower stock against European competitors. In the 1930s and early 1940s the need for social reform was counterpoised to threats from fascist regimes. And today we tend to forget how often social reform initiatives in the late 1950s and early 1960s were grounded in hawkish Cold War claims of standing up to the Russians. Today there is no dramatic foreign threat pressuring us to act on our interests as one people. As we will see in a moment, the slow-motion challenge of harsher economic competition with other democratic nations is not quite the same thing.

Another obvious difference is that in the 1960s there was an immense confidence in the ability of government to solve problems. Those over forty-five can probably remember the faith in "systematic thinking for social action," the self-assured way each problem had a program for an answer (usually of a self-implementing nature), how Rand-style policy sciences would be switched from problems of missile deployment to attacks on urban policy. By now we have had a generation of government-bashing and hard experience with the intractability of many social problems. People have become inured to the idea that government policies backfire, creating more problems than they solve. Government is said to be just another special interest. Significantly, there is evidence that those who are most inclined to think there is a collective responsibility to address social welfare problems are precisely the ones who now have the least confidence in government and participate the least politically (Bobo, 1991).

Then too in the 1960s, at least for a while, there was still an afterglow of the civil rights movement. Blacks and whites of goodwill had come together and were righting the self-evident wrong of publicly sanctioned segregation. By the end of the 1960s much of that glow had been consumed in the larger fires burning in the nation's inner cities. If anything, the events in Los Angeles in late spring 1992 were an even more bitter convulsion. But again there is a counterpoint.

A less superficial faith in the power of government to fix deep-seated social problems may help prevent the political over-promising that corrodes realistic faith, a promising that occurred too easily in the 1960s. Though many are more bitter after the events of the last thirty years, perhaps many are also less naive about racial integration and can begin to see the magnitude of the country's racial problem. Seeing the truth of the bitterness may start a more authentic healing process than does pretending a dream.

Finally, the political gears linking ordinary people and public policymakers seem broken in the 1990s in a way that was not true in the 1960s. This sounds odd when one thinks back to the protests and demonstrations of those times. But such then-unconventional practices were expressing their own form of hope that ordinary citizens could make a difference in the larger political system. In the last thirty years, one of the clearest trends in opinion polling is the growth of the real majority party in the country—the party of the withdrawn, people who sense that what they think and want plays little part in how things get done. In the 1980s, for the first time since such data began to be gathered in the 1950s, people's overall partisan identification ceased to track with their policy "mood" regarding what policymakers should be doing (Stimson, 1991, pp. 93–94). Quite possibly this was a reflection of people's sense that something was disconnected, unable to transmit motion from citizens through the machinery of an insider system.

Some would attribute all this to the growing role of money in politics. Others point to the increasingly sophisticated use of the media, or the slick candidate packaging and issue positioning of campaigns by political consultants. These critics contend that American democracy has become a focus group writ large, where people are not consulted as citizens but probed and tested as consumers to discover what will "sell" politically. Still others fault the highly credentialed journalists, policy experts, and political insiders who carry on the public debate in an echo chamber that leaves the average citizen voiceless. A few even suggest that the problem lies with an increasingly rootless citizenry governed by whims and wishful thinking to which politicians respond only too well (Dionne, 1991; Ehrenhalt, 1992; Greider, 1992).

No doubt there are many forces at work. The point is that advocates of antipoverty policy face a political setting in which many people see politics as shrinking in meaning. It seems a realm of tactical calculation and smallness of spirit, in which the truth is not so much considered and rejected as not even regarded as relevant. Many ordinary people wonder how they can renew from the outside an insiders' system that cannot renew itself. Americans have never had much faith in government, but they have traditionally had a good deal of faith in their politics, for that has seemed, with all its warts, to be their own handiwork of self-government. This feeling of ownership over the political process has greatly diminished since the 1960s.

A New Beginning?

All of this matters because antipoverty policy is an act of collective self-confidence. It asks of people that they feel not only dissatisfied with the way things are but also convinced that something positive can be done about impoverished lives. History suggests that such dissatisfaction, conviction, and the will to stick to the difficult task does not come from more and better social science findings about poverty conditions. Continually documenting the social decay may even be a desensitizing process ("What, another report on child poverty?"). Not

being self-interpreting, facts acquire force only through a political struggle of mo-
bilizing, organizing, and alliance building—struggles where history is often made
by some people winning and others losing. Similarly moral suasion, as Martin
Luther King, Jr., eventually concluded, can only take an antipoverty movement
so far. The resistance offered by privilege and indifference has to be politically
engaged. That is why the poor, being weak, have to be part of a larger coalition—
whether within the Democratic or Republican party or some new political formation—seeking a politics of inclusion.

Given this situation, the Clinton presidency as a focus for antipoverty leadership finds itself in a peculiar position. On the one hand the Democrats' 1992 campaign captured the public mood for change. It seemed to affirm and renew an
activist approach to economic and social problems.

On the other hand, people's distrust of government and social tinkering has
remained strong, and the new president did not enter Washington with an effective public mandate. For all his attacks on Reaganomics, candidate Clinton could
never launch a thoroughgoing attack on the prevailing political order commensu-
rate with the popular revulsion against that order. This is because Clinton, his
colleagues in the Democratic Congressional Leadership Council, the myriad affiliated interest groups, consultants, lobbyists, and Democratic congressional
leadership are themselves a major part of the received order. Hence Clinton's
prospect for achieving major policy changes rests on traditionally weak grounds,
not simply because he received only 43 percent of the vote but, more important,
because he leads no popular movement to "throw the bums out" and transform
policy and politics as usual.

By all accounts President Clinton and his advisors enjoy policy analysis and
thinking through government strategies to deal with social problems. They have
shown themselves adept at designing new proposals based on the most progressive social science research, and some of the leading social policy researchers in
the country have taken prominent policymaking positions in the administration.
Proposed reforms in health insurance, child support enforcement, and the Earned
Income Tax Credit will help many of the poor who do not fall into the underclass
and welfare dependent categories. On welfare reform, in particular, the administration's agenda embraces the leading academic ideas of the last fifteen years:
supporting families who leave welfare with child care, transportation, education,
and training for specific jobs in return for a maximum time limit on how long an
able-bodied parent may remain on welfare. But Clinton's skill and interest in
dealing with complex policy issues may be a toxic aptitude unless the larger political case can be made for doing such things. And this implies a motive force
more like a red-blooded political movement than a policy seminar. Why should
Americans feel antipoverty efforts are worth fighting for, paying taxes for, and
sticking with over the long run? In short, why should they care?

Two prudential answers are the ones that are most frequently given: one based on economics, the other on social stability. The economic rationale cites our competitive need for a fully productive work force, a work force increasingly non-white and increasingly under global pressure to improve all its human resources (Reich, 1991). There is also the generational economic argument that retiring Baby Boomers in the next century will be dependent in their old age on the productive power of a relatively smaller number of workers paying social security taxes. The argument for antipoverty policy on grounds of social stability is equally obvious. A great deal of the crime and other antisocial behavior threatening the rest of society is the natural by-product of deprived and desperate living conditions.

Neither of these prudential appeals to enlightened self-interest strikes me as a particularly powerful way of energizing political commitments to antipoverty policy, however. Economically, it appears that many Americans can prosper very nicely in the international economy while other Americans live in a virtual Third World economy. The lack of any shared economic stake is precisely what is revealed in the growing income inequality of the last twenty years. Unless Americans are already predisposed to understand themselves and the nation's problems as being part of a single society—a society of people mutually concerned about each other—the foreign economic challenge has at least as much potential for pulling us apart as for pulling us together. And to ask people to invest in poor people now because of Social Security revenue and spending projections twenty to thirty years from now is asking for an uncommonly large dose of enlightenment in enlightened self-interest.

When it comes to ensuring social stability, the prospects for antipoverty policy are not more promising. Attacking the conditions that breed riots and non–white collar crime is a slow and expensive process. The much easier and therefore more likely answer is to insist on better ways of protecting "us" from "them." The turmoil produced by clashes among groups of have-nots is not something that usually reaches the suburbs, and the indirect psychological threat it poses is more likely to be met by privileged persons' redoubled efforts to buy physical protection for themselves. In any case, fear-inspired social reforms are always a dubious basis for building social cohesion.

Knowing ever more facts about social marginalization, prudential reasoning about self interest—this does not get to the heart of poverty politics. Why should we do anything about these facts? If we can get by or do well without these other strangers who are Americans, why shouldn't we? The basic question is, why should we care about each other, care in any concrete, action-forcing way? These "why should" questions ultimately find answers only within the moral will of a political community.[6] It is "moral" because the questions are about valuations, not facts, about judgments of worthiness applied not only to individuals but also to how a society comports itself. It is "political" because we are the subject, a collective enterprise aimed at expressing itself through joint action.

If antipoverty policy does not come from some larger framework within which we understand ourselves, then we will be left with shallow gestures. The truth is that many people care not at all whether single mothers enter the work force and get their lives together for their children, but only that they not absorb tax dollars on welfare. Many care less that young black men in inner cities have jobs that can support a family than that these young men not loot or shoot people outside the inner cities. Many who doing well are not interested in lifting others as they climb. Only the deeply engaged moral commitment of a political community can sustain antipoverty efforts through the inevitable policy frustrations. Without it, why try anything until we are sure what works? Without it, every policy evaluation of program failure will be an excuse for giving up rather than a reason for trying harder.

The problem is that we have come to a point where any talk of "moral commitment in a political community" sounds like pure bromide to modern ears. In part this reflects the continuing reverberations from America's particularly devastating experiences from the Kennedy through the Nixon years. It was an experience of high hopes and assassinations, promises and lies that made many people wonder and keep wondering if they really knew themselves. And it is many of the same people, now in their middle years and running much of society, who will have trouble responding to any call of moral leadership. Against the assiduous cadence of self-doubt, any high-sounding talk of morality is suspect, the very language trivialized and demeaned in modern political campaigns.

The difficulty is more than generational or confined to the 1960s hangover, however. Whether we use the term secularization, the modern identity, "culture wars," or some other phrase, the fact is that during this century our society, like others in the West, has been changing in a way that makes it extremely awkward to have any public conversation about the moral foundations of social reform (Neuhaus, 1984; Turner, 1985; Hunter, 1991; Wuthnow, 1991). It is as if there is no center, no frame of shared assumptions to argue through the politics of inclusion. Even that sounds too sermonic, for many Americans seem to think that "shared vision" must be a code word for imposing values and oppression. Instead, membership in racial, ethnic, and gender groups is thought by many to constitute the most fundamental truth of each person's experience.

A hundred or more years ago the "old paternalists" were more sure about their moral bearings. Their preaching of moral values to the poor was part of a larger preaching throughout society, including the social gospel and the stewardship of wealth doctrine to the rich. Today's "new paternalists" lack both that sense of righteousness that would apply norms of responsibility to the well-off and the deference that was once forthcoming from the poorly off. Therefore tough love will probably not go as far as the conservatives hope and the liberals fear. Clearly we are much more interested in preaching to "them" about proper behavior than to ourselves about the irresponsibility of a larger society celebrating vulgar sexuality, violence, and self-indulgence. Perhaps it is hidden recognition of this hypocrisy—one of the few things still capable of embarrassing modern sensitivities—that keeps us from preaching to the poor with much conviction. Paternalism is not what it used to be.

The civil rights movement culminating in the 1960s certainly drew on this older tradition of religious and moral commitment to shape claims for political action. Perhaps so much of poverty policy became translated into a civil rights agenda because it has been the only claim energized with moral force in recent times. But for many people that force now seems expended and transformed into special group pleading.

We know we cannot go back to that time. And the history seems too heavy to keep carrying. There are no new beginnings, but can we act as if we are making a new beginning? There is authenticity in that question asked by another Mr. King, a badly beaten, "underclass" black man: "Can't we get along?" A new beginning? Moral commitments to a politics of inclusion and antipoverty policy will have to grow from inside our national life, and cannot be remembered, shamed, or blamed into being. Are there still the wellsprings in modern American society for a genuine renewal from within? Social science is mute on such questions.

CHAPTER SIXTEEN

The Nature, Causes, and Cures of Poverty: Accomplishments from Three Decades of Poverty Research and Policy

ROBERT HAVEMAN

The chapters in this volume describe the major developments in poverty research over the past three decades; they stand as a clear statement of what we have learned in a variety of areas. They also contain suggestions regarding what we should do, based upon what we have learned. Here I summarize and assess these contributions.[1]

Lessons Learned

The major lessons of this book can be briefly summarized as follows.

Rising poverty rates. The nation has experienced two decades of stagnant earnings and family incomes, and growing inequality in both. As a result, we have witnessed secularly rising poverty rates (irrespective of how poverty is measured). For some groups—primarily the elderly and college-educated workers—poverty has fallen; for other groups—primarily less-educated workers, mother-only families, and children—the poverty problem has become more serious. Growing earnings inequality has had particularly deleterious effects on young workers and those with little education, decreasing their incentive to work. And we have observed a decline in the work effort of young men.

The nation's response has grown, but is directed more at symptoms. The nation's efforts to reduce poverty have grown substantially over the past twenty years, and massive public expenditures are now undertaken on behalf of the poor. In real terms, expenditures on means-tested programs increased fourfold from 1965 to 1980. After a budgetary retrenchment in the early 1980s, outlays have again risen. Most of the growth in social welfare spending has been in the form of social insurance benefits to elderly and disabled people, or in the form of in-kind benefits, Medicare and Medicaid in particular. Since 1980 federal investment in education and training has fallen substantially, even though these would seem to be both popular and effective strategies for reducing *pre*transfer poverty. Because of the imbalance between income transfers and investments in people, the nation has done more to relieve the symptoms than to cure the problem of poverty.

Lack of progress against poverty. The antipoverty policies emphasized during the 1965–1975 period, together with strong economic growth, reduced poverty. Since then, however, and especially since 1980, slower economic growth—together with rising earnings inequality, a slowdown in spending on social welfare programs, and accelerated growth in mother-only families—caused the poverty rate to stagnate, and then to rise.

The efficiency costs of social welfare expenditures. The efficiency costs of social welfare expenditures are significant. They take the form of reduced labor supply, reduced savings, and other distorted choices. Of every $1 spent on the poor, as little as $.50 may actually end up as a net increase in their income. The evidence from other industrialized nations, in contrast, suggests that these countries do substantially more to reduce poverty and social inequities, with little adverse effect on their economic growth rates.

Mobility in and out of poverty. The bulk of poverty and welfare spells are short, and there is substantial mobility in and out of both poverty and welfare recipiency. This mobility has been fairly constant over time, and at about the same level as in other industrialized countries. However, there is a group of hard-core disadvantaged people—teen nonmarried mothers, high school dropouts, those with criminal records—who experience long stays either in poverty and/or on welfare. There is some intergenerational poverty and welfare dependence—children of poor or welfare-receiving parents have a higher probability of themselves being poor or on welfare—but growing up in a welfare-receiving family appears to have relatively small effects on children's attainments.

The growth of single-parent families. The poverty rate has been pushed steadily upward by the growth of single-parent families. In 1960, about 8 percent of all families with children were headed by single mothers; by 1990 that figure was nearly 25 percent; and demographers estimate that about half of all children born in the 1980s will live in a mother-only family before the age of 18. About half of mother-only families have incomes below the poverty line, and research over the 1980s shows that, compared with children in two-parent families, children from these families are less likely to graduate from high school, more likely to become teen parents, and less likely to be employed. Single-mother families in the United States are much worse off than single-mother families in other Western industrialized countries, primarily because those nations provide more generous assistance to such families. Although many people believe that the U.S. welfare system has contributed importantly to the growth of single-parent families, research evidence indicates that it has played a minor role, accounting for no more than 15 percent of the overall growth in female headship and 30 percent of the growth in female headship among the low-income population.

The "underclass" concept. Although the concept of the "underclass" has deep historical roots, efforts to measure and quantify it have not produced a consensus. Most of the estimates, however, find that the underclass is a small, though growing, group. The underclass concept has moved poverty research beyond income measures and has rekindled interest in neighborhoods, in behavior, and in the social context of individual decision making. Although changes in the economy have reduced the demand for unskilled labor with devastating consequences for young men residing in inner-city communities, there is little evidence that male joblessness is the primary reason for the growth of single-parent families. Migration of jobs from inner-city neighborhoods, in combination with high levels of racial segregation, has contributed to the social isolation and concentration of poor blacks, and this isolation may have affected certain labor market and parenting behaviors.

Economic growth is no panacea. The conventional belief that time, in association with a growing economy, can erode the official poverty rate seems today to be quite wrong. For one thing, growth has been slow, and there is little anticipation that this will change. For another, growth no longer reduces poverty to the same degree that it once did. The tide isn't rising much (and isn't likely to), and as a result of changes in the structure of the family and the economy, some boats are becoming more leaky.

Immigrants and poverty. The rate of immigration to the United States rose rapidly after the 1960s, increasing the share of the foreign-born population to 7 percent in 1990 (still well below the 14 percent share recorded at the turn of the century). Immigrants are an increasingly diverse group in terms of both nation of origin and skill levels, but are more likely to be poor upon arrival than thirty years ago. The flow of legal immigrants has been augmented by a flow of undocumented immigrants (primarily from Mexico) and political refugees (primarily from Asia). Initially poor immigrants tend to work more, and use welfare less, than the native-born poor. Most appear to move up the economic ladder quite rapidly. Although a number of studies find that immigrants do not adversely affect the employment and wages of native workers with whom they compete, other studies come to the opposite conclusion. The controversies have not yet been resolved.

Educational needs. The growing gap between the wages of college graduates and high school dropouts (or graduates) suggests that poor and minority children, especially those with limited basic skills, will not do well in the labor market of the future. Because these groups will make up an increasing share of the nation's future work force, we need to give high priority to finding ways to improve their skills and to assist them in their transition from school to work by better integrating vocational and academic training. Although the need in this area is large, the federal role in elementary and secondary education has contracted.

School choice. One widely touted education policy strategy is "school choice." Parental choice might improve student achievement, but evidence to support the spending of public monies to open choices to all public and private schools does not exist. One simulation model, discussed in this book, suggests that a large-scale movement to "school choice" would not yield the positive effects for poor children or for educational opportunity that its advocates suggest. More research is needed to resolve this issue.

Health care. Although the poor utilize the health care system as much as the nonpoor, their more severe and more numerous health problems leave many of them less than adequately served. This is less true of those poor who are covered by Medicaid, which, in many states, provides substantial coverage. The mentally disabled, however, are a poor group that falls through the safety net; many of them are homeless and drug and/or alcohol dependent.

Employment. Much of the rhetoric in the nation's antipoverty efforts has emphasized work. Although the economy has generated many "jobs," their wages and benefits often are not sufficient to lift a family out of poverty. Creating jobs and increasing incomes are thus quite distinct goals. In recent years, programs have sought to increase work among single mothers by providing job search and job training for them. The equally serious problem of joblessness among low-wage males has not been addressed. Only the expansion of the Earned Income Tax Credit has sought to reward the work effort of low-wage family heads, both male and female.

Urban policy. In the wake of recent urban riots, policy directed at American cities is back on the national agenda. Many urban programs, such as "enterprise zones," are spatially targeted, although neither the theoretical nor the empirical justifications for place-oriented rather than people-oriented policies are strong. Enterprise zones, for example, exist in thirty-seven states and the District of Columbia, but evaluations suggest that they have done little, if anything, to increase employment among zone residents. Similarly, some efforts to increase employment directly—for example, through public service employment or employer-based tax credits for hiring disadvantaged workers—have a spotty record of success. And public housing subsidies have kept the poor locked in neighborhoods with multiple social problems and few jobs.

Public attitude. A major barrier to a new attack on poverty and racial inequalities is public attitude. Although Americans are less supportive of social welfare policies than people in other Western industrialized countries, their attitude toward the poor and welfare do not seem to have become more conservative over time. Support for helping blacks as a group is relatively low overall; there is an enormous gap between minority and white Americans on this issue. Support for affirmative action depends on whether it is viewed as "compensatory," as in the case of special recruitment efforts, or "preferential," as in the case of hiring quotas. Given existing attitudinal, political, and economic constraints, it seems unlikely that the country is willing to embark on any major new initiatives to narrow racial income differences or to reduce poverty. Moreover, whatever we do will probably have a good dose of "tough love" attached to it.

Policy Implications

The most important of these lessons concern (1) the economy and its relationship to the poor; (2) the nation's political and social values toward and expectations of the poor; (3) trends in aggregate social welfare spending and the effects of these policies on poverty, inequality, and efficiency; (4) the underlying determinants of poverty and dependency; (5) the nature and effectiveness of policy initiatives over past decades in a variety of areas—taxes, transfers, education, health, housing, and employment; and (6) the dim prospects for a new wave of social policy legislation designed to reduce poverty and its destructive correlates.

Do these lessons carry with them any implicit suggestions for policy? What might the authors of these chapters say to the President, were he to ask for their advice? To begin with, they would surely tell him that ideally they would like to know more before making any recommendations. Recognizing that policymaking cannot wait for complete information, however, and that what is now known leaves analysts relatively more confident than they were a decade ago, they might offer a number of specific suggestions.

Reduce unemployment. An initial suggestion is to attempt to reduce the unemployment rate to about 5 percent by making appropriate appointments to the Federal Reserve Board and by vetoing any attempt to enact a balanced budget amendment. Although economic growth may not have the antipoverty punch that it once had, it is still the best way to afford opportunities to those with few skills and even less hope.

Health care reform. Health care reform is already a top domestic priority. It is such a complicated issue, however, that a more modest recommendation can be made should an overall reform plan not be enacted by Congress. The adoption of a "healthy kid" program would cover all children through a system of community health centers, financed by limiting the tax deductibility of employer-paid health insurance premiums. Although such a child-focused health program would not reduce income poverty in the short run, it would be relatively inexpensive, would improve children's health, and would enable us to learn more about operating a public insurance program covering large numbers of people.

Educational reform. Federal education policy should support school-based re-forms, designed to change the way teachers and students in individual schools interact, as well as more systemic reforms that are aimed at setting standards, assessing whether students achieve them, and creating incentives that improve performance. The federal role should be to ensure that poor students receive the quantity and quality of instruction needed to meet the new standards. Preschool programs and compensatory education should be expanded, as already proposed, but with attention to the quality of both the Head Start program and the design of Chapter 1. The transition from school to work can be addressed through experi-ments with promising initiatives such as career academies, youth apprenticeships, and the President's national service program, all of which promote academic and vocational skills. The federal government should also provide incentives to recruit talented teachers (especially from minority groups) to work in urban schools.

Public sector jobs programs. The contributors are divided in their assessment of the effectiveness of a public sector jobs program. Some believe that low skills and poor preparation for work are more of a problem than a lack of jobs. A dem-onstration program in a few cities, however, targeted on disadvantaged family heads or absent fathers and offering a minimum-wage job for a year, should show whether there are large numbers of people whom employers will not hire, even at low wages.

Support for children. The nation's children are its most valuable resource, and the collective responsibility that we all have for their nurture and development should be publicly acknowledged. A number of initiatives would make this re-sponsibility real. These could include refundable tax credits, of, say, $1,000 per child, as a replacement for the child exemption in the current tax code, and a child support assurance system (CSAS) in which the government would both require all nonresident parents to share a portion of their income with their children and ensure a minimum child support benefit in cases where the father's income is inadequate. These initiatives would be very costly, but could significantly in-crease the incomes of families headed by mothers who work at minimum wage.

The Earned Income Tax Credit. The large increase in the EITC, enacted in August 1993, is an important contribution for the working poor. Although it may diminish slightly the incentive to work for some of the employed, it sends the right overall message about the value of work. It will help to offset the decline in earnings among younger and less-educated workers that not only has contributed to poverty but has discouraged people from working at all. The utilization of the advanced-payment feature of the EITC, which allows people to secure income support prior to filing their tax return, should also be increased. This provision is now available, but either lack of information or confusion has caused it to be underused.

Training programs. More training programs for adults, including but not limited to mothers on welfare, are also recommended. There is evidence that such programs produce modest gains in earnings for important target groups, and that they pass a benefit-cost test. Funds could be shifted from existing employment programs serving youth, some of which appear to be less effective.

Inner cities. With respect to the problems of the inner cities, the contributors remain divided on whether to recommend people- or place-specific policies. On the one hand, the fear is that place-specific policies will be both ineffective and subject to political logrolling; moreover, it seems important that people have the choice to live, work, and educate their children wherever they wish. On the other hand, there is merit in co-locating services where families with multiple problems are concentrated and in rebuilding community institutions in these areas. A more comprehensive urban policy could include both housing subsidies designed to enhance residential mobility and access to jobs and further experimentation with job-creation programs targeted on inner-city areas. The states and local governments also have a responsibility to invest in the social infrastructure of such areas.

Immigration. What is needed is not an *immigration* policy but an *immigrant* policy. The former would be appropriate if immigrants were harming native workers, but there is currently little strong evidence of that. An immigrant policy would help to integrate new arrivals more quickly into national life and, it is hoped, reduce poverty in the process. Federal policy has been much more generous in dealing with political than with economic migrants (witness the 1986 five-year moratorium on the receipt of welfare benefits among newly legalized immigrants). Many believe that a more uniform and generous policy of social assistance for immigrants should be adopted, including eliminating such moratoriums, providing help similar to that available to minorities in starting small businesses, and targeting immigrants for training, language instruction, and other services.

Antidiscrimination policy. There is clear evidence that employment discrimination and housing segregation continue to limit opportunities for minorities; vigorous enforcement of existing antidiscrimination laws is still needed.

Further investigation. Although these recommendations would make a contribution to reducing poverty and improving the lives of the poor, more efforts are needed. The already appointed urban policy and welfare reform task forces, each charged to consider bolder initiatives and to plan and fund new demonstration projects, deserve full support and a full commitment of resources.

Other Issues

Although these chapters teach us a great deal, some issues and ideas regarding the nation's social problems could not be covered. Because they arise in current debates over poverty policy, however, we note them here.

The problem of homelessness is the most visible manifestation of the nation's poverty problem—perhaps its most destructive and embarrassing manifestation. Although the anatomy of the problem is still not clearly understood, and no consensus on an effective policy approach to it exists, this is perhaps one area where policy may not be able to wait for more research and evaluation.

Another issue of concern is the character of the nation's intergenerational imbalance: the way we treat our children relative to our elderly. As recognized in the preceding chapters, the nation's elderly population has fared rather well, largely owing to the Social Security and Medicare programs. The chapters also emphasize the astoundingly high level of children's poverty rates and the need for improvements in education, health care, and other resources as well as family income. Another step would be explicit discussion of the alternative strategies available for righting the imbalance between services to young and old. The lack of reliable evaluation and analysis of policies directed toward children, along with the enormous expenditures that may be required, are daunting, to be sure. The onerous task of informing the nation's higher-income taxpayers, both middle-aged and elderly, that some sacrifice is needed in order to support investment in the nation's children also inhibits explicit discussion of this issue.

Addressing the underlying causes of a range of dysfunctional behaviors among the poor, often the poor concentrated in large urban ghettos, also looms on the poverty agenda. This issue clearly separates conservatives from liberals today, and it is an issue on which current data, research, and analysis are mostly silent. For example, why do drug use, violent behavior, and rejection of accepted legal and institutional structures seem to be so prevalent in inner-city communities? Is the increase in the prevalence of low birthweight babies in some large American cities due to maternal behavior or to a lack of access to medical and social services? Similarly, why has the prevalence of child inoculations against common diseases declined?

Particularly because of the recent urban disturbances and their aftermath, another important policy issue concerns the standing of the poor and minorities before the courts and the police, and the implications of the calls for more stringent social and police control. The rate of incarceration of young black men is terrifyingly high, and the implications of this for their future are grim. This very high rate of imprisonment of young minorities is visible evidence that something is tragically wrong in our policies. It seems counterproductive to be spending enormous sums on the construction and operation of prisons necessary to confine young black and Hispanic people, while their families are impoverished and their neighborhoods are breeding places for illegal activities.

It is also important to continue to compare the dimensions of the poverty and social policy situation in the United States with those in other industrialized nations. Particular attention should be given to the apparent differences in the effectiveness of U.S. efforts relative to those abroad. For example, why do Americans not consider social and antipoverty policy in the context of "social solidarity," unlike nearly all other industrialized nations?

Alternative Policy Strategies

There also exist certain additional untested policy strategies—perhaps bolder and more draconian—that might change the way people behave, aspire, and attain. In spite of the paucity of experimental results and reliable research findings, the severity of the problems associated with poverty—especially the grinding poverty seen in the nation's urban ghettos—calls for a broader vision of possible policy responses. Even though research has not addressed the possibilities inherent in bold new initiatives, policy-oriented scholars can offer their best judgments as to their efficacy.

Are there alternative ways of organizing social policy, for example, so as to redirect and reorient the 700 billion dollars that we now spend publicly on such measures—reorientations that might result in less poverty and less inequality at lower social cost? It seems worthwhile to lay out a few of these more broad and far-reaching policy ideas: ideas that claim to be able to buy us gains in equity, efficiency, self-sufficiency, responsibility, and dignity all at the same time. On the basis of the decades of poverty research that now lie behind us and the numerous findings from interventions that have been tested, policy-oriented scholars may have something important to say about which strategies have potential and which do not, which should be undertaken—at least experimentally—and which should not.

First, many have suggested that major gains in equity, efficiency, and self-sufficiency would result from abolishing the welfare system as we know it—AFDC and other means-tested transfers—and substituting for it a quite different set of programs with superior incentives, higher expectations of recipients, and increased adequacy. The *package* of alternative programs—available to all of the poor—might include support for the purchase of child care services, governmentally enforced child support, job training and job-finding services, a guaranteed income floor, and wage subsidies to able-bodied adults—and perhaps long-term public employment, if nothing else works.[2] Do we at least know enough to try the most appealing of the options in large-scale demonstrations?

Second, programs designed to increase the ability of the poor to better control their own economic futures have been suggested at both ends of the political spectrum. These include home ownership strategies (for example, the privatizing of public housing); personal and publicly subsidized asset accounts as a substitute for welfare; targeted or universal youth capital accounts, either means tested or not. Do such approaches create incentives or open opportunities that would warrant major public investments in either new programs or, initially, major experiments?

Third, today we confront the daunting task of reducing the size of the nation's largest employer—the military. Would not a far-sweeping policy designed to use the skills and talents of these people be superior to releasing them unsupported to the vagaries of an unfettered labor market in a stagnant economy? Surely we should be thinking through the merits—and demerits—of a National Urban Corps established to utilize the thousands of soon-to-be released military personnel. Can they be effectively used in training and organizing nonemployed youths in the nation's inner cities for increasing neighborhood safety, containing drug trafficking, providing job training, or clearing debris? Given the seriousness of both the nation's urban problems and the difficulties likely to be confronted by those released from the military, wouldn't our past experience with the G.I. Bill warrant initiating a program similar in scope and objectives today?

Fourth, over the years, the government has intervened in the nation's labor markets in a number of ways and researchers have studied the results of these interventions. Is our insight into the operation of low-wage labor markets sufficient to warrant proceeding with interventions designed to increase both work incentives and job opportunities for low-skilled workers? I refer to proposals involving a sizable wage rate subsidy for low-skilled workers and employer-based marginal employment subsidies, perhaps in combination with a low-level refundable tax credit—financed at least in part by elimination of a variety of existing means-tested cash and in-kind transfer programs.

Fifth, the need for a redirection of policies toward investment in children and away from programs that support the incomes of the relatively well-to-do—both middle-aged and elderly—or those that encourage consumption seems widely accepted. Serious consideration might be given to major reorientations designed to accomplish these objectives, even though the economic, social, and political consequences of such a change in public priorities may not yet be fully understood. A policy that combined, say, enriched parent-involved schools, fully funded Head Start, and high-quality child care, coupled with the elimination of tax provisions whose benefits accrue to high-income citizens and perhaps a scaling back of Social Security over time into a poverty-line program (together with generous tax subsidies and information provision for private provision for retirement), might be attractive.

Sixth, there is a need for a bold, multifaceted attack on the many dimensions of poverty. What if a jolt of job training by itself—or a jolt of day care by itself, or housing, or job creation, or police protection, or health care, or income support—yields little if any impact on poverty, as many evaluations have found? But, conversely, what if a major dose of a constellation of these measures, taken together, could yield major increases in esteem, productivity, responsibility, and income among the poor? What if such a constellation could loosen the grip of those schools and neighborhoods that seem to pull down those who might want to, and otherwise be able to, escape? And what if a major multipronged approach would not only exploit these synergies but, in addition and at the same time, also change the parameters in the production function—change tastes, motivations, and hopes? Henry Aaron (1992) has made a similar point, and in powerful words. With reference to Lafayette and Pharaoh Rivers and their mother LaJoe in Alex Kotlowitz's *There Are No Children Here,* he stated:

> Many interventions may fail because we change only one thing at a time. We provide school counselling for children who are acting out, but do little to change the social and family environments that shape these children's behavior. We offer welfare recipients job training, but do nothing to increase demand for the skills they are acquiring or to assure that completion of training and successful employment will bring added income. In short, some interventions show up as ineffective because we have changed only one factor when we need to change many to succeed . . . The problems in the Henry Horner Homes are hard to solve in large part because each resident of those projects lives in a sea of crime, truancy, and unemployment, in which stable families are oddities and a sense of community is absent . . . By concentrating behaviors regarded as aberrant when diluted these projects made drugs, murder, unemployment, truancy, and despair the normal everyday experience of all who lived within them.

The changes prescribed here and in the rest of this volume are not out of the question—indeed, some are likely to take place. What is certain is that we cannot discover the full potential of our prescriptions for confronting poverty unless we take bold action.

Notes
References
Contributors
Index

Notes

1. Introduction

1. President Carter's Program for Better Jobs and Income actually proposed both to make cash welfare universally available *and* to provide minimum-wage public service jobs for adults with children in one- and two-parent families who were "expected to work" but who could not find a regular private or public sector job.

2. The Historical Record

The authors thank June O'Neill, Robert Plotnick, and Christopher Jencks for helpful comments and Maria Cancian and Luise Cunliffe for research assistance.

1. This section draws on research in progress by Danziger and Peter Gottschalk. See also Danziger and Gottschalk (1993) and Gottschalk and Danziger (1985).
2. These reports are based on interviews each March with roughly sixty thousand families and unrelated individuals. Respondents are asked the sources and amount of income they received during the previous calendar year. The Current Population Survey of March 1992 thus reports the demographic characteristics of the family as of the interview date, and the 1991 incomes of those currently residing at the address.
3. Smeeding (1982) developed the earliest estimates of poverty adjusted for noncash transfers received and taxes paid. His results for the 1968–1979 period, however, are not consistent with the post-1979 Census series reviewed below.
4. Problems arose with the CPI-U in the 1970s because of the way it reflected changes in the costs of home ownership. In this period of rising home prices and interest rates, too large a weight was given to home ownership costs, particularly mortgage interest rates, leading to an overstatement of inflation. As a result, a new price index, the CPI-U-X1, was adopted in 1983. It is less affected by current housing prices and mortgage interest rates because it estimates the cost of renting and not purchasing a home. Use of the CPI-U thus overstates inflation and understates income growth during the period when income growth slowed. For example, between 1973 and 1982, the CPI-U rose by 117 percent, while the CPI-U-X1 rose by 103 percent. Real median income fell by 10.5 percent, if the CPI-U is used to

measure inflation; it fell by 4 percent if the CPI-U-X1 is used. We incorporate the CPI-U-X1 as far back as 1968 in Table 2.1.

5. The official dating of the post–World War II recessions by the National Bureau of Economic Research are as follows: 11 months, from November 1948 to October 1949; 10 months, from July 1953 to May 1954; 8 months, from August 1957 to April 1958; 10 months, from April 1960 to February 1961; 11 months, from December 1969 to November 1970; 16 months, from November 1973 to March 1975; 6 months, from January to July 1980; 16 months, from July 1981 to November 1982; and 9 months, from July 1990 to March 1991.

6. The data in Table 2.1 are computed only for families, defined as "a group of two or more persons related by birth, marriage, or adoption and residing together." They do not incorporate changes in the living standards of a substantial and rapidly increasing portion of the population—unrelated individuals, defined as "persons who are not living with any relatives." The Census Bureau also publishes a time series on household income for the 1967–1992 period. Households are defined to include unrelated individuals as well as families. That series shows income trends that are quite similar to those shown in Figure 2.1. Another series, on per capita income, both includes unrelated individuals and adjusts for average household size. Because household size has fallen over time, the per capita income series shows a more rapid rate of income growth than either the family or the household income series. Nonetheless, each series shows a much slower rate of growth in the two decades following 1973 than in the prior two decades.

7. There is some mobility of families across quintiles over time. For example, Short and Shea (1991) report that about 19 percent of families moved down one or more quintiles, and about 13 percent moved up one or more quintiles between 1987 and 1988. Duncan, Smeeding, and Rodgers (1991), however, find that mobility across income classes was lower in the 1980s than it was in the 1970s. See also Sawhill and Condon (1992).

8. Jantti (1992) and Cutler and Katz (1991) estimate regression models to explain the trends in the income shares of each of the quintiles. Both papers control for cyclical fluctuations and find that the share of the richest fifth increased and that of the other four decreased during the 1980s.

9. The Tax Reform Act of 1986 and the Omnibus Reconciliation Act of 1990 did make some progressive changes in the federal personal income tax, notably an expansion of the Earned Income Tax Credit. Nonetheless, federal income and payroll taxes were less progressive in 1990 than they were at the beginning of the 1980s.

10. Jenkins (1991) points out that a Gini coefficient of .400 can be interpreted to mean that the expected difference in family income between two families drawn at random from the income distribution is 40 percent.

11. The trend in inequality of household income is similar to that of family income (data are not shown). In any year there is more inequality in the household distribution, because the relatively low incomes of unrelated individuals are included in this series. The percentage increase in inequality, however, is not quite as rapid. For example, the household Gini in 1992 was 10.8 percent above the 1969 level, while the family Gini increased by 15.5 percent over the same period.

12. All of the increased inequality between 1982 and 1989 was accounted for by the income gains of the richest 5 percent of families. Their income share increased by 1.9 percent of total family income. The share of the lowest quintile fell by 0.1 percent, that of the second,

third, and fourth quintiles each fell by 0.6 percent, and that of the next 15 percent was constant. Inequality seems to have stopped increasing after 1989, as the 1992 Gini coefficient is not statistically greater than the 1989 level. But it is difficult to predict whether this marks a return to stability in the distribution of income. It is clear that only dramatic changes in the economy and/or public policies could lower inequality to the levels of the late 1960s.

13. Ruggles (1990) argues that the Orshansky (1963, 1965) line reflected an absolute minimum thirty years ago, but not today. She proposes an updated poverty threshold based on a new market basket that reflects a broader number of necessities; she would reevaluate this basket every decade to reflect changes in society's notion of a minimum standard of living. Ruggles presents several alternative poverty line estimates, including one that incorporates a minimum housing consumption standard and one that updates the Orshansky method using more recent family budgets and food shares. She concludes that "poverty standards today, to be comparable in terms of their consumption implications to the original Orshansky thresholds, would have to be at least 50 percent higher than the official thresholds" (1990, p. 167).

14. Until 1981, there were separate poverty lines for farm and nonfarm families and for families headed by males and females. These differences resulted from the different food requirements for men and women and because farm families were assumed to grow some of their own food.

15. If per capita income had been chosen as an equivalence scale, then a family of four (two adults and two children) would have a poverty line twice as large as that of a nonelderly couple. The official poverty line assumes that children consume less than adults. As a result, the official poverty line for this family of four is 1.51 times that of the couple. Likewise, the poverty line for an elderly couple would be the same as that for a nonelderly couple if per capita income were used. The official line, however, is based on the finding that the elderly consume less food than the nonelderly, so the poverty line for an elderly couple is 0.9 times that of the nonelderly couple. Ruggles (1990) argues that this equivalence scale is not appropriate for the elderly, and that if the scales were based on a broader range of consumption items, the line for the elderly would not be lower than that of the nonelderly. Orshansky did introduce an arbitrary upward adjustment in the thresholds for one- and two-person families.

16. The Census Bureau does publish a poverty rate for persons with incomes below 125 percent of the poverty line (see Figure 2.3). Coincidentally, in 1992 this cutoff was about 50 percent of median family income. The official rate in 1992 was 14.5 percent, and 19.4 percent were below this "relative" threshold.

17. The lack of progress during the 1970s can largely be attributed to the lack of growth in real median income, though if inflation is taken into account (using the CPI-U-X1), poverty would have been as low in the late 1970s as in 1973 (see Weicher [1987] and Table 2.2, column 3).

18. The adjusted poverty series in columns 2 and 4 of Table 2.2 excludes the net imputed return on home equity. If this were included, the 1992 poverty rate would be reduced still further, to 10.4 percent.

19. The concept behind fungible value is simple: Medicare and Medicaid benefits are counted as income *only* to the extent that they free up other resources that might have been spent on medical care. Medicare and Medicaid have full income value (estimated as the mean

government subsidy for families of a given risk class) only if the family's other income exceeds the sum of basic food and housing requirements plus the estimated value of the health benefit. (The cost of basic food requirements is determined by the Agriculture Department's Thrifty Food Plan; the cost of housing by the Housing and Urban Development Department's Fair Market Rents). If the family's income is less than this minimum, the fungible value of the health benefits will be reduced, possibly to zero if the family's other income is insufficient to cover even the basic food and housing costs. (The fungible value of medical benefits received is thus correlated with the family's income.) See Weinberg and Lamas (1991).

20. An alternative method, suggested by Aaron and Burtless (in U.S. Bureau of the Census, 1986), is to consider someone not poor only if he or she had adequate medical coverage. The poverty thresholds would presumably then be adjusted to exclude medical costs.

21. To place these exclusions in context, note that because the poverty rate is estimated from a survey, there is a standard error associated with its measurement. The standard error of the poverty rate in 1990, about 523,000 persons, or 0.2 percentage points, is about the same size as the estimate of the homeless population. There are other exclusions as well—the nursing home and mental hospital populations, whose inclusion would raise the poverty rate, and the armed forces, whose inclusion would lower it.

22. Ross, Danziger, and Smolensky (1987) and Smolensky, Danziger, and Gottschalk (1988) examine trends in poverty for various demographic groups from 1939 to the present. They extend the official poverty measure back to 1949 using the CPI, and report poverty rates of about 40 percent for all persons, 49 percent for children, and 60 percent for the elderly.

23. The CPS does not have a sample large enough to estimate group-specific poverty rates for persons who report their race as other (for example, Asian Americans, American Indians).

24. The typical demographic standardization relies on the assumption that changes in population shares are independent of changes in the group-specific poverty rates, and vice versa. Such standardizations are also very sensitive to the number and nature of the demographic groups. Ryscavage, Green, and Welniak (1992) present a standardization that deals with a related set of economic and demographic changes, including changes in the industrial mix and in the educational distribution of the population.

25. As mentioned in note 24, these simulations are extremely sensitive to the number of groups used. For example, our simulation asks, "What would poverty be like if the percentage of children living in female-headed families was the same in 1973 as in 1990, *but* the poverty rate for female-headed families remained at the 1990 level?" The problem is that the 1990 poverty rate for female heads of families would be different if the characteristics of female heads had not changed over the period. For example, Gottschalk and Danziger (1993) show that female family heads today have more education and fewer children than their 1973 counterparts. These changes in the characteristics of female heads were poverty-reducing and offset, to a great extent, the poverty-increasing effects of the increased numbers of children living in such families. Thus the simulation reported in the text overstates the poverty increase due to demographic change.

26. During this period, the number of elderly did increase much faster than the number of children—23 versus 3 percent. The number of poor children, however, increased by 29 percent.

27. In 1974 SSI replaced three programs—Old Age Assistance, Aid to the Blind, and Aid to

the Permanently and Totally Disabled. These separate programs still continue in Guam, Puerto Rico, and the Virgin Islands. Of 4.8 million persons receiving SSI in September 1990, 30.5 percent were elderly, 67.8 percent, disabled, and 1.8 percent, blind. For individuals receiving only the federal SSI benefit in 1990, the benefits received were 73.9 percent of the poverty threshold. Combined Social Security and SSI benefits were 77.7 percent of poverty, and adding Food Stamps to the other two raised the combined benefit to 84.8 percent of poverty. The corresponding figures for couples in 1990 were 87.9 percent, 90.9 percent, and 100.4 percent.

28. Food Stamps, SSI, and AFDC all have assets tests in addition to income tests. For example, an elderly widow receiving only a few thousand dollars in social security will be ineligible for SSI if she has more than $2,000 in liquid assets.

29. The Survey of Income and Program Participation (SIPP) is more comprehensive and covers more programs than the Current Population Survey (CPS), but not all of the program benefits are assigned a cash value there as yet. In contrast, the special CPS analysis file prepared by the Census Bureau for their reports (see, for example, U.S. Bureau of the Census, 1992c) has estimated values for benefits in the key noncash programs—Food Stamps, School Lunch, Medicaid, Medicare, and housing assistance. For an analysis of multiple program participation using the SIPP data, see Weinberg (1987).

Even if the CPS showed that all transfers were received by the nonpoor, this would not necessarily mean that benefits were mistargeted. There is no strict match between the annual incomes reported by the CPS and program rules on the eligible assistance unit (for example, a destitute elderly person could validly receive SSI and still reside with nonpoor relatives) or the accounting period (for example, a female householder with a child could receive AFDC for part of a year, then get married). Finally, income could be underreported to the CPS (showing a family to be poor when it is not) or to a program (making it eligible for benefits when it is not). Underreporting of transfer income can lead to systematic underestimation of the antipoverty effectiveness of transfers.

30. Pretransfer poverty overstates the extent to which private market incomes fail to keep people out of poverty. Transfers induce some persons to work less than they would have if they had not been eligible for transfers. As a result, private income in the absence of transfers would exceed pretransfer income as measured here. The literature suggests that this poverty-increasing effect of income transfers is rather small (see Moffitt, 1992).

31. More detailed tables that present transfer receipt for the elderly and other demographic groups are available from the authors. We have also analyzed the data on transfer receipt for unrelated individuals. About one-third of all unrelated individuals and about two-thirds of the pretransfer poor received a social insurance transfer. As with families, Social Security was the most effective transfer, removing 35 percent of pretransfer poor individuals from poverty and reducing their poverty deficit by 52 percent.

32. This is equivalent to beginning with pretransfer income, as in Table 2.5, and then adding cash social insurance payments. About 45 percent of unrelated individuals receive means-tested transfers; about 80 percent of these transfers are received by the prewelfare poor. Only 17 percent of them, however, escape poverty through transfers.

33. While pretransfer income does not count any money income from government programs, prewelfare income includes all money income except that from cash public assistance (welfare) programs—for example, AFDC, Supplemental Security Income, and General

Assistance. The antipoverty impact of government transfers can thus be broken down into three separate components. The percentage of persons removed from poverty by cash social insurance can be approximately measured as the difference between the pretransfer and the prewelfare poverty rates; the percentage removed by cash welfare, by the difference between the prewelfare and the official rates; and the net percentage removed by noncash transfers and taxes, by the difference between the official and adjusted rates. The pretransfer poverty series shown in Table 2.2, column 5, was initially developed by Robert Plotnick (Plotnick and Skidmore, 1975). It treats the pensions of government employees in the same manner as Social Security benefits—as government cash social insurance transfers. The Census Bureau has published a pretransfer poverty series for recent years (U.S. Bureau of the Census, 1992c) that treats government pensions in the same manner as private pensions—as market income. The Census Bureau pretransfer poverty rate is thus about one percentage point lower than the series shown in Table 2.2. The Census Bureau definition of private money income is used in Tables 2.5 and 2.6.

34. The calculations of antipoverty impacts in Table 2.7 are sequential, so that all social insurance benefits are first added to pretransfer incomes, yielding the prewelfare poverty rate in column 2. Welfare transfers are then added, yielding the official poverty rate in column 3. The antipoverty impact of social insurance is then defined as the percentage difference between the rates in columns 2 and 1 expressed as a percentage of the pretransfer poverty rate (column 1). The antipoverty impact of welfare is defined as the percentage difference between the rates in columns 3 and 2 expressed as a percentage of the rate in column 1. These antipoverty impacts are shown in columns 4 and 5.

3. Public Spending on the Poor

The author is indebted to Sheldon Danziger, Christopher Jencks, Gary Sandefur, Eugene Smolensky, and Daniel Weinberg for helpful suggestions. Suzanne Smith of Brookings provided superb research assistance.

1. Unless otherwise stated, all spending amounts are calculated as federal fiscal year totals measured in constant 1990 dollars. Spending totals include estimates of state and local as well as federal outlays. Current dollars are deflated using the personal consumption expenditure deflator, the deflator used by the U.S. Office of Management and Budget to deflate payments to individuals.

2. In fiscal year 1991, the total amount of the EITC was estimated to be $8.75 billion (U.S. House of Representatives, 1991, p. 901); public outlays on AFDC benefits amounted to $20.7 billion.

3. Medicaid eligibility is linked to actual or potential eligibility for benefits under the AFDC or SSI programs. Between 1975 and 1988, the AFDC need standard in nearly all states rose more slowly than the rate of change in prices (U.S. House of Representatives, 1991, pp. 601–603). Families were effectively required to have lower incomes in order to qualify for AFDC and Medicaid.

4. Weinberg measured household income in a way that included the cash-equivalent value of in-kind benefits.

5. Unemployment insurance, like workers' compensation, offers protection only to wage and

salary workers. The other social insurance programs insure self-employed as well as wage and salary workers.

6. In a recent survey of the nonexperimental evidence about the effects of public assistance, Moffitt (1992) reaches a similar conclusion.

7. Two-parent families enrolled in the experimental NIT plans received average transfer payments that were about $2,700 larger than the transfer payments received by similar families in the control group (that is, the group of families who were not offered eligibility in the experimental plans). The combined earnings reduction of husbands and wives in the experimental plans was almost $1,800. In essence, the experiment spent nearly $2,700 on additional transfers, caused earnings reductions of two-thirds that amount, and succeeded in raising net family income by only about $900—one-third the amount of added taxpayer spending (Burtless, 1987, p. 28).

8. The well-being of poor families might be raised by more than $1.00, that is, by more than their increase in net income. One reason that women may have reduced their paid work in the NIT experiments was to spend more time in caring for their children. These women gave up some of the potential income gains they could have obtained from the generous NIT in order to improve child rearing. Taxpayers, of course, are unlikely to value this kind of improvement in well-being very much because it is notoriously difficult to observe or measure.

9. This estimate is based on the labor supply responses observed in the Seattle and Denver experiments (see Burtless, 1987, pp. 40–45). It excludes the earnings losses, if any, that taxpayers would sustain in responding to higher taxes. For example, if higher income taxes are imposed to finance more generous transfers, some high-income earners might reduce their work effort and earnings. However, the Seattle and Denver results suggest that such responses would be small, and might even *raise* the pretax earnings of high-income taxpayers.

4. The Dynamics and Intergenerational Transmission of Poverty and Welfare Participation

The authors wish to thank Christopher Jencks and Sheldon Danziger for very useful comments on a previous draft.

1. Annual income would be the proper measure if people could only save or borrow to smooth income within each year.

2. Note that this argument implicitly assumes that people can smooth their consumption by either saving or borrowing against future income. The argument for extending the accounting period beyond a year becomes much weaker if many poverty spells occur early in life when income smoothing through saving may not be possible.

3. This view is still often reflected in public statements. For example, in his famous "Murphy Brown" speech, Vice President Dan Quayle stated that "the intergenerational poverty that troubles us so much today is predominantly a poverty of values." *Boston Globe,* May 21, 1992.

4. We find more one-year spells than reported in Bane and Ellwood (1986). This reflects our use of the official poverty line rather than 125 percent of the official thresholds, our inclu-

sion of post-1982 data, our inclusion of persons over sixty-five, and their exclusion of some one-year spells. Using their procedure reduces the frequency of one-year spells by .084.

5. Ruggles defines monthly poverty as having monthly income below one-twelfth of the annual poverty line.

6. The shorter one makes the period, the more mobility one will find by construction. Ruggles (1990, p. 94) finds that almost twice as many families are poor in at least one month than the number whose annual incomes are less than their annual poverty lines.

7. The anomaly is a result of the sampling method. If spells in progress are sampled, then the long-term spells have a higher probability of being included because they are more likely to be still in progress when the sample is taken. In our example there is always one short spell and one long spell in progress at any moment in time. If new poverty spells are sampled as in Figure 4.1, however, then all spells have equal probabilities of being included. In our example, 90 percent of new spells are short.

8. Any family with an income/needs ratio less than 1.0 in both 1986 and 1987 was poor in both years.

9. See Levy and Murnane (1992) for a review of the literature on changes in wage inequality and Danziger and Gottschalk (1993) for a review of the literature on family income inequality.

10. Adjacent three-year periods are measured by comparing three-year moving averages of family income and poverty lines for each person. This widening of the accounting period eliminates some temporary movements across the poverty line.

11. Data presented in Duncan and Rodgers (1991) also suggests that the probability of remaining persistently poor changed relatively little over the 1980s.

12. To escape from the lowest decile a family's income must be 20 percent higher than the top cutoff of the lowest decile, according to their definition.

13. These data compare family income positions at two points in time, usually one year apart.

14. This question differs from the question that asks how long spells currently in progress will last.

15. Our results differ from those of Ellwood (1986a) who used fewer years of data and who looked only at spells of both receiving AFDC and being a female head of household.

16. Blank (1989a) finds somewhat shorter durations because she uses monthly data.

17. Although AFDC receives by far the most attention, the Food Stamp program provides assistance to a much larger caseload. Burstein and Visher (1989) show that there is even more turnover in the Food Stamp caseload than in the AFDC caseload. At the end of one year, roughly two-thirds of all Food Stamp cases have been closed. If long-term recipiency is defined as a Food Stamp spell that lasts for three years or more, then only 15 percent of all Food Stamp cases could be classified as long term.

18. Because AFDC is available to pregnant women, we include the year prior to birth and the following nine years in the ten-year window.

19. These data are generated by estimating discrete time duration models for spells on and off of welfare and simulating the predicted spell durations over the ten-year period. The data on the first spell differ from the data in Figure 4.4, which samples all spells.

20. Duncan, Laren, and Yeung (1991) examined families in the PSID that received AFDC at least once during the first eighteen years of their child's life. Although their conclusions

are based on smaller samples that do not allow for disaggregation, they find similar overall patterns.

21. See Duncan et al. (1991), table 3. Two-parent families show similar patterns.

22. Similar patterns are found if we follow all persons who received assistance in at least one of the last three years and ask whether they will receive assistance in all three of the next three years.

23. There have been a small number of social experiments in which benefits were set at different levels for experimental groups and the control group.

24. Note that none of this evidence can be used to estimate how people would have behaved had there been no welfare system for single parents, because data for such an "experiment" are not available. The extreme position that eliminating public assistance would change behavior substantially therefore remains untested.

25. Furthermore, a focus on the association in income across generations may be more informative, as individuals who experience childhood poverty may experience near-poverty as adults. They would not be counted as poor, but analyzing income, rather than poverty status, overcomes the problem of living standards above the poverty line.

26. Becker and Tomes (1986) concluded that the intergenerational correlation in income was somewhere around .17, based on their review of some early studies. This finding suggests a fairly small effect of parental income on the income of children later as adults.

27. If the intergenerational correlation in income were zero, the probability that the child of a poor family would fall into poverty would be the same as the probability for the child of a rich family, namely .20.

28. These findings do not mean that intergenerational occupational mobility increased throughout the 1962–1990 period. Although occupational mobility did increase between 1962 and 1973, Michael Hout (1988) points out that intergenerational mobility did not increase for men observed in 1982–1985 relative to those observed in 1972–1975, because the occupational structure changed less between the early 1970s and the early 1980s than between the early 1960s and the early 1970s. Thus "structural mobility [i.e., mobility due to changes in the occupational distribution over time] did not disappear, but it declined enough to offset the increased openness of the class structure" (Hout, 1988, p. 1390).

29. These studies measure mobility after adjusting for differences in the distribution of occupations across countries.

30. For a review of this literature, see McLanahan and Booth (1989).

31. These patterns are attenuated but not eliminated after controlling for a large number of factors that may also affect the daughter's participation.

32. Gottschalk (1992) finds some evidence that the relationship is not just spurious.

5. The Underclass

An earlier draft of this chapter was a product of the Underclass Research Project at the Urban Institute. The author thanks Flona Mincy for research assistance, help in preparation of the manuscript, and dialogue that contributed to ideas expressed. The author also thanks Erol Ricketts for similar conversations, and Reginald Clark, Robinson Hollister, Christopher Jencks, Melvin Oliver, Isabelle Sawhill, Susan Wiener, Franklin Wilson, and the editors of this volume for comments on an earlier draft.

1. See Katz (1989) for an extended historical discussion of the political history of the poverty debate in economics, law, philosophy, and political science.

2. The Social Science Citation Index in 1992 listed 355 papers citing Wilson's book *The Truly Disadvantaged: The Inner City, the Underclass, and Public Policy* (1987).

3. The displacement of low-skilled workers by structural economic changes is what Myrdal (1963) had in mind when he introduced the term "underclass" to American social policy debates.

4. Wilson also mentioned demographic changes, especially increases in the number of women entering the labor force. This created a labor surplus economy in which employers could be selective about whom they hired. Given their low skills, black males were less able to compete.

5. Gramlich and Laren (1991) actually studied the migration patterns of persons in persistently poor, middle-income, and rich families. A family was persistently poor if a three-, five-, or seven-year average of its income-to-needs ratio fell below 1.25. A family was persistently middle class if a three-, five-, or seven-year average of its income-to-needs ratio fell between 1.24 and 3.00. A family was persistently rich if a three-, five-, or seven-year average of its income-to-needs ratio exceeded 3.00. Neighborhood classifications were based on Census definitions. A poor neighborhood had a poverty rate of 30 percent or more; a middle-class neighborhood had a poverty rate between 10 and 30 percent; a rich neighborhood had a poverty rate below 10 percent.

6. For example, although out-of-wedlock birth rates are rising, most children are born to married couples. Never-married single mothers may therefore prefer to claim that they are widows or divorcees. And because marriage rates among white women, educated women, and higher-income women are higher, and these women are more likely to have the resources for abortions, the tendency to misreport out-of-wedlock fertility may be higher among these women.

7. Anderson (1990) uses the term "decent" to describe families with two parents, or families with a strong single mother and supportive relatives, who strictly supervise their children from early childhood through adolescence. "Fast girls" refers to girls who are socialized in a street peer group and who have sexual intercourse early in their adolescence.

8. Aponte (1988) would prefer to limit the underclass concept to material deprivation caused by structural unemployment. He argues that this was the tendency prior to a few widely read and sensationalist journalists' accounts between 1977 and 1980. One-dimensional discussions of social disadvantage, however, were a relatively recent and short-lived perspective (Wilson, 1991c).

9. I thank Susan Wiener for permission to use Tables 5.1 and 5.2.

10. For example, Mincy (1991) showed that the vast majority of the Hispanic poverty area population lived in metropolitan areas with over 2 million people. Two of these metropolitan areas were New York and Chicago. Many Hispanics in these areas are Puerto Ricans. These metropolitan areas were also highly segregated.

11. Ricketts and Sawhill (1988) used four social problems: (1) households headed by females with children; (2) households receiving public assistance; (3) males working fewer than twenty-six weeks during the year, their proxy for weak attachment to the labor force; (4) teenagers who dropped out of high school. A census tract had to score at least one standard deviation above the national average on all four of these problems to be included among underclass areas.

12. Several experiments with measures of the underclass area population show these varia-tions. Hughes (1989) excluded the high school dropout component, which had the smallest correlation with the other components of the Ricketts and Sawhill measure. In another experiment, Hughes weighted the four Ricketts and Sawhill social problems using a differ-ent scheme. Finally, Ricketts and Mincy (1988) estimated the growth in the underclass area population using national averages of social problems in 1970 for both decades and averages of social problems in the Census year (1970 or 1980). These results showed that estimates of size and growth of population in underclass areas (or Hughes's "impacted ghettos") are sensitive to these changes.

13. Jencks's comment on this point is part of a larger criticism that the social problems linked in the underclass literature are driven by different social processes having different policy implications. See Jencks's comments cited in Aponte (1988) and Prosser (1991).

14. There is some support for the view that poverty concentration is a sufficient proxy for the concentration of other social problems linked to the underclass. Earlier studies have found that poverty area residents exhibit high rates of social problems, and 61 percent of the underclass area identified by Ricketts and Sawhill were also extreme poverty areas. Under-class areas are more restrictive, however, because 72 percent of the poverty areas were not underclass areas.

15. Montgomery (1989) and Hoffman, Duncan, and Mincy (1991) are recent attempts to in-corporate the effects of peers and neighbors on preferences, demonstrating how difficult these questions really are.

16. I use "detachment" as an abbreviation for individuals with little or no attachment to the labor force and individuals who participate in the labor force inconsistently.

17. To be fully consistent, we should use the spelling "under class."

18. Having explained my understanding of the term *underclass* and why I think it is appropri-ate, I will continue to use the term, with the awareness that others may disagree.

19. Since few Hispanics or whites lived in extreme poverty areas, Fernandez and Harris re-stricted their analysis to blacks. Their study therefore tells us about the social networks available to black poverty area residents, but nothing about the social networks available to black, white, and Hispanic residents of nonpoverty areas.

20. Space does not permit a more detailed discussion of these recommendations. In the context of helping young black males, Mincy (forthcoming) contains extended discussions of these issues by specialists in youth development and youth programming.

21. In Chapter 7 Blank discusses employment policies that are closely related to the fairness and opportunity themes in the following discussion, which includes comments on her work.

22. My thanks to Greg Patton of the Philadelphia Children's Network for sharing his experi-ence with me as a counselor in the Philadelphia site.

6. Poverty in Relation to Macroeconomic Trends, Cycles, and Policies

The author is very grateful to Yale undergraduate research assistants for dedicated and expert help: Mitch-ell Tobin (no relation) and Vassil Konstantinov for work specifically on an earlier draft of this chapter during the academic year 1991–92; Greg Back and Andrew Metrick for useful related calculations four years earlier incident to my participation in the National Academy of Sciences' study on the status of black Americans.

7. The Employment Strategy

The author thanks Yasuyo Abe, Susan Lloyd, Rebecca London, and Meredith Phillips for research assistance and the Center for Urban Affairs and Policy Research at Northwestern University for research support. Judith Gueron, Robinson Hollister, Christopher Jencks, Larry Mead, Isaac Shapiro, Ernst Stromsdorfer, and the editors of this volume provided useful comments.

1. In this chapter, I do not address poverty among the aged or the disabled.
2. These calculations are based on total civilian employment among workers aged sixteen and over.
3. For a more thorough review of these trends, see Katz and Murphy (1992) or Karoly (1993). Note that the use of weekly wages in Table 7.2 is not contaminated by changes in hours, because weekly hours for male workers have changed little since 1960 (Coleman and Pencavel, 1992).
4. A growing body of research provides a thorough discussion of these facts and investigates causal hypotheses. See Blackburn, Bloom, and Freeman (1990), Davis and Haltiwanger (1991), Levy and Murnane (1992), Bound and Johnson (1992), and Murphy and Welch (1993).
5. David Ellwood (1988) is generally credited with popularizing this phrase.
6. This tabulation includes all poor and many near-poor families. The years 1969, 1979, and 1989 are relatively comparable years. The years 1969 and 1989 are the last years of an extended economic expansion. The year 1979 is the peak year of a shorter expansion. In 1989 families (as defined in Table 7.3) in the bottom 20 percent had incomes below $12,497; the mean in that year was $41,446.
7. Tabulations by race are available for Table 7.3 from the author.
8. Mead (1992) argues that the increase in nonwork among men reflects a change in the learned behavior and psychology of the poor.
9. Table 7.3 shows only whether women ever work and obscures the increases in hours and weeks of work among employed women. For more extensive discussion of these trends, see Cancian, Danziger, and Gottschalk (1993).
10. Private correspondence from Burtless. These tables can be obtained from the author upon request.
11. Most research seems to indicate that mother's employment, per se, does not have a negative effect on children (Blau and Ferber, 1992, pp. 276–277).
12. Very few nonelderly married or single men have access to income assistance programs, unless they are disabled or temporarily unemployed.
13. Over the 1970s, legislative changes made it easier for eligible AFDC households to receive food stamps, so that food stamp recipiency in the AFDC population increased even though average real benefit levels were constant.
14. This finding is consistent with other evidence that concludes that most women would still retain eligibility for AFDC if they were forced off the rolls. Their hours of work and earnings would be so low that their family income would still be below the AFDC eligibility maximum. For a review of this research, see Moffitt (1992).
15. Several states, for example, have proposed excluding children born after a woman becomes an AFDC recipient from AFDC benefits.
16. Not surprisingly, given the low AFDC benefit levels and the high tax rate on earnings after

four months, there is evidence that a substantial number of AFDC families have unreported earnings (Jencks and Edin, 1990), although the amounts are typically quite low. High tax rates may have a greater effect on income reporting than they do on actual work behavior.

17. For a discussion of the effects of child care costs on women's labor market behavior, see Connelly (1991).

18. For a discussion of the impact of Medicaid eligibility on AFDC participation and work, see Blank (1989b) or Winkler (1991).

19. See Nathan (1993) for an extensive discussion of the structural design issues involved in state work-welfare programs.

20. For a further discussion of program evaluation issues and the costs and benefits of random assignment experimentation, see Nathan (1988) and Manski and Garfinkel (1992).

21. For a thorough discussion of the results summarized here, see U.S. General Accounting Office (1987), Gueron (1990), and Gueron and Pauly (1991). For a critical review of these evaluations, see Greenberg and Wiseman (1992).

22. For a discussion of the political story behind the passage of FSA, see the symposium on this topic in *Journal of Policy Analysis and Management* 10 (1991): 588–666.

23. For a review of the implementation issues in JOBS programs, see Hagen and Lurie (1992). For discussion of how states have structured their JOBS programs, see Greenberg (1992).

24. For a review of recent tax changes, see Steuerle (1992).

25. Eligible families can receive advance payment of their refund, so they do not have to wait until April of the following year.

26. Studies are lacking in part because the major source of EITC data is tax records, which are not publicly available. (Scholz [1993] is an exception.) There is some evidence of significant errors in EITC claims. There is also evidence that participation rates in EITC among eligible households are reasonably high (Scholz, 1990, 1993).

27. Some families would not use the Dependent Care Credit even if it were refundable, because the child care worker must be named and some number of families purchase child care "off the books."

28. For example, some analysts argue that minority youth, particularly males, are viewed with suspicion by employers and have difficulty getting hired and acquiring job experience (Kirschenman and Neckerman, 1991). In this case, some time in a public sector job might produce useful work experience and job recommendations.

29. For a review of the international evidence on widening wage inequality, see Davis (1992) or Freeman and Katz (1993).

30. Because most states have balanced-budget requirements in their constitutions, they are not able to fund countercyclical programs.

31. The effects of such a change are discussed in Robins (1990a).

8. Single-Mother Families, Economic Insecurity, and Government Policy

1. The definition of single mother used in this chapter includes mothers who are divorced, separated, widowed, and never married.

2. Note that poverty is here defined as having income less than 50 percent of the median family income.

3. Improvements in employment opportunities for women appear to be the single most important factor.

4. That Sweden has a lower proportion of single-parent families than the United States may come as a surprise. This is because of the confusion between marital status and residence patterns. Children who live with unmarried mothers are frequently included in the Swedish count of single-mother families. About half of these children, however, are living with their natural fathers and therefore should be counted as two-parent families (Gustafson, 1991).

5. Until early in the twentieth century, poor single mothers, predominantly widows, were expected to work and earn income. But for the most part the work was in the home—taking in boarders, doing laundry, and baking. In difficult times, these women usually received poor relief to supplement their earnings. Unlike most other poor relief recipients, widows with children throughout most of our history received relief in their own homes. During the late nineteenth century, however, poor relief in general was attacked for creating dependence, and access to it was substantially curtailed. This led to the widespread practice of taking children away from their destitute mothers and placing them in orphanages so that the mothers would be free to find work outside their homes in the new industrial work world. In the early twentieth century, those responsible for administering these policies—juvenile court judges and social workers—concluded that the children would be better off in their own homes, cared for by their mothers, rather than by employees in public orphanages. Because most married mothers did not work, it seemed obvious that a single parent could not be expected to be both a homemaker and a breadwinner. Juvenile court judges and social workers therefore led the fight for the creation of mothers' or widows' pensions. By 1909 they had enlisted the support of President Theodore Roosevelt, who sponsored the first national Conference on Children, at which mothers' pensions were discussed in great detail. In the next decade, forty states enacted mothers' pension programs.

6. See Table 8.1. These data omit health insurance and child care benefits and thereby understate the real differences between the United States and the other countries with respect to reliance upon income-tested beliefs. But they also omit some tax relief benefits, such as the child care tax credit and the child deduction in the United States, which overstates the real differences. On balance, we feel fairly confident that more comprehensive measures would not change the qualitative picture conveyed by the Luxembourg Income Study data: the United States relies much more heavily upon income-tested benefits than do Canada, France, and Sweden.

7. Some policies for increasing earning capacity, such as reforms of the public education system, fall outside the realm of income transfer policy, narrowly construed. Others, like general employment and training, which were never really very important relative to cash assistance and which were cut to the bone during the Reagan administration, are discussed in detail in Chapter 7.

8. Some form of national health insurance is also a critical component of increasing public responsibility for children. Currently, health insurance coverage for most working parents is provided by the employer. Many single mothers who work outside the home are not covered, however, either because they work part time or because their jobs do not provide medical benefits. Single mothers on welfare are covered through Medicaid, which is in-

come tested. The income test provides a strong disincentive for leaving welfare and going to work. Medicaid is part of the "poverty trap" mentioned earlier. Single mothers with low earning capacity cannot afford to leave welfare and give up their Medicaid benefits, yet staying on welfare means staying below the poverty line. National health insurance is discussed in Chapter 10.

9. Six different financing packages were suggested, but none was endorsed.

9. Updating Urban Policy

The research for this chapter was supported by the Institute for Research on Poverty, at the University of Wisconsin–Madison; by the Research and Training Program on Poverty, the Underclass, and Public Policy, at the University of Michigan; and by the William Cook Research Trust, at the University of Michigan Law School. The author is grateful to Sheldon Danziger, Diane Lehman, William Prosser, Erol Ricketts, and Gary Sandefur for their helpful criticisms of prior drafts, as well as to participants in a workshop at Yale University's Institution for Social and Policy Studies.

1. In 1987 Congress authorized HUD to designate one hundred zones nationally on the basis of measures of economic distress, but put very few dollars behind the designation— merely funding priority under programs such as Urban Development Action Grants and Community Development Block Grants. The authority lapsed without being exercised.

2. Such a zone/community must consist of no more than three parcels of land, situated in no more than two contiguous states, and encompassing no more than 20 square miles. For cities with a population of more than 2,000,000, the zone/community may have a population of no more than 200,000; for cities with a population of 500,000 to 2,000,000, the zone/community may have a population of no more than 10 percent of the city; for cities with a population of less than 500,000, the zone/community may have a population of no more than 50,000.

   Every census tract in a zone/community must have a poverty rate of at least 20 percent; at least 90 percent of the tracts must have poverty rates of at least 25 percent, and at least 50 percent of the tracts must have poverty rates of at least 35 percent. Central business districts must have poverty rates of at least 35 percent (for empowerment zones) or at least 30 percent (for enterprise communities). In the case of enterprise communities, these requirements may be relaxed to a limited extent by the Secretary of HUD.

3. The groups are "(A) a vocational rehabilitation referral, (B) an economically disadvantaged youth, (C) an economically disadvantaged Vietnam-era veteran, (D) an SSI recipient, (E) a general assistance recipient, (F) a youth participating in a cooperative education program, (G) an economically disadvantaged ex-convict, (H) an eligible work incentive employee, (I) an involuntarily terminated CETA employee, or (J) a qualified summer youth employee" (I.R.C. §51(d)(1)).

4. Kaus estimates that his subminimum wage positions would cost "at least $10,000 per job" (1992, p. 134). In 1985, Baumer and Van Horn (1985, p. 172) put the cost of public service jobs at $10,000 per job and the cost of "public works" (construction-oriented) jobs at $30,000 per job.

5. Title II of CETA, the direct successor to the Emergency Employment Act of 1971, was justified as a source of "transitional" jobs for unemployed victims of "structural" unemployment. Title VI, added at the end of 1974, was justified as a "countercyclical" response

to recession. In practice, however, there were no significant differences between participants in the two types of PSE program—for the most part, they were nondisadvantaged
adult white males who had been unemployed for relatively short durations (Mucciaroni,
1992).

6. To be sure, this argument leaves open the possibility that *some* forms of statistical discrimination might be morally tolerable. We do not always fault people who harm others
   through actions based on generalizations that are *almost always* true. To criticize such
   forms of statistical discrimination, one would need to rely on one of the other arguments
   made in the text.

10. Reform of Health Care for the Nonelderly Poor

The author gratefully acknowledges helpful contributions from Gina Livermore and Robert Haveman; the editors of this volume; and discussants at the IRP Conference, Katherine Swartz and Mary Fennell.

1. According to a recent OECD study (Schieber and Poullier, 1989) that used 1987 data to
   compare medical care expenditures per capita across the OECD countries, the United
   States spends far more per person than any other OECD country. The values are compared
   by assigning the United States per capita expenditure a value of 100 percent; the next
   highest value among the OECD countries was Canada at 72 percent. Switzerland was at 60
   percent along with Sweden; France was at 54, Germany at 53, and the Netherlands at 51
   percent. Except for Norway, all others were below 50 percent.

2. The increase has several causes, including the aging of the population (older persons use
   far more medical care than younger persons); improvements in technology, which extend
   life and improve the quality of life but are expensive in terms of real resources; and the
   third-party-payer system (see text), which sets the conditions for the rapid spread of new
   technology but reduces the incentive for consumers to search for lower prices of care and
   increases the probability that they will demand care for any given health problem.

3. As of October 1993, the Congressional Budget Office projects that health care expenditures will rise to 18 percent of gross domestic product by the year 2000 (U.S. Congressional Budget Office, 1993). Their 1993 estimate is $898 billion, or 14.3 percent of GDP.

4. In terms of forgone taxes (tax expenditures), the value of this subsidy is expected to be $56
   billion in 1992 for the federal government and an additional $12 billion for states. Of
   course, a number of tax rates are increased to compensate for these subsidies (Steuerle,
   1991).

5. Persons on end-stage renal dialysis are also eligible.

6. It is difficult for firms to reduce nominal wages. Hence, if there is little growth in productivity or little increase in prices, firms are constrained in their ability to shift the burden of
   paying for increases in health insurance to employees.

7. Of the nonelderly population, there was a decline in the percentage covered by another
   family member's employer-based plan from 34.3 percent in 1979 to 31.4 percent in 1986
   (U.S. House of Representatives, 1991, p. 313).

8. Another aspect of health care costs that has become increasingly important to U.S. firms is
   the liability to pay for health care benefits promised to retirees. Beginning in 1992, firms
   have had to report the unfunded liability of health insurance benefits promised on their

financial statements. One early estimate is a $227 billion liability in 1988 dollars (U.S. General Accounting Office, 1991a).

9. This does not include health care coverage of public-sector employees.

10. The measure of inadequate coverage that is used in the literature is coverage that leaves a person at risk of spending more than 10 percent of income on medical care in the event of a major illness. Using this definition, an estimated 20 million people had a 1 percent or greater risk of spending more than 10 percent of their income on health care in 1987 (Pepper Commission, 1990, pp. 23, 45). Most of these individuals have insurance plans that do not have caps on the amount the individual pays in the event of high medical care costs and may include exclusion waivers that omit prior conditions from coverage.

11. The service sector includes the following industries: personal services, retail trade, entertainment and recreational services, construction, business and repair services, and agriculture, forestry, and fishing. The extent to which such a shift has contributed to the growth in the uninsured is not known and may be small.

12. The other aspect of this is the growth of charity of uncompensated care. When individuals are very ill and require hospitalization, care is generally provided. Part of this is covered by state and local tax appropriations but some is not covered (unsponsored care). According to the American Hospital Association, uncompensated care was about 5.2 percent of all hospital expenses in the early 1980s and about 6.2 percent in the late 1980s; about 4 percent was unsponsored care in the earlier period compared with about 4.8 percent in the later period. As of 1989 this amounted to $8.9 billion.

13. See Pepper Commission (1990), tables 1–2.

14. Swartz and McBride (1990) also found that half of all spells of being uninsured last less than four months and that only 15 percent last longer than two years.

15. According to a survey by the Robert Wood Johnson Foundation (1987), in 1986 a million people were turned away from hospitals because they could not pay.

16. Rates of poor or fair health are also greater among blacks than whites—15.9 compared to 8.2 percent; this holds after controlling for broad income categories. The percentages for 1985–1987 were 18 percent of blacks and 11.1 percent of whites with family incomes less than $10,000 (National Center for Health Statistics, 1990).

17. To the extent that some health problems are linked to poverty, and the research on them does not control for poverty, the link between race and health may really be a link between poverty and health. See Keil et al. 1992).

18. Simple data on the relationship between utilization and insurance coverage may overstate the extent of the relationship. This occurs because we expect those with greater expected utilization to be more likely to purchase (or apply for) health insurance (that is, having coverage may be endogenous). Even taking such endogeny into account, however, persons with coverage have higher utilization than those without coverage once health, age, gender, income, and so on are taken into consideration.

19. Official data may overstate physician refusal to provide care to Medicaid patients: paperwork requirements tied to such reimbursement lead some physicians to treat Medicaid recipients but forgo Medicaid reimbursement for their services. Hence surveys of physicians regarding the nature of their practice (source of revenues or types of patients) and official data from Medicaid will both be incorrect. (I thank Katherine Swartz for pointing this out to me.)

20. As of 1993, the requirement to cover premiums extended to those elderly with incomes less than 110 percent of the poverty line; in 1995, the income limit increases to 120 percent of the poverty line.

21. Some hospitals are closing emergency rooms, which are frequented by the poor and tend to attract the medically indigent. This reduces availability and increases the indirect costs of receiving care (Pepper Commission, 1990, p. 37).

22. As of 1988, 111 nonmetropolitan counties had no physician; 1,473 had no obstetrician and 1,488 had no pediatrician (Summer, 1991).

23. The use of self-reported measures of health (the presence of a condition that led to a limitation) may mean that the poor report fewer conditions and hence that the use of care may still not reflect "equal care for equal needs."

24. Low-income workers are more likely to be docked pay for time missed at work than higher-paid salaried workers.

25. Cocaine causes a decreased flow of blood to the fetus and with it, a decrease in nutrients. It may also have a direct effect on cell growth. Cocaine use is also associated with the use of other substances such as cigarettes, marijuana, and alcohol, all of which may negatively influence birth outcomes including birth weight and the size of the brain (Zuckerman, 1991).

26. By the end of the first year of life, a low-birth-weight infant has a relative risk 1.6 times that of a normal-weight baby of having a congenital anomaly or developmental delay; for very low birth weight infants, the relative risk is 3.3 times that of normal-weight infants (McCormick, 1985, p. 88).

27. As of 1985, the relative risk of infant mortality was about forty times higher for an infant born weighing twenty-five hundred grams (five pounds) or less and two hundred times greater for those born with very low birth weights than for normal-weight infants (McCormick, 1985, p. 84).

28. This estimate is from Joyce, Racine, and Mocan (1992); it is based on the distribution of weights of low-birth-weight infants where drug use of the mother is established, times the average medical care costs for neonatal care only, for infants of that weight.

29. But the percentage reductions differ by education: 11 percent for those with more than twelve years of education, 20 percent for those with twelve years, and 35 percent for those with less than twelve years of education (Kleinman and Madans, 1985).

30. See the last section of this chapter.

31. Because of low reimbursement rates, physicians may spend less time per visit with each Medicaid-insured patient than with privately insured patients. One way physicians accomplish this is to require a separate visit for any medical need—preventive or curative.

32. In 1989 the monthly poverty line for a three-person family was $824.

33. When this is combined with medical school training that emphasizes the "technological imperative"—do all that is technologically possible for one's patients—and the difficulty of knowing what consumers would choose were they fully informed, the expectation is that more care will be provided than would be the case if the consumer were well informed.

34. A recent large-scale study, the Rand Health Insurance Experiment, provides rather convincing evidence that the elasticity of demand for medical care is positive and hence that more is demanded when individuals have greater insurance coverage (and thus pay a smaller share) than when they have less coverage. See Manning et al. (1987).

35. This phrase is placed in quotes because most economists believe that, with the exception of workers at a mandated minimum wage, employees bear the bulk of the cost of insurance in terms of forgone earnings. If there is a sudden increase in coverage, however, it may take time for the full share to be shifted to employees. This occurs because wages tend to be hard to reduce.

36. The public sector would also provide a subsidy toward the purchase of health insurance for those with low incomes. If the "pay" part of the pay or play plan were large enough, however, this would not be necessary. Recent versions of pay or play include Medicaid recipients but replace Medicaid with access to the new public plan. The pay, or public, portion would cover both individuals whose employer chose to pay and the poor.

37. States may find the expansion of Medicaid preferable to state-based strategies, as the cost is shared with the federal government, an administrative structure is in place, and certain cost-containment strategies may be more easily employed than in alternative plans. As of 1987, twenty states had expended Medicaid as a means of reducing the number of uninsured.

38. Extending such benefits may increase employment—and reduce the need for other transfer payments. For example, people with a paralysis may need special equipment (such as a motorized wheelchair and/or a specially equipped vehicle) in order to function independently. With these aids they can often be employed.

39. The ideas is that if these costly employees were removed, insurers' fear of adverse selection might be reduced and hence the premiums offered to small firms would be reduced. This effect is likely to be small, however.

40. The current tax incentives include a tax subsidy for the purchase of employer-based coverage; this subsidy is in the form of omitting the employer's contribution to health insurance from an employee's income and hence eliminating both payroll and income taxes on this component of compensation. A second tax subsidy is also included in the federal income tax. One can claim a tax deduction for medical care expenditures (including privately paid insurance premiums), above 7.5 percent of adjusted gross income.

41. The formation of risk pools is another alternative that is sometimes discussed in conjunction with refundable tax credits. Single individuals, families, and small firms generally must pay far more for the same insurance coverage than persons in large groups. Risk pools combine groups of individuals or small groups of employees to reduce the surcharge insurance companies charge small groups and individuals. (The surcharge reflects the higher costs of selling to small groups and the fear of adverse selection—that only those with the greatest expected medical expenditures will purchase individual policies.)

42. A proposal to reduce the tax subsidy to high-income persons is a more limited form of such policies.

43. A third alternative would combine employer-based insurance with a high deductible (say, $3,000 per family) with an employer contribution to a medical IRA (tax-free allowances) to cover deductibles and other health costs. The funds could be used for deductibles, for premiums should the individual not be employed, or for long-term care. The employee would keep any IRA amounts not spent, subject to certain limitations on withdrawals.

44. Danzon (1992) analyzes the difference in overhead in the United States and Canada and finds a far smaller difference than is commonly acknowledged. She starts with the United States' 11.7 percent of benefit payments compared with Canada's figure of 0.9 and then

(1) nets taxes, returns on capital, and investment income out of private insurers' overhead premium, reducing the 11.7 to 7.6 percent; and (2) estimates the hidden costs, which include patient time costs for multiple visits because less time is spent per visit by the provider in response to low fees; productivity losses as patients wait for services but have difficulty carrying on their work and other normal activities; and excess burdens due to higher tax rates to finance the system. When all of these are included, the Canadian system may have higher overhead costs than the U.S. system.

45. Numerous studies of such systems, including those of Canada and Great Britain, find evidence of substantial differences in care provided to those of differing income or socioeconomic groups. Those with more resources always appear favored.

46. These contributions have a ceiling.

47. Along with the national health system, which covers all citizens, is a small but growing private sector used primarily by those with higher incomes. The private insurance is primarily used for elective procedures, for which a wait would be required within the national system.

48. Some reorganization of the labor market might also occur under a pay-or-play plan. With a proportional tax, the insurance of low earners would be subsidized while high earners would be penalized. High earners are likely to prefer firms with private "play" plans; low earners, firms which participate in the pay, or public sector, aspect. (See Steuerle, 1991.) Firms may also establish subsidiaries in order to take advantage of any subsidies based on firm size.

49. This is likely to occur because firms will want to establish how much they will contribute under any new financing plan, and may seek to establish alternative fringe benefits to advance employee loyalty. Both of these will be viewed as part of employee compensation and will reduce the amount firms are willing to offer employees as cash compensation.

50. The plan had to be approved (granted a waiver) at the federal level before it could be put into effect. This was granted in 1993.

51. The providers in the community care center would be either private providers who contract to provide care at the center as well as manage all additional care for the children served by the center or, in certain limited cases, publicly employed providers.

52. Such a response, termed "moral hazard" in the literature, also includes an incentive to take fewer precautions to avoid the need for medical care as well as a reduction of the incentive to search for a lower-priced provider.

53. These chronic conditions would be limited and might include certain cancers, AIDS, and a few other conditions. The adjustment would be a multiplicative factor, such as 1.5 times the basic prepayment.

54. Including *all* children and pregnant women rather than only those below some income cutoff should also reduce the potential problem of underservice.

55. A relative value scale is an index based on the characteristics of the care provided, such as effort and/or training required. It is used to create a fee schedule for payment. It may include cost considerations, such as the cost of offices in the particular community in which a service is provided.

56. An example of this is the Japanese medical system, which compensates physicians according to a fee schedule that pays more if a prescription is given than if not. The result is that Japanese have the most prescriptions written (and filled) per capita!

57. This figure is an overestimate, because it does not subtract other programs that provide

services to low-income children, such as WIC, state programs for children with incomes below a variety of cutoffs, block grants to Community Health Centers, or special programs targeted at low-income pregnant women, and those programs mentioned in this paragraph.

58. For private insurance companies, Healthy-Kid may represent a tradeoff: a loss of the market for children and pregnant women but an increase in the market for private coverage of adults.

59. This would be greatly encouraged if the remaining subsidy was tied to a requirement that policies either be managed care or require coinsurance up to a maximum payment per capita that might be linked to income.

60. Some adjustment for mid-year changes might be included in this plan to provide a work incentive for Medicaid recipients.

61. HMOs would also be required to participate, offering a basic package to a specified minimum number of families, set to reflect each HMO's share of the insurance market in the state in the prior year. The share of insurance companies would also be set according to their share of the health insurance market in the state for the prior year. New entry and exit of insurers would also influence the actual shares.

62. The cost of treating all AIDS patients in one year, 1992, was estimated to be $7.5 billion (Hellinger, 1988).

63. Eligibility for Medicare begins twenty-four months after entitlement to cash benefits under the disability program.

64. The Catastrophic Coverage Act of 1988, repealed in 1989, would have provided unlimited days of coverage as well as more extensive nursing home and hospice benefits.

65. These fee schedules are based on a relative value scale similar to that recently introduced for Medicare. The actual schedule differs across regions and is the result of negotiations between regional associations of physicians and of sickness funds. They can be lowered toward the end of the year if expenditures on physicians are high relative to a goal or cap.

66. These rates are based on annual global (all-inclusive) budgets set for each hospital, the result of negotiations between each hospital, and the regional association of sickness funds.

67. The private system has been somewhat controversial—patients may be hospitalized in public hospitals and cared for by the Chiefs or senior M.D.s, who serve both types of patients. This takes resources from the public sector to provide additional care for the privately insured who tend to be in a higher social class.

11. Education and the Well-Being of the Next Generation

This chapter draws on Murnane (1988) and Murnane and Levy (1992). The author appreciates the permission of the Brookings Institution to use material from these publications.

1. See Levy and Murnane (1992) for a discussion of trends in the distribution of earnings.

2. As explained in Murnane, Willett, and Levy (1993), the relationships between test scores and subsequent wages were estimated in models that controlled for family background and postsecondary educational attainments.

3. Half of all dropouts—more than 500,000 a year—do eventually earn a high school equivalency diploma by passing the General Educational Development (GED) test, which is used in all fifty states. No one would dispute the importance of providing dropouts a sec-

ond chance, but holders of the GED earn considerably less than high school graduates. For evidence on males, see Cameron and Heckman (1991). For evidence on females, see Maloney (1991).

4. These percentages, reported in Danziger and Danziger (1992), come from U.S. Censuses of Population and from the March 1991 Current Population Survey.

5. For more information on school-based reforms and systemic reform efforts, see Murnane and Levy (1992).

6. Participation in compensatory preschool education programs does not appear to have lasting effects on IQ. Opponents of devoting more governmental resources to such programs emphasize this pattern, rather than the evidence of long-term effects on other outcomes. Barnett (1992) discusses possible explanations for the sensitivity of findings to the choice of outcome measure.

7. I am indebted to Sheldon White for helping me to understand the evidence on the effects of early childhood intervention programs.

8. The process by which Chapter 1 funds are distributed has several steps. Funds are distributed to counties primarily on the basis of counts of low-income children. The state is then responsible for allocating the funds to local districts based on counts of low-income children. At the district level, schools are selected for Chapter 1 services based on their relative poverty levels. Within individual schools, children are eligible for Chapter 1 services if their educational achievements are below those appropriate for children their age. Most Chapter 1 programs concentrate services on students in grades one through six (Sinclair and Gutmann, 1992).

9. In 1991–92, 74 percent of elementary school principals reported using the pullout model to comply with Chapter 1. This proportion was a decline from 84 percent six years earlier (U.S. Department of Education, 1993).

10. This is one of the recommendations of the congressionally mandated Independent Review Panel of the National Assessment of Chapter 1.

11. As this volume went to press, Congress had begun reauthorizing Chapter 1, and the recommendations made here may have become part of the revised Chapter 1 program.

12. I am indebted to Stephen Hamilton and Larry Rosenstock for many of the ideas on improving school-to-work transition.

13. See Murnane and Raizen (1988) for ideas concerning the content of a monitoring system.

12. Systemic Educational Reform and Social Mobility

This work was supported by grant 87ASPE041A from the Office of the Assistant Secretary for Planning and Evaluation, U.S. Department of Health and Human Services. The author is grateful to Tom Corbett, Bill Prosser, and John Witte for their comments and to Ted Shen for his expert programming assistance. An earlier version, published in the *Economics of Education Review* (Manski 1992), provides a detailed technical description of the simulation model applied here. Portions of this article reprinted by permission of Elsevier Science Ltd., Oxford, England.

13. Poverty and Immigration in Policy Perspective

Manuscript preparation for this chapter was supported by a grant (HD-25588) from the Center for Population Research to the University of Chicago. The authors gratefully acknowledge able research assistance from Patrick Phillips and institutional support from the Population Center of NORC and the University of Chicago. Alejandro Portes and the volume editors provided excellent comments on an early draft.

1. Contrary to popular belief, the Immigration Reform and Control Act of 1986 (IRCA) was not the first act of Congress that granted amnesty to unauthorized migrants. The 1986 program is the largest amnesty program in U.S. immigration history, however, and is certainly the most debated. Most other acts granting amnesty were targeted at specific groups.

2. For example, Jasso and Rosenzweig (1990, p. 195) note that the backlog for fifth-preference visas (siblings of U.S. citizens) increased from approximately half a million in 1980 to nearly 1.5 million in 1989.

3. Immigration statistics have been kept since they were congressionally mandated in 1819, that is, from 1820 to the present. Much of the federal legislation governing immigration prior to 1819 focused on regulations about naturalization, requirements for reporting passengers on arriving vessels, the safeguard of passengers, and the establishment of a Commissioner of Immigration.

4. At least one restrictive measure occurred prior to this time, however. The Immigration Act of 1862 prohibited the transportation of Chinese "coolies" on American vessels, but not necessarily on foreign vessels.

5. Lawmakers came to realize the discriminatory underpinnings of the 1924 act, and the benchmark for establishing quotas was modified in 1929 to use the 1920 rather than the 1890 census. The change was too late, however, to have much influence on the composition of newcomers because immigration all but stopped following the stock market crash of 1929. A less well known fact about the 1929 legislation is that it enacted the first legalization program by qualifying for permanent resident status all individuals who had entered the United States before June 3, 1921. This represents a somewhat longer waiting period than was stipulated by the 1986 IRCA legislation—8 years versus 5 years, respectively. In the same year, 1929, many Mexicans were repatriated to Mexico, including those who had been born in the United States.

6. Table 13.1 lists the "Bracero Program" as if it were a single act of Congress. Actually this program was initiated in 1942 as a series of bilateral agreements with several countries before it was ratified by Congress in 1943. This formal statutory program, which was formally terminated in 1947, continued informally and without regulation until 1951. Reconstituted as Public Law 78 in response to labor shortages stemming from the Korean conflict, the Bracero program was reformalized from 1951 to 1964. It continued informally for several years beyond this, and provided the economic and political foundation for the provisions in the IRCA legislation that governed special agricultural workers and replenishment agricultural workers.

7. The alien address reporting requirement was discontinued in 1980.

8. The 1978 Amendment to the Immigration and Nationality Act brought both hemispheres under a single worldwide ceiling of 290,000. Mexico, the largest single contributor to undocumented immigration, was the country most affected by the 1976 legislation.

9. Hereafter we use interchangeably the terms labor migrants and economic migrants, and the terms refugees and political migrants. The distinction between political and economic migrants is not as clear-cut as legal divisions might suggest, however. See Portes and Bach (1985).

10. "Refugees" are persons who reside outside of their home country and are unable or unwilling to return due to a well-founded fear of persecution. Those given asylum ("asylees") satisfy the definitions of refugees, but are residing within the United States or at a port of entry, and are pending formal admission. Parolees are persons who are otherwise inadmissible to the United States, but may be allowed to enter under emergency or humanitarian conditions. Both refugees and asylees can adjust their lawful status to permanent resident after only one year of continuous presence in the United States. These admissions are exempt from the worldwide limitation of 270,000, but the 1952 Immigration and Nationality Act only permits 5,000 asylees to adjust per fiscal year (INS, 1991).

11. Between 1961 and 1974 the federal government allocated an estimated $1 billion in various forms of resettlement assistance to Cuban refugees, and this would pale by comparison with the assistance later received by Southeast Asian refugees.

12. Cubans who entered during the "Mariel crisis" were not officially recognized as refugees, but were rather designated "entrants" until a special act could be passed to regularize their status as refugees.

13. This belief was articulated at all levels, from the President to news television programs and magazines. In 1984 then President Reagan was quoted in *Newsweek* as saying, "The simple truth is that we've lost control of our own borders and no nation can do that and survive" (INS, 1991, p. 30).

14. Much of the literature on undocumented migration uses the term "illegal" to identify migrants who are not authorized to be in the United States, but we prefer the terms "undocumented" and "unauthorized" migrants, which are more neutral in connotation than terms like "illegal," "deportable," and "aliens."

15. The imposition of sanctions on employers who hired undocumented immigrants also eliminated the peculiar clause in the 1952 act that protected employers who hired undocumented immigrants while making it a felony to be an undocumented migrant.

16. Findings from various studies are at variance with one another, however. For example, using INS apprehension data, analysts at the Urban Institute find that IRCA has reduced the volume of undocumented Mexican migration (Espenshade et al., 1990). Studies based on community-level data from Mexico suggest otherwise (Cornelius, 1990; Donato, Durand, and Massey, 1992).

17. Although there is general agreement that the size of the undocumented population grew between 1960 and 1980 (Passel and Woodrow, 1984; Warren and Passel, 1987; Vernez and Ronfeldt, 1991), there is far less consensus about the absolute size and relative growth over the period.

18. Approximately 1.3 million undocumented immigrants applied for amnesty under the Special Agricultural Worker (SAW) program of IRCA. About 82 percent of these were of Mexican origin. However, the eligibility criteria for SAWs were considerably more lenient than those used for the general program, and hence there need not be any connection between these two estimates.

19. Goza (1987) is a possible exception, except that his voluntary immigrants comparison was a cross-sectional sample.

20. Although we believe that issues of cultural pluralism are themselves worthy of discussion in their own right, we focus here on economic considerations.

21. These general issues apply to undocumented migrants as well, but we raise them in this

section so that our discussion of undocumented and legalized immigrants can address issues that are unique to them.

22. The emerging consensus seems to be that migration is simultaneously a cause and a consequence of employment, namely, that high levels of immigration create jobs and that this job creation continues to draw migrants (see Greenwood and McDowell, 1986; Massey, 1990b). In the case of New York, Waldinger (1989) and Stern (1990) have argued that New York City would have suffered worse economic declines were it not for the enterprising economic activity of recent immigrants.

23. In deriving estimates of the rate of assimilation from cross-sectional data, Chiswick assumed that the high earnings of early cohorts can be used to represent the future earnings of recent cohorts.

24. Of course, the direction of bias depends on the selection mechanisms governing emigration.

25. LaLonde and Topel also used a wider age spectrum—sixteen to sixty-four versus eighteen to fifty-four—in their assessment, and it is unclear what share of the observed differences in their conclusions might be attributed to this change. In any event, this difference is not likely to be great.

26. Borjas and Tienda (1987) have pointed out that two false assumptions are built into the displacement arguments. One is that the number of jobs in the economy is fixed. This assumption ignores the underpinnings of employment theory that show that employment levels result from the interaction of supply and demand. A second false assumption is that natives and foreigners are perfect substitutes in production.

27. These authors arrived at this powerful conclusion not from direct estimates of the impact of immigration but, rather, from the assumption that immigration necessarily shifts the supply curve to the right. Using approximate estimates of the demand for labor based on other studies, Borjas, Freeman, and Katz (1991) derived negative effects of immigration on employment.

28. These authors also determined that the presence of a large number of Mexican immigrants has served to lower the prices of labor-intensive goods and services consumed within the state. Unfortunately, secondary consumption issues are rarely considered in the economic balance sheets used to evaluate immigration.

29. Unfortunately, Jensen included Puerto Ricans in his assessment of Hispanic immigrant poverty. Because Puerto Ricans technically are not immigrants and because they have unusually high poverty rates (Tienda and Jensen, 1988), it is not possible to ascertain a pure immigrant effect on poverty for this regional origin group.

30. These averages do not indicate whether working poverty was more prevalent among some groups, nor do they speak to the duration of poverty.

31. For example, Stern (1990) documented that immigrants avoid filing for unemployment insurance. How immigrants' legal status influences this tendency is unclear, however.

32. Borjas and his associates have attributed ethnic differences in welfare participation rates to intergenerational transmission processes, but the evidence marshalled in support of this thesis is weak. It is not clear to what extent Borjas and Trejo's detection of an increased use of entitlement programs captures the change in eligibility after three years of U.S. residence. Furthermore, estimates simulated from synthetic cohort comparisons cannot address protracted economic dependency, the major issue causing political excitement.

33. This concept was developed after an examination of the Cuban refugee experience (see Portes, 1969, and Pedraza-Bailey, 1985).
34. Permanent authority for the Cuban Refugee Program was provided by the Migration and Refugee Assistance Act, which not only provided direct financial assistance to needy refugees but also reimbursed state and local agencies that provided assistance. Also provided by the program were transportation costs to leave Cuba, resettlement assistance outside of Miami, and employment and language training courses for refugees, including professionals and highly skilled workers.
35. There are several additional but smaller categorical programs authorized by the act, including Refugee Health and national discretionary projects. In 1990 the discretionary projects designed to improve refugee resettlement operations totaled about $12 million. The Refugee Health allocation is used to monitor overseas screening of prospective refugees, to inspect admissions at port of entry, and to subsidize local health departments for their involvement in health assessments of refugees.
36. In our judgment, however, the official position is more positive than assessments conducted by private researchers indicate.
37. Bach and Aguiros did not consider the prevalence of welfare recidivism, which is an important topic for further research given the apparent prevalence of working poverty in California.
38. The numerous labor market studies compiled by Bach and Brill (1991) and by the "Changing Relations Project" (Bach, 1991) underscore the importance of taking into account social context in deciphering the economic impacts of immigration.
39. This is a reasonable assumption, although we are not aware of any studies that have compared the prevalence of working poverty among immigrant and native populations of various national origins.
40. Categorical programs to reduce poverty through tax credits, such as the Earned Income Tax Credit, are probably the only proposals likely to obtain political support under the political climate of the 1990s.

14. Antipoverty Policy, Affirmative Action, and Racial Attitudes

The authors wish to thank the editors and Jennifer L. Hochschild for their comments on an earlier draft of this paper, and Betty Evanson for making sure that it was completed in a timely way.

1. Welfare reform has also been the subject of a ballot initiative in California. In 1992 Californians rejected Proposition 165, a welfare reform measure that would have reduced benefit levels and imposed work requirements.
2. In this regard we should note that an individual's prior attitudes and values are important contributors to willingness to participate in collective action (Walsh and Warland, 1983). For example, several studies have identified racial attitudes as contributors to anti–school busing protest involvement (Begley and Alker, 1982; D. Taylor, 1986; Useem, 1980).
3. Public attitudes are not fixed and given. Instead, they are socially created and learned responses to social stimuli. Such attitudes are acquired, used, tested, and reinforced or modified by ongoing social experience (H. Kelman, 1974). In addition, public opinion, even within the delimited domain of antipoverty and race-based social policy, is complex,

sometimes internally contradictory, and loosely structured at best. In a copious review of the public opinion literature, Kinder and Sears (1985) noted that American political thinking is not highly constrained and consistent as though tightly organized around a well understood liberal-conservative ideological continuum. There are, nonetheless, reasonably clear patterns and regularities revealed in the literature. Below we will review data and research on the social and psychological sources of public opinion on antipoverty and race-based policy issues.

4. The data are taken from the General Social Survey (J. Davis and Smith, 1990), which samples between 1,400 and 1,500 persons. The figures show the percentage of respondents who placed themselves on a scale point of 1 or 2 for the Help Poor, Help Sick, Help Not, and Equal Wealth questions.

5. This trend is a departure from patterns observed by earlier analysts. For instance, Coughlin noted that "while there is no sign of any mass-based health-care 'back-lash,' neither is there a concerted push for expanded government intervention" (1979, p. 21). Survey data over the past decade show a steady rise in support for greater social spending on health care.

6. To be sure, exact wording matters for understanding responses to survey questions. Sometimes seemingly trivial differences in wording can produce substantial differences in levels of support and can on occasion alter relationships to other variables (for example, time and education; see Schuman and Presser, 1981). These apparent "artifacts" of exact question wording can yield important insight into the contours of public opinion on the question under investigation; that is, they are often informative rather than being misleading or grounds for doubting the value of surveys (Schuman, 1980).

7. Lipset and Schneider (1978, p. 43) note that the history of social change in America has been marked by a "shifting back and forth between these core values as a period of obsessive concern with quality and social reform is followed by a period emphasizing individual achievement and upward mobility."

8. We use multiple ordinary least squares regressions to assess the relative effects of race, socioeconomic status, and other attitudinal variables on individual's social welfare and racial policy preferences. An excellent nontechnical discussion of the use of regression by social scientists can be found in Tufte (1974), and more technical but accessible introductions can be found in Achen (1982) and Weisberg (1980).

9. The demographic variables included in each model are age, sex, years of education, family income, occupational prestige, and residence in a southern state.

10. These measures include self-designation on a continuum running from extremely liberal through middle of the road to extremely conservative; commitment to equity notions of reward based on merit, ability, and effort; individualistic perceptions of the causes of poverty; and structural perceptions of the causes of poverty.

11. The same patterns emerged in Lipset and Schneider's (1978) detailed review of public opinion polls reaching back to 1935.

15. Poverty Politics

The author wishes to thank Lawrence Mead for his extensive and invariably helpful comments on this chapter.

1. Not many, however, were as explicit as Governor Eugene Talmadge of Georgia. In attacking New Deal legislation, and the Social Security Act in particular, Talmadge complained: "The Federal (Social Security) Board in Washington is going to make them add on nearly every Negro of a certain age in the county to this pauper's list. What will become of your farm labor—your wash-woman, your cooks, your plowhands?" (Hanson, 1992, p. 21).

2. A fuller historical account would show that for at least six hundred years reformers in Western societies have been trying to rationalize public assistance to help the truly needy while denying a free ride to undeserving, work-shy persons (Heclo, 1992; Mollat, 1986).

3. Stimson, for example, calculates mood by using a set of 871 readings on domestic issues drawn from questions asked more than once by virtually all the major survey organizations between 1956 and 1989. The issues cover a full range of public views on everything from gun control and the size of government to the environment, health care, race relations, and so on. Questions on abortion, which follow a unique and often misleading pattern, are the only major domestic area excluded (Stimson, 1991, app. 3).

4. Although perhaps unconstitutional under the Supreme Court's 1969 *Shapiro v. Thompson* decision, state legislatures in California, Maine, and Wisconsin were seriously considering such proposals in early 1992.

5. Wisconsin received permission for a five-year experiment in four counties. The experiment will require parenting classes and high school attendance, permit married couples to receive AFDC and earn up to $14,000 without loss of benefit, cut benefits in half for a second child, and eliminate benefits for any additional children born while the mother is on welfare.

6. As if on belated cue from a deteriorating civil order, social scientists have recently emphasized the moral dimension as part of social reality (March and Olsen, 1989; Selznick, 1992; J. Q. Wilson, 1993).

16. The Nature, Causes, and Cures of Poverty

1. This chapter reflects the comments of Isabel Sawhill, who served as a co-rapporteur with Robert Haveman at the conference that resulted in this volume.

2. The New Hope program (now being tried in Milwaukee, Wisconsin) is a prototype of such an approach. It is based on the proposition that by simultaneously intervening in several dimensions that constrain many poor families—and providing them with the economic and social arrangements that more affluent families have—we can effectively test the proposition that the poor can, like the rest of us, become self-sufficient and independent.

References

Aaron, Henry J. 1978. *Politics and the Professors: The Great Society in Perspective.* Washington, D.C.: Brookings Institution.

—— 1982. *Economic Effects of Social Security.* Washington, D.C.: Brookings Institution.

—— 1992. "Strategy versus Tactics in Designing Social Policy." Speech delivered at Brandeis University. Brookings Institution, Washington, D.C. Mimeo.

Abbott, Edith. 1937. *Some American Pioneers in Social Welfare.* Chicago: University of Chicago Press.

Abrahamse, Allan F., Peter Morrison, and Linda J. Waite. 1988. "Beyond Stereotypes: Who Becomes a Teenage Mother?" RAND Corporation, Santa Monica, Calif. Mimeo.

Abrams, Elliot, and Franklin Abrams. 1975. "Immigration Policy—Who Gets In and Why?" *Public Interest* 38 (Winter): 3–29.

Achen, Christopher H. 1982. *Interpreting and Using Regression.* Beverly Hills, Calif.: Sage Publications.

Adams, Terry K., Greg J. Duncan, and Willard L. Rodgers. 1988. "The Persistence of Urban Poverty." In *Quiet Riots: Race and Poverty in the United States,* ed. Fred R. Harris and Roger W. Wilkins. New York: Pantheon Books.

Akerlof, George. 1985. "Discriminatory, Status-Based Wages among Tradition-Oriented, Stochastically Trading Coconut Producers." *Journal of Political Economy* 93: 265–276.

Aleinikoff, T. Alexander. 1992. "The Constitution in Context: The Continuing Significance of Racism." *University of Colorado Law Review* 63: 325–373.

Alliance Housing Council. 1988. *Housing and Homelessness.* Washington, D.C.: National Alliance to End Homelessness.

Altonji, Joseph, and David Card. 1991. "The Effects of Immigration on the Labor Market Outcomes of Less-Skilled Natives." In *Immigration, Trade, and the Labor Market,* ed. John M. Abowd and Richard B. Freeman. Chicago: University of Chicago Press.

Anderson, Elijah. 1989. "Sex Codes and Family Life among Poor Inner-City Youths." *Annals of the American Academy of Political and Social Science* 501 (January): 59–78.

—— 1990. *Streetwise: Race, Class, and Change in an Urban Community.* Chicago: University of Chicago Press.

Aponte, Robert. 1988. "Conceptualizing the Underclass: An Alternative Perspective." Paper presented at the annual meetings of the American Sociological Association, August 26, Atlanta.

Apostle, Richard, Charles Y. Glock, Thomas Piazza, and Marijean Suzele. 1983. *The Anatomy of Racial Attitudes.* Berkeley: University of California Press.

Arfin, D. M. 1986. "The Use of Financial Aid to Attract Talented Students to Teaching: Lessons from Other Fields." *Elementary School Journal* 86: 405–423.

Arrow, Kenneth. 1971. "The Theory of Discrimination." In *Discrimination in Labor Markets,* ed. Orley Ashenfelter and Albert Rees. Princeton, N.J.: Princeton University Press.

Atkinson, Anthony B. 1992. "Poverty, Statistics, and Progress in Europe." The Welfare State Programme, Suntory-Toyota International Centre for Economics and Related Disciplines. No. WSP/60. London School of Economics. April.

Auletta, Ken. 1982. *The Underclass.* New York: Random House.

Bach, Robert L. 1988. "State Intervention in Southeast Asian Refugee Resettlement in the United States." *Journal of Refugee Studies* 1 (1): 38–56.

———— 1991. "Changing Relations: Newcomers and Established Residents in U.S. Communities." Final Report of the National Board of Changing Relations Project. Department of Sociology, SUNY-Binghamton. Mimeo.

Bach, Robert L., and Rita Aguiros. 1991. "Economic Progress among Southeast Asian Refugees in the United States." In *Refugee Policy: Canada and the United States,* ed. Howard Adelman. Toronto: York Lanes Press.

Bach, Robert L., and Howard Brill. 1991. "Impact of the IRCA on the U.S. Labor Market." Final Report to the U.S. Department of Labor, Washington, D.C. Mimeo.

Bach, Robert L., and Marta Tienda. 1984. "Contemporary Immigration and Refugee Movements and Employment Adjustment Policies." In *Immigration: Issues and Policy,* ed. Vernon M. Briggs, Jr., and Marta Tienda. Salt Lake City, Utah: Olympus Press.

Bailey, Thomas, and Donna Merritt. 1992. "School to Work Transition and Youth Apprenticeship in the United States." Draft discussion paper, Teachers College and Conservation of Human Resources, Columbia University, New York.

Baily, Martin N., and Alok K. Chakrabarti. 1988. *Innovation and the Productivity Crisis.* Washington, D.C.: Brookings Institution.

Bane, Mary Jo, and David T. Ellwood. 1986. "Slipping into and out of Poverty: The Dynamics of Spells." *Journal of Human Resources* 21 (Winter): 1–23.

Bane, Mary Jo, and Paul A. Jargowsky. 1988. "Urban Poverty Areas: Basic Questions Concerning Prevalence, Growth, and Dynamics." Center for Health and Human Resources Policy Discussion Paper Series, Harvard University.

Banfield, Edward C. 1958 (2nd ed., 1970). *The Unheavenly City.* Boston: Little, Brown.

Barnett, W. Stephen. 1992. "Benefits of Compensatory Preschool Education." *Journal of Human Resources* 27 (Spring): 279–312.

Barnow, Burt S. 1987. "The Impact of CETA Programs on Earnings: A Review of the Literature." *Journal of Human Resources* 22 (Spring): 157–193.

Bassi, Laurie J. 1983. "The Effect of CETA on the Postprogram Earnings of Participants." *Journal of Human Resources* 18: 539–556.

Bassi, Laurie J., and Orley Ashenfelter. 1986. "The Effect of Direct Job Creation and Training Programs on Low-Skilled Workers." In *Fighting Poverty: What Works and What*

Doesn't, ed. Sheldon H. Danziger and Daniel H. Weinberg. Cambridge, Mass.: Harvard University Press.

Bates, Timothy, and Constance R. Dunham. 1992. "Facilitating Upward Mobility through Small Business Ownership." In *Urban Labor Markets and Job Opportunity*, ed. George E. Peterson and Wayne Vroman. Washington, D.C.: Urban Institute Press.

Baumer, Donald, and Carl Van Horn. 1985. *The Politics of Unemployment*. Washington, D.C.: C. Q. Press.

Bean, Frank D., B. Lindsay Lowell, and Lowell J. Taylor. 1988. "Undocumented Mexican Immigrants and the Earnings of Other Workers in the United States." *Demography* 25: 35–52.

Bean, Frank D., and Marta Tienda. 1987. *The Hispanic Population of the United States*. New York: Russell Sage Foundation.

Bean, Frank D., George Vernez, and Charles Keely. 1989. *Opening and Closing the Doors: Evaluating Immigration Reform and Control*. Santa Monica, Calif.: Rand Corporation.

Becker, Gary S. 1957. *The Economics of Discrimination*. Chicago: University of Chicago Press.

——— 1964. (2nd ed., 1975). *Human Capital*. New York: Columbia University Press.

Becker, Gary S., and Nigel Tomes. 1986. "Human Capital and the Rise and Fall of Families." *Journal of Labor Economics* 4 (2, pt. 2): S1–S39.

Begley, Thomas M., and Henry Alker. 1982. "Anti-Busing Protest: Attitudes and Actions." *Social Psychology Quarterly* 45: 187–197.

Behrman, Jere R., and Paul Taubman. 1990. "The Intergenerational Correlation between Children's Adult Earnings and Their Parents' Income: Results from the Michigan Panel Study of Income Dynamics." *Review of Income and Wealth* 36: 115–127.

Belknap, Joanne, Merry Morash, and Robert Trojanowicz. 1987. "Implementing a Community Policing Model for Work with Juveniles: An Exploratory Study." *Criminal Justice and Behavior* 14: 211–245.

Berrueta-Clement, John R., L. Schweinhart, W. Barnett, A. Epstein, and D. Weikart. 1984. *Changed Lives: The Effects of the Perry Preschool Program on Youths through Age 19*. Ypsilanti, Mich.: High/Scope Press.

Bird, Kevin D. 1989. "Bringing New Life to Enterprise Zones: Congress Finally Takes the First Step with the Housing and Community Development Act of 1987." *Washington University Journal of Urban and Contemporary Law* 35: 109–125.

Birdsong, Bret. 1989. "Federal Enterprise Zones: A Poverty Program for the 1990s?" Working Paper, Urban Institute, Washington, D.C.

Bishop, John, and Suk Kang. 1991. "Applying for Entitlements: Employers and the Targeted Jobs Tax Credit." *Journal of Policy Analysis and Management* 10: 24–45.

Blackburn, McKinley L., David E. Bloom, and Richard B. Freeman. 1990. "Why Has the Economic Position of Less-Skilled Workers Deteriorated in the United States?" In *A Future of Lousy Jobs*, ed. Gary Burtless. Washington, D.C.: Brookings Institution.

Blakely, Edward. 1989. "Theoretical Approaches for a Global Community." In *Community Development in Perspective*, ed. James Christenson and Jerry Robinson. Ames: Iowa State University Press.

Blank, Rebecca M. 1989a. "Analyzing the Length of Welfare Spells." *Journal of Public Economics* 39: 245–273.

———— 1989b. "The Effect of Medical Need and Medicaid on AFDC Participation." *Journal of Human Resources* 24: 55–87.

———— 1991. "Why Were Poverty Rates So High in the 1980s?" Working Paper no. 3878, National Bureau of Economic Research, Cambridge, Mass., October.

———— 1993. "Why Were Poverty Rates So High in the 1980s?" In *Poverty and Prosperity in the USA in the Late Twentieth Century,* ed. Dimitri B. Papadimitriou and Edward N. Wolff. New York and London: Macmillan.

Blank, Rebecca M., and Alan Binder. 1986. "Macroeconomics, Income Distribution, and Poverty." In *Fighting Poverty: What Works and What Doesn't,* ed. Sheldon H. Danziger and Daniel H. Weinberg. Cambridge, Mass.: Harvard University Press.

Blau, Francine D. 1984. "The Use of Transfer Payments by Immigrants." *Industrial and Labor Relations Review* 37 (2): 222–239.

Blau, Francine D., and Marianne A. Ferber. 1992. *The Economics of Women, Men, and Work.* 2nd ed. Englewood Cliffs, N.J.: Prentice-Hall.

Blau, Peter M., and Otis D. Duncan. 1967. *The American Occupational Structure.* New York: John Wiley.

Blendon, Robert, and Karen Donelan. 1991. "National Health Insurance: Does the Public Buy It?" *Public Perspective* 2: 5–10.

Bloom, Howard S., Larry L. Orr, George Cave, Stephen H. Bell, and Fred Doolittle. 1993. "The National JTPA Study." Report to the U.S. Department of Labor. Bethesda, Md.: Abt Associates.

Bobo, Lawrence. 1988. "Attitudes toward the Black Political Movement: Trends, Meaning, and Effects on Racial Policy Preferences." *Social Psychology Quarterly* 51: 287–302.

———— 1991. "Social Responsibility, Individualism, and Redistributive Policies." *Sociological Forum* 6 (1): 71–92.

Bobo, Lawrence, and James R. Kluegel. 1993. "Opposition to Race Targeting: Self-Interest, Stratification Ideology, or Racial Attitudes?" *American Sociological Review* 58:443–464.

Boeck, David. 1984. "The Enterprise Zone Debate." *Urban Lawyer* 16: 71–173.

Borjas, George J. 1985. "Assimilation, Changes in Cohort Quality, and the Earnings of Immigrants." *Journal of Labor Economics* 3: 463–489.

———— 1986. "The Sensitivity of Labor Demand Functions to Choice of Dependent Variable." *Review of Economics and Statistics* 68 (February): 58–66.

———— 1987. "Immigrants, Minorities, and Labor Market Competition." *Industrial and Labor Relations Review* 40 (3): 382–392.

———— 1990. *Friends or Strangers: The Impact of Immigrants on the U.S. Economy.* New York: Basic Books.

Borjas, George J., Richard B. Freeman, and Lawrence Katz. 1991. "On the Labor Market Effects of Immigration and Trade." Working Paper, National Bureau of Economic Research, Cambridge, Mass.

Borjas, George J., and Marta Tienda. 1987. "The Economic Consequences of Immigration." *Science* 235: 645–651.

———— 1993. "Employment and Wages of Legalized Immigrants." *International Migration Review.* 27 (4): 712–747.

Borjas, George J., and Stephen J. Trejo. 1991. "Immigrant Participation in the Welfare System." *Industrial and Labor Relations Review* 44 (2): 195–211.

Bosco, J. J., and L. R. Harring. 1973. "Afloat on the Sea of Ambiguity: The Teacher Corps Experience." *Education and Urban Society* 15: 331–349.

Bosworth, Barry, and Gary Burtless. 1992. "The Effects of Tax Reform on Labor Supply, Investment, and Saving." *Journal of Economic Perspectives* 6: 3–26.

Bound, John, and Richard B. Freeman. 1990. "What Went Wrong? The Erosion of the Relative Earnings and Employment of Young Black Men in the 1980s." National Bureau of Economic Research, Cambridge, Mass., November. Mimeo.

Bound, John, and George Johnson. 1992. "Changes in the Structure of Wages in the 1980s: An Evaluation of Alternative Explanations." *American Economic Review* 82: 371–392.

Bourgois, Philippe. 1991. "In Search of Respect: The New Service Economy and the Crack Alternative in Spanish Harlem." Russell Sage Foundation, New York, May. Mimeo.

Bouvier, Leon F., and Robert W. Gardner. 1986. "Immigration to the U.S.: The Unfinished Story." *Population Bulletin* 41 (4): 1–50.

Bradbury, Kathryn, and Anthony Downs, eds. 1981. *Do Housing Allowances Work?* Washington, D.C.: Brookings Institution.

Brest, Paul. 1976. "The Supreme Court, 1975 Term—Foreword: In Defense of the Antidiscrimination Principle." *Harvard Law Review* 90: 1–54.

Brooks-Gunn, Jeanne, Greg J. Duncan, Pam Kato, and Naomi Sealand. 1991. "Do Neighborhoods Influence Child and Adolescent Behavior?" Paper presented at the biennial meeting of the Society for Research on Child Development, April, Seattle.

Brounstein, Paul J., Harry P. Hatry, David M. Altschuler, and Louis H. Blair. 1990. "Substance Abuse and Delinquency among Inner-City Adolescent Males." Urban Institute Report 90-3, Washington, D.C.

Brown, Clair, and Michael Reich. 1988. "When Does Union-Management Cooperation Work? A Look at Nummi and GM-Van Nuys." Paper prepared for the conference "Can California Be Competitive and Caring?" University of California, Los Angeles.

Brown, Michael K., and Steven P. Erie. 1981. "Blacks and the Legacy of the Great Society: The Economic and Political Impact of Federal Social Policy." *Public Policy* 29 (3, Summer): 299–330.

Bumpass, Larry. 1984. "Children and Marital Disruption: A Replication and Update." *Demography* 21: 93–116.

Burghardt, John, Ann Rangarajan, Anne Gordon, and Ellen Kisker. 1992. *Evaluation of the Minority Female Single Parent Demonstration: Summary Report.* Vol. 1. New York: Rockefeller Foundation.

Burke, Vee. 1992. "State Innovations in Aid to Families with Dependent Children." *CRS Report for Congress.* No. 92-601. Washington, D.C.: Congressional Research Service.

Burkhauser, Richard V., Robert H. Haveman, and Barbara L. Wolfe. 1992. "How People with Disabilities Fare when Public Policies Change." Discussion Paper no. 974-92, Institute for Research on Poverty, University of Wisconsin–Madison.

Burstein, Nancy R., and Mary G. Visher. 1989. "The Dynamics of Food Stamp Program Participation." U.S. Department of Agriculture, Food and Nutrition Service, Washington, D.C. March. Mimeo.

Burstein, Paul. 1979. "Public Opinion, Demonstrations, and the Passage of Antidiscrimination Legislation." *Public Opinion Quarterly* 79: 157–172.

———— 1985. *Discrimination, Jobs, and Politics.* Chicago: University of Chicago Press.

Burt, Martha. 1992. *Over the Edge: The Growth of Homelessness in the 1980s.* New York: Russell Sage Foundation.

Burtless, Gary. 1984. "Unemployment Insurance and Poverty." In U.S. House of Representatives, Committee on Ways and Means, *Poverty Rate Increase Hearings,* Serial 98-55. Washington, D.C.: U.S. Government Printing Office.

—— 1985. "Are Targeted Wage Subsidies Harmful? Evidence from a Wage Voucher Experiment." *Industrial and Labor Relations Review* 39: 105–114.

—— 1986. "The Work Response to a Guaranteed Income: A Survey of Experimental Evidence." In *Lessons from the Income Maintenance Experiments,* ed. Alicia A. Munnell. Boston: Federal Reserve Bank of Boston.

—— 1987. "The Work Response to a Guaranteed Income: A Survey of Experimental Evidence." In *The Income Maintenance Experiments: Lessons for Welfare Reform,* ed. Alicia Munnell. Boston: Federal Reserve Bank of Boston.

—— 1991a. "Is Unemployment Insurance Ready for the 1990s?" In *Social Insurance Issues for the Nineties,* ed. Paul N. van de Water. Dubuque, Iowa: Kendall/Hunt.

—— 1991b. "Supply-Side Legacy of the Reagan Years: Effects on Labor Supply." In *The Economic Legacy of the Reagan Years: Euphoria or Chaos?* ed. A. P. Sahu and Ronald L. Tracy. New York: Praeger.

Butler, Stuart M. 1981. *Enterprise Zones: Greenlining the Inner Cities.* New York: Universe Books.

Caftel, Brad. 1992. *Counseling Organizations in Community Economic Development.* Berkeley, Calif.: National Economic Development and Law Center.

Cain, Glen G., and Ross E. Finnie. 1990. "The Black-White Difference in Youth Employment: Evidence for Demand-Side Factors." *Journal of Labor Economics* 8 (1, pt. 2): S364–S395.

Cain, Glen G., and Arthur Goldberger. 1983. "Public and Private Schools Revisited." *Sociology of Education* 56: 208–218.

Cameron, Steven, and James J. Heckman. 1991. "The Nonequivalence of High School Equivalents." University of Chicago, Department of Economics. Mimeo.

Cancian, Marcia, Sheldon Danziger, and Peter Gottschalk. 1993. "The Changing Contributions of Men and Women to the Level and Distribution of Family Income, 1968–88." In *Poverty and Prosperity in the USA in the Late Twentieth Century,* ed. Dimitri B. Papadimitriou and Edward N. Wolff. New York and London: Macmillan.

Caplan, Nathan, John Whitmore, and Quang Bui. 1985. "Southeast Asian Refugee Self-Sufficiency Study." Prepared for the Office of Refugee Resettlement, U.S. Department of Health and Human Services, Washington, D.C.

Card, David. 1990. "The Impact of the Mariel Boatlift on the Miami Labor Market." *Industrial and Labor Relations Review* 43: 245–257.

—— 1992a. "Do Minimum Wages Reduce Employment? A Case Study of California, 1987–89." *Industrial and Labor Relations Review* 46: 38–54.

—— 1992b. "Using Regional Variation in Wages to Measure the Effects of the Federal Minimum Wage." *Industrial and Labor Relations Review* 46: 22–37.

Carmines, E. G., and J. A. Stimson. 1989. *Issue Evaluation: Race and the Transformation of American Politics.* Princeton, N.J.: Princeton University Press.

Case, Anne C., and Lawrence F. Katz. 1990. "The Company You Keep: The Effects of Family and Neighborhood on Disadvantaged Youths." National Bureau of Economic Research, Cambridge, Mass., July. Mimeo.

Cassetty, Judith. 1978. *Child Support and Public Policy: Securing Support from Absent Fathers.* Lexington, Mass.: Heath.

Cave, George, Hans Bos, Fred Doolittle, and Cyril Roussaint. 1993. *JOBSTART Final Report.* New York: Manpower Development Research Corporation.

Center for the Study of Public Policy. 1970. *Education Vouchers: A Report on Financing Elementary Education by Grants to Parents.* Cambridge, Mass.: Center for the Study of Public Policy.

Center on Budget and Policy Priorities. 1991. *The States and the Poor.* Washington, D.C.: Center on Budget and Policy Priorities.

Center on Social Welfare Policy and Law. 1992a. "Impact of Termination of General Assistance Benefits for Employables in Massachusetts, Michigan, and Pennsylvania." Publication no. 805, Center on Social Welfare Policy and Law, New York.

———— 1992b. "1991: The Poor Got Poorer as Welfare Programs Were Slashed." Publication no. 165, Center on Social Welfare Policy and Law, New York.

Centers for Disease Control. 1991. *Measles—United States, 1990.* Hyattsville, Md.: U.S. Public Health Service.

Chambers, David. 1979. *Making Fathers Pay: The Enforcement of Child Support.* Chicago: University of Chicago Press.

Cherlin, Andrew J., Frank F. Furstenberg, P. Lindsay Chase-Lansdale, Kathleen E. Kiernan, Philip K. Robins, Donna Ruane Morrison, and Julien O. Teitler. 1991. "Longitudinal Studies of Effects of Divorce on Children in Great Britain and the United States." *Science* 252 (June): 1386–1389.

Children's Defense Fund. 1989. *The Health of America's Children.* Washington, D.C.: Children's Defense Fund.

Chiswick, Barry R. 1978. "The Effect of Americanization on the Earnings of Foreign-born Men." *Journal of Political Economy* 86: 897–921.

Chubb, John, and Terry M. Moe. 1990a. *Politics, Markets, and America's Schools.* Washington, D.C.: Brookings Institution.

———— 1990b. "Choice *Is* a Panacea." *Brookings Review,* Summer, pp. 4–12.

Citrin, Jack, and Donald Philip Green. 1990. "The Self-Interest Motive in American Public Opinion." *Research in Micropolitics* 3: 1–28.

Clairmont, Don. 1991. "Community-Based Policing: Implementation and Impact." *Canadian Journal of Criminology* 33: 469–484.

Clark, Kenneth B. 1965. *Dark Ghetto: Dilemmas of Social Power.* New York: Harper and Row.

Clark, Rebecca L., and Douglas A. Wolf. 1992. "Do Neighborhoods Matter?: Dropping Out among Teenage Boys." Urban Institute, Washington, D.C. Mimeo.

Coalition on Human Needs. N.d. *How the Poor Would Remedy Poverty.* Washington, D.C.: Coalition on Human Needs.

Cohen, David K., and Eleanor Farrar. 1977. "Power to the Parents? The Story of Education Vouchers." *Public Interest* 48: 72–97.

Coleman, James S., et al. 1966. *Equality of Educational Opportunity.* Washington, D.C.: U.S. Department of Health, Education, and Welfare.

Coleman, James, and Thomas Hoffer. 1987. *Public and Private High Schools.* New York: Basic Books.

Coleman, James, Thomas Hoffer, and Sally Kilgore. 1982. *High School Achievement.* New York: Basic Books.

Coleman, Mary T., and John Pencavel. 1992. "Changes in Work Hours of Male Employees since 1940." Department of Economics, Stanford University. Mimeo.

Comer, James P. 1980. *School Power: Implications of an Intervention Project.* New York: Free Press.

Committee for Economic Development (CED). 1991. *An Assessment of American Education: The View of Employers, Higher Educators, and the Public, Recent Students and Their Parents.* New York: CED.

Connelly, Rachel. 1991. "The Importance of Child Care Costs to Women's Decision Making." In *The Economics of Child Care,* ed. David Blau. New York: Russell Sage Foundation.

Cook, Fay Lomax. 1990. "Congress and the Public: Convergent and Divergent Opinions on Social Security." In *Social Security and the Budget,* ed. Henry J. Aaron. New York: University Press of America.

Cook, Fay Lomax, and Edith J. Barrett. 1992. *Support for the American Welfare State.* New York: Columbia University Press.

Coons, John E., and Stephen D. Sugarman. 1978. *Education by Choice: The Case for Family Control.* Berkeley: University of California Press.

Corcoran, Mary, Roger H. Gordon, Deborah Laren, and Gary Solon. 1987. "Intergenerational Transmission of Education, Income, and Earnings." University of Michigan, Institute of Public Policy Studies. Mimeo.

———— 1990. "Effects of Family and Community Background on Men's Economic Status." Paper presented at the Joint Center for Political and Economic Studies/HHS Forum on Models of the Underclass, March 8–9, Washington, D.C.

Cornelius, Wayne A. 1990. "The Impact of the 1986 U.S. Immigration Law on Emigration from Rural Mexican Sending Communities." In *Undocumented Migration to the United States: IRCA and the Experience of the 1980s,* ed. Frank D. Bean, Barry Edmonston, and Jeffrey Passel. Washington, D.C.: Urban Institute Press.

Coughlin, Richard M. 1979. "Social Policy and Ideology: Public Opinion in Eight Nations." *Comparative Social Research* 2: 3–40.

Crane, Jonathan. 1991. "The Epidemic Theory of Ghettos and Neighborhood Effects on Dropping Out and Teenage Childbearing." *American Journal of Sociology* 96 (5, March): 1126–1159.

Cross, Harry, Genevieve Kenney, Jane Mell, and Wendy Zimmerman. 1990. "Employer Hiring Practices: Differential Treatment of Hispanic and Anglo Job Seekers." Report no. 90-4, Urban Institute, Washington, D.C.

Cutler, David M., and Lawrence F. Katz. 1991. "Macroeconomic Performance and the Disadvantaged." *Brookings Papers on Economic Activity* 2: 1–74.

Dallek, Robert. 1991. *Lone Star Rising.* New York: Oxford University Press.

Danziger, Sandra K., and Sheldon Danziger. 1992. "Child Poverty and Public Policy: Toward a Comprehensive Antipoverty Agenda." Unpublished paper, Institute of Public Policy Studies, University of Michigan. September.

Danziger, Sheldon, and Peter Gottschalk. 1985. "The Poverty of *Losing Ground.*" *Challenge* (May–June): 32–38.

Danziger, Sheldon, and Peter Gottschalk, eds. 1993. *Uneven Tides: Rising Inequality in the 1980s.* New York: Russell Sage Foundation.

Danziger, Sheldon, Robert Haveman, and Robert Plotnick. 1981. "How Income Transfer Programs Affect Work, Savings, and the Income Distribution: A Critical Review." *Journal of Economic Literature* 19 (September): 975–1028.

————— 1986. "Antipoverty Policy: Effects on the Poor and Nonpoor." In *Fighting Poverty: What Works and What Doesn't,* ed. Sheldon H. Danziger and Daniel H. Weinberg. Cambridge, Mass.: Harvard University Press.

Danziger, Sheldon H., and Daniel H. Weinberg, eds. 1986. *Fighting Poverty: What Works and What Doesn't.* Cambridge, Mass.: Harvard University Press.

Danzon, Patricia. 1992. "Hidden Overhead Costs: Is Canada's System Really Less Expensive?" *Health Affairs* 11 (Spring): 21–43.

Darden, Joseph. 1987. "Choosing Neighbors and Neighborhoods: The Role of Race in Housing Preference." In *Divided Neighborhoods: Changing Patterns of Racial Segregation,* ed. Gary Tobin. Newbury Park, Calif.: Sage.

Darity, William A., Jr., and Samuel L. Myers, Jr. 1983. "Changes in Black Family Structure: Implication for Welfare Dependency." *American Economic Review* 73 (May): 59–64.

Darity, William A., Jr., Samuel L. Myers, Jr., William Sabol, and Emmet D. Carson. 1990. "Microeconomic vs. Structural Models of the Underclass." Paper presented at the Joint Center for Political and Economic Studies/HHS Forum on Models of the Underclass, March 8–9, Washington, D.C.

Darity, William A., Jr., Samuel L. Myers, Jr., William Sabol, and Emmet D. Carson. Forthcoming. *Race and Unwantedness: Essays on the Black Underclass.* New York: Garland Publications.

Datcher, Linda. 1982. "Effects of Community and Family Background on Achievement." *Review of Economics and Statistics* 64: 32–41.

Davis, James A., and Tom W. Smith. 1990. *The General Social Survey: Cumulative Codebook and Data File.* Chicago: National Opinion Research Center and University of Chicago.

Davis, Karen. 1975. "Equal Treatment and Unequal Benefits: The Medicare Program." *Milbank Memorial Fund Quarterly* 53 (3): 449–488.

————— 1989. "A Critique of the Kane Proposal for the U.S. Health Care System." In *Changing America's Health Care System,* ed. Shelah Leader and Marilyn Moon. Washington, D.C.: American Association of Retired Persons.

Davis, Steven J. 1992. "Cross-Country Patterns of Change in Relative Wages." Working Paper no. 4085, National Bureau of Economic Research, Cambridge, Mass.

Davis, Steven J., and John Haltiwanger. 1991. "Wage Dispersion between and within U.S. Manufacturing Plants, 1963–1986." In *Brookings Papers on Economic Activity: Microeconomics,* ed. Martin N. Baily and Clifford Winston. Washington, D.C.: Brookings Institution.

DeFreitas, Gregory, and Adriana Marshall. 1984. "Immigration and Wage Growth in U.S. Manufacturing in the 1970s." In *Industrial Relations Research Association Series, Proceedings of the Thirty-Seventh Annual Meeting.* Madison, Wis.: Industrial Relations Research Association.

deHaven-Smith, Lance. 1983. "Evidence on the Middle Management Principle of Program Design: Implementation of the Targeted Jobs Credit." *Journal of Politics* 45: 711–730.

Denison, Edward. 1974. *Accounting for U.S. Economic Growth: 1929–1964.* Washington, D.C.: Brookings Institution.

——— 1985. *Trends in American Economic Growth.* Washington, D.C.: Brookings Institution.

Derthick, Martha. 1979. *Policymaking for Social Security.* Washington, D.C.: Brookings Institution.

Dewar, Margaret. 1990. "Tax Incentives, Public Loans, and Subsidies: What Difference Do They Make in Nonmetropolitan Economic Development?" In *Financing Economic Development,* ed. Richard D. Bingham, Edward W. Hill, and Sammis B. White. Newbury Park, Calif.: Sage.

Dionne, E. J. 1991. *Why Americans Hate Politics.* New York: Simon and Schuster.

Donato, Katharine M., Jorge Durand, and Douglas S. Massey. 1992. "Stemming the Tide? Assessing the Deterrent Effects of the Immigration Reform and Control Act." *Demography* 29: 139–157.

Donohue, John. 1986. "Is Title VII Efficient?" *University of Pennsylvania Law Review* 134: 1411–1431.

Doolittle, Fred. 1986. "Ronald Reagan and Conservative Welfare Reform." Manpower Demonstration Research Corporation, New York. Mimeo.

Dossey, John A., et al. 1988. *The Mathematics Report Card: Are We Measuring Up?* Report 17-M-01. Princeton, N.J.: Educational Testing Service.

Downs, Anthony. 1990. "A Strategy for Designing a Fully Comprehensive National Housing Policy for the Federal Government of the United States." In *Building Foundations,* ed. Denise DiPasquale and Langley Keyes. Philadelphia: University of Pennsylvania Press.

——— 1991. "The Advisory Commission on Regulatory Barriers to Affordable Housing: Its Behavior and Accomplishments." *Housing Policy Debate* 2: 1095–1137.

——— 1992. "Policy Directions Concerning Racial Discrimination in U.S. Housing Markets." *Housing Policy Debate* 3: 685–745.

Duncan, Greg J., B. Gustafsson, Robert M. Hauser, G. Schmaus, S. Jenkins, H. Messinger, R. Muffels, B. Nolan, J. C. Ray, and W. Voges. 1991. "Poverty and Social-Assistance Dynamics in the United States, Canada, and Europe." Paper presented at the Joint Center for Political and Economic Studies, Washington, D.C. September.

Duncan, Greg J., Martha S. Hill, and Saul D. Hoffman. 1988. "Welfare Dependence within and across Generations." *Science* 239: 467–471.

Duncan, Greg J., and Saul D. Hoffman. 1985. "A Reconsideration of the Economic Consequences of Marital Dissolution." *Demography* 22: 485–498.

Duncan, Greg J., Deborah Laren, and W. J. J. Yeung. 1991. "How Dependent Are America's Children on Welfare? Recent Findings from the PSID." Institute for Social Research, University of Michigan, Ann Arbor. Mimeo.

Duncan, Greg J., and Willard Rodgers. 1991. "Has Children's Poverty Become More Persistent?" *American Sociological Review* 56: 538–550.

Duncan, Greg J., Timothy Smeeding, and Willard Rodgers. 1991. "Whither the Middle Class? A Dynamic View." Institute for Social Research, University of Michigan, Ann Arbor. Mimeo.

duRivage, Virginia L. 1992. "Flexibility Trap: The Proliferation of Marginal Jobs." *American Prospect* 9 (Spring): 84–93.

Economic Report of the President. 1964. Washington, D.C.: U.S. Government Printing Office.

Economic Report of the President. 1967. Washington, D.C.: U.S. Government Printing Office.

Edin, Kathryn, and Christopher Jencks. 1992. "Reforming Welfare." In Jencks, *Rethinking Social Policy: Race, Poverty, and the Underclass.* Cambridge, Mass.: Harvard University Press.

Edsall, Thomas Byrne, and Mary Edsall. 1991a. *Chain Reaction: The Impact of Race, Rights, and Taxes on American Politics.* New York: Norton.

———— 1991b. "When the Official Subject is Presidential Politics, Taxes, Welfare, Crime, Rights, or Values . . . The Real Subject Is Race." *Atlantic Monthly* 269: 53–86.

Ehrenhalt, Alan. 1992. *The United States of Ambition: Politicians, Power, and the Pursuit of Office.* New York: Random House.

Ellwood, David T. 1986a. *Targeting "Would-Be" Long-Term Recipients of AFDC.* Princeton, N.J.: Mathematica Policy Research.

———— 1986b. "The Spatial Mismatch Hypothesis: Are There Teenage Jobs Missing in the Ghetto?" In *The Black Youth Employment Crisis,* ed. Richard B. Freeman and Harry J. Holzer. Chicago: University of Chicago Press.

———— 1988. *Poor Support: Poverty in the American Family.* New York: Basic Books.

———— 1989. "The Origins of Dependency: Choice, Confidence, or Culture?" *Focus* (newsletter of the Institute for Research on Poverty) 12 (1, Spring–Summer): 6–13.

Ellwood, David T., and Jonathan Crane. 1990. "Family Change among Black Americans." *Journal of Economic Perspectives* 4 (4, Fall): 65–84.

Ellwood, David T., and David T. Rodda. 1991. "The Hazards of Work and Marriage: The Influence of Male Employment on Marriage Rates." Malcolm Wiener Center for Social Policy, John F. Kennedy School of Government, Harvard University, March. Mimeo.

Employee Benefit Research Institute. 1992. "EBRI Issue Brief: Health Care Reform: Tradeoffs and Implications." Washington, D.C., April. Mimeo.

Epstein, Richard. 1992. *Forbidden Grounds: The Case against Employment Discrimination Laws.* Cambridge, Mass.: Harvard University Press.

Erikson, Robert, and John H. Goldthorpe. 1985. "Are American Rates of Social Mobility Exceptionally High? New Evidence on an Old Issue." *European Sociological Review* 1: 1–22.

Ermisch, John. 1990. "Demographic Aspects of the Growing Number of Lone-Parent Families." In *Lone-Parent Families: The Economic Challenge,* ed. Elizabeth Duskin. OECD Social Policy Study, no. 8. Paris: Organisation for Economic Co-Operation and Development.

Espenshade, Thomas J., Frank Bean, Tracy Ann Goodis, and Michael J. White. 1990. "Immigration Policy in the United States: Future Prospects for the Immigration and Reform and Control Act of 1986." In *Population Policy: Contemporary Issues and Problems,* ed. Godfrey Roberts. New York: Praeger.

Fagan, Jeffery. 1992. "Drug Selling and Licit Income in Distressed Neighborhoods: The Economic Lives of Street-Level Drug Users and Sellers." In *Drugs, Crime, and Social Isolation: Barriers to Urban Opportunity,* ed. Adele V. Harrell and George E. Peterson. Washington, D.C.: Urban Institute Press.

Farkas, George, Robert P. Grobe, Daniel Sheehan, and Yuan Shuan. 1990. "Cultural Resources and School Success: Gender, Ethnicity, and Poverty Groups within an Urban School District." *American Sociological Review* 55 (February): 127–142.

Farley, Reynolds. 1991. "Residential Segregation of Social and Economic Groups among Blacks, 1970–80." In *The Urban Underclass,* ed. Christopher Jencks and Paul E. Peterson. Washington, D.C.: Brookings Institution.

Farley, Reynolds, and Walter Allen. 1987. *The Color Line and the Quality of Life in America.* New York: Russell Sage Foundation.

Feagin, Joe R. 1972. "America's Welfare Stereotypes." *Social Science Quarterly* 52: 921–933.

———— 1975. *Subordinating the Poor: Welfare and American Beliefs.* Englewood Cliffs, N.J.: Prentice-Hall.

Featherman, David L., and Robert M. Hauser. 1978. *Opportunity and Change.* New York: Academic Press.

Feder, Judith, Jack Hadley, and Ross Mullner. 1984. "Falling through the Cracks: Poverty, Insurance Coverage, and Hospital Care for the Poor, 1980 and 1982." *Milbank Memorial Fund Quarterly* 62 (4): 544–566.

Feldman, S. 1984. "Economic Individualism and American Public Opinion." *American Politics Quarterly* 11: 3–29.

Feldstein, Martin S. 1974. "Social Security, Induced Retirement, and Aggregate Capital Accumulation." *Journal of Political Economy* 82 (September–October): 905–926.

Ferguson, Ronald. 1990. "The Case for Community-Based Programs That Inform and Motivate Black Male Youth." Draft paper, Urban Institute, Washington, D.C.

Fernandez, Roberto, and David Harris. 1992. "Social Isolation and the Underclass." In *Drugs, Crime, and Social Isolation: Barriers to Urban Opportunity,* ed. Adele V. Harrell and George E. Peterson. Washington, D.C.: Urban Institute Press.

Finn, Chester E., Jr. 1987. "The High School Dropout Puzzle." *Public Interest* 87: 3–22.

Firebaugh, Glenn, and Kenneth E. Davis. 1988. "Trends in Antiblack Prejudice, 1972–1984: Region and Cohort Effects." *American Journal of Sociology* 94: 251–272.

Form, William, and Claudia Hanson. 1985. "The Consistency of Stratal Ideologies of Economic Justice." *Research in Social Stratification and Mobility* 4: 239–269.

Franklin, Grace, and Randall Ripley. 1984. *CETA: Politics and Policy, 1973–1982.* Knoxville: University of Tennessee Press.

Frazier, E. Franklin. 1939. *The Negro in the United States.* Chicago: University of Chicago Press.

———— 1962. *Black Bourgeoisie.* New York: Collier Books.

Freeman, Howard E., Linda H. Aiken, Robert J. Blendon, and Christopher R. Covey. 1990. "Uninsured Working-Age Adults: Characteristics and Consequences." *Health Services Research* 24 (February): 811–824.

Freeman, Richard B. 1991. "Employment and Earnings of Disadvantaged Young Men in a Labor Shortage Economy." In *The Urban Underclass,* ed. Christopher Jencks and Paul E. Peterson. Washington, D.C.: Brookings Institution.

———— 1992. "Crime and the Employment of Disadvantaged Youths." In *Urban Labor Markets and Job Opportunity,* ed. George E. Peterson and Wayne Vroman. Washington, D.C.: Urban Institute Press.

Freeman, Richard B., and Harry Holzer. 1991. "The Deterioration of Employment and Earnings Opportunities for Less Educated Young Americans: A Review of the Evidence." Department of Economics, Harvard University. Mimeo.

Freeman, Richard B., and Lawrence F. Katz. 1993. "Rising Wage Inequality: The United

States vs. Other Advanced Countries." Conference paper, National Bureau of Economic Research, Cambridge, Mass.

Freibert, H. J. 1981. "The Federal Government as a Change Agent: Fifteen Years of the Teacher Corps." *Journal of Education for Teaching* 7: 231–245.

Frieden, Bernard, and Marshall Kaplan. 1975. *The Politics of Neglect: Urban Aid from Model Cities to Revenue Sharing.* Cambridge, Mass.: MIT Press.

Friedlander, Daniel, James Riccio, and Stephen Freedman. 1993. *GAIN: Two-Year Impacts in Six Countries.* New York: Manpower Demonstration Research Corporation.

Friedman, Joseph, and Daniel H. Weinberg. 1982. *The Economics of Housing Vouchers.* New York: Academic Press.

Friedman, Milton. 1955. "The Role of Government in Education." In *Economics and the Public Interest,* ed. Robert Solo. New Brunswick, N.J.: Rutgers University Press.

—— 1962. *Capitalism and Freedom.* Chicago: University of Chicago Press.

Fuchs, Victor. 1992. "Poverty and Health: Asking the Right Questions." Paper presented at Cornell University Health Policy Conference, New York, N.Y., February.

Galster, George C. 1986. "More Than Skin Deep: The Effect of Housing Discrimination on the Extent and Pattern of Racial Segregation in the United States." In *Housing Desegregation and Federal Policy,* ed. John Goering. Chapel Hill: University of North Carolina Press.

—— 1991. "Housing Discrimination and Urban Poverty of African Americans." *Journal of Housing Research* 2 (2): 87–122.

Gamoran, Adam. 1992. "Social Factors in Education." In *Encyclopedia of Educational Research.* 6th ed. New York: Macmillan.

Gamson, William A., and Kathryn E. Lasch. 1983. "The Political Culture of Social Welfare Policy." In *Evaluating the Welfare State: Social and Political Perspectives,* ed. Shimon E. Spiro and Ephraim Yuchtman-Yaar. New York: Academic Press.

Gamson, William A., and Andre Modigliani. 1987. "The Changing Culture of Affirmative Action." In *Research in Political Sociology,* ed. R. G. Braungart and M. M. Braungart. Greenwich, Conn.: JAI Press.

Gans, Herbert J. 1968. "Culture and Class in the Study of Poverty: An Approach to Anti-Poverty Research." In *On Understanding Poverty: Perspectives from the Social Sciences,* ed. Daniel P. Moynihan. New York: Basic Books.

—— 1990. "Deconstructing the Underclass." *APA Journal* 56 (271, Summer): 1–7.

Ganzeboom, Harry B. G., Donald J. Treiman, and Wout C. Ultee. 1991. "Comparative Intergenerational Stratification Research: Three Generations and Beyond." *Annual Review of Sociology,* vol. 17, ed. W. Richard Scott and Judith Black.

Garfinkel, Irwin. 1992. *Assuring Child Support: An Extension of Social Security.* New York: Russell Sage Foundation.

Garfinkel, Irwin, Charles F. Manski, and Charles Michalopolous. 1992. "Micro Experiments and Macro Effects." In *Evaluating Welfare and Training Programs,* ed. Charles F. Manski and Irwin Garfinkel. Cambridge, Mass.: Harvard University Press.

Garfinkel, Irwin, and Sara S. McLanahan. 1986. *Single Mothers and Their Children: A New American Dilemma.* Washington, D.C.: Urban Institute Press.

Garfinkel, Irwin, and Marygold Melli, eds. 1982. "Child Support: Weakness of the Old and Features of a Proposed New System." Special Report nos. 32A, 32B, 32C, Institute for Research on Poverty, University of Wisconsin–Madison.

Garfinkel, Irwin, and Daniel Oellerich. 1989. "Noncustodial Fathers' Ability to Pay Child Support." *Demography* 26: 219–233.

Garfinkel, Irwin, and Annemette Sørensen. 1982. "Sweden's Child Support System: Lessons for the United States." *Social Work* 27: 509–515.

Gilder, George. 1981. *Wealth and Poverty.* New York: Basic Books.

Gilens, Martin I. 1991. "Radical Attitudes and Opposition to the American Welfare State." Paper presented at the 46th annual conference of the American Association for Public Opinion Research.

Ginzberg, Eli. 1980. *Employing the Unemployed.* New York: Basic Books.

Glasgow, Douglas G. 1980. *The Black Underclass: Poverty, Unemployment, and Entrapment of Ghetto Youth.* San Francisco: Jossey-Bass.

Glazer, Nathan. 1975. *Affirmative Discrimination: Ethnic Inequality and Public Policy.* New York: Basic Books.

——— 1978. "Why *Bakke* Won't End Reverse Discrimination: 2." *Commentary* 66: 36–41.

Goodwin, Leonard. 1983. *Causes and Cures of Welfare: New Evidence on the Social Psychology of the Poor.* Lexington, Mass.: D. C. Heath.

Gottschalk, Peter. 1992. "Is the Correlation in Welfare Participation across Generations Spurious?" Department of Economics, Boston College. Mimeo.

Gottschalk, Peter, and Sheldon Danziger. 1985. "A Framework for Evaluating the Effects of Economic Growth and Transfers on Poverty." *American Economic Review* 74 (March): 153–161.

——— 1986. "Poverty and the Underclass." Testimony before the Select Committee on Hunger, U.S. Congress, August. Mimeo.

——— 1993. "Family Structure, Family Size, and Family Income: Accounting for Changes in the Economic Well-Being of Children, 1968–1986." In *Uneven Tides: Rising Inequality in America,* ed. Danziger and Gottschalk. New York: Russell Sage Foundation.

Gottschalk, Peter, and Mary Joyce. 1992. "Changes in Earnings Inequality: An International Perspective." Department of Economics, Boston College. Mimeo.

Gottschalk, Peter, and Barbara Wolfe. 1992. "How Equal Is the Utilization of Medical Care in the United States?" Boston College, Department of Economics. Mimeo.

Goza, Franklin William. 1987. "Adjustment and Adaptation among Southeast Asian Refugees in the United States." Ph.D. dissertation, Department of Sociology, University of Wisconsin–Madison.

Gramlich, Edward M. 1986. "Evaluation of Educational Projects: The Case of the Perry Preschool Program." *Economics of Education Review* 5: 17–24.

Gramlich, Edward M., Richard Kasten, and Frank Sammartino. 1993. "Growing Inequality in the 1980s: The Role of Federal Taxes and Cash Transfers." In *Uneven Tides: Rising Inequality in America,* ed. Sheldon Danziger and Peter Gottschalk. New York: Russell Sage Foundation.

Gramlich, Edward, and Deborah Laren. 1991. "Geographical Mobility and Persistent Poverty." Paper presented at the Conference on Urban Labor Markets and Labor Mobility, Airlie House, Va., March 7–8.

Green, Jack R., and Stephen D. Mastrofski, eds. 1988. *Community Policing: Rhetoric or Reality?* New York: Praeger.

Green, Jesse, and Peter S. Arno. 1990. "The 'Medicalization' of AIDS." *Journal of the American Medical Association* 264 (10): 1261–1266.

Greenberg, David, and Michael Wiseman. 1992. "What Did the Work-Welfare Demonstrations Do?" Discussion Paper no. 969-92, Institute for Research on Poverty, University of Wisconsin–Madison.

Greenberg, Mark. 1992. *Welfare Reform on a Budget: What's Happening in JOBS.* Washington, D.C.: Center for Law and Social Policy.

Greene, Richard. 1991. "Poverty Area Diffusion: The Depopulation Hypothesis Examined." *Urban Geography* 12 (6, November–December): 526–541.

Greenstein, Robert. 1991. "Universal and Targeted Approaches to Relieving Poverty: An Alternative View." In *The Urban Underclass,* ed. Christopher Jencks and Paul E. Peterson. Washington, D.C.: Brookings Institution.

Greenwood, Michael, and John McDowell. 1986. "Factor Market Consequences of U.S. Immigration." *Journal of Economic Literature* 26: 1738–1772.

Greider, William. 1992. *Who Will Tell the People? The Betrayal of American Democracy.* New York: Simon and Schuster.

Gueron, Judith M. 1987. *Reforming Welfare with Work.* New York: Russell Sage Foundation.

———— 1990. "Work and Welfare: Lessons from Employment Programs." *Journal of Economic Perspectives* 4: 79–98.

Gueron, Judith M., and Edward Pauly. 1991. *From Welfare to Work.* New York: Russell Sage Foundation.

Gustafson, Sigrid. 1991. "Single Mothers in Sweden: Why Is Poverty Less Severe?" Paper presented at the Joint Center for Political and Economic Studies, Washington, D.C., September 20–21.

Guttentag, Marcia, S. Salassin, and Deborah Belle. 1980. *The Mental Health of Women.* New York: Academic Press.

Guyer, Bernard. 1990. "Medicaid and Prenatal Care: Necessary But Not Sufficient." *Journal of the American Medical Association* 264 (17): 2264–2265.

Haar, Charles M. 1975. *Between the Idea and the Reality: A Study in the Origin, Fate, and Legacy of the Model Cities Program.* Boston: Little, Brown.

Hagedorn, John M. 1988. *People and Folks: Gangs, Crime, and the Underclass in a Rustbelt City.* Chicago: Lake View Press.

Hagen, Jan L., and Irene Lurie. 1992. *Implementing JOBS: Initial State Choices.* Albany, N.Y.: Nelson A. Rockefeller Institute of Government.

Hamilton, Richard F. 1972. *Class and Politics in the United States.* New York: John Wiley.

Handler, Arden, Naomi Kristin, Faith Davis, and Cynthia Ferré. 1991. "Cocaine Use during Pregnancy: Perinatal Outcomes." *American Journal of Epidemiology* 133: 818–825.

Hanson, Russell L. 1992. "Liberalism and the Course of American Social Welfare Policy." Indiana University, Department of Political Science. Mimeo.

Harrington, Michael. 1962. *The Other America: Poverty in the United States.* New York: Macmillan.

Harrison, Bennett, and Barry Bluestone. 1988. *The Great U-Turn.* New York: Basic Books.

Hartman, Chester. 1964. "The Housing of Relocated Families." *Journal of the American Institute of Planners* 30: 266–286.

Harvey, P. 1989. *Securing the Right to Employment.* Princeton, N.J.: Princeton University Press.

Hasenfeld, Yeheskel, and Jane A. Rafferty. 1989. "The Determinants of Public Attitudes toward the Welfare State." *Social Forces* 67: 1027–1048.

Hauser, Robert M., and John Allen Logan. 1992. "How Not to Measure Intergenerational Occupational Persistence." *American Journal of Sociology* 97 (6): 1689–1711.

Haveman, Robert H., ed. 1977. *A Decade of Federal Antipoverty Programs: Achievements, Failures, and Lessons.* New York: Academic Press.

Haveman, Robert H. 1987. *Poverty Policy and Poverty Research: The Great Society and the Social Sciences.* Madison: University of Wisconsin Press.

Haveman, Robert, Barbara Wolfe, Brent Kreeder, and Mark Stone. 1993. "Market Work, Wages, and Men's Health." *Journal of Health Economics* 13 (1).

Haveman, Robert H., Barbara L. Wolfe, and Jennifer L. Warlick. 1984. "Disability Transfers, Early Retirement, and Retrenchment." In *Retirement and Economic Behavior,* ed. Henry J. Aaron and Gary Burtless. Washington, D.C.: Brookings Institution.

Hayek, Friedrich A. 1976. *Law, Legislation, and Liberty.* Vol. 2. Chicago: University of Chicago Press.

Hebel, J. Richard, Patricia Nowicki, and Mary Sexton. 1985. "The Effect of an Antismoking Intervention during Pregnancy: An Assessment of Interaction with Maternal Characteristics." *American Journal of Epidemiology* 122: 135–148.

Heclo, Hugh. 1986a. "The Political Foundations of Antipoverty Policy." In *Fighting Poverty: What Works and What Doesn't,* ed. Sheldon H. Danziger and Daniel H. Weinberg. Cambridge, Mass.: Harvard University Press.

———. 1986b. "Two Concepts of Welfare." *Political Science Quarterly* 101 (2): 179–196.

———. 1992. "America's Welfare Legacy." *The World & I,* September, pp. 60–75.

Hellinger, Fred J. 1988. "National Forecasts of the Medical Care Costs of AIDS: 1988–1992." *Inquiry* 25 (Winter): 469–484.

Himmelstein, Jerome, and James A. McRae. 1988. "Social Issues and Socioeconomic Status." *Public Opinion Quarterly* 52: 492–512.

Hochschild, Jennifer L. 1981. *What's Fair? American Beliefs about Distributive Justice.* Cambridge, Mass.: Harvard University Press.

Hoffman, Saul D., Greg J. Duncan, and Ronald B. Mincy. 1991. "Marriage and Welfare Use among Young Women: Do Labor Market, Welfare, and Neighborhood Factors Account for Declining Rates of Marriage among Black and White Women?" Paper presented at the annual meetings of the American Economic Association, New Orleans, December.

Hoffman, Saul D., and Laurence S. Seidman. 1990. *The Earned Income Tax Credit: Antipoverty Effectiveness and Labor Market Effects.* Kalamazoo, Mich.: Upjohn Institute for Employment Research.

Hogan, Dennis P., and Evelyn M. Kitagawa. 1985. "The Impact of Social Status, Family Structure, and Neighborhood on the Fertility of Black Adolescents." *American Journal of Sociology* 90: 825–855.

Holden, Karen C., and Pamela J. Smock. 1991. "The Economic Costs of Marital Dissolution: Why Do Women Bear a Disproportionate Cost?" *Annual Review of Sociology* 17: 51–78.

Hollister, Robinson G., Jr., Peter Kemper, and Rebecca A. Maynard. 1984. *The National Supported Work Demonstration.* Madison: University of Wisconsin Press.

Holzer, Harry J. 1991. "The Spatial Mismatch Hypothesis: What Has the Evidence Shown?" *Urban Studies* 28 (4, February): 104–122.

Horrigan, Michael W., and Ronald B. Mincy. 1993. "The Minimum Wage and Earnings and

Income Inequality." In *Uneven Tides: Rising Inequality in America,* ed. Sheldon Danziger and Peter Gottschalk. New York: Russell Sage Foundation.

Hout, Michael. 1988. "More Universalism, Less Structural Mobility: The American Occupational Structure in the 1980s." *American Journal of Sociology* 93: 1358–1400.

Howard, Christopher. 1992. "Sowing the Seeds of 'Welfare': The Transformation of Mothers' Pensions, 1900–1940." *Journal of Political History* 4 (2): 188–227.

Howe, Neil, and Phillip Longman. 1992. "The Next New Deal." *The Atlantic* 269 (April): 88–99.

Huber, Joan, and William H. Form. 1973. *Income and Ideology: An Analysis of the American Political Formula.* New York: Free Press.

Hughes, Mark Alan. 1989. "Misspeaking Truth to Power: A Geographical Perspective on the Underclass Fallacy." *Economic Geography* 65: 187–207.

Hunter, James Davison. 1991. *Culture Wars: The Struggle to Define America.* New York: Basic Books.

Hurd, Michael D., and John B. Shoven. 1985. "The Distributional Effects of Social Security." In *Pensions, Labor, and Individual Choice,* ed. David Wise. Chicago: University of Chicago Press.

Hutchens, Robert M. 1986. "The Effects of the Omnibus Budget Reconciliation Act of 1981 on AFDC Recipients: A Review of Studies." In *Research in Labor Economics,* ed. Ronald G. Ehrenberg, vol. 8, pt. B. Greenwich, Conn.: JAI Press.

Ihlanfeldt, Keith R., and David L. Sjoquist. 1989. "The Impact of Job Decentralization on the Economic Welfare of Central City Blacks." *Journal of Urban Economics* 26: 110–130.

Immigration and Naturalization Service (INS). 1991. *1990 Statistical Yearbook of the Immigration and Naturalization Service.* Washington, D.C.: U.S. Government Printing Office, for the U.S. Department of Justice.

Iyengar, Shanto. 1987. "Television News and Citizens' Explanations of National Issues." *American Political Science Review* 81: 815–832.

———— 1989. "How Citizens Think about Political Issues: A Matter of Responsibility." *American Journal of Political Science* 33: 878–900.

———— 1990. "Framing Responsibility for Political Issues: The Case of Poverty." *Political Behavior* 12: 19–40.

James, Franklin. 1991. "The Evaluation of Enterprise Zone Programs." In *Enterprise Zones: New Directions in Economic Development,* ed. Roy Green. Newbury Park, Calif.: Sage.

Jantti, Markus. 1992. "A More Efficient Estimate of the Effects of Macroeconomic Activity on the Distribution of Income." Abo Akademi University, Abo, Finland. Mimeo.

Jargowsky, Paul A. 1991. "Ghetto Poverty: Economic vs. Spatial Factors." Paper presented at the annual meeting of the Association for Public Policy Analysis and Management, Bethesda, Md., October.

Jargowsky, Paul A., and Mary Jo Bane. 1991. "Ghetto Poverty in the United States, 1970–1980." In *The Urban Underclass,* ed. Christopher Jencks and Paul E. Peterson. Washington, D.C.: Brookings Institution.

Jarret, Robin L. 1990. "A Comparative Examination of Socialization Patterns among Low-Income African Americans, Chicanos, Puerto Ricans, and Whites: A Review of the Ethnographic Literature." Social Science Research Council, New York, May. Mimeo.

Jasso, Guillermina, and Mark Rosenzweig. 1990. *The New Chosen People.* New York: Russell Sage Foundation.

Jaynes, Gerald, and Robin Williams, eds. 1989. *A Common Destiny: Blacks and American Society.* Washington, D.C.: National Academy Press.

Jencks, Christopher. 1966. "Is the Public School Obsolete?" *Public Interest* 2: 18–27.

—— 1988. "Deadly Neighborhoods." *New Republic* (June): 23–32.

—— 1991. "Is the American Underclass Growing?" In *The Urban Underclass,* ed. Christopher Jencks and Paul E. Peterson. Washington, D.C.: Brookings Institution.

—— 1992. *Rethinking Social Policy: Race, Poverty, and the Underclass.* Cambridge, Mass.: Harvard University Press.

Jencks, Christopher, and Kathryn Edin. 1990. "The Real Welfare Problem." *American Prospect* 1: 31–50.

Jencks, Christopher, and Susan Mayer. 1990. "Residential Segregation, Job Proximity, and Black Job Opportunities." In *Inner-City Poverty in the United States,* ed. Lawrence E. Lynn, Jr., and Michael G. H. McGeary. Washington, D.C.: National Academy Press.

Jencks, Christopher, and Paul E. Peterson, eds. 1991. *The Urban Underclass.* Washington, D.C.: Brookings Institution.

Jencks, Christopher, Marshall Smith, Henry Acland, Mary Jo Bane, David Cohen, Herbert Gintis, Barbara Heyns, and Stephan Michelson. 1972. *Inequality.* New York: Basic Books.

Jenkins, Stephen. 1991. "Recent Trends in UK Income Inequality." In *Research on Economic Inequality,* ed. Daniel Slottje. Greenwich, Conn.: JAI Press.

Jensen, Leif. 1988. "Poverty and Immigration in the United States: 1960–1980." In *Divided Opportunities: Minorities, Poverty, and Social Policy,* ed. Gary D. Sandefur and Marta Tienda. New York: Plenum Press.

—— 1989. *The New Immigration: Implications for Poverty and Public Assistance Utilization.* New York: Greenwood Press.

Job Training Longitudinal Survey Research Advisory Panel. 1985. *Recommendations of the Job Training Longitudinal Survey Research Advisory Panel.* Report prepared for the Office of Strategic Planning and Policy Development, Employment and Training Administration, U.S. Department of Labor. Washington, D.C.: U.S. Department of Labor.

Johnson, A. Sidney. 1992. "Testimony before the Senate Finance Subcommittee on Social Security and Family Policy." U.S. Senate, Washington, D.C. Mimeo.

Johnson, James H., and Melvin L. Oliver. 1991. "Economic Restructuring and Black Male Joblessness in U.S. Metropolitan Areas." *Urban Geography* 12 (6): 542–562.

Johnson, Lyndon. 1964. Letter of Transmittal. In *Economic Report of the President, 1964.* Washington, D.C.: U.S. Government Printing Office.

Jones, Jacqueline. 1992. *The Dispossessed: America's Underclasses from the Civil War to the Present.* New York: Basic Books.

Journal of Policy Analysis and Management. 1991. "A Symposium on the Family Support Act of 1988." 10: 588–666.

Joyce, Theodore, Andrew D. Racine, and Naci Mocan. 1992. "The Consequences and Costs of Maternal Substance Abuse in New York City: A Pooled Time-Series, Cross-Section Analysis." *Journal of Health Economics* 11 (3): 297–314.

JTLSR Advisory Panel. *See* Job Training Longitudinal Survey Research Advisory Panel.

Judd, Dennis. 1988. *The Politics of American Cities: Private Power and Public Policy.* Glenview, Ill.: Scott, Foresman.

Juhn, Chinhui. 1992. "The Decline of Male Labor Market Participation: The Role of Declining Market Opportunities." *Quarterly Journal of Economics* 107: 79–122.

Juhn, Chinhui, Kevin M. Murphy, and Brooks Pierce. 1989. "Wage Inequality and the Rise in Returns to Skill." Department of Economics, University of Chicago. Mimeo.

Kaestle, Carl F., and Michael S. Smith. 1982. "The Federal Role in Elementary and Secondary Education, 1940–1980." *Harvard Educational Review* 52: 384–408.

Kain, John. 1968. "Housing Segregation, Negro Unemployment, and Metropolitan Decentralization." *Quarterly Journal of Economics* 82: 175–197.

Kamerman, Sheila B. 1991. "Child Care Policies and Programs: An International Overview." *Journal of Social Issues* 47 (2): 179–196.

Kaplan, Marshall. 1990. "National Urban Policy: Where Are We Now? Where Are We Going?" In *The Future of National Urban Policy,* ed. Marshall Kaplan and Franklin James. Durham, N.C.: Duke University Press.

Kaplan, Marshall, and Franklin James, eds. 1990. *The Future of National Urban Policy.* Durham, N.C.: Duke University Press.

Karoly, Lynn A. 1993. "The Trend in Inequality among Families, Individuals, and Workers in the United States: A Twenty-Five Year Perspective." In *Uneven Tides: Rising Inequality in America,* ed. Sheldon Danziger and Peter Gottschalk. New York: Russell Sage Foundation.

Kasarda, John D. 1988. "Jobs, Migration, and Emerging Urban Mismatches." In *Urban Change and Poverty,* ed. Michael G. H. McGeary and Lawrence E. Lynn, Jr. Washington, D.C.: National Academy Press.

—— 1989. "Urban Industrial Transition and the Underclass." *Annals of the American Academy of Political and Social Science* 501 (January): 26–47.

—— 1990. "Structural Factors Affecting the Location and Timing of Urban Underclass Growth." *Urban Geography* 11: 234–264.

—— 1992. "The Severely Distressed in Economically Transforming Cities." In *Drugs, Crime, and Social Isolation: Barriers to Urban Opportunity,* ed. Adele V. Harrell and George E. Peterson. Washington, D.C.: Urban Institute Press.

Katz, Lawrence F., and Alan B. Krueger. 1992. "The Effect of the Minimum Wage on the Fast Food Industry." *Industrial and Labor Relations Review* 46: 6–21.

Katz, Lawrence F., and Kevin M. Murphy. 1990. "Changes in Relative Wages, 1963–1987: Supply and Demand Factors." National Bureau of Economic Research, Cambridge, Mass., April. Mimeo.

—— 1992. "Changes in Relative Wages, 1963–1987: Supply and Demand Factors." *Quarterly Journal of Economics* 107: 35–78.

Katz, Michael B. 1986. *In the Shadow of the Poorhouse: A Social History of Welfare in America.* New York: Basic Books.

—— 1989. *The Undeserving Poor: From the War on Poverty to the War on Welfare.* New York: Pantheon Books.

Kaus, Mickey. 1992. *The End of Equality.* New York: New Republic Books.

Kavee, Andrew, and Michael J. White. 1990. "The Outmigration of Educated Blacks from Inner Cities." Paper presented at the annual meeting of the Association for Public Policy Analysis and Management, San Francisco, October.

Keely, Charles B. 1974. "Immigration Composition and Population Policy." *Science* 185: 587–593.

Keil, Julien E., Susan E. Sutherland, Rebecca Knapp, and Herman A. Tyroler. 1992. "Does Equal Socioeconomic Status in Black and White Men Mean Equal Risk of Mortality?" *American Journal of Public Health* 82 (8): 1133–1136.

Kelman, Herbert C. 1974. "Attitudes Are Alive and Well and Gainfully Employed in the Sphere of Action." *American Psychologist* 29: 310–324.

Kelman, Mark. 1991. "Concepts of Discrimination in 'General Ability' Job Testing." *Harvard Law Review* 104: 1158–1247.

Kenney, Martin, and Richard Florida. 1992. "The Japanese Transplants: Production Organization and Regional Development." *Journal of the American Planning Association* 58: 21–38.

Kinder, Donald R., and Lynn M. Sanders. 1987. "Pluralistic Foundations of American Opinion on Race." Paper presented at the annual meeting of the American Political Science Association, Chicago, September 3–6.

———— 1990. "Mimicking Political Debate with Survey Questions: The Case of White Opinion on Affirmative Action for Blacks." *Social Cognition* 8: 73–103.

Kinder, Donald R., and David O. Sears. 1981. "Prejudice and Politics: Symbolic Racism versus Racial Threats to the Good Life." *Journal of Personality and Social Psychology* 40: 414–431.

———— 1985. "The Public Opinion and Political Action." In *Handbook of Social Psychology,* ed. Gardner Lindzey and Elliot Aronson. 3rd ed., vol. 2. New York: Random House.

Kindig, David, Harmoz Movassaghi, Nancy Cross Dunham, Daniel I. Zwick, and Charles M. Taylor. 1987. "Trends in Physician Availability in 10 Urban Areas from 1963 to 1980." *Inquiry* 24 (2): 136–146.

Kirsch, Irwin S., and Ann Jungeblut. 1986. *Literacy: Profiles of America's Young Adults—Final Report.* Princeton, N.J.: Educational Testing Service.

Kirschenman, Joleen. 1991. "Gender within Race in the Labor Market." Paper presented at the Urban Poverty and Family Life Conference, University of Chicago, October 10–12.

Kirschenman, Joleen, and Kathryn M. Neckerman. 1991. "'We'd Love to Hire Them, But . . .': The Meaning of Race for Employers." In *The Urban Underclass,* ed. Christopher Jencks and Paul E. Peterson. Washington, D.C.: Brookings Institution.

Kleinman, Joel C., and J. H. Madans. 1985. "The Effects of Maternal Smoking, Physical Stature, and Educational Attainment on the Incidence of Low Birth Weight." *American Journal of Epidemiology* 121: 843–855.

Kluegel, James R. 1987. "Macro-economic Problems, Beliefs about the Poor, and Attitudes toward Welfare Spending." *Social Problems* 34, no. 1.

———— 1988. "Economic Problems and Socioeconomic Beliefs and Attitudes." In *Research in Social Stratification and Mobility,* ed. Arne Kalleberg. Vol. 7, pp. 273–302.

———— 1990. "Trends in Whites' Explanations of the Gap in Black-White Socioeconomic Status, 1977–1989." *American Sociological Review* 55: 512–525.

Kluegel, James R., and Eliot R. Smith. 1983. "Affirmative Action Attitudes: Effects of Self-Interest, Racial Affect, and Stratification Beliefs on Whites' Views." *Social Forces* 61: 3.

———— 1986. *Beliefs about Inequality: Americans' Views of What Is and What Ought to Be.* New York: Aldine de Gruyter.

Knoke, D., L. E. Raffalovich, and W. Erskine. 1987. "Class, Status, and Economic Policy Preferences." *Social Stratification and Mobility* 6: 141–158.

Kochan, Thomas, and Paul Osterman. 1994. *Human Resource Development and Training: Is There Too Little in the U.S.?* Prepared for the American Council on Competitiveness. Cambridge, Mass.: Harvard Business School Press.

Krafcik, J. F. 1986. "Learning from Nummi: International Motor Vehicle Program." Working Paper, Department of Economics, Massachusetts Institute of Technology.

Kushner, James. 1988. "An Unfinished Agenda: The Federal Fair Housing Enforcement Effort." *Yale Law and Policy Review* 6: 348–392.

―――― 1992. "Enforcement and Review of the Fair Housing Amendments Act of 1988." *Housing Policy Debate* 3: 537–599.

Ladd, Everett C. 1991. "American Values in Comparative Perspective." *Public Perspective* 3 (1): 5–8.

―――― 1992. "*E Pluribus Unum* Still: The Unity of America." *Public Perspective* 3 (4): 3–11.

LaLonde, Robert J., and Robert H. Topel. 1990. "The Assimilation of Immigrants in the U.S. Labor Market." Working Paper no. 3573, National Bureau of Economic Research, Cambridge, Mass.

―――― 1991. "Labor Market Adjustment to Increased Immigration." In *Immigration, Trade, and the Labor Market,* ed. John M. Abowd and Richard B. Freeman. Chicago: University of Chicago Press.

Lampman, Robert. 1971. *Ends and Means of Reducing Income Poverty.* Chicago: Markham.

Lau, Richard R., and David O. Sears. 1981. "Cognitive Links between Economic Grievances and Political Responses." *Political Behavior* 3: 279–302.

LaWare, J. P. 1992. "Statement." *Federal Reserve Bulletin* 78: 193–194.

Lawrence, Charles. 1987. "The Id, the Ego, and Equal Protection: Reckoning with Unconscious Racism." *Stanford Law Review* 39: 317–388.

Lee, Lung Fei. 1982. "Health and Wage: A Simultaneous Equation Model with Multiple Discrete Indicators." *International Economic Review* 23: 199–221.

Lehman, Jeffrey S. 1991. "To Conceptualize, to Criticize, to Defend." *Yale Law Journal* 101 (3): 685–727.

Lehman, Jeffrey S., and Rochelle Lento. 1992. "Law School Support for Community-Based Economic Development in Low-Income Urban Neighborhoods." *Journal of Urban and Contemporary Law* 42: 65–84.

Leighton, Barry. 1991. "Visions of Community Policing: Rhetoric and Reality in Canada." *Canadian Journal of Criminology* 33: 485–522.

Lemann, Nicholas. 1991. *The Promised Land: The Great Black Migration and How It Changed America.* New York: Knopf.

Leonard, Paul, and Robert Greenstein. 1993. *The New Budget Reconciliation Law: Progressive Deficit Reduction and Critical Social Investments.* Washington, D.C.: Center on Budget and Policy Priorities.

Lerman, Robert I. 1989. "Employment Opportunities of Young Men and Family Formation." *American Economic Review* 79 (May): 62–66.

Levin, Henry M. 1968. "The Failure of the Public Schools and the Free Market Remedy." *Urban Review* 2: 32–37.

―――― 1988. "Accelerated Schools for At-Risk Students." Center for Policy Research in Education, Report Series RR-010, Rutgers University, New Brunswick, N.J.

———— 1991. "The Economics of Educational Choice." *Economics of Education Review* 10: 137–158.

Levitan, Sar A. 1985. *Programs in Aid of the Poor.* Baltimore: Johns Hopkins University Press.

Levitan, Sar, and Frank Gallo. 1987. "The Targeted Jobs Tax Credit: An Uncertain and Unfinished Experiment." *Labor Law Journal* 38: 641–647.

Levitan, Sar, and Elizabeth Miller. 1992. "Enterprise Zones: A Promise Based on Rhetoric." Center for Social Policy Studies, Washington, D.C. Mimeo.

Levy, Frank. 1987. *Dollars and Dreams: The Changing American Income Distribution.* New York: Russell Sage Foundation.

Levy, Frank, and Richard J. Murnane. 1992. "U.S. Earnings Levels and Earnings Inequality: A Review of Recent Trends and Proposed Explanations." *Journal of Economic Literature* 30: 1333–1381.

Lewis, Oscar. 1961. *The Children of Sanchez.* New York: Random House.

———— 1966. "The Culture of Poverty." *Scientific American* 215: 19–25.

Lieberson, Stanley. 1980. *A Piece of the Pie: Black and White Immigrants since 1980.* Berkeley: University of California Press.

Lipset, Seymour Martin. 1979. *The First New Nation: The United States in Historical and Comparative Perspectives.* New York: Norton.

Lipset, Seymour Martin, and William Schneider. 1978. "The *Bakke* Case: How Would It Be Decided at the Bar of Public Opinion?" *Public Opinion,* March/April, pp. 38–48.

Littman, Mark S. 1989. "Poverty in the 1980s: Are the Poor Getting Poorer?" *Monthly Labor Review* (June): 13–18.

———— 1991. "Poverty Areas and the 'Underclass': Untangling the Web." *Monthly Labor Review* (March): 19–32.

Long, Sharon. 1990. *Children and Welfare.* Washington, D.C.: Urban Institute Press.

Lowi, Theodore J. 1986. "The Welfare State: Ethical Foundations and Constitutional Remedies." *Political Science Quarterly* 101: 197–220.

Lowry, Ira. 1983. *Experimenting with Housing Allowances.* Cambridge: Oelgeschlager, Gunn, and Hain.

Luft, Harold. 1975. "The Impact of Poor Health on Earnings." *Review of Economics and Statistics* 57: 43–57.

Macdonald, Dwight. 1963. "Our Invisible Poor." *New Yorker,* January 19, pp. 82–132.

Majors, Richard, and Janet Mancini Billson. 1992. *Cool Pose: The Dilemmas of Black Manhood in America.* New York: Lexington Books.

Maloney, Timothy. 1991. "Estimating the Returns to a Secondary Education for Female Dropouts." Discussion Paper no. 737-91, Institute for Research on Poverty, University of Wisconsin–Madison.

Manning, Willard G., Joseph P. Newhouse, Niahua Duan, Emmett B. Keeler, Arleen Leibowitz, and M. Susan Marquis. 1987. "Health Insurance and the Demand for Medical Care: Evidence from a Randomized Experiment." *American Economic Review* 77 (3): 251–277.

Manski, Charles F. 1992. "Schooling *Choice* (Vouchers) and Social Mobility." *Economics of Education Review* 4: 351–369.

Manski, Charles F., and Irwin Garfinkel, eds. 1992. *Evaluating Welfare and Training Programs.* Cambridge, Mass.: Harvard University Press.

Manski, Charles F., Gary D. Sandefur, Sara S. McLanahan, and David Powers. 1992. "Alternative Estimates of the Effects of Family Structure during Childhood on High School Graduation." *Journal of the American Statistical Association* 87: 25–37.

Manski, Charles F., and Theodore Shen. 1992. "EDCHOICE: Schooling Equilibrium Simulation." FORTRAN Code and Documentation, Institute for Research on Poverty, University of Wisconsin–Madison.

March, James S., and John P. Olsen. 1989. *Rediscovering Institutions: The Organizational Basis of Politics.* New York: Free Press.

Mare, Robert D., and Christopher Winship. 1991. "Socioeconomic Change and the Decline of Marriage for Blacks and Whites." In *The Urban Underclass,* ed. Christopher Jencks and Paul E. Peterson. Washington, D.C.: Brookings Institution.

Marmor, Theodore R. 1973. *The Politics of Medicare.* Chicago: Aldine.

Marmor, Theodore R., Jerry L. Mashaw, and Philip L. Harvey. 1990. *America's Misunderstood Welfare State: Persistent Myths, Enduring Realities.* New York: Basic Books.

Massey, Douglas S. 1981. "Dimensions of the New Immigration to the U.S. and the Prospects for Assimilation." *Annual Review of Sociology* 7: 57–85.

——— 1990a. "American Apartheid: Segregation and the Making of the Underclass." *American Journal of Sociology* 96 (2): 329–357.

——— 1990b. "Social Structure, Household Strategies, and the Cumulative Causation of Migration." *Population Index* 56 (1): 3–25.

Massey, Douglas S., Rafael Alarcon, Jorge Durand, and Humberto Gonzalez. 1987. *Return to Aztlan.* Berkeley: University of California Press.

Massey, Douglas S., and Nancy A. Denton. 1988. "The Dimensions of Residential Segregation." *Social Forces* 67: 281–315.

——— 1993. *American Apartheid: Segregation and the Making of the Underclass.* Cambridge, Mass.: Harvard University Press.

Massey, Douglas S., and Mitchell L. Eggers. 1990. "The Ecology of Inequality: Minorities and the Concentration of Poverty." *American Journal of Sociology* 95: 1153–1188.

Massey, Douglas S., and Andrew Gross. 1991. "Explaining Trends in Racial Segregation, 1970–80." *Urban Affairs Quarterly* 27: 13–35.

Mayer, Neil. 1984. *Neighborhood Organizations and Community Development: Making Revitalization Work.* Washington, D.C.: Urban Institute Press.

Mayer, Susan. 1991. "Are There Economic Barriers to the Use of Physician Services?" University of Chicago, Harris Graduate School of Public Policy Studies. Mimeo.

Mayer, William G. 1992. *The Changing American Mind: How and Why American Public Opinion Changed between 1960 and 1988.* Ann Arbor: University of Michigan Press.

McCarthy, Kevin F., and Robert Burciaga Valdez. 1986. *Current and Future Effects of Mexican Immigration in California.* Santa Monica, Calif.: Rand Corporation.

McClosky, Herbert, and John Zaller. 1984. *The American Ethos: Public Attitudes toward Capitalism and Democracy.* Cambridge, Mass.: Harvard University Press.

McCormick, Marie. 1985. "The Contribution of Low Birth Weight to Infant Mortality and Childhood Morbidity." *New England Journal of Medicine* 312 (2): 82–90.

McLanahan, Sara S. 1983. "Family Structure and Stress: A Longitudinal Comparison of Two-Parent and Female-Headed Families." *Journal of Marriage and the Family* 45: 347–357.

———— 1985. "Family Structure and the Reproduction of Poverty." *American Journal of Sociology* 90: 873–901.

———— 1988. "Family Structure and Dependency: Early Transitions to Female Household Headship." *Demography* 25: 1–16.

McLanahan, Sara S., and Karen Booth. 1989. "Mother-Only Families: Problems, Prospects, and Politics." *Journal of Marriage and the Family* 51: 557–580.

McLanahan, Sara S., and Irwin Garfinkel. 1991. "Single-Mother Families and Social Policy: Lessons for the U.S. from Canada, France, and Sweden." Paper presented at the Joint Center for Political and Economic Studies, Washington, D.C., September 20–21.

McLanahan, Sara S., Irwin Garfinkel, and Dorothy Watson. 1987. "Family Structure, Poverty, and the Underclass." In *Contemporary Urban Problems,* ed. Mike McGeary and Lawrence Lynn. Washington, D.C.: National Academy Press.

McLanahan, Sara S., and Gary D. Sandefur. 1994. *Uncertain Childhood, Uncertain Future.* Cambridge, Mass.: Harvard University Press.

Mead, Lawrence M. 1986. *Beyond Entitlement: The Social Obligations of Citizenship.* New York: Free Press.

———— 1988. "The Hidden Jobs Debate." *Public Interest* 91 (Spring): 40–58.

———— 1989. "Interview." *GAO Journal* (Spring), pp. 15–22.

———— 1992. *The New Politics of Poverty: The Working Poor in America.* New York: Basic Books.

Medoff, James L. 1992. "The New Unemployment." Paper prepared for the Subcommittee on Economic Growth, Trade, and Taxes of the Joint Economic Committee, U.S. Congress, April.

Melnick, R. Shep. 1991. "The Politics of the New Property." Reprint no. 443, Brookings Institution Series, Washington, D.C.

Melville, Keith, and John Doble. 1988. *The Public's Perspective on Social Welfare Reform.* New York: Public Agenda Foundation.

Michel, Richard C. 1980. "Participation Rates in the AFDC Programs." Working Paper no. 1387-02, Urban Institute, Washington, D.C.

Michel, Richard C., and Frank Levy. 1986. "Work for Welfare." *American Economic Review* 76 (2): 399–404.

Miller, Warren E. 1991. *National Election Studies/Center for Political Studies.* Ann Arbor: Center for Political Studies, University of Michigan.

Mincy, Ronald B. 1990. "Raising the Minimum Wage: Effects on Family Poverty." *Monthly Labor Review* 113 (July): 18–25.

———— 1991. "Underclass Variations by Race and Place: Have Large Cities Darkened Our Picture of the Underclass?" Urban Institute, Washington, D.C., February. Mimeo.

Mincy, Ronald B., ed. Forthcoming. *Nurturing Young Black Males: Challenges to Agencies, Programs, and Social Policy.* Washington, D.C.: Urban Institute Press.

Mincy, Ronald B., and Susan E. Hendrickson. 1988. "AIDS and the Underclass." Statement before the Presidential Commission on the Human Immunodeficiency Virus Epidemic, Washington, D.C., April. Mimeo.

Mincy, Ronald B., Isabel V. Sawhill, and Douglas A. Wolf. 1990. "The Underclass: Definition and Measurement." *Science* 248: 450–453.

Mincy, Ronald B., and Susan Wiener. 1990. "A Mentor, Peer Group, and Incentive Model for Helping Underclass Youth." Draft paper, Urban Institute, Washington, D.C., September.

Mirengoff, William. 1980. *The New CETA: Effect on Public Service Employment Programs.* Washington, D.C.: National Academy Press.

———. 1982. *CETA: Accomplishments, Problems, Solutions.* Kalamazoo, Mich.: Upjohn Institute for Employment Research.

Mishel, Lawrence, and J. Bernstein. 1992. "Declining Wages for High School *and* College Graduates." Briefing Paper, Economic Policy Institute, Washington, D.C.

Mitchell, Janet B. 1991. "Physician Participation in Medicaid Revisited." *Medical Care* 29 (July): 645–653.

Moffitt, Robert. 1987. "Historical Growth in Participation in Aid to Families with Dependent Children." *Journal of Post-Keynesian Economics* 9: 347–363.

———. 1992. "Incentive Effects of the U.S. Welfare System: A Review." *Journal of Economic Literature* 30: 1–61.

Moffitt, Robert, and Barbara Wolfe. 1990. "The Effect of the Medicaid Program on Welfare Participation and Labor Supply." Department of Economics, Brown University. Mimeo.

———. 1992. "The Effect of the Medicaid Program on Welfare Participation and Labor Supply." *Review of Economics and Statistics* 74 (4): 615–626.

Mollat, Michel. 1986. *The Poor in the Middle Ages: An Essay in Social History.* Trans. Arthur Goldhammer. New Haven: Yale University Press.

Monroe, A. D. 1983. "American Party Platforms and Public Opinion." *American Journal of Political Science* 27: 27–42.

Montgomery, James D. 1989. "Is Underclass Behavior Contagious? A Rational Choice Analysis." Department of Economics, Northwestern University. Mimeo.

Morris, Charles. 1980. *The Cost of Good Intentions.* New York: McGraw-Hill.

Moss, Philip, and Christopher Tilly. 1991. "Why Black Men Are Doing Worse in the Labor Market: A Review of Supply-Side and Demand-Side Explanations." Social Science Research Council, New York. Mimeo.

Moynihan, Daniel Patrick. 1969. *Maximum Feasible Misunderstanding.* New York: Random House.

———. 1992. "How the Great Society 'Destroyed the American Family.' " *Public Interest* 108 (Summer): 53–64.

Mucciaroni, Gary. 1992. *The Political Failure of Employment Policy, 1945–1982.* Pittsburgh: University of Pittsburgh Press.

Muller, Thomas, and Thomas J. Espenshade. 1985. *The Fourth Wave: California's Newest Immigrants.* Washington, D.C.: Urban Institute Press.

Mullis, Ina V. S., J. Dossey, M. Foertsch, L. Jones, and C. Gentile. 1991. *Trends in Academic Progress.* Washington, D.C.: U.S. Department of Education.

Murnane, Richard J. 1988. "Education and the Productivity of the Work Force: Looking Ahead." In *American Living Standards: Threats and Challenges,* ed. Robert E. Litan, Robert Z. Lawrence, and Charles L. Schultze. Washington, D.C.: Brookings Institution.

Murnane, Richard J., and David K. Cohen. 1986. "Merit Pay and the Evaluation Problem: Why Most Merit Pay Plans Fail and a Few Survive." *Harvard Educational Review* 56: 1–17.

Murnane, Richard J., and Frank Levy. 1992. "Education and Training." In *Setting Domestic*

Priorities: What Can Government Do? ed. Henry J. Aaron and Charles L. Schultze. Washington, D.C.: Brookings Institution.

Murnane, Richard J., and Senta A. Raizan, eds. 1988. *Improving Indicators of the Quality of Science and Mathematics Education in Grades K–12.* Washington, D.C.: National Academy Press.

Murnane, Richard J., J. D. Singer, J. B. Willett, J. J. Kemple, and R. J. Olsen. 1991. *Who Will Teach? Policies That Matter.* Cambridge, Mass.: Harvard University Press.

Murnane, Richard J., J. B. Willett, and Frank Levy. 1993. "The Growing Importance of Cognitive Skills in Wage Determination." Working Paper, Graduate School of Education, Harvard University.

Murphy, Kevin M., and Finis Welch. 1989. "Wage Premiums for College Graduates: Recent Growth and Possible Explanations." *Educational Researcher* 18 (4): 17–26.

———— 1993. "Industrial Change and the Rising Importance of Skill." In *Uneven Tides: Rising Inequality in America,* ed. Sheldon Danziger and Peter Gottschalk. New York: Russell Sage Foundation.

Murray, Charles. 1984. *Losing Ground: American Social Policy, 1950–1980.* New York: Basic Books.

Myrdal, Gunnar. 1957. *Economic Theory and Under-Developed Regions.* London: Duckworth.

———— 1963. *The Challenge to Affluence.* New York: Pantheon.

Nathan, Richard P. 1986. "The Underclass: Will It Always Be with Us?" Paper presented to a symposium at the New School for Social Research, New York, November.

———— 1988. *Social Science in Government: Uses and Misuses.* New York: Basic Books.

———— 1990. "No More Mr. Nice Guy: The Implementation of New-Style Workfare." Manuscript prepared for the Twentieth Century Fund, New York.

———— 1993. *Turning Promises into Performance.* New York: Columbia University Press.

National Center for Education Statistics (NCES). 1991a. *Digest of Educational Statistics, 1991.* NCES 91-660, Office of Educational Research and Improvement. Washington, D.C.: U.S. Department of Education.

———— 1991b. *The State of Mathematics Achievement: NAEP's 1990 Assessment of the Nation and the Trial Assessment of the States.* Washington, D.C.: U.S. Department of Education.

National Center for Health Statistics. 1990. *Health of Black and White Americans, 1985–87.* Series 10, no. 171. Hyattsville, Md.: U.S. Public Health Service.

———— 1991. *Health, United States, 1990.* Hyattsville, Md.: U.S. Public Health Service.

National Commission on Children. 1991. *Beyond Rhetoric: A New American Agenda for Children and Families.* Washington, D.C.: National Commission on Children.

National Commission on Excellence in Education. 1983. *A Nation at Risk: The Imperative for Educational Reform.* Report to the nation and the Secretary of Education. Washington, D.C.: National Commission on Excellence in Education.

National Commission on Interstate Child Support Enforcement. 1992. *Supporting Our Children: A Blueprint for Reform.* Final Report of the National Commission on Interstate Child Support. Washington, D.C.: U.S. Government Printing Office.

National Council of La Raza (NCLR). 1990. *Hispanic Education: A Statistical Portrait, 1990.* Washington, D.C.: NCLR.

National Head Start Association. 1989. *Head Start: The Nation's Pride, a Nation's Challenge.* Report of the Silver Ribbon Panel. Alexandria, Va.: National Head Start Association.

National Institute of Mental Health. 1987. *Mental Health, United States, 1987.* Washington, D.C.: U.S. Government Printing Office.

―――― 1991. *Caring for People with Severe Mental Disorders: A National Plan of Research to Improve Services.* Washington, D.C.: U.S. Government Printing Office.

National Science Board. 1987. *Science and Engineering Indicators.* Washington, D.C.: National Science Board.

NCES. *See* National Center for Education Statistics.

Nelson, Melvin D., Jr. 1992. "Socioeconomic Status and Childhood Mortality in North Carolina." *American Journal of Public Health* 82 (8): 1131–1133.

Nelson, Richard R., and Edmund S. Phelps. 1966. "Investment in Humans, Technological Diffusion, and Economic Growth." *American Economic Review* 56 (May): 69–75.

Neuhaus, Richard John. 1984. *The Naked Public Square: Religion and Democracy in America.* Grand Rapids, Mich.: Eerdmans.

Nichols-Casebolt, Ann, and Irwin Garfinkel. 1991. "Trends in Paternity Adjudications and Child Support Awards." *Social Science Quarterly* 72: 83–97.

Niemi, Richard G., John Mueller, and Tom W. Smith. 1989. *Trends in Public Opinion: A Compendium of Survey Data.* New York: Greenwood Press.

Oakes, Jeannie. 1990. *Multiplying Inequalities: The Effects of Race, Social Class, and Tracking on Opportunities to Learn Mathematics and Science.* Santa Monica, Calif.: Rand Corporation.

OECD (Organisation for Economic Co-Operation and Development). 1983. *The Growth of Social Expenditure: Recent Trends and Implications for the 1980s.* Paris: OECD, Directorate for Social Affairs, Manpower, and Education.

―――― 1986. *Historical Statistics, 1960–84.* Paris: OECD.

―――― 1992. *Historical Statistics, 1960–1990.* Paris: OECD.

Office of Refugee Resettlement (ORR). 1991. *Report to the Congress: Refugee Resettlement Program.* Washington, D.C.: U.S. Department of Health and Human Services, Administration for Children and Families.

Office of Technology Assessment. 1992. *Technology and the American Economic Transition: Choices for the Future.* OTA-TET-238. Washington, D.C.: U.S. Government Printing Office.

O'Hare, William P., and Brenda Curry-White. 1992. "The Rural Underclass: Examination of Multiple-Problem Populations in Urban and Rural Settings." Population Reference Bureau, Washington, D.C., January. Mimeo.

Okun, Arthur. 1975. *Equality and Efficiency: The Big Tradeoff.* Washington, D.C.: Brookings Institution.

O'Neill, June. 1992. "Testimony before the U.S. House of Representatives, Committee on Ways and Means." September 10. Mimeo.

Orfield, Gary. 1986. "The Movement for Housing Integration." In *Housing Desegregation and Federal Policy,* ed. John Goering. Chapel Hill: University of North Carolina Press.

Organisation for Economic Co-Operation and Development. *See* OECD.

Orshansky, Mollie. 1963. "Children of the Poor." *Social Security Bulletin* 26 (July): 3–13.

―――― 1965. "Counting the Poor." *Social Security Bulletin* 28 (January): 3–29.

Osterman, Paul. 1991. "Is There a Problem with the Youth Labor Market; and If So, How Should We Fix It?" Sloan School of Management, Massachusetts Institute of Technology. Mimeo.

Oxley, Howard, and John P. Martin. 1991. "Controlling Government Spending and Deficits: Trends in the 1980s and Prospects for the 1990s." *OECD Economic Studies* 17 (Autumn): 145–189.

Page, Benjamin I., and Robert Y. Shapiro. 1983. "Effects of Public Opinion on Policy." *American Political Science Review* 77: 175–190.

―――― 1992. *The Rational Public: Fifty Years of Trends in Americans' Policy Preferences.* Chicago: University of Chicago Press.

Papke, Leslie. 1991. "Tax Policy and Urban Development: Evidence from an Enterprise Zone Program." Working Paper no. 3945, National Bureau of Economic Research, Cambridge, Mass.

Passel, Jeffrey S., and Barry Edmonston. 1992. *Immigration and Race in the United States.* Washington, D.C.: Urban Institute Press.

Passel, Jeffrey S., and Karen A. Woodrow. 1984. "Geographic Distribution of Undocumented Immigrants: Estimates of Undocumented Aliens Counted in the 1980 Census." *International Migration Review* 18 (Fall): 642–671.

Patterson, James T. 1986. *America's Struggle against Poverty, 1900–1985.* 2nd ed. Cambridge, Mass.: Harvard University Press.

Pauly, Mark, Patricia Danzon, Paul Feldstein, and John Hoff. 1991. "A Plan for Responsible Health Insurance." *Health Affairs* (Spring): 5–25.

Pedder, Sophie. 1991. "Social Isolation and the Labour Market: Black Americans in Chicago." Paper presented at the Urban Poverty and Family Life Conference, University of Chicago, October 10–12.

Pedraza-Bailey, Silvia. 1985. *Political and Economic Migrants in America.* Austin: University of Texas Press.

Pencavel, John. 1986. "Labor Supply of Men: A Survey." In *Handbook of Labor Economics,* vol. 1, ed. Orley Ashenfelter and Richard Layer. Amsterdam and New York: North-Holland.

Pepper Commission. 1990. *A Call for Action.* U.S. Bipartisan Commission on Comprehensive Health Care, Final Report. Washington, D.C.: U.S. Government Printing Office.

Peterson, Paul E., Barry G. Rabe, and Kenneth K. Wong. 1986. *When Federalism Works.* Washington, D.C.: Brookings Institution.

Peterson, Paul E., and Mark C. Rom. 1990. *Welfare Magnets: A New Case for National Standards.* Washington, D.C.: Brookings Institution.

Phibbs, Ciaran S. 1991. "The Economic Implications of Substance Abuse." *The Future of Children* 1 (1): 113–120.

Phibbs, Ciaran S., David A. Bateman, and Rachel M. Schwartz. 1991. "The Neonatal Costs of Maternal Cocaine Use." *Journal of the American Medical Association* 266: 1521–1526.

Pitts, Jennifer. 1992. "Twilight Zone." *New Republic,* September 7, pp. 25–28.

Plotnick, Robert, and Felicity Skidmore. 1975. *Progress against Poverty: A Review of the 1964–1974 Decade.* New York: Academic Press.

Portes, Alejandro. 1969. "Dilemmas of a Golden Exile: Integration of Cuban Refugee Families in Milwaukee." *American Sociological Review* 34 (4): 505–518.

―――― 1992. "Comments on Tienda and Liang's 'Horatio Alger Fails: Poverty and Immigration in Policy Perspective.' " Presented at the conference Poverty and Public Policy: What Do We Know? What Should We Do? Madison, Wis., May 25–27.

Portes, Alejandro, and Robert Bach. 1985. *Latin Journey: Cuban and Mexican Immigrants in the United States.* Berkeley: University of California Press.

Portes, Alejandro, and Ruben G. Rumbaut. 1990. *Immigrant America.* Berkeley: University of California Press.

Portes, Alejandro, and Alex Stepick. 1985. "Unwelcome Immigrants." *American Sociological Review* 50 (4): 493–515.

Portes, Alejandro, and Min Zhou. 1991. "Gaining the Upper Hand: Old and New Perspectives in the Study of Ethnic Minorities." Paper presented at Urban Poverty Workshop, Northwestern University, Evanston, Ill.

Prosser, William R. 1991. "The Underclass: Assessing What We Have Learned." *Focus* (newsletter of the Institute for Research on Poverty) 13 (2, Summer): 1–18.

Rainwater, Lee. 1968. "The Problem of Lower-Class Culture and Poverty—War Strategy." In *On Understanding Poverty: Perspectives from the Social Sciences,* ed. Daniel P. Moynihan. New York: Basic Books.

——— 1982. "Stigma in Income-Tested Programs." In *Income-Tested Transfer Programs: The Case For and Against,* ed. Irwin Garfinkel. New York: Academic Press.

Rainwater, Lee, and William L. Yancey. 1967. *The Moynihan Report and the Politics of Controversy.* Cambridge, Mass.: MIT Press.

Reagan, Ronald. 1982. Remarks before the National Black Republican Council, September 14, 1982. *Weekly Compilation of Presidential Documents* 18: 1152–1157. Washington, D.C.: U.S. Government Printing Office.

Reich, Robert. 1991. *The Work of Nations: Preparing Ourselves for Capitalism in the 21st Century.* New York: Knopf.

Reinhardt, Uwe. 1989. "Toward a Fail-Safe Health-Insurance System." *Wall Street Journal,* January 11.

Reischauer, Robert D. 1987. "The Size and Characteristics of the Underclass." Paper presented at the annual meeting of the Association for Public Policy Analysis and Management, Bethesda, Md., October.

Resnick, Lauren B. 1987. "Learning in School and out." *Educational Researcher* 16: 13–20.

Reuman, David. 1989. "How Social Comparison Mediates the Relation between Ability-Grouping Practices and Students' Achievement Expectancies in Mathematics." *Journal of Educational Psychology* 81: 178–189.

Reuter, Peter, Robert McCoun, and Patrick Murphy. 1990. *Money from Crime: A Study of the Economics of Drug Dealing in Washington, D.C.* Santa Monica, Calif.: Rand Corporation.

Riccio, James, and Daniel Friedlander. 1992. *GAIN: Program Strategies, Participation Patterns, and First-Year Impacts in Six Counties.* New York: Manpower Demonstration Research Corporation.

Ricketts, Erol R., and Ronald B. Mincy. 1988. "Growth of the Underclass, 1970–1980." Working Paper, Urban Institute, Washington, D.C.

Ricketts, Erol R., and Isabel V. Sawhill. 1988. "Defining and Measuring the Underclass." *Journal of Policy Analysis and Management* 7 (2): 316–325.

Ries, Peter W. 1990. *Americans Assess Their Health: United States, 1987.* National Center for Health Statistics, series 10, no. 174. Hyattsville, Md.: U.S. Public Health Service.

Robert Wood Johnson Foundation. 1987. *Access to Health Care in the United States: Results of a 1986 Survey.* Special Report no. 2. Princeton, N.J.: Robert Wood Johnson Foundation.

Robins, Philip. 1990a. "Federal Financing of Child Care: Alternative Approaches and Economic Implications." *Population Research and Policy Review* 9: 65–90.

―――― 1990b. "Explaining Recent Declines in AFDC Participation." *Public Finance Quarterly* 18: 236–255.

Rosenbaum, James. 1991. "Black Pioneers—Do Their Moves to the Suburbs Increase Economic Opportunity for Mothers and Children?" *Housing Policy Debate* 2: 1179–1213.

Rosenbaum, James, Marilyn Kulieke, and Leonard Rubinowitz. 1988. "White Suburban Schools' Response to Low-Income Black Children: Sources of Success and Problems." *Urban Review* 20: 28–41.

Rosenbaum, James, and Susan J. Popkin. 1991. "Employment and Earnings of Low-Income Blacks Who Move to Middle-Class Suburbs." In *The Urban Underclass,* ed. Christopher Jencks and Paul E. Peterson. Washington, D.C.: Brookings Institution.

Ross, Christine, Sheldon Danziger, and Eugene Smolensky. 1987. "The Level and Trend of Poverty in the United States, 1939–1979." *Demography* 24 (November): 587–600.

Ross, David, and Peter Usher. 1986. *From the Roots Up: Economic Development as if Community Mattered.* Croton-on-Hudson, N.Y.: Bootstrap Press.

Roth, Byron. 1990. "Social Psychology's Racism." *Public Interest* 98: 26–36.

Rubin, Barry, and Margaret Wilder. 1989. "Urban Enterprise Zones: Employment Impacts and Fiscal Incentives." *APA Journal* 418 (Autumn): 418–431.

Rubin, Marilyn, and Edward Trawinski. 1991. "New Jersey's Urban Enterprise Zones: A Program That Works." *Urban Lawyer* 23: 461–471.

Ruggles, Patricia. 1990. *Drawing the Line: Alternative Poverty Measures and Their Implications for Public Policy.* Washington, D.C.: Urban Institute Press.

Ruggles, Patricia, and William P. Marton. 1986. "Measuring the Size and Characteristics of the Underclass: How Much Do We Know?" Urban Institute, Washington, D.C. Mimeo.

Ryscavage, Paul, Gordon Green, and Edward Welniak. 1992. "The Impact of Demographic, Social, and Economic Change on the Distribution of Income." In *Studies in the Distribution of Income.* U.S. Bureau of the Census, Current Population Reports, Consumer Income, P-60, no. 183. Washington, D.C.: U.S. Government Printing Office.

Rytina, Steve. 1992. "Scaling the Intergenerational Continuity of Occupation: Is Occupational Inheritance Ascriptive After All?" *American Journal of Sociology* 97 (6): 1658–1688.

Sabol, William L. Forthcoming. "The Underclass and Crime: An Explanatory Framework." In *Race and Unwantedness: Essays on the Black Underclass,* ed. William A. Darity, Jr., Samuel L. Myers, Jr., William L. Sabol, and E. M. Carson. New York: Garland Publications.

Sampson, Robert. 1987. "Urban Black Violence: The Effect of Male Joblessness and Family Disruption." *American Journal of Sociology* 93: 348–382.

Saunders, Peter. 1984. "Evidence on Income Redistribution by Governments." Paper no. 11, OECD, Economics and Statistics Department, Paris.

Sawhill, Isabel V., ed. 1988. *Challenge to Leadership: Economic and Social Issues for the Next Decade.* Washington, D.C.: Urban Institute Press.

Sawhill, Isabel V., and Mark Condon. 1992. "Is U.S. Income Inequality Really Growing?" Policy Bits, no. 13, Urban Institute, Washington, D.C.

Schafer, Robert, and Helen Ladd. 1981. *Discrimination in Mortgage Lending.* Cambridge, Mass.: MIT Press.

Schelling, Thomas. 1972. "A Process of Residential Segregation: Neighborhood Tipping." In *Racial Discrimination in Economic Life,* ed. Anthony Pascal. Lexington, Mass.: Lexington Books.

Schieber, George, and Jean-Pierre Poullier. 1989. "Overview of International Comparisons of Health Care Expenditures." *Health Care Financing Review,* Annual Supplement.

Schill, Michael. 1990. "Privatizing Federal Low Income Housing Assistance: The Case of Public Housing." *Cornell Law Review* 75: 878–882.

_____ 1992a. "Deconcentrating the Inner City Poor." Paper presented at the John M. Olin Foundation Conference on the Law and Economics of Urban Issues, University of Virginia School of Law, November 8–9.

_____ 1992b. "The Federal Role in Reducing Regulatory Barriers to Affordable Housing in the Suburbs." Draft paper, March 1.

Scholz, John Karl. 1990. "The Participation Rate of the Earned Income Tax Credit." Discussion Paper no. 928-90, Institute for Research on Poverty, University of Wisconsin–Madison.

_____ 1993. "The Earned Income Tax Credit: Participation, Compliance, and Antipoverty Effectiveness." Discussion Paper no. 1020-93, Institute for Research on Poverty, University of Wisconsin–Madison.

Schorr, Lisbeth B. 1988. *Within Our Reach: Breaking the Cycle of Disadvantage.* New York: Anchor Press/Doubleday.

Schramm, Richard. 1987. "Local, Regional, and National Strategies." In *Beyond the Market and the State: New Directions in Community Development,* ed. Severyn Bruyn and James Meehan. Philadelphia: Temple University Press.

Schultz, Theodore W. 1963. *The Economic Value of Education.* New York: Columbia University Press.

Schuman, Howard. 1980. "Artifacts Are in the Mind of the Beholder." Paper presented at the annual meeting of the American Sociological Association, New York, August 27.

Schuman, Howard, and Stanley Presser. 1981. *Questions and Answers in Attitude Surveys.* New York: Academic Press.

Schuman, Howard, Charlotte Steeh, and Lawrence Bobo. 1988. *Racial Attitudes in America: Trends and Interpretations.* Cambridge, Mass.: Harvard University Press.

Schwarz, John E., and Thomas J. Volgy. 1992. *The Forgotten Americans.* New York: Norton.

Schweinhart, Lawrence J., and David P. Weikart. 1986. "What Do We Know So Far? A Review of the Head Start Synthesis Project." *Young Children* (January), pp. 49–55.

Scribner, Sylvia. 1986. "Thinking in Action: Some Characteristics of Practical Thought." In *Practical Intelligence: Nature and Origins of Competence in the Everyday World,* ed. R. J. Sternberg and R. K. Wagner. New York: Cambridge University Press.

Sears, David O., and Jack Citrin. 1985. *Tax Revolt: Something for Nothing in California.* Cambridge, Mass.: Harvard University Press.

Sears, David O., and Carolyn L. Funk. 1991. "The Role of Self-Interest in Social and Political Attitudes." *Advances in Experimental Social Psychology* 24: 1–91.

Secretary's Commission on Achieving Necessary Skills (SCANS). 1991. *What Work Requires of Schools.* Washington, D.C.: U.S. Department of Labor.

Selznick, Phillip. 1992. *The Moral Commonwealth.* Berkeley: University of California Press.

Shapiro, Isaac, Mark Sheft, Julie Strawn, Laura Summer, Robert Greenstein, and Steven D. Gold. 1991. *The States and the Poor: How Budget Decisions in 1991 Affected Low-Income People.* Washington, D.C.: Center on Budget and Policy Priorities; and Albany, N.Y.: Center for the Study of the State. December.

Shapiro, Robert Y., and J. T. Young. 1989. "Public Opinion and the Welfare State: The United States in Comparative Perspective." *Political Science Quarterly* 104: 59–87.

Shklar, Judith N. 1991. *American Citizenship: The Quest for Inclusion.* Cambridge, Mass.: Harvard University Press.

Short, Kathleen, and Martina Shea. 1991. *Transitions in Income and Poverty Status: 1987–88.* U.S. Bureau of the Census, Current Population Reports, series P-70, no. 24. Washington, D.C.: U.S. Government Printing Office.

Short, Pamela. 1990. *Estimates of the Uninsured Population, Calendar Year 1987.* DHHS Publication no. (PHS) 90-3469. National Medical Expenditure Survey Data Summary 2, Agency for Health Care Policy and Research. Rockville, Md.: Public Health Service.

Simon, Julian. 1984. "Immigrants, Taxes, and Welfare in the United States." *Population and Development Review* 10 (1): 55–69.

—— 1989. *The Economic Consequences of Immigration.* Oxford: Basil Blackwell.

Simon, Rita J. 1985. *Public Opinion and the Immigrant: Print Media Coverage, 1880–1980.* Lexington, Mass.: Lexington Books.

Sinclair, B., and Babette Gutmann. 1992. "A Summary of State Chapter 1 Participation and Achievement Information: LEA Grant and State Neglected and Delinquent Programs—1989–90." Westat, Inc., prepared for U.S. Department of Education, Office of Policy and Planning, Washington, D.C.

Sizer, Theodore R. 1992. *Horace's School: Redesigning the American High School.* Boston: Houghton Mifflin.

Skocpol, Theda. 1991. "Targeting within Universalism: Politically Viable Policies to Combat Poverty in the United States." In *The Urban Underclass,* ed. Christopher Jencks and Paul E. Peterson. Washington, D.C.: Brookings Institution.

—— 1992. *Protecting Soldiers and Mothers: The Political Origins of Social Policy in the United States.* Cambridge, Mass.: Harvard University Press.

Skolnick, Jerome, and David Bayley. 1988. *Community Policing: Issues and Practices around the World.* Washington, D.C.: U.S. Department of Justice.

Slavin, Robert E., Nancy L. Karweit, and Nancy A. Madden. 1989. *Effective Programs for Students at Risk.* Boston: Allyn and Bacon.

Slavin, Robert E., and Nancy A. Madden. 1991. "Modifying Chapter 1 Program Improvement Guidelines to Reward Appropriate Practices." *Educational Evaluation and Policy Analysis* 13: 369–379.

Smeeding, Timothy. 1982. "The Antipoverty Effects of In-Kind Transfers." *Policy Studies Journal* 10: 499–521.

—— 1992. "Why the U.S. Antipoverty System Doesn't Work Very Well." *Challenge* 35 (January–February): 30–35.

Smeeding, Timothy, and Lee Rainwater. 1991. "Cross-National Trends in Income Poverty and Dependency: The Evidence for Young Adults in the Eighties." Paper presented at the Joint Center for Political and Economic Studies, Washington, D.C., September 20–21.

Smith, Kevin B. 1985. "I Made It Because of Me: Beliefs about the Causes of Wealth and Poverty." *Sociological Spectrum* 5: 255–267.

Smith, Mark D., Drew Altman, Robert Leitman, Thomas Moloney, and Humphrey Taylor. 1992. "Taking the Public's Pulse on Health System Reform." *Health Affairs* (Summer): 125–133.

Smith, Tom W. 1987. "That Which We Call Welfare by Any Other Name Would Be Sweeter." *Public Opinion Quarterly* 51: 75–83.

Smolensky, Eugene, Sheldon Danziger, and Peter Gottschalk. 1988. "The Declining Significance of Age in the United States: Trends in the Well-Being of Children and the Elderly since 1939." In *The Vulnerable,* ed. John Palmer, Timothy Smeeding, and Barbara Torrey. Washington, D.C.: Urban Institute Press.

Snow, C. E., W. Barnes, J. Chandler, L. Hemphill, and I. Goodman. 1991. *Unfulfilled Expectations: Home and School Influences on Literacy.* Cambridge, Mass.: Harvard University Press.

Solon, Gary. 1992. "Intergenerational Income Mobility in the United States." *American Economic Review* 82 (3): 393–408.

Steeh, Charlotte, and Howard Schuman. 1992. "Young White Adults: Did Racial Attitudes Change in the 1980s?" *American Journal of Sociology* 98: 340–367.

Stegman, Michael A. 1972. *Housing Investment in the Inner City: The Dynamics of Decline—A Study of Baltimore, Maryland, 1968–1970.* Cambridge, Mass.: MIT Press.

Stern, Anna. 1990. "Immigrants and Refugees: Some Considerations for Training the Workforce of the Future." Paper prepared for National Commission for Employment Policy, Annual Conference on Training a Diverse Work Force, Washington, D.C.

Steuerle, C. Eugene. 1991. "Finance-Based Reform: The Search for Adaptable Health Policy." Paper presented at American Enterprise Institute conference American Health Policy: Critical Issues for Reform. Washington, D.C. October.

——— 1992. *The Tax Decade.* Washington, D.C.: Urban Institute Press.

Stimson, James A. 1991. *Public Opinion in America: Moods, Cycles, and Swings.* Boulder, Colo.: Westview Press.

Stockman, David. 1984. "Statement." In U.S. House of Representatives, Committee on Ways and Means, *Poverty Rate Increase Hearings,* serial 98-55. Washington, D.C.: U.S. Government Printing Office.

Strauss, David. 1991. "The Law and Economics of Racial Discrimination in Employment: The Case for Numerical Standards." *Georgetown Law Journal* 79: 1619–1657.

Struyk, Raymond, and Marc Bendick, eds. 1981. *Housing Vouchers for the Poor: Lessons from a National Experiment.* Washington, D.C.: Urban Institute Press.

Struyk, Raymond, Sue Marshall, and Larry Ozanne. 1978. *Housing Policies for the Urban Poor: A Case for Local Diversity in Federal Programs.* Washington, D.C.: Urban Institute Press.

Sullivan, Mercer L. 1989. "Absent Fathers in the Inner City." *Annals of the American Academy of Political and Social Science* 501 (1, January): 48–58.

Summer, Laura. 1991. *Limited Access: Health Care for the Rural Poor.* Washington, D.C.: Center on Budget and Policy Priorities.

Sumner, William Graham. 1982 (first published 1883). *What the Social Classes Owe to Each Other.* Caldwell, Idaho: Caxton Printers.

Sundquist, James, and David Davis. 1969. *Making Federalism Work.* Washington, D.C.: Brookings Institution.

Swartz, Katherine, and Timothy McBride. 1990. "Spells without Health Insurance: Distributions of Durations and Their Link to Point-in-Time Estimates of the Uninsured." *Inquiry* 27: 281–288.

Task Force on Homelessness and Severe Mental Illness. 1992. *Outcasts on Main Street.* Washington, D.C.: U.S. Public Health Service.

Taub, Richard. 1988. *Community Capitalism.* Boston: Harvard Business School Press.

—— 1991. "Differing Conceptions of Honor and Orientations toward Work and Marriage among Low-Income African-Americans and Mexican-Americans." Paper presented at the Urban Poverty and Family Life Conference, University of Chicago, October 10–12.

Taylor, Carl S. 1989. *Dangerous Society.* East Lansing: Michigan State University Press.

Taylor, D. Garth. 1986. *Public Opinion and Collective Action.* Chicago: University of Chicago Press.

Teitelbaum, Michael. 1980. "Right versus Right: Immigration and Refugee Policy in the United States." *Foreign Affairs* 59 (1): 21–59.

Testa, Mark. 1991. "Male Joblessness, Nonmarital Parenthood, and Marriage." Paper presented at the Urban Poverty and Family Life Conference, University of Chicago, October 10–12.

Thernstrom, Stephen, ed. 1980. *Harvard Encyclopedia of American Ethnic Groups.* Cambridge, Mass.: Harvard University Press.

Tienda, Marta, George J. Borjas, Hector Cordero-Guzman, Kristin E. Neuman, and Manuela Romero. 1991. "The Demography of Legalization: Insights from Administrative Records of Legalized Aliens." Final Report to the Office of the Assistant Secretary for Planning and Evaluation, U.S. Department of Health and Human Services. September.

Tienda, Marta, and Leif I. Jensen. 1986. "Immigration and Public Assistance: Dispelling the Myth of Dependency." *Social Science Research* 15 (4): 372–400.

—— 1988. "Poverties and Minorities: A Quarter Century Profile of Color and Socioeconomic Disadvantage." In *Divided Opportunities: Minorities, Poverty, and Social Policy,* ed. Gary D. Sandefur and Marta Tienda. New York: Plenum Press.

Tienda, Marta, and Audrey Singer. 1992. "Wage Mobility of Legalized Immigrants." Paper presented at the annual meetings of the American Sociological Association, Pittsburgh, August.

Tienda, Marta, and Haya Stier. 1991a. "Joblessness and Shiftlessness: Labor Force Activity in Chicago's Inner City." In *The Urban Underclass,* ed. Christopher Jencks and Paul E. Peterson. Washington, D.C.: Brookings Institution.

—— 1991b. "Makin' a Livin': Color and Opportunity in the Inner City." Paper presented at the Urban Poverty and Family Life Conference, University of Chicago, Chicago, Ill., October 10–12.

Tocqueville, Alexis de. 1969 (1840). *Democracy in America.* New York: Harper and Row.

Tollet, Kenneth S. 1991. "Racism and Race-Conscious Remedies." *American Prospect* (Spring): 91–93.

Treiman, Donald J., and Robert M. Hauser. 1977. "Intergenerational Transmission of Income: An Exercise in Theory Construction." In *The Process of Stratification: Trends and Analyses,* ed. Robert M. Hauser and David L. Featherman. New York: Academic Press.

Tufte, Edward R. 1974. *Data Analysis for Politics and Policy.* Englewood Cliffs, N.J.: Prentice-Hall.

Turner, James. 1985. *Without God, without Creed: The Origins of Unbelief in America.* Baltimore, Md.: Johns Hopkins University Press.

Turner, Margery A. 1991. *Opportunities Denied, Opportunities Diminished: Discrimination in Hiring.* Washington, D.C.: Urban Institute Press.

————. 1992. "Discrimination in Urban Housing Markets: Lessons from Fair Housing Audits." *Housing Policy Debate* 3: 185–215.

Turner, Margery A., Maris Mikelsons, and John G. Edwards. 1991. "Housing Discrimination Study: Analyzing Racial and Ethnic Steering." U.S. Department of Housing and Urban Development, Office of Policy Development and Research, Washington, D.C. Mimeo.

Turner, Margery A., Raymond Struyk, and John Yinger. 1991. "Housing Discrimination Study: Synthesis." Urban Institute Research Paper, Washington, D.C.

U.S. Advisory Commission on Regulatory Barriers to Affordable Housing. 1991. *"Not in My Back Yard": Removing Barriers to Affordable Housing.* Washington, D.C.: U.S. Government Printing Office.

U.S. Bureau of the Census. 1985. *1980 Census of the Population,* vol. 2: *Poverty Areas in Large Cities,* Subject Reports PC 80-2-8D. Washington, D.C.: U.S. Government Printing Office.

————. 1986. "Conference on the Measurement of Noncash Benefits: Proceedings, Volume 1." Washington, D.C.: U.S. Government Printing Office.

————. 1991a. *Money Income of Households, Families, and Persons: 1990.* Current Population Reports, series P-60, no. 174. Washington, D.C.: U.S. Government Printing Office.

————. 1991b. *Households, Families, and Persons in the United States: 1990.* Current Population Reports, series P-60, no. 175. Washington, D.C.: U.S. Government Printing Office.

————. 1991c. *Measuring the Effect of Benefits and Taxes on Income and Poverty: 1990.* Current Population Reports, series P-60, no. 176-RD. Washington, D.C.: U.S. Government Printing Office.

————. 1991d. *Poverty in the United States: 1990.* Current Population Reports, series P-60, no. 175. Washington, D.C.: U.S. Government Printing Office.

————. 1991e. *Statistical Abstract of the United States: 1991.* Washington, D.C.: U.S. Government Printing Office.

————. 1992a. *Money Income of Households, Families, and Persons: 1991.* Current Population Reports, series P-60, no. 180. Washington, D.C.: U.S. Government Printing Office.

————. 1992b. *Poverty in the United States: 1991.* Current Population Reports, series P-60, no. 181. Washington, D.C.: U.S. Government Printing Office.

————. 1992c. *Measuring the Effect of Benefits and Taxes on Income and Poverty: 1979–1991.* Current Population Reports, series P-60, no. 182. Washington, D.C.: U.S. Government Printing Office.

————. 1993. *Poverty in the United States: 1992.* Current Population Reports, series P-60, no. 185. Washington, D.C.: U.S. Government Printing Office.

U.S. Congress. 1992. *H. Rept. 102-1034: Conference Report on Revenue Act of 1992 (H.R.11).* Washington, D.C.: U.S. Government Printing Office.

————. 1993. "Ways and Means Committee Print 103-11, Fiscal Year 1994 Budget Reconciliation Recommendations of the Committee on Ways and Means." Washington, D.C.: U.S. Government Printing Office.

U.S. Congressional Budget Office. 1993. *Projections of National Health Expenditures: 1993 Update.* October. Washington, D.C.: CBO Publications Office.

U.S. Congressional Budget Office and National Commission for Employment Policy (NCEP). 1982. *CETA Training Programs—Do They Work for Adults?* Washington, D.C.: U.S. Government Printing Office.

U.S. Council of Economic Advisers. 1964. *Economic Report of the President, 1964.* Washington, D.C.: U.S. Government Printing Office.

U.S. Department of Education. 1991. *America 2000 Sourcebook.* Washington, D.C.: U.S. Department of Education.

U.S. Department of Education, Office of Policy and Planning. 1993. *Reinventing Chapter 1: The Current Chapter 1 Program and New Directions—Executive Summary.* Washington, D.C.: U.S. Department of Education. February.

U.S. Department of Health, Education, and Welfare. 1971. *Expenditures for Assistance and Administrative Costs in Public Assistance and Medicaid: Fiscal Years 1936 to Present.* Washington, D.C.: U.S. Government Printing Office.

U.S. Department of Health and Human Services. 1976. *The Measure of Poverty: A Report to Congress.* Washington, D.C.: Department of Health and Human Services.

———— 1991. *Health Care Financing Program Statistics: Medicare and Medicaid Data Book, 1990.* Baltimore, Md.: Health Care Financing Administration. March.

U.S. Department of Health and Human Services, Health Care Financing Administration (HCFA). 1991. *Health Care Financing Program Statistics: Medicare and Medicaid Data Book, 1990.* Baltimore, Md.: Health Care Financing Administration, Office of Research and Demonstrations.

U.S. Department of Health and Human Services, Public Health Service. 1990. *Healthy People 2000.* Washington, D.C.: U.S. Government Printing Office.

U.S. Department of Health and Human Services, Social Security Administration. 1984. *Social Security Bulletin, Annual Statistical Supplement.* January. Washington, D.C.: U.S. Government Printing Office.

———— 1991. *Social Security Bulletin, Annual Statistical Supplement.* January. Washington, D.C.: U.S. Government Printing Office.

U.S. Department of Labor. 1993. *Employment and Earnings.* January. Washington, D.C.: U.S. Government Printing Office.

U.S. Department of Labor, Office of Policy Planning and Research. 1965. *The Negro Family: The Case for National Action.* Daniel Patrick Moynihan. Washington, D.C.: U.S. Government Printing Office.

U.S. General Accounting Office. 1987. *Work and Welfare: Current AFDC Work Programs and Implications for Federal Policy.* Washington, D.C.: GAO.

———— 1988. *Enterprise Zones: Lessons from the Maryland Experience.* Washington, D.C.: U.S. Government Printing Office.

———— 1990. *Immigration Reform: Employer Sanctions and the Question of Discrimination.* Washington, D.C.: U.S. Government Printing Office.

———— 1991a. "Medicaid Expansions: Coverage Improves but State Fiscal Problems Jeopardize Continued Progress." GAO/HRD-91-78. June. Washington, D.C.

———— 1991b. *The Changing Workforce.* GAO/GGD-92-38. Washington, D.C.: U.S. General Accounting Office.

U.S. House of Representatives, Committee on Ways and Means. 1984. *Background Material and Data on Programs within the Jurisdiction of the Committee on Ways and Means.* Washington, D.C.: U.S. Government Printing Office.

———— 1990. *1990 Green Book.* Washington, D.C.: U.S. Government Printing Office.

———— 1991. *1991 Green Book.* Washington, D.C.: U.S. Government Printing Office.

———— 1992. *1992 Green Book.* Washington, D.C.: U.S. Government Printing Office.

U.S. Office of Management and Budget. Various years. *Budget of the United States Government.* Washington, D.C.: U.S. Government Printing Office.

———— 1988. *Historical Tables, Budget of the U.S. Government, FY 1989.* Washington, D.C.: U.S. Government Printing Office.

———— 1991. *Budget of the United States Government: Fiscal Year 1992.* Washington, D.C.: U.S. Government Printing Office.

U.S. Senate, Subcommittee on Social Security and Family Policy. 1992. "Hearings on the Recent State Welfare Reform Plans." U.S. Senate. Mimeo.

Useem, Bert. 1980. "Solidarity Model, Breakdown Model, and the Boston Anti-Busing Movement." *American Sociological Review* 45: 357–369.

Valentine, Charles A. 1968. *Culture and Poverty: Critique and Counter-Proposals.* Chicago: University of Chicago Press.

van Doorslaer, Eddy, Adam Wagstaff, and Frans Rutten, eds. 1993. *Equity in the Finance and Delivery of Health Care.* Oxford: Oxford University Press.

Van Haitsma, Martha. 1989. "A Contextual Definition of the Underclass." *Focus* (newsletter of the Institute for Research on Poverty) 12 (1, Spring–Summer): 27–31.

———— 1991. "Attitude, Social Context, and Labor Force Attachment: Blacks and Immigrant Mexicans in Chicago Poverty Areas." Paper presented at the Urban Poverty and Family Life Conference, University of Chicago, October 10–12.

Venezky, Richard L., Carl F. Kaestle, and Andrew M. Sum. 1987. *The Subtle Danger: Reflections on the Literacy Abilities of America's Young Adults.* Princeton, N.J.: Educational Testing Service.

Vernez, George, and David Ronfeldt. 1991. "The Current Situation in Mexican Immigration." *Science* 251: 1189–1193.

Vladeck, Bruce. 1990. "Health Care and the Homeless: A Political Parable for Our Time." *Journal of Health, Politics, Policy and Law* 15 (2): 305–317.

Waldinger, Roger. 1985. "Immigration and Industrial Change in the New York City Apparel Industry." In *Hispanics in the U.S. Economy,* ed. George J. Borjas and Marta Tienda. Orlando, Fla.: Academic Press.

———— 1989. "Immigration and Urban Change." *Annual Review of Sociology* 15: 211–232.

Walsh, Edward J., and Rex H. Warland. 1983. "Social Movement Involvement in the Wake of a Nuclear Accident: Activists and Free Riders in the TMI Area." *American Sociological Review* 48: 764–780.

Warren, Elizabeth. 1988. *The Legacy of Judicial Policy-Making.* Lanham, Md.: University Press of America.

Warren, Robert, and Jeffrey Passel. 1987. "A Count of the Uncountable: Estimates of Undocumented Aliens Counted in the 1980 United States Census." *Demography* 24: 375–393.

Warren, Roland, Stephen Rose, and Ann Bergunder. 1974. *The Structure of Urban Reform.* Lexington, Mass.: Lexington Books.

Weicher, John C. 1987. "Mismeasuring Poverty and Progress." *Cato Journal* 6 (3): 215–230.

—— 1990. "The Voucher/Production Debate." In *Building Foundations,* ed. Denise DiPasquale and Langley Keyes. Philadelphia: University of Pennsylvania Press.

Weinberg, Daniel H. 1987. "Filling the 'Poverty Gap,' 1979–1984." *Journal of Human Resources* 22 (Fall): 563–573.

—— 1991. "Poverty Dynamics and the Poverty Gap, 1984–86." *Journal of Human Resources* 26 (Summer): 535–544.

Weinberg, Daniel H., and Enrique J. Lamas. 1991. "The History and Current Issues of U.S. Poverty Measurement." Paper presented at the International Scientific Conference on Poverty Measurement for Economies in Transition in Eastern European Countries, Warsaw, Poland, October.

Weir, Margaret. 1992. *Politics and Jobs: The Boundaries of Employment Policy in the United States.* Princeton, N.J.: Princeton University Press.

Weisberg, Sanford. 1980. *Applied Linear Regression.* New York: John Wiley.

Weissberg, Robert. 1991. "The 'Politics' of the Study of Race." Paper presented at the meetings of the Midwest Political Science Association, Chicago.

Welch, Finis. 1970. "Education in Production." *Journal of Political Economy* 78: 35–59.

West, E. G. 1967. "Tom Paine's Voucher Scheme for Public Education." *Southern Economic Journal* 33: 378–382.

Wiebe, Robert H. 1967. *The Search for Order: 1877–1920.* New York: Hill and Wang.

Wiener, Joshua M., and Jeannie Engel. 1991. *Improving Access to Health Services for Children and Pregnant Women.* Washington, D.C.: Brookings Institution.

Wiener, Susan. 1988. "How Much Do Definitions and Data Sources Matter in Conclusions about the Size and Growth of the Underclass?" Urban Institute, Washington, D.C. Mimeo.

Wienk, Ronald. 1992. "Discrimination in Urban Credit Markets: What We Don't Know and Why We Don't Know It." *Housing Policy Debate* 3: 217–240.

Williams, Terry M., and William Kornblum. 1985. *Growing up Poor.* Lexington, Mass.: Lexington Books.

Williamson, John B. 1974. "The Stigma of Public Dependency: A Comparison of Alternative Forms of Public Aid." *Social Problems* 21: 213–228.

Wilson, James Q. 1993. "The Moral Sense." *American Political Science Review* 87 (1): 1–11.

Wilson, William Julius. 1987. *The Truly Disadvantaged: The Inner City, the Underclass, and Public Policy.* Chicago: University of Chicago Press.

—— 1988. "The American Underclass: Inner-City Ghettos and the Norms of Citizenship." Godkin Lecture, presented at the John F. Kennedy School of Government, Harvard University, April.

—— 1991a. "Poverty, Joblessness, and Family Structure in the Inner City: A Comparative Perspective." Paper presented at the Urban Poverty and Family Life Conference, University of Chicago, October 10–12.

—— 1991b. "Response." *American Prospect* (Spring): 93–96.

—— 1991c. "Studying Inner-City Social Dislocations: The Challenge of Public Agenda Research—1990 Presidential Address." *American Sociological Review* 56 (February): 1–14.

Wilson, William Julius, and Lawrence M. Mead. 1987. "The Obligation to Work and the Availability of Jobs: A Dialogue between Lawrence M. Mead and William Julius Wilson." *Focus* (newsletter of the Institute for Research on Poverty) 10 (2, Summer): 11–19.

Wilson, William Julius, and Kathryn M. Neckerman. 1986. "Poverty and Family Structure: The Widening Gap between Evidence and Public Policy Issues." In *Fighting Poverty: What Works and What Doesn't,* ed. Sheldon H. Danziger and Daniel H. Weinberg. Cambridge, Mass.: Harvard University Press.

Winkler, Anne E. 1991. "The Incentive Effects of Medicaid on Women's Labor Supply." *Journal of Human Resources* 26: 308–337.

Wiseman, Michael. 1991. "A Symposium on the Family Support Act of 1988." *Journal of Policy Analysis and Management* 10 (4): 588–632.

Witte, John. 1990a. "Choice in American Education." Appalachia Educational Laboratory, Charleston, W.V. Mimeo.

———— 1990b. "Understanding High School Achievement: After a Decade of Research, Do We Have Any Confident Policy Recommendations?" Department of Political Science, University of Wisconsin–Madison. Mimeo.

Wolfe, Barbara, and Steven Hill. 1993. "The Health, Earnings Capacity, and Poverty of Single-Mother Families." In *Poverty and Prosperity in the USA in the Late Twentieth Century,* ed. Dimitri B. Papadimitriou and Edward N. Wolff. New York and London: Macmillan.

Wong, Raymond S. K. 1990. "Understanding Cross-National Variation in Occupational Mobility." *American Sociological Review* 55: 560–573.

Wong, Yin-Ling Irene, Irwin Garfinkel, and Sara S. McLanahan. 1993. "Single-Mother Families in Eight Countries: Economic Status and Social Policy." *Social Science Review* 67 (June): 177–197.

Wuthnow, Robert. 1991. *Acts of Compassion: Caring for Others and Helping Ourselves.* Princeton, N.J.: Princeton University Press.

Yinger, John. 1976. "Racial Prejudice and Racial Residential Segregation in an Urban Model." *Journal of Urban Economics* 3: 383–396.

———— 1979. "Prejudice and Discrimination in the Urban Housing Market." In *Current Issues in Urban Economics,* ed. Peter Mieszkowski and Mohlon Straszheim. Baltimore, Md.: Johns Hopkins University Press.

Zigler, Edward F. 1989. "Addressing the Nation's Child Care Crisis: The School of the Twenty-First Century." *American Journal of Orthopsychiatry* 59: 484–491.

Zigler, Edward F., and Susan Muenchon. 1992. *Head Start: The Inside Story of America's Most Successful Educational Experiment.* New York: Basic Books.

Zuckerman, Barry. 1991. "Drug-Exposed Infants: Understanding the Medical Risk." *Future of Children* 1 (1): 26–35.

Contributors

REBECCA M. BLANK, Department of Economics and Center for Urban Affairs and Policy Research, Northwestern University, Evanston, Illinois

LAWRENCE BOBO, Department of Sociology, University of California, Los Angeles, California

GARY BURTLESS, The Brookings Institution, Washington, D.C.

SHELDON H. DANZIGER, School of Social Work, Institute of Public Policy Studies, and Population Studies Center, University of Michigan, Ann Arbor, Michigan

IRWIN GARFINKEL, School of Social Work, Columbia University, New York, New York; Institute for Research on Poverty, University of Wisconsin, Madison, Wisconsin

PETER GOTTSCHALK, Department of Economics, Boston College, Boston, Massachusetts; Institute for Research on Poverty, University of Wisconsin, Madison, Wisconsin

ROBERT HAVEMAN, Department of Economics, La Follette Institute of Public Affairs, and Institute for Research on Poverty, University of Wisconsin, Madison, Wisconsin

HUGH HECLO, Department of Public Affairs, George Mason University, Fairfax, Virginia

JEFFREY S. LEHMAN, School of Law and Institute of Public Policy Studies, University of Michigan, Ann Arbor, Michigan

ZAI LIANG, Department of Sociology, Hunter College, New York, New York

CHARLES F. MANSKI, Department of Economics and Institute for Research on Poverty, University of Wisconsin, Madison, Wisconsin

SARA MCLANAHAN, Department of Sociology and Office of Population Research, Princeton University, Princeton, New Jersey; Institute for Research on Poverty, University of Wisconsin, Madison, Wisconsin

RONALD B. MINCY, The Ford Foundation, New York, New York

RICHARD J. MURNANE, Graduate School of Education, Harvard University, Cambridge, Massachusetts

GARY D. SANDEFUR, Department of Sociology and Institute for Research on Poverty, University of Wisconsin, Madison, Wisconsin

RYAN A. SMITH, Department of Sociology, University of California, Los Angeles, California

MARTA TIENDA, Department of Sociology and Population Research Center, University of Chicago, Chicago, Illinois

JAMES TOBIN, Cowles Foundation for Economic Research, Yale University, New Haven, Connecticut

DANIEL H. WEINBERG, U.S. Bureau of the Census, Washington, D.C.

BARBARA L. WOLFE, Department of Economics, Department of Preventive Medicine, La Follette Institute of Public Affairs, and Institute for Research on Poverty, University of Wisconsin, Madison, Wisconsin

Index